RRB Junior Engineer

Information Technology (IT) : CBT-1

Latest Edition
Practice Kit

15 Tests
15 Mock Test

Based On Real Exam Pattern

✓ Thoroughly Revised and Updated

✓ Detailed Analysis of all MCQs

Title	: RRB Junior Engineer Information Technology (IT) : CBT-1
Author Name	: Mr. Rohit Manglik
Published By	: EduGorilla Community Pvt. Ltd.
Publishers Address	: 12/651, First Floor Opp. Arvindo Park, Near Jama Masjid, Indira Nagar, Lucknow, Uttar Pradesh-226016, India

Copyright EduGorilla

Disclaimer EduGorilla

ROHIT MANGLIK
CEO, EduGorilla

Dear Applicants,

People say *"Success comes to those who work hard."* But I've seen people working hard for their exams day in and day out for marginal success. While others succeed in their examinations by putting in just half the work. So are they God Gifted? No! I believe that it's because they work *smart* and not just *hard*. Similarly, for your exams, you should strategize your preparation so as to increase the likelihood of success. Well with EduGorilla get ready to increase your *chances of selection* in your exam by *16x*.

EduGorilla helps you in not only working *hard* but also working in a *smart and strategic* manner. With EduGorilla's preparation package, you get a chance to make your exam preparation easy, and a fun learning path towards selection. Finding the right path to your preparations can be difficult if you don't know in which direction to head. Don't worry, we have you covered! EduGorilla will be your guide to success in your journey. With our Preparation Package, you can prepare strategically and beat the exam in just one attempt.

EduGorilla's Preparation Package includes-

• **Test Series**　　　　　• **Books**

Our preparation package is handcrafted as per the latest changes, expert opinions, and students' discretion. Thus, enabling you to get through each stage of the selection process for your exam.

Our Books are designed by the teachers and experts of the respective exam with a combined 150+ years of experience; to provide you with easy, efficient, and effective learning. Our books are smart, in the sense that not only do they give you the answers to the questions but also provide similar questions for practice.

EduGorilla's competent Test Series gives you real-time experience and confidence through which you can clear your offline or online exam in just one attempt. We currently host 83,000+ mock tests for 1,440+ competitive and academic exams.

Thus, EduGorilla misses no chance to assist you in your preparation and covers all stages of the exam, so that you don't have to look anywhere else.

We provide complete preparation packages for defense, banking, teaching, and other National & State-Level exams. Hence, it doesn't matter which exam you aspire to because you will reach your success.

ALL THE BEST !
Let EduGorilla be your Guide to Success.

Rohit Manglik,
Founder and CEO, EduGorilla

INTRODUCTION

EduGorilla focuses on guiding students to succeed in their examinations. With that in mind, our book, titled "RRB Junior Engineer : Information Technology (IT) : CBT-1", has been drafted through the collective efforts of our distinguished experts with 150+ years of combined experience. This book consists of questions that are created following the latest changes in the syllabus and exam pattern. We compiled the book on the basis of questions that are most likely to appear in the RRB JE IT (Information Technology). Through EduGorilla's "RRB Junior Engineer : Information Technology (IT) : CBT-1" your chances of success will increase 16x.

EduGorilla does this through our Complete Preparation Package. This package consists of well-conceptualized and structured content in the form of questions that are tailor-made according to your needs and will help you practice for exams in a smart way by pinpointing all the necessary information. It also provides hints and solutions, along with a smart answer sheet for your self-evaluation. You can assess your shortcomings and work accordingly on areas that may require more of your attention.

EduGorilla promises to help you succeed in your examination and accomplish your dream goals. We believe in our aspirants and see them at the top of the merit list. And the first step towards the top is to start preparing with us. EduGorilla's "RRB Junior Engineer : Information Technology (IT) : CBT-1" includes the following attributes.

➤ Well-Researched Content

➤ Top-Notch Quality

➤ Detailed Answers and Analysis

➤ Smart Answer Sheet

➤ Exam Relevant Questions

Therefore, EduGorilla fortifies your preparation and makes it durable enough to help you stand tall and beat the examination.

RRB JE IT (Information Technology)
Scan QR code for Eligibility, Exam Pattern, Syllabus and more.

Book ID: 0381

TABLE OF CONTENTS

Mock Test	1-248
Mock Test - 1	1-20
Mock Test - 2	21-38
Mock Test - 3	39-53
Mock Test - 4	54-70
Mock Test - 5	71-85
Mock Test - 6	86-102
Mock Test - 7	103-119
Mock Test - 8	120-134
Mock Test - 9	135-149
Mock Test - 10	150-165
Mock Test - 11	166-179
Mock Test - 12	180-194
Mock Test - 13	195-213
Mock Test - 14	214-231

Mathematics

Q.1 In a school, 1000 chocolates were distributed in such a way that each student gets chocolates equal to 10% of the total students. Find the number of chocolates that each student gets

A. 30 **B.** 60 **C.** 80 **D.** 10

Q.2 If the cost price of 12 pen is same as the selling price of 15 pen. What is the percentage of gain or loss?

A. 10% , loss **B.** 20%, loss **C.** 25% gain **D.** 20% gain

Q.3

The following table represents marks obtained by four students in five subjects and maximum marks of each subject.

Students	Maths (200)	Science (150)	Hindi (50)	English (100)	Computer (200)
Ankit	120	100	30	70	100
Vishal	150	120	35	75	120
Sushil	60	140	25	60	190
Sujal	180	80	40	90	150
Manav	160	90	45	100	160

Find the respective ratio of overall percentage of marks obtained by Ankit in all the five subjects and overall percentage of marks obtained by Sujal in all the five subjects

A. 4:5 **B.** 3:4 **C.** 7:9 **D.** 6:7

Q.4 Area of rhombus is $(7 + 6.5\sqrt{5})$ cm² and length of its one diagonal is $(3 + 2\sqrt{5})$ cm, then what is the length of its second diagonal?

A. $(8 + \sqrt{5})$ cm **B.** $(6 - 2\sqrt{5})$ cm
C. $(8 + 3\sqrt{5})$ cm **D.** $(8 - \sqrt{5})$ cm

Q.5 Solve the following expression: $(\sqrt[3]{42875} \div \sqrt{49}) + (15^2 - 21 \times 10) - \sqrt{625}$.

A. 0 **B.** -5 **C.** 5 **D.** -10

Q.6 A set of 7 pipes can fill 70% of a vessel in 7 minutes. Another set of 5 pipes can fill 2/5th of the vessel in 5 minutes. A third set of 10 pipes can empty 1/3rd of the tank in 10 minutes. How much time (in minutes) will it take to fill the entire tank if all the pipes are opened at the same time?

A. 75/13 **B.** 85/13 **C.** 75/11 **D.** 7

Q.7 What is the mass number of Gold?

A. 20 **B.** 108 **C.** 23 **D.** 197

Q.8 If an article is sold for a gain of 7% instead of selling it at a loss of 13%, a trader gets Rs.1080 more. What is the selling price of the article, when the article is sold at a profit of 25%?

A. Rs. 6750 **B.** Rs. 3600 **C.** Rs. 5400 **D.** Rs. 4500

Q.9 There are total 10 students whose marks in an exam are 45, 65, 56, (P + 16), (2P + 3), 78, 24, (4P - 8), 44 and 48 respectively and mean marks of first 5 students is 49, then what is mean marks of last 5 students?

A. 72.2 **B.** 53.2 **C.** 64.2 **D.** 48.2

Q.10 Select the odd one out: (6×10^{-3}), $\sqrt{[(5^2 + 11) \times 10^{-6}]}$, $(0.06 \div 10^2)$ and $\sqrt{0.000036}$.

A. (6×10^{-3}) **B.** $\sqrt{[(5^2 + 11) \times 10^{-6}]}$
C. $(0.06 \div 10^2)$ **D.** $\sqrt{0.000036}$

Q.11 There is a fraction such that if we add 11/30 to it then it gets reverted. Further if we subtract 1 from numerator then the fraction becomes 2/3. What is the fraction?

A. 13/18 **B.** 7/9 **C.** 5/6 **D.** 8/11

Q.12

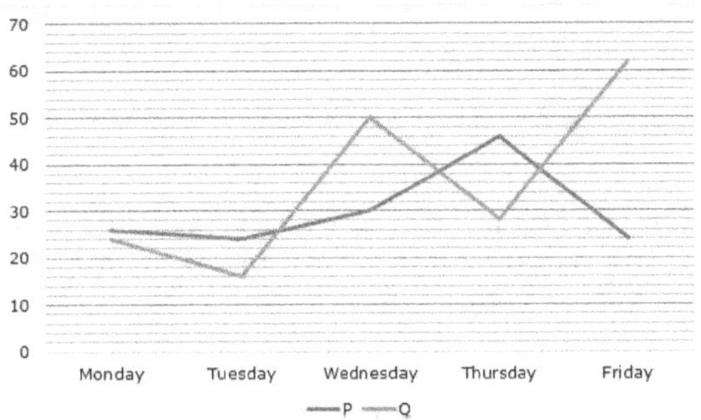

A. 2 **B.** 3 **C.** 1 **D.** 4

Q.13 Ramesh and Suresh invested same amount of money in two banks for 2 years which offer interest at the same rate, but Ramesh invested in a bank which offers compound interest and Suresh invested in a bank which offers simple interest. After two years Ramesh got Rs. 525 as interest and Suresh got Rs. 500 as interest. What is the rate of interest offered by the banks?

A. 12% **B.** 10% **C.** 5% **D.** 12.5%

Q.14 Line graph given below shows the total number of presence of employees in two different companies P and Q on five different working days from Monday to Friday.

What is the sum of the average number of presence of employees in company P and average number of presence of employees in company Q on all the five working days?

A. 66 **B.** 72 **C.** 58 **D.** 74

Q.15 If $[(0.09)^2 \times (0.3)^8 \times (0.027) \times 10^{12}]/[3^{12} \times (0.3)^x] = 1$, then what is the value of x?

A. 3 **B.** 4 **C.** 2 **D.** 1

Q.16 In one revolution, the object travels_____ distance.

A. $2\pi r$ **B.** $3\pi r$ **C.** $4\pi r$ **D.** πr

Q.17 Sita buys a parker pen at Rs. 100 and sell it to Geeta at Rs. 120. Geeta sells this pen to Radha at a price of Rs. 80. Radha sells it back to Sita at Rs. 90. Sita sells it to Roma at Rs. 150. What is Sita's profit/loss %?

A. 70% **B.** 50% **C.** 60% **D.** 80%

Q.18 Mahesh is travelling at a distance of 1200 km in Japan by Bullet train. Due to some technical fault in the engine of the train, speed of the train was reduced by 100 km/hr thus overall time of his journey increased by 24 minutes. What was the normal speed of the bullet train?

A. 400 km/hr   **B.** 500 km/hr
C. 600 km/hr   **D.** 450 km/hr

Q.19 If $4x - 1/3x = 9$, then what is the value of $(144x^4 - 1)/(27x^2 + 2x)$?

A. 9   **B.** 1   **C.** 27   **D.** 54

Q.20 What is the simplified value of $(\cos^3 x/\sin x) + (\cos^2 x.\cot^3 x)$?

A. $\cos^3 x$ **B.** $\sec^3 x$ **C.** $\cot^3 x$ **D.** $\tan^3 x$

Q.21 If 25% of (A+B) is 30% of (A-B), then B is what percent of A?

A. 100/11%   **B.** 100/9%   **C.** 99/121%   **D.** 101/9%

Q.22 What is the ∠SRO if O is the centre of circle, ∠SPO = 55⁰ and ∠POR = 115⁰

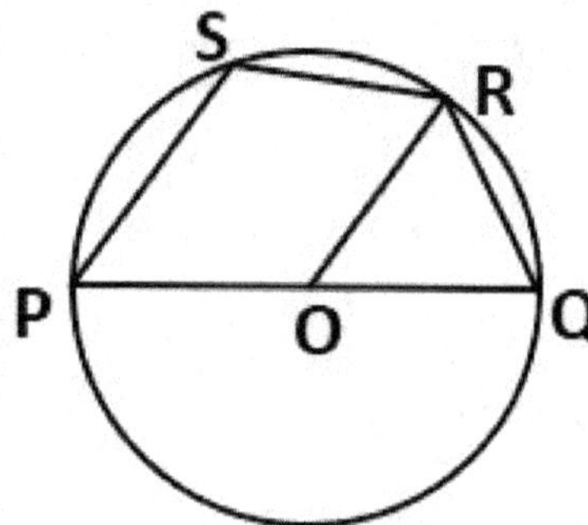

A. 57.5⁰   **B.** 62.5⁰   **C.** 67.5⁰   **D.** 72.5⁰

Q.23 A number 135 is split into three parts in such a way that all the three parts are in increasing Arithmetic Progression. The Product of the two largest parts is 2160, then what is the ratio of the smallest part to the highest part?

A. 8:9   **B.** 7:8   **C.** 6:7   **D.** 9:10

Q.24 Simplify the value of $3[\{1/(\sqrt{9} - \sqrt{8})\} - \{1/(\sqrt{9} + \sqrt{8})\}] + (2 - 3\sqrt{2})^2$.

A. 22   **B.** 24   **C.** 33   **D.** 36

Q.25 There are 7 students in a class whose weights are: 54 kg, 45 kg, 48 kg, A kg, 42 kg, 50 kg and 55 kg. If the mean of their weights is 49 kg, then what is the median of their weights?

A. 48 kg   **B.** 49 kg   **C.** 50 kg   **D.** 45 kg

Q.26 The LCM of two numbers is 2376 and their HCF is 22. Find their difference, if the sum of numbers is 682.

A. 516   **B.** 253   **C.** 506   **D.** 108

Q.27 60 liters of first mixture of milk and water is mixed with another 40 liters mixture of milk and water. After mixing the mixture, the mixture is sold at the cost of pure milk, then what is the percent profit gained if ratio of milk to water in first and second mixture is 7:5 and 3:5 respectively?

Given below are the steps involved. Arrange them in the sequential order.

A) Amount of milk and water in first mixture is 60 x (7/12) = 35 liters and 60 x (5/12) = 25 liters respectively.

B) Total amount of milk and water is final mixture is (35 + 15) = 50 liters and (25 + 25) = 50 liters respectively.

C) Percent profit earned = [(100 - 50)/50] x 100 = 100%

D) Amount of milk and water in second mixture is 40 x (3/8) = 15 liters and 40 x (5/8) = 25 litres respectively.

E) Cost price of final mixture = 50 x 1 = 50 and selling price of final mixture = 100 x 1 = 100

A. BADEC   **B.** ADBEC   **C.** ADCEB   **D.** ADECB

Q.28 If cosec θ = x + 1/4x, then the value of cosec θ + cot θ is:

A. -2x   **B.** 2x   **C.** 1/2x   **D.** −1/2x

Q.29 At present, the sum of ages of R and K is 63 years. The ratio of their ages after 7 years will be 7:4 , what is the present age of R ?

A. 40 years   **B.** 42 years   **C.** 29 years   **D.** 34 years

Q.30 If 5 girls can embroider a dress in 9 days, then the number of days taken by 3 girls will be ____.

A. 14 days   **B.** 10 days   **C.** 20 days   **D.** 15 days

General Intelligence & Reasoning

Q.31 Argument and which is a 'weak' argument and choose the corresponding option as your answer.

Should religion be taught in schools in a secular state?

I. No, because in a secular state, indoctrination of children would be wrongful.

II. Yes, religion helps in inculcating moral values in a child.

A. Only I is strong
B. Only II is strong
C. Both I and II are strong
D. Neither I nor II are strong

Q.32 Identify the diagram that best represents the relationship among the given classes.

Toys, plastic, wood

(1)

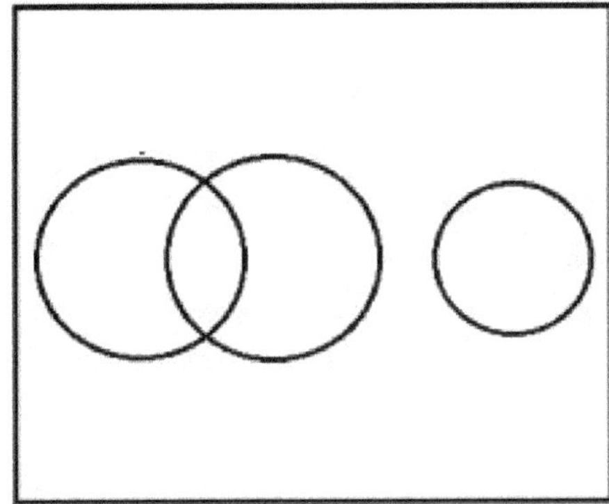

(2)

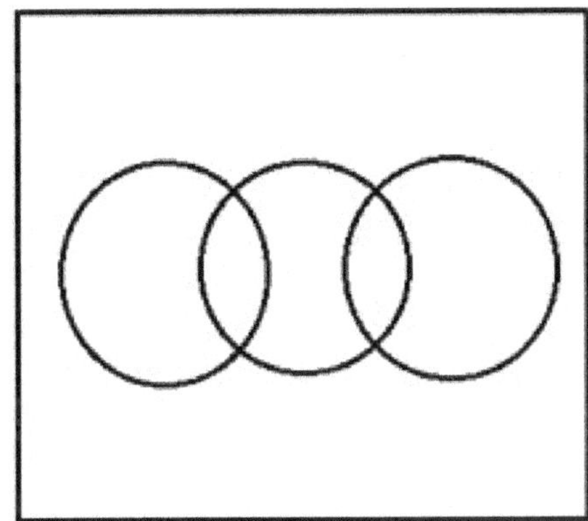

(3)

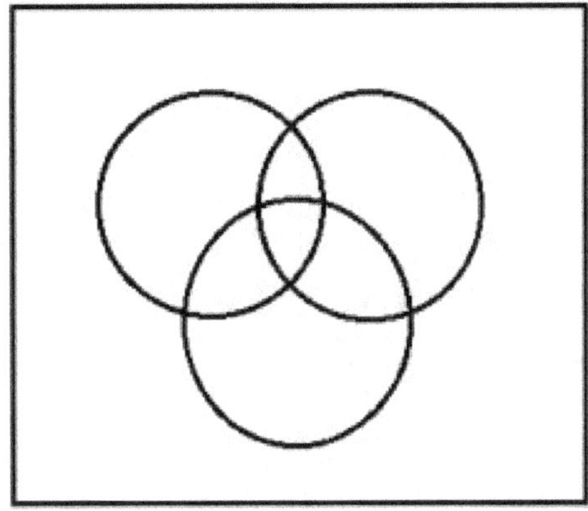

(4)

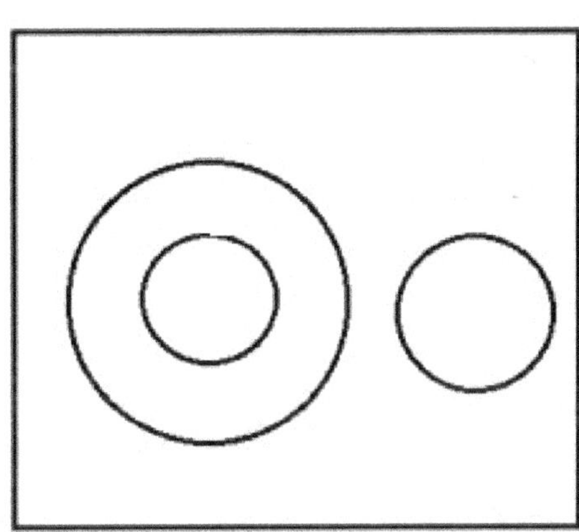

A. 1   **B.** 2   **C.** 3   **D.** 4

Q.33 Three years ago, the average age of a family of 5 members was 17 years. The current average age of the family is equal to the average age of the family 3 years ago, due to the birth of a child. What is the present age of the child?

A. 3 years   **B.** 1.5 years   **C.** 2 years   **D.** 2.5 years

Q.34 Seven people A, B, C, D, E, F, G were standing in a row according to their age in decreasing order such that the eldest person was standing in the front. Further it is known that G who was elder to F was standing adjacent to A. C was second youngest and was standing just behind E. F was not the youngest while D was standing at the front. A was not standing adjacent to D. How many people were standing between A and B?

A. 2   **B.** 3   **C.** 1   **D.** 4

Q.35 If AMPHIBIOUS is written as MAHPBIOISU then how will ANTIBIOTIC be written as?

A. NATIIBTOCI   **B.** NAITITBOCI

C. NIATIBTOCI   **D.** NAITIBTOCI

Q.36 Which of the following will be the mirror image of the given question figure, if a mirror is placed along the line MN.

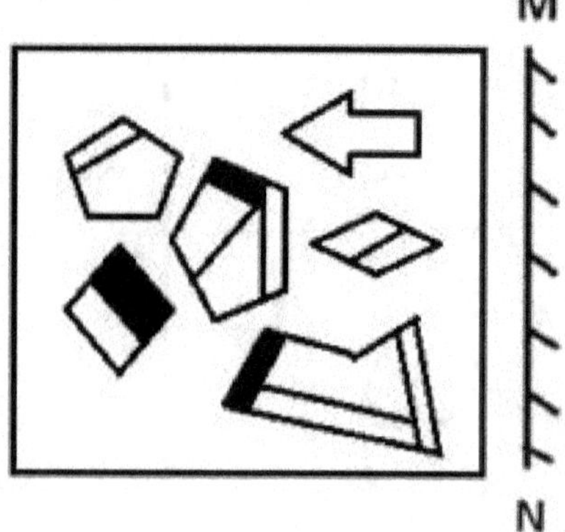

a)

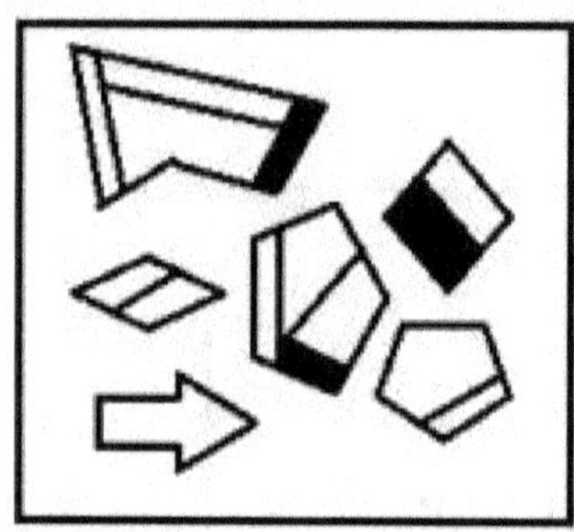

b)

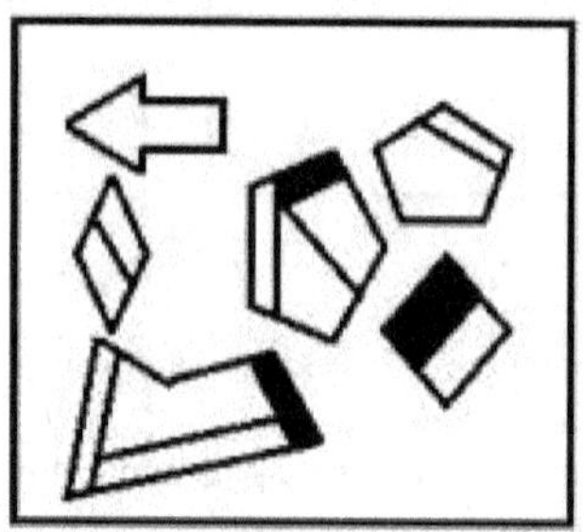

c)

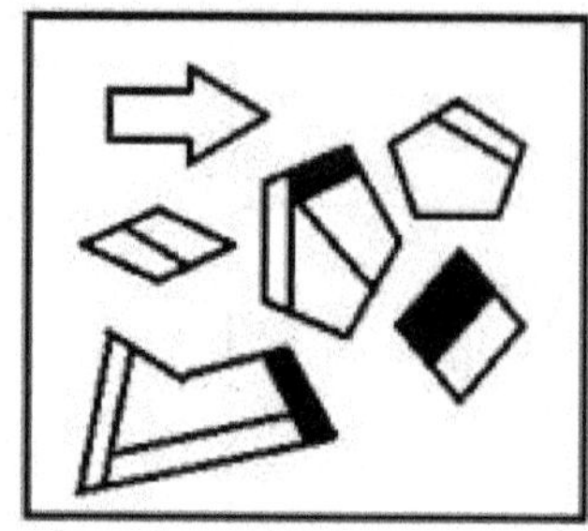

d)

A. a   **B.** b   **C.** c   **D.** d

Q.37 In each of the questions below, an assertion (a) is given, followed by a reason (R) which may or may not explain the assertion. From the given options, choose the right answer.

A: When we chew rice for a long time, it begins to taste sweet.

R: Ptyalin, an enzyme contained in saliva, breaks down starch into glucose.

A. Both A and R are true, and R is the correct explanation for A

B. Both A and R are true, but R is not the correct explanation for A

C. A is true, while R is false

D. A is false, while R is true

Q.38 A boy started walking straight for 5 kms. Then he took a right turn and walked for 2 kms. Then he again turned right and walked for 10 kms. Then he turned to his left and walked for 3 kms. It was the time for sunset and he observed that his shadow falls to his left. In which direction was he facing when he started walking from the starting point?

A. South   **B.** North   **C.** West   **D.** East

Q.39 A two digit number is 20% more than the number which is reverse of that number. What is the number?

A. 45   **B.** 54   **C.** 50   **D.** 36

Q.40 F is the brother of A. C is the daughter of A. K is the sister of F, G is the brother of C. who is the uncle of G ?

A. A   **B.** C   **C.** K   **D.** F

Q.41 Mark the correct option based on which statement/statements are sufficient to answer the question.

How many sisters does Ramya have?

I. Antara is the sister of Ramya and is the youngest in the family

II. Ramya who is Sita's sister, has two siblings

A. Both the statements are sufficient to answer the question

B. Only II is sufficient to answer the question

C. Only I is sufficient to answer the question

D. Both the statements together also are not sufficient to answer the question.

Q.42 In each of the questions below, two statements are given, followed by two conclusions. You have to consider the given statements as true, even if they are at variance from commonly known facts. From the given options, choose the one that provides the correct combination of conclusions that follow/ can be derived from the given statements.

Statement A: Vineyards flourish, and wine is made in all parts of the kingdom.

Statement B: But that wine which is imported so largely into England, is made only from the grapes grown on the steep hillsides, as they are the finest of the lot.

Conclusions:

I: Only the wine made from the finest grapes is imported largely into England from the kingdom.

II: Wine is made only from grapes grown on steep hillsides.

A. Only I   **B.** Only II

C. Both I and II   **D.** Neither I nor II

Q.43 Find the odd one.

A. 68 - 99   **B.** 73 - 104   **C.** 54 - 85   **D.** 63 - 84

Q.44 In each of the following questions, select a figure from amongst the four alternatives, which when placed in the blank space of figure (X) would complete the pattern.
Identify the figure that completes the pattern.

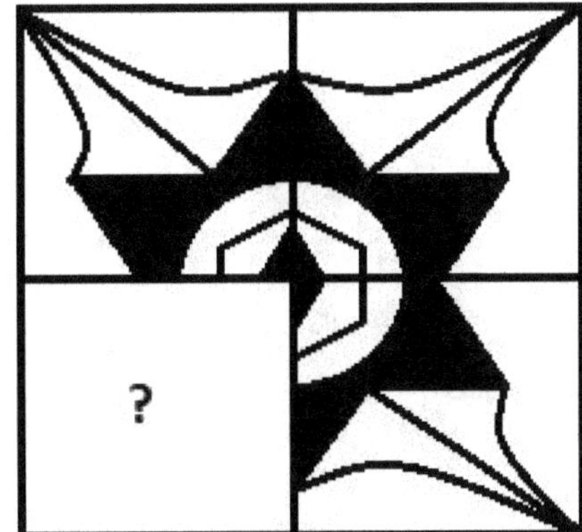

a)

b)

c)

d)

A. a   **B.** b   **C.** c   **D.** d

Q.45 In the following question, which one set of letters when sequentially placed at the gaps in the given letter series shall complete it?

b _ d e _ b c _ e f _ c _ _ f b _ d _ f

A. cfddebce   **B.** cfdbdece   **C.** cdfdebce   **D.** cedefbee

Q.46 A is the father of C and D is son of B. E is brother of A. If C is sister of D, how is B related to E?

A. Brother

B. Sister

C. Brother-in-law

D. Sister-in-law

Q.47 In the following question, four figures marked A, B, C and D, are given. Among these, three figures follow the same pattern and remaining one figure doesn't follow that pattern and hence, is odd. Mark the option which denotes the odd figure.

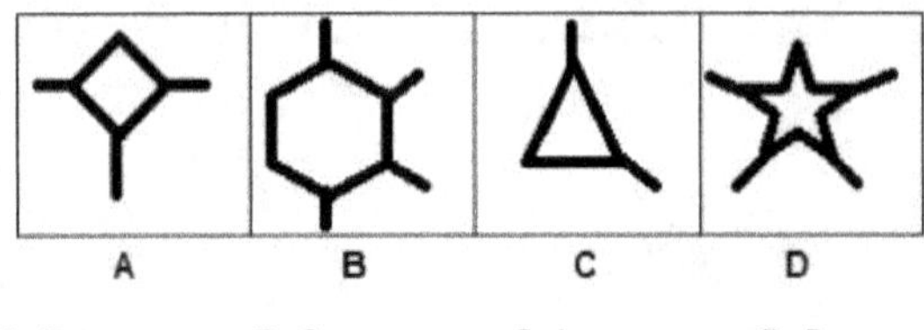

A. B   **B.** C   **C.** A   **D.** D

Q.48 In each of the questions below are given some statements followed by two conclusions numbered I and II. You have to take the given statements to be true even if they seem to be at variance from commonly known facts.

Read all the conclusions and then decide which of the given conclusions logically follows from the given statements disregarding commonly known facts.

Statements:

Some petals are corals.

No coral is a deal.

No petal is a steel.

Conclusions:

I. No deal is a coral.

II. Some deals are steels.

A. if only conclusion I follows.

B. if only conclusion II follows.

C. if neither conclusion I or II follows.

D. if both conclusions I and II follow.

Q.49 How many triangles are present in the given figure?

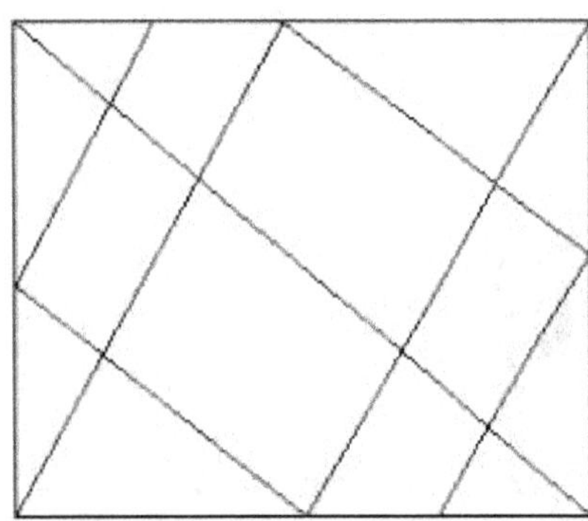

A. 15   **B.** 18   **C.** 22   **D.** 25

Q.50 Select the answer figure from the given alternatives, which can be formed by folding the given question figure?
Question Figure:

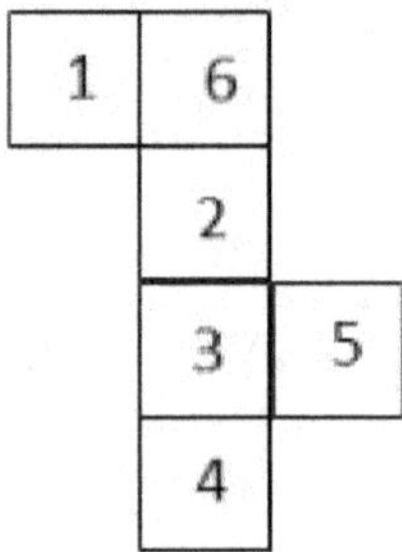

Answer Figure:

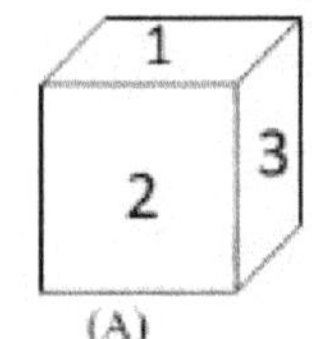

(A)

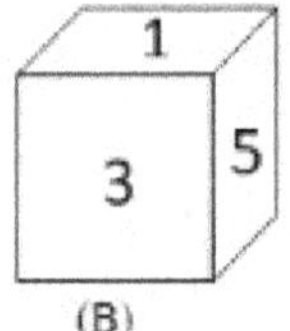

(B)

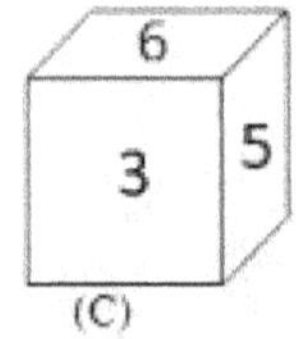

(C)

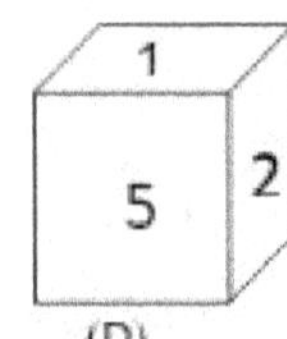

(D)

A. A   **B.** B   **C.** C   **D.** D

Q.51 A class consists of 180 students, 50 % passed in Maths, 10% students failed in Maths and English and 20% students passed in both Math's and English. Find the number of students passed only in English

A. 50   **B.** 60   **C.** 45   **D.** 72

Q.52

A piece of paper is folded and cut as shown in the figure.

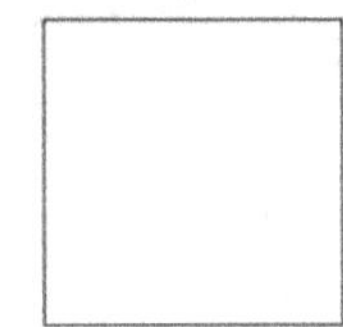 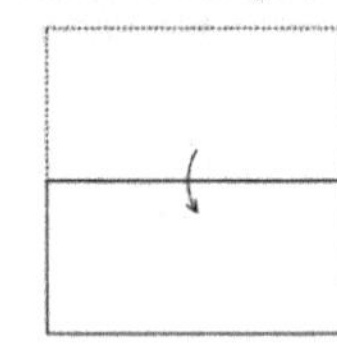 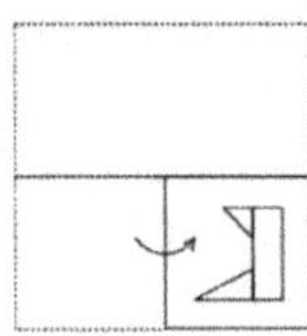

How will it appear when it is unfolded?

(A)

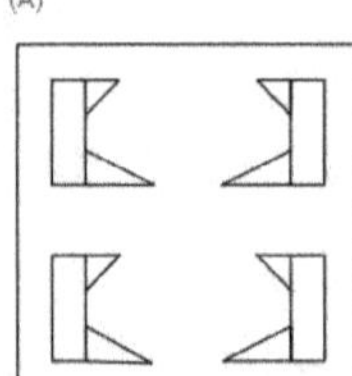

(B)

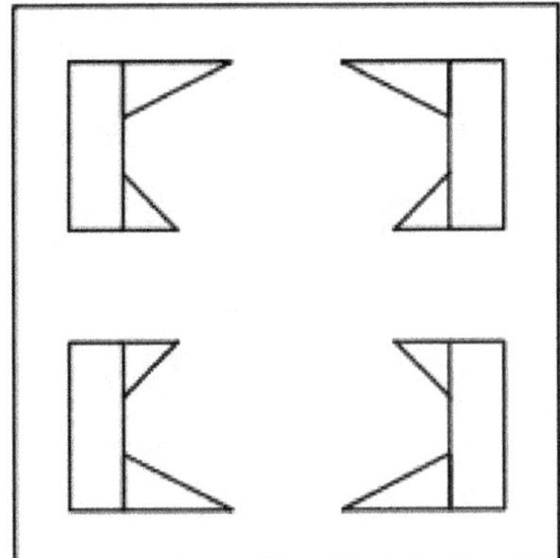

(C)

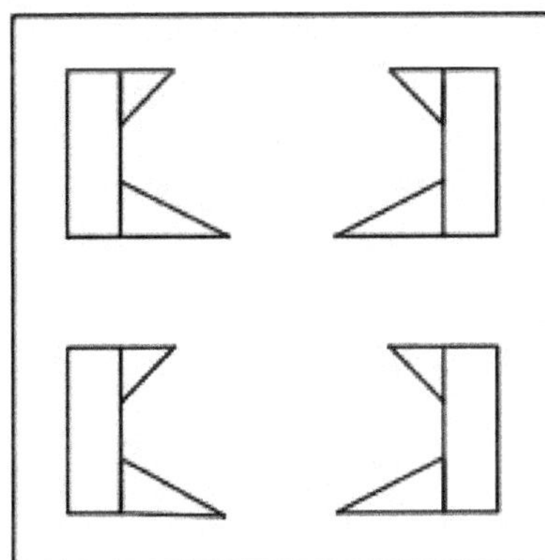

(D)

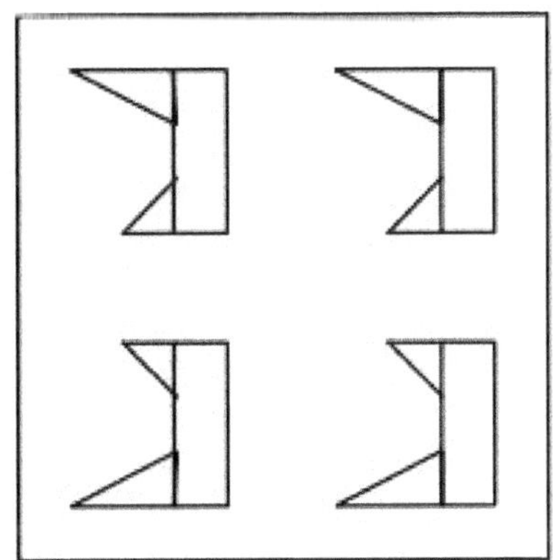

A. A   **B.** B   **C.** C   **D.** D

Q.53 The series is given, with one term missing. Choose amongst the given responses and complete the series.

AZP, CWR, ETT, GQV, __.

A. INX   **B.** JMY   **C.** ISX   **D.** JMX

Q.54 If A is directly proportional to square of B, B is inversely proportional to square of C and C is directly proportional to D, then what will be the change in value of A if value of D is increased by 200%?

A. (1/80) times.   **B.** (1/36) times.
C. (1/81) times.   **D.** 81 times.

Q.55 In each of the following questions, you are given a figure (X) followed by four alternative figures (a), (b), (c) and (d) such that figure (X) is embedded in one of them. Trace out the alternative figure which contains fig. (X) as its part.

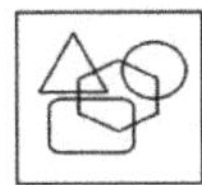 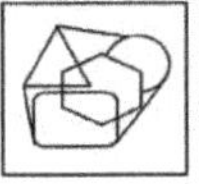 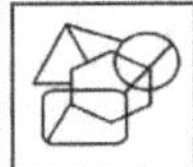 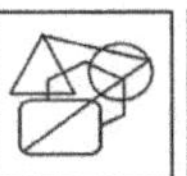 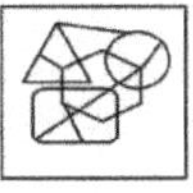

A. a   **B.** b   **C.** c   **D.** d

General Awareness

Q.56 All India Muslim league was set up in the year________.
A. 1906   **B.** 1909   **C.** 1919   **D.** 1927

Q.57 India's First Global Skills Park will be established in________.
A. Madya Pradesh   **B.** Gujarat
C. Uttarakhand   **D.** Bihar

Q.58 Which of the following countries, recently rolled out the world's first hydrogen-powered train.?
A. China   **B.** Japan
C. India   **D.** Germany

Q.59 What was the original name of Nur Jahan?
A. Zeb-un-Nisa   **B.** Fatima Begum
C. Mehr-un-Nisa   **D.** Jahanara

Q.60 How many schedules are there in Indian constitution?
A. 8   **B.** 9   **C.** 11   **D.** 12

Q.61 _________ five-year plan was based on the P.C Mahalanobis Model.
A. First   **B.** Second   **C.** Third   **D.** Sixth

Q.62 Wold Oceans day is observed every year on______.
A. June 8   **B.** May 3
C. April 7   **D.** March 22

Q.63 The 6th RCEP Trade Ministers Meeting took place in______
A. Singapore   **B.** New Delhi
C. Mumbai   **D.** Shanghai

Q.64 Who among the following discovered dynamite?
A. Max Plank   **B.** Alfred Nobel
C. Lee de forest   **D.** John Dalton

Q.65 _________ clinched the Davis cup, 2018 title.
A. France   **B.** Croatia
C. Serbia   **D.** Switzerland

Q.66 Kalinga cup is associated with the game of _________.
A. Hockey   **B.** Cricket
C. Football   **D.** Badminton

Q.67 Who among the following has been sworn in as new president of Brazil?

A. Juscelino Kubitschek
B. Pedro Aleixo
C. Jair Bolsonaro
D. Tancredo Neves

Q.68 Who among the following is an author of book 'War and Peace'?

A. Adam smith
B. Leo Tolstoy
C. John Milton
D. Charles Dickens

Q.69 In each of the questions below, two statements are given, followed by two assumptions on which the passage may or may not lie. From the options below, choose the one that reflects the correct choice of assumptions that follow.
Ramesh's teachers suspect that he is facing child abuse at home, since his grades have dropped significantly.
I. The home environment of a child has the capacity to affect a child's school grades.
II. Children who face child abuse often fare poorly in academics.

A. Only I
B. Only II
C. Both I and II
D. Neither I nor II

Q.70 _______ has been adjudged the most liveable city in 2018.
A. Vienna
B. Melbourne
C. Indore
D. Damascus

General Science

Q.71 Which of the following plant hormones plays main role in separation of leaves?

A. Florigens
B. Abscisic acid
C. Ethylene
D. Cytokinin

Q.72 What is the escape velocity for moon?
A. 2.4
B. 11.2
C. 3.6
D. 5.4

Q.73 Which of the following falls under the category of Abiotic components of environment ?
A. Birds
B. Plants
C. Sunlight
D. Fungi

Q.74 A car accelerates to a speed of 17 m/s over a distance of 25 m. The uniform acceleration of the car will be _______.
A. 3.66 m/s^2
B. 4.67 m/s^2
C. 5.78 m/s^2
D. 6.34 m/s^2

Q.75 What is the mass number of Gold ?
A. 20
B. 108
C. 23
D. 197

Q.76 Feldspar is an ore of _______.
A. Aluminium
B. Zinc
C. Copper
D. Lead

Q.77 _______ is a constituent of ear drop.
A. Oxalic acid
B. Boric acid
C. Formic acid
D. Carbonic acid

Q.78 _______ is not an example of monocotyledon plant.
A. Barley
B. Coconut
C. Onion
D. Cabbage

Q.79 Which of the following is often regarded as the purest form of carbon?
A. Graphite
B. Coke
C. Charcoal
D. Diamond

Q.80 Which is the second largest gland of Human body?
A. Liver
B. Large Intestine
C. Thorax
D. Pancreas

Q.81 _________ states that, properties of elements are a periodic function of their atomic weight.
A. Mendeleev's periodic law
B. Modern Periodic law
C. Newlands's law of octaves
D. None of the above

Q.82 _________ is the process in which a material changes from a frozen solid to a gas without passing through the intermediate liquid state.
A. Evaporation
B. Condensation
C. Sublimation
D. Decantation

Q.83 Which of the following statements in context of electromagnetic waves is/are not true?
A. They are neutral
B. They propagate as transverse wave
C. They propagate with velocity more than speed of light
D. X-ray is a type of electromagnetic wave

Q.84 Kelvin is an SI Unit of _______.
A. Temperature
B. Mass
C. Length
D. Luminous Intensity

Q.85 Which of the following is a water-soluble vitamin?
A. Vitamin B
B. Vitamin A
C. Vitamin D
D. Vitamin K

Q.86 One mole of oxygen atoms contains _________ oxygen atoms.
A. 6.023×10^{23}
B. 6.023×10^{20}
C. 6.023×10^{21}
D. 6.023×10^{27}

Q.87 A player serves a table tennis ball with a velocity of 25 m/s. If the ball has a mass of 300 g, what is the kinetic energy (KE) in Joule of the ball?
A. 77.55
B. 93.75
C. 88.35
D. 99.55

Q.88 One-watt hour is equivalent to_______ Joule.
A. 746
B. 3600
C. 6.67×10^{11}
D. 1800

Q.89 Momentum is the property of a moving body is defined as the product of mass & _______.
A. Velocity
B. Acceleration
C. Displacement
D. Time

Q.90 Hydraulic press & Hydraulic brake work on the principle of _______.
A. Snell's law
B. Pascal's law

C. Newton's First law of motion

D. Stefan's Law

Q.91 Oiled paper is an example of __________ material.

A. Translucent **B.** Transparent

C. Opaque **D.** None of the above

Q.92 Kepler's __________ law states that square of the period of any planet is proportional to the cube of the semimajor axis of its orbit.

A. First **B.** Second **C.** Third **D.** Fourth

Q.93 For a non-polar covalent compound, the value of electronegativity is _____.

A. Zero **B.** Infinite

C. One **D.** Greater than 1.7

Q.94 Chickenpox is caused by __________.

A. Orthomixovirus **B.** Rhino Virus

C. Varicella Virus **D.** Enterovirus

Q.95 A fog is an aerosol of _____ particles.

A. Solid **B.** Liquid

C. Gas **D.** None of the above

Q.96 __________ do not fall under the category of Metals.

A. Iron **B.** Copper

C. Phosphorus **D.** Zinc

Q.97 The longest cells in the human body are_____.

A. Fat cells **B.** Skin cells

C. Nerve cells **D.** Blood cells

Q.98 What is the scientific name of peacock?

A. Pavo cristatus **B.** Nelumbo nucifera

C. Orzya Sativa **D.** Panthera tigris

Q.99 What is the largest source of power in India?

A. Solar **B.** Wind **C.** Thermal **D.** Nuclear

Q.100 Speed of sound is the greatest in __________.

A. Water **B.** Air **C.** Glass **D.** Glycerin

// Smart Answer Sheet //

Correct Percentage of students who answered correctly. **Skipped** Percentage of students who skipped.

Q.	Ans.	Correct / Skipped
1	D	84.14 % / 15.04 %
2	B	81.12 % / 11.31 %
3	C	83.38 % / 13.71 %
4	D	88.3 % / 11.13 %
5	B	80.71 % / 18.37 %
6	C	87.69 % / 10.07 %
7	D	89.4 % / 10.3 %
8	A	84.71 % / 11.57 %
9	B	77.36 % / 16.45 %
10	C	86.43 % / 11.96 %
11	C	83.73 % / 12.84 %
12	C	87.64 % / 11.41 %
13	B	76.81 % / 13.62 %
14	A	79.45 % / 11.8 %
15	A	82.23 % / 10.65 %
16	A	79.15 % / 10.38 %
17	D	77.66 % / 18.11 %
18	C	81.37 % / 14.82 %
19	C	82.0 % / 13.45 %
20	C	80.51 % / 13.83 %
21	A	86.02 % / 11.03 %
22	C	88.21 % / 11.34 %
23	B	89.28 % / 10.28 %
24	A	86.14 % / 12.72 %
25	B	77.18 % / 12.21 %
26	C	79.08 % / 11.53 %
27	B	89.33 % / 10.27 %
28	B	79.08 % / 12.83 %
29	B	89.88 % / 10.09 %
30	D	78.31 % / 18.15 %
31	B	88.94 % / 10.09 %
32	B	88.44 % / 10.95 %
33	C	85.25 % / 11.97 %
34	B	77.39 % / 22.54 %
35	D	87.34 % / 10.49 %
36	C	88.2 % / 10.17 %
37	A	81.69 % / 14.88 %
38	D	78.47 % / 21.18 %
39	B	82.06 % / 16.87 %
40	D	88.25 % / 10.37 %
41	D	77.03 % / 15.71 %
42	A	89.9 % / 10.03 %
43	D	87.44 % / 11.01 %
44	B	83.9 % / 14.12 %
45	B	89.83 % / 10.1 %
46	D	89.03 % / 10.74 %
47	A	79.67 % / 12.71 %
48	A	79.1 % / 11.83 %
49	C	85.95 % / 13.09 %
50	A	80.48 % / 17.18 %
51	D	82.71 % / 13.4 %
52	B	77.29 % / 21.87 %
53	A	82.8 % / 10.22 %
54	C	88.92 % / 10.25 %
55	D	78.59 % / 18.81 %
56	A	85.06 % / 12.61 %
57	A	79.74 % / 10.42 %
58	D	86.82 % / 10.55 %
59	C	76.73 % / 13.28 %
60	D	79.07 % / 20.6 %
61	B	89.47 % / 10.06 %
62	A	88.91 % / 10.18 %
63	A	79.98 % / 16.55 %
64	B	82.43 % / 14.09 %
65	B	89.31 % / 10.55 %
66	C	77.59 % / 22.04 %
67	C	89.15 % / 10.24 %
68	B	83.46 % / 13.94 %
69	C	89.15 % / 10.71 %
70	A	77.21 % / 19.73 %
71	B	87.64 % / 11.23 %
72	A	83.53 % / 13.15 %
73	C	80.52 % / 16.08 %
74	C	81.02 % / 18.34 %
75	D	87.9 % / 12.08 %
76	A	76.01 % / 19.46 %
77	B	80.84 % / 15.91 %
78	D	83.58 % / 16.34 %
79	D	86.83 % / 12.81 %
80	D	86.12 % / 11.98 %

Q.	Ans.	Correct		Q.	Ans.	Correct		Q.	Ans.	Correct		Q.	Ans.	Correct		Q.	Ans.	Correct
		Skipped				Skipped				Skipped				Skipped				Skipped
81	A	77.41 %		85	A	84.48 %		89	A	80.74 %		93	A	76.75 %		97	C	85.1 %
		20.46 %				14.25 %				19.07 %				22.96 %				13.4 %
82	C	86.12 %		86	A	87.88 %		90	B	83.85 %		94	C	87.37 %		98	A	89.09 %
		10.28 %				10.61 %				11.4 %				11.34 %				10.09 %
83	C	88.12 %		87	B	82.66 %		91	A	78.16 %		95	B	76.38 %		99	C	86.38 %
		10.11 %				12.86 %				17.26 %				22.88 %				11.86 %
84	A	82.42 %		88	B	86.92 %		92	C	89.2 %		96	C	84.07 %		100	C	80.48 %
		11.15 %				10.05 %				10.2 %				11.09 %				13.06 %

//Hints and Solutions//

1. Let the number of students = s

10 x s x s/100 = 1000

$s^2 = 10,000$

s = 100

Each student got 10x100/100

=> 10 chocolates

2.

CP of 12 pen= SP of 15 pen

CP X 12 = SP X 15

$\Rightarrow \frac{CP}{SP} = \frac{5}{4} \ldots \ldots (1)$

From equation (1) we can see that CP > SP , therefore there will be loss.

Let the CP = 5 and SP = 4

Then Loss = 1

$Loss\% = \frac{Loss}{CP} \times 100$

$= \frac{1}{5} \times 100$

= 20% loss

3. Total marks in all subjects = 200 + 150 + 50 + 100 + 200 = 700

Overall percentage of marks obtained by Ankit in all the five subjects

= (120 + 100 + 30 + 70 + 100)/700 x 100

= 420/700 x 100

= 60%

Overall percentage of marks obtained by Sujal in all the five subjects

= (180 + 80 + 40 + 90 + 150)/700 x 100

= 540/700 x 100

= 540/7%

Required ratio = 60 : 540/7

= 420 : 540

= 7:9

4. Area of rhombus = (First diagonal x Second diagonal) / 2

2 x Area of rhombus = (First diagonal x Second diagonal)

Let its second diagonal = (a + b√5) cm

(14 + 13√5) = (3 + 2√5) x (a + b√5)

(14 + 13√5) = (3a + 3b√5 + 2a√5 + 10b)

After comparing-

(3a + 10b) = 14 ...... (1)

(2a + 3b) = 13 .... (2)

From (1) and (2)-

a = 8 and b = -1

Length of second diagonal = (a + b√5) = (8 - √5) cm

5. = ($\sqrt[3]{42875} \div \sqrt{49}$) + ($15^2$ - 21 x 10) - $\sqrt{625}$

= (35 ÷ 7) + (225 - 210) - 25

= 5 + 15 - 25

= -5

6. 7 pipes of first set can fill $7/10^{th}$ of the vessel in 7 minutes.

Hence, 7 pipes of first set can fill $1/10^{th}$ of the vessel in 1 min.

5 pipes of second set can fill $2/5^{th}$ of the vessel in 5 minutes

Hence, 5 pipes of second set can fill $2/25^{th}$ of the vessel in 1 min.

10 pipes of third set can empty $1/3^{rd}$ of the vessel in 10 minutes.

Hence, 10 pipes of third set can empty $1/30^{th}$ of the vessel in 1 min

So, if all the pipes are open in one minute 1/10 + 2/25 - 1/30 = $11/75^{th}$ of the vessel is filled up.

Hence, to fill up the whole vessel, time required= 75/11 minutes.

7. The mass number of Gold is 197. Mass number is the sum of the numbers of protons and neutrons present in the nucleus of an atom.

Mass numbers of some common elements-

Neon- 20

Sodium- 23

Silver- 108

8.

Let cost price of article be Rs x

(13 + 7)% of x = 1080

20% of x = 1080

x = 5400

SP = 125% of 5400 = 6750

9. Mean marks of first 5 students = [45 + 65 + 56 + (P + 16) + (2P + 3)]/5 = 49

185 + 3P = 245

3P = 60

P = 20

Mean marks of first 5 students = [78 + 24 + (4P - 8) + 44 + 48]/5 = (186 + 4P)/5 = 266/5

= 53.2

10. (6 x 10^{-3}) = 0.006

$\sqrt{[(5^2 + 11) \times 10^{-6}]}$ = 6 x 10^{-3} = 0.006

(0.06 ÷ 10^2) = 0.0006

$\sqrt{0.000036}$ = 0.006

11. Let the fraction = m/n

According to the 1st condition; m/n + 11/30= n/m ...(1)

According to the 2nd condition; (m-1)/n=2/3

=> 3m - 3 = 2n

=>3m - 2n = 3 ...(2)

By solving equation 1,

=> $30m^2 + 11mn - 30n^2 = 0$

=> (6m-5n)(5m+6n)=0

we get the value of m/n = 5/6,-6/5

applying condition(2),

m/n = (5-1)/6 = 4/6 = 2/3

Hence the required fraction = m/n = 5/6

12.

$\sqrt[3]{(3^5 * 24)} = \sqrt[3]{(3^5 * 3 * 2^3)} = 3^2 * 2 = 18$ = (Rational)

$\sqrt{[12^3 - (2^6 * 11)]} = \sqrt{[1728 - 704]} = \sqrt{1024} = 32$ = (Rational)

$\sqrt[5]{\dfrac{10^3}{10.24}} = \sqrt[5]{\dfrac{10^5}{1024}} = \sqrt[5]{\dfrac{10^5}{4^5}}$ = 10/4 = 5/2 = (Rational)

$\sqrt[3]{(13.31 \div 10)} = \sqrt[3]{1.331} = 1.1 = 11/10$ = (Rational)

13. In case of simple interest we get the same amount of interest each year.

Hence amount of interest Suresh will get in first year = 500/2 = Rs. 250

If the same amount is invested and interest rate is same then in first year the interest obtained is same whether it is simple interest or compound interest.

Hence compound Interest obtained in 1st year = Rs. 250

Therefore amount of interest obtained in the 2nd year = Rs. (525 - 250) = Rs. 275

Hence rate of interest = 100 x (275 - 250)/250 = 10%

14. Average number of presence of employees in company P on all the five working days = 26 + 24 + 30 + 46 + 24 = 150

Average = 150/5 = 30

Average number of presence of employees in company Q on all the five working days = 24 + 16 + 50 + 28 + 62 = 180

Average = 180/5 = 36

Required sum = 30 + 36 = 66

15. $[(0.09)^2 \times (0.3)^8 \times (0.027) \times 10^{12}]/[3^{12} \times (0.3)^x] = 1$

$[(0.09)^2 \times (0.3)^8 \times (0.027) \times 10^{12}] = [3^{12} \times (0.3)^x]$

$[(0.3)^4 \times (0.3)^8 \times (0.3)^3] = [(0.3)^{12} \times (0.3)^x]$

$(0.3)^{15}/(0.3)^{12} = (0.3)^x$

$(0.3)^3 = (0.3)^x$

x = 3

16. In one revolution, the object travels 2πr distance. Revolution means a circular motion around an axis, located outside the object. For e.g. Rounding a curve in a car, merry go round etc.

17. C.P. of pen for Sita = Rs 100

S.P. of pen for Sita = Rs 150-90+120 = 180

Profit % = [(180-100)/100] x 100 = 80%

18. Let the normal speed of the bullet train is N km/hr and the corresponding time taken is A hours.

Hence; 1200/N = A .. (1)

According to the 2nd condition; 1200/(N-100) = A + 2/5 .. (2)

Equation (2) - Equation (1); 1200/(N-100)-1200/N=2/5

If we will try to solve this equation then it will become too lengthy. Hence such questions we should solve by using the options.

Out of the given options, option (c) satisfies above equation.

Hence; N = 600 km/hr

19. $(12x^2 - 1)/3x = 9$

=> $(12x^2 - 1)/3x = 9$

=> $12x^2 - 1 = 27x$ ------- (i)

Now,

$(144x^4 - 1)/(27x^2 +2x)$

= $[(12x^2 - 1)(12x^2 + 1)]/[x(27x + 2)]$ ------- $[(a^2 - b^2 = (a - b)(a + b)]$

= $[27x(27x -1 + 1 +1)]/[x(27x + 2)]$ ---- {Putting the value of equation (i)]

= $[27x(27x + 2)]/[x(27x + 2)]$

= 27

20. $\cos^3 x/\sin x + \cos^2 x \cot^3 x$

= $(\cos^3 x/\sin^3 x) \sin^2 x + \cos^2 x \cot^3 x$

= $\cot^3 x \sin^2 x + \cos^2 x \cot^3 x$

= $\cot^3 x (\sin^2 x + \cos^2 x)$

= $\cot^3 x$

21. => 25/100(A+B) = 30/100(A-B)

=> 5A+5B= 6A-6B

=> A= 11B

=> Let p% of B is equal to A

=> p/100 x B= A

=> But B= 11A

22.

In quadrilateral PQRS, $\angle SRQ = 180^0 - \angle SPQ = 180^0 - 55^0 = 125^0$ [Sum of opposite angle of a cyclic quadrilateral is 180^0]

$\angle ROQ = 180^0 - \angle POR = 180^0 - 115^0 = 65^0$

In $\triangle QOR$, $\angle OQR = \angle ORQ$ [Angles opposite of same side]

$\angle ROQ + \angle OQR + \angle ORQ = 180^0$

$65^0 + \angle ORQ + \angle ORQ = 180^0$

$\angle ORQ = (180^0 - 65^0)/2 = 57.5^0$

$\angle SRO = \angle SRQ - \angle ORQ = 125^0 - 57.5^0 = 67.5^0$

23. Let the three numbers are: (a - d), a, (a + d) respectively.

According to questions-

a(a + d) = 2160 ...... (1)

(a - d) + a + (a + d) = 135

a = 45

From equation (1)-

45(45 + d) = 2160

(45 + d) = 48

d = 3

Required ratio = (a - d):(a + d) = 42:48 = 7:8

24. $= 3[\{1/(\sqrt{9} - \sqrt{8})\} - \{1/(\sqrt{9} + \sqrt{8})\}] + (2 - 3\sqrt{2})^2$

$= 3[\{(\sqrt{9} + \sqrt{8}) - (\sqrt{9} - \sqrt{8})\}/(\sqrt{9} - \sqrt{8})(\sqrt{9} + \sqrt{8})] + (2 - 3\sqrt{2})^2$

$= 3[2\sqrt{8}] + (2 - 3\sqrt{2})^2$

$= 6\sqrt{8} + (4 + 18 - 12\sqrt{2})$

$= 12\sqrt{2} + (22 - 12\sqrt{2})$

$= 22$

25. Mean of their weights = (54 + 45 + 48 + A + 42 + 50 + 55)/7 = 49

294 + A = 343

A = 49 kg

Arrange the weights in ascending order = 42, 45, 48, 49, 50, 54, 55

Median of their weights = 4th term in series = 49 kg

26. Let the number be 22x and 22y

22x + 22y = 682

x + y = 31 → (1)

22x x 22y = 2376 x 22

xy = 108 → (2)

Solving (1) and (2), we get

x = 27 and y = 4

Difference = 22x - 22y

= 22(27 - 4)

= 22 x 23

= 506

27. The correct arrangement is:

A) Amount of milk and water in first mixture is 60 x (7/12) = 35 litres and 60 x (5/12) = 25 liters respectively.

D) Amount of milk and water in second mixture is 40 x (3/8) = 15 liters and 40 x (5/8) = 25 liters respectively.

B) Total amount of milk and water is final mixture is (35 + 15) = 50 litres and (25 + 25) = 50 liters respectively.

E) Cost price of final mixture = 50 x 1 = 50 and selling price of final mixture = 100 x 1 = 100

C) Per cent profit earned = [(100 - 50)/50] x 100 = 100%

28. Let $\csc \theta + \cot \theta = k$

$\Rightarrow \csc \theta - \cot \theta = 1/k$

On adding, we get

$2 \csc \theta = k + 1/k = 2(x+1/4x) = k+1/k$

$\Rightarrow x+1/2x = k+1/k \Rightarrow k=2x$

29. Let the present age of R is x

$\Rightarrow$ present age of K is 63-x

7 years later

R's age = x + 7

K's age = 63-x+7= 70-x

$\Rightarrow$ (x+7)/(70-x) = 7/4

$\Rightarrow$ 4x+28= 490-7x

$\Rightarrow$ 11x= 462

$\Rightarrow$ x = 42 years

therefore present age of R= 42 years

30. Days taken by 5 girls to embroider a dress = 9 days

Days taken by 1 girl to embroider a dress = 9 x 5 days

Days taken by 3 girls to embroider a dress = 9×5/3 days = 15 days

31. I is a weak argument as it is taking about indoctrination of children. In a secular state, all religions are given equal status, and choosing to teach or learn any religion should be allowed. 'Indoctrination' is a strong word to be used to define teaching of a religion. II is a strong argument, as it gives a benefit of teaching religion. B is the right answer.

32. Some toys are of wood and some toys are of plastic. No plastic is wood

33. Total age of the family 3 years ago = 17 x 5 = 85 years
Total age of the family now = 17 x 6 = 102 years
Total age of the family excluding the child now = 85 + 15 = 100 years
Age of the child = 2 years

34. D was standing at the front, so D was the eldest. C was second youngest and was standing just behind E, so E was third youngest.
D > __ >__>__> E > C> __
Now G was elder to F and adjacent to A. Also A was not seated

adjacent to D.
D > G > A > ___ >E > C >___
Since F was not the youngest. Hence
D > G > A > F > E > C > B.
So three people were seated between A and B.

35. The word is divided into 5 groups of 2 letters. The letters in each group is written in the reverse order. Thus, ANTIBIOTIC will be written as NAITIBTOCI

36.

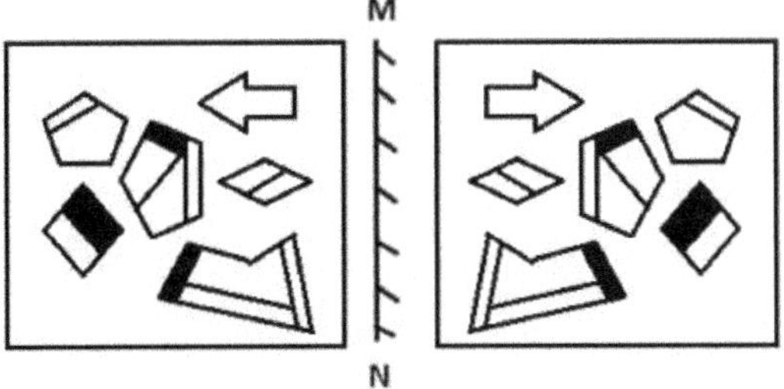

37. R is the correct reason for A, as this enzyme breaks down starch, which is contained in rice, into glucose which leads to its sweet taste. (A) is the right answer.

38.
At sunset, the shadow falls to the east. We have the path traversed by the boy as:

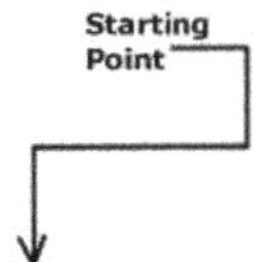

39. Let the number be 10a+b
The reverse number is 10b+a
10a+b= (10b+a) [1+(20/100)]
10a+b= (10b+a) [6/5]
50a+5b= 60b+6a
44a= 55b
4a= 5b
a/b = 5/4
Hence the number is 10a+b = 10x5+4 = 54

40.

$$K(-) — F(+) — A$$
$$C(-) — G(+)$$

(+) = Male
(-) = Female

41.
From I,

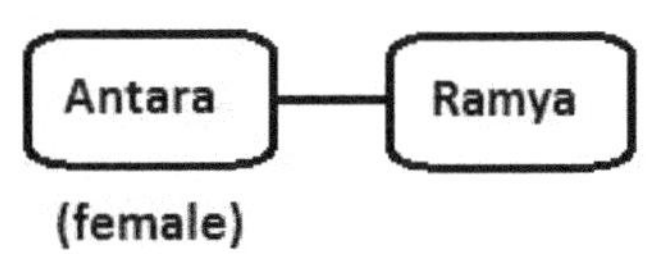

So statement I only is not sufficient to answer the question.

From II,

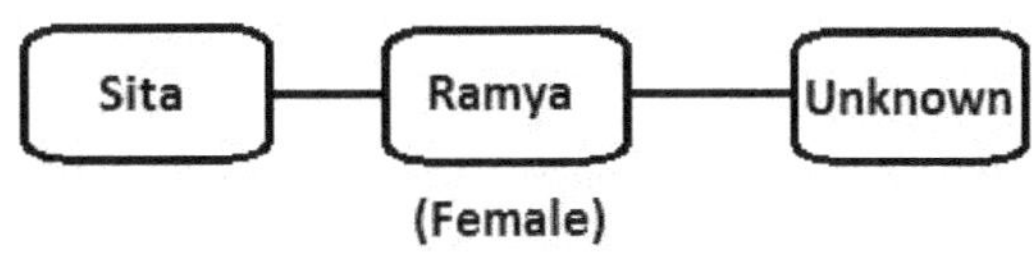

So statement II only is not sufficient to answer the question.

From I and II,

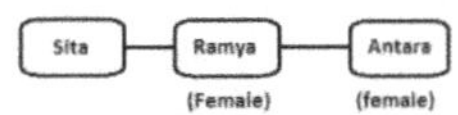

So we cannot answer how many sisters Ramya has because we do not know the gender of Sita.
Please note in reasoning questions one cannot assume the genders of person even if they have names that are very commonly used for a male or female.
So, option d is the correct answer.

42. Statement B mentions that the grapes grown on steep hillsides are the finest of the lot, which is why they are used to make the wine which is imported into England. So, this confirms I. II is incorrect, as the statements together imply that wine is made in all parts of the kingdom, not only on steep hillsides. A is the right answer, as only I follows.

43. 68 + 31 = 99

73 + 31 = 104

54 + 31 = 85

63 + 21 = 84

44.

45. b c d e f / b c d e f / b c d e f / b c d e f

46.

We get the following family tree:

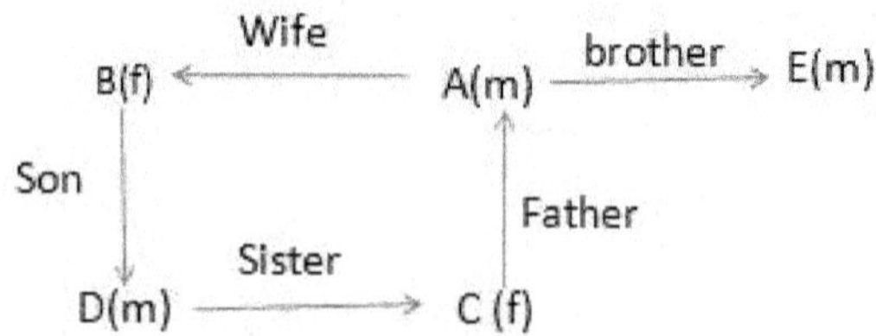

Clearly B is the sister - in - law of E.

47. Figure B is odd as, rest others have number of lines which drawn from the vertices are one less than the number of vertices of respective diagram. Figure B have 6 vertices with 4 lines drawn from the vertices.

48.

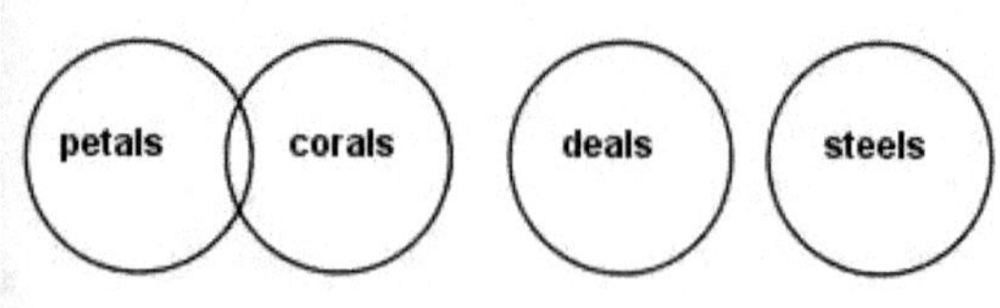

Conclusion I follows

49.

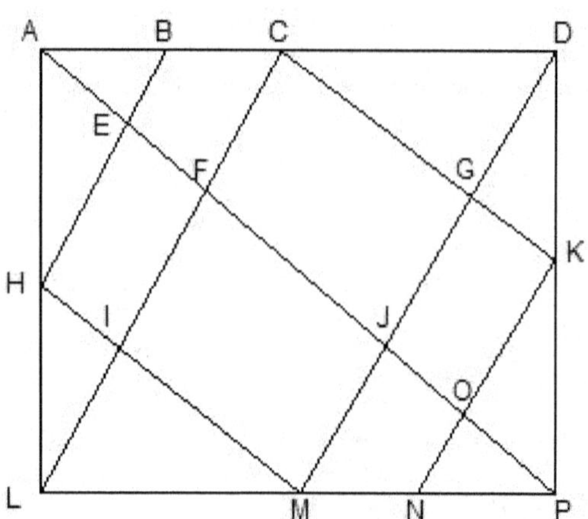

On one side of diagonal AP triangles are- ABE, ACF, ADJ, ADP, CDG, CDK, DGK, DJP, KOP = 9 triangles

So, on both sides = 2x9= 18 triangles.

But, apart from these 18, we have-

ABH, ACL, PNK, PMD = 4 triangles.

Thus, we have total triangles = 18+4= 22 triangles in the given figure.

50.

After folding the figure:

6 lies opposite 3.

2 lies opposite 4.

1 lies opposite 5.

1 and 5 cannot be on the adjacent faces.

6 and 3 cannot be on the adjacent faces.

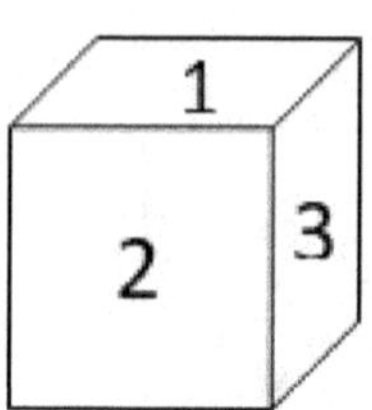

51. Total students = 180

Failed in both = 10% of 180

=> 18

=> Passed in both = 20% of 180

=> 36

=> Passed in maths = 50% 0f 180

=> 90

=> Passed only in math = 90-36

=> 54

=> Passed only in English = 180 - (54 + 36 + 18)

=> 72

52.

After 1st unfolding:

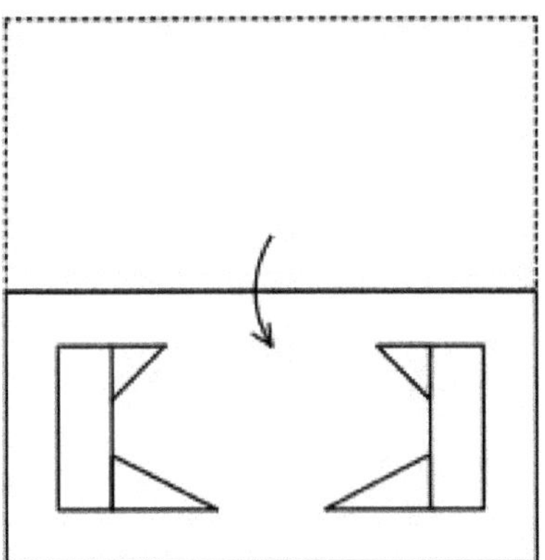

After 2nd unfolding:

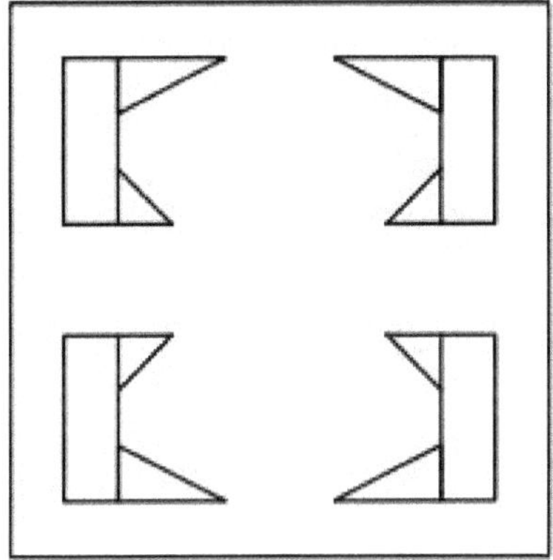

So, option 2 is the correct answer.

53. 1st letter of each term is shown by a line from A to F.

2nd letter of each term is shown by a line from Z to N.

3rd letter of each term shown by dotted line from P to X.

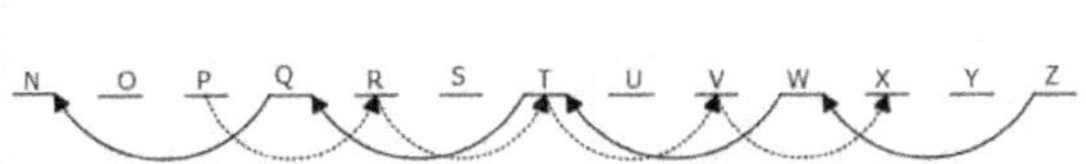

So, INX is the correct answer.

54. As per given information in the question

C is directly proportional to D

D increases by 200% so it becomes 3 times

So, C becomes 3 times.

B is directly proportional $(1/C^2) = 1/9$

B becomes (1/9) times

A is directly proportional $B^2 = (1/9)^2 = (1/81)$ times

A becomes (1/81) times.

55.

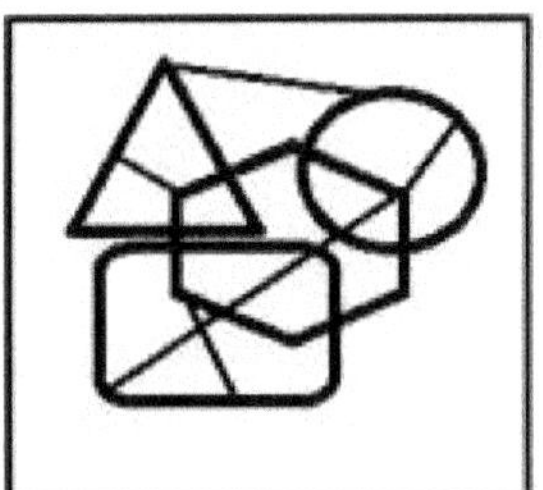

56.

All India Muslim league was set up in the year **1906** at Dhaka.

Founders of All India Muslim League- Khwaja Salimullah, Vikar-ul-Mulk, Syed Amir Ali, Syed Nabiullah.

Events	Year
1909	Morley Minto reforms
1919	Jallianwala Bagh Massacre
1927	Simon Commission

57. Asian Development Bank (ADB) and Government of India signed a $150 million loan agreement to establish a Global Skills Park (GSP) in Madhya Pradesh i.e. first Multi-Skills Park in India, to enhance the quality of technical and vocational education.

58. Germany rolled out the world's first hydrogen-powered train. It uses fuel cells that produce electricity through a combination of hydrogen and oxygen, leaving behind water and steam. It is built by French TGV-maker Alstom.

59. Noor Jehan (1577-1645) was an empress who belonged to the great Mughal Dynasty. Noor Jehan was the favourite wife of the Mughal Emperor Jahangir. Her real name was Mehr-un-Nisa.

60. There are twelve schedules in Indian constitution. Schedules are lists in the constitution which categorise and tabulate bureaucratic activity and government policy. It is an appendix or annexure highlighting lists or details mentioned in its main text.

61. Second Five-year plan was based on the P.C Mahalanobis Model.

The second Five Year Plan centered on a shift towards developing capital goods and heavy industry for long-term economic benefit. During that period, agriculture spending fell from 37 percent of public spending to 20.9 percent, while industry allocation increased from 4.9 to 24.1 percent.

62.

Wold Oceans day is observed every year on 8th of June.

Date	Day observed
May 3	World press freedom day
April 7	World health day
March 22	World Water day

63. The 6th RCEP Trade Ministers' Meeting took place in Singapore. It consists of 10 ASEAN countries and six ASEAN FTA partners namely, India, China, Japan, Korea, Australia and New Zealand. RCEP-Regional Comprehensive Economic Partnership. Suresh prabhu represented India.

64.

The dynamite was discovered by **Alfred Nobel.**

Discovery	Scientist
Quantum Theory	Max Plank
Triode Bulb	Lee de Forest
Atom	John Dalton

65. Marin Cilic clinched Croatia's second Davis Cup title beating France's Lucas Pouille. The 2018 Davis Cup was the 107th edition of the Davis Cup, a tournament between national teams in men's tennis. Croatia clinched the title 13 years after the first title.

66. Kalinga cup is associated with the game of Football.

Duleep trophy- Cricket

Aga Khan Cup- Hockey

Badminton- Uber Cup

67. Jair Bolsonaro has been sworn in as new president of Brazil, after a controversial, polarizing campaign to radically change the center-left path taken by Latin America's biggest country over the last 15 years.

68. The book 'War and Peace' has been written by Leo Tolstoy.

Book - Author

Wealth of Nations - Adam Smith

Paradise Lost - John Milton

Oliver Twist - Charles Dickens

69. I follows as only if I is assumed, can Ramesh's teachers' suspicion hold true and have substance. II also follows, as if true, then the teachers' suspicion can be said to be valid. C is the right answer.

70. According to Economist Intelligence Unit's Global Liveability Index, Vienna has been adjudged the most liveable city in 2018 followed by Melbourne. Damascus retained last place, followed by the Bangladeshi capital Dhaka.

71. Abscisic acid plays main role in separation of leaves.
Florigens - blooming of flowers
Ethylene - Ripening of fruits
Cytokinin - Cell division

72. Escape velocity for moon is 2.4 Km/s. For earth it is around 11.2 Km/s. Escape velocity is the speed that an object needs to be traveling to break free of a planet or moon's gravity well and leave it without further propulsion.

73. Sunlight is an example of Abiotic component.
Abiotic factors refer to non-living physical and chemical elements in the ecosystem.
Biotic factors are living or once-living organisms in the ecosystem.

74. v_i = 0 m/s, v_f = 17 m/s

S= 25 m

$v_f^2 = v_i^2 + 2as$

$(17)^2 = (0)^2 + 2(a)(25 \text{ m})$

$289 = 0 + (50)a$

$289 = (50)a$

$a = 289/50$

$a = 5.78 \text{ m/sec}^2$

75. The mass number of Gold is 197. Mass number is the sum of the numbers of protons and neutrons present in the nucleus of an atom.
Mass numbers of some common elements-
Neon- 20
Sodium- 23
Silver- 108

76.

Feldspar is an ore of **Aluminium.**

Metal	Ore
Zinc	Zinc Blende
Copper	Copper glance
Lead	Galena

77.

Boric acid is a constituent of ear drop.

Acid	Use/Found in
Oxalic acid	Tomato
Carbonic acid	Aerated drinks
Formic acid	Red ants
Acetic acid	Vinegar

78. Cabbage is not an example of monocotyledon plant it is a dicotyledon. The Dicotyledons have two lateral cotyledons in each seed while Monocotyledon have one cotyledon, with a terminal position.

79. Diamond is often regarded as the purest form of carbon. In its purest form diamond is colourless, lustrous, Crystalline solid, It is a bad conductor of heat and electricity because it lacks free electrons. It also has a very high melting point.

80. After liver the second largest gland is Pancreas

81. Mendeleev's periodic law states that properties of elements are a periodic function of their atomic weight. Modern periodic law-The physical and chemical properties of elements are periodic functions of their atomic number. Newlands's law of octaves-if the chemical elements are arranged according to

increasing atomic weight, those with similar physical and chemical properties occur after each interval of seven elements.

82. Sublimation is the process in which a material changes from a frozen solid to a gas without passing through the intermediate liquid state.

Condensation is the process by which water vapor in the air is changed into liquid water.

Evaporation is the process by which water changes from a liquid to a gas or vapor.

Decantation is a process to separate mixtures by removing a liquid layer that is free of a precipitate.

83. Electromagnetic waves propagate with the speed of light. Transmission of energy through a vacuum or using no medium is accomplished by electromagnetic waves. It is caused by the oscillation of electric and magnetic fields

84.
The SI Unit **of temperature** is Kelvin.

Quantity	SI Unit
Mass	Kilogram
Length	Metre
Luminous Intensity	Candela

85. Vitamin B is a water-soluble vitamin. A vitamin that can dissolve in water. Water-soluble vitamins are carried to the body's tissues but are not stored in the body.
Vitamin A, D, E & K are fat soluble vitamins.

86. One mole of oxygen atoms contains 6.023×10^{23} oxygen atoms

A mole corresponds to the mass of a substance that contains 6.023×10^{23} particles of the substance. The mole is the SI unit for the amount of a substance and its symbol is mol.

Definition of mole- 1 mol of carbon-12 has a mass of 12 grams and contains $6.022140857 \times 10^{23}$ of carbon atoms.

87. Given-

Velocity(V)= 25 m/s

Mass(M)= 300g or 0.3 Kg

K.E $=1/2$ M x V^2

K.E$=1/2$x0.3x25^2

K.E= 93.75 J

88. One-watt hour is equivalent to 3600 Joule. The watt-hour (Wh) is a unit of energy equivalent to one watt (1 W) of power expended for one hour (1 h) of time. It is commonly used in electrical applications.

1 Kilowatt-hour = 3.6×10^6 joule

89. Momentum is the property of a moving body & is defined as the product of mass & velocity. The standard unit of momentum magnitude is the kilogram-metre per second.

Newton's second law , illustrates the concept of momentum i.e. The rate of change of momentum of an object is directly proportional to the resultant force applied and is in the direction of the resultant force. The resultant force is equal to the rate of change of momentum.

90. Hydraulic press & Hydraulic brake work on the principle of Pascal's law. Pascal's law states that when there is an increase in pressure at any point in a confined fluid, there is an equal increase at every other point in the container.

91. Oiled paper is an example of Translucent material. A translucent material lets light pass through, but objects on the other side can't be seen clearly while a transparent material allows us to clearly see the objects on the other side.

92. Kepler's third law states that square of the period of any planet is proportional to the cube of the semimajor axis of its orbit.

First law i.e. Law of Orbits: All planets move in elliptical orbits, with the sun at one focus.

Second Law i.e. Law of Areas: A line that connects a planet to the sun sweeps out equal areas in equal times.

93. For a non-polar covalent compound , the value of electronegativity is Zero. Electronegativity is a measure of an atom's ability to attract the shared electrons of a covalent bond to itself.

94.
Chickenpox is caused by Varicella Virus.

Virus	Disease
Orthomixovirus	Influenza Flu
Rhino Virus	Common cold
Enterovirus	Polio

95. A fog is an aerosol of liquid particles, in particular a low cloud.
Aerosols are dispersions in gases. In aerosols the particles often exceed the usual size limits for colloids. If the dispersed particles are solid, it is called aerosols of solid particles, if they are liquid, they are called aerosols of liquid particles.

96. Phosphorus is a non-metal. It is a chemical element with symbol P and atomic number 15. Elemental phosphorus exists in two major forms, white phosphorus & red phosphorus. It is an important constituent of bones and teeth, and it is essential to the growth of living organisms.

97. The longest cells in the human body are the nerve cells . The cell bodies of Nerve cells are located in the base of your spinal cord and their axons run down to the ends of your toes. They are approximately 1 meter long.

98. Pavo cristatus is the scientific name of peacock.

Lotus- Nelumbo nucifera

Rice- Orzya Sativa

Tiger- Panthera tigris

99. Thermal power is the "largest" source of power in India. There are different types ofthermal power plants based on the fuel used to generate the steam such as coal, gas, and Diesel. About 71% of electricity consumed in India are generated bythermal power plants.

100. Sound travels faster in liquids and non-porous solids than it does in air. It travels about 4.3 times as fast in water (1,484 m/s), and nearly 15 times as fast in iron (5.120 m/s), than in air at 20 degrees Celsius. Sound waves in solids are composed of compression waves (just as in gases and liquids), but also exhibit a different type of sound wave called a shear wave, which occurs only in solids. The speed of sound is the distance travelled during a unit of time by a sound is the distance travelled during a unit of time by a sound wave propagating through an elastic medium. In dry air at 20°/C (68 °F), the speed of sound is 343.2 meters per second (1,126 ft/s). This is 1,236 kilometers per hour (768 mph), or about one kilometer in three seconds or approximately one mile in five seconds.

Mathematics

Q.1 Two trains 165 m and 175 m long run at the speed of 50 km/h and 52 km/h respectively in opposite directions on parallel tracks. What is the time (in seconds) they take to cross each other?

A. 9   **B.** 9.6   **C.** 10   **D.** 12

Q.2 If two equations: $2x^2 - Ax - 20 = 0$ and $2x^2 - 11x + 12 = 0$ have one root in common, then what is the value of 'A' if the value of A is positive?

A. 3   **B.** 2   **C.** 4   **D.** 5

Q.3 Divya has 3 types of coins having denomination of 20p, 10p and 5p. Their numbers are in the ratio of 1 : 2 : 3. If Divya has total money of Rs. 44 then how many 5p coins are there?

A. 240   **B.** 120   **C.** 210   **D.** 180

Q.4 The difference between 42% and 23% of a number is 304. What is 72% of that number?

A. 1650   **B.** 1536   **C.** 1265   **D.** 1152

Q.5 What is the value of $60 \div [\{21 \div 7 \times \sqrt{(\sqrt{625} + \sqrt{121})} - 6] \times 5 - 42 \div 3 \times 2 = ?$

A. 2   **B.** -3   **C.** -4   **D.** -1

Q.6 Three pipes x, y and z can fill a water tanker in 20, 25 and 30 minutes respectively. All the three pipes are opened to fill the tanker and if the pipe y is closed 2 minutes before the water tanker gets filled, then in how much time will the tank get filled?

A. 8 minutes   **B.** 10 minutes
C. 324/37 minutes   **D.** 312/37 minutes

Q.7 If $[4x - (1/12x) = 8]$, then what is the value of $[x^2 + \{1/(2304x^2)\}]$?

A. 97/24   **B.** 93/22   **C.** 85/14   **D.** 87/16

Q.8 A boy throws a ball of mass 4 kg vertically downwards for a height of 20 metres. What is the velocity of the ball which touches the ground? (Take g= 10 m/s^2)

A. 20 m/s   **B.** 25 m/s   **C.** 30 m/s   **D.** 18 m/s

Q.9 Express 0.78414141.. into (p/q) form.

A. 7763/9900   **B.** 7736/9900
C. 7772/9990   **D.** 7774/9990

Q.10 Nidhi borrowed Rs. 10000 from a bank for a period of two years at the rate of 10% per annum. From that amount, she invested Rs. 3500 in another bank which offers simple interest @12.5% per annum and remaining amount she invested into a chit fund which offers compound interest of 10% per annum. What is the profit obtained by Nidhi at the end of two years?

A. Rs. 120   **B.** Rs. 240   **C.** Rs. 350   **D.** Rs. 280

Q.11 A book was marked initially at Rs. 500 which A purchased at 8% discount. He marked up the price by 15% on his purchased price and sold after Rs. 20 discount to B. B marked up the price by 20% above his purchased price and sold to C after allowing Rs. 50.9 discount. What is the percent profit gained by B when sold to C?

Given below are the steps involved. Arrange them in the sequential order.

(A) Initial marked price of book = Rs. 500 and purchased price for A = 92% of 500 = Rs. 460

(B) Purchased price of book by B = 529 - 20 = Rs. 509

(C) Per cent profit = [(559.9 - 509)/509] x 100 = 10%

(D) Marked price of book by A = 115% of 460 = Rs. 529

(E) Marked price of book by B = 120% of 509 = Rs. 610.8 and purchased price of book by C = 610.8 - 50.9 = Rs. 559.9

A. ADBEC   **B.** ABEDC   **C.** BAEDC   **D.** AEDBC

Q.12 Seema purchased an item for Rs.9,600 and sold it for a loss of 5 percent. From that money she purchased another item and sold it for a gain of 5 percent. What is her overall gain/loss?

A. Loss of Rs.36   **B.** Loss of Rs.24
C. Loss of Rs.54   **D.** None of these

Q.13 What is the angle between the hands of a clock at 8:30 a.m.?

A. 85°   **B.** 90°   **C.** 105°   **D.** 75°

Q.14 Following data given below shows the sex ratio of India in last 10 years. Find the mode of sex ratio in India.

976, 979, 1084, 993, 1084, 993, 935, 979, 991, 979

A. 976   **B.** 979   **C.** 993   **D.** 1084

Q.15 If $7x^5 - 2x^4 + 3x^3 - 4x^2 + 6x + 2k$ is divisible by (x + 1), then what is the value of k?

A. 13   **B.** 9   **C.** 11   **D.** 7

Q.16 The ratio of two numbers is 7:5 and their H.C.F. is 6. What is their L.C.M.?

A. 148   **B.** 156   **C.** 210   **D.** 270

Q.17 From an external point O, a secant is drawn on a circle which meets the circle at points A and B respectively, if OA = 4 cm and AB = 60 cm. The length of the tangent drawn on circle from point O is (in cm)

A. 16 cm   **B.** 12 cm   **C.** 13 cm   **D.** 14 cm

Q.18 A copper-wire when bent in the form of a square enclose an area of 121 cm^2. If the same wire is bent in the form of a circle, then the area of the circle is

A. 121 cm^2 **B.** 242 cm   **C.** 154 cm^2 **D.** 60 cm

Q.19 Table given below shows the total number of employees of four different grades in a department and average age of employees in those difference grades.

Grade	Department P	Average age (Years)
A	25	28
B	40	24
C	15	32
D	20	22

Table given below shows the total number of employees of four different grades in a department and average age of employees in those difference grades.

A. 23.4 years **B.** 22.6 years
C. 26.2 years **D.** 25.8 years

Q.20 What will be the percentage profit after selling an article at a certain price if there is a loss of 12.5% when the article is sold at half of the previous selling price?

A. 50% **B.** 45% **C.** 75% **D.** 60%

Q.21 If α, $3\alpha+6$, and 71α are in arithmetic progression, then find the value of α.

A. 7/11 **B.** 23/99 **C.** 71/55 **D.** 2/11

Q.22 One-fourth of Lainey's savings in Kisan Vikas Patra is equal to one-fifth of her savings in Employee Provident Fund. How much has she saved in Employee Provident Fund, if she has a total savings of ₹ 180,000?

A. ₹ 100,000 **B.** ₹ 95,000
C. ₹ 85,000 **D.** ₹ 80,000

Q.23 When 20% of 40% of half of a number 'm' is added to 3/4th of 20% of itself, then a second number is obtained which is 21 less than the 40% of m. What is the difference between first and second number?

A. 76 **B.** 81 **C.** 72 **D.** 70

Q.24 What will come in place of (?) in this equation?
125% of [{? + 200 ÷ (16 ÷ 2 x 4 x (1/8))} ÷ 7.5 x 8 ÷ (18 ÷ 3 - 50% of 4)] = ?

A. 15 **B.** 20 **C.** 25 **D.** 30

Q.25 If $\cos(90^0 - \theta)/\cos(30^0 + \theta) = 1$, then the value of $\sin\theta + \cos 2\theta$

A. 0 **B.** 1 **C.** $\sqrt{2}$ **D.** $\sqrt{3}$

Q.26 A fraction is such that if it is squared and then the numerator is divided by 2, while the denominator is increased by 25%, the new fraction thus obtained is 4 times the original fraction. What is the new fraction?

A. 8 **B.** 10
C. 50 **D.** None of these

Q.27 What should come in place of question mark (?) in the following series?
15, 17, 23, 35, 55, (?)

A. 60 **B.** 72 **C.** 85 **D.** 98

Q.28 How much does a watch lose per day, if its hands coincide every 65 minutes?

A. 10(21/143) minutes **B.** 10(21/143) minutes

C. 10(10/143) minutes **D.** 15(10/143) minutes

Q.29 Fifteen years hence, the ratio of the ages of a man and his son will be 2:1. If the present age of the man is 45, then what is his son's present age?

A. 30 **B.** 25 **C.** 15 **D.** 20

Q.30 Ramesh can do 20% more work as Mohan can do in same time. If Mohan can finish the work in 30 hours then Ramesh with the help of Mohan, can finish the same work in how many hours ?

A. 110/25 hours **B.** 150/11 hours
C. 140/9 hours **D.** 130/12 hours

General Intelligence & Reasoning

Q.31 In each of the following questions, select a figure from amongst the four alternatives, which when placed in the blank space of figure (X) would complete the pattern. Identify the figure that completes the pattern.

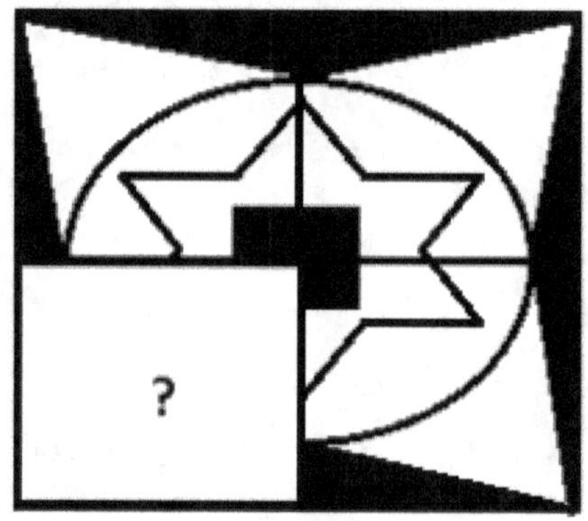

(x)

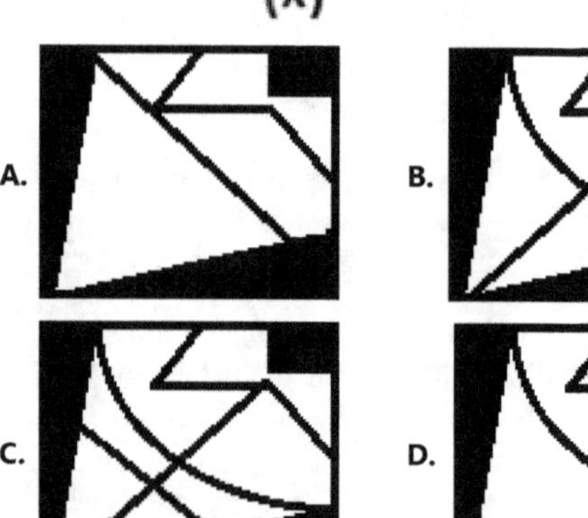

A. B.
C. D.

Q.32 Find out from amongst the four alternatives as to how the pattern would appear on the sheet when the sheet is folded at the dotted line and is punched as given

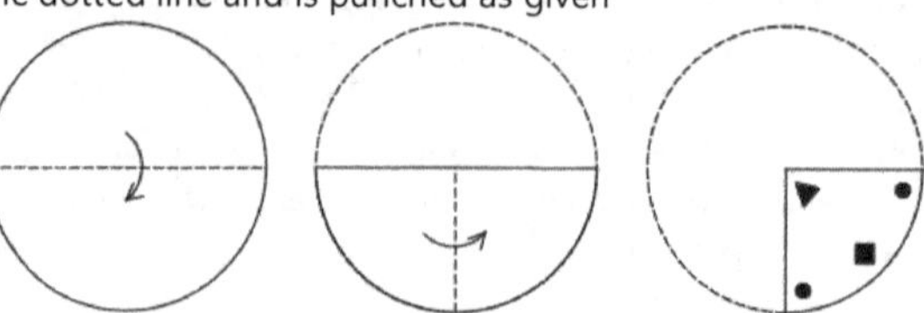

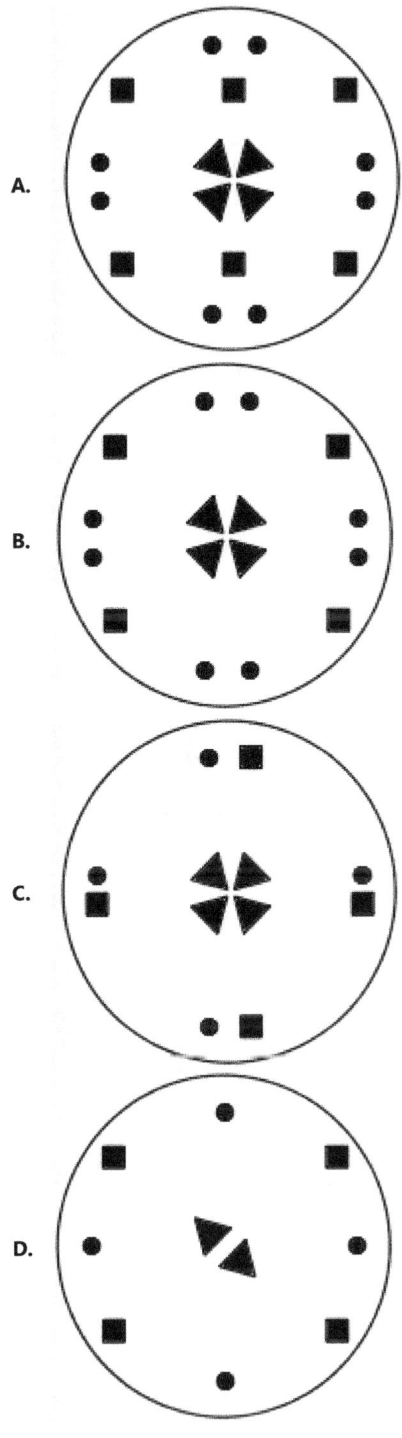

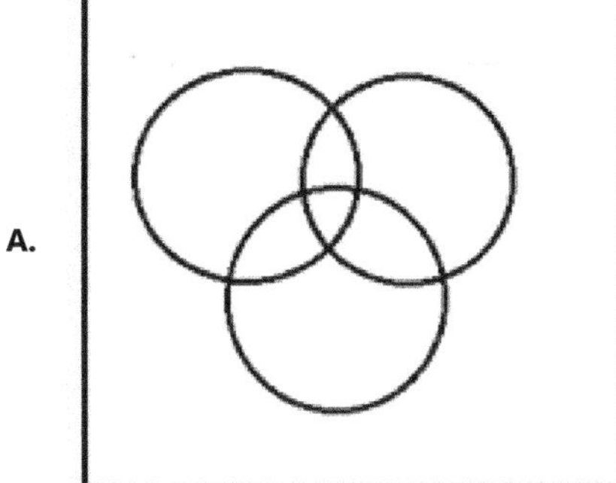

A.

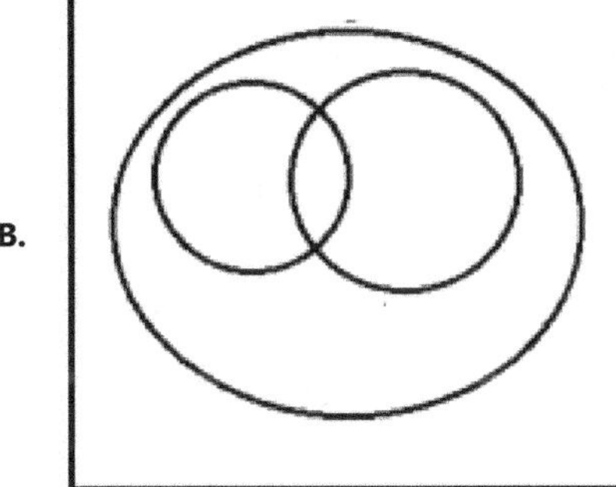

B.

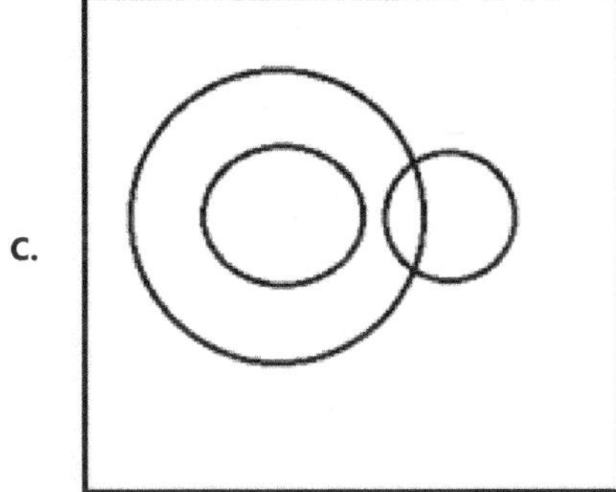

C.

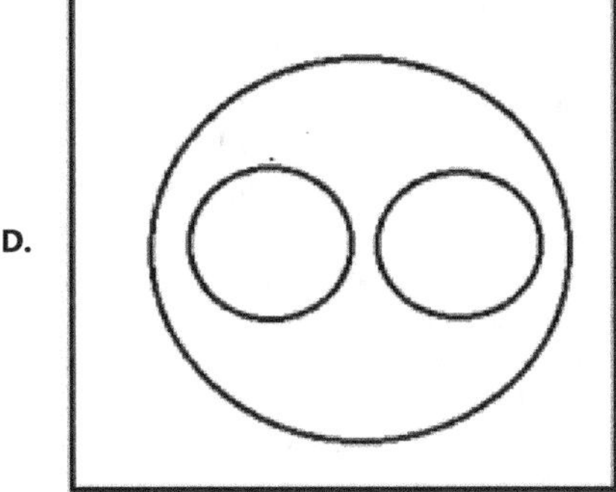

D.

Q.33 In the following question, which one set of letters when sequentially placed at the gaps in the given letter series shall complete it?

k d _ w _ k _ h w e _ d _ w _

A. whedke   **B.** hdekhk   **C.** kehdhe   **D.** hedkhe

Q.34 Identify the diagram that best represents the relationship among the given classes.

Integers, prime numbers, even numbers

Q.35 Find the odd one out.

A. 28 + 42   **B.** 45 + 25   **C.** 51 + 32   **D.** 36 + 34

Q.36 In the following question, a figure (x) is given having a pattern which is embedded in one or more than one of the given patterns (i), (ii), (iii) and (iv). Select the option in which the pattern (x) is embedded.

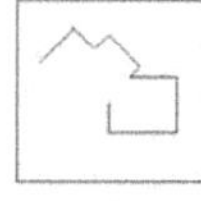

(x)

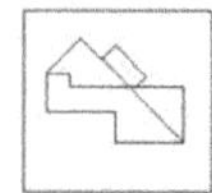 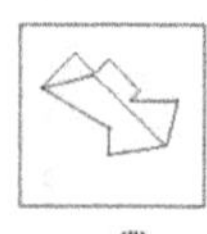 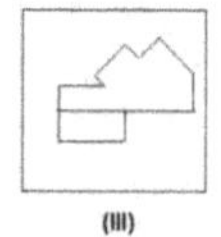 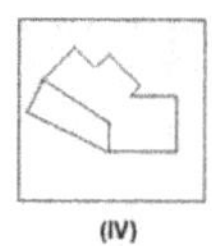

(I)　　　　(II)　　　　(III)　　　　(IV)

A. Only III
C. Both II and III
B. Both I and IV
D. All the given

Q.37 A conclusion is followed by two statements which give us data for the conclusion. Study that data and the conclusion on and mark the correct answer.

Conclusion: Education has become notoriously poor.

Statements: 1. Education should be rich.

2. Poor Education is not good.

A. If statement 1 alone can bring us to the conclusion.

B. If statement 2 alone can bring us to the conclusion.

C. If both the statements 1 and 2 taken together can bring us to the conclusion.

D. If the statements taken separately or together cannot bring us to the conclusion.

Q.38 If today is Thursday then what will the day after 415 weeks and 5 days?

A. Tuesday
C. Wednesday
B. Monday
D. Sunday

Q.39 Each of the questions below consists of a question and two statements numbered I and II given below it. You have to decide whether the data provided in which of the statements are sufficient to answer the question. Choose your answer from the options based on this.

What is the code for '%$&#'?

I. In a certain code 'PLAY' is written as '&#*$'.

II. In a certain code 'AWAY' is written as '#%&#'

A. If the data in statement I alone are sufficient to answer the question, while the data in statement II alone are not sufficient to answer the question.

B. If the data in statement II alone are sufficient to answer the question, while the data in statement I alone are not sufficient to answer the question.

C. If the data either in statement I alone or in statement II alone are sufficient to answer the question.

D. If the data in both the statements I and II together are not sufficient to answer the question.

Q.40 Which of the following will be the mirror image of the given question figure (x), if the mirror is placed along the line MN. Choose the correct mirror image among (I), (II), (III) and (IV) given.

(x)

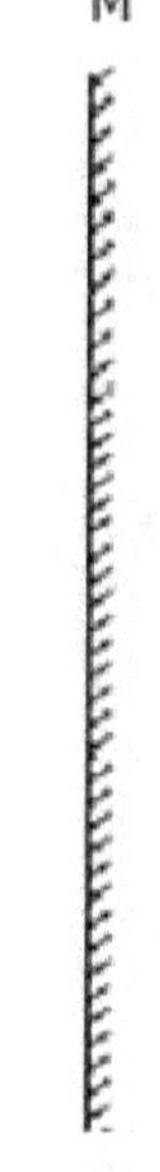

M

N

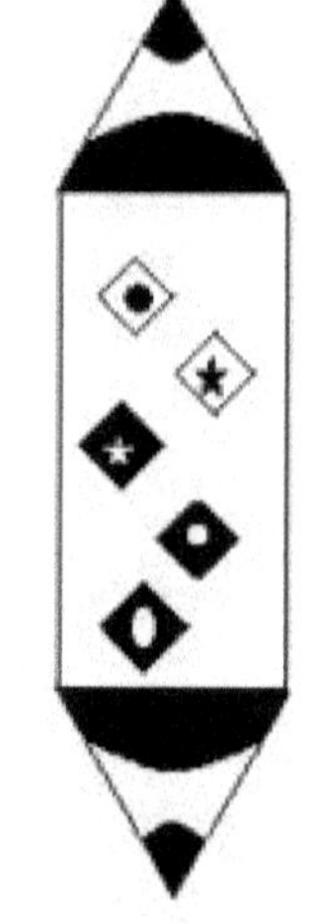

A.

I

B.

II

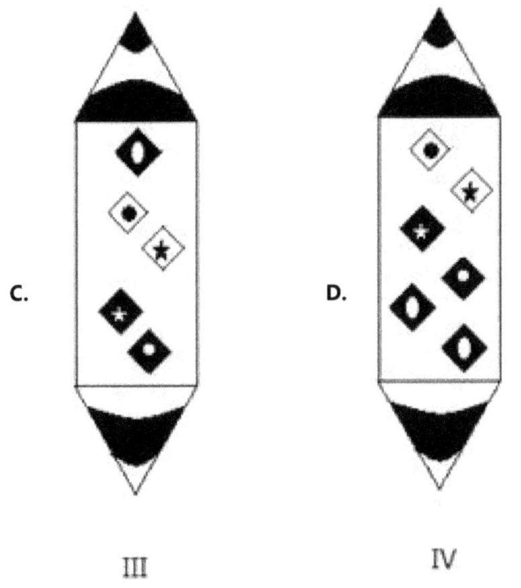

C.   **D.**

III   IV

Q.41 Two positions of a same cube are shown below. What is the colour of face opposite to 'red' coloured face?

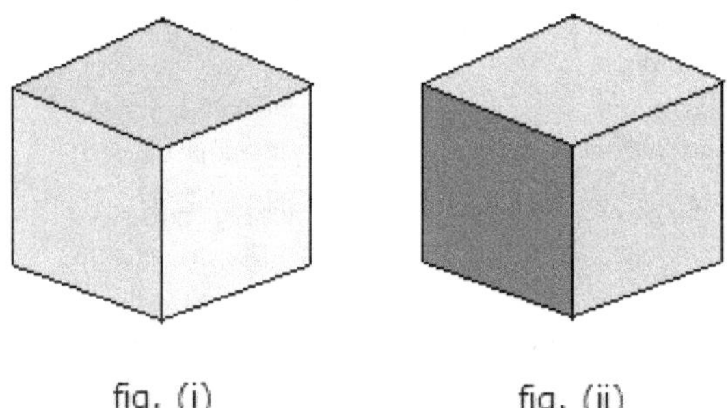

fig. (i)   fig. (ii)

A. Green
B. Yellow
C. Grey
D. Cannot be determined

Q.42 Six persons A, B, C, E, F and G, are having different weights. C is lighter than only one person, who is neither E nor B. A is the lightest one and F is not the heaviest one. E is lighter than B. F is lighter than at least three persons. B is lighter than how many persons?

A. One
B. Two
C. Three
D. Either (a) or (b)

Q.43 Answer the following question based on the information given below.

Among P, Q, R, S and T, who is the shortest?

I. P is shorter than Q but taller than T.

II. S is taller than R but shorter than P.

A. If the data in Statement I alone is sufficient to answer the question, while the data in Statement II alone is not sufficient to answer the question.

B. If the data in Statement II alone is sufficient to answer the question, while the data in Statement I alone is not sufficient to answer the question.

C. If the data in Statement I alone or in Statement II alone is sufficient to answer the question

D. If the data in both the Statements I and II together are not sufficient to answer the question.

Q.44 How many triangles are present in the given figure?

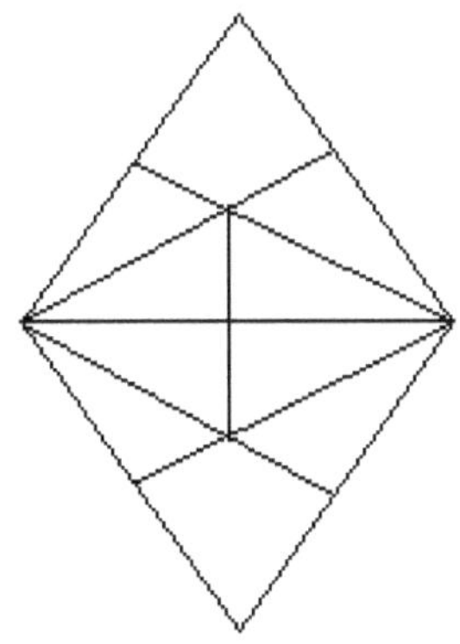

A. 21   **B.** 22   **C.** 20   **D.** 19

Q.45 In the following question, select the related letters from the given alternatives.
MQY:OU :: BFN: ?

A. CI   **B.** CJ   **C.** DJ   **D.** DI

Q.46 In each of the questions below are given some statements followed by two conclusions numbered I and II. You have to take the given statements to be true even if they seem to be at variance from commonly known facts.

Read all the conclusions and then decide which of the given conclusions logically follows from the given statements disregarding commonly known facts.

Statements:

All jets are sacks.

No sack is a tiger.

Some tigers are fins.

Conclusions:

I. No jet is a tiger.

II. No fins are sacks.

A. If only conclusion I follows.

B. If only conclusion II follows.

C. If either conclusion I or conclusion II follows.

D. If neither conclusion I nor conclusion II follows.

Q.47 F is to the west of E. P is to the west of L, K is to the south-west of P. If E is to the north-west of P then towards which direction F must go so as to reach L ?

A. South-east   **B.** East
C. South   **D.** Can't be determined

Q.48 W is the mother of T. V is the father of F. P is the mother of F. If F is the niece of W then how is T related to F ?

A. Sister   **B.** Brother
C. Cousin   **D.** Can't be determined

Q.49 In a certain code BERTH is coded as SVKFJ. What will be the code for SHRUB?

A. SWEWM   **B.** SEWMW

C. SEMWW   **D.** SWEMW

Q.50 Arrange the given words in a meaningful sequence.
1. Thursday
2. Monday
3. Sunday
4. Friday
5. Tuesday

A. 1, 2, 4, 5, 3   **B.** 3, 4, 1, 5, 2
C. 3, 4, 1, 2, 5   **D.** 2, 5, 4, 1, 3

Q.51 In each of the questions below, a statement/passage is given. From the options below, choose the one that reflects the correct choice of assumption(s) that follows/follow.

Many social media sites, forums, and message boards allow users to post using only a username that is virtually impossible to trace back to their real-life identity.

I. Some social media sites, forums take pride in preserving the absolute anonymity of their users.

II. It's important for social media sites to maintain the privacy of their users.

A. Only I   **B.** Only II
C. Both I and II   **D.** Neither I nor II

Q.52 Each question given below consists of a statement, followed by two arguments I and II. You have to decide which of the arguments is a 'strong' argument and which is a 'weak' argument.

Statement: Should all education be made free for girls and women of all ages in India?

Arguments:

I. No, this will weaken our present social structure.

II. Yes, this is the only way to bring back glory to Indian womanhood.

A. if only argument I is strong.
B. if only argument II is strong.
C. if either I or II strong.
D. if neither I nor II strong.

Q.53 In a certain code language, 315 means 'play is fun', 324 means 'game is nice', 614 means 'fun and nice'. Find the code for 'and'.

A. 6   **B.** 7   **C.** 9   **D.** 4

Q.54 In each of the following questions, select the one which is different from the others.
(A) Pant   (B) Coat
(C) Shirt   (D) Sweater

A. A   **B.** B   **C.** C   **D.** D

Q.55 In each of the following questions, a series is given with one term missing. Choose the correct alternatives from the given ones that will complete the series.
-9, -2, ?, 15, 25

A. 0   **B.** 4   **C.** 6   **D.** 8

General Awareness

Q.56 India's 1st National Sports University to be set up in __________.

A. Kohima, Nagaland   **B.** Imphal, Manipur
C. Gangtok, Sikkim   **D.** Guwahati, Assam

Q.57 Who was recently appointed as the first Woman Chief Economist at International Monetary Fund
A. Indira Nooyi
B. Anindita Chakraborty
C. Gita Gopinath
D. Jaya Jaitley

Q.58 Based on a study by the Global Carbon Project released on December 5 2018, India ranks as ___ highest carbon emitter in the world.
A. 4th   **B.** 3rd   **C.** 1st   **D.** 5th

Q.59 Who is the current Chief of Army Staff?
A. Gen. Dalbir Singh
B. Gen. Sam Manekshaw
C. Gen. Bipin Rawat
D. Gen. V.K. Singh

Q.60 __________ is an initiative of Government to introduce school students to all 22 languages in Schedule 8 of Indian Constitution.
A. Bhasha Saar   **B.** Bhasha Sangam
C. Bhasha Ekta   **D.** Shrestha Bhasha

Q.61 Which of these Indian Cricketer recently announced his retirement from all forms of the game in December 2018?
A. Anil Kumble   **B.** Virendra Sehwag
C. Narayan Karthick   **D.** Gautam Gambhir

Q.62 Who became the 1st female boxer to win 6 gold medals at World Boxing Championships 2018?
A. Hanna Okhota   **B.** Hyang Mi Kim
C. Mary Kom   **D.** Sarina Wavrinka

Q.63 Water Literacy Campaign, "Jala saksharatha" was recently launched by which Indian State?
A. Karnataka   **B.** Tamil Nadu
C. Goa   **D.** Kerala

Q.64 Where is the headquarters of Indian Space Research Organisation?
A. New Delhi
B. Mumbai, Maharashtra
C. Chennai, Tamil Nadu
D. Bengaluru, Karnataka

Q.65 Under the newly launched PM-JAY, also known as Ayushman Bharat, Government provides health insurance cover of up to _______ per family per year
A. Rs. 2 Lakh   **B.** Rs. 10 Lakh
C. Rs. 5 Lakh   **D.** Rs. 1 Lakh

Q.66 Where is Sariska Tiger Reserve situated?
A. Pune, Maharashtra   **B.** Imphal, Manipur
C. Thrissur, Kerala   **D.** Alwar, Rajasthan

Q.67 In 1942, during which popular movement of freedom struggle did Mahatma Gandhi gave the call, "to do or die"?

A. Sepoy Mutiny

B. Chalo Delhi movement

C. Royal Navy Mutiny

D. Quit India Movement

Q.68 Sangai Festival is an annual celebration of which Indian State?

A. Meghalaya
B. Sikkim
C. Nagaland
D. Manipur

Q.69 Human Rights Day is celebrated annually across the globe on which date?

A. 11th September
B. 12th February
C. 10th December
D. 5th January

Q.70 Who among the following won her 4th term as Prime Minister of Bangladesh?

A. Abdul Hamid
B. Sheikh Hasina
C. Mehbooba Mufti
D. Fathima Sheikh

General Science

Q.71 Statement: No Heat Engine can operate with 100% efficiency (convert heat energy to mechanical work). The given statement is__________.

A. TRUE in all conditions

B. FALSE in all conditions

C. TRUE If the engine is in vacuum

D. FALSE If the engine is in vacuum

Q.72 Which among the following is also called "Artificial sugar"?

A. Glucose
B. Fructose
C. Cellulose
D. Saccharin

Q.73 Dynamo is an instrument which works on the process of transforming __________ Energy to __________ Energy.

A. Chemical, Heat

B. Sound, Electrical

C. Electrical, Mechanical

D. Mechanical, Electrical

Q.74 Bauxite is an ore of ________ metal.

A. Aluminium
B. Copper
C. Gold
D. Silver

Q.75 ________ are atoms of the elements having the same atomic number but different mass numbers.

A. Isobars
B. Isotones
C. Isotopes
D. Isoelectronic

Q.76 Study of virus is called _______.

A. Virothesis
B. Microbiology
C. Virology
D. Morphology

Q.77 Which of these is/are plant hormone(s)?

A. Auxins
B. Cytokinin
C. Gibberellin
D. All of the above

Q.78 ________ is a radioactive process in which the nucleus of an atom splits into smaller parts.

A. Nuclear fission
B. Nuclear fusion
C. Nuclear Activity
D. Atomic fusion

Q.79 Which of the following is/are not a property of a covalent bond?

A. Having high boiling points

B. Generally Bad conductor of Heat

C. Generally insoluble in water

D. All of the above

Q.80 Which of the following are part of group 17 of periodic table, also called "halogens"?

A. Bromine
B. Chlorine
C. Argon
D. Both 1 & 2

Q.81 Vulcanisation is a process associated with which of the following materials?

A. Cotton
B. Iron
C. Gold
D. Rubber

Q.82 Thyroid gland is associated with which of the following parts in a human body?

A. Shoulders
B. Neck
C. Thigh
D. Chest

Q.83 Lactic Acid is found in which of the following ?

A. Fruits
B. Milk
C. Tomatoes
D. Vinegar

Q.84 Which of the following makes up to 60%-75% by mass of human body?

A. Magnesium
B. Air
C. Bones
D. Water

Q.85 For a pendulum in Simple Harmonic Motion, Time period (t) is __________ to Acceleration due to gravity (g).

A. Inversely proportional

B. Directly proportional

C. Equal

D. Depends on Material of pendulum

Q.86 __________ is a process in which two or more metal items are joined together.

A. Soldering
B. Smelting
C. Forging
D. None of these

Q.87 Current in a 60 W light bulb when it is connected to a 240 V power supply is________.

A. 0.26
B. 0.28
C. 0.25
D. 1.25

Q.88 __________ is a thermodynamic process in which there is no heat transfer into or out of a system and is generally obtained by surrounding the entire system with a strongly insulating material.

A. Isothermal process

B. Adiabatic Process

C. Hyperthermal Process

D. Kelvin Process

Q.89 Medulla is part of _______ in the human body.

A. Heart   **B.** Skin
C. Intestines   **D.** Brain

Q.90 __________ is a measuring instrument used to measure the current in a circuit.
A. Voltmeter   **B.** Ammeter
C. Seismometer   **D.** Odometer

Q.91 Which of the following are TRUE regarding the variation of "g "(acceleration due to gravity)?
A. g is maximum at poles
B. g is minimum at equator
C. g decreases due to rotation of the Earth
D. All of the above

Q.92 Which of the following is related to the statement that "For a given colour of light, the ratio of sine of angle of incident and angle of refraction is same"?
A. Kirchoff's Law   **B.** Snell's Law
C. Stefan's law   **D.** Sine Law

Q.93 Plasma is a component of which among the following part of human body?
A. Liver   **B.** Lungs   **C.** Blood   **D.** Brain

Q.94 Which of the following is defined as the amount of energy released during the formation of one mole of ionic compound from its constituent ions?
A. Lattice Energy   **B.** Escape Energy
C. Hydration Energy   **D.** Evolution Energy

Q.95 __________ is the speed that an object needs to be traveling to break free of a planet or moon's gravity well and leave it without further propulsion.
A. Kinetic Energy   **B.** Potential Energy
C. Dynamic Energy   **D.** Escape Velocity

Q.96 __________is the study of humans and human behaviour and societies in the past and present.
A. Seismology   **B.** Anthropology
C. Virology   **D.** Psychology

Q.97 Which of these is/are applications of Ultrasonic Waves ?
A. Measuring depth of sea
B. Cleaning cloths and Machinery parts
C. Sterilizing a liquid
D. All of the above

Q.98 Which of the following have a pH value less than 7?
A. Saliva   **B.** Vinegar
C. Milk   **D.** Both B & C

Q.99 Lakes and forests are best classified as examples of __________

A. Artificial ecosystem   **B.** Natural ecosystem
C. Natural Biosphere   **D.** Artificial Biosphere

Q.100 Gammaxene, D.D.T. and Bleaching powder are important compounds of :
A. Sulphur   **B.** Nitrogen
C. Chlorine   **D.** Phosphorus

// Smart Answer Sheet //

Correct — Percentage of students who answered correctly.   **Skipped** — Percentage of students who skipped.

Q.	Ans.	Correct / Skipped
1	D	80.98 % / 17.94 %
2	A	85.54 % / 14.22 %
3	A	80.08 % / 17.22 %
4	D	76.81 % / 19.4 %
5	B	87.94 % / 10.19 %
6	C	89.4 % / 10.02 %
7	A	79.72 % / 18.83 %
8	A	89.64 % / 10.12 %
9	A	79.55 % / 12.72 %
10	B	78.45 % / 19.67 %
11	A	87.2 % / 10.34 %
12	B	76.92 % / 14.71 %
13	D	76.64 % / 21.99 %
14	B	77.41 % / 11.35 %
15	C	79.0 % / 14.23 %
16	C	83.19 % / 10.88 %
17	A	86.07 % / 11.28 %
18	C	88.31 % / 11.13 %
19	D	78.0 % / 13.84 %
20	C	89.09 % / 10.29 %
21	D	81.77 % / 16.42 %
22	A	82.27 % / 10.58 %
23	B	78.85 % / 21.02 %
24	C	83.0 % / 13.36 %
25	B	78.33 % / 20.24 %
26	D	80.53 % / 13.18 %
27	C	85.4 % / 11.81 %
28	C	83.66 % / 11.48 %
29	C	89.23 % / 10.12 %
30	B	89.55 % / 10.39 %
31	D	79.18 % / 11.55 %
32	B	85.57 % / 10.17 %
33	D	89.97 % / 10.02 %
34	B	89.71 % / 10.2 %
35	C	76.94 % / 10.09 %
36	B	82.19 % / 16.52 %
37	D	84.37 % / 10.37 %
38	A	89.31 % / 10.1 %
39	D	85.57 % / 11.54 %
40	C	76.26 % / 10.8 %
41	B	85.99 % / 11.5 %
42	B	87.58 % / 10.23 %
43	D	86.09 % / 10.43 %
44	B	85.08 % / 11.51 %
45	C	88.14 % / 11.7 %
46	A	85.4 % / 10.73 %
47	A	76.86 % / 14.16 %
48	C	85.45 % / 11.23 %
49	A	83.83 % / 13.1 %
50	B	86.06 % / 11.64 %
51	B	82.34 % / 11.73 %
52	D	80.76 % / 12.87 %
53	A	78.29 % / 21.37 %
54	A	81.3 % / 14.75 %
55	C	89.07 % / 10.26 %
56	B	78.5 % / 13.56 %
57	C	78.67 % / 16.56 %
58	A	79.75 % / 13.21 %
59	C	78.64 % / 11.2 %
60	B	80.54 % / 11.6 %
61	D	87.84 % / 11.31 %
62	C	85.37 % / 12.34 %
63	D	79.29 % / 14.98 %
64	D	84.37 % / 15.15 %
65	C	82.77 % / 16.97 %
66	D	83.81 % / 11.48 %
67	D	83.17 % / 12.08 %
68	D	77.8 % / 14.64 %
69	C	80.92 % / 15.23 %
70	B	82.19 % / 13.66 %
71	A	79.28 % / 12.68 %
72	D	77.45 % / 12.46 %
73	D	76.55 % / 13.13 %
74	A	79.61 % / 18.31 %
75	C	77.54 % / 14.93 %
76	C	88.47 % / 10.74 %
77	D	86.06 % / 10.89 %
78	A	83.48 % / 13.03 %
79	A	88.05 % / 10.09 %
80	D	81.42 % / 14.89 %

Q.	Ans.	Correct		Q.	Ans.	Correct		Q.	Ans.	Correct		Q.	Ans.	Correct		Q.	Ans.	Correct
		Skipped				Skipped				Skipped				Skipped				Skipped
81	D	78.8 %		85	A	77.34 %		89	D	78.47 %		93	C	83.86 %		97	D	89.74 %
		10.15 %				12.61 %				14.23 %				14.57 %				10.09 %
82	B	80.69 %		86	A	86.06 %		90	B	78.78 %		94	A	81.1 %		98	D	87.68 %
		15.51 %				12.56 %				13.33 %				10.37 %				12.25 %
83	B	81.23 %		87	C	85.76 %		91	D	85.54 %		95	D	77.08 %		99	B	86.31 %
		18.18 %				14.05 %				10.8 %				11.98 %				11.12 %
84	D	87.99 %		88	B	82.8 %		92	B	78.47 %		96	B	83.18 %		100	C	76.93 %
		10.7 %				15.38 %				13.71 %				14.79 %				12.49 %

//Hints and Solutions//

1. Relative speed = (50 + 52) km/h = (102 x 5/18) m/s = (255/9) m/s.

Distance covered in crossing each other = (165 + 175) = 340 m.

∴ Required time = (340 x 9/255) = 12 s.

2. $2x^2 - 11x + 12 = 0$

$(2x - 3)(x - 4) = 0$

x = 1.5 and 4

Since both the equations have one root in common-

Case 1: When x = 1.5 is common-

$2(1.5)^2 - A(1.5) - 20 = 0$

3. Since the ratio between the numbers of coins of 20p, 10p and 5p is 1 : 2 : 3 So let us assume the number of 20p coins = a

Then number of 10p coins is 2a and number of 5p coins is 3a.

Total worth of 20p coins = number of coins X worth of each coin = a X (1/5) = Rs (a/5)

Total worth of 10p coins = 2a X (1/10) = Rs (a/5)

Similarly total worth of 5p coins = 3a X (1/20) = Rs (3a/20)

Since total money with the Divya is Rs 44 hence

a/5 + a/5 + 3a/20 = 44 => 2a/5 + 3a/20 = 44

=> 8a/20 + 3a/20=44 => 11a/20 =44 => a = 80

So the number of 5p coins = 3a = 80 x 3 = 240

4. Let the number be 100x.

∴ 42x - 23x = 304

=> 19x = 304

=> x = 16

∴ The number is 100 x 16 = 1600.

=> 72% of the number = 0.72 x 1600 = 1152

5. $60 \div [\{21 \div 7 \times \sqrt{(\sqrt{625} + \sqrt{121})}\} - 6] \times 5 - 42 \div 3 \times 2$

$= 60 \div [\{3 \times \sqrt{(25 + 11)}\} - 6] \times 5 - 14 \times 2$

$= 60 \div [\{3 \times \sqrt{(36)}\} - 6] \times 5 - 28$

$= 60 \div [\{3 \times 6\} - 6] \times 5 - 28$

$= 60 \div [18 - 6] \times 5 - 28$

$= 60 \div 12 \times 5 - 28$

$= 5 \times 5 - 28$

$= -3$

6. Let the time after which the water tanker gets filled be 't' minutes.

In one minute pipe x can fill 1/20 part.

In t minutes, pipe x can then fill t/20 part.

Therefore, t/20 + t-2/25 + t/30 = 1

On solving, we get t = 324/37 minutes.

7. 4x - 1/12x = 8

=> 4(x - 1/48x) = 8

=> x - 1/48x = 2 ------ (i)

Squaring both sides, we get

$(x - 1/48x)^2 = 4$

=> $x^2 + 1/(2304x^2) - 2x/48x = 4$ ------ [$(a - b)^2 = a^2 + b^2 - 2ab$]

$x^2 + 1/2304\ x^2 = 4 + 1/24 = 97/24$

8. According to question,

Mass of ball = m = 4 kg, elevation from ground= h= 20 m; v= velocity at touch point

So, mgh = ½ (mv^2)

Gives v= 20 m/s

mg = 1/2 (mv^2)

$2gh = v^2$

$v^2 = 2 \times 10 \times 20 = 400$

v = 20 m/sec

9. Let x = 0.78414141..

=> 100x = 78.414141.. (I)

=> 10000x = 7841.414141.. (II)

(II) - (I) gives,

9900x = 7763

=> x = 7763/9900

10. Total interest that Nidhi has to pay after 2 years = Rs. (10000 x 2 x 10)/100 = Rs. 2000

Interest obtained by Nidhi from the bank = Rs. (3500 x 2 x 12.5)/100 = Rs. 875

Interest obtained by Nidhi from Chit fund = 6500(1 + 0.1)2 - 6500 = Rs. 1365

So total interest obtained by Nidhi = Rs. (875 + 1365) = Rs. 2240

Profit = Rs. (2240 - 2000) = Rs. 240

11. The correct order is:

(A) Initial marked price of book = Rs. 500 and purchased price for A = 92% of 500 = Rs. 460

(D) Marked price of book by A = 115% of 460 = Rs. 529

(B) Purchased price of book by B = 529 - 20 = Rs. 509

(E) Marked price of book by B = 120% of 509 = Rs. 610.8 and purchased price of book by C = 610.8 - 50.9 = Rs. 559.9

(C) Per cent profit = [(559.9 - 509)/509] x 100 = 10%

12.

$$SP = 9600 \times \frac{95}{100} = Rs.9,120$$
$$Second \ S.P. = 9120 \times \frac{105}{100} = Rs.9,576$$
$$Loss = 9600 - 9576 = 24$$

13. At 8:30 a.m. minute hand points at 6 and and hour hand points exactly between 8 and 9.

So these two hands are apart by 2.5 blocks.

We know that the difference of angle of one block is 30°.

Hence the angle between the hands = 2.5 X 30° = 75°

14. The mode is a statistical term that refers to the most frequently occurring number found in a set of numbers.

Since, 979 is occurring frequently and number of occurrence of 979 is 3.

Hence mode of sex ratio in India in last 10 years is 979.

15. Since, $7x^5 - 2x^4 + 3x^3 - 4x^2 + 6x + 2k$ is divisible by $(x + 1)$

=> x = -1 must satisfy the given equation

=> $7(-1)^5 - 2(-1)^4 + 3(-1)^3 - 4(-1)^2 + 6(-1) + 2k = 0$

=> -7 - 2 - 3 - 4 - 6 + 2k = 0

=> 2k = 22

=> k = 11

16. Let the numbers be 7x and 5x.

as, 7 and 5 are co-prime pairs.

∴ Their H.C.F. = x = 6 (given).

=> The numbers are 42 and 30.

L.C.M. of 42 and 30 = 210.

17.

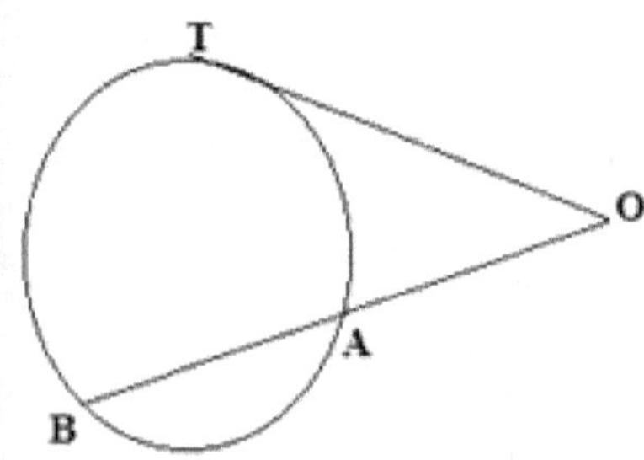

Let the tangent be T

OT_2 = OA.OB

=> OA = 4

=> OB = OA + AB

=> 4+60

=> 64

OT_2 = 4x64

=> 256

=> OT = 16 cm

18. Side of square = √121 = 11 cm

Length of wire = circumference of circle.

44 = 2 π r or r = (44 x 7)/(2 x 22) = 7 cm

Hence, area of circle = πr^2 = 22/7 x 7 x 7 = 154 cm²

19. Sum of ages of all employees in grade A = 25 x 28 = 700 years

Sum of ages of all employees in grade B = 40 x 24 = 960 years

Sum of ages of all employees in grade C = 15 x 32 = 480 years

Sum of ages of all employees in grade D = 20 x 22 = 440 years

Sum of ages of all the employees of the department P = 700 + 960 + 480 + 440 = 2580 years

Total employees in department P = 25 + 40 + 15 + 20 = 100

Average age of the employees of department P = 2580/100 = 25.8 years

20. Suppose the previous selling price = Rs. x

Selling price = Rs. x/2

There is a loss of 12.5% when selling price is Rs. x/2.

Cost Price = x/2 x 100/(100-12.5)= (100 x)/175= 4x/7

Now, when selling price is Rs. x, % profit =[(x-(4x/7))/(4x/7)] x 100 = (3x/4x) x 100 = 75%

21. α, 3α + 6, and 71α are in arithmetic progression.

=> 3α + 6 - α = 71α - 3α - 6 = common difference of the arithmetic progression.

=> 2α = 68α - 6 - 6

=> 66α = 12

=> α = 12/66 = 2/11

22. Let her savings in Employee Provident Fund be ₹ x.

∴ Her savings in Kisan Vikas Patra = ₹ (180,000 - x)

∴ (180,000 - x)/4 = x/5

=> 900,000 - 5x = 4x

=> x = ₹ 100,000

23. First number = m

Second number = (40% of m) - 21

According to the question:

20% of 40% of (m/2) + (3/4) x 20% of m = (40% of m) - 21

m = 100

Second number = (40% of m) - 21 = 40% of 100 - 21 = 19

Difference = 100 - 19 = 81

24. Let '?' be denoted by 'a'.

125% of [{a + 200 ÷ (16 ÷ 2 x 4 x (1/8))} ÷ 7.5 x 8 ÷ (18 ÷ 3 - 50% of 4)] = a

=> 125% of [{a + 200 ÷ (8 x 4 x (1/8))} ÷ 7.5 x 8 ÷ (6 - 2)] = a

=> 125% of [{a + 200 ÷ 4} ÷ 7.5 x 8 ÷ 4] = a

=> 125% of [{a + 50} ÷ 7.5 x 2] = a

=> 125% of 2(a + 50)/7.5 = a

=> (5/4) x 2(a + 50)/7.5 = a

=> a + 50 = 3a

=> a = 25

25. $\cos(90^0 - \theta)/\cos(30^0 + \theta) = 1$

$\sin \theta = \cos(30^0 + \theta)$

$\sin \theta = \sin(90^0 - 30^0 - \theta)$

$\theta = 90^0 - 30^0 - \theta$

$\theta = 30^0$

$= (\sin \theta + \cos 2\theta)$

$= \sin 30^0 + \cos 60^0$

$= 1/2 + 1/2$

$= 1$

26. Let the original fraction be x/y

According to given condition,

$$\frac{x^2 \times \frac{1}{2}}{y^2 \times 1.25} = 4 \times \frac{x}{y}$$

i.e. $\dfrac{x^2 \times 2}{y^2 \times 5} = \dfrac{4x}{y}$

27. 15 + (1 x 2) = 17

17 + (2 x 3) = 23

23 + (3 x 4) = 35

35 + (4 x 5) = 55

55 + (5 x 6) = 85

28. For a regular clock, we know that the hands of a watch meet after every 65(5/11) minutes.

Hence loss in 65 minutes = 65(5/11) - 65 = (5/11) minutes

Hence loss in 24 hours = (5 x 24 x 60) / (11 x 65) = 10(10/143) minutes

29. Fifteen years hence the ration of age = 2:1.

Let the present age of the son be 'x'.

(45+15)/(x+15) = 2/1

2x + 30 = 60

x = 15

So, the present age of son is 15 years

30. Mohan can complete a work in 30 hours.

Ramesh can do 6/5 work in 30 hours.

So Ramesh can complete the work in 30 x (5/6) = 25 hours.

Together they can finish 1/30 + 1/25 of work in 1 hour i.e., 11/150.

So in 150/11 hours, they will finish the work together.

31.

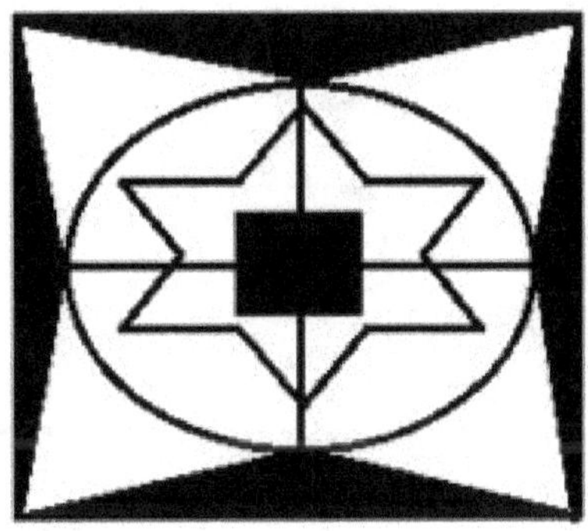

32. The paper when opened would look like the one given in figure b

33. k d **h** w **e**/ k **d** h w e/ **k** d h w **e**

34. All prime numbers and even numbers are integers, 2 is prime as well as even.

35. 28+42= 70

45+25= 70

51+32= 83 not 70

36+34= 70.

36. (x) is embedded in both I and IV.

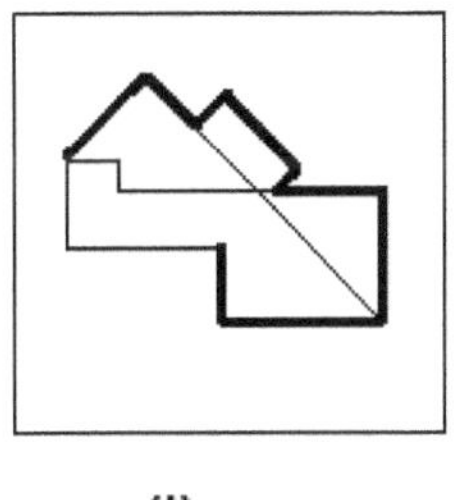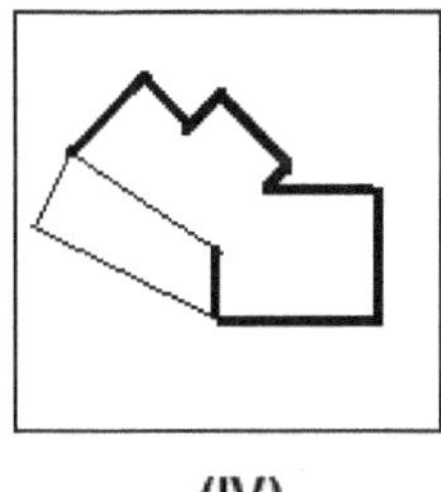

(I)   (IV)

37. Neither of the statements, taken in isolation or together, will lead us to the conclusion that education has become poor, or, that it has deteriorated.

38. Total number of odd days in the given period = 5

Hence required day = Thursday + 5 days = Tuesday

39. The solution can't be obtained even if we combine the two statements since A=#, Y=&, W=%, and P/L = $/*.

40. Image III is the correct mirror image of (x).

(x)

41. Yellow is opposite to red face.

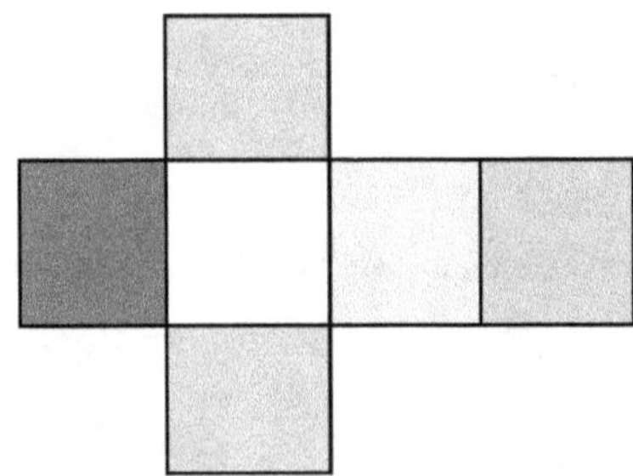

From different positions, cube faces are as follows:

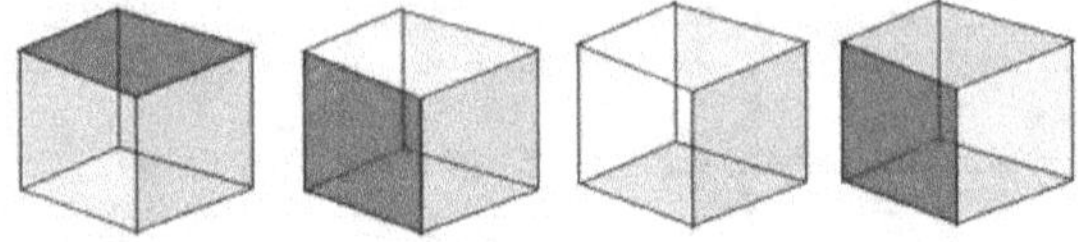

42. C is lighter than only one person, who is neither E nor B.

Thus, we get,

_ < _ < _ < _ < C < _

since,

A is the lightest one and F is not the heaviest one.

Thus, G is the heaviest.

We get,
A < _ < _ < _ < C < G

Now,

E is lighter than B.

F is lighter than at least three persons.

We get two possibilities:

A < E < F < B < C < G

Or

A < F < E < B < C < G

In both the possible cases, B is lighter than 2 persons. Hence, option (b).

43. Using statement I alone:

T< P < Q

No information is given about S and R.

Thus, the question cannot be answered using Statement I alone.

Using statement II alone:

P > S > R

No information is given about Q and T.

Thus, the question cannot be answered using Statement II alone.

Using both statements I and II together:

Q is the tallest and P is the second tallest.

But the shortest person cannot be determined.

Thus, the question cannot be answered using both statements I and II together.

Hence, option d is correct

44. 22 triangles are present in the given figure

45. O comes exactly in between M and Q; U comes exactly in between Q and Y

Similarly, D comes exactly in between B and F; J comes exactly in between F and N

46. A possible representation is:

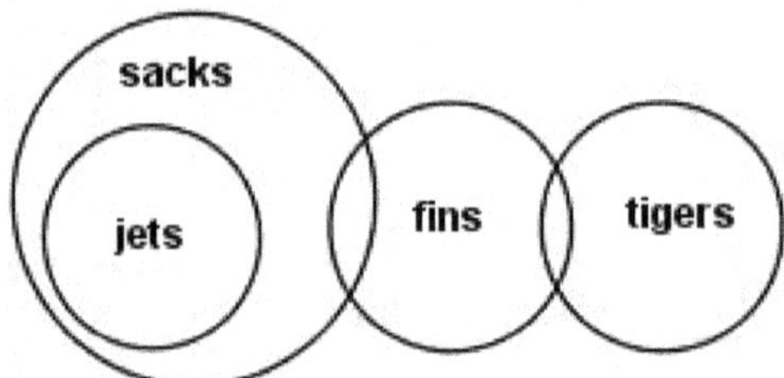

Conclusion I follows.

47.

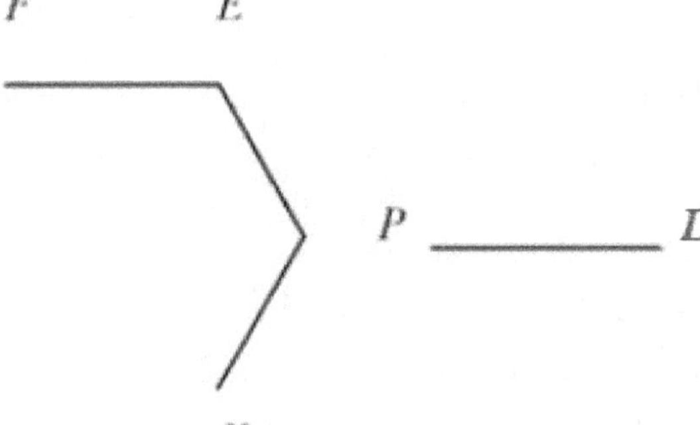

48.

49. The first two letters of the word are placed at the last places from the left and then arranged in the following manner.

SHRUB= RUBSH

RUBSH= SWEWM

50. These are arranged in reverse order of weekdays.

51. II- it's an implicit assumption for the given statement as it talks about the importance of maintaining users' privacy. I- it cannot be said to be an assumption as whether social media sites etc take pride in preserving the anonymity is open to interpretation.

52. II is weak because of the term only in that argument. Free education may weaken the economic condition of a country. Talking about weakening of social structure by giving free education to women and girl is senseless.

53. 3 = is, 4 = nice, 1 = fun then 'and' = 6

54. Except pant, rest of the three wear above the part of the body.

55.

$$-9 \xrightarrow{+7} -2 \xrightarrow{+8} 6 \xrightarrow{+9} 15 \xrightarrow{+10} 25$$

56. 1st National Sports University is all set to come up in Imphal, Manipur. The university aims to fill the void in various areas such as sports science, sports technology and high-performance training.

The Campus is Slated to have - An exhaustive library, with material across formats, Mental health student services and counselling, Guest lecture facility, Ample campus space/tie-ups with stadiums and a dedicated centre for food and nutritional sciences among various other facilities.

57. Gita Gopinath, professor at Harvard University, has been appointed as the chief economist of the International Monetary Fund (IMF).

Ms. Gopinath, alumni of Delhi School of Economics hold a Ph.D. in economics from Princeton University. She has previously worked as a co-director of the International Finance and Macroeconomics Program at the National Bureau of Economic Research.

58. India ranked as 4th highest emitter of carbon dioxide in the world, accounting for 7% of global emissions in 2017.

were China (27%), the US (15%), the European Union (10%) and India (7%), according to the projection by the Global Carbon Project.

The rest of the world contributed 41% in 2017.

59. General Bipin Rawat is the 27th Chief of Army Staff of the Indian Army. He assumed office on 31 December 2016.

Rawat was inducted into the 5th battalion of 11 Gorkha Rifles on 16 December 1978, the same unit as his father. He is highly experienced in high altitude warfare and spent 10 years conducting counter insurgency operations.

60. The Objective of the initiative BHASHA SANGAM is introduce school students to all the 22 Indian Languages of Schedule VIII of the Constitution of India and enhance linguistic tolerance and respect, and promote national integration.

The Initiative will be run by the respective State/UT Department of School Education, using Digital platforms.

61. Gautam Gambhir, an aggressive opener was India's top-scorer in the finals of the 2007 World T20 in South Africa and the 2011 ODI World Cup, both of which the country won.

Being an Opener for Indian side Gautam Gambhir, played a pivotal role in India's two World Cup triumphs.

62. Mary Kom won a silver at the inaugural women's world championships in 2001, kickstarting her international career.

She went on to win gold in each of the next five world championships. In 2010, Mary Kom won the gold medal at the Asian Women's Boxing Championship in Kazakhstan, Women's World Boxing Championship in Barbados, her 5th consecutive gold at the championship.

63. Kerala unveiled a major drive" Jala saksharatha" (water literacy) to create awareness among the public on the need to conserve water bodies in the state. Kerala is famously known for its abundance of rivers, backwaters, waterfalls, streams and ponds.

64. Since its inception in Bengaluru, Karnataka, ISRO has upheld its mission of bringing space to the service of the common man, to the service of the Nation. In the process, it has become one of the six largest space agencies in the world. ISRO maintains one of the largest fleets of communication satellites (INSAT) and remote sensing (IRS) satellites, that cater to the ever-growing demand for fast and reliable communication and earth observation respectively

65. (PM-JAY) would provide financial protection (Swasthya Suraksha) to 10.74 crore poor, deprived rural families and identified occupational categories of urban workers' families as per the latest Socio-Economic Caste Census (SECC) data (approx. 50 crore beneficiaries). It will have offered a benefit cover of Rs. 5 lakh per family per year (on a family floater basis).

Priority would be given to girl child, women and senior citizens. Free treatment available at all public and empanelled private hospitals in times of need. Covers secondary and tertiary care hospitalization.

66. Sariska Tiger Reserve in the Alwar district of Rajasthan is well nestled in the Aravalli Hills covering 800 sq. km area divided into the grasslands, dry deciduous forests, sheer cliffs and rocky landscape.

Sariska park is home to numerous carnivores including Leopard, Wild Dog, Jungle Cat, Hyena, Jackal, and Tiger.

67. In August 1942, Gandhiji started the 'Quit India Movement' and decided to launch a mass civil disobedience movement 'Do or Die' call to force the British to leave India. The movement was followed by large-scale violence directed at railway stations, telegraph offices, government buildings, and other emblems and institutions of colonial rule. There were widespread acts of sabotage, and the government held Gandhi responsible for these acts of violence, suggesting that they were a deliberate act of Congress policy.

68. Every year the State of Manipur celebrates the "Manipur Sangai Festival". The 'Festival' is named after the State animal, Sangai, the brow-antlered deer found only in Manipur.

It started in the year 2010 and has grown over the years into a big platform for Manipur to showcase its rich tradition and culture to the world. The festival helps promote Manipur as a world class tourism destination.

Festival showcases the tourism potential of the state in the field of Arts & Culture, Handloom, Handicrafts, Indigenous Sports, Cuisine, Music and Adventure sports of the state etc.

69. Human Rights Day is observed every year on 10 December. The United Nations General Assembly in 1948 adopted the Universal Declaration of Human Rights.

In 2018, Human Rights Day marked the 70th anniversary of the Universal Declaration of Human Rights, a milestone document that proclaimed the inalienable rights which everyone is inherently entitled to as a human being - regardless of race, colour, religion, sex, language, political or other opinion, national or social origin, property, birth or other status.

70. On December 30, Sheikh Hasina's party Awami League won the 11th parliamentary elections with a landslide victory.

Sheikh Hasina was first elected prime minister in 1996 and then again in 2008 and 2014.

71. It is not possible to construct an engine which does nothing but convert heat into useful work.

If some of the heat must go into raising the temperature of a sink, not all of it can be converted into work.

if work is being done by the heat engine, the object on which work is being done is not isolated from the heat engine. Unless it is at the same temperature as the heat source, heat will flow in a conventional manner from the heat source to the object on which work is being done, and the object's temperature will rise.

72. Saccharin is used to sweeten low-calorie candies, jams, jellies and cookies. Saccharin is a zero-calorie artificial sweetener. It is 300 - 400 times sweeter than sugar and commonly used as a replacement.

Saccharin is often blended with other artificial sweeteners to compensate for each sweetener's weaknesses.

73. Dynamo is an Electrical generator that works on the process of transforming Mechanical Energy to Electrical Energy.

The electric dynamo uses rotating coils of wire and magnetic fields to convert mechanical rotation into a pulsing direct electric current through Faraday's law of induction

74. Bauxite: Of all the aluminum ores, bauxite is the chief ore of aluminum.

Chalcopyrite is the chief ore of copper.

Most common silver-bearing minerals recovered by flotation are argentiferous galena, native silver, argentite (Ag_2S) and tetrahedrite (Cu, Fe, Ag) Sb_4S_3).

75. Isotopes are atoms having same atomic number but different mass numbers. Examples Carbon with atomic number 6 occurs in three forms with mass numbers 12, 13 & 14.

Isobars are atoms having same mass number but different atomic numbers.

Isotones are atoms of different elements having same number of neutrons.

76. Virology is the study of viruses and virus-like agents, including (but not limited to) their taxonomy, disease-producing properties, cultivation and genetics.

Microbiology is the study of microscopic organisms, such as bacteria, viruses, archaea, fungi and protozoa. This discipline includes fundamental research on the biochemistry, physiology, cell biology, ecology, evolution and clinical aspects of microorganisms (of which Virology may be a part of)

Morphology is the study of forms and features of different part of plants like roots, stems, leaves flowers etc.

77. Auxin is a plant hormone produced in the stem tip that promotes cell elongation, resulting in plant growth

Cytokinins are a class of plant growth hormones that promote cell division, in plant roots and shoots. They affect apical dominance, axillary bud growth, and leaf senescence

Gibberellin is type of plant and fungal hormone. Gibberellin can overcome dormancy in seeds, extend the length of cells and encourage division, and even has hormonal and signalling roles in the fruiting and senescence processes

78. Nuclear fission is a process in nuclear physics in which the nucleus of an atom splits into two or more smaller nuclei as fission products, and usually some by-product particles.

For Example- The Sun is a main-sequence star, and thus generates its energy by nuclear fusion of hydrogen nuclei into helium. In its core, the Sun fuses 620 million metric tons of hydrogen each second.

79. A covalent bond in chemistry is a chemical link between two atoms or ions in which the electron pairs are shared between them. Covalent compounds usually have low melting points. They have low boiling points and insoluble in water.

These compounds are non-conductors of electrical charge due to the absence of charged ions.

They are bad conductors of heat also. Their molecules lack free electrons and that obstructs the flow of heat energy.

80. Halogen element, any of the six non-metallic elements that constitute Group 17 (7a) of the periodic table. The halogen elements are fluorine (F), chlorine (Cl), bromine (Br), iodine (I), astatine (At), and tennessine (Ts).

81. Vulcanization, chemical process by which the physical properties of natural or synthetic rubber (which are generally very soft) are improved; finished rubber has higher tensile strength and resistance to swelling and abrasion and is elastic over a greater range of temperatures.

82. The thyroid gland lies in the front of the neck region in a position just below the Adam's apple.

The thyroid makes two hormones that it secretes into the blood stream.

These hormones are necessary for all the cells in your body to work normally.

83.

Substance	Acid
Fruits	Citric Acid
Milk	Lactic Acid
Tomatoes	Oxalic Acid
Vinegar	Acetic Acid

84. Up to 60%- 75% of the human adult body is water.

The brain and heart are composed of 73% water, and the lungs are about 83% water. The skin contains 64% water, muscles and kidneys are 79%, and even the bones are watery: 31%.

Water serves several essential functions to keep us all going:

- A vital nutrient to the life of every cell, acts first as a building material.

- It regulates our internal body temperature by sweating and respiration

- The carbohydrates and proteins that our bodies use as food are metabolized and transported by water in the bloodstream;

- It assists in flushing waste mainly through urination

- acts as a shock absorber for brain, spinal cord, and foetus, forms saliva & lubricates joints

85. A simple pendulum is one which can be a point mass suspended from a string or rod of negligible mass. It is a resonant system with a single resonant frequency. For small amplitudes, the period of such a pendulum can be approximated by:

$T = 2\pi\sqrt{(l/g)}$

86. Soldering is a process in which two or more metal items are joined together by melting and then flowing a filler metal into the joint - the filler metal having a relatively low melting point. Soldering is used to form a permanent connection between electronic components.

87. According to Ohm's law, Ohm's law equation (formula): V = I X R and the power law equation (formula): P = I x V.

P = power

So, 60 = I x 240

I = 60/240

Therefore, I = 0.25 A

88. An adiabatic process is a thermodynamic process in which there is no heat transfer into or out of a system and is generally obtained by surrounding the entire system with a strongly insulating material or by carrying out the process so quickly that there is no time for a significant heat transfer to take place.

A system that expands under adiabatic conditions does positive work, so the internal energy decreases, and a system that contracts under adiabatic conditions does negative work, so the internal energy increases.

89. Medulla oblongata, also called medulla, the lowest part of the brain and the lowest portion of the brainstem. The medulla oblongata is connected by the pons to the midbrain and is continuous posteriorly with the spinal cord, with which it merges at the opening (foramen magnum) at the base of the skull.

90. The instrument which measures the flows of current in ampere is known as ampere meter or ammeter.

A voltmeter is an electronic instrument used to measure potential between any two points in an electric or electronic circuit in volts

Odometers are used to calculate distance travelled in a vehicle, used along speedometers

91. Acceleration due to gravity is zero at the centre of earth. The value of g is least at the equator and maximum at the poles. It means the value of acceleration due to gravity increases as we go from equator to the poles.

The acceleration due to gravity:

- Decreases on account of rotation of earth.

- Increases with the increase in latitude of the place.

92. Snell's law, in optics, a relationship between the path taken by a ray of light in crossing the boundary or surface of separation between two contacting substances and the refractive index of each. It states that for a given color of light, ratio of sine of angle of incident and angle of refraction is same.

Kirchhoff's current law states that current flowing into a node (or a junction) must be equal to current flowing out of it. This is a consequence of charge conservation. Kirchhoff's voltage law states that the sum of all voltages around any closed loop in a circuit must equal zero.

Stefan-Boltzmann law, statement that the total radiant heat energy emitted from a surface is proportional to the fourth power of its absolute temperature.

93. Plasma is the largest component of your blood, making up about 55% of its overall content. When isolated on its own, blood plasma is a light-yellow liquid, similar to the color of straw. Along with water, plasma carries salts and enzymes.

The primary purpose of plasma is to transport nutrients, hormones, and proteins to the parts of the body that need it. Cells also deposit their waste products into the plasma. The plasma, in turn, helps remove this waste from the body. Blood plasma also ushers the movement of all the elements of blood through the circulatory system.

94. Lattice Energy is defined as the amount of energy released during the formation of one mole of ionic compound from its constituent ions.

Lattice energy is relevant to many practical properties including solubility, hardness, and volatility.

Hydration energy is the amount of energy released when one mole of ions undergo hydration which is a special case of solvation. It is a special case of dissolution of energy, with the solvent being water.

95. Escape velocity is the speed that an object needs to be traveling to break free of a planet or moon's gravity well and leave it without further propulsion. For example, a spacecraft leaving the surface of Earth needs to be going 7 miles per second, or nearly 25,000 miles per hour to leave without falling back to the surface or falling into orbit.

Since escape velocity depends on the mass of the planet or moon that a spacecraft is blasting off of, a spacecraft leaving the moon's surface could go slower than one blasting off of the Earth, because the moon has less gravity than the Earth.

96. Anthropology is the study of people throughout the world, their evolutionary history, how they behave, adapt to different environments, communicate and socialise with one another. The study of anthropology is concerned both with the biological features that make us human (such as physiology, genetic makeup, nutritional history and evolution) and with social aspects (such as language, culture, politics, family and religion).

Seismology is the study of earthquakes and seismic waves that move through and around the earth

Psychology is the scientific study of the mind and behaviour. Psychology is a multifaceted discipline and includes many sub-fields of study such areas as human development, sports, health, clinical, social behavior and cognitive processes.

97. Sound waves with frequencies higher than the upper audible limit of human hearing are called ultrasound. The limit varies from person to person but is approximately 20,000 Hertz. The physical properties of ultrasound are like the normal audible sound

Applications include-

- Measuring depth of sea (SONAR)

- Sterilizing Medical equipment

- Cleaning the various industry specific Machinery parts

98.

Substance	pH
Saliva	7.4
Vinegar	2.4
Milk	6.7 - 6.5
Soaps	>9

99. A natural ecosystem is the result of interactions between organisms and the environment. For example, an ocean, lakes, forests etc.

An artificial ecosystem is not self-sustaining, and the ecosystem would perish without human assistance. For example, a farm, an aquarium etc.

The biosphere is a global ecosystem composed of living organisms (biota) and the abiotic (non-living) factors from which they derive energy and nutrients extending from a few kilometres into the atmosphere to the deep-sea vents of the ocean.

100. These are the compounds of chlorine.

Mock Test 03

Mathematics

Q.1 If cosec θ = x + 1/4x, then the value of cosec θ + cot θ is:

A. -2x   **B.** 2x   **C.** 1/2x   **D.** – 1/2x

Q.2 AB = 8 cm and CD = 6 cm are parrellel chords on the same side of the center of a circle. The distance between them is 1cm. The radius of the circle is:

A. 5 cm   **B.** 4 cm   **C.** 3 cm   **D.** 2 cm

Q.3 Find the area between two concentric circles of circumference 88 cm and 132 cm.

A. 780 cm²   **B.** 770 cm²   **C.** 715 cm²   **D.** 660 cm²

Q.4 At present, the sum of ages of R and K is 63 years. The ratio of their ages after 7 years will be 7:4 , what is the present age of R ?

A. 40 years   **B.** 42 years   **C.** 29 years   **D.** 34 years

Q.5 If 5 girls can embroider a dress in 9 days, then the number of days taken by 3 girls will be ____.

A. 14 days   **B.** 10 days   **C.** 20 days   **D.** 15 days

Q.6 The total annual CO_2 emissions from various sectors are 5 mmt. In the pie chart given below, the percentage distribution to CO_2 emission from various sectors are indicated.

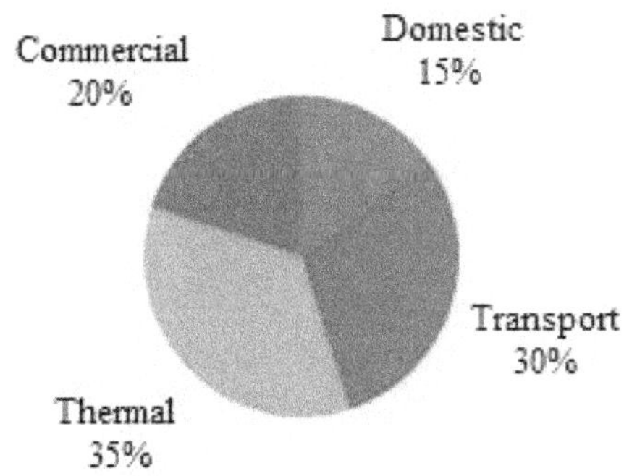

Which of the following sectors have emission difference of 1 mmt between them?

A. Domestic and Commercial
B. Transport and Commercial
C. Thermal and Domestic
D. Thermal and Transport

Q.7 The total annual CO_2 emissions from various sectors are 5 mmt. In the pie chart given below, the percentage distribution to CO_2 emission from various sectors are indicated.

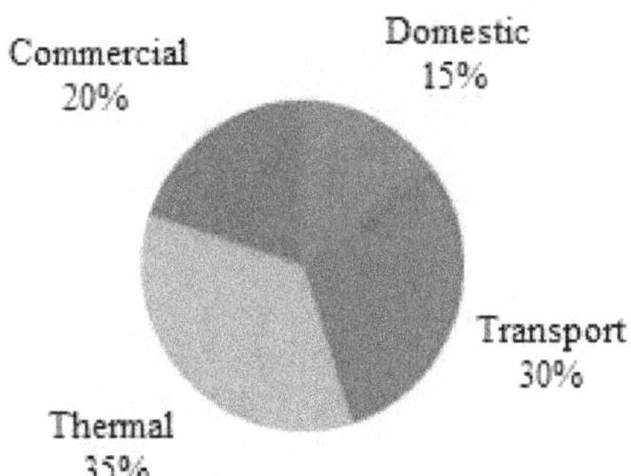

Emission of Domestic sector is how much % of transport and commercial sector combined?

A. 20%   **B.** 15%   **C.** 30%   **D.** 35%

Q.8 In the figure AB ∥ CD, ∠DPL= 1/2∠NPO, OP is the perpendicular on MN, the value of x° is :

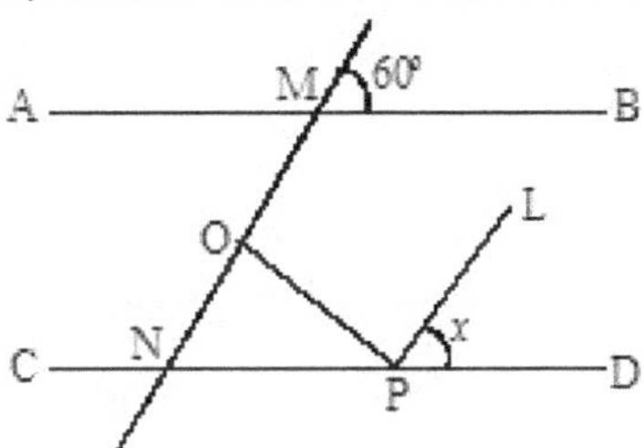

A. 30°   **B.** 40°   **C.** 15°   **D.** 25°

Q.9 Two trains travelling in the same direction at 40 kmph. and 22 kmph. completely pass off another in 1 minute. If the length of the first train is 125 metres, what is the length of the second train?

A. 125 metres   **B.** 150 metres
C. 175 metres   **D.** 185 metres

Q.10 A dress is sold at profit of 25%. If both the cost price and selling price are ₹ 100 less, the profit would be 35%. Find its cost price?

A. ₹ 250   **B.** ₹ 300   **C.** ₹ 350   **D.** ₹ 400

Q.11 The ratio between the ages of a father and a son at present is 5: 2 respectively. Four years hence the ratio between the ages of the son and his mother will be 1: 2 respectively. What is the ratio between the present ages of the father and the mother respectively?

A. 3:4   **B.** 5:4
C. 4:3   **D.** Can't be determined

Q.12 A man moving at a speed of 36 kmph covered the shadow of a tower of height 75 m in 3 seconds. If the height of the person is 1.75 m, the length of the shadow cast by the man in meters is:

A. 1.5   **B.** 0.7   **C.** 1   **D.** 0.5

Q.13 In the given figure AB ‖ CD ‖ EF ‖ GH and BH = 100 cm. Find the value of DF.

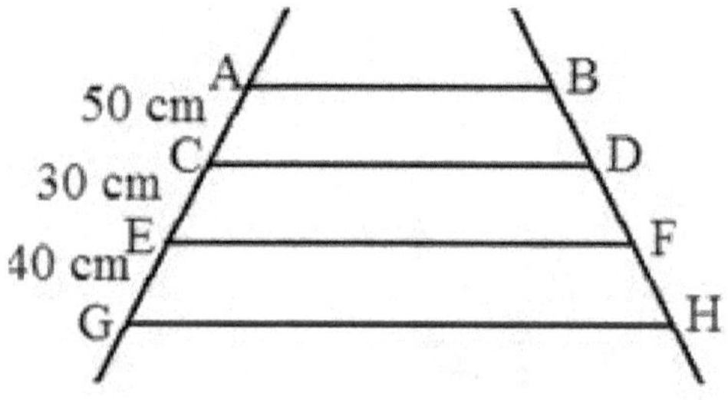

A. 26 cm   **B.** 40 cm   **C.** 25 cm   **D.** 24 cm

Q.14 The speed of a car during the second hour of its journey is thrice that in the first hour. Also its third hours speed is the average speed of the first two hours. Had the car travelled at the second hour's speed during all the first three hours, then it would have travelled 150 km more. Find the percentage reduction in time if the original distance covered by second hour's speed:

A. 331/3%   **B.** 40%   **C.** 25%   **D.** 50%

Q.15 A sum of Rs. 210 was taken as a loan. This is to be paid back in two equal installments. If the rate of interest be 10% compounded annually, then the value of each installment is

A. Rs. 127   **B.** Rs. 121   **C.** Rs. 210   **D.** Rs. 225

Q.16 If A+B = 45°, then find the value of tan A + tan B + tan A tan B.

A. -1   **B.** 1/2   **C.** √3   **D.** 1

Q.17 If sin (10° 6′ 32″) = a, then the value of cos (79° 53′ 28″) + tan (10° 6′ 32″) is:

A. $\dfrac{a\left(1 + \sqrt{1 - a^2}\right)}{\sqrt{1 - a^2}}$

B. $\dfrac{1 + \sqrt{1 - a^2}}{\sqrt{1 - a^2}}$

C. $\dfrac{\sqrt{1 - a^2} + a}{\sqrt{1 - a^2}}$

D. $\dfrac{a\sqrt{1 - a^2} + 1}{\sqrt{1 - a^2}}$

Q.18 Base of a right pyramid is a square of area 324 sqm. If the volume of the pyramid is 1296 cu.m., then the area (in m²) of the slant surface is:

A. 360   **B.** 432   **C.** 540   **D.** 1080

Q.19 Twenty per cent of Anuj's annual salary is equal to seventy five per cent of Raj's annual salary. Raj's monthly salary is 60% of Ravi's monthly salary. If Ravi's annual salary is Rs. 1.44 lacs, what is Anuj's monthly salary?

A. Rs. 2,70,000   **B.** Rs. 27,000
C. Rs. 3,24,000   **D.** Rs. 5,400

Q.20 If a + b +c = 13, what is the maximum value of (a -3)(b -2)(c + 1) ?

A. 26   **B.** 27   **C.** 30   **D.** 19

Q.21 If P = sin θ (sin θ + sin 3θ), then

A. P ≥ 0 only when θ ≥ 0
B. P ≤ 0 for all real θ
C. P ≥ 0 for all real θ
D. P ≤ 0 only when θ ≤ 0

Q.22 The difference between simple and compound interest for the fourth year is ₹ 7280 at 20% p.a. What is the sum?

A. ₹ 10,000   **B.** ₹ 50,000
C. ₹ 1,00,000   **D.** ₹ 40,000

Q.23 A tank that would normally be filled in 8 hours is now taking 2 hours more because of a leak. In how much time, will the leak empty the full tank?

A. 32 hours   **B.** 40 hours   **C.** 45 hours   **D.** 42 hours

Q.24 The length of three medians of a triangle are 9 cm, 12 cm and 15 cm. The area (in sq. cm) of the triangle is:

A. 48   **B.** 144   **C.** 24   **D.** 72

Q.25

The value of the expression:

$$\frac{4^n \times 20^{m-1} \times 12^{m-n} \times 15^{m+n-2}}{16^m \times 5^{2m+n} \times 9^{m-1}}$$

A. 500   **B.** 1   **C.** 200   **D.** 1/500

Q.26 How many metres length of cloth 10 m wide will be required to make a conical tent with base radius of 14 m and height is 48 m?

A. 110 m   **B.** 55 m   **C.** 77 m   **D.** 220 m

Q.27 If $x^4 + 1/x^4 = 119$ and x > 1, then the value of $x^3 - 1/x^3$ is:

A. 54   **B.** 18   **C.** 72   **D.** 36

Q.28 The floor of a room is of size 4 m x 3 m and its height is 3 m. The walls and ceiling of the room require painting. The area to be painted is

A. 66 m²   **B.** 54 m²   **C.** 43 m²   **D.** 33 m²

Q.29 Perimeter of an equilateral triangle is equal to the circumference of a circle. The ratio of their areas is :
(Use π= 22/7)

A. 22:212√   **B.** 22:213√
C. 21:223√   **D.** 21:222√

Q.30 The product of two successive numbers is 4032. Which is the greater of the two numbers?

A. 63   **B.** 64   **C.** 65   **D.** 66

General Intelligence & Reasoning

Q.31 In questions given below, select the number from the given alternatives.

1:8 :: 4: ?

A. 64   **B.** 512   **C.** 125   **D.** 361

Q.32 Select the odd letter/word/number from the given alternatives.

A. YWU   **B.** NLJ   **C.** KIF   **D.** VTR

Q.33 DIRECTIONS: Arrange the following in a logical order:

(i) Collector

(ii) Governor

(iii) Chief Secretary

(iv) President

(v) Clerk

A. (i), (ii), (iii), (iv), (v)

B. (v), (i), (iii), (ii), (iv)

C. (v), (i), (iii), (iv), (ii)

D. (v), (i), (iv), (iii), (ii)

Q.34 What should come at the place of question mark?

N_5V, K_7T, ?, $E_{14}P$, $B_{19}N$

A. H_9R **B.** $H_{10}Q$ **C.** H10R   **D.** $I_{10}R$

Q.35 What should come at the place of question mark?

KM_5, IP_8, GS_{11}, EV_{14}, ?

A. BX_{17} **B.** GY_{17} **C.** CY_{17} **D.** CY_{18}

Q.36 How many rural uneducated people are employed?

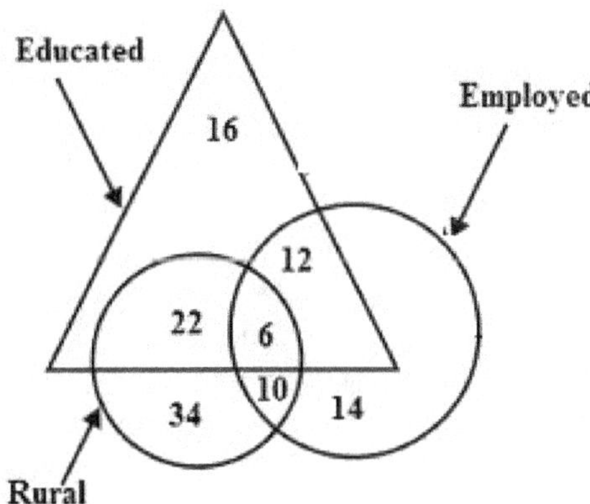

A. 10   **B.** 6   **C.** 12   **D.** 14

Q.37 Find out missing number from the following given figures.

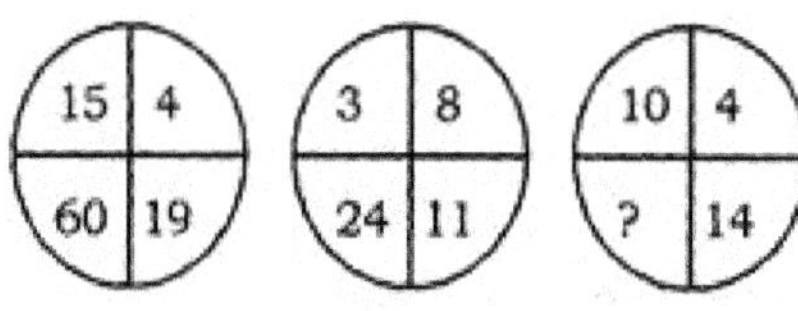

A. 117   **B.** 40   **C.** 61   **D.** 81

Q.38 Complete the given series:

6, 12, 30, 56, ?

A. 132   **B.** 102   **C.** 98   **D.** 108

Q.39 In each of the questions given below which one of the five answer figures on the right should come after the problem figures on the left, if the sequence were continued?

Problem Figures

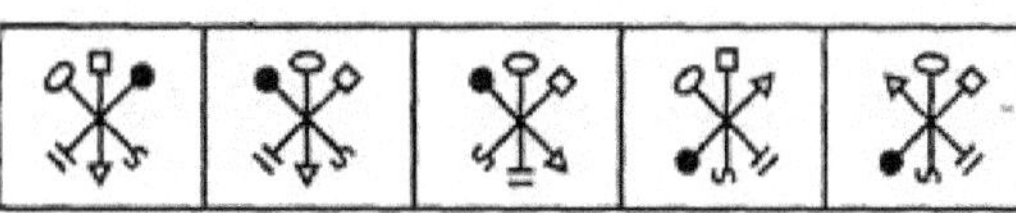

Answer Figures

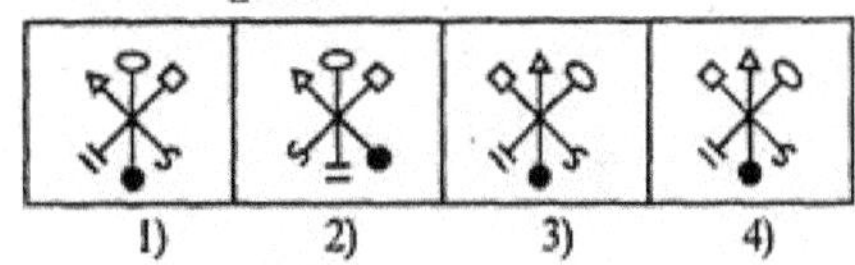

A. 1   **B.** 2   **C.** 3   **D.** 4

Q.40 Vivek and Ashok start from a fixed point. Vivek moves 3 km north and turns right and then covers 4 km. Ashok moves 5 km west and turns right and walks 3 km. How far are they apart?

A. 10 km.   **B.** 9 km.   **C.** 8 km.   **D.** 6 km.

Q.41 In the following letter series, some of the letters are missing which are given in that order one of the alternatives below it. Select the correct alternative.

a_ab_bcbc_caca_

A. ccba   **B.** acba   **C.** bccb   **D.** bcab

Q.42 In an examination in English, Harsh obtained more marks than total of marks obtained by Kunal and Debu. The total of marks obtained by Kunal and Shankar were more than Harsh. Sonal obtained more marks than Shankar. Neha obtained more marks than Harsh. Who amongst them obtained highest marks?

A. Harsh   **B.** Neha

C. Sonal   **D.** Data inadequate

Q.43 If the 3rd day of a month is Monday, which day will fall on the 5th day after the 21st of that month?

A. Thursday   **B.** Monday

C. Wednesday   **D.** Tuesday

Q.44 Find the odd word from the given alternatives

A. Turmeric   **B.** Gourd

C. Potato   **D.** Carrot

Q.45 Select the related word/ number form the give alternatives.

MANISH : JDKLPK :: SANJOG : ?

A. KELMQR   **B.** PDMKLJ

C. PDKMLJ   **D.** JLMKDP

Q.46 Select the related word/ number form the give alternatives.

(7, 27, 55)

A. (9, 35, 71)   **B.** (8, 32, 64)

C. (8, 16, 24)   **D.** (9, 36, 74)

Q.47 From the given alternative words, select the word which cannot be formed using the letters of the given word.

How many such pairs are letters are there in the word 'OVERWHELM ' each of which has as many letters between them in the word as in the English alphabet?

A. None
B. One
C. Two
D. More than three

Q.48 In the question, select the related letters from the given alternatives.

REASON : SBFLXC :: STAIRS : ?

A. T F Q B A H
B. T Q F B A H
C. T Q A B S T
D. H A B F Q T

Q.49 Rajiv is the brother of Arun. Sonia is the sister of Sunil. Arun is the son of Sonia. How is Rajiv related to Sunil?

A. Son
B. Brother
C. Father
D. Nephew

Q.50 Choose the odd one out from the given alternatives.

A. Shirt
B. Shoe
C. Chair
D. Cobbler

Q.51 In each of the questions given below which one of the five answer figures on the right should come after the problem figures on the left, if the sequence were continued?

Problem Figure

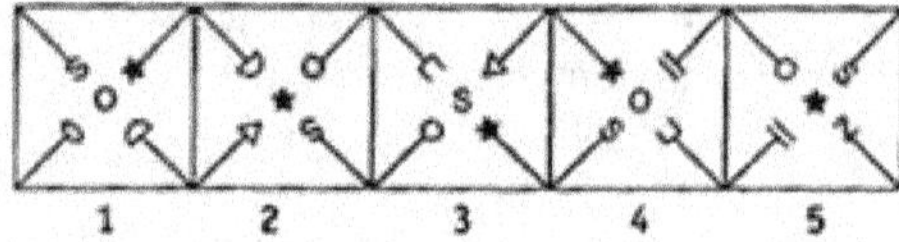

Answer Figure

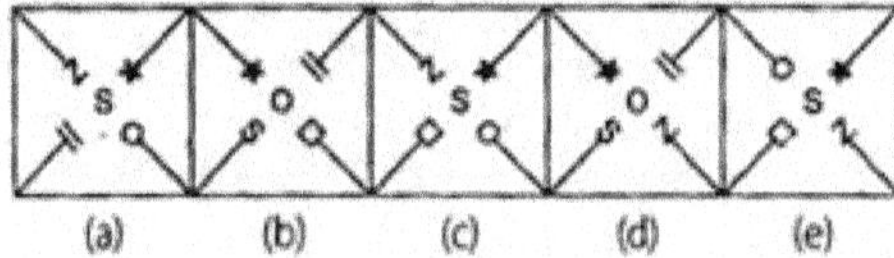

A. a
B. b
C. c
D. d

Q.52 A word is represented by only one set of numbers as given in anyone of the alternatives. The set of numbers given in the alternatives are represented by two classes of alphabets as in the 2 matrices given below. The columns and rows of Matrix I are from 0 to 4 and that of Matrix II from 5 to 9. A letter can be represented first by its row and next by its column number. e.g., 'C' can be represented by 02, 21, etc. 'T' can be represented by 65, 96 etc. Similarly, you have to identify the correct set for the word given below.

"ADJUST"

Matrix I

	0	1	2	3	4
0	D	V	C	P	M
1	P	M	D	V	C
2	V	C	P	M	D
3	M	D	V	C	P
4	C	P	M	D	V

Matrix II

	5	6	7	8	9
5	S	A	U	T	J
6	T	J	S	A	U
7	A	U	T	J	S
8	J	S	A	U	T
9	U	T	J	S	A

A. 87, 31, 66, 69, 54, 89
B. 68, 12, 66, 58, 86, 65
C. 87, 31, 66, 69, 86,89
D. 75, 43, 97, 69, 86,79

Q.53 How many such letters are there in the word BEACON each of which is as far away from the beginning is the word as when they are arranged in alphabetical order?

A. None
B. One
C. Two
D. Three

Q.54 Four of the following five pair have same relation between their elements and hence form a group. Which one does not belong to that group?

A. Bull-Calf
B. Cat-Kitten
C. Chitah-Cub
D. Tiger-Tigress

Q.55 In question given below, an unfolded dice is given while four answer choices are given in the form of complete dices. Select the correct answer which is formed by folding the unfolded dice.

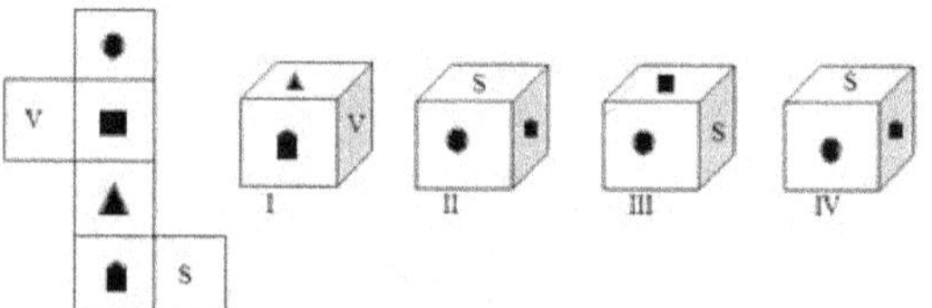

A. Only I
B. II and III
C. I, II and III
D. I, II, III & IV

General Awareness

Q.56 Where was the eleventh session of India – Czech Republic Joint Commission on Economic Cooperation (JCEC) held on 22nd – 23rd October 2018?

A. Prague
B. Ostrava
C. New Delhi
D. Hyderabad

Q.57 First Swachh Survekshan was conducted in:

A. 2014   B. 2015   C. 2016   D. 2017

Q.58 Gulmarg is a hill station in __________.

A.   Himachal Pradesh
B.   Jammu and Kashmir
C.   Maharashtra
D.   Tamil Nadu

Q.59 Which one of the following is the longest river?

A. Chenab   B. Jhelum   C. Ravi   D. Satluj

Q.60 Who is considered as the Architect of the India Constitution?

A. Mahatma Gandhi   B. B.R. Ambedkar
C. Jawaharlal Nehru   D. B.N. Rao

Q.61 Dr K Sivan is the Chairman of:

A.   RBI
B.   Human Rights Commission
C.   ISRO
D.   DRDO

Q.62 Right to education to all children between the age of 6 to 14 years is?

A.   Included in the Directive Principle of State Policy.
B.   A fundamental Right.
C.   A Statutory Right.
D.   None of the above.

Q.63 Every year Earth Day is observed on ....

A. April 21   B. April 22   C. April 23   D. April 24

Q.64 Gross Domestic Product (GDP) is defined as the value of all

A.   Goods produced in an economy in a year
B.   Goods and services in an economy in a year
C.   Final goods produced in an economy in a year
D.   Final goods and services produced in an economy in a year

Q.65 The Battle of Plassey was fought in -

A. 1757   B. 1830   C. 1880   D. 1890

Q.66 With which of these countries has India signed 17 agreements for cooperation in various sectors like areas of defence, space, health and agriculture?

A. Uzbekistan   B. Kazakhstan
C. Sudan   D. Algeria

Q.67 Blue Revolution is related to__________.

A. fish production   B. milk production
C. oil production   D. food production

Q.68 Recently, COP 24 is in news. It is related with:

A. Refugee issue   B. Climate change
C. Human rights   D. AIDS campaign

Q.69 Who has been appointed as new CM of Madhya Pradesh?

A. Viraj Thakral   B. Jyotiraditya Scindia
C. Kamalnath   D. Sudeep Singh

Q.70 "Hand in Hand" joint military exercise concluded between which of the following countries?

A. India and Russia   B. India and China
C. India and Australia   D. India and Maldives

General Science

Q.71 The average distance of the earth from the sun is .... Km.

A. 1.495×10^{11} B. 1.495×10^{12}
C. 1.495×10^{13} D. 1.495×10^{14}

Q.72 What is the largest source of power in India?

A. Solar   B. Wind   C. Thermal   D. Nuclear

Q.73 The percentage composition of carbon in urea, $CO(NH_2)_2$ is __________

A. 40 %   B. 30 %   C. 20 %   D. 10 %

Q.74 Speed of sound is the greatest in__________.

A. Water   B. Air   C. Glass   D. Glycerin

Q.75 Nuclear reactors used to produce electricity are based on__________ .

A. nuclear fission   B. nuclear fusion
C. cold fusion   D. superconductivity

Q.76 The study of fossils is called ....

A. Phylogeny   B. Palaeontology
C. Cycadofilicales   D. Biogeography

Q.77 Which is the part of digestive system of human?

A. Buccal cavity   B. Alimentary canal
C. Teeth   D. All of these

Q.78 What is the mass of 0.5 mole of ozone molecule?

A. 8 g   B. 16 g   C. 24 g   D. 48 g

Q.79 Weight of the body is ________ ?

A.   Minimum at the equator.
B.   Maximum at the equator.
C.   Minimum at the poles.
D.   Same everywhere.

Q.80 Which of the following has least penetrating power?

A.   Alpha particles
B.   Beta particles
C.   Gamma particles
D.   All have same power

Q.81 Ribosomes are made up of-

A.   DNA, RNA and Proteins
B.   DNA and proteins
C.   RNA and protein
D.   Nucleoproteins

Q.82 Which of the following is used as a moderator in nuclear reactor ?

A. Ordinary water   B. Radium
C. Thorium   D. Graphite

Q.83 Which variety of coal contains the highest percentage of carbon?

A. Anthracite
B. Peat
C. Bituminous
D. Lignite

Q.84 The size of a cell depends upon

A. Regulation ability of its nucleus
B. Its mineral requirements
C. Its oxygen requirements
D. All of the above

Q.85 In which following processes light energy is converted into chemical energy ?

A. Respiration
B. Fermentation
C. Photosynthesis
D. Photorespiration

Q.86 The value of gravitational constant represented by G is:

A. 6.67×10^{-9}
B. 6.67×10^{-10}
C. 6.67×10^{-11}
D. 6.67×10^{-12}

Q.87 PWM switching is preferred in voltage source inverters for the purpose of:

A. Controlling output voltage
B. Reducing filter size
C. All the above
D. None of the above

Q.88 When a bullet is fired upward vertically, it gains ______.

A. Speed
B. Acceleration
C. Kinetic energy
D. Potential energy.

Q.89 Tuberculosis is a _____.

A. viral disease
B. bacterial disease
C. protozoan disease
D. fungal disease

Q.90 A person can jump higher on the moon's surface than on the earth because:

A. The Moon has no atmosphere.
B. The Moon is cooler than earth.
C. The Moon surface is rough.
D. The acceleration due to gravity in moon is smaller than that on the earth.

Q.91 The unit of luminous intensity is ....

A. Mole
B. Candela
C. Kelvin
D. pH

Q.92 According to Avogadro's law which one of the following is correct?

A. $V \propto 1/p$
B. $V \propto T$
C. $V \propto n$
D. All of the above

Q.93 The acceleration due to gravity on the moon is approximately ______ .

A. 4.9 m/s^2
B. 3.3 m/s^2
C. 2.4 m/s^2
D. 1.6 m/s^2

Q.94 When something is dropped it does not fall with uniform ....

A. Speed
B. Acceleration
C. Velocity
D. None of the above

Q.95 Electromagnetic radiation is emitted by_____.

A. X-rays
B. Electrons
C. Ultrasonic
D. Protons

Q.96 Which mirror forms virtual image?

A. Concave mirror
B. Convex mirror
C. Plane mirror
D. All of the above

Q.97 Atom bomb is made on the basis of —

A. Nuclear fusion
B. Nuclear fission
C. Both (A) & (B)
D. None of these

Q.98 Who discovered X-rays?

A. Land
B. Roentgen
C. Eastman
D. Kodak

Q.99 Malaria is a disease caused by ________.

A. virus
B. bacteria
C. fungi
D. protozoa

Q.100 It is difficult to walk on sand than on a concrete road because?

A. Sand is soft.
B. There is less friction.
C. There is more friction.
D. None of the above.

// Smart Answer Sheet //

Correct — Percentage of students who answered correctly.　**Skipped** — Percentage of students who skipped.

Q.	Ans.	Correct / Skipped
1	B	85.14 % / 10.17 %
2	A	77.49 % / 10.78 %
3	B	79.45 % / 20.33 %
4	B	81.16 % / 13.85 %
5	D	79.3 % / 11.85 %
6	C	79.14 % / 14.0 %
7	C	79.22 % / 20.21 %
8	C	81.67 % / 12.93 %
9	C	76.07 % / 11.98 %
10	C	77.45 % / 11.04 %
11	D	78.01 % / 11.3 %
12	B	79.06 % / 12.2 %
13	C	78.37 % / 14.8 %
14	A	78.71 % / 13.41 %
15	B	89.37 % / 10.52 %
16	D	86.42 % / 11.76 %
17	A	87.2 % / 12.75 %
18	C	86.57 % / 13.06 %
19	B	81.38 % / 10.92 %
20	B	87.89 % / 11.99 %
21	C	81.13 % / 13.12 %
22	B	81.48 % / 16.75 %
23	B	79.29 % / 20.13 %
24	D	85.2 % / 10.6 %
25	D	78.52 % / 11.33 %
26	D	87.32 % / 10.14 %
27	D	81.55 % / 16.62 %
28	B	88.27 % / 10.4 %
29	B	77.56 % / 14.73 %
30	B	87.99 % / 11.4 %
31	B	85.93 % / 12.53 %
32	C	78.3 % / 18.27 %
33	B	80.74 % / 16.85 %
34	C	78.11 % / 20.85 %
35	C	86.34 % / 10.23 %
36	A	78.04 % / 10.11 %
37	B	83.44 % / 14.51 %
38	A	81.48 % / 15.57 %
39	A	78.03 % / 12.48 %
40	B	87.75 % / 10.22 %
41	D	81.05 % / 13.88 %
42	D	79.44 % / 15.43 %
43	C	80.59 % / 14.44 %
44	B	81.77 % / 17.35 %
45	C	85.31 % / 13.45 %
46	A	88.6 % / 11.36 %
47	D	80.02 % / 10.75 %
48	B	83.5 % / 12.56 %
49	D	78.97 % / 14.98 %
50	D	87.36 % / 10.23 %
51	C	77.37 % / 20.66 %
52	C	80.65 % / 18.31 %
53	A	78.63 % / 13.15 %
54	A	89.24 % / 10.14 %
55	D	86.47 % / 12.14 %
56	A	80.23 % / 17.3 %
57	C	78.74 % / 11.12 %
58	B	89.65 % / 10.32 %
59	D	80.54 % / 18.55 %
60	B	80.25 % / 14.16 %
61	C	82.53 % / 13.44 %
62	B	81.1 % / 13.15 %
63	B	76.14 % / 16.02 %
64	D	87.25 % / 11.43 %
65	A	89.51 % / 10.33 %
66	A	76.63 % / 17.88 %
67	A	78.45 % / 14.65 %
68	B	80.66 % / 17.85 %
69	C	82.6 % / 11.53 %
70	B	88.54 % / 11.34 %
71	A	82.93 % / 10.04 %
72	C	86.34 % / 12.11 %
73	C	77.55 % / 17.79 %
74	C	84.54 % / 10.36 %
75	A	86.71 % / 13.15 %
76	B	88.15 % / 10.88 %
77	D	78.35 % / 18.49 %
78	C	83.62 % / 11.35 %
79	A	82.06 % / 17.83 %
80	A	85.75 % / 13.84 %

Q.	Ans.	Correct		Q.	Ans.	Correct		Q.	Ans.	Correct		Q.	Ans.	Correct		Q.	Ans.	Correct
		Skipped				Skipped				Skipped				Skipped				Skipped
81	C	89.91 %		85	C	89.7 %		89	B	76.33 %		93	D	89.44 %		97	B	80.24 %
		10.02 %				10.03 %				21.12 %				10.17 %				11.36 %
82	D	80.43 %		86	C	82.89 %		90	D	83.38 %		94	C	86.59 %		98	B	82.22 %
		19.32 %				14.82 %				11.34 %				12.24 %				16.64 %
83	A	82.65 %		87	A	85.14 %		91	B	77.78 %		95	A	83.18 %		99	D	88.94 %
		11.97 %				12.61 %				20.57 %				13.06 %				10.95 %
84	D	76.12 %		88	D	86.09 %		92	C	89.81 %		96	B	85.03 %		100	C	79.25 %
		12.74 %				13.0 %				10.13 %				10.74 %				15.09 %

//Hints and Solutions//

1. Let cosec θ + cot θ = k

$\Rightarrow$ cosec θ - cot θ = 1/k

On adding, we get

2 cosec θ = k + 1/k = 2(x+1/4x) = k+1/k

$\Rightarrow$ 2x+1/2x = k+1/k $\Rightarrow$ k = 2x

2.

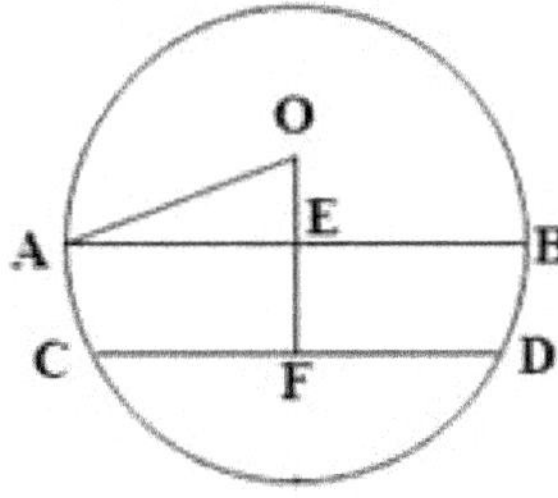

Let OE= x

OF = x+1, OA=OC= r

AE= 4cm, CF= 3cm

From Δ OAE

$r^2 = 16+x^2$

$x^2 = r^2 - 16$ ------(1)

From Δ OCF

$(x+1)^2 = r^2 - 9$ ------ (2)

By equation (2) - (1)

x = 3cm

r = 5cm

3. Let the radius of the inner circle be r_1 and the radius of the outer circle be r_2.

A.T.Q.,

$$2\pi r_1 = 88 \Rightarrow r_1 = \frac{88}{2\pi} \text{ and } 2\pi r_2 = 132 \Rightarrow r_2 = \frac{132}{2\pi}$$

Area between the two circles = $\pi(r_1^2 \sim r_2^2)$

$$= \pi \left[\left(\frac{88}{2\pi}\right)^2 \sim \left(\frac{132}{2\pi}\right)^2 \right] = \frac{1}{4\pi}\left[132^2 - 88^2\right]$$

$$= \frac{1}{4\pi} \times 220 \times 44 = \frac{7}{22 \times 4} \times 220 \times 44 = 770 \text{ cm}^2$$

4. Let the present age of R is x

$\Rightarrow$ present age of K is 63 - x

7 years later

R's age = x+7

K's age = 63-x+7 = 70-x

$\Rightarrow$ (x+7)/(70-x) = 7/4

$\Rightarrow$ 4x+28 = 490-7x

$\Rightarrow$ 11x = 462

$\Rightarrow$ x = 42 years

therefore present age of R= 42 years

5. Days taken by 5 girls to embroider a dress = 9 days

Days taken by 1 girl to embroider a dress = 9 x 5 days

Days taken by 3 girls to embroider a dress = 9×5/3 days = 15 days

6. 1 mmt = 20% = Thermal – Domestic

7. 15/50 × 100 = 30%

8.

$$\angle ONP = 60°$$

$$\angle OPN = 90° - \angle ONP = 90^0 - 60^0$$

$$\Rightarrow OPN = 30^0$$

$$\angle DPL = \frac{1}{2} \angle NPO = \frac{1}{2}(30)^0$$

$$\Rightarrow \angle DPL = 15^0 \qquad\qquad \Rightarrow x = 15^0$$

9. Distance traveled by the relative speed of (40-22) kmph i.e. 18 kmph

In 1 minute= 18×1000/60 = 300 m

∴ Length of second train = (300-125) = 175 m

10. C.p = (Initial profit + increase in profit %)/Increase in profit%×Amount

C.P = 25+10/10×100

= ₹ 350

11. Let the present ages of father and son be '5x' and '2x' years respectively.

After 4 years, Son's age = (2x + 4) years

According to question

After 4 years

$$\frac{\text{age of son}}{\text{age of mother}} = \frac{1}{2}$$

$$\Rightarrow \frac{(2x+4)}{\text{age of mother}} = \frac{1}{2}$$

$$\Rightarrow \text{Age of mother} = 2 \times (2x+4) = 4x+8 \text{ years}$$

Present age of Mother = 4x + 8 - 4

= 4x + 4

Ratio between the present age of the father and mother = 5x: (4x + 4)

∴ We cannot find the exact value of ratio.

12.

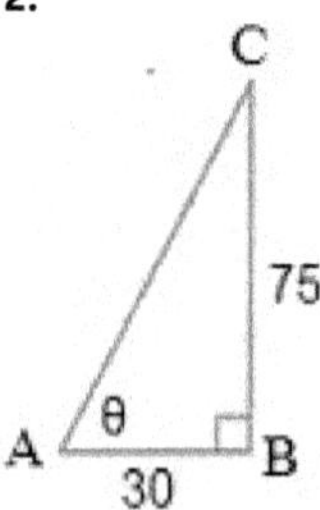

Distance traveled in 3 seconds with a speed of 36 kmph is =

$(5/18) \times (3) \times (36) = 30$m.

From the figure tan θ = BC/AB = 75/30 = 5/2

The height of the person is 1.75 m

Let the length of the shadow be x m.

tan θ = 1.75/x ⇒ 52 = 1.75/x

⇒ x = 1.75/5(2) = 0.7

13. AG/BH=CE/DF

120/100=30/DF⇒DF=100×30/120=25

14.

	First	Second	Third	Total
		hour	hour	hour
Initial speed	x	3x	2x	6x
New speed	3x	3x	3x	9x

∴ Percentage increase in speed = 3x/6x × 100 = 50%

Since speed is increased by (50%) 1/2

Therefore, time will reduce by (33.33%) 1/3

15.

Let x be the value of installment.

Principal = Present value of x for 1 year + Present value of x for 2 years

$$210 = \frac{x}{\left(1+\frac{R}{100}\right)} + \frac{x}{\left(1+\frac{R}{100}\right)}$$

$$\Rightarrow 210 = \frac{x}{1+\frac{1}{10}} + \frac{x}{\left(1+\frac{1}{10}\right)^2}$$

$$\Rightarrow 210 = \frac{x}{\frac{11}{10}} + \frac{x}{\left(\frac{11}{10}\right)^2}$$

$$\Rightarrow 210 = \frac{10x}{11} + \frac{100x}{121}$$

$$210 = \frac{110x + 100x}{121}$$

$$210 = \frac{210x}{121}$$

$$121 = \frac{210}{210}x$$

$$x = 121.$$

16. A+B = 45°

tan (A+B) = tan 45°

tan A +tan B1−tan A .tan B=1

tan A + tanB + tanAtanB = 1

17.

cos 79° 53' 28" + tan 10° 6' 32"

$$= \sin 10° 6' 32" + \frac{\sin 10° 6' 32"}{\cos 10° 6' 32"}$$

$$a + \frac{a}{\sqrt{1-a^2}} = \frac{a\left(1+\sqrt{1-a^2}\right)}{\sqrt{1-a^2}}$$

18.

Height of pyramid = $\frac{1296}{324} \times 3 = 12$ mtr.

Slant height = $\sqrt{12^2 + 9^2} = 15$ [∵ Side of square = 18 m]

Area of slant surface = $4 \times \frac{1}{2} 18 \times 1515 = 540$ m^2

19.

Monthly salary of Raj

$$= \frac{1.44 \times 60}{12 \times 100} = ₹0.072 \text{ lakh}$$

∴ Anuj's monthly salarly × $\frac{1}{5}$

= Raj's monthly salary × $\frac{3}{4}$

⇒ Anuj's monthly salary = ₹ $\left(0.072 \times \frac{3}{4} \times 5\right)$ lakh

= ₹27,000

20. if x+y +z is constant, the product xyz takes maximum value when each of x, y, z takes equal value.

∵ a + b +c = 13

∴ (a -3) + (b -2) + (c + 1) = 13 − 3 − 2 + 1 = 9

For the maximum value of (a -3)(b -2) (c + 1)

= (a -3)= (b -2)= (c + 1)= 9/3 = 3

So, (a -3)(b -2) (c + 1) = 3 × 3 × 3 = 27

21. We have

P = sin θ (sin θ + sin 3θ)

= sin θ (2sin 2θ. cos θ)

[∵ sin C + sin D = 2sin (C+D/2).cos (C−D/2)]

⇒ P = sin 2θ (2sin θ. cos θ)

= sin 2θ.sin 2θ = sin² 2θ

P = sin² 2θ ≥ 0

for all real θ

22.

Difference between CI and SI for n^{th} year

$$= \frac{Pr}{100}\left[\left(1 + \frac{r}{100}\right)^{n-1} - 1\right]$$

$$7280 = \frac{P \times 20}{100}\left[(1.2)^3 - 1\right]$$

$$\Rightarrow P = 50,000$$

Alternatively:

	Initially	Ist Year	IInd Year	IIIrd year	IVth year
SI	10000	12000	14000	16000	18000
CI	10000	12000	14400	17280	20736

CI for 4th year = 20736—17280 = 3456

SI for 4th year = 2000

Difference between CI and SI = 1456 for ₹10000

So, the difference of ₹7280 is for ₹50,000

23. Time taken by the inlet pipe to fill the tank = 8 h

Time taken to fill the tank due to leak = 8 + 2 = 10 h

Let the leak take x hours to empty the filled tank.

Now, according to the question:

$$\frac{1}{8} - \frac{1}{x} = \frac{1}{10}$$

$$\frac{1}{8} - \frac{1}{10} = \frac{1}{x}$$

$$\frac{5 - 4}{40} = \frac{1}{x}$$

$$\frac{1}{x} = \frac{1}{40}$$

Time taken by leak to empty the tank = X = 40 hours

24. Area of triangle = 43× Area of triangle formed by taking median as a side of triangle

A= 9, B=12, C=15

Side = A+B+C2 = 9+12+152 = 18

area of triangle
=43 $\sqrt{S(S-a)(S-b)(S-c)}$ - - - - - - - - - - - - - - - - - - -

$\sqrt{4318 \times 9 \times 6 \times 3}$ - - - - - - - - - - - -

=43×9×3×2=72

25.

$4^{(n+m-1+m-n-2m)} \times 5^{(m-1+m+n-2-2m-n)} \times 3^{(m-n+m+n-2-2m+2)}$

$=4^{-1} \times 5^{-3} \times 3^0$

$= 1/4 \times 1/125 \times 1 = 1/500$

26. Slant height of a cone: (l) = √(r2 + h2)

= √(142 + 482)

= √196 + 2304

= √2500

l = 50 m

Lateral surface area of a cone = πrl

=227×14×50= 2200 m2

Hence length of cloth= 220010

= 220 m

27.

$$x^4 + \frac{1}{x^4} = 119$$

$$\Rightarrow \left(x^2 + \frac{1}{x^2}\right)^2 - 2 = 119$$

$$\Rightarrow \left(x^2 + \frac{1}{x^2}\right)^2 = 121$$

$$\Rightarrow x^2 + \frac{1}{x^2} = 11$$

$$\Rightarrow \left(x - \frac{1}{x}\right)^2 + 2 = 11$$

$$\Rightarrow \left(x - \frac{1}{x}\right)^2 = 9 \Rightarrow x - \frac{1}{x} = 3$$

Cubing both sides,

$$\left(x - \frac{1}{x}\right)^3 = 27$$

$$\Rightarrow x^3 - \frac{1}{x^3} - 3\left(x - \frac{1}{x}\right) = 27$$

$$\Rightarrow x^3 - \frac{1}{x^3} - 3 \times 3 = 27$$

$$\Rightarrow x^3 - \frac{1}{x^3} = 27 + 9 = 36$$

28. Area of the four walls of the room

=2 x height (length + breath)

= 2 x 3(4+3) = 42 sq. metre

Area of ceiling = 4 x 3

= 12 sq. metre

Required area = 42 + 12

= 54 sq. metre

29.

According to the question,

$$3a = 2\pi r$$

$$\Rightarrow a = \frac{2}{3}\pi r$$

Area of an equilateral triangle:

$$= \frac{\sqrt{3}}{4} \times a^2$$

$$= \frac{\sqrt{3}}{4} \times \left(\frac{2}{3}\pi r\right)^2$$

$$= \frac{\sqrt{3}}{4} \times \frac{4}{9}\pi^2 r^2$$

$$= \frac{\pi^2 r^2}{3\sqrt{3}} \text{ sq. units.}$$

Area of circle:

$$= \pi r^2$$

$$\therefore \text{ Required ratio } = \frac{\pi^2 r^2}{3\sqrt{3}} : \pi r^2$$

$$= \pi : 3\sqrt{3}$$

$$= \frac{22}{7} : 3\sqrt{3} = 22 : 21\sqrt{3}$$

30. 63 x 64 = 4032

$$1 \quad : \quad 8 \quad :: \quad 4 \qquad \mathbf{512}$$

$$(1)^3 \times 8 = 8 \qquad (4)^3 \times 8 = 512$$

31.

32. In all other groups of words there is a gap of one letter as in the alphabet between second and third letter.

33. Meaningful order of the words in ascending order is as follows:

Clerk → Collector → Chief → Secretary → Governor → President

34. N−→−3K−→−3[H]−→−3E−→−3B

5−→+27−→+3[10]−→+414−→+519

V−→−2T−→−2[R]−→−2P−→−2N

35. K−→−2I−→−2G−→−2E−→−2[C]

M−→+3P−→+3S−→+3V−→+3[Y]

5−→+38−→+311−→+314−→+3[17]

36. There are 10 who are rural uneducated people who are employed.

37. In figure I = 15 × 4 = 60,

15+4 = 19

In figure II = 3 x 8 = 24,

3 + 8=11

Then missing number is = 10 × 4

= 40

38. The given series follows the pattern:

(prime number)2 + (prime number)

So, 22+2=4+2=6,

32+3=9+3=12,

52+5=25+5=30,

72+7=49+7=56,

112+11=121+11=132.

Hence required term will be 132.

39. From figure 1 to fig.2, lower part is kept fixed and upper half is rotated clockwise. from 2 to 3 upper part is kept fixed and lower half is rotated anticlockwise.from fig.3 to 4, whole structure is rotated 1 step anticlockwise.again from 4 to 5 fig. lower part is fixed and upper part clockwise so for next fig it should be upper part fixed and lower part anticlockwise

40.

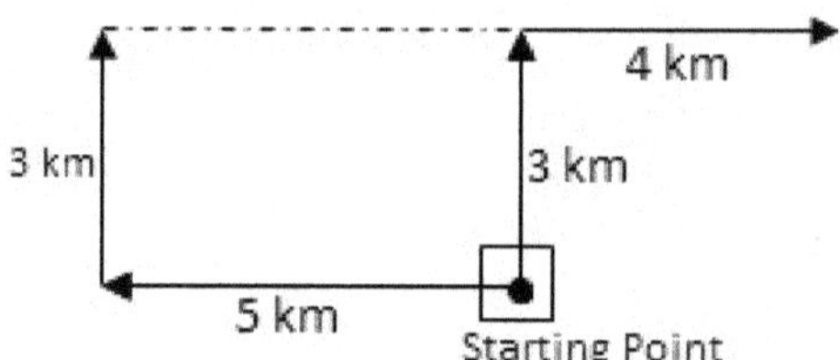

Required distance = 5 + 4 = 9 km

41.

$$a\boxed{b}\,a\,b\,\boxed{c}\;/\;bc\,bc\,\boxed{a}\;/\;caca\,\boxed{b}$$

42. According to the question,

Kunal + Debu < Harsh...(1)

Kunal + Shankar > Harsh ...(2)

Sonal > Shankar

Neha > Harsh

From (1) and (2)

Kunal + Debu < Harsh < Kunal + Shankar

Therefore, data is inadequate to answer who got the highest marks.

43. The 3rd day is Monday. So, the 10th and 17th days are also Mondays.

Thus, the 21st day is Friday.

∴. The fifth day from the 21st will be Wednesday.

44. Except Gourd, all others are grown underground.

45.

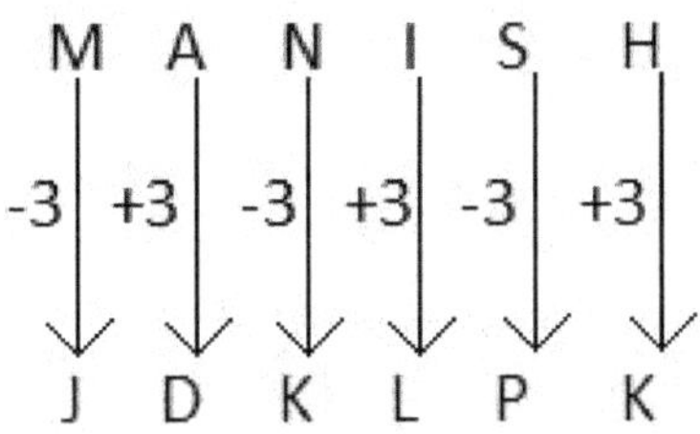

Similarly

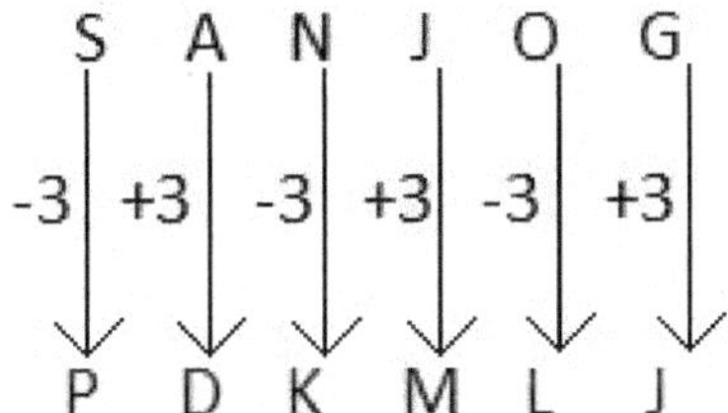

46. Given

7, 7×4 = 28−1 = 27, 7×8 = 56−1= 55

Same way

(9, 9×4 = 36−1 = 35, 9×8 = 72−1 = 71)

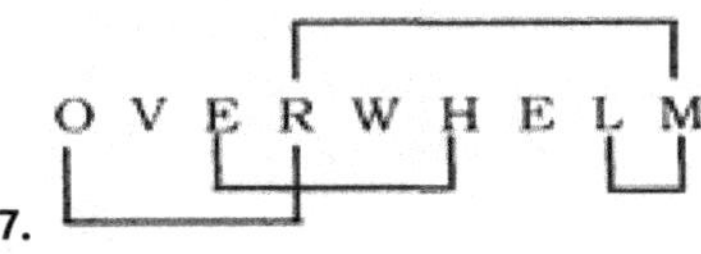

47.

Alternate solution:

OVERWHELM

In Forward direction:

OPQR = OVER (OR has as many letters between them in the word as in the English alphabet)

ERWH = EFGH (EH has as many letters between them in the word as in the English alphabet)

LM = LM (LM has as many letters between them in the word as in the English alphabet)

In Reverse direction:

RWHELM = RQPONM(RM has as many letters between them in the word as in the English alphabet)

So, Required number of pairs of letters is 4. So, More than three is correct.

48.

Given ,

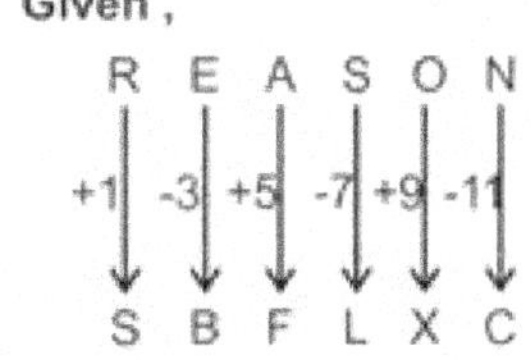

Similarly ,

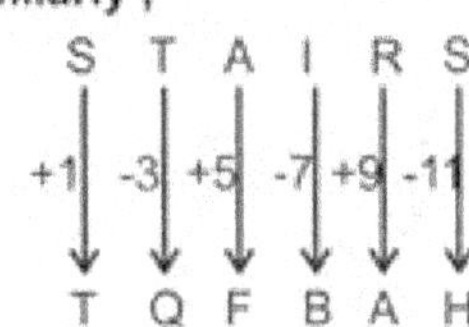

49.

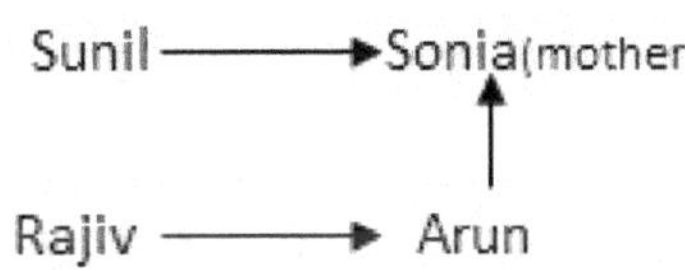

Rajiv and Arun are sons of Sonia. Therefore, Rajiv is nephew of Sunil.

50. Cobbler is human being while all other are used by human beings.

51. The sequence of problem figures is

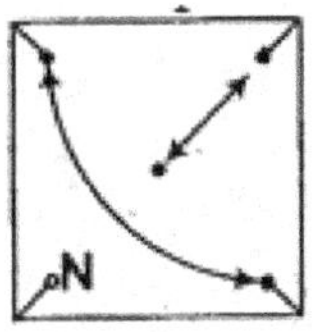

N = New design

and the whole figure rotates by 90° clockwise.

52. According to the question,

A = 75, 56, 87, 68, 99

D = 00, 31, 12, 43, 24

J = 85, 66, 97, 78, 59

U = 95, 76, 57, 88, 69

S = 55, 86, 67, 98, 79

T = 65, 96, 77, 58, 89

So, ADJUST = 87, 31, 66, 69, 86, 89

53. Original word: B E A C O N

On Arranging: A B C E N O

Required letters = None

54. Only the tiger and the tigress hold the male and female relationship, while the remaining hold the parent and offspring relationship.

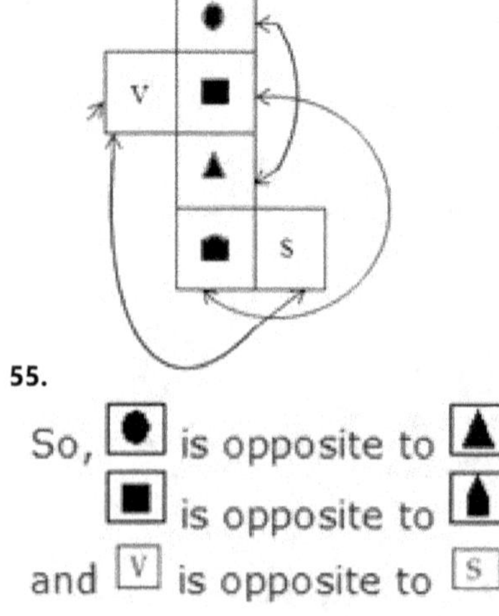

55.

So, ● is opposite to ▲

■ is opposite to ◭

and V is opposite to S

Now, it is clear that all cubes I, II, III & IV can be formed by folding the dice

56. The eleventh session of India – Czech Republic Joint Commission on Economic Cooperation (JCEC) was held on 22nd – 23rd October 2018 at Prague.

57. As a prelude to encouraging cities to improve urban sanitation, the Ministry of Housing and Urban Affairs (MoHUA) had conducted 'Swachh Survekshan-2016' survey for ranking 73 cities in January 2016.

58. Jammu and Kashmir. Gulmarg ("Meadow of Flowers") is a town, a hill station, a popular skiing destination and a notified area committee in Baramula district in the Indian state of Jammu and Kashmir. The town is sitiuated in the Pir Pinjal range in the western the Himalayas and is within miles of the Line of Control between India and Pakistan.

59. The longest river Satluj.

60. The chief architect of the Indian constitution was B.R. Ambedkar. The Indian constitution which was drafted by Ambedkar has been described as first and foremost a social document. The majority of India's constitutional provisions are either directly arrived at furthering the aim of social revolution or attempt to foster this revolution by establishing conditions necessary for its achievement by Granville Austin.

61. Indian Space Research Organisation (ISRO) Chairman Dr K Sivan has said that the Union Government has allocated 10,900 crore rupees for the development of 40 satellite launch vehicles in the next four years.

62. The 86th Amendment Act 2002 had made the following changes in our constitution: Change in Fundamental Rights: A new article 21A was inserted below the Article 21 which made Right to Education a Fundamental Right for children in the range of 6-14 years. This article reads: "The State shall provide free and compulsory education to all children of the age of six to fourteen years in such manner as the State may, by law, determine". It made education for all children below 6 years a Directive Principle for State Policy (DPSP). It made the opportunities for education to child a Fundamental duty of the parents of the children

63. Every year Earth Day is observed on April 22.

64. The gross domestic product (GDP) is one of the primary indicators used to gauge the health of a country's economy. It represents the total dollar value of all goods and services produced over a specific time period; you can think of it as the size of the economy.

65. The Battle of Plassey was fought in 1757.

66. India and Uzbekistan inked 17 agreements on Monday, including in the areas of defence, space, health and agriculture.

67. The water equivalent of the green revolution is Blue revolution and on primary basis it is referred to as the management of water resources that can steer humanity to achieve drinking water and crop irrigation security. In other contexts, it refers to aquaculture or fish farming. The term "blue revolution is referred to as the remarkable emergence of aquaculture as an important and highly productive agricultural activity. All forms of active culturing of aquatic animals and plants, occurring in marine, brackish, or fresh waters is generally referred to as "Aquaculture".

68. The Union Cabinet chaired by Prime Minister Shri Narendra Modi has given its ex-post facto approval to the negotiating stand of India at the 24th Conference of Parties (COP) to the United Nations Framework Convention on Climate Change (UNFCCC) held in Katowice, Poland from 2-15 December 2018.

69. Kamalnath is the new CM of Madhya Pradesh.

70. "Hand in Hand" joint military exercise concluded between India and China.

71. The average distance of the earth from the sun is 1.495×10^{11}

72. Thermal power is the "largest" source of power in India. There are different types ofthermal power plants based on the fuel used to generate the steam such as coal, gas, and Diesel. About 71% of electricity consumed in India are generated bythermal power plants.

73. Formula of Urea is $CO(NH_2)_2$

60 gm of urea contains 12 g of carbon-

$$\text{Mass percentage of Carbon in Urea} = \frac{\text{Molar mass of Carbon}}{\text{Molar mass of Urea}} \times 100$$
$$= \frac{12}{60} \times 100$$
$$= 20\%$$

74. Sound travels faster in liquids and non-porous solids than it does in air. It travels about 4.3 times as fast in water (1,484 m/s), and nearly 15 times as fast in iron (5.120 m/s), than in air at 20 degrees Celsius. Sound waves in solids are composed of compression waves (just as in gases and liquids), but also exhibit a different type of sound wave called a shear wave, which occurs only in solids. The speed of sound is the distance travelled during a unit of time by a sound is the distance travelled during a unit of time by a sound wave propagating through an elastic medium. In dry air at 20°/C (68°F), the speed of sound is 343.2 meters per second (1,126 ft/s). This is 1,236 kilometers per hour (768 mph), or about one kilometer in three seconds or approximately one mile in five seconds.

75. A nuclear reactor is a device to initiate and control a sustained nuclear chain reaction. Most commonly they are used for generating electricity and for the propulsion of ships. Usually heat from nuclear fission is passed to a working fluid (water or gas), which runs through turbines that power either ship's propellers or generator. Some produce isotopes for medical and industrial use, and some are run only for research. Just as conventional power stations generate electricity by harnessing the thermal energy released from burning fossil fuels, nuclear reactors convert the thermal energy released from nuclear fission.

76. The study of fossils is called Palaeontology.

77. The human digestive system consists of the gastrointestinal tract plus the accessory organs of digestion (the tongue, salivary glands, pancreas, liver, and gallbladder). In this system, the process of digestion has many stages, the first of which starts in the mouth.

78.
$$1\,mole\ of\ ozone\ (O_3) = 48\,g$$
$$0.5\,mole\ of\ (O_3) = ?$$
$$0.5\,mole\ of\ ozone\ (O_3) = \frac{0.5 \times 48}{1} = 24\,g$$

79. Minimum at the equator

80. Alpha particles

81. RNA and proteins

82. Graphite

83. Anthracite, often referred to as hard coal, is a hard, compact variety of coal that has a submetallic luster. It has the highest carbon content, the fewest impurities, and the highest energy density of all types of coal except for graphite and is the highest ranking of coal.

84. All of the above

85. Photosynthesis

86. The value of gravitational force represented by G is 6.67 x 10^{-11}

87. PWM switching is preferred in voltage source inverters for the purpose of Controlling output voltage.

88. Potential energy-If a bullet is shot STRAIGHT up (90 degrees to the ground), gravity will convert nearly all of its kinetic energy to potential energy. Falling back to earth, though, does not bring it back to the same velocity. At some point it will hit terminal velocity, slowed by air friction and it will hit the ground at a fraction of its starting speed . In other words, all of its kinetic energy is converted to potential energy in its rise, but much of the potential energy is converted to forms of energy (heat, sound) other than velocity on its return.

89. Tuberculosis disease is caused by Mycobacterium tuberculosis, a rod-shaped bacterium.

90. The acceleration due to gravity in moon is smaller than that on the earth.

91. In photometry, luminous intensity is a measure of the wavelength-weighted power emitted by a light source in a particular direction per unit solid angle, based on the luminosity function, a standardized model of the sensitivity of the human eye. The unit of luminous intensity is Candela.

92. According to Avogadro Law, Volume of gas is directly proportional to number of molecules.

93. The acceleration due to gravity on the moon is one-sixth of the acceleration due to gravity on the earth (9.8 m/s^2)

94. When something is dropped it does not fall with uniform velocity. They are under the constant acceleration of the gravitational force.

95. X-rays

96. Convex mirrors form a virtual image, since the focal point (F) and the centre of curvature (2F) are both imaginary points "inside" the mirror, that cannot be reached.

97. Nuclear fission

98. Roentgen

99. Malaria is a disease caused by infection with single-celled parasites of the genus Plasmodium. Anopheles mosquitoes transmit these parasites from one person to another in their bites.

100. There is more friction It is difficult to walk on sand than on concrete road because there is more friction.

Mathematics

Q.1 Read the following bar graph which represent a company's manufacturing and selling(in lakh) of product from 2002 to 2008 and answer the following questions.

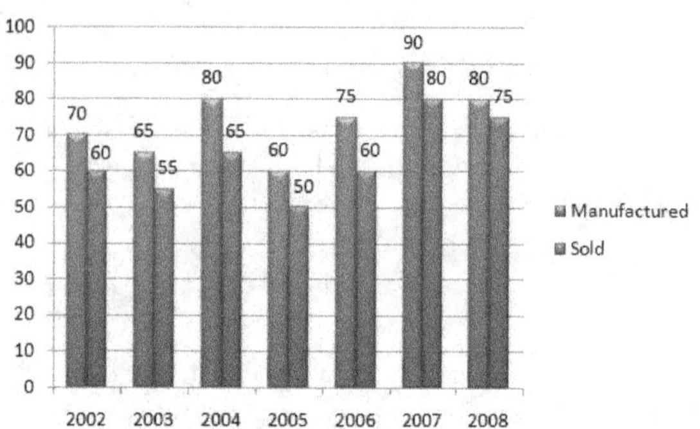

Approximately what is the average number of items unsold for all the years together?

A. 10,50,000

B. 10,55,000

C. 10,43,000

D. 10,70,000

Q.2 Read the following bar graph which represent a company's manufacturing and selling(in lakh) of product from 2002 to 2008 and answer the following questions.

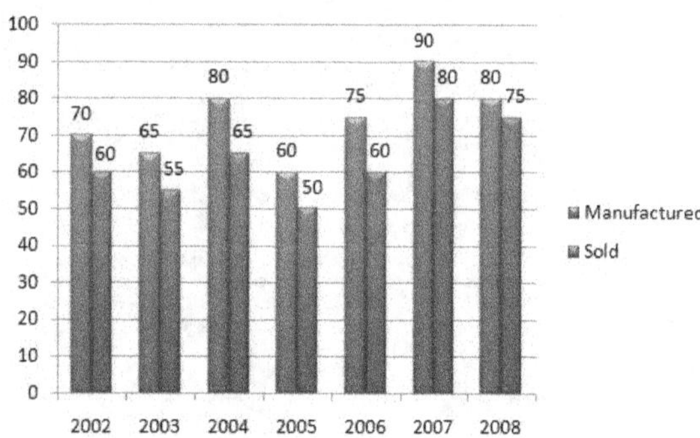

Approximately what is the average number of items sold for all the years together?

A. 60 lakhs.　　**B.** 61 lakhs.　　**C.** 63 lakhs.　　**D.** 67 lakhs.

Q.3 Read the following bar graph which represent a company's manufacturing and selling(in lakh) of product from 2002 to 2008 and answer the following questions.

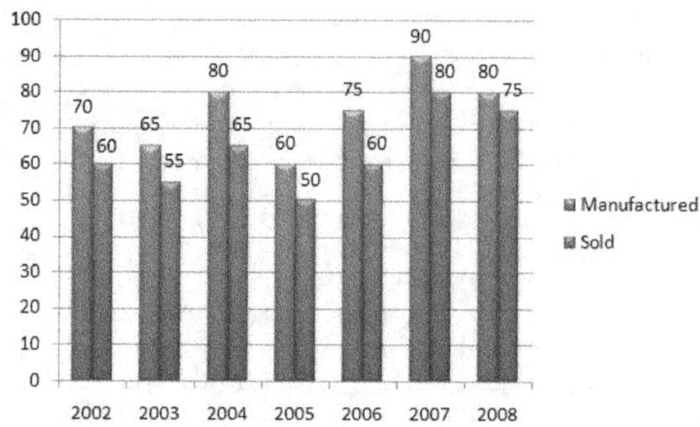

Number of items manufactured in 2007 is what percent of the total number of items manufactured in all the years together? (Rounded off to two digits after decimal)?

A. 17.31　　**B.** 13.71　　**C.** 17.03　　**D.** 13.97

Q.4 Read the following bar graph which represent a company's manufacturing and selling(in lakh) of product from 2002 to 2008 and answer the following questions.

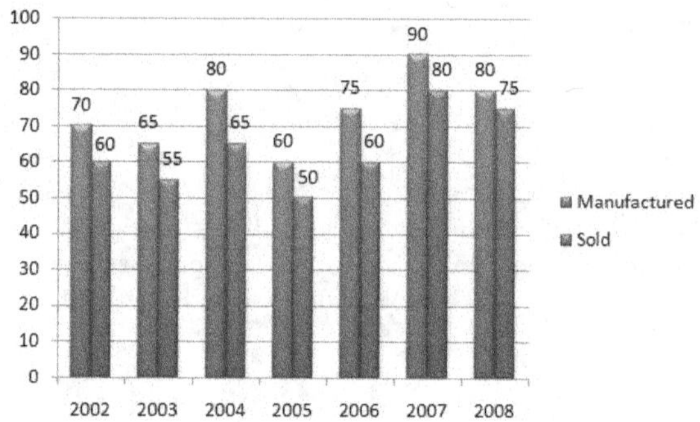

During which year the percentage of items unsold was the highest?

A. 2004　　**B.** 2006　　**C.** 2008　　**D.** 2002

Q.5 What should come in place of the question mark (?)?

$(833.25 - 384.45) \div 24 = ?$

A. 1.87　　**B.** 20.1　　**C.** 2.01　　**D.** 18.7

Q.6 If a = 12, b = 13 and c = 14, then the value of $b^2 c^2 + c^2 a^2 + a^2 b^2 - a^4 - b^4 - c^4$ is.

A. −2029　　**B.** −2050　　**C.** −1859　　**D.** −2129

Q.7 A certain sum, invested at 4% per annum at compound interest, compounded half-yearly, amounts to Rs. 7,803 at the end of one year. Find the sum.

A. Rs. 7,000

B. Rs. 7,200

C. Rs. 7,500

D. Rs. 7,700

Q.8 Distance between the parallel lines 3x + 4y − 15 = 0 and 9x + 12y − 20 = 0 is

A. 1 unit

B. 5/3 units

C. 10/3 units

D. 3 units

Q.9 If sin (10° 6′ 32″) = a, then the value of cos (79° 53′ 28″) + tan (10° 6′ 32″) is:

A. $\dfrac{a\left(1 + \sqrt{1 - a^2}\right)}{\sqrt{1 - a^2}}$

B. $\dfrac{1 + \sqrt{1 - a^2}}{\sqrt{1 - a^2}}$

C. $\dfrac{\sqrt{1 - a^2} + a}{\sqrt{1 - a^2}}$

D. $\dfrac{a\sqrt{1 - a^2} + 1}{\sqrt{1 - a^2}}$

Q.10 In a container of 56 litres the ratio of petrol to oil is 6:1. How much oil must be added to the mixture to make this ratio 2:1?

A. 14 Litre.   **B.** 16 Litre.   **C.** 18 Litre.   **D.** 19 Litre.

Q.11 Find the measures of an angle which is complement of 50°.

A. 40°   **B.** 30°   **C.** 45°   **D.** 50°

Q.12 A room 8 m long, 6 m broad and 3 m height has two windows 1 1/2 m × 1 m and a door 2 m × 1 1/2 m. Find the cost of papering the walls with paper 50 cm wide at 25 paise per meter.

A. 39   **B.** 37   **C.** 33   **D.** 35

Q.13 If cos T = 3/5 and if sin R = 8/17, where T is in the fourth quadrant and R is in second quadrant, then cos (T-R) is equal to:

A. 77/85   **B.** 13/85

C. $-\dfrac{13}{85}$ **D.** $-\dfrac{77}{85}$

Q.14 A mixture of 40 litres of milk and water contains 10% water. How much water must be added to make water 20% in the new mixture?

A. 10 litres   **B.** 7 litres   **C.** 5 litres   **D.** 3 litres

Q.15 There are 13 white and 7 black balls in a bag. Two balls are drawn at random. What is the probability that they are of same colour?

A. 99/190   **B.** 5/13   **C.** 19/90   **D.** 189/90

Q.16 Two circle with radii R and r touch each other externally. A direct common tangent with length l is drawn to the circles. Which is true?

A. l = R² + r²   **B.** l = R² – r²

C. $l = 2\sqrt{Rr}$ **D.** l = 3 R² r²

Q.17 A, B and C can finish a work in 8 days, 10 days and 12 days respectively. They worked together and get Rs. 740. How much each of them will get?

A.   Rs. 200, Rs. 240, Rs. 200
B.   Rs. 300, Rs. 240, Rs. 200
C.   Rs. 100, Rs. 200, Rs. 300
D.   Rs. 340, Rs. 100, Rs. 200

Q.18 The midpoint of the line segment joining (3,-8) and (x + 2, -2) is (4, -5). What is the value of X?

A. 3   **B.** 1   **C.** 2   **D.** 5

Q.19 The ratio between the angles of a quadrilateral is 3:4:6:7. Half of the smallest angle of quadrilateral is the angle of cyclic quadrilateral. Find another angle of cyclic quadrilateral?

A. 97°   **B.** 86°   **C.** 112°   **D.** 153°

Q.20 Walking at 6/7th of his usual speed, a man is 12 minutes late. The usual time taken by him to cover that distance is-

A.   1 hr   **B.**   1 hr 12 min
C.   1 hr 15 min   **D.**   None of these

Q.21 The average weight of 8 persons increases by 2.5 kg, when one person whose weight is 65 kg is replaced by a new person. What Is the weight of the new person?

A. 78 kg   **B.** 82 kg   **C.** 85 kg   **D.** 80 kg

Q.22 Area of circle is equal to the area of a rectangle having perimeter of 100 cm and length is more than the breadth by 6 cm. What is the diameter of the circle?

A. 14 cm   **B.** 28 cm   **C.** 22 cm   **D.** 24 cm

Q.23 A, B and C divide an amount of Rs. 9,915 amongst themselves in the ratio 3:5:7 respectively. What is the C's share in the amount?

A.   Rs. 4,627   **B.**   Rs. 5,627
C.   Rs. 6,627   **D.**   Rs. 7,627

Q.24 In selling an article for ₹ 76, there is a profit of 52%, if it is sold for ₹ 75, then the profit percent will be.

A. 44%   **B.** 46%   **C.** 48%   **D.** 50%

Q.25 The average of three numbers is 135. The largest number is 195 and the difference between the other two is 20. The smallest number is:

A. 65   **B.** 95   **C.** 105   **D.** 115

Q.26 'A' starts business with ₹ 3,500 and after 5 months, B joins with A as his partner. After a year, the profit is divided in the ratio 2:3 what is B's contribution in the capital?

A. ₹ 7,500   **B.** ₹ 8,000   **C.** ₹ 8,500   **D.** ₹ 9,000

Q.27 60 boys working 7 hours a day can do a work in 18 days. In how many days will 28 boys working 9 hours a day do the same work?

A. 25 days.   **B.** 20 days.   **C.** 30 days.   **D.** 40 days.

Q.28 The lines x + 3y = 4 and 3x – y = 6 intersect the y – axis at A and B respectively. AB = ?

A.   22/3 Units   **B.**   26/3 Units
C.   29/3 Units   **D.**   32/3 Units

Q.29 A man saves 25% of his salary. If due to price rise he increases his monthly expenses by 25% and he is able to save only Rs. 25 per month. Find his monthly salary.

A. Rs .400　　　**B.** Rs. 500　　　**C.** Rs. 600　　　**D.** Rs. 650

Q.30 Seema purchased an item for Rs.9,600 and sold it for a loss of 5 percent. From that money she purchased another item and sold it for a gain of 5 percent. What is her overall gain/ loss?

A. Loss of Rs.36　　　　**B.** Loss of Rs.24

C. Loss of Rs.54　　　　**D.** None of these

General Intelligence & Reasoning

Q.31 'Suma' is shorter than 'Uma', 'Neha is taller then 'Suma', 'Sudha' is taller than 'Uma' but shorter than 'Hema'. 'Uma' is taller than 'Neha'. Who is the tallest among them?

A. Hema　　　**B.** Uma　　　**C.** Sudha　　　**D.** Neha

Q.32 In the following questions, find out the answer figure which completes the problem figure matrix.

Problem Figures

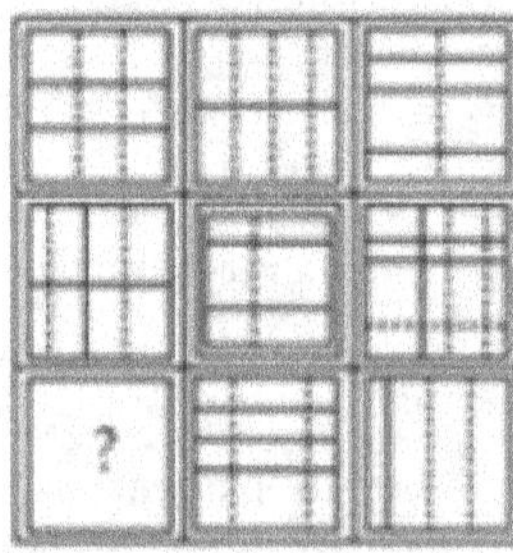

Answer Figures

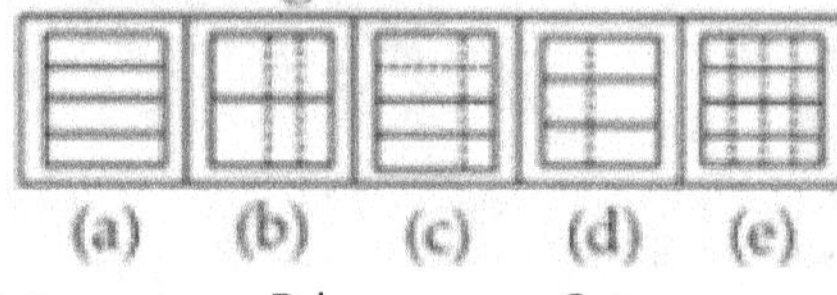

A. a　　　**B.** b　　　**C.** c　　　**D.** d

Q.33 Select the related word from the give alternatives.

BCG : URP :: LMQ : ???

A. FGI　　　**B.** XUS　　　**C.** SUX　　　**D.** CEH

Q.34 How many hexagons are their in the figure given below?

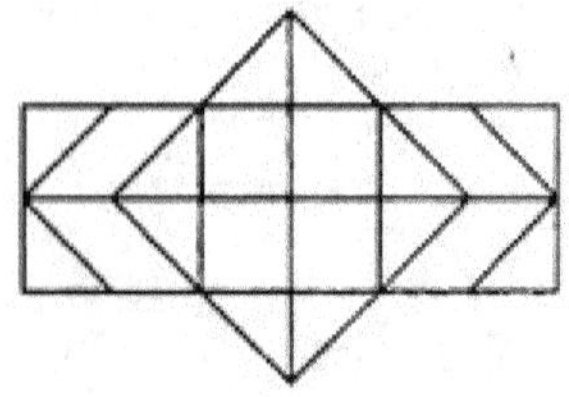

A. 4　　　**B.** 5　　　**C.** 11　　　**D.** 8

Q.35 Mohan starts walking East and walked 30 metres, then he turned right and walked 50 metres and he again turned left and walked 40 metres. Again he turned left and walked 50 metres. Now, how far is he from his starting point?

A. 170 meters.　　　　**B.** 70 meters.

C. 120 meters.　　　　**D.** 110 meters.

Q.36 A and B are sisters. R and S are brothers. A's daughter is R's sister. What is B's relation to S?

A. Mother.　　　　**B.** Grandmother.

C. Sister.　　　　**D.** Aunt.

Q.37 Choose the odd one out from the given alternatives.

A. HDF　　　**B.** WSU　　　**C.** RPN　　　**D.** LHJ

Q.38 Find the odd one out from the given alternatives.

A. NKMJ　　　**B.** FCEB　　　**C.** URTQ　　　**D.** TQRP

Q.39 Three of the following four are alike in a certain way and hence form a group. Which is the one that does not belong to that group?

A. JHUM　　　**B.** TRAW　　　**C.** MKOP　　　**D.** DFPG

Q.40 What should come at the place of question mark?

2, A, 9, B, 6, C, 13, D, ?

A. 9　　　**B.** 10　　　**C.** 12　　　**D.** 19

Q.41 If HOSPITAL is written as 32574618 in a certain code, how would POSTAL be written in that code ?

A. 752618　　　**B.** 725618　　　**C.** 725168　　　**D.** 725681

Q.42 Choose the odd one out of the given alternatives.

A. LNJ　　　**B.** RTP　　　**C.** NPK　　　**D.** FHD

Q.43 In the question below, there are few statements followed by few conclusions. You have to take the given statements to be true even if they seem to be at variance with commonly known facts and then decide which of the given conclusion logically follow(s) from the given statements.

Statements:

1. Some books are pens.

2. Some pens are pencils.

3. All pencils are rubber.

Conclusions:

I. Some books are pencils.

II. No book is a pencil.

A.　If only conclusion I follows

B.　If only conclusion II follows

C.　If either conclusion I or II follows

D.　If neither conclusion I nor II follows

Q.44 In the questions given below, some relationship has been expressed through symbols as shown below. Based on the meaning of these symbols and choose the correct answer.

φ means 'less than'

Δ means 'not greater than'

- means 'equal to'

+ means 'not equal to'

× means 'not less than'

= means 'greater than'

X - Y = Z implies

A. X + Y + Z　　　　**B.** X Δ Y × Z

C. X + Y φ Z　　　　**D.** X + Y × Z

Q.45 Identify the diagram that best represents the relationship among Iron, Lead, Nitrogen.

Choose the correct venn diagram.

 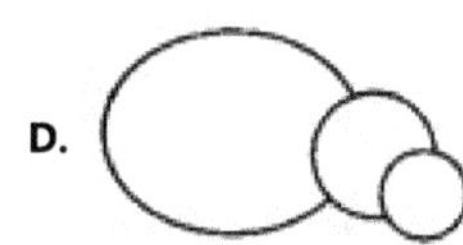

Q.46 DRIVEN is related to EIDRVN in the same way as BEGUM is related to ________.

A. BGMEU
B. BGMUE
C. EUBGM
D. MGBEU

Q.47 A word is represented by only one set of numbers as given in anyone of the alternatives. The set of numbers given in the alternatives are represented by two classes of alphabets as in the 2 matrices given below. The columns and rows of Matrix I are from 0 to 4 and that of Matrix II from 5 to 9. A letter can be represented first by its row and next by its column number. e.g., 'C' can be represented by 02, 21, etc. 'T' can be represented by 65, 96 etc. Similarly, you have to identify the set of words for 'STAMP'.

Matrix I

	0	1	2	3	4
0	D	V	C	P	M
1	P	M	D	V	C
2	V	C	P	M	D
3	M	D	V	C	P
4	C	P	M	D	V

Matrix II

	5	6	7	8	9
5	S	A	U	T	J
6	T	J	S	A	U
7	A	U	T	J	S
8	J	S	A	U	T
9	U	T	J	S	A

A. 55, 77, 56, 12, 41
B. 67, 96, 58, 30, 42
C. 79, 58, 68, 04, 02
D. 98, 89, 75, 23, 34

Q.48 There are two sets of figures namely problem Figure containing five figures 1, 2, 3, 4, 5 and answer figures (a), (b), (c), (d). You have to select one Figure from the answer set which will continue the same series as given in problem set figures.

Problem figure

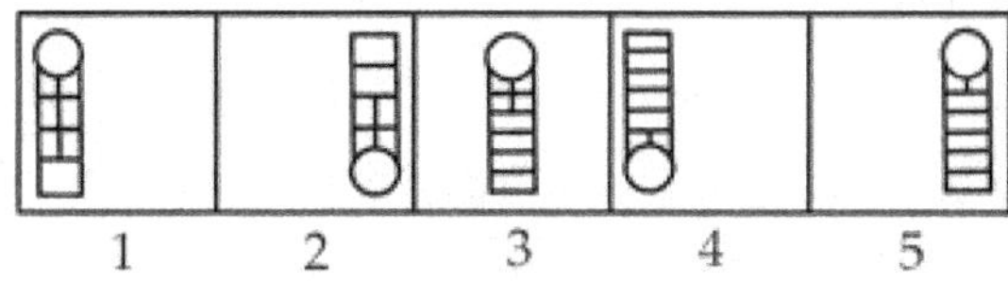

Answer figure

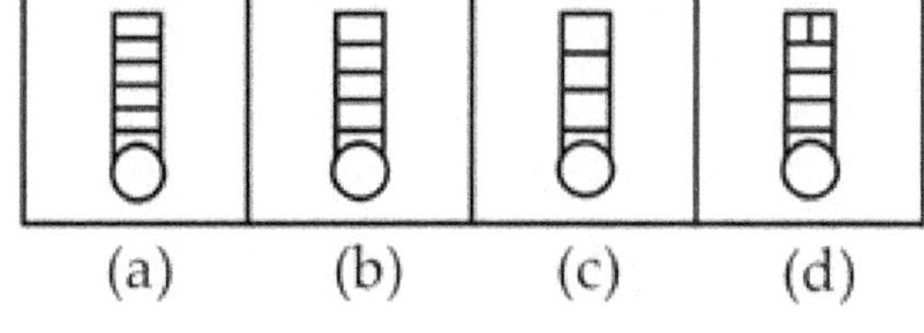

A. (a)
B. (b)
C. (c)
D. (d)

Q.49 In the following questions a word is followed by five other words, one of which cannot be formed by using the letters of the given word. Find this word

CLASSIFICATION

A. FICTION
B. ACTION
C. NATION
D. LIAISON

Q.50 D said A's father is the only brother of my sister's son. How is A's father related to D?

A. Cousin
B. Nephew
C. Aunt
D. Data Inadequate

Q.51 Find the missing term.

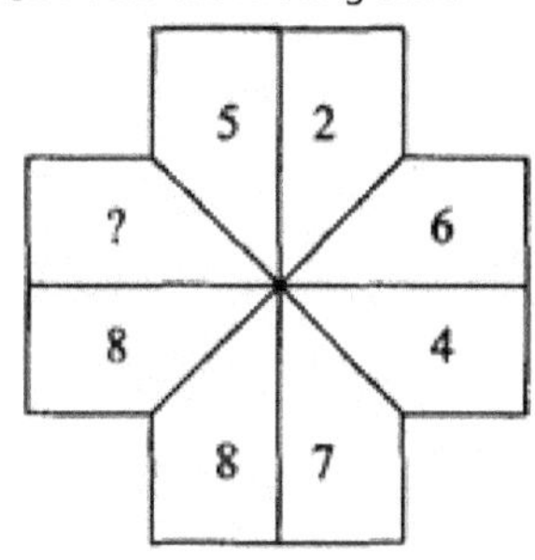

A. 10
B. 14
C. 16
D. 18

Q.52 Study the following diagram and answer the questions that follow.

a. The rectangle represents men.
b. The Circle represents graduates.
c. Triangle represents skilled persons.
d. Square represents employed persons.

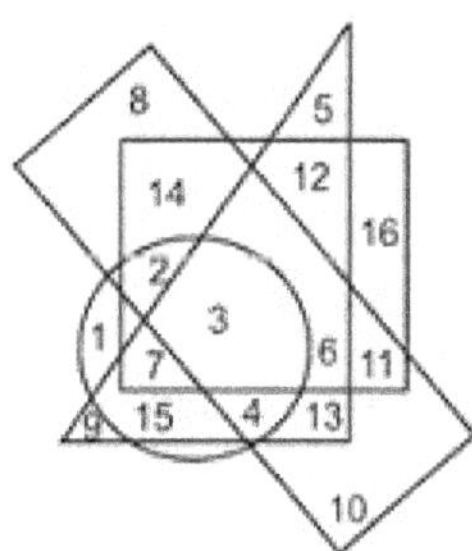

The skilled employed women who are graduates are-

A. 3 and 4
B. Only 7
C. 7 and 3
D. Only 8

Q.53 If in a certain code language 'CONTROL' is written as 'DMQPWIS', then how will 'BROTHQR' be written in that code?

A. CPRPMYK
B. YRPMKP
C. CPRPMKY
D. CPMPRKY

Q.54 In the given sequence how many such symbols and numbers are there which are either immediately preceded or immediately followed by the letters which is from the first half of the English alphabet?

2 L K @ 8 $ P B 1 V # 6 % G W 9 J C D 4 © 7 F R 4 A

A. 6
B. 7
C. 5
D. 8

Q.55 Solve the following series?

B2F, G4K, L12P, Q38U, ?

A. V118Z   **B.** V108Z   **C.** U118Z   **D.** Z108V

General Awareness

Q.56 Who invaded India seventeen times?
A. Muhammad Ghori.
B. Muhammad Ghaznavi.
C. Timur.
D. Ahmad Shah Abdali.

Q.57 India's largest Cancer Institute, National Cancer Institute (NCI) has opened in -

A. Jhajjar   **B.** Rohtak   **C.** Sonipat   **D.** Hisar

Q.58 Under the Constitution of India, which one of the following is not a fundamental duty?
A. To vote in public elections
B. To develop the scientific temper
C. To safeguard public property
D. To abide by the Constitution and respect its ideals

Q.59 Who is the Information and Broadcasting Minister of India?
A. Suresh Prabhu
B. Piyush Goyal
C. Rajyavardhan Rathode
D. Nirmala Sitharaman

Q.60 Which is the Tallest Dam of India?
A. Tehri Dam, Uttaranchal
B. Bhakra Nangal Dam, Himachal Pradesh
C. Andhra Pradesh, Himachal Pradesh
D. Nagarjuna Sagar Dam, Andhra Pradesh

Q.61 The traditional Indian folk dance 'Ghoomar' was developed in the Indian State of:
A. Haryana   **B.** Madhya Pradesh
C. Punjab   **D.** Rajasthan

Q.62 Where is the head quarter of "European Bank for Reconstruction and Development"?
A. Belgium   **B.** Paris
C. London   **D.** Rome

Q.63 Election of Rajya Sabha is held after?
A. 1 yr   **B.** 2 yrs   **C.** 6 yrs   **D.** 5 yrs

Q.64 A member of Parliament will lose his membership of Parliament if he is continuously absent from Sessions for-
A. 45 days   **B.** 60 days   **C.** 90 days   **D.** 365 days

Q.65 Who is the governor of Tripura?
A. Kaptan Singh Solanki
B. Suraj Singh
C. Sahil Kumar
D. Swapnil Rao

Q.66 Prime Minister Shri Narendra Modi has become the ____ recipient to receive Seoul Peace Prize 2018.
A. Fifth   **B.** Sixth

C. Ninth   **D.** Fourteenth

Q.67 Which of the following is called "Blue Planet"?
A. Saturn   **B.** Earth   **C.** Jupiter   **D.** Mars

Q.68 Amongst the following which state in India has the longest coastline?
A. Andhra Pradesh   **B.** Gujarat
C. Kerala   **D.** Maharashtra

Q.69 Govind Rao Commmittee has been set up for:
A. Service tax
B. Small savings
C. Reforms in banking infrastructure
D. All of these

Q.70 National Rural Health Mission (NRHM) was launched in the year :-
A. 2003   **B.** 2004   **C.** 2005   **D.** 2006

General Science

Q.71 For the reversibility of a cycle, there should be
A. loss of energy   **B.** no loss of energy
C. gain of energy   **D.** no gain of energy

Q.72 How many periods are there in the Periodic Table?
A. 6   **B.** 7   **C.** 8   **D.** 9

Q.73 A family consumes 40 kg. of fuel in 20 days. Calculate the average energy consumed per day (calorific value of fuel = 40 KJ/g).
A. 8×10^2 KJ   **B.** 8×10^4 KJ
C. 16×10^6 KJ   **D.** 16×10^4 KJ

Q.74 Solids which conduct electricity at higher temperature but not at lower temperature are called
A. super-conductor   **B.** metallic-conductor
C. semi-conductor   **D.** Insulator

Q.75 When a helium atom loses an electron it becomes:
A. An alpha particle.
B. A positive helium ion.
C. A negative helium ion.
D. A proton.

Q.76 When 1 mol of a gas is heated at constant volume, temperature is raised from 298 to 308 K. Heat supplied to the gas is 500 J. Then which statement is correct?
A. $q = W = 500$ J, $dU = 0$
B. $q = dU = 500$ J, $W = 0$
C. $q = W = 500$, $dU = 0$
D. $dU = 0$, $q = W = -500$ J

Q.77 A sudden fall in the level of mercury in a barometer indicates.
A. fair weather   **B.** stormy weather
C. cold weather   **D.** hot weather

Q.78 Which of the following applications don't use the Bernoulli's principal?

A. Aero plane taking off
B. Carburetor in reciprocating engine
C. Boat floating on water
D. None of these

Q.79 Surface tension in a liquid is due to __________.
A. Adhesive force between molecules
B. Cohesive force between molecules
C. Gravitational force between molecules
D. Electrical force between molecules.

Q.80 Which of the following is called the 'Kitchen of the Cell'?
A. Chromoplast
B. Chloroplast
C. Chlorophyll
D. None of these

Q.81 Which of the following law states that, "When a body is wholly or partially immersed in a fluid, it experience an upthrust equal to the weight of the fluid displaced"?
A. Bernoulli's Theorem.
B. Archimedes Principle.
C. Both of the above.
D. None of these.

Q.82 Which of the following is an example of inertia?
A. Passengers bend backward when car or train starts suddenly
B. Dust particles are removed when a coat is beaten
C. Both of the above
D. None of the above

Q.83 According to Dalton's atomic theory the smallest particle which can exist independently is —
A. An atom
B. A molecule
C. A cation
D. An anion

Q.84 Longest cell in human body is
A. Muscle cell
B. Blood cell
C. Bone cell
D. Nerve cell

Q.85 How many chromosomes pairs are in a human body?
A. 19
B. 22
C. 23
D. 24

Q.86 Communication satellites are used to:
A. Receive communication signal only
B. Receive and redirect communication signal
C. Provide information of natural resources only
D. Transmit communication signal only

Q.87 The minimum velocity which must be attained by a rocket to leave the earth's atmosphere is known as escape velocity. Its value is
A. 8 km/s
B. 9 km/s
C. 10.5 km/s
D. 11.2 km/s

Q.88 If you run on a horizontal road, the work done by gravity force is equal to—
A. Product of your weight and distance through which you run
B. Your weight
C. Product of your mass and distance through which you run
D. Zero

Q.89 Combustion is the process in which —
A. Heat is produced
B. Light is produced
C. Heat and Light is produced
D. None of these

Q.90 Which one of the following is true about the center of gravity if a body is in unstable equilibrium?
A. The center of gravity of the body should be as low as possible.
B. The center of gravity should be as high as possible.
C. The center of gravity of the body is not affected.
D. The center of gravity should be in the mid of the body.

Q.91 Woolen clothes keep us warm in winter because:
A. they give heat to body
B. they protect the heat of body from escaping
C. they protect the cold from entering the body
D. None of these

Q.92 For instant energy, athletes take:
A. Sucrose
B. Vitamin C
C. Sodium chloride
D. Glucose

Q.93 which of the following is chemical change?
A. wood burning in a fireplace
B. ice melting to water
C. chopping wood for a fire
D. sewing a button on a shirt

Q.94 How many Newton's Laws of Motion are there?
A. 2
B. 3
C. 4
D. 5

Q.95 The smallest living organisms with cell wall are-
A. Cyanobacteria
B. Bacteria
C. Yeast
D. Algae

Q.96 The SI unit of impulse is -
A. Ns
B. Ns2
C. Nms
D. Nms2

Q.97 Which law states that at a constant temperature, the volume of a definite mass of a gas is inversely proportional to pressure?
A. Avogado's Gas Law
B. Charles Law
C. Gay-Lussac's Law
D. Boyle's Law

Q.98 Which of the following will be displaced by the other three in its salt solution?
A. Magnesium
B. Iron
C. Copper
D. Zinc

Q.99 When gold is melted and formed in a mold to make a piece of jewelry, what type of change is taking place?
A. a chemical change
B. a change of size
C. evaporation
D. physical change

Q.100 Which of the following is an Ideal Fluid?
A. Fluids which show streamline flow
B. A fluid with the least Terminal Velocity

C. A fluid with zero viscosity

D. None of these

// Smart Answer Sheet //

Correct — Percentage of students who answered correctly. **Skipped** — Percentage of students who skipped.

Q.	Ans.	Correct / Skipped	Q.	Ans.	Correct / Skipped	Q.	Ans.	Correct / Skipped	Q.	Ans.	Correct / Skipped	Q.	Ans.	Correct / Skipped
1	D	88.15 % / 10.88 %	17	B	89.41 % / 10.34 %	33	B	79.98 % / 19.71 %	49	C	81.73 % / 18.02 %	65	A	87.5 % / 12.03 %
2	C	89.94 % / 10.01 %	18	A	78.71 % / 13.79 %	34	B	78.48 % / 16.43 %	50	B	80.47 % / 18.28 %	66	D	78.06 % / 15.0 %
3	A	82.8 % / 13.86 %	19	D	89.98 % / 10.01 %	35	B	84.14 % / 12.28 %	51	C	89.33 % / 10.53 %	67	B	89.43 % / 10.4 %
4	B	86.69 % / 11.46 %	20	B	77.94 % / 21.6 %	36	D	88.76 % / 10.79 %	52	B	86.79 % / 11.93 %	68	B	84.26 % / 10.78 %
5	D	88.73 % / 10.92 %	21	C	78.89 % / 17.24 %	37	C	81.72 % / 16.78 %	53	C	80.88 % / 18.54 %	69	C	79.24 % / 15.68 %
6	A	80.83 % / 10.47 %	22	B	85.79 % / 12.63 %	38	D	87.41 % / 10.43 %	54	D	87.53 % / 10.85 %	70	C	80.67 % / 17.6 %
7	C	76.67 % / 12.44 %	23	A	80.61 % / 17.74 %	39	D	89.4 % / 10.21 %	55	A	80.21 % / 18.02 %	71	B	88.98 % / 10.34 %
8	B	79.91 % / 12.59 %	24	D	82.4 % / 15.26 %	40	B	86.14 % / 13.84 %	56	B	84.99 % / 13.36 %	72	B	78.88 % / 13.25 %
9	A	89.06 % / 10.73 %	25	B	76.47 % / 17.08 %	41	B	80.56 % / 18.06 %	57	A	87.79 % / 10.42 %	73	B	82.79 % / 12.21 %
10	B	79.1 % / 12.87 %	26	D	83.68 % / 15.79 %	42	C	89.19 % / 10.58 %	58	A	83.48 % / 14.41 %	74	C	76.97 % / 14.15 %
11	A	81.31 % / 11.18 %	27	C	83.95 % / 12.47 %	43	C	84.14 % / 10.34 %	59	C	80.36 % / 10.84 %	75	B	77.11 % / 22.68 %
12	A	80.78 % / 17.21 %	28	A	80.85 % / 19.14 %	44	B	89.79 % / 10.07 %	60	A	78.51 % / 19.45 %	76	B	78.34 % / 14.0 %
13	D	85.45 % / 12.23 %	29	A	81.4 % / 12.58 %	45	B	84.95 % / 14.97 %	61	D	82.25 % / 14.95 %	77	B	79.8 % / 17.02 %
14	C	85.02 % / 14.07 %	30	B	82.15 % / 16.37 %	46	D	85.97 % / 13.08 %	62	C	82.1 % / 15.09 %	78	C	83.26 % / 15.82 %
15	A	83.74 % / 14.58 %	31	A	88.41 % / 10.54 %	47	D	76.96 % / 14.47 %	63	B	78.35 % / 16.77 %	79	B	80.68 % / 12.27 %
16	C	79.46 % / 16.01 %	32	C	83.79 % / 11.65 %	48	A	89.63 % / 10.23 %	64	B	88.73 % / 10.19 %	80	B	79.8 % / 11.22 %

Q.	Ans.	Correct / Skipped
81	B	82.78 %
		13.97 %
82	C	80.77 %
		18.55 %
83	A	82.85 %
		10.64 %
84	D	79.29 %
		16.67 %

Q.	Ans.	Correct / Skipped
85	C	77.0 %
		11.26 %
86	B	85.43 %
		13.59 %
87	D	83.85 %
		12.58 %
88	B	87.76 %
		11.27 %

Q.	Ans.	Correct / Skipped
89	C	87.97 %
		10.57 %
90	B	84.59 %
		11.44 %
91	B	84.11 %
		13.79 %
92	D	83.57 %
		13.23 %

Q.	Ans.	Correct / Skipped
93	A	87.73 %
		10.07 %
94	B	83.64 %
		15.39 %
95	B	85.63 %
		10.51 %
96	A	87.21 %
		11.53 %

Q.	Ans.	Correct / Skipped
97	D	79.78 %
		15.04 %
98	C	82.35 %
		12.19 %
99	D	76.25 %
		22.56 %
100	C	78.92 %
		17.86 %

//Hints and Solutions//

1. Average = (10+10+15+10+15+10+5)/7 = 75/7 lakh

≈ 1,07,000 lakh(Aprx)

2. Average = (60+55+65+50+60+80+75)/7 = 445/7 = lakh

≈ 63 lakh(Appx.)

3.

$$\text{Reqd.}\% = \left\{ \frac{(90 \times 100)}{520} \right\}\% = 17.307\% = 17.31\% \text{ (Appx.)}$$

4.

$$\% \text{ in } 2002 = \left\{ \frac{(10 \times 100)}{70} \right\}\% = 14.3\%;$$

$$\% \text{ in } 2003 = \left\{ \frac{(10 \times 100)}{65} \right\}\% = 15.38\%;$$

$$\% \text{ in } 2004 = \left\{ \frac{(15 \times 100)}{80} \right\}\% = 18.75\%;$$

$$\% \text{ in } 2005 = \left\{ \frac{(10 \times 100)}{60} \right\}\% = 16.67\%;$$

$$\% \text{ in } 2006 = \left\{ \frac{(15 \times 100)}{75} \right\}\% = 20\%;$$

$$\% \text{ in } 2007 = \left\{ \frac{(10 \times 100)}{90} \right\}\% = 11.11\%$$

$$\text{and } \% \text{ in } 2008 = \left\{ \frac{(5 \times 100)}{80} \right\}\% = 6.25\%.$$

It was the highest in 2006.

5. Ans: (d) ?= (833.25–384.45)/24 = 448.8/24 = 18.7

6. $b^2 c^2 + c^2 a^2 + a^2 b^2 - a^4 - b^4 - c^4$

$= -12(2a^4 + 2b^4 + 2c^4 - 2a^2 b^2 - 2b^2 c^2 - 2c^2 a^2)$

$= -12[(a^2 - b^2)^2 + (b^2 - c^2)^2 + (c^2 - a^2)^2]$

$= -12[(144 - 169)^2 + (169 - 196)^2 + (196 - 144)^2]$

$= -12[(-25)^2 + (27)^2 + (52)^2] = -2029$

7.

Let the sum be Rs.P.

As, the interest is compounded half-yearly,

∴ R = 2%, T = 2 half years

$$\therefore A = P\left(1 + \frac{R}{100}\right)^T$$

$$\Rightarrow 7803 = P\left(1 + \frac{2}{100}\right)^2$$

$$\Rightarrow 7803 = P\left(1 + \frac{1}{50}\right)^2$$

$$\Rightarrow 7803 = P \times \frac{51}{50} \times \frac{51}{50}$$

$$\Rightarrow P = \frac{7803 \times 50 \times 50}{51 \times 51} = Rs.7500$$

Alternatively :-

If interest is compounded half- yearly rate will be 2%

C.I. for 2 years = 4.04%

$$\text{Principal} = \frac{7803}{104.04} \times 100 = Rs.7500$$

8.

$3x + 4y - 15 = 0$

Or $9x + 12y - 45 = 0$ ---------(1)

and $9x + 12y - 20 = 0$ ---------(2)

The distance between two parallel lines

$ax + by + c_1 = 0$ and $ax + by + c_2 = 0$ is $\dfrac{|c_1 - c_2|}{\sqrt{a^2 + b^2}}$

$$= \frac{|-20 + 45|}{\sqrt{9^2 + 12^2}} = 25/15 = 5/3 \text{ units}$$

9.

$$\cos 79° \, 53' \, 28'' + \tan 10° \, 6' \, 32''$$

$$= \sin 10° \, 6' \, 32'' + \frac{\sin 10° \, 6' 32'}{\cos 10° \, 6' 32'}$$

$$a + \frac{a}{\sqrt{1 - a^2}} = \frac{a\left(1 + \sqrt{1 - a^2}\right)}{\sqrt{1 - a^2}}$$

10. Quantity of petrol = (6/7) x 56 = 48 Litre

Quantity of oil = (1/7) x 56 = 8 litre

Given, New Ratio = 48/8+x=12

$48 = 16 + 2x$

$2x = 48 - 16$

$2x = 32$

$x = 16$

16 litre is to be added

11. Let the measure of angle = x°

measure of its complement = 50°

∴ x° + 50°= 90° ⇒ x° = 40°

12.

Area of walls = 2(length + breadth) × height

$= 2(8 + 6) \times 3 = 84m^2$

Area of two windows and a door = $(1 \frac{1}{2} \times 1) + (2 \times 1 \frac{1}{2}) = 6m^2$

∴ Area to be covered = 84 − 6

$= 78m^2$

∴ Area of paper = Area to be covered = 78

⇒ (length × breadth) of paper 78

⇒ length of paper = $\frac{78}{50} \times 100m$

= 156 m

∴ cost = $\frac{156 \times 25}{100}$ = Rs.39

13.

We have

$\cos T = \dfrac{3}{5}$

$\sin T = \sqrt{1 - \dfrac{3^2}{5^2}}$

$= \sqrt{1 - \dfrac{9}{25}}$

$= \sqrt{\dfrac{16}{25}} = -\dfrac{4}{5}$ (since T is in IV quadrant)

$\sin R = \dfrac{8}{17}\Big|$

$\cos R = \sqrt{1 - \dfrac{8^2}{17^2}}$

$= \sqrt{1 - \dfrac{64}{289}}$

$= \sqrt{\dfrac{225}{289}} = -\dfrac{15}{17}$ (since R is in II quadrant)

Now, cos (T-R) =cos T cos R + sin T sin R

$= \dfrac{3}{5} \times \dfrac{-15}{17} + \dfrac{-4}{5} \times \dfrac{8}{17}\Big|$

$= \left[\dfrac{-45 - 32}{85}\right] = -\dfrac{77}{85}$

14. Milk =90/100 × 40 = 36 litres

water = 5 litres

$$\frac{x+4}{40+x} \times 100 = 20$$

$$\frac{x+4}{40+x} = \frac{1}{5}$$

$$\therefore 5x + 20 = 40 + x$$

$$x = 5$$

15. Probability that both balls are of same colour =

$$\frac{^{13}C_2 + {}^{7}C_2}{^{20}C_2} = \frac{99}{190}$$

16. Length of direct common tangent $l^2 = d^2 - (R - r)^2$

Here, d = R + r

Therefore, $l^2 = (R + r)^2 - (R - r)^2 = 4Rr$

$$l = 2\sqrt{Rr}$$

17.

Given,

1 day work of A, B & C is $\frac{1}{8}, \frac{1}{10}$ & $\frac{1}{12}$ respectively

therefore, Their shares in money = $\frac{1}{8} : \frac{1}{10} : \frac{1}{12} = 15 : 12 : 10$

Sum of their share = 15+12+10=37

Now, A's share = ₹740 $\times \frac{15}{37} = $ ₹300

B's share = ₹740 $\times \frac{12}{37} = $ ₹240

C's share = ₹740 $\times \frac{10}{37} = $ ₹200

18. Midpoint of (x_1, y_1) and (x_2, y_2)

$X = (x_1 + x_2)/2$

$4 = (3 + x + 2)/2$

$\Rightarrow (x+5)/2 = 4 \Rightarrow x = 3$

19. Let smallest angle is 3x

So,

$3x + 4x + 6x + 7x = 360°$

Smallest angle = 54°

According to given condition one angle of Cyclic quadrilateral = 27°

Another = 180 – 27 = 153°

20.

$$S_1 : S_2 = 6 : 7$$

$$T_1 : T_2 = 7 : 6 \ (S \propto \frac{1}{T})$$

Difference between

T_1 & $T_2 = 1 \ (7 - 6 = 1)$

If $1 = 12$min.

then $6 = 72$ min. = 1 hrs 12min.

21. Total increase in weight due to addition of new persons = 2.5 × 8 = 20 kg

Weight of new person = 65 + 20 = 85 kg

22.

Let breadth = x, then length

= (x + 6)

$\therefore 2(x + x + 6) = 100$

$\Rightarrow 2x + 6 = 50$

$\Rightarrow x = 22$ cm

$\therefore$ breadth = x = 22 cm & length

= 22 + 6 = 28 cm

$\therefore$ Area of circle = Area of rectangle

$\Rightarrow \pi r^2 = 22 \times 28$

$$\Rightarrow r^2 = \frac{22 \times 28}{22} \times 7 = 7 \times 4 \times 7$$

$\Rightarrow 7 \times 2 = 14$ cm

$\therefore$ Diameter = 2r = 28 cm

23. A : B : C

3 : 5 : 7

Sum of their ratio − 3 + 5 + 7

= 15 units

Share of C = 7/15 × 9915 = 4,627

24.

152% = 76

$$100\% = \text{Cost price} = \frac{76}{152} \times 100$$

C.P = Rs.50

New selling price = 75

$$\therefore \% \text{ profit} = \frac{75 - 50}{50} \times 100\%$$

$$= \frac{25}{50} \times 100\% = 50\%$$

25.
According to the question,

$195 + x + x + 20 = 135 \times 3$

$\Rightarrow 2x + 215 = 405$

$\Rightarrow 2x = 405 - 215 = 190$

$\therefore x = \dfrac{190}{2} = 95$

= smallest number

26.
Let B's investment be Rs x then

$$\dfrac{3500 \times 12}{x \times 7} = \dfrac{2}{3}$$

$\Rightarrow 6000 \times 3 = 2x$

$\Rightarrow x = ₹9,000$

27. Using the formula $M_1D_1H_1W_2 = M_2D_2H_2W_1$

Since work is same for the two cases

$M_1D_1H_1 = M_2D_2H_2$

$$\Rightarrow D_2 = \dfrac{M_1D_1H_1}{M_2H_2} = \dfrac{60 \times 7 \times 18}{28 \times 9} = 30 \; days.$$

28.

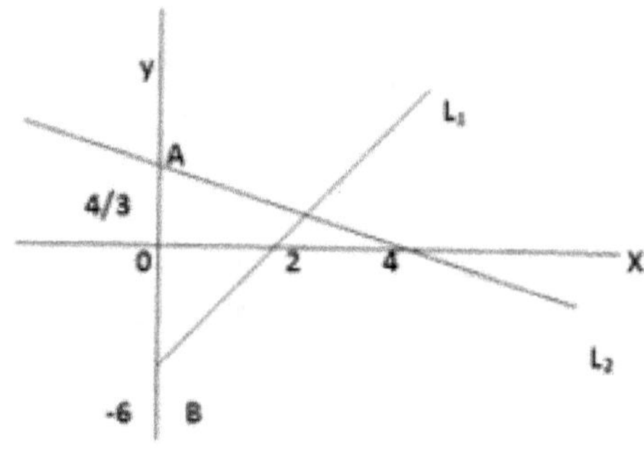

$x + 3y = 4$ --------- $L_1 \, L_1$

L_1 cuts y axis at A $(0, \dfrac{4}{3})$

L_2 cuts y axis at B $(0, -6)$

$AB = \dfrac{4}{3} + 6 = \dfrac{4 + 18}{3} = \dfrac{22}{3}$ units

$3x - y = 6$ ----------- L_2

29.
Expenses before price rise = 100-25=75

25% increase in expenses=100+25

= Rs. 125

Monthly expenses = $\dfrac{(75 \times 125)}{100}$

$= \dfrac{375}{4}$

Saving = $100 - \dfrac{375}{4} = \dfrac{25}{4}$

If saving is $\dfrac{25}{4}$ then salary = 100

If saving is 25 then salary

$= \dfrac{(100 \times 25 \times 4)}{25}$

= Rs. 400

30.

SP = $9600 \times \frac{95}{100} = Rs.9,120$

Second $S.P. = 9120 \times \frac{105}{100} = Rs.9,576$

Loss = 9600 - 9576 = 24

31. Uma > Suma --------------- (i)

Neha > Suma ------------------(ii)

Hema > Sudha > Uma > Neha ---------(iii)

On combining above statement,

Hema > Sudha > Uma >Neha> Suma

Therefore, Hema is the tallest among all.

32. Each row and column contains six complete lines and six broken lines.

33. The series will be:

$$B \xrightarrow{+1} C \xrightarrow{+4} G$$
$$U \xrightarrow{-3} R \xrightarrow{-2} P$$

Same way,

$$L \xrightarrow{+1} M \xrightarrow{+4} Q$$
$$X \xleftarrow{-3} U \xrightarrow{-2} S$$

34.

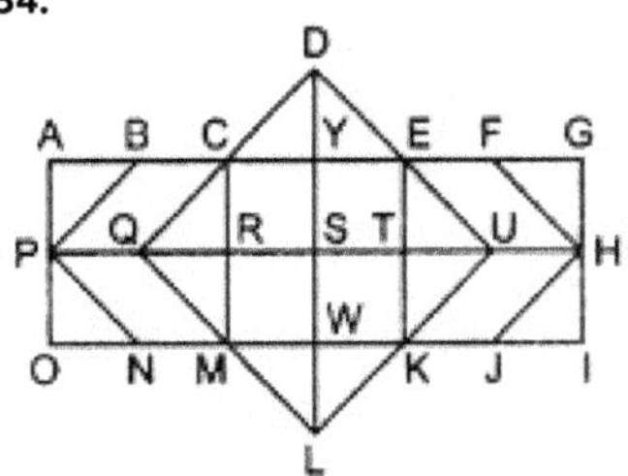

∴ Total hexagons= CDEKLM, CEUKMQ, CFHJMQ, BEUKNP, BFHJNP = 5

35.

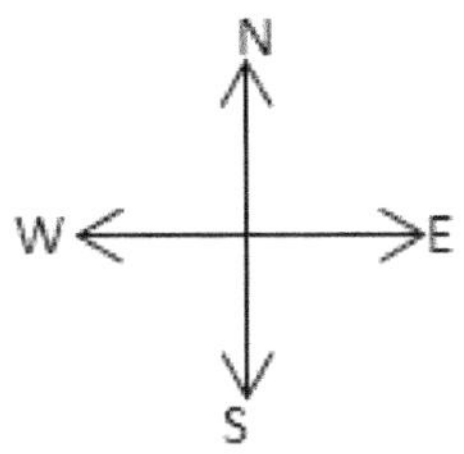

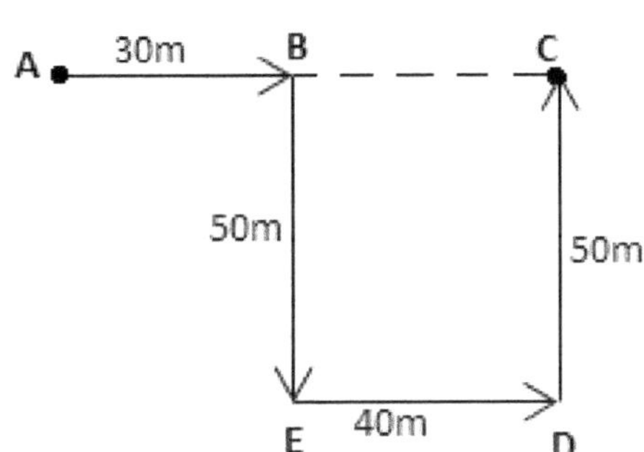

Start point is A

End point is C

AC = AB + BC

= 30 + 40

= 70 (BC = ED)

36.

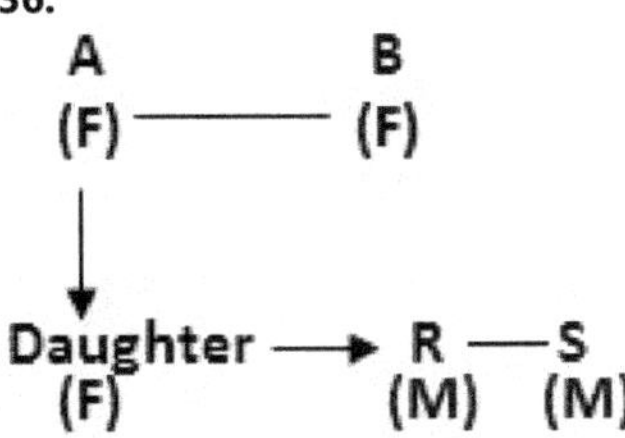

Clearly B is the aunt of S.

37.

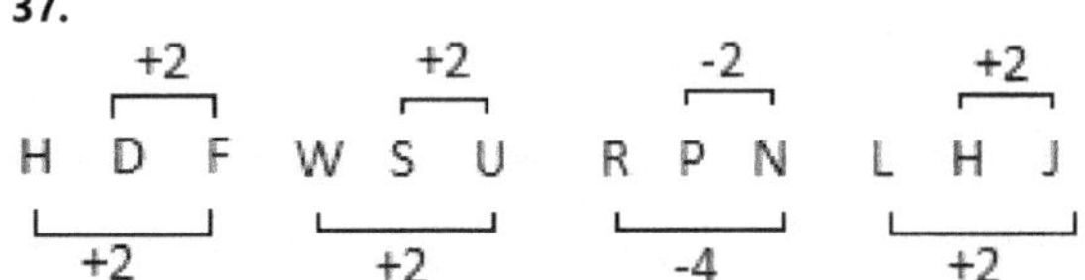

38. In all other groups there is a gap of two letters as in alphabet between third and fourth letter.

39.

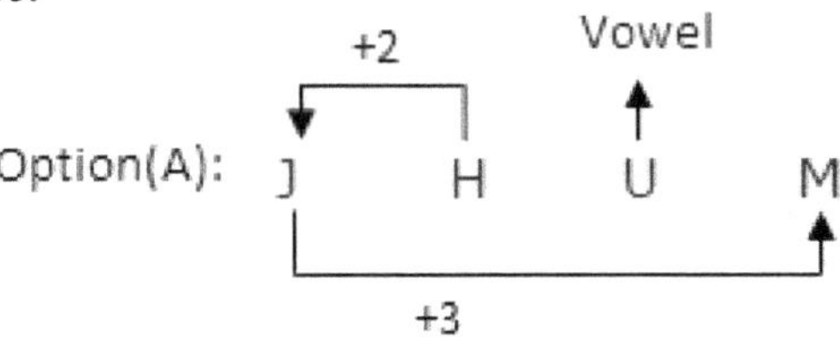

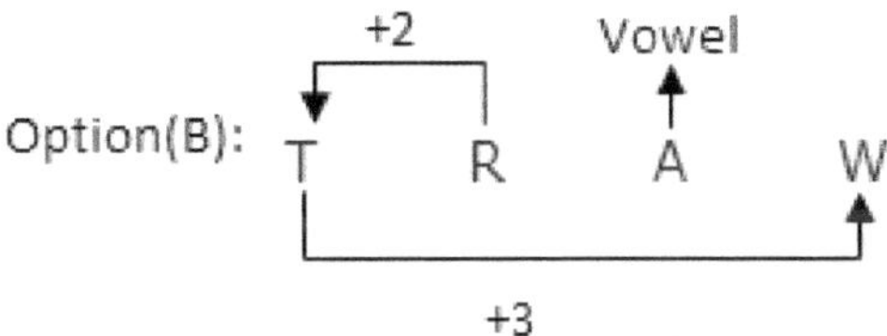

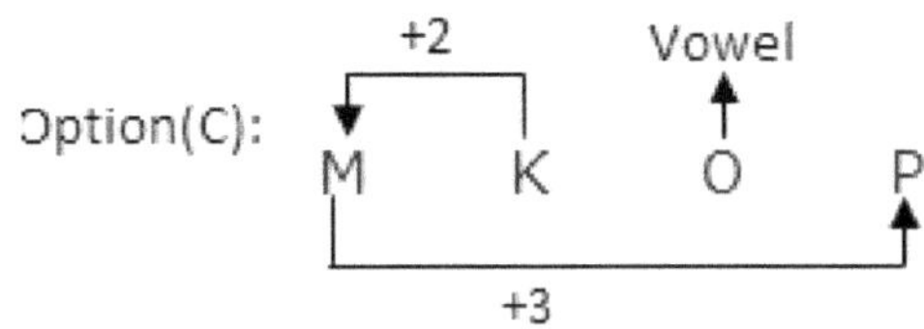

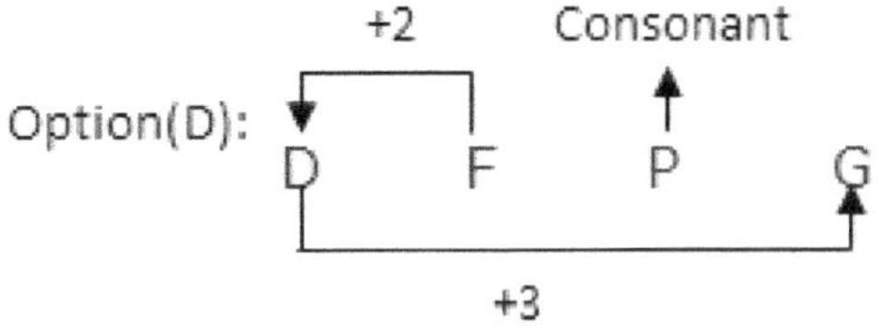

Here option (D) does not belong to the group.

40.

Here,

Series I = 2, 9, 6, 13, ?

Series II = A, B, C, D

In Series I,

$$2 \xrightarrow{+7} 9 \xrightarrow{-3} 6 \xrightarrow{+7} 13 \xrightarrow{-3} 10$$

41.

```
H   O   S   P   I   T   A   L
↓   ↓   ↓   ↓   ↓   ↓   ↓   ↓
3   2   5   7   4   6   1   8
```

So,

```
P   O   S   T   A   L
↓   ↓   ↓   ↓   ↓   ↓
7   2   5   6   1   8
```

42. In all other groups there is a gap of one letter as in the alphabet between first and third letter.

43. Either conclusion I or II follows.

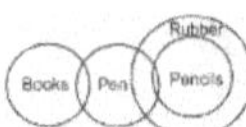

44.

Clearly, the meaning of the given symbols

$X - Y = Z \Rightarrow X = Y > Z$

Using the proper notations/symbols in option (b), we get

$X \vartriangle Y \times Z \Rightarrow X \leq Y \geq Z \Rightarrow X = Y > Z$

Therefore, $X - Y = Z \Rightarrow X \vartriangle Y \times Z$.

45. There is no relation between iron, lead and nitrogen.

So,

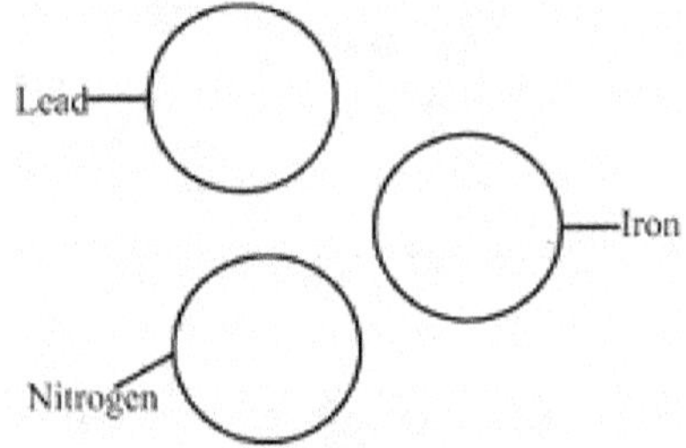

46.

As,

```
1   2   3   4   5   6
D   R   I   V   E   N

E   I   D   R   V   N
5   3   1   2   4   6
```

Similarly,

```
1   2   3   4   5
B   E   G   U   M

M   G   B   E   U
5   3   1   2   4
```

47. According to the matrices,

$$S = 55, 86, 67, \boxed{98}, 79$$
$$T = 65, 96, 77, 58, \boxed{89}$$
$$A = \boxed{75}, 56, 87, 68, 99$$
$$M = 30, 11, 42, \boxed{23}, 04$$
$$P = 10, 41, 22, 03, \boxed{34}$$

∴ Stamp = 98, 89, 75, 23, 34

48. Problem figure 2 is reverse of figure 1 with same number of horizontal lines and vertical lines decreases by one row. Similarly, Figure 4 is revers of figure 3 and symmetrical changes in pattern of lines. Therefore, answer figure (a) is reverse of problem figure 5.

49. As there is only one 'N' letter in the given word

50.

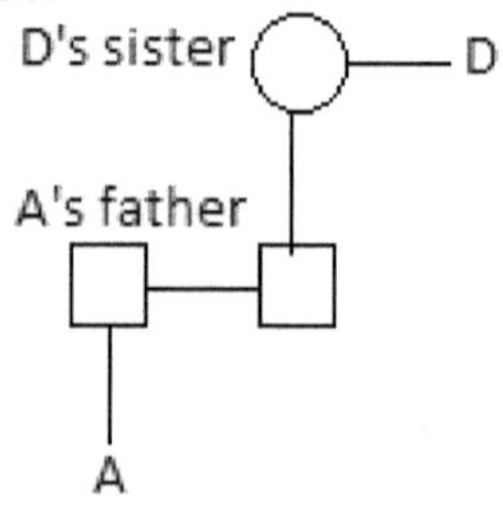

A's father is the nephew of D. Hence option (b) is correct.

51. There are two alternate series.

1st series: 5, 6, 7, 8, 9, ... and so on.

2nd series: 2 (×2) , 4 (×2), 8 (×2) ... and so on.

52. Only 7

53.

```
3  15 14 20 18 15 12
C  O  N  T  R  O  L
+1 -2 +3 -4 +5 -6 +7
D  M  Q  P  W  I  S
4  13 17 16 23 9  19
```

Similarly,

```
2  18 15 20 8  17 18
B  R  O  T  H  Q  R
+1 -2 +3 -4 +5 -6 +7
C  P  R  P  M  K  Y
3  16 18 16 13 11 25
```

54. Such combinations are :

2L, K@, B1, %G, 9J, D4, 7F, 4A,

55. The series is as follows:

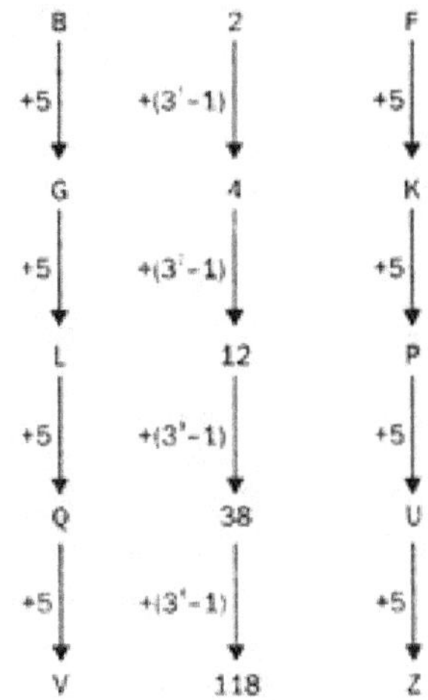

V118Z will come in place of '?'.

56. Muhammad Ghaznavi. In 998 AD, the Turkish conqueror, Mahmud of Ghazni, succeeded his father, and established a huge empire in Central Asia, with capital at Ghazni, the present-day South Kabul. He was 27 years old then and the first ruler to get the title as "Sultan", which means authority, thereby implying his power and strength. For 17 times, he attacked India during the period between 1000 and 1027 AD.

57. India's largest Cancer Institute, National Cancer Institute (NCI) has opened in Jhajjar.

58. To vote in public elections

59. Rajyavardhan Singh Rathode is the Information and Broadcasting Minister of India.

60. The Tehri Dam is the tallest dam in India and one of the tallest in the world. It is a multi-purpose rock and earth-fill embankment dam on the Bhagirathi River near Tehri in Uttarakhand, India. It is the primary dam of the THDC India Ltd. and the Tehri hydroelectric complex.

61. Rajasthan

62. The headquarter of European Bank for Reconstruction and Development is in London, England.

63. One-third Members of Rajya Sabha retire after every second year. A member who is elected for a full term serves for a period of six years. The election held to fill a vacancy arising otherwise than by retirement of a member on the expiration of his term of office is called 'Bye-election'.

64. The Constitution provides that if for a period of sixty days a member of either House of Parliament is without permission of the House absent from all meetings thereof, the House may declare his seat vacant. In computing the said period of sixty days. however. no account is taken of any period during which the House is prorogued or is adjourn for more than four consecutive days. The period of sixty days referred to in the Constitution means a single unbroken period of sixty days and for invoking the provision of the Constitution, the absence has to be continuous.

65. Kaptan Singh Solanki is the governor of Tripura.

66. The Seoul Peace Prize Committee has decided to confer the 2018 Seoul Peace Prize on Prime Minister Shri Narendra Modi. He is the fourteenth recipient of this award.

67. Earth is known as a Blue planet due to the vast encompass of oceans on its surface. From space the ocean combined with the atmosphere makes the planet look blue. The abundance of water on Earth's surface is the unique feature which distinguishes it from the rest planets of the solar system.

68. Gujarat state in India has the longest coastline

69. Reforms in banking infrastructure.

70. The National Rural Health Mission (NRHM) is an initiative undertaken by the government of India to address the health needs of under-served rural areas. Launched in April 2005 by Indian Prime Minister Manmohan Singh, the NRHM was initially tasked with addressing the health needs of 18 states that had been identified as having weak public health indicators.

71. For the reversibility of a cycle, there should be no loss of energy

72. There are 7 Periods in the Periodic Table.

73. Mass of fuel consumed in

20 days = 40 kg. = 40000g.

Energy liberated by 1 g. of fuel

= 40 KJ.

Energy liberated by 40000 g. of fuel = 40 × 40000 KJ Average energy consumption

$= (40 \times 40000)/20 = 80000$ K J

$= 8 \times 10^4$ KJ

74. Semiconductors are insulators at low temperatures and reasonably good conductors at higher temperatures. As temperature incresses, the Semiconductor material becomes a better and better conductor.

75. A positive helium ion.

76. At constant volumes, dV = 0. Hence W = 0. Further

$dU = q + w$ As W = 0, $dU = q = 500$ J

77. stormy weather- A sudden fall in the mercury level in a barometer indicates stormy weather.

78. Boat floating on water can be described by Archimedes principal.

79. Surface tension is a contractive tendency of the surface of a liquid that allows it to resist an external force. This property is caused by cohesion of similar molecules, and is responsible for many of the behaviors of liquids. It is revealed, for example, in the floating of some objects on the surface of water, even though they are denser than water, and in the ability of some insects (e.g. water striders) to run on the water surface.

80. The Chloroplast is called the Kitchen of the Cell as it is the green pigment found in green plants involved in the photosynthesis.

81. Archimedes Principle.

82. Both of the above are examples of inertia

83. An atom

84. Nerve cell (Neuron) is the longest cell in human body, with a length of 90-100 cm. Its jointed the Central Nervous system to other parts of body.

85. In humans, each cell normally contains 23 pairs of chromosomes, for a total of 46. Twenty-two of these pairs, called autosomes, look the same in both males and females. The 23rd pair, the sex chromosomes, differ between males and females

A chromosome is a deoxyribonucleic acid (DNA) molecule with part or all of the genetic material (genome) of an organism. Most eukaryotic chromosomes include packaging proteins which, aided by chaperone proteins, bind to and condense the DNA molecule to prevent it from becoming an unmanageable tangle.

Chromosomes are normally visible under a light microscope only when the cell is undergoing the metaphase of cell division (where all chromosomes are aligned in the center of the cell in their condensed form). Before this happens, every chromosome is copied once (S phase), and the copy is joined to the original by a centromere, resulting either in an X-shaped structure (pictured to the right) if the centromere is located in the middle of the chromosome or a two-arm structure if the centromere is located near one of the ends. The original chromosome and the copy are now called sister chromatids. During metaphase the X-shape structure is called a metaphase chromosome. In this highly condensed form chromosomes are easiest to distinguish and study. In animal cells, chromosomes reach their highest compaction level in anaphase during chromosome segregation.

Chromosomal recombination during meiosis and subsequent sexual reproduction play a significant role in genetic diversity. If these structures are manipulated incorrectly, through processes known as chromosomal instability and translocation, the cell may undergo mitotic catastrophe. Usually, this will make the cell initiate apoptosis leading to its own death, but sometimes mutations in the cell hamper this process and thus cause progression of cancer.

86. A communication satellite is basically a self-contained communications system with the ability to receive signals from Earth and to retransmit those signals back with the use of a transponder-an integrated receiver and transmitter of radio signals.

87. 11.2 km/s-The minimum velocity which must be attained by a rocket to leave the earth's atmosphere is known as escape velocity and its value is 11.2 km/s.

88. Your weight

89. Heat and Light is produced

90. The center of gravity should be as high as possible. The center of gravity is a geometric property of any object the center of gravity is the average location of the weight of an object.

91. Cotton clothes are thin and do not have space in which air can be trapped. Thus, cotton clothes do not prevent heat coming out of our body. Woollen clothes keep us warm during winter because wool is a poor conductor of heat and it has air trapped in between the fibres.

92. Glucose readily mixes in the blood and gives energy, thus it is the go-to for athleteThe digestive system breaks down carbohydrates in foods and drinks into simple sugars, mainly glucose. For example, both rice and soft drink will be broken down to simple sugars in your digestive system. This simple sugar is then carried to each cell through the bloodstream.

The pancreas secretes a hormone called insulin, which helps the glucose to migrate from the blood into the cells. Once inside a cell, the glucose is 'burned' along with oxygen to produce energy. Our brain, muscles and nervous system all rely on glucose as their main fuel to make energy.

The body converts excess glucose from food into glycogen. Glycogen acts as a storage form of glucose within the muscle tissue and the liver. Its role is to supplement blood sugar levels if they drop between meals or during physical activity.

93. wood burning in a fireplace Chemical change is any change that results in the formation of new chemical substances. At the molecular level, chemical change involves making or breaking of bonds between atoms. These changes are chemical: iron rusting (iron oxide forms)

94. There are 3 Newton's Laws of Motion

95. Bacteria are the smallest single-celled prokaryotes with cell walls. Cyanobacteria (blue-green algae), yeast and algae are all larger than bacteria.

96. It is Newton Seconds, Ns

97. Boyle's Law states that at a constant temperature, the volume of a definite mass of a gas is inversely proportional to pressure

98. Less reactive metal will be displaced by more reactive metal in its salt solution.

99. Physical change- When gold is melted and formed in a mold to make a piece of jewelry. It is a physical change.

100. A fluid with zero viscosity is called an Ideal Fluid. It doesn't exist in reality .

Mathematics

Q.1 If '-' stands for division, '+' for multiplication, ' ÷ ' for subtraction and 'x' for addition, which one of the following equations is correct?

A. $18 ÷ 3 × 2 + 8 - 6 = 10$

B. $18 - 3 + 2 × 8 ÷ 6 = 14$

C. $18 - 3 ÷ 2 × 8 + 6 = 17$

D. $18 × 3 + 2 ÷ 8 - 6 = 15$

Q.2 Concentrations of three solutions A, B and C are 20%, 30% and 40% respectively. They are mixed in the ratio 3 : 5 : x resulting in a solution of 30% concentration. Find x

A. 5   **B.** 2   **C.** 3   **D.** 4

Q.3 Mahesh grows potatoes in his backyard which is in the shape of a square. Each potato takes 1 cm^2 in his backyard. This year, he has been able to grow 137 more potatoes than last year. The shape of the backyard remained a square. How many potatoes did Mahesh produce this year?

A. 6400   **B.** 3049   **C.** 4761   **D.** 6325

Q.4 With the increase in the price of pressure cooker by 20%, its sale decreases by 50%. How much of a shopkeeper will earn less or more income from the past?

A. 30%   **B.** 55%   **C.** 40%   **D.** 25%

Q.5 D is 4 years younger than B and C is 4 years older than A. A and B are twins. If the average age of all the four boys is 11 years, then the sum of the ages of the youngest and the oldest boy is

A. 22 years   **B.** 20 years   **C.** 24 years   **D.** 18 years

Q.6 Marked price of articles 'P' and 'Q' are Rs. 50 and Rs. 35 respectively. With every article of 'P', 2 pencils worth Rs. 3 each are given free and with every article of 'Q', 3 pens worth Rs. 5 each are given free. If a customer buys 3 articles of 'P' and 2 articles of 'Q', then what is the approximate discount percentage?

A. 10%   **B.** 12%   **C.** 16%   **D.** 18%

Q.7

$S = 14132×152 + 16152×172 + 18172×192 + 20192×212 + 22212×232f$

Find S.

A. $90/299^2$ **B.** $45/299^2$ **C.** $90/315^2$ **D.** $45/315^2$

Q.8 Present age of Ajit and Amar are in the ratio of 8 : 7 and after four years ratio of their ages will be 9 : 8. Find the present age of Amar?

A. 30 years   **B.** 48 years   **C.** 28 years   **D.** 21 years

Q.9 In how many years will 800 rupees 10% annual compound interest rate be 926.10, if interest is biannually combined?

A. 212year   **B.** 112year   **C.** 213year   **D.** 113year

Q.10 Read the following information carefully and answer the question given below-

In the CBSE Board exams last year, 53% passed in Biology, 61% percent passed in English, 60% in Social Studies, 24% in Biology and English, 35% in English and Social Studies, 27% in Biology and Social Studies and 5% in none.

If the number of students in the class is 200, how many passed in only one subject?

A. 48   **B.** 46

C. More than 50   **D.** Less than 40

Q.11 The dimensions of a luggage box are 80 cm, 60 cm and 40 cm. How many sq. cm of cloth is required to cover the box?

A. 10400 sq. cm   **B.** 20800 sq. cm

C. 20400 sq. cm   **D.** 10200 sq. cm

Q.12 A number consists of two digits. If the digits interchange places and the new number is added to the original number, then the resulting number will be divisible by:

A. 10   **B.** 7   **C.** 11   **D.** 9

Q.13 A shopkeeper earns a profit of 12% on selling a book at 10% discount on the printed price. The ratio of the cost price and the printed price of the book is

A. 45 : 56   **B.** 45 : 51   **C.** 47 : 56   **D.** 47 : 51

Q.14 There are some rabbits and some pigeons in a zoo. If their heads and feet are counted, the number of heads is 90 and their feet are counted, then their number of feet is received 224. Tell me how many rabbits are there in this zoo?

A. 9   **B.** 25   **C.** 48   **D.** 22

Q.15 What is the mode of the following list of numbers: 52, 54, 55, 56, 55, 54, 53, 55, 53, 51, and 57 ?

A. 53   **B.** 54   **C.** 55   **D.** 52

Q.16 The sum of the 28th, 29th and 30th terms of an Arithmetic Progression, which has 57 terms, is 111. Find the arithmetic mean of the progression.

A. 37   **B.** 31

C. 43   **D.** Data insufficient

Q.17 From a container, 5 litres of wine was drawn out and was replaced by soda. Again 5 litres of mixture was drawn out & replaced by the soda. Thus the quantity of wine and soda in the container after these two operation is 9:16. The quantity of mixture is

A. 10.5 litres   **B.** 13.5 litres

C. 11.5 litres   **D.** 12.5 litres

Q.18 The cash difference between the selling price of an article at a profit of 2% and 12% is Rs. 3. The ratio of two selling prices is:

A. 51 : 56   **B.** 51 : 53   **C.** 52 : 53   **D.** 55 : 56

Q.19 In an election, there were only two candidates. One of the candidates secured 40% of votes and is defeated by the other candidate by 298 votes. The total number of votes polled is?

A. 1490   **B.** 2490   **C.** 1500   **D.** 1800

Q.20 A 6 m-long vertical pole casts a shadow of 4 m. At the same time, a tower casts a shadow 25 m long on the ground. The height of the tower is :

A. 45.5 m   **B.** 40.5 m   **C.** 37.5 m   **D.** 32.5 m

Q.21 A shopkeeper marks the price of an article at Rs. 320. Find the cost price if after allowing a discount of 10%, he still gains 20% on the cost price.

A. Rs. 240   **B.** Rs. 280   **C.** Rs. 300   **D.** Rs. 264

Q.22

In which of the following is p > q ?
I.$(0.9)p > (0.9)q$
II.$(1.8)p < (1.8)q$
III.$(8.5)p > (8.5)q$
IV.$(12)p < (12)q$

A. I and IV   **B.** II and III
C. III and IV   **D.** II and IV

Q.23

If $sinx = 45$, then $sec2x - 1 = ?$
A. 16/25   **B.** 25/9   **C.** 9/16   **D.** 16/9

Q.24 Two circles of radius 37 cm and 20 cm intersect each other at P and Q. O and O' are the centers of the circles. If the length of PQ is 24 cm, then the distance between their center is:

A. 35 cm   **B.** 51 cm   **C.** 21 cm   **D.** 16 cm

Q.25 Find the LCM of the following fractions : 2/3, 8/9, 16/27, 32/81

A. 32/81   **B.** 81/32   **C.** 32/3   **D.** 11/41

Q.26 Read the following graph carefully and answer the question given below.

The number of mobile sim cards in 4 states are given in multiple bar diagrams.

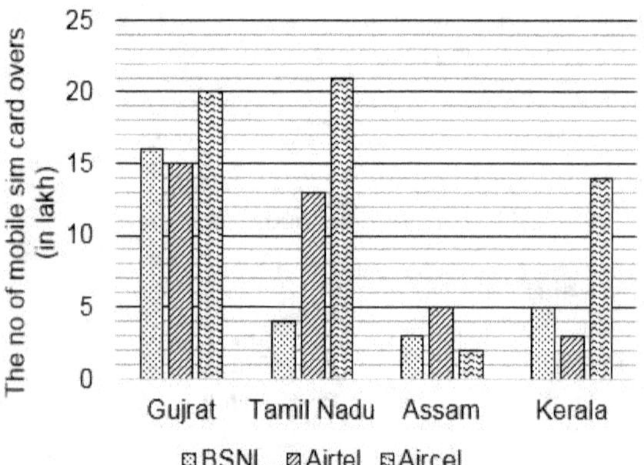

In Which state are there the largest number of owners of Airtel sim card?

A. Gujarat   **B.** Kerala
C. Assam   **D.** Tamil Nadu

Q.27 Read the following graph carefully and answer the question given below.

The number of mobile sim cards in 4 states are given in multiple bar diagrams.

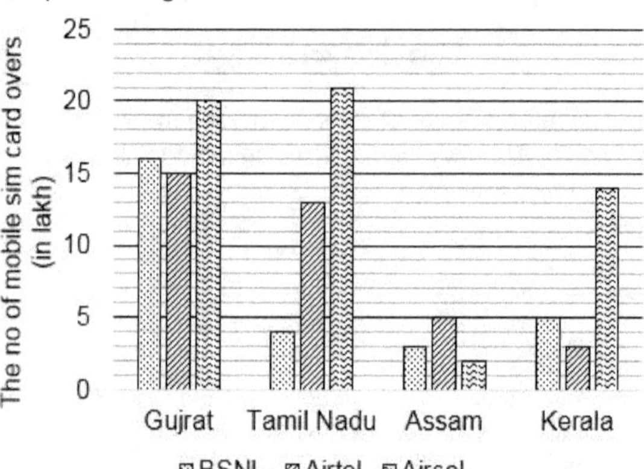

In Assam, the ratio of Aircell sim card and Artel Sim card sold is:

A. 2 : 5   **B.** 5 : 2   **C.** 2 : 3   **D.** 3 : 2

Q.28 Read the following graph carefully and answer the question given below.

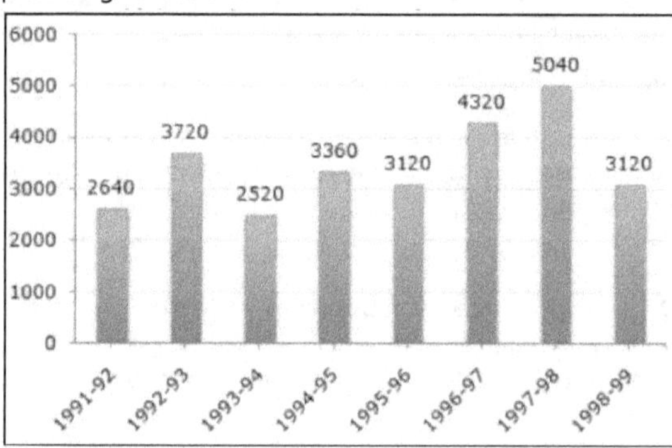

For which year, the percent increase of foreign exchange reserves over the previous year, is the highest?

A. 1992-93   **B.** 1993-94   **C.** 1994-95   **D.** 1996-97

Q.29 Read the following graph carefully and answer the question given below.

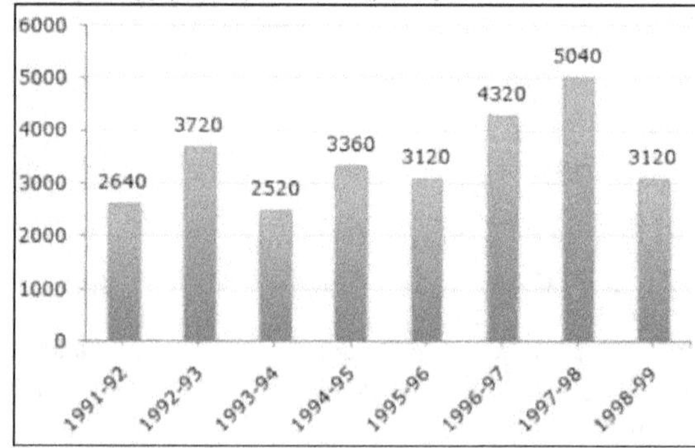

The foreign exchange reserves in 1997-98 was how many times that in 1994-95?

A. 0.7   **B.** 1.2   **C.** 1.4   **D.** 1.5

Q.30 Read the following graph carefully and answer the question given below.

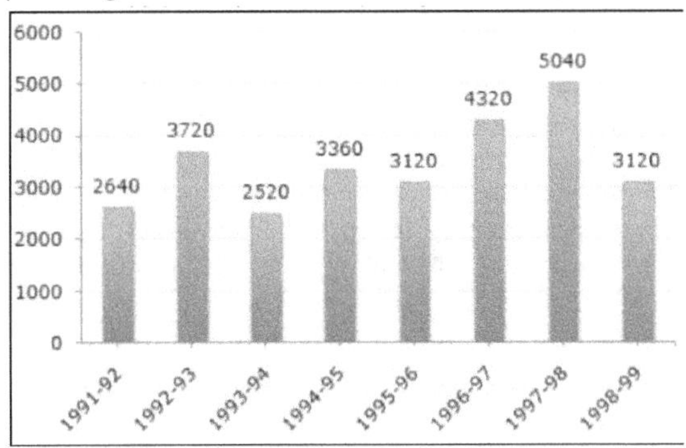

The ratio of the number of years, in which the foreign exchange reserves are above the average reserves, to those in which the reserves are below the average reserves is?

A. 2 : 6   **B.** 3 : 4   **C.** 3 : 5   **D.** 4 : 4

General Intelligence & Reasoning

Q.31 Choose the one which is different or odd from the following.

A. Aluminium   **B.** Iron

C. Copper   **D.** Brass

Q.32 If South West becomes North, North East becomes South and so on, what will East become?

A. West   **B.** North West

C. South West   **D.** South East

Q.33 In a code language, A is written as B, B is written as C, C is written as D and so on, then how will STUDY be written in that code language ?

A. TUVEZ   **B.** SVVFZ   **C.** TYBSU   **D.** SNBRU

Q.34 How many meaningful english words of three or more letters, can be formed from the words "TONE" beginning with "N" and without repeating any letter ?

A. 3   **B.** 1

C. 2   **D.** 4 or more

Q.35 A, B, C, D and E each has different heights. D is only shorter than B. E is shorter than A and C. Who is the shortest of them?

A. E   **B.** A

C. C   **D.** Data inadequate

Q.36 In these questions, statements are given followed by two conclusions I and II. You have to consider both the statements to be true even if they seem to be at variance from commonly known facts. You have to decide which of the given conclusions is/are definitely drawn from the given statements. Select answer as: (A) If only I follows (B) If only II follows (C) If neither I nor II follows (D) If both I and II follows

Statements :

All boys are girls.

No girl is a father.

Conclusions :

I. All girls are boys.

II. No boy is a father

A. A   **B.** B   **C.** C   **D.** D

Q.37 Arrange the given words in the sequence in which they occur in the dictionary.

1. Waste

2. Wrong

3. Witty

4. Worcester

5. Warlike

A. 51324   **B.** 13452   **C.** 51342   **D.** 15342

Q.38 Which answer figure will complete the pattern in the question figure ?

Question figure:

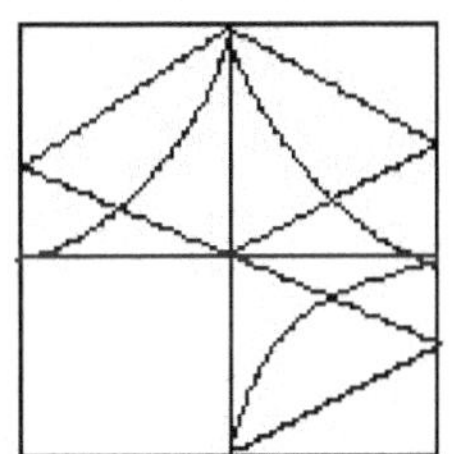

Answer figure :

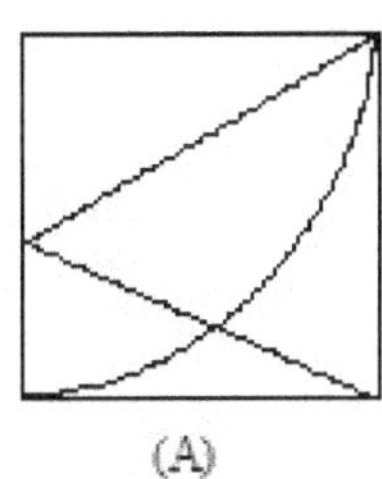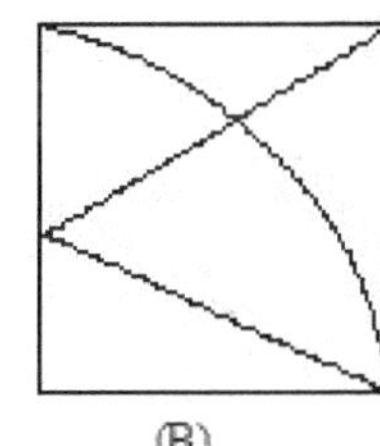
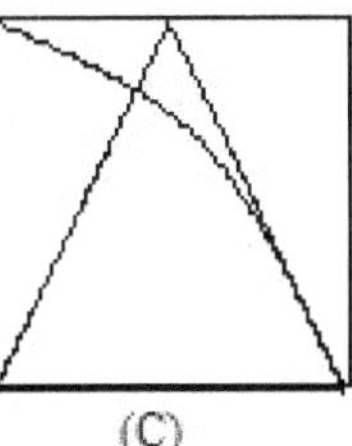

(A)   (B)

(C)   (D)

A. A   **B.** B   **C.** C   **D.** D

Q.39 In the following questions below are given some statements followed by some given conclusions. You have to take the given statements to be true even if they seem to be at variance with commonly known facts. Read all the conclusions and then decide which of the given conclusions logically follows from the given statements, disregarding commonly known facts. Give answer:

Statement:

1. Due to contamination of water, large number of people were admitted to hospital.

2. The symptoms were of Typhoid.

Conclusions:

I. Contamination of water may lead to Typhoid.

II. Typhoid is a contagious disease.

A. Only conclusions I is true

B. Only conclusions II is true

C. Both conclusions I and II are true

D. Both conclusions I and II are false

Q.40 6 days from today, it will be 20th of the month, then what was the date before yesterday?

A. 11th   **B.** 12th   **C.** 13th   **D.** 14th

Q.41 Pointing to a boy in a photograph, Rani said, "His mother's only daughter is my mother". How is Rani related to that boy?

A. Wife

B. Sister

C. Either Niece or Nephew

D. Nephew

Q.42 In the given figure, the Circle represents Indian, Square represents Dancer and triangle represents Musicians. Find the region of Indian Musicians.

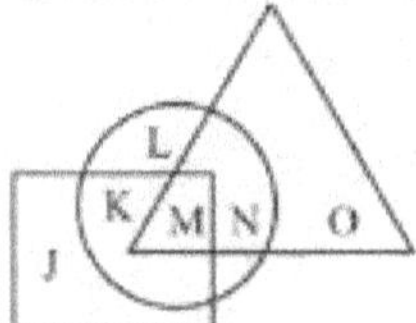

A. M   **B.** L   **C.** K   **D.** N

Q.43 A piece of paper is folded and cut as shown below in the question figures. From the given answer figures, indicate how it will appear when opened.

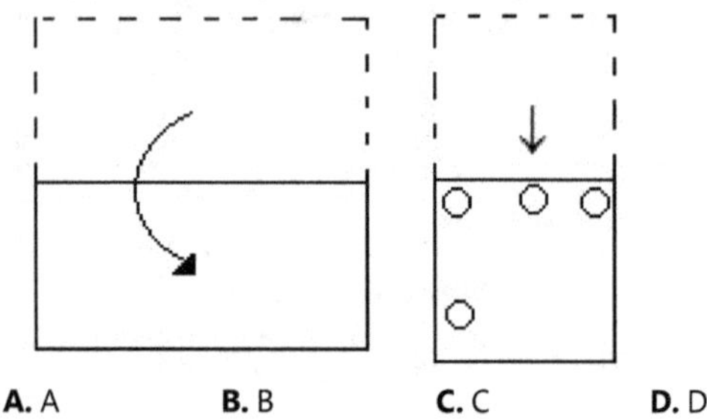

A. A   **B.** B   **C.** C   **D.** D

Q.44 In the following questions below are given some statements followed by some given conclusions. You have to take the given statements to be true even if they seem to be at variance with commonly known facts. Read all the conclusions and then decide which of the given conclusions logically follows from the given statements, disregarding commonly known facts. Give answer:

Statement

No lion is dog.

No dog is hen.

Conclusion

I. No lions are hen.

II. Some lions are hens

A. Only conclusion I follows

B. Only conclusion II follows

C. Either conclusion I or conclusion II follow

D. Neither I nor II conclusions follow

Q.45 In each of the questions given below, a statement has been given, then two preconceptions under which the numbers I and II have been given. A pre-conceived or perceived assumption is called prediction. You have to consider the statements and the assumptions given below and then decide which pre-concepts are contained in the statement. Please give - (A) if only I is implicit. (B) if only II is implicit. (C) if neither I nor II is implicit. (D) if both I and II are implicit.

Statement:

Profit from the investment in shares of company X happened by serendipity.

Assumptions:

I. Luck can play a role in deciding the fate of shares of X.

II. Luck is a must when it comes to investment in shares.

A. A   **B.** B   **C.** C   **D.** D

Q.46 The option which is the water reflection of the word given below-

QUESTION FIGURE

MIXTURE

ANSWER FIGURE

ƎЯUTXIM
(A)

MIXTURE
(B)

MIXTUᴚE
(C)

ƎЯUTXIM
(D)

A. A   **B.** B   **C.** C   **D.** D

Q.47 Which one of the following diagrams represent the correct relationship between DOCTORS, SURGEONS and NURSES.

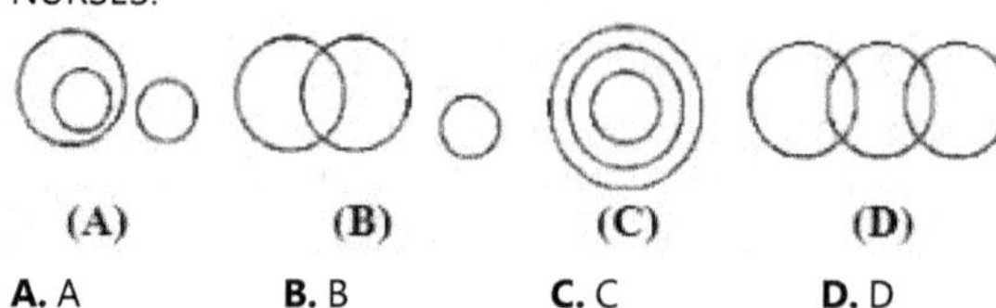

(A)   **(B)**   **(C)**   **(D)**

A. A   **B.** B   **C.** C   **D.** D

Q.48 If every Sunday of any month is on fourth, eleventh eighteenth and twenty fifth, then which day will be the last day of the month if first day of the month is Thursday ?

A. Saturday   **B.** Tuesday

C. Thursday   **D.** Data insufficient

Q.49 In the following questions below are given some statements followed by some given conclusions. You have to take the given statements to be true even if they seem to be at variance with commonly known facts. Read all the conclusions and then decide which of the given conclusions logically follows from the given statements, disregarding commonly known facts. Give answer:

Statements:

Some sword are knife.

All knife are weapon.

Conclusions:

I. Some weapon are sword.

II. Some knife are sword.

A. Only I   **B.** Only II

C. Both I and II   **D.** Nether I nor II

Q.50 What will come in place of the question mark (?) in the following number series?

34, 203, 428, 717, ?

A. 1315   **B.** 1223   **C.** 1078   **D.** 1090

Q.51 Which of the following figure is the correct mirror image of the given figure?

Question figure

Answer figures

(A) (mirror image of TR5D6P7S)

(B) (mirror image of TR5D6P7S)

(C) (mirror image of TR5D6P7S)

(D) (mirror image of TR5D6P7S)

A. A   **B.** B   **C.** C   **D.** D

Q.52 In each of the following questions, select the related word/letters/number from the given alternatives.

Encouragement : Victory : : Frustration : ?

A. Stalemate   **B.** Anger

C. Failure   **D.** Anxiety

Q.53 In each of the following questions, select the one which is different from the others.

(A) Nose   (B) Ear

(C) Tongue (D) Teeth

A. A   **B.** B   **C.** C   **D.** D

Q.54 Given below is a statement followed by 2/3 Assumptions. An assumption is something not written directly but can be considered as the implicit understanding before writing any text, document or writing. Choose the implicit assumption in the following question:

Statements:

1. India is manufacturing a much greater number of two wheelers than it did a decade back.

2. The quality has also improved quite a lot.

Assumption :

I. We are exporting two wheelers.

II. Our two-wheeler industry has made commendable progress.

A. Only I follows

B. Only II follows

C. Both I & II follows

D. Neither I nor II follows

Q.55 Which one of the given responses would be a meaningful order of the following ?

1- Wall

2- Clay

3- House

4- Room

5- Bricks

A. 5, 2, 1, 4, 3   **B.** 2, 5, 4, 1, 3

C. 2, 5, 1, 4, 3   **D.** 1, 2, 3, 4, 5

General Awareness

Q.56 Nallamalai, Veliconda are associated with which of the following?

A. Western Ghat   **B.** Eastern Ghat

C. Deccan Plateau   **D.** Aravali

Q.57 In which of the following Indian state are you likely to see Salher range?

A. Maharashtra   **B.** Karnataka

C. Kerala   **D.** Andhra Pradesh

Q.58 When was Civil Disobedience withdrawn?

A. Dec, 1931   **B.** Feb, 1933

C. May, 1934   **D.** April, 1934

Q.59 In a code language, A is written as B, B is written as C, C is written as D and so on, then how will STUDY be written in that code language ?

A. TUVEZ   **B.** SVVFZ   **C.** TYBSU   **D.** SNBRU

Q.60 Budapest city is located on the banks of which river?

A. Volga river   **B.** Danube River

C. Elbe River   **D.** Loire River

Q.61 With reference to the religious practices in India, the "Sthanakvasi" sect belongs to:

A. Buddhism   **B.** Jainism

C. Vaishnavism   **D.** Shaivism

Q.62 Who was the British Governor General during Third Anglo-Mysore War?

A. Lord Cornwallis

B. Lord Dalhousie

C. Lord Warren Hastings

D. Lord Wellesley

Q.63 The term polyarchy was used by Robert Dahl to describe a form of government in which?

A. It reduces the multitudinous differences of opinion to relatively simple alternatives

B. It takes individual as the basic unit of democratic model

C. People can participate through their representations

D. People act both through the electoral system and the group process

Q.64 If the posts of the President and Vice-president fall vacant, who will act as the President of India?

A. Speaker of LokSabha
B. Prime Minister of India
C. Chief Justice of India
D. Union Council of Ministers

Q.65 Dispersion of seeds can be done by ...?

A. Wind
B. Water
C. Animal
D. All of these

Q.66 Under which Article of the constitution of India, can the fundamental rights of member of the Armed Forces be specially restricted ?

A. Article 19
B. Article 21
C. Article 25
D. Article 33

Q.67 What is the rank of India in terms of genetically modified crops worldwide?

A. First
B. Second
C. Fifth
D. Seventh

Q.68 Lala Lajpat Rai was associated with the following newspapers-

1. Kohinoor
2. The Punjabi
3. Vande Mataram
4. The Pupil

A. 1, 2 and 4
B. 2, 3 and 4
C. 2 and 4
D. All of the above

Q.69 Finance Commisson is included in________of Indian Constitution.

A. Article 340
B. Article 280
C. Article 360
D. Article 390

Q.70 Who among the following artist has been conferred with Tansen Samman for 2018?

A. Manju Mehta
B. Alka Yagnik
C. Saroj Khan
D. Preeti Mallick

General Science

Q.71 The SI unit of power—

A. Joule
B. Watt
C. Newton
D. Dyne

Q.72 What happens If an egg with shell is placed in a microwave oven?

A. The egg shell will explode
B. The egg shell becomes yellow
C. The egg will not get warmed
D. The egg will get cooked slowly similar to a boiled egg

Q.73 Choose the one which is different or odd from the following.

A. Aluminium
B. Iron
C. Copper
D. Brass

Q.74 Which of the following enzyme is not secreted in small intestine?

A. Bile
B. Trypsin
C. Lactase
D. Pepsin

Q.75 Which of the following type of rays does NOT penetrate Earth's atmosphere?

A. Visible Light
B. X-Rays
C. Ultraviolet Rays
D. Radio Waves

Q.76 Which of the following is the parasitic plant?

A. Marchantia
B. Kelp
C. Mushroom
D. Pteris

Q.77 The life span of RBC is:

A. 30 days
B. 60 days
C. 90 days
D. 120 days

Q.78 Farad is associated with....?

A. Resistance
B. Conductance
C. Capacitance
D. None of these

Q.79 Why the clear nights are cooler than the cloudy nights?

A. Conductance
B. Condensation
C. Radiation
D. Insulation

Q.80 The resistance of a conductor is inversely proportional to:

A. Length
B. Its area of cross
C. Density
D. Melting point

Q.81 A person bakes a cake. It turns out to be hard and small in size. Which ingredient has he forgotten to add that would have caused the cake to rise and become light?

A. Cooking oil
B. Baking powder
C. Bleaching powder
D. Sugar

Q.82 The unit of Young's Modulus of Elasticity in MKS system is?

A. Nm^{-2}
B. N/cm^2
C. Dynes/cm
D. $Dynes/cm^2$

Q.83 Melting point of cast iron (in °C) is in the range of

A. 1450-1600
B. 1800-1900
C. 1150-1300
D. 600-700

Q.84 If a bus starts from rest then the passenger will ....?

A. Fall forward
B. Fall backward
C. Will remain the same
D. None of these

Q.85 Candela is the unit of-

A. Electric current
B. Thermodynamic Temperature
C. Luminous intensity
D. Length

Q.86 What is an electrical fuse used to _______?

A. interrupt excessive Resistance
B. interrupt excessive Voltage
C. interrupt excessive Inductance
D. interrupt excessive Current

Q.87 The nitride ion will have-

A. 10 protons and 7 electrons
B. 7 protons and 10 electrons

C. 4 protons and 7 electrons
D. 4 protons and 10 electrons

Q.88 Which of the following substance is also called brain alcohol?
A. Methanol
B. Ethanal
C. Amyl Alcohol
D. Ethyl Alcohol

Q.89 Which acid is used to remove stains?
A. Boric Acid
B. Oxalic Acid
C. Tartaric Acid
D. Formic Acid

Q.90 The addition of a neutron to the nucleus of an atom-
A. increases the atomic mass of the atom
B. decreases the atomic mass of the atom
C. increases the charge on the nucleus
D. decreases the charge on the nucleus

Q.91 Lucas Test is associated with....?
A. Amines
B. Alcohol
C. Ether
D. Halides

Q.92 When a Red Glass Plate and a Blue Glass plate combined, it will transmit _____?
A. Blue Light
B. Green Light
C. No Light
D. Red light

Q.93 Where shall the water boil at the lowest temperature?
A. New Delhi
B. Kochi
C. Ooty
D. Mount Abu

Q.94 Which catalyst is used in conversion of sucrose into glucose and fructose?
A. Mycoderma aceti
B. Lactase
C. Invertase
D. Pepsin

Q.95 Quartz is a metamorphic rock. What is the chemical name of quartz?
A. Silicon dioxide
B. Potassium hydroxide
C. Calcium hydroxide
D. None of these

Q.96 Graphite and heavy water are two common moderators used in a nuclear reactor. The function of the moderator is to:
A. Slow down neutrons
B. Absorb neutrons
C. Cool the reactor
D. Arrest the chain reaction

Q.97 The Chemical formula of Caustic Soda is-
A. $Na(OH)_2$
B. Na_2CO_3
C. $NaOH$
D. $NaCl$

Q.98 Which of the following belong to phylum coelenterata?
A. Hydra
B. Jelly fish
C. Sea anemone
D. All of these

Q.99 Which mosquito is responsible for Japanese encephalitis?
A. Andes
B. Anopheles
C. Culex
D. None of these

Q.100 Which of the following is not a colloid?
A. Chlorophyll
B. Smoke
C. Ruby glass
D. Milk

// Smart Answer Sheet //

Correct Percentage of students who answered correctly. **Skipped** Percentage of students who skipped.

Q.	Ans.	Correct / Skipped	Q.	Ans.	Correct / Skipped	Q.	Ans.	Correct / Skipped	Q.	Ans.	Correct / Skipped	Q.	Ans.	Correct / Skipped
1	B	78.28 % / 16.45 %	17	D	86.24 % / 10.25 %	33	A	88.58 % / 10.07 %	49	C	88.42 % / 10.96 %	65	D	82.24 % / 10.84 %
2	C	84.83 % / 10.63 %	18	A	87.91 % / 12.03 %	34	D	86.42 % / 12.48 %	50	C	89.27 % / 10.71 %	66	D	80.16 % / 18.7 %
3	C	78.58 % / 15.03 %	19	A	86.31 % / 10.05 %	35	A	83.53 % / 16.4 %	51	A	87.83 % / 10.42 %	67	C	89.27 % / 10.02 %
4	C	82.02 % / 16.85 %	20	C	80.51 % / 18.32 %	36	B	89.26 % / 10.66 %	52	C	77.99 % / 18.9 %	68	C	78.74 % / 20.83 %
5	A	85.79 % / 10.38 %	21	A	76.04 % / 18.02 %	37	C	85.66 % / 12.74 %	53	D	77.2 % / 15.2 %	69	B	78.58 % / 17.44 %
6	D	81.21 % / 17.73 %	22	C	87.69 % / 10.36 %	38	B	89.11 % / 10.86 %	54	B	88.51 % / 10.09 %	70	A	86.25 % / 12.67 %
7	A	88.82 % / 10.76 %	23	D	85.78 % / 12.17 %	39	A	81.23 % / 12.25 %	55	C	80.84 % / 11.82 %	71	B	86.46 % / 11.75 %
8	C	81.34 % / 17.25 %	24	B	78.46 % / 20.64 %	40	B	77.47 % / 17.4 %	56	B	87.35 % / 11.63 %	72	A	77.09 % / 19.39 %
9	B	83.29 % / 15.33 %	25	C	85.42 % / 12.02 %	41	C	76.37 % / 17.83 %	57	A	80.86 % / 18.79 %	73	D	79.1 % / 16.93 %
10	B	86.23 % / 12.8 %	26	D	76.85 % / 19.79 %	42	D	77.33 % / 16.82 %	58	C	88.1 % / 11.3 %	74	D	76.04 % / 10.26 %
11	B	86.13 % / 13.67 %	27	A	82.1 % / 10.89 %	43	C	84.59 % / 12.53 %	59	A	83.34 % / 13.72 %	75	B	80.33 % / 14.87 %
12	C	81.37 % / 14.83 %	28	A	84.7 % / 11.53 %	44	C	76.68 % / 10.47 %	60	B	78.3 % / 12.37 %	76	C	84.8 % / 10.7 %
13	A	76.28 % / 17.85 %	29	D	82.54 % / 11.65 %	45	A	81.03 % / 15.23 %	61	B	77.81 % / 22.04 %	77	D	78.18 % / 12.1 %
14	D	85.65 % / 14.03 %	30	C	77.63 % / 13.51 %	46	C	76.04 % / 17.1 %	62	A	83.04 % / 12.8 %	78	C	86.05 % / 12.87 %
15	C	81.5 % / 11.25 %	31	D	87.04 % / 11.93 %	47	A	79.64 % / 14.93 %	63	D	80.57 % / 14.35 %	79	C	79.39 % / 17.0 %
16	A	86.06 % / 11.89 %	32	C	83.78 % / 15.87 %	48	D	88.45 % / 10.73 %	64	C	79.16 % / 18.31 %	80	B	83.39 % / 13.0 %

Q.	Ans.	Correct		Q.	Ans.	Correct		Q.	Ans.	Correct		Q.	Ans.	Correct		Q.	Ans.	Correct
		Skipped				Skipped				Skipped				Skipped				Skipped
81	B	84.59 % 15.3 %		85	C	85.47 % 12.12 %		89	B	87.47 % 11.85 %		93	C	81.79 % 10.52 %		97	C	82.76 % 10.13 %
82	A	78.39 % 21.51 %		86	D	88.66 % 10.8 %		90	A	87.82 % 11.27 %		94	C	77.52 % 13.76 %		98	D	84.68 % 12.13 %
83	C	84.56 % 14.75 %		87	B	83.45 % 16.28 %		91	B	88.22 % 11.3 %		95	A	84.55 % 13.76 %		99	C	88.53 % 11.35 %
84	B	85.86 % 13.92 %		88	D	76.37 % 20.08 %		92	C	85.7 % 13.79 %		96	A	82.66 % 10.3 %		100	A	86.34 % 12.78 %

//Hints and Solutions//

1. $18-3+2\times8\div6 = 14$

After replacing signs,

$18\div3\times2+8-6$

$\Rightarrow 18/3\times2+8-6$

$\Rightarrow 12+8-6$

$\Rightarrow 14$

2. $3 \times 0.2 + 5 \times 0.3 + x \times 0.4 = 0.3\,(3+5+x)$

$\Rightarrow 2.1 + 0.4x = 0.3(8+x)$

$\Rightarrow 2.1 + 0.4x = 2.4 + 0.3x$

or, $x = 3$

3. Let the area of backyard be x^2 this year and previous year was y^2

$x^2-y^2 = 137$

$(x+y)\,(x-y) = 137 \times 1$

$x + y = 137$ ---- (i)

$x - y = 1$ ---- (ii)

On solving eq. (i) & (ii), we get

$x = 69,\ y = 68$

No of potatoes produced this year $= 69^2 = 4761$

4. Percentincreaseinearningsdecrease$=(20-50)-20\times50100$
$= -30 - 10$
$= -40\%$
Percentage decrease in income $= 40\%$

5. Let the age of A = B = y years

Age of D = y-4 years

Age of C = y+4 years

Then,

$y-4+y+y+y+4 = 4\times11$

$y = 11$

Sum of ages of the youngest and oldest boy = 7+15 = 22 years

6. With 3 articles of P, 6 pencils are given free

Total price = 50 x 3 + 6 x 3 = Rs. 168

With 2 articles of Q, 6 pens are given free

Total price = 35 x 2 + 6 x 5 = Rs. 100

Total Price of all product = Rs 268

Discount given = 18+30 = Rs 48

Discount Percentage = 48/268×100 ≈ 18%

7.

Consider $\dfrac{14}{13^2\times15^2}$

$$\frac{14}{13^2\times15^2} = \frac{1}{4}\left(\frac{56}{13^2\times15^2}\right) = \frac{1}{4}\left(\frac{15^2-13^2}{13^2\times15^2}\right) = \frac{1}{4}\left(\frac{1}{13^2} - \frac{1}{15^2}\right)$$

Similar expressions can be written for other terms as well.

$$S = \frac{1}{4}\left(\frac{1}{13^2} - \frac{1}{15^2} + \frac{1}{15^2} - \frac{1}{17^2} + \frac{1}{17^2} - \frac{1}{19^2} + \frac{1}{19^2} - \frac{1}{21^2} + \frac{1}{21^2} - \frac{1}{23^2}\right)$$

$$S = \frac{1}{4}\left(\frac{1}{13^2} - \frac{1}{23^2}\right) = \frac{1}{4}\left(\frac{23^2-13^2}{23^2\times13^2}\right) = \frac{90}{299^2}$$

8.

Let present age of Ajit and Amar be $8x$ and $7x$

according to question,

$$\frac{8x+4}{7x+4} = \frac{9}{8}$$

$$64x + 32 = 63x + 36$$

$$\Rightarrow x = 4$$

so,

Present age of Ajit = 8 x 4 = 32 years

Present age of Amar = 7 x 4 = 28 years

9.

Supposed t is half yearly year

$$\therefore\ \text{rate} = \frac{10}{2} = 5\%$$

$$\because\ 800\left(1 + \frac{5}{100}\right)^t = 926.10$$

$$\text{or, } 800\left(\frac{21}{20}\right)^t = 926.10$$

$$\text{or, } \left(\frac{21}{20}\right)^t = \frac{926.10}{800}$$

$$= \frac{9261}{8000} = \left(\frac{21}{20}\right)^3$$

$$t = 3$$

$$\text{Hence required year} = \frac{3}{2} = 1.5year$$

10.

Let people who passed all three be x. Then:

53 + 61 + 60 − 24 − 35 − 27 + x = 95

x=7

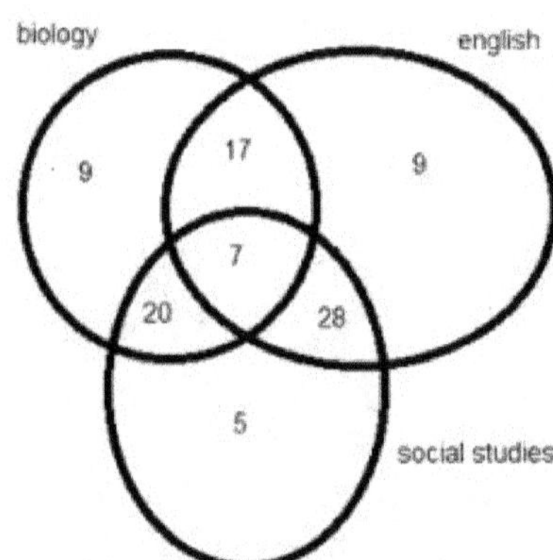

Percentage of student passed only in 1 subject
=9+9+5=23%

Now 23% of 200=46 students

11. Surface area of a cuboid= 2(lb+bh+lh),

where l= length,

b= breadth,

h= height of the cuboid

Let the length, breadth and height of the luggage be l , b, h respectively

Here, l= 80 cm, b= 60 cm, h= 40 cm

Therefore, area= 2(80 x 60+60 x 40+40 x 80) cm²

= 2(4800+2400+3200) cm²

= 2 x 10400 cm²

=20800 cm²

20800sq. cm of cloth is required to cover the box

12. Let the ten's digit be x and unit's digit be y.

Then, number = 10x + y.

Number obtained by interchanging the digits = 10y + x.

∴ (10x + y) + (10y + x) = 11(x + y), which is divisible by 11.

13.

Let the CP be Rs. 100.

∴   SP = Rs. 112

If the marked price be Rs. x, then

90% of x = 112

$$x = \frac{112 \times 100}{90} = Rs. \frac{1120}{9}$$

Required Ratio $= 100 : \frac{1120}{9}$

= 900 : 1120 = 45 : 56

14.

Average number of feet $= \frac{224}{90} = \frac{112}{45}$

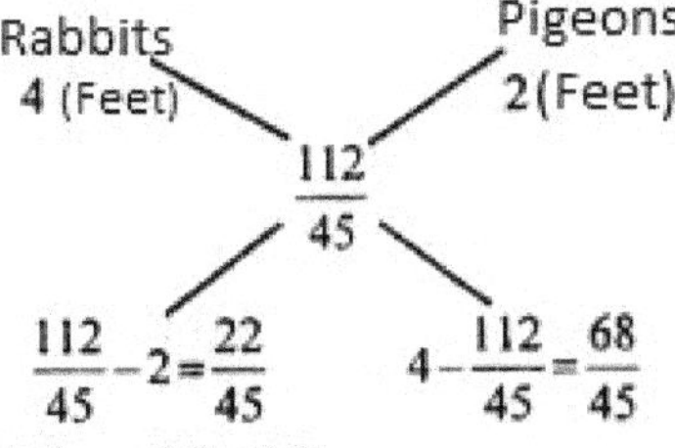

Ratio = 22 : 68

That is, the number of rabbits is 22.

15. The "mode" is the value that occurs most often. If no number in the list is repeated, then there is no mode for the list.

So 55 is the mode as it comes 3 times.

16. Since the progression has an odd number of the terms, the average of the three middle most terms will its arithmetic mean.

$$= \frac{111}{3} = 37$$

Hence, the required mean

17.

$$\frac{9}{25} = \left(1 - \frac{5}{K}\right)^2$$

$$\frac{3}{5} = 1 - \frac{5}{K}$$

$$-\frac{2}{5} = -\frac{5}{K}$$

K = 12.5 litres

18.

Let CP of article be 100 units

Then

SP_1 = 102 units

SP_2 = 112 units

Now difference between SP =10units

A.T.Q

10 units =Rs. 3

1 unit $= \frac{3}{10}$

$SP_1 = \frac{3}{10} \times \frac{102}{100}$

and $SP_2 = \frac{3}{10} \times \frac{112}{100}$

ratio of $\frac{SP_1}{SP_2} = \frac{3 \times 102}{3 \times 112} = \frac{51}{56}$

19.

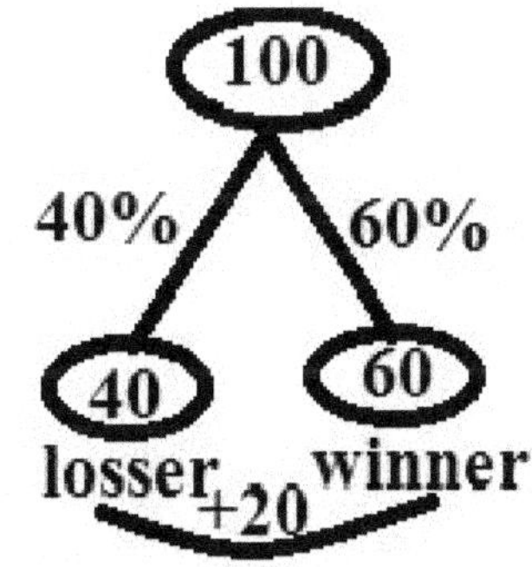

Let the total number of votes =100

20 units=298

1 unit $= \frac{298}{20}$

100 units $= \frac{298}{20} \times 100$

=1490

20.

Let the angle of elevating of the top of the tower from the end point of the shadow be θ

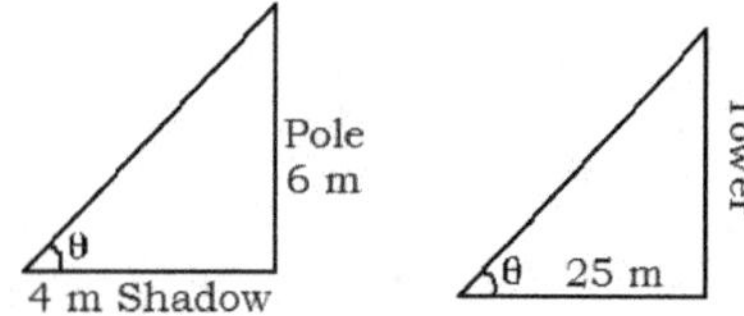

Then,

$tan\theta = \frac{6}{4} = \frac{3}{2}$

$\therefore$ Height of the tower $= \frac{3}{2} \times 25 = 37.5\ m$

21.

Let cost price of the article = Rs.x

A shopkeeper marks the price of an article at Rs.320

Therefore, SP of the article after a discount of 10%.$= 320 \times \frac{100-10}{100} = Rs.288$

CP of the article with a profit of 20%

$x \times \frac{100+20}{100} = Rs.288$

x = Rs. 240

CP of the article = Rs.240

22.

Use the following results.

If $(N)^p > (N)^q$ when N > 0 and positive integral

=p > q

If $(N)^p > (N)^q$ when N > 0 and fractional

= p < q

If $(N)^p < (N)^q$ when N > 0 and positive integral

=p < q

If $(N)^p < (N)^q$ when N > 0 and fractional

= p > q

Using these results we get option C is the correct answer.

23.

$sin\ x = \frac{4}{5}$

$cos\ x = \sqrt{1 - sin^2 x}$

$cos\ x = \sqrt{1 - \left(\frac{4}{5}\right)^2}$

$cos\ x = \sqrt{1 - \frac{16}{25}}$

$cos\ x = \sqrt{\frac{25-16}{25}}$

$cos\ x = \sqrt{\frac{9}{25}} = \frac{3}{5}$

and $sec\ x = \frac{1}{cos\ x}$

$sec\ x = \frac{1}{\frac{3}{5}}$

$sec\ x = \frac{5}{3}$

$\therefore sec^2 x - 1 = \left(\frac{5}{3}\right)^2 - 1$

$= \frac{25-9}{9} = \frac{16}{9}$

24.

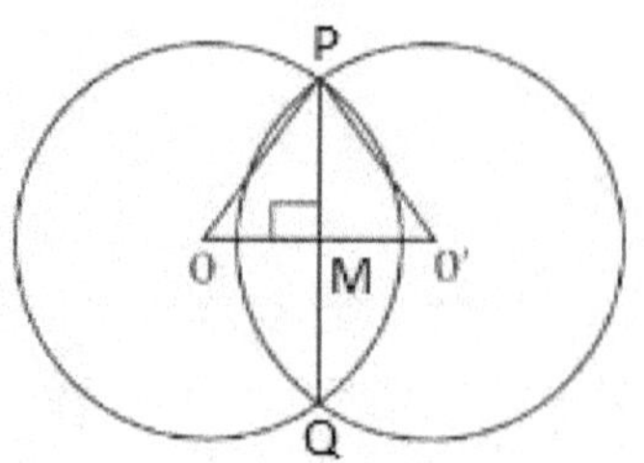

OP = 37 cm and O'P = 20 cm

PQ = 24 cm

PM = MQ = 12 cm

$OM = \sqrt{37^2 - 12^2}$

OM = 35 cm

$O'M = \sqrt{20^2 - 12^2}$

O'M = 16 cm

OO' = OM +O'M

OO' = 35 + 16 = 51 cm

25.

LCM of the following fractions: $\frac{2}{3}, \frac{8}{9}, \frac{16}{27}, \frac{32}{81}$

$Lcm = \frac{lcm\ of\ numerators}{hcf\ of\ denominator}$

Therefore lcm of 2,8,16,&32=32

hcfof 3,9,27,81=3

therefore lcm of the above fractions $= \frac{32}{3}$

26. Largest No. of owners of Airtel simcards= 13 lakhs

(Tamil Nadu)

27. In Assam, Aircel sim cards sold = 2 lakhs

In Assam, Airtel sim cards sold = 5 lakhs

The Ratio of Aircel and Airtel sim cards sold = 2/5 = 2:5

28.

% Increase in 1992-93 = $\frac{3720-2640}{2640} \times 100 = 40.99\%$

% Increase in 1994-95 = $\frac{3360-2520}{2520} \times 100 = 33.33\%$

% Increase in 1996-97 = $\frac{4320-3120}{3120} \times 100 = 38.46\%$

% Increase in 1997-98 = $\frac{5040-4320}{4320} \times 100 = 16.66\%$

So maximum is in 1992-93.

29. Required ratio = 5040/3360 =1.5

30. Average foreign exchange reserves over the given period = 3480 million US $.

The country had reserves above 3480 million US $ during the years 1992-93, 1996-97 and 1997-98, i.e., for 3 years and below 3480 million US $ during the years 1991-92, 1993-94, 1994-95, 1995-56 and 1998-99 i.e., for 5 years.

Hence, required ratio = 3 : 5.

31. Except aluminum, iron and copper, Brass is an alloy of copper and zinc.

32.

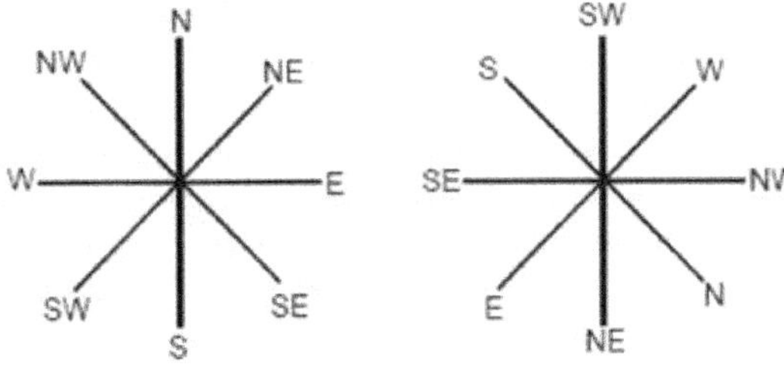

33. The letters are coded by moving them 1 step forward.

34. TON, NOTE, NOT and NET, These are meaningful word can be formed from the given word "TONE".

35. According to the question,

B > D

A/C > E

B > D > A/C > E

Clearly, shortest = E

36.

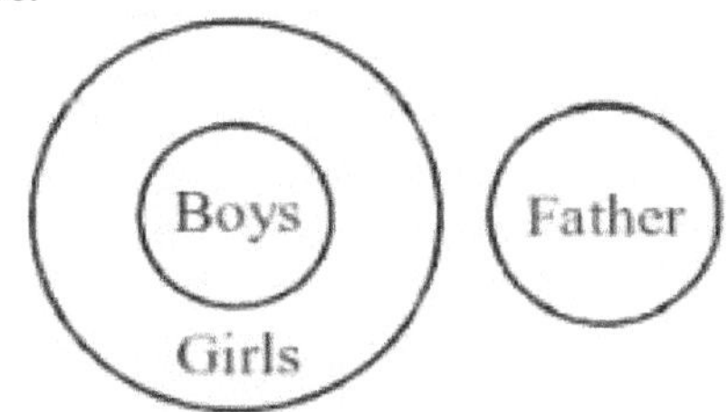

As per the above Venn Diagram, only conclusion II follow because all boys are girls and no girl is father, therefore no boy is father is a definite case.

37. (5) Warlike, (1) Waste, (3) Witty, (4) Worcester, (2) Wrong

38.

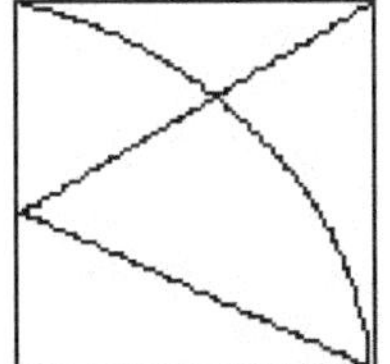

39. From statement, it is not clear that Typhoid is contagious. Hence, only conclusion 1 is true.

40. before ----- 12th

yesterday---13th

today--------14th

1-------------15th

2-------------16th

3-------------17th

4-------------18th

5-------------19th

6-------------20th

41.

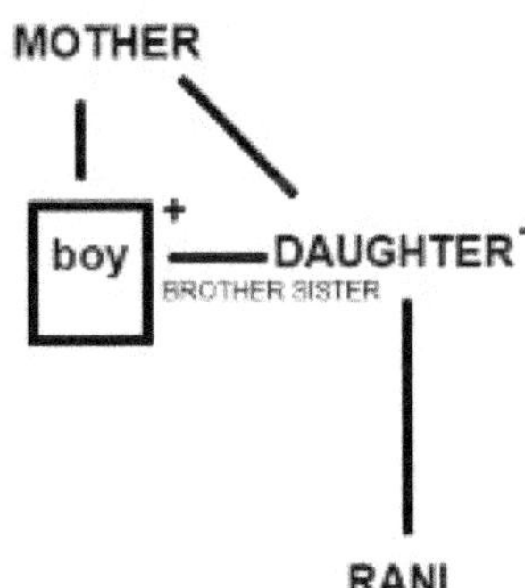

Rani is the neice of boy.

42. As, Circle represents Indian and triangle represents Musicians so the only N is common in both and it is the answer. So the answer is (D).

43.

44.

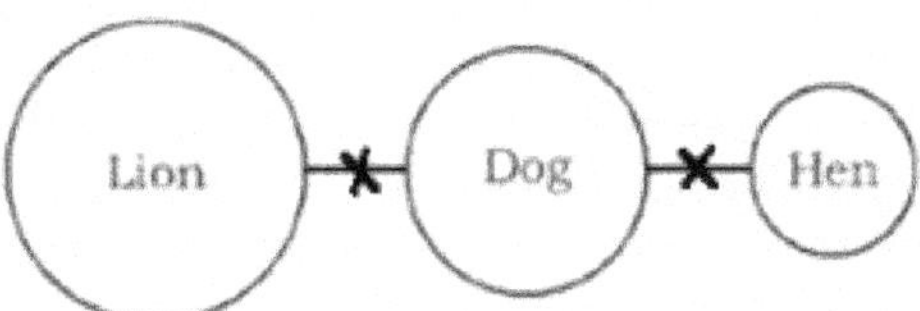

Both I and II conclusions are false but are complementary pairs, hence either I or II follows.

45. Assumption I is implicit since the statement clearly states that the profit happened by serendipity (i.e luck). Hence assumption I is implicit.

Assumption II is not implicit since the statement does not state if luck is a mandatory thing for profit in shares.

46. option (C) is right answer.

47.

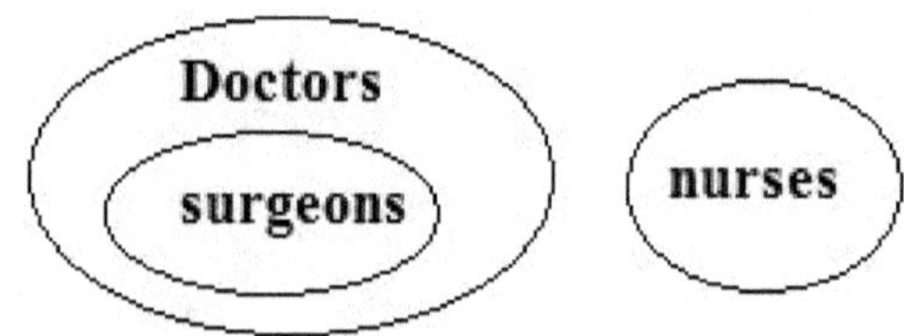

48. First day is thursday means 3rd 10th ,17th, 24th and 30th day will be sunday,We can not determine the last day of the month as we don't have information regarding i.e whether given month have 30 or 31 days.

49.

As per the above Venn diagram, both conclusion I and II is a definite case hence both follow.

50. $34 + 13^2 = 203$

$203 + 15^2 = 428$

$428 + 17^2 = 717$

$717 + 19^2 = 1078$

51.

52. Encouragement related to Victory same way Frustration related to Failure

53. Nose, ear and tongue are sense organs.

Teeth is not a sense organ

54. From above statement it can be said that two-wheeler industry has made commendable progress as manufacturing of two wheeler vehicle has been increased significantly but does not mean they are exporting two wheeler vehicles.

55. 2- Clay

5- Bricks

1-Wall

4- Room

3- House

56. The Nallamalas (also called the Nallamalla Range) are the section of the Eastern Ghats which stretch primarily over Kurnool, Nellore, Guntur, Prakasam, Kadapa and Chittoor districts of the state of Andhra Pradesh and Mahabubnagar, Nalgonda districts of the state of Telangana, in India.

57. Salher range is a part of western ghat with its extension in Maharshtra.

58. The Civil Disobedience movement was withdrawn in May 1934.

59. The letters are coded by moving them 1 step forward.

60. Budapest is the perfect tourist destination in Europe. Budapest is the capital city of Hungary i.e., made up of Buda and Pest, with the Danube River flowing past them, along a stretch of 28 kilometers.

61. Sthānakavāsī is a sect of Śvētāmbara Jainism founded by a merchant named Lavaji in 1653 AD. It believes that idol worship is not essential in the path of soul purification and attainment of Nirvana.

62. Lord Cornwallis was the British Governor General during Third Anglo-Mysore War.

63. The term polyarchy was used by Robert Dahl to describe a form of government in whichPeople act both through the electoral system and the group process. Polyarchy, concept coined by the American political scientist Robert Dahl to denote the acquisition of democratic institutions within a political system that leads to the participation of a plurality of actors.

64. If the post of president and vice president fall vacant then chief justice of india will act as the president of india as prescribed in the constitution of india. If chief justice is also not present then senior most judge of supreme court will act as president.

This Precedence has happened only once in Indian Political timeline when Md. Hidayatullah (then CJI) became President after death of Zakir hussain and subsequent resignation of VV Giri in 1969.

65. Wind, water, and animals are the mediums to carry the seed from one place to another.

66. Article 33 & 34 empower the Parliament to restrict, modify or abrogate the fundamental rights to the members of armed forces, para-military forces, police forces, members of intelligence agencies or similar services.

67. Indian ranked fifth in terms of area in genetically modified crops worldwide.

68. Both the Pupil and Punjabi newspaper started by Lala Lajpat Rai, whereas, Vande Matram is started by Bipin Chandra Pal and Kohinoor by Munshi Harsukh Rai.

69. The Finance Commission came into existence in 1951. It was established under Article 280 of the Indian Constitution by the President of India.

70. Noted sitar player Manju Mehta has been conferred with the 'Tansen Samman' for 2018 by the Madhya Pradesh government for her contribution in the field of music.

71. The SI unit of power is the watt (W), which is equal to one joule per second.

72. If an egg with shell is placed in a microwave oven, the egg shell will explode. It is because there is no control on the rise of temperature while heating in microwave and the water content in albumen (actually yolk also contains water but it is mainly fat. Albumen has relatively more water content) gets converted into steam and the pressure inside the shell increases. Hence it explodes

73. Except aluminium, iron and copper, Brass is an alloy of copper and zinc.

74. Pepsin is secreted in stomach which converts protein into peptones.

75. X-Rays are not able to penetrate earth's thick atmosphere. Hence to image X-rays from celestial bodies, we are sending X-ray telescopes to outer space.

76. A parasitic plant is a plant that derives some or all of its nutritional requirements from another living plant.

77. Human red blood cells are formed mainly in the bone marrow and have an average lifespan of approximately 120 days.

78. Farad is the unit of capacitance. 1 Farad is the capacitance if a charge of 1C increases potential difference by 1 volt

79. Clouds are made of tiny droplets of liquid or frozen water. Clouds act like blankets which prevent heat energy stored in the air and soil from leaving the Earth in the form of infrared radiation.

80. The resistance of a wire is proportional to its length and inversely proportional to its cross-sectional area. The constant of proportionality is called the resistivity of the material making up the wire.

81. Baking powder is a dry chemical leavening agent, a mixture of a carbonate or bicarbonate and a weak acid and is used for increasing the volume and lightening the texture of baked goods.

82. Young's modulus is the ratio of stress (which has units of pressure) to strain (which is dimensionless), and so Young's modulus has units of pressure. Its SI unit is therefore the pascal (Pa or N/m^2 or kg).

83. Cast Iron melting point range 1150-1300 °C

84. Due to the inertia of rest passenger sitting on a motion less bus will move backward as the bus starts

85. The luminous intensity, in a given direction, of a source that emits monochromatic radiation of frequency 540×1012 hertz and that has a radiant intensity in that direction of 1/683 watts per steradian.

86. In electronics and electrical engineering, a fuse is an electrical safety device that operates to provide overcurrent protection of an electrical circuit.

87. A nitride ion has 7 protons, 8 neutrons, and 10 electrons.

88. Ethyl Alcohol is an intoxicant which is formed by the anaerobic respiration of yeast and is also called brain alcohol

89. Oxalic Acid is used to remove the stain and it is mainly the constituent of tomato.

90. The addition of a neutron to the nucleus of an atom, will increase the atomic mass of the atom.

91. Lucas test is performed to difference among primary, secondary and tertiary alcohol

92. When a Red Glass Plate and a Blue Glass plate combined, it will transmit No Light.

93. Water to get boil, its vapour pressure must reach to its surrounding pressure. In a pressure cooker, it boils at the highest temperature. Elevation of Kochi is 0 m, Ooty is 2,486 m, Mount Abu is 1,200 m, New Delhi is 216 m, and Shimla is 2,205 m. So comparing all of them, water will boil at lowest temperature at Ooty, followed by Shimla, Mount Abu , New Delhi and Kochi. This is because, higher we go lower is the atmospheric pressure and lower is the point where water's vapour pressure gets equal to the atmospheric pressure.

94. Invertase is an enzyme that catalyzes the hydrolysis of sucrose into fructose and glucose. The resulting mixture of fructose and glucose is called inverted sugar syrup.

95. Quartz is a metamorphic form of sand stone which is chemically known as silicon dioxide.

96. Heavy water is basically used as a moderator in nuclear reactors to slow down the neutrons so that they are captured and become effective to bring about the fission reaction. The main reason why heavy water is used as a moderator is because it captures less neutrons than the normal water.

97. Sodium hydroxide, also known as lye and caustic soda, is an inorganic compound with the formula NaOH.

98. Animals belonging to coelenterata have thread like structures called tentacles and hydra, jelly fish and sea anemone belongs to this.

99. Culex mosquito is active in tropical and subtropical region and is responsible for Japanese encephalitis.

100. Chlorophyll is a green pigment essential for photosynthesis. And it is not a colloid

Mathematics

Q.1 Read the following graph carefully and answer the question given below.

The bar-graph given above shows the percentage of marks obtained by six students namely P, Q, R, S, T and U in a class test. There were three class tests viz. Hindi, English and Science and each test were of 20 marks. Any student scoring less than 58% marks is considered failed in the exams.

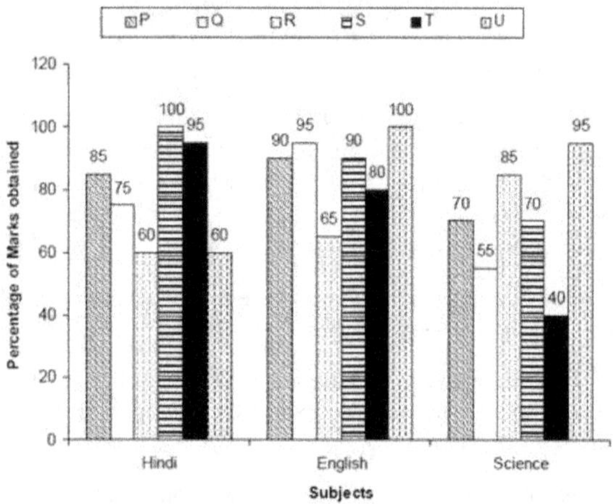

What is the average score of the class in these three tests?

A. 15.9

B. 17.8

C. 18.4

D. Cannot be determined

Q.2 Read the following graph carefully and answer the question given below.

The bar-graph given above shows the percentage of marks obtained by six students namely P, Q, R, S, T and U in a class test. There were three class tests viz. Hindi, English and Science and each test was of 20 marks. Any student scoring less than 58% marks is considered failed in the exams.

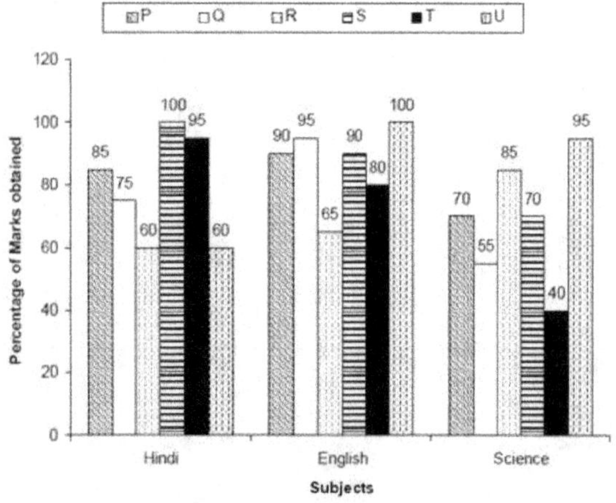

By what percentage, the marks scored by P in Hindi more or less than that scored by T in Science?

A. 112.5 %   **B.** 52.94 %

C. 136.67 %   **D.** 109.5 %

Q.3 Read the following graph carefully and answer the question given below.

Three different companies of bikes used by persons (in lacs)

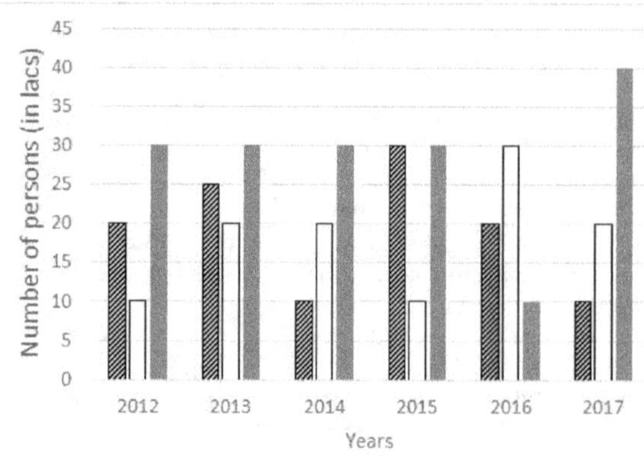

Find out the percentage increase or decrease in the number of persons using Hero from 2014 to 2015?

A. 100 %   **B.** 150 %   **C.** 200 %   **D.** 250 %

Q.4 Read the following graph carefully and answer the question given below.

Three different companies of bikes used by persons (in lacs)

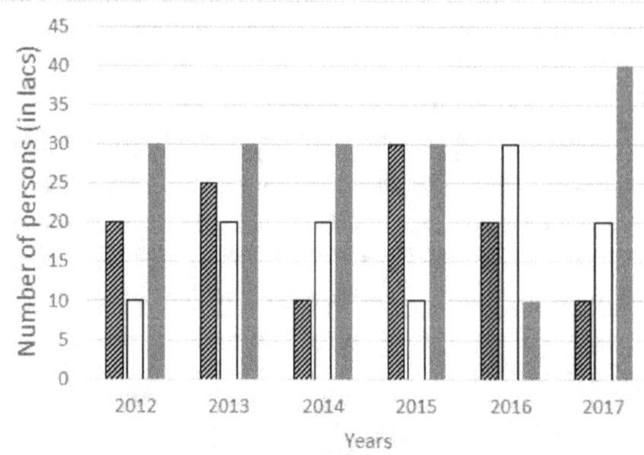

Find the ratio of average of hero bikes used in the 2012 and 2017 and average of Honda bikes used in the same years.

A. 2 : 5   **B.** 3 : 4   **C.** 5 : 7   **D.** 3 : 7

Q.5 Read the following graph carefully and answer the question given below.

3 different products (in Thousands) produced by a company in five different years

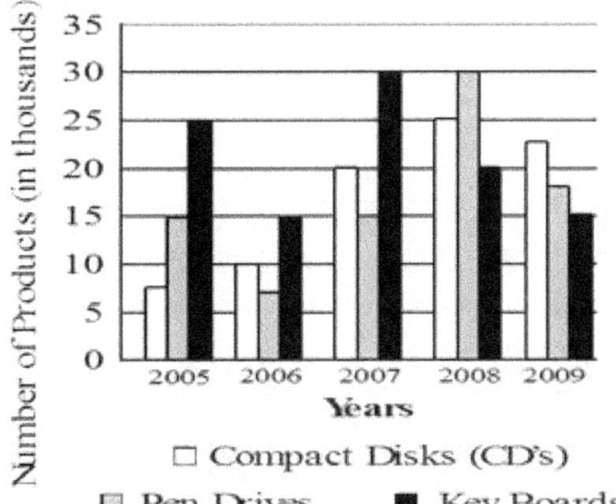

What was the total number of all the products produced by the company in the year 2005 and 2007 together?

A. 112500

B. 11250000

C. 11250

D. 121500

Q.6 What percentages of numbers from 1 to 80 have 1 or 9 in the unit's digit?

A. 14 **B.** 16 **C.** 18 **D.** 20

Q.7 Ria was one more than eleven times as old as Sandhya in January, 2000 and seven more than three times as old as her in January, 2009. How old was Ria in January, 2000?

A. 28 years **B.** 30 years **C.** 34 years **D.** 38 years

Q.8

What is the positive square root of $[19+421--\sqrt{}]$?

A. $\sqrt{7} + 2\sqrt{3}$ **B.** $\sqrt{3} + 2\sqrt{7}$

C. $\sqrt{2} + 3\sqrt{7}$ **D.** $\sqrt{7} + 3\sqrt{3}$

Q.9 The median of six numbers 6, 7, x – 5, x – 3, 17 and 19, in ascending order, is 11. The value of x is:

A. 10 **B.** 12 **C.** 15 **D.** 16

Q.10 In triangle PQR, A is the point of intersection of all the altitudes and B is the point of intersection of all the angle bisectors of the triangle. If ∠PBR = 105°, then what is the value of ∠PAR?

A. 150° **B.** 100° **C.** 105° **D.** 115°

Q.11 If $\tan^2\theta + \cot^2\theta = x$, what is the value of $1/\cos\theta.\sin\theta$ = ?

A. x^2 **B.** x **C.** $\sqrt{x}$ **D.** $\sqrt{2} + x$

Q.12 Amit and Bhanu invest in a business in the ratio 3 : 2. If 5% of the total profit goes to charity and Amit's share is Rs. 8550, then find the profit share of Bhanu.

A. Rs. 5370 **B.** Rs. 6450 **C.** Rs. 5700 **D.** Rs. 5740

Q.13 Seats for Science, Arts and Commerce in a school are in the ratio 6:9:10. There is a proposal to increase these seats by 30%, 20% and 65% respectively. What will be the ratio of increased seats?

A. 26 : 36 : 55 **B.** 36 : 23 : 65

C. 26 : 12 : 65 **D.** 6 : 3 : 5

Q.14 The average monthly income of A and B is Rs 7760. The average monthly income of B and C is Rs. 10990 and that of C and A is Rs. 9070. What is the annual income of B?

A. Rs. 120240 **B.** Rs. 124480

C. Rs. 112360 **D.** Rs. 116160

Q.15 What is the difference between CI and SI, if sum is Rs. 8,000 for 4 years at a rate of 4%?

A. Rs. 21.32 **B.** Rs. 25.42

C. Rs. 27.27 **D.** Rs. 38.91

Q.16 If a shopkeeper sells a TV at a discount of 42%, he loses 13%. At what discount should he sell the TV to earn a profit of 5%?

A. 25% **B.** 42% **C.** 30% **D.** 70%

Q.17 50% of a class of 120 students passed in physics and only 20% not passed in chemistry. The maximum possible number of students who can neither passed in physics nor in chemistry is?

A. 24 **B.** 30 **C.** 36 **D.** 40

Q.18 Three-fourth part of a tank is filled with water. 50% of the water is removed from the tank and 60 liters of pure milk is added to it. If now the ratio of milk-water in the tank becomes 5:4, then the capacity of the tank will be:

A. 120 liters **B.** 128 liters

C. 112 liters **D.** 136 liters

Q.19 What is the unit digit in $(7^{95} - 3^{57})$?

A. 0 **B.** 1 **C.** 3 **D.** 4

Q.20 The profit obtained by selling an article for Rs. 856 is twice the loss incurred when the article is sold for Rs. 760. The cost price of the article is?

A. 783 **B.** 792 **C.** 801 **D.** 810

Q.21 If length, breadth and height of a cuboid is increased by a%, b% and c% respectively, then its volume is increased by-

A. $\left(a + b + c + \dfrac{ab+bc+ca}{100} + \dfrac{abc}{100}\right)\%$

B. $\left(a + b + c + \dfrac{ab+bc+ca}{100} + \dfrac{abc}{(100)^2}\right)\%$

C. $\left(a + b + c + \dfrac{ab+bc+ca}{100} + \dfrac{abc}{(100)^3}\right)\%$

D. $\left(a + b + c + \dfrac{ab+bc+ca}{100}\right)\%$

Q.22 One glass has wine and soda in the ratio 4:3 while other same quantity of glass has in the ratio 3:2. If both glasses poured in a vessel, then what will be final ratio of soda to wine in the vessel?

A. 41 : 35 **B.** 41 : 29 **C.** 29 : 41 **D.** 35 : 41

Q.23 Two poles of the height 12 m and 17 m stand vertically upright on a plane ground. If the distance between their feet is 12 m, find the distance between their tops.

A. 11 m **B.** 12 m **C.** 13 m **D.** 14 m

Q.24 The length of two parallel chords of a circle of radius 5cm are 6 cm and 8 cm in the same side of the centre. The distance between them is-

A. 2 cm　　　**B.** 1 cm　　　**C.** 1.5 cm　　　**D.** 3 cm

Q.25 Surendra started a mock tail (soft drink + soda) counter. Initially, he had 140 liters mocktail which had 30% soda in it. He sold 20 liters of the mocktail. Then he added equal amount of soft drink and soda. Now the ratio of soda to soft drink became 2:3. How much soda was added later on?

A. 40　　　**B.** 60　　　**C.** 45　　　**D.** 55

Q.26 If $\tan\theta = p/q$, then the value of $p\cos 2\theta + q\sin 2\theta$ is:

A. p

B. q

C. $p(3q^2+p^2)/p^2+q^2$

D. $p(3q^2-p^2)/p2+q2$

Q.27 The product of two numbers is 108 and the sum of their squares is 625. The sum of the number is:

A. 29　　　**B.** 27　　　**C.** 33　　　**D.** 37

Q.28 P and Q are standing at a distance of 350 m from each other on a straight road such that P is to the west of Q. Both of them start walking simultaneously towards each other and cover a distance of 50 m each. Thereafter, P turns to his left and walks 290 m while Q turns to his right and walks 80 m. At the end both of them turn to their left such thatP covers a distance of 50 m while Q covers a distance of 100 m. How far and in which direction is Q from P?

A. 270 m, North-East

B. 240 m, East

C. 290 m, South-East

D. None of these

Q.29 Find the remainder in the expression $557\times653\times672/9$.

A. 0　　　**B.** 3　　　**C.** 5　　　**D.** 6

Q.30 A sum of Rs. 4000 becomes Rs. 5800 in 3 years, when invested in a scheme of simple interest. If the same sum is invested in a scheme of compound interest with same yearly interest rate (compounding of interest is done yearly), then what will be the amount (in Rs) after 2 years?

A. 4430　　　**B.** 5450　　　**C.** 5290　　　**D.** 4970

General Intelligence & Reasoning

Q.31 In a certain code language RECTORY is written as UMUSHAN. How will VIADUCT be written in that code language?

A. PFSCYLR

B. XAWEZFZ

C. PSFCYLR

D. UDVEBJW

Q.32 In these questions, statements are given followed by two conclusions I and II. You have to consider both the statements to be true even if they seem to be at variance from commonly known facts. You have to decide which of the given conclusions is/are definitely drawn from the given statements. Select answer as: (A) If only I follows (B) If only II follows (C) If neither I nor II follows (D) If both I and II follow

Statements:
A. All tables are books.
B. All pens are books
Conclusions:

I. All tables are pens.
II. All pens are tables.

A. A　　　**B.** C　　　**C.** B　　　**D.** D

Q.33 'Anvil' is used in the work of

A. Welding

B. Forging

C. Fitting

D. Machining

Q.34 Five bells commence tolling together and toll at intervals of 4, 6, 8 10 and 12 seconds respectively. In 30 minutes, how many times do they toll together?

A. 12　　　**B.** 14　　　**C.** 15　　　**D.** 16

Q.35 In this question, choose the correct water image of figure (X) from amongst the 4 alternatives.

Question Figure

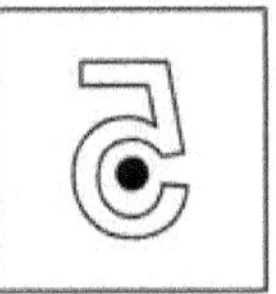

Answer Figure

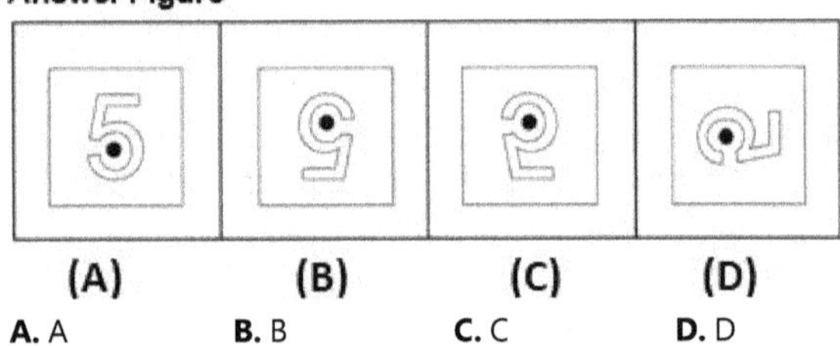

(A)　　　(B)　　　(C)　　　(D)

A. A　　　**B.** B　　　**C.** C　　　**D.** D

Q.36 In a family of Six members, A, B, C, D, E and F. A and B are married, A is a male member. D is the son of C, who is the brother of A. E is the sister of D. B is the daughter-in-law of F, whose husband has died.

How is C related to B?

A. Brother

B. Brother-in-law

C. Father-in-law

D. Father

Q.37 In these questions, statements are given followed by two conclusions I and II. You have to consider both the statements to be true even if they seem to be at variance from commonly known facts. You have to decide which of the given conclusions is/are definitely drawn from the given statements. Select answer as: (A) If only I follows (B) If only II follows (C) If neither I nor II follows (D) If both I and II follow

Statements :
All goats are wolves.
Some wolves are tigers.

Conclusions :
I. Some goats are tigers.
II. Some tigers which are wolves are not goats.

A. A　　　**B.** B　　　**C.** D　　　**D.** C

Q.38 Read the following information carefully and answer the question given below-

Eight person F, G, H, I, J, K, L and M all are sitting around a rectangular table facing the center. In which four are sitting on the corner and four are middle at the line. All are liked different colour Red, Blue, Brown, Yellow, Green, Grey, pink and purple. (Not necessary in the same order).

F is sitting third to the right of I and third to the left of K. The person who likes red colour is the neighbour of J. The person who likes grey colour is sitting second to the right of F and second to the left of L. Green is the neighbour of grey. K likes pink colour. Blue and brown colour are not the neighbours of purple and pink. F likes purple colour. I likes blue colour. G does not like green, grey and brown colour. M does not like green colour. M sits at the corner.

Which of the following options denoted the group of persons are sitting at the corner of the rectangular table?

A. K, I, G and H   **B.** M, H, F and G

C. M, L, J and F   **D.** L, J, I and F

Q.39 Read the following information carefully and answer the question given below-

Eight persons F, G, H, I, J, K, L and M all are sitting around a rectangular table facing the centre. In which four are sitting on the corner and four are middle at the line. All are liked different colour Red, Blue, Brown, Yellow, Green, Grey, pink and purple. (Not necessary in the same order).

F is sitting third to the right of I and third to the left of K. The person who likes red colour is the neighbour of J. The person who likes grey colour is sitting second to the right of F and second to the left of L. Green is the neighbour of grey. K likes pink colour. Blue and brown colour are not the neighbours of purple and pink. F likes purple colour. I likes blue colour. G does not like green, grey and brown colour. M does not like green colour. M sits at the corner.

Which of the following colours is liked by M?

A. Blue   **B.** Grey   **C.** Red   **D.** Yellow

Q.40 In each of the following questions, select the related word/letters/number from the given alternatives.

Clock : Time : : Calorimeter : ?

A. Energy   **B.** Heat

C. Temperature   **D.** Radiation

Q.41 In the question, a piece of paper is folded and cut as shown below in the questions figures. From the given option figure, indicates how it will appear when opened.

Question figure

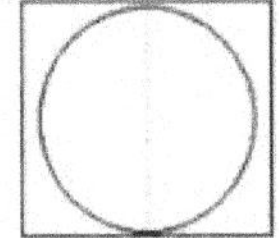 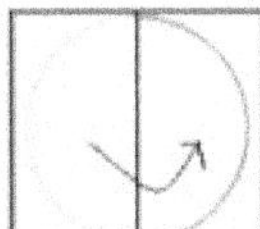 

Answer figure

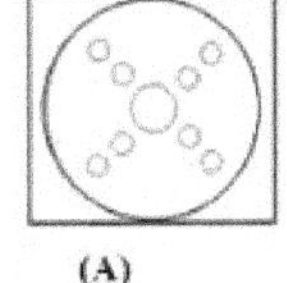 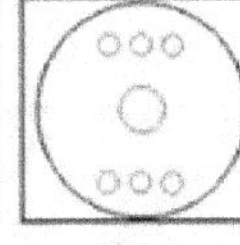 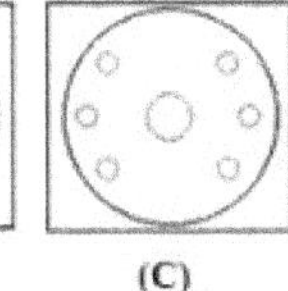 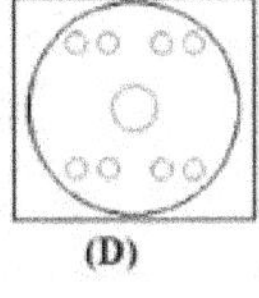

   (A)   (B)   (C)   (D)

A. A   **B.** B   **C.** C   **D.** D

Q.42 How many such pairs of letters are there in the word ESTABLISHMENT each of which has as many letters between them in the word as in the English alphabet?

A. 3   **B.** 4   **C.** 5   **D.** 6

Q.43 How many meaningful English words can be made with the letters 'P E A R' using each letter only once in each word?

A. One   **B.** Two

C. More than 3   **D.** Three

Q.44 In the following problems, there is one question and some statements given below the question. You have to decide whether the data given in the statements is sufficient to answer the question. Read all the statements carefully and find out which of the statements is/are sufficient to answer the given question. Choose the correct alternative for each question.

Find Ratnesh's present age, if

I. Five years ago, Ratnesh's age was double that of his daughter's age at that time.

II. Present ages of Ratnesh and his daughter are in the ratio of 11:6 respectively.

III. Five years hence, the respective ratio of Ratnesh's age and his daughter age will become 12:7.

A. Only I and II

B. Only II and III

C. Only I and III

D. Any two of the three

Q.45 If DEAR is written as EDFEBASR, then MUST can be written as:

A. MNUVSTTO   **B.** MNVUTSTU

C. NMVUTSUT   **D.** NMVTUUST

Q.46 Question : In which year was Neha born ?

Statement I : Neha at present is 20 years younger to her mother.

Statement II.: Neha"s brother, who was born in 1970, is 25 years younger to his mother.

A. Only statement I is sufficient to answer the question but statement II not.

B. Only statement II is sufficient to answer the question but statement I not.

C. Both statement I and II sufficient to answer the question

D. None of the statement is sufficient to answer the question.

Q.47 iven below is a statement followed by 2/3 Assumptions. An assumption is something not written directly but can be considered as the implicit understanding before writing any text, document or writing. Choose the implicit assumption in the following question:

Statement: TATA passenger bus manufacturing company announced a sharp reduction in the prices of their luxury Buses.

Assumptions:

I. There may be an increase in the sale of their luxury buses.

II. The other such bus manufacturers will also reduce their prices.

A. only assumption I is implicit.

B. only assumption II is implicit.

C. both I and II are implicit.

D. neither I nor II is implicit.

Q.48 Seats for Science, Arts and Commerce in a school are in the ratio 6 :9 : 10. There is a proposal to increase these seats by

30%, 20% and 65% respectively. What will be the ratio of increased seats?

A. 26 : 36 : 55   **B.** 36 : 23 : 65
C. 26 : 12 : 65   **D.** 6 : 3 : 5

Q.49 In the following problems, there is one question and some statements given below the question. You have to decide whether the data given in the statements are sufficient to answer the question. Read all the statements carefully and find out which of the statements is/are sufficient to answer the given question. Choose the correct alternative for each question.

How Monika related to Praveen?

Statement I: Ramesh is father of Praveen and Monika is Granddaughter of Sima.

Statement II: Ramesh is only one son of Sima

A. Statement I alone is sufficient to answer the question

B. Statement II alone is sufficient to answer the question

C. Statement I and II together required to answer the question

D. The data given in both statements are not sufficient to answer the question.

Q.50 Which answer figure will complete the pattern in the question figure ?

Question figure:

Answer figures:

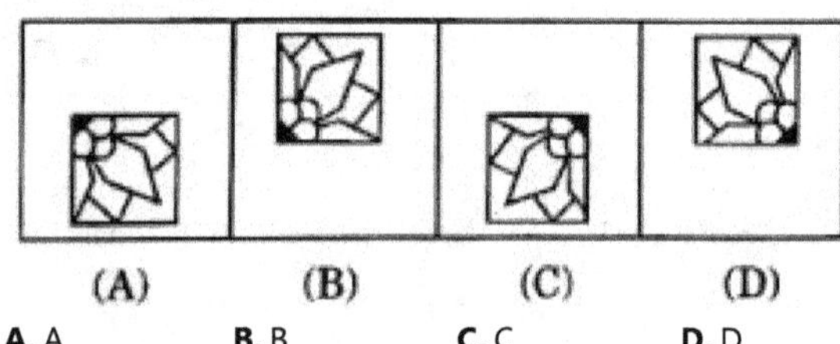

(A)   (B)   (C)   (D)

A. A   **B.** B   **C.** C   **D.** D

Q.51 In the following questions below are given some statements followed by some given conclusions. You have to take the given statements to be true even if they seem to be at variance with commonly known facts. Read all the conclusions and then decide which of the given conclusions logically follows from the given statements, disregarding commonly known facts. Give answer:

Statements:

Some pens are blue.

Some pencils are pens.

Conclusions:

I. Some pens are green.

II. Pencil is blue.

A. Only (I) conclusion follows

B. Only (II) conclusion follows

C. Either (I) or (II) follows

D. Neither (I) nor (II) follows

Q.52 In these questions, statements are given followed by two conclusions I and II. You have to consider both the statements to be true even if they seem to be at variance from commonly known facts. You have to decide which of the given conclusions is/are definitely drawn from the given statements. Select answer as: (A) If only I follows (B) If only II follows (C) If neither I nor II follows (D) If both I and II follow

Statements:

A. Most lilies are roses.

B. Some roses are daffodils.

Conclusions:

I. Some daffodils are roses.

II. Some lilies are daffodils.

A. A   **B.** B   **C.** C   **D.** D

Q.53 Which of the following expression will be true if the given equation 5x - 8 < 12 is definitely true ?

A. X > 4   **B.** X < 4   **C.** X = 4   **D.** x ≤ 4

Q.54 In the given figure, how many red are pens?

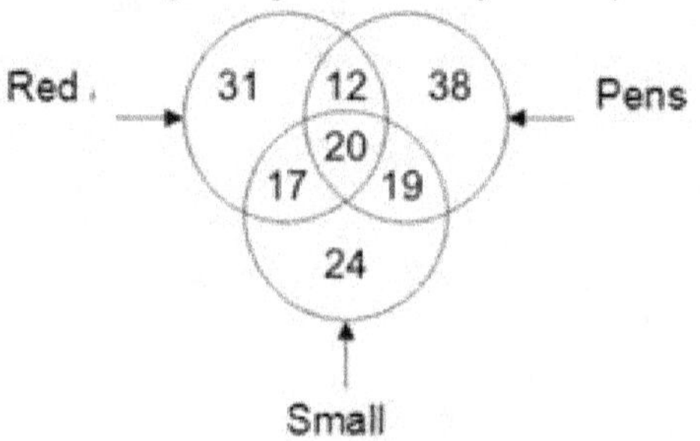

A. 12   **B.** 32   **C.** 20   **D.** 29

Q.55 Choose the alternative which is closely resembles the mirror image of the given figure.

Question figure \प्रश्न आकृति

Answer figure \उत्तर आकृति

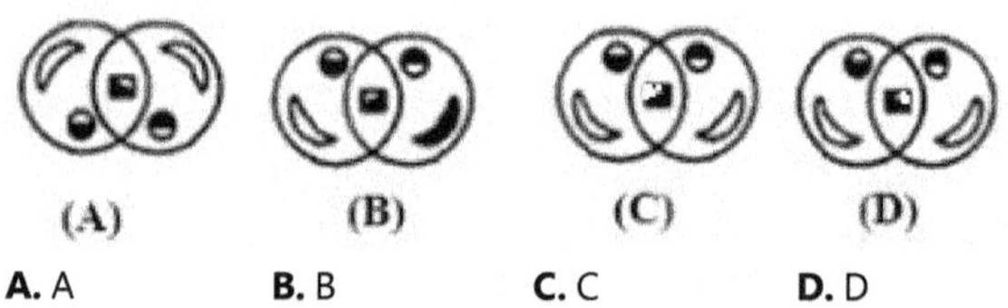

(A)   (B)   (C)   (D)

A. A   **B.** B   **C.** C   **D.** D

General Awareness

Q.56 India is a secular state defined by___?

A. Fifth schedule

B. Preamble of the constitution

C. Directive principles of state policy

D. Fundamental rights

Q.57 When was Delhi annexed by the Britishers for the first time?

A. 1803   **B.** 1806
C. 1857   **D.** None of these

Q.58 In context of Indian agriculture which irrigation system is most prominent in Andhra Pradesh?

A. Tank irrigation   **B.** Canal irrigation
C. Well irrigation   **D.** Drip irrigation

Q.59 In which state of India the Thattekkad Bird Sanctuary is located?

A. Arunachal Pradesh   **B.** Kerala
C. Andhra Pradesh   **D.** Tamil Nadu

Q.60 Which among the following amendments of the Constitution of India, Delhi was designated as National Capital Territory (NCT)?

A. 64th Amendment Act
B. 69th Amendment Act
C. 71st Amendment Act
D. 73rd Amendment Act

Q.61 Which two countries' Prime Ministers have been nominated for Nobel Peace Prize 2019 for signing the Prespa Agreement?

A. Greece and Turkey
B. Greece and Macedonia
C. Serbia and Kosovo
D. Uganda and Rwanda

Q.62 Kerala is famous for the cultivation of

1. Coconut   2. Black pepper   3. Rubber   4. Rice

A. 1, 2 and 4   **B.** 2, 3 and 4
C. 1 and 4   **D.** 1, 2 and 3

Q.63 Find the odd one out.

A. South America – French Guiana
B. North America – Panama
C. Africa - Bahamas
D. Asia – Japan

Q.64 Who formed the Satyagarh Sabha in Bombay?

A. Ali Zinna   **B.** Tilak
C. Gandhiji   **D.** Nehru

Q.65 The post of Vice President has been inspired by the constitution of

A. Australia   **B.** Canada   **C.** Ireland   **D.** US

Q.66 During which dynasty, Mahabalipuram temple was constructed?

A. Gupta Dynasty   **B.** Pallava Dynasty
C. Chola Dynasty   **D.** Chalukya Dynasty

Q.67 What is the minimum age of Joining Atal Pension Yojana?

A. 21 years   **B.** 18 years   **C.** 15 years   **D.** 25 years

Q.68 What is the literal meaning of the term "Quo-Warranto"?

A. We command

B. To forbid
C. By what authority (or) warrant
D. None of these

Q.69 About 50% of the World population is concentrated between the latitudes of____?

A. 40° N and 60° N   **B.** 20° N and 40°N
C. 30° S and 40° S   **D.** 5° N and 20° N

Q.70 What will be the day of the week 15th August, 2010?

A. Thursday   **B.** Sunday
C. Monday   **D.** Saturday

General Science

Q.71 Which is the largest phylum in animal kingdom?

A. Arthropod   **B.** Reptile
C. Protoctista   **D.** Plantae

Q.72 What is the flavor of amyl acetate?

A. Banana   **B.** Orange
C. Apple   **D.** Pineapple

Q.73 'Anvil' is used in the work of

A. Welding   **B.** Forging
C. Fitting   **D.** Machining

Q.74 Solenoid is a-

A. Shaft
B. Hollow tube
C. Tube on which wire is coiled
D. Cell

Q.75 Who discovered the basic structure of atom?

A. Madam Curie   **B.** Rutherford
C. J J Thomson   **D.** James Chadwick

Q.76 On which of the following factor does the working of optical fibre depends?

A. Reflection
B. Interference
C. Diffraction
D. Total Internal Reflection

Q.77 A White Vitriol is __________?

A. Zinc oxide   **B.** Zinc Chloride
C. Zinc Sulphate   **D.** Zinc Phosphate

Q.78 Carborundum is another name of which of the following?

A. Nitrous oxide   **B.** Silicon carbide
C. Calcium carbide   **D.** Calcium oxide

Q.79 Depending upon the chemical nature butter can be called as...?

A. Gel   **B.** Foam
C. Emulsion   **D.** None of these

Q.80 At which angle are the two plane mirror inclined to each other in periscope?

A. 90 Degree   **B.** 60 Degree
C. 45 Degree   **D.** None of these

Q.81 In a nuclear power station, which one of the following is commonly used as a fuel for producing heat?

A. Iron   B. Coal   C. Zinc   D. Uranium

Q.82 Light waves projected on oil surface shows many colours due to-`

A. Reflection   B. Refraction
C. Polarization   D. Interference

Q.83 What is the pigment that is responsible for absorption of light in plants?

A. Stoma   B. Chlorophyll
C. Xylem   D. Phloem

Q.84 Which of the following is natural fiber ?

A. Silk   B. Rayon
C. Nylon   D. Polyester

Q.85 Of which of the following factor is the speed of sound independent?

A. Pressure
B. Temperature
C. Quality of the medium
D. All of these

Q.86 Which of the following is used in purification of water?

A. Zeolite   B. Sodium hydroxide
C. Calcium oxide   D. All of these

Q.87 What is the nature of an air bubble trapped in water?

A. Convex lens   B. Concave lens
C. Bifocal lens   D. Cylindrical lens

Q.88 Which of the following is the common name of Phosgene ?

A. Carbonyl chloride
B. Phosphine
C. Carbon tetrachloride
D. Phosphorus trichloride

Q.89 Which cell organelles possess another set of DNA inside the cell body?

A. Ribosome   B. Golgi Bodies
C. Mitochondria   D. Chloroplast

Q.90 Which of the following is the product of the process of photosynthesis?

A. Ammonia   B. Chlorine
C. Oxygen   D. Carbon Dioxide

Q.91 Which of the following statements is true ?

A. Lead is the most hazardous metal pollutant of automobile exhaust.
B. The toxic effect of Carbon Monoxide is due to its greater affinity for haemoglobin as compared to oxygen.
C. Photochemical smog always contains Ozone.
D. All options are correct.

Q.92 The nerves which are attached to the brain and emerge from the skull is________?

A. Sacral Nerves   B. Thoracic Nerves
C. Spinal Nerves   D. Cranial Nerves

Q.93 Which of the following is not true about electromagnetic waves?

A. These waves are produced by accelerating charged particles
B. Electric and magnetic fields in electromagnetic waves are perpendicular to each other
C. The change in electric and magnetic field is not sinusoidal but random
D. These waves do not require any medium to propagate

Q.94 Which one of the following types of medicines is used for treating indigestion?

I. Antibiotic
II. Analgesic
III. Antacid
IV. Antiseptic

A. I   B. II   C. III   D. IV

Q.95 When Bleaching Powder is mixed in water which gas is released?

A. Oxygen   B. Carbon Dioxide
C. Nitrogen   D. Chlorine

Q.96 Producer gas mainly constitutes up of ....?

A. Carbon dioxide and Nitrogen
B. Carbon dioxide and Oxygen
C. Carbon monoxide and Oxygen
D. Carbon monoxide and Nitrogen

Q.97 Fermi-Kurie plot is used for the study of which one of the physical properties?

A. Beta Decay   B. Internal Conversion
C. Cluster Decay   D. Alpha Decay

Q.98 The buckling loads depend upon-

A. slenderness ratio
B. cross-sectional area
C. modulus of elasticity
D. All of the above

Q.99 The SI unit of power—

A. Joule   B. Watt   C. Newton   D. Dyne

Q.100 What happens If an egg with shell is placed in a microwave oven?

A. The egg shell will explode
B. The egg shell becomes yellow
C. The egg will not get warmed
D. The egg will get cooked slowly similar to a boiled egg

// Smart Answer Sheet //

Correct — Percentage of students who answered correctly.   **Skipped** — Percentage of students who skipped.

Q.	Ans.	Correct / Skipped
1	D	89.5 % / 10.13 %
2	A	78.37 % / 17.9 %
3	C	79.43 % / 19.28 %
4	D	77.76 % / 12.06 %
5	A	86.85 % / 12.32 %
6	D	76.64 % / 20.79 %
7	C	88.4 % / 10.52 %
8	A	80.83 % / 18.55 %
9	C	78.5 % / 14.25 %
10	A	86.57 % / 10.15 %
11	D	82.04 % / 17.19 %
12	C	77.32 % / 19.41 %
13	A	88.28 % / 10.29 %
14	D	82.33 % / 16.94 %
15	D	83.57 % / 14.43 %
16	C	86.63 % / 11.31 %
17	A	79.65 % / 20.1 %
18	B	85.49 % / 11.45 %
19	A	80.67 % / 12.1 %
20	B	87.11 % / 10.27 %
21	B	79.54 % / 17.43 %
22	C	77.31 % / 13.71 %
23	C	85.94 % / 13.43 %
24	B	78.91 % / 10.24 %
25	B	86.42 % / 12.08 %
26	D	86.01 % / 13.96 %
27	A	79.39 % / 16.86 %
28	C	80.45 % / 12.5 %
29	D	80.59 % / 17.12 %
30	C	83.78 % / 15.12 %
31	C	88.3 % / 10.22 %
32	B	83.09 % / 14.2 %
33	B	80.21 % / 14.3 %
34	D	87.29 % / 11.13 %
35	B	79.23 % / 17.96 %
36	B	77.92 % / 14.24 %
37	D	88.95 % / 11.03 %
38	C	78.68 % / 14.27 %
39	B	81.36 % / 15.03 %
40	B	80.19 % / 14.47 %
41	D	87.53 % / 11.77 %
42	C	80.37 % / 15.23 %
43	C	85.61 % / 14.03 %
44	D	86.95 % / 11.6 %
45	C	84.92 % / 10.18 %
46	C	89.97 % / 10.02 %
47	A	82.88 % / 14.02 %
48	A	77.21 % / 16.04 %
49	C	77.04 % / 16.78 %
50	D	79.96 % / 12.29 %
51	D	84.95 % / 11.57 %
52	A	88.76 % / 10.93 %
53	B	80.75 % / 10.16 %
54	B	87.66 % / 10.78 %
55	D	87.31 % / 12.68 %
56	B	84.97 % / 10.24 %
57	A	88.22 % / 11.42 %
58	A	77.27 % / 18.05 %
59	B	89.88 % / 10.08 %
60	B	88.83 % / 10.39 %
61	B	84.43 % / 13.77 %
62	D	78.96 % / 13.98 %
63	C	89.06 % / 10.43 %
64	C	77.39 % / 16.68 %
65	D	85.24 % / 12.16 %
66	D	80.07 % / 13.35 %
67	B	82.14 % / 11.2 %
68	C	78.2 % / 20.94 %
69	B	82.18 % / 10.22 %
70	B	88.64 % / 10.07 %
71	A	77.03 % / 18.39 %
72	A	80.16 % / 16.24 %
73	B	84.86 % / 15.02 %
74	C	86.56 % / 12.07 %
75	B	87.45 % / 11.04 %
76	D	83.3 % / 13.37 %
77	C	77.99 % / 15.41 %
78	B	80.48 % / 17.85 %
79	A	83.22 % / 13.75 %
80	C	84.05 % / 11.07 %

Q.	Ans.	Correct / Skipped
81	D	84.46 %
		15.46 %
82	D	83.56 %
		13.92 %
83	B	89.77 %
		10.15 %
84	A	86.0 %
		11.71 %

Q.	Ans.	Correct / Skipped
85	A	80.46 %
		14.3 %
86	A	81.23 %
		10.91 %
87	B	85.32 %
		10.23 %
88	A	84.5 %
		14.59 %

Q.	Ans.	Correct / Skipped
89	C	85.33 %
		10.5 %
90	C	82.86 %
		15.88 %
91	D	76.51 %
		16.56 %
92	D	77.31 %
		11.8 %

Q.	Ans.	Correct / Skipped
93	C	87.69 %
		11.65 %
94	C	88.3 %
		10.61 %
95	D	84.54 %
		13.47 %
96	D	83.21 %
		11.36 %

Q.	Ans.	Correct / Skipped
97	A	82.76 %
		14.57 %
98	D	89.89 %
		10.11 %
99	B	86.18 %
		13.04 %
100	A	86.0 %
		10.45 %

//Hints and Solutions//

1. As we don't know the total number of student in the class. Hence, we cannot determine the average of marks of the class.

2. Marks scored by P in Hindi = 20 × 0.85 = 17

Marks scored by T in science = 20 × 0.40 = 8

Percentage value

= 17−8/8 × 100 = 112.5%

3. Number of persons using Hero bikes in 2014 = 1000000

Number of persons using Hero bikes in 2014 = 3000000

Required percentage increase =

3000000−1000000/1000000×100

= 2000000/1000000×100 = 200%

= 200 %

4. Average of hero bikes used in 2012 and 2017 = 2000000+1000000/2 = 1500000

Average of honda bikes using in 2012 and 2017 = 3000000+4000000/2 = 3500000

Required ratio = 1500000/3500000 = 3 : 7

5. Required number of all products = (7.5+15+25+20+15+30) thousand

= 112500

6. Numbers from 1 to 80 have 1 or 9 in the unit's digit

1, 9, 11, 19, 21, 29, 31, 39, 41, 49, 51, 59, 61, 69, 71, 79

Number of such number = 16

Required percentage = (16/80 × 100) = 20%

7. Let Ria's and Sandhya's age in January 2000 be X years and Y years resp.

According to Question-

X= 1+11Y---------- (1)

In January 2009, Ria's age was (X+9) years and Sandhya's was (Y+9) years.

So,

X+9 = 7+3(Y+9)

X = 25+3Y------------(2)

On Solving(1) and (2)

X = 34 and Y = 3

Hence. In January 2000 Ria was 34 Years old.

8.

$$[19 + 4\sqrt{21}]$$
$$= (\sqrt{7})^2 + (2\sqrt{3})^2 + 2 \times 2\sqrt{3} \times \sqrt{7}$$

Which is a perfect square,

$$= (\sqrt{7} + 2\sqrt{3})^2$$

its square root $= \sqrt{7} + 2\sqrt{3}$

9. The median of six number

= (x−5) + (x−3)/2

= 2x − 8/2

= x − 4

According to Question-

x - 4 = 11

x = 15

10.

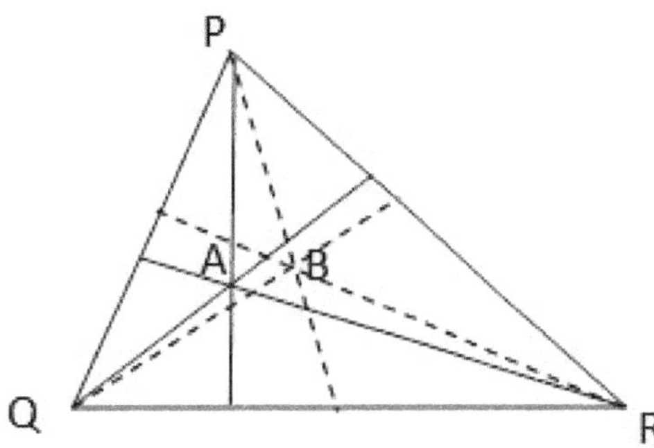

$$\angle PBR = 90^0 + \frac{\angle Q}{2}$$
$$105^0 - 90^0 = \frac{\angle Q}{2}$$
$$\angle PQR = 30^0$$
$$\angle PAR = 180^0 - 30^0 = 150^0$$

11.

$$tan^2\theta + cot^2\theta = x$$
$$\frac{sin^2\theta}{cos^2\theta} + \frac{cos^2\theta}{sin^2\theta} = x$$
$$\frac{sin^4\theta + cos^4\theta}{cos^2\theta.sin^2\theta} = x$$
$$\frac{(sin^2\theta + cos^2\theta)^2 - 2cos^2\theta sin^2\theta}{cos^2\theta.sin^2\theta} = x$$
$$1 - 2cos^2\theta sin^2\theta = xcos^2\theta.sin^2\theta$$
$$1 = (2 + x)cos^2\theta.sin^2\theta$$
$$\frac{1}{cos^2\theta.sin^2\theta} = 2 + x$$
$$\frac{1}{cos\theta.sin\theta} = \sqrt{2 + x}$$

12. Let the total profit be Rs. 100.

After paying to charity, Amit's share = Rs. ($95 \times 3/5$) = Rs. 57

If Amit's share is Rs. 57, total profit = Rs. 100

If Amit's share is Rs. 8550 then total profit = $8550 \times 100/5$

= 15000

Bhanu's share = ($15000 \times 95/100 \times 25$) = Rs. 5700

13. Originally, let the number of seats for Science, Arts and Commerce be 6x, 9x and 10x respectively.

Number of increased seats are (130% of 6x), (120% of 9x) and (165% of 10x).

($130/100 \times 6x$) : ($120/100 \times 9x$) : ($165/100 \times 10x$)

= 78x : 108x : 165x

= 26 : 36 : 55

14. Total income of A and B = 2 x 7760

So, A+B = 15520 ... (i)

Similarly,

B +C = 10990 x 2 = 21980... (ii)

and A+C = 9070 x 2 = 18140 ... (iii)

Adding Eqs. (i), (ii) and (iii),

2(A + B + C) = 55640

$\Rightarrow$ A+B + C =27820 ... (iv)

Subtracting Eq. (iii) from Eq. (iv),

B = 27820 – 18140 = 9680

Hence, annual income of B = 9680 x 12 = Rs. 116160

15. Difference between SI and CI = Sum $\times r^2 \times$ (300+r)/100^3

= $8000 \times 4^2 \times$ (300+4)/100^3

= 38912000/1000000 = 38.91

16. SP= (1−42/100) MP= (1−13/100) CP

MP= $0.87 \times$ CP/0.58= $1.5 \times$ CP

To earn profit of 5%, let the discount be D%.

New SP= (1+5/100) CP = (1−D/100) MP

1.05CP = (1−D/100) $\times$ 1.5 $\times$ CP

D= 30%

Short trick:

$100 - D_1/100 - D_2 = 100 + P_1/100 + P_2$

$58/100 - D_2 = 87/105$

$\Rightarrow D_2 = 100 - 70 = 30\%$

17. Number of students does not pass in physics = 50% of 120 = 60

Number of students does not pass in chemistry = 20% of 120

= $20/100 \times 120 = 24$

So, the maximum possible number of students who can neither passed in physics nor in chemistry is = 24

18. As the new ratio of milk and water is 5:4

The quantity of milk = 60 liters and hence the quantity of water has to be 48 liters.

Now, 1/2 of 3/4th of the capacity of tank =48 liters

So, capacity of the tank = $48 \times 2 \times 4/3 = 128$ liters

19. Unit digit in 7^{95} = Unit digit in $[(7^4)^{23} \times 7^3]$

= Unit digit in [(Unit digit in (2401))^{23} × (343)]

= Unit digit in $(1^{23} \times 343)$

= Unit digit in (343)

= 3

Unit digit in 3^{57} = Unit digit in

=$[(3^4)^{14} \times 3^1]$ = Unit digit in [Unit digit in (81)^{14} × 3]

= Unit digit in $[(1)^{14} \times 3]$

= Unit digit in (1 x 3)

= Unit digit in (3)

= 3

Unit digit in ($7^{95} - 3^{57}$) = Unit digit in (343 - 3) = Unit digit in (340) = 0.

20. Let 'C' be the cost price of the article.

$\Rightarrow$ (856 - C) = 2(C - 760)

$\Rightarrow$ 3C = 856 + 1520

$\Rightarrow$ 3C = 2376

$\Rightarrow$ C = 792

$\therefore$ The cost price of the article = 792

21. Let us suppose that each side of the cuboid be 100 units. Then its volume 100^3 units

Now new sides of the cuboid are: (100 + a), (100 + b) and (100 + c)

Then its new volume = (100 + a)(100 + b)(100 + c)

= $100^3 + 100^2(a+b+c) + 100(ab+bc+ca) + abc$

Then % change in volume

= $100^2(a+b+c) + 100(ab+bc+ca) + abc/100^3) \times 100$

= $(a+b+c + ab+bc+ca/100 + abc/(100)^2)\%$

22. Glass 1 : Wine : soda = 4 : 3

Glass 2 : Wine : soda =3 : 2

Vessel Wine = Glass 1 + Glass 2 = 4/7+3/5 = 41/35

Vessel soda = Glass 1 + Glass 2 = 3/7+2/5 = 29/35

Soda to wine ratio = 29/35 : 41/35 = 29 : 41

23.

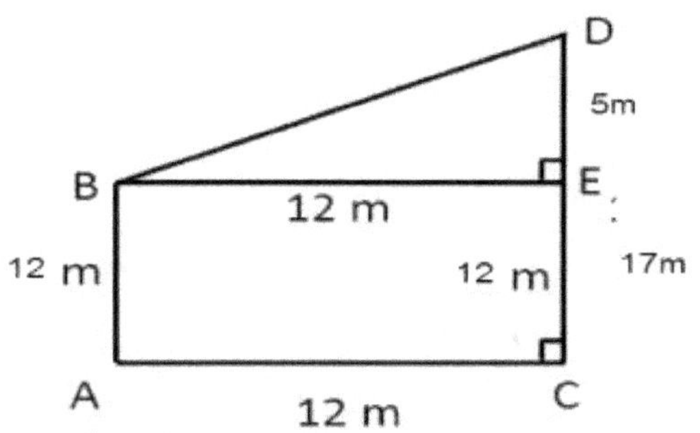

In triangle BDE ,
$$BD^2 = BE^2 + DE^2$$
$$= 5^2 + 12^2 = 144 + 25 = 169$$
BD = 13m

24. Here, O is the centre of the circle of radius 5 cm and AB and CD are two chord of length 8 cm and 6 cm respectively.

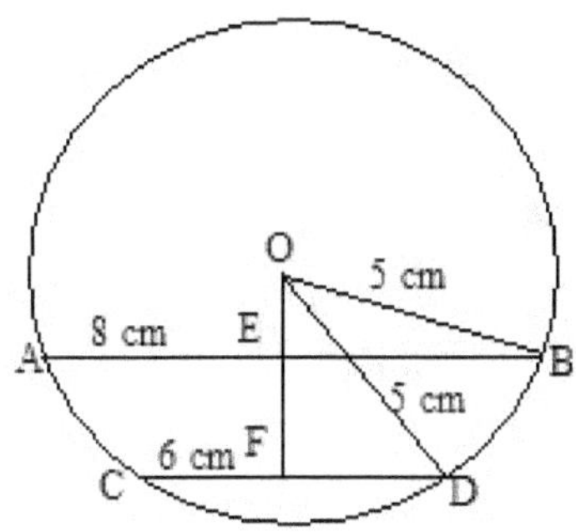

∵ ∵ Perpendicular drawn from the centre of a circle to the chord bisects the chord.

∴ ∴ EB = 4 cm and FD = 3 cm

Now, In Δ Δ OEB

OB2=OE2+EB2

25. Initial amount of soft drink = 100% mock tail – 30% soda = 70% soft drink

Surendra sold 20 liter mock tail, so now he has 140 - 20 = 120 liters mocktail

In this 120l mock tail, the ratio will be same i.e., 30% soda and 70% soft drink

So, amount of soft drink = 70% of 120 = 84 liters

So, Amount of soda = 120 – 84 = 36 liters

Now, let Surendra add x liters of soft drink and x liters of soda

36+x/84+x = 23

108 + 3x = 168 + 2x

x = 60 liters =amount of soda added

26.
$$p\,\cos 2\theta + q\sin 2\theta = p\left(\frac{1-\tan^2\theta}{1+\tan^2\theta}\right) + q\left(\frac{2\tan\theta}{1+\tan^2\theta}\right)$$

$$= p\left(\frac{1-\frac{p^2}{q^2}}{1+\frac{p^2}{q^2}}\right) + q\left(\frac{\frac{2p}{q}}{1+\frac{p^2}{q^2}}\right)$$

$$= p\left(\frac{q^2-p^2}{q^2+p^2}\right) + \left(\frac{2pq^2}{q^2+p^2}\right) = \frac{p(q^2-p^2+2q^2)}{p^2+q^2}$$
$$= \frac{p(3q^2-p^2)}{p^2+q^2}$$

27. Let the Numbers be P and Q.

PQ= 108, P²+Q² = 625

(P+Q)² = P²+Q²+2PQ

(P+Q)² = 625+2×108

(P+Q)² = 841

P+Q = 29

28.

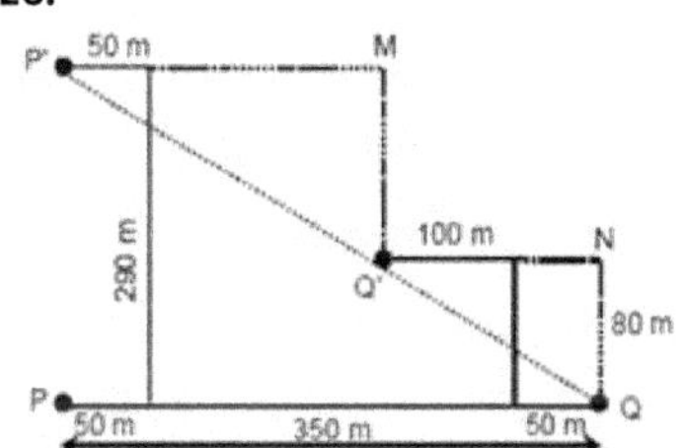

Shortest Distance between P and Q =P'Q'=
$$\sqrt{(P'M')^2 + (Q'M)^2}$$
$$= \sqrt{200^2 + 210^2}$$
$$= 290m$$

Hence Q is 290m from P and in the South- East Direction.

29. 557×653×672/9

557 is divided by 9, remainder = 8

653 is divided by 9, remainder = 5

672 is divided by 9, remainder = 6

So, now multiplication of remainders 8×5×6 = 240 is divided by 9, find the required remainder.

Required remainder = 6

30.

$$\therefore S.I. = \frac{P \times R \times R}{100}$$

$$\therefore 5800 - 4000 = \frac{4000 \times 3 \times R}{100}$$

$$R = \frac{1800 \times 100}{4000 \times 3}$$

$$= 15\%$$

Amount of C.I.

$$A = P\left[1 + \frac{R}{100}\right]^n$$

$$A = 4000\left[1 + \frac{15}{100}\right]^2$$

$$= 4000 \times \frac{115 \times 115}{100 \times 100}$$

$$= 4000 \times \frac{23 \times 23}{20 \times 20}$$

$$= Rs. = 5290$$

31.

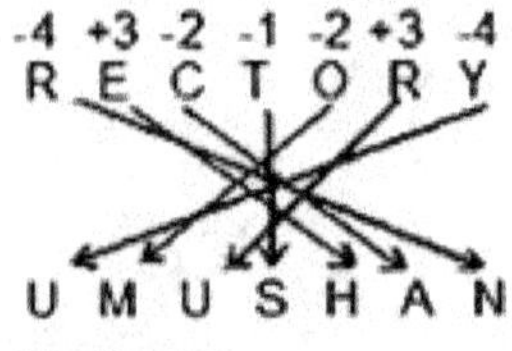

Similarly,

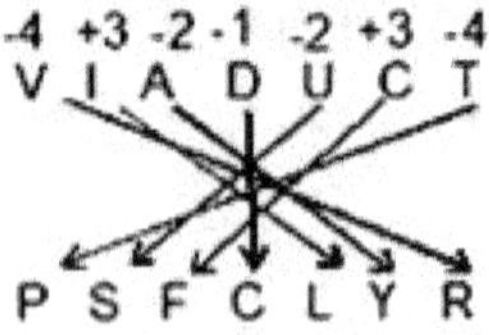

32.

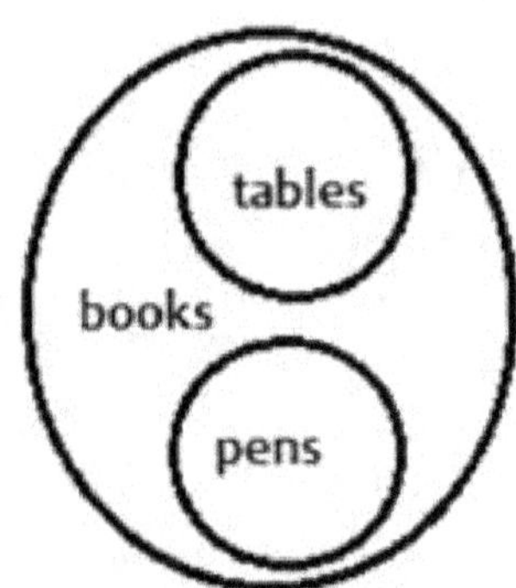

36.

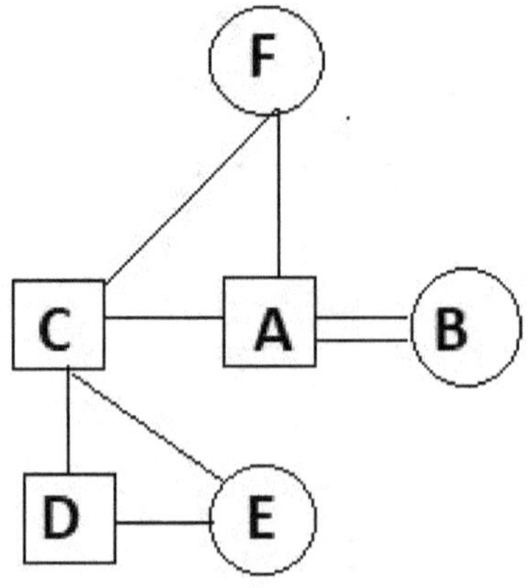

C is Brother in -law of B.

37.

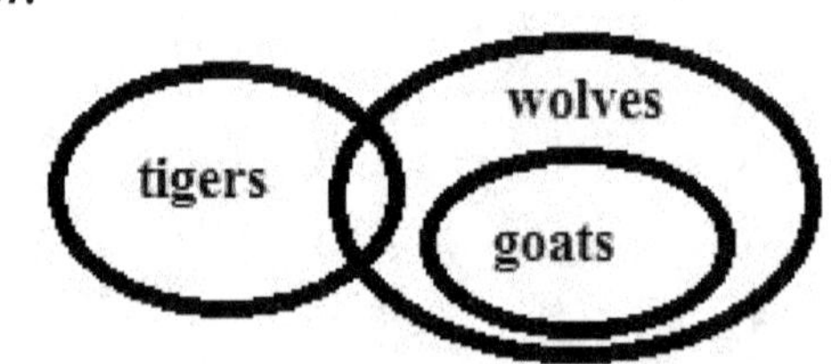

neither I nor II follows

38.

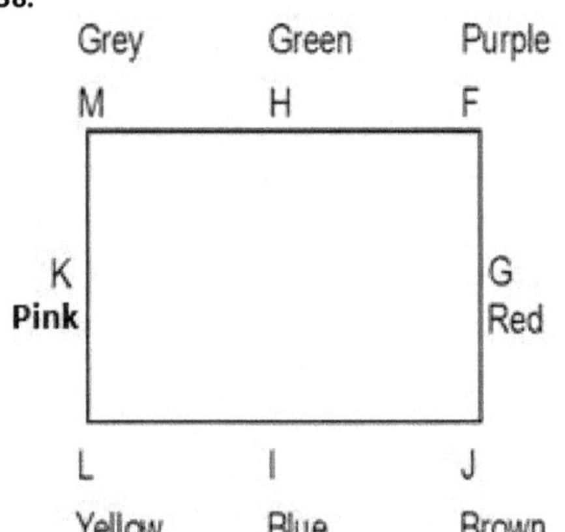

33. Anvils are as massive as they are practical, because the higher their inertia, the more efficiently they cause the energy of striking tools to be transferred to the work piece. In most cases the anvil is used as a forging tool.

34. L.C.M. of 4, 6, 8, 10, and 12 is 120.
So, the bells will toll together after every 120 seconds (2 minutes). In 30 minutes, they will toll together 30/2 + 1 = 16 times.

35. Figure (B) is exactly invert of figure (x) so it is water image.

39.

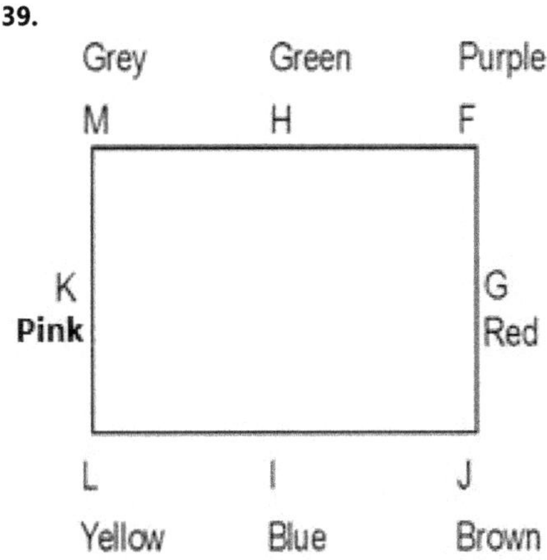

40. First is an instrument to measure the second. Calorimeter is the instrument for measuring absorbed or involved heat.

41.

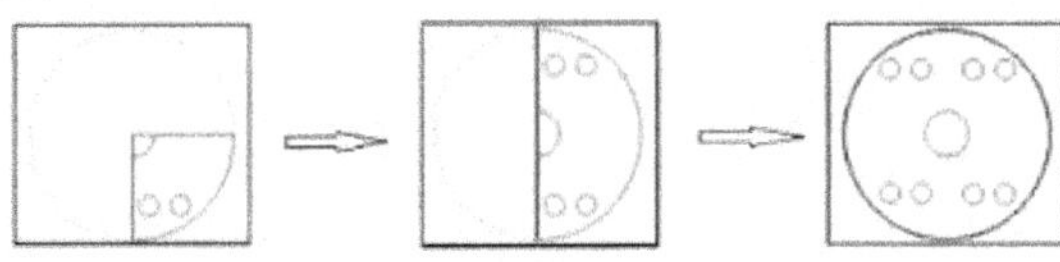

42.

43. There are four words form from the letters 'P E A R' i.e., Pare, Pear, Reap & Rape.

44. 1) Present ages of Ratnesh and his daughter will be 11x and 6x years respectively.

2) 5 years ago, Ratnesh's age = 2 x His daughter's age

3) 5 years hence, Ratnesh's age/daughter's age = 12/7

Clearly, any two of the above will give Ratnesh's present age Therefore, correct answer is (D).

45. The next letter in the English alphabet is added before each letter of DEAR i.e. E is added before D, F is added before E and so on.

Therefore, MUST can be written as NMVUTSUT

46. Age of mother be = x

Age of Neha = x -20

Age of Neha's brother = x+25

Difference between age of Neha and Neha's brother = x-20-x+25

= 5 years

Thus, Neha is 5 years younger to her brother

Therefore, Neha was born in 1965.

So both the statement I and II are required.

47. The price of any product is lowered assuming that its demand will increase. Therefore, assumption I is implicit in the statement.

48. Originally, let the number of seats for Science, Arts and Commerce be 6x, 9x and 10x respectively.

Number of increased seats are (130% of 6x), (120% of 9x) and (165% of 10x).

$(130/100 \times 6x) : (120/100 \times 9x) : (165/100 \times 10x)$

$= 78x : 108x : 165x$

$= 26 : 36 : 55$

49.

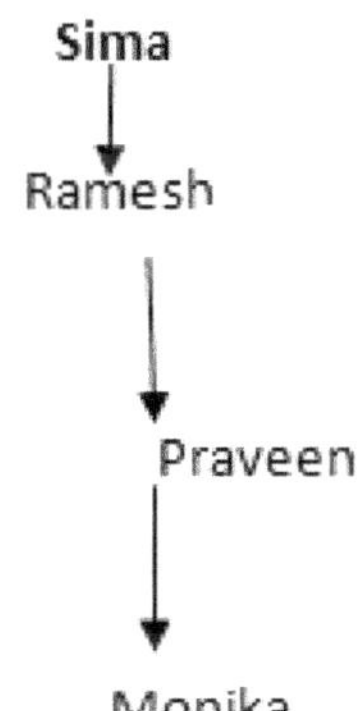

Statement I and II together required to answer the question

50.

51.

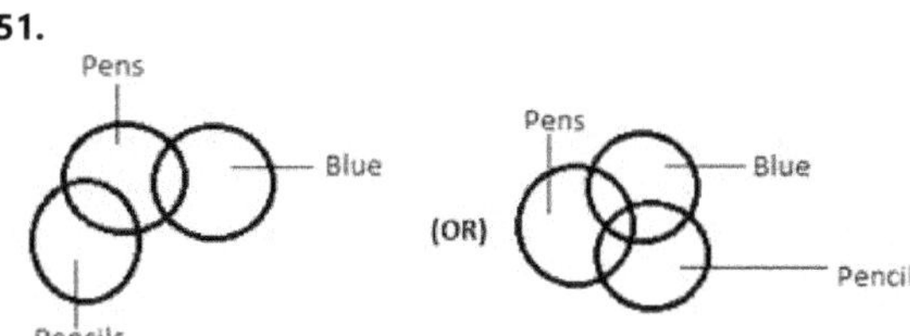

None of the two conclusions follow.

52.

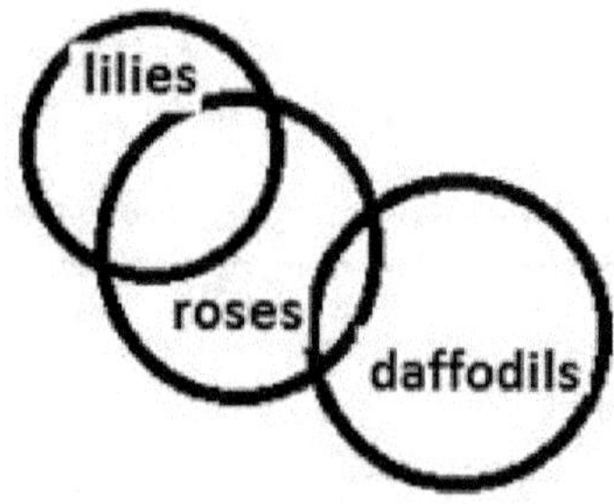

53. 5x - 8 + 8 < 12 + 8

5x < 20

x < 4

54. No. of red that are pens are 12 + 20 = 32.

55.

(D)

56. Secularism in India means equal treatment of all religions by the state. With the 42nd Amendment of the Constitution of India enacted in 1976, the Preamble to the Constitution asserted that India is a secular nation. However, neither India's constitution nor its laws define the relationship between religion and state.

57. After the second Anglo-Maratha war the then powerful Maratha Confederacy was defeated. And it ensured that n reasonal power was capable of having control over Delhi. And for the first time it was annexed by Lord Lacke in 1803.

58. Andhra Pradesh is leading in tank irrigation with 28.8% of total agricultural land of India followed by Tamil Nadu.

59. The Thattekkad Bird Sanctuary, covering an area of barely 25 km^2 , and located about 12 km from Kothamangalam (Kerala state, India), was the first bird sanctuary in Kerala.

60. According to article 239 of India constitution Union territory shall be administered by the President. Article 239AA of the Indian Constitution, enacted as per 69th Amendment Act of 1991, confers special previsions for National Capital Territory of Delhi.

61. The Prime ministers of Macedonia and Greece, Zoran Zaev and Alexis Tsipras, are nominated for the 2019 Nobel Peace Prize for signing the Prespa Agreement between the two countries.

62. Kerala is famous for the cultivation of coconut, tea, coffee, cashew and spices.

63. Except option 3, remaining are correct combinations. Bahamas is a North American country.

64. In February 1919 Gandhiji founded the Satyagraha Sabha to protest against the Rowlatt Act.

65. The Vice President shall be ex-officio chairman of the Rajya Sabha or the Council of States. The election of this post is conducted by the Election Commission where an electoral college consisting of the members of both houses of parliament in accordance with the system of proportional representation can vote. The post has been inspired by the US constitution

66. Mahabalipuram templeis also called as The Shore Temple (built in 700–728 AD). The Shore Temple is located in Mahabalipuram of Tamil Nadu. This temple is a fine specimen of Dravid architecture and is built with a block of granite.The Shore Temple is considered one of the oldest temples of south India, which is related to the eighth century. At the time of its creation, the site was a busy port during the reign of Narasimhavarman II of the Pallava dynasty. There are three temples within the Shore Temple. There is Lord Vishnu's temple in between; Shiva temple is on both sides of it.

67. Minimum age of Joining Atal Pension Yojana is 18 years. APY was announced in Finance Budget of 2015-16. The existing subscribers of Swavalamban Scheme would be automatically migrated to APY, unless they opt out.

68. Quo Warranto: A legal proceeding during which an individual's right to hold an office or governmental privilege is challenged.

69. Most populous countries like China, India, USA and North African countries are situated between 20° N and 40° N.

70. 15th Aug 2010 = (2009 years + period from 1-Jan-2010 to 15-Aug-2010)

We know that number of odd days in 400 years = 0

Hence the number of odd days in 2000 years = 0 (Since 2000 is a perfect multiple of 400)

Number of odd days in the period 2001-2009 = 7normal years + 2leap year

= 7 x 1 + 2 x 2 = 11 = (11 - 7x1) odd day = 4 odd day

Days from1-Jan-2010 to15-Aug-2010 = 31 (Jan) + 28 (Feb) + 31 (Mar) + 30 (Apr) + 31(may) +

30(Jun) +31(Jul) + 15(Aug) = 227

227days = 32weeks + 3day =3 odd days

Total number of odd days = (0 + 4 + 3) = 7 odd days = 0 odd day

0 odd day = Sunday. Hence 15th August, 2010 is Sunday.

71. Arthropoda, the largest phylum in the animal kingdom, which includes such familiar forms as lobsters, crabs, spiders, mites, insects, centipedes, and millipedes. About 84 percent of all known species of animals are members of this phylum.

72. Amyl acetate is used to give banana flavor to the food product and it belongs to ester group.

73. Anvils are as massive as they are practical, because the higher their inertia, the more efficiently they cause the energy of striking tools to be transferred to the work piece.In most cases the anvil is used as a forging tool.

74. A solenoid is a coil of insulated or enameled wire wound on a rod-shaped form made of solid iron, solid steel, or powdered iron. Devices of this kind can be used as electromagnets, as inductors in electronic circuits, and as miniature wireless receiving antennas.

75. Ernest Rutherford established that atoms have nuclei which are made up of Neutron and Proton, and electrons revolve around it.

76. Optical fibre is a thin flexible fibre which is used to transmit light signal and it works on total internal reflection

77. Zinc sulphate is an inorganic compound and dietary supplement. As a supplement it is used to treat zinc deficiency and to prevent the condition in those at high risk.

78. Silicon carbide (SiC), also known as carborundum is a compound of silicon and carbon with chemical formula SiC.

79. Butter is a gel which is a colloidal solution in which dispersed phases liquid and dispersed medium is solid.

80. Periscope is a device which is used in submarine in order to view the moment at sea surface and in this two plane mirror inclined to each other at 45 Degree.

81. Fuel is a complex mixture of the fission products, uranium, plutonium, and transplutonium metals.

82. This is known as thin-film interference, because it is the interference of light waves reflecting off the top surface of a film with the waves reflecting from the bottom surface.

83. Chlorophyll is the pigment that is responsible for absorption of light in plants.

84. Natural fibres are defined as substances produced by plants and animals that can be spun into filament, thread or rope and further be woven, knitted, matted or bound. The most viable structural fibres typically derive from specifically grown textile plants and fruit trees. Natural fibers are good sweat absorbents and can be found in variety of textures.Natural fibers have advantages such as lower density, better thermal insulation, and reduced skin irritation.

Silk, animal fibre produced by certain insects and arachnids as building material for cocoons and webs, some of which can be used to make fine fabrics. In commercial use, silk is almost entirely limited to filaments from the cocoons of domesticated silkworms. the production of raw silk by means of raising caterpillars (larvae), particularly those of the domesticated silkworm is called sericulture.

Rayon was the first synthetic fabric ever created. It was developed as a less-expensive alternative to silk fabric and, appropriately, was dubbed artificial silk.

Rayon is a versatile fiber and is widely claimed to have the same comfort properties as natural fibers, although the drape and slipperiness of rayon textiles are often more like nylon. It can imitate the feel and texture of silk, wool, cotton and linen. The fibers are easily dyed in a wide range of colors.

Nylon was the first commercially successful synthetic thermoplastic polymer. Nylon is made of repeating units linked by amide links[12] similar to the peptide bonds in proteins.

Polyester is a generalised term for any fabric or textile, which is made using polyester yarns or fibres. It is a shortened name for a synthetic, man-made polymer, which, as a specific material, is most commonly referred to as a type called polyethylene terephthalate (PET). It is made by mixing ethylene glycol and terephthalic acid.

85. Speed of sound remains unchanged with the increase or decrease in the pressure.

86. Zeolite is used to purify water using permutit method.

87. An air bubble trapped in water seems to be a convex lens but works as concave lens which means that it is diverging in nature not the converging one.

88. Phosgene is the chemical compound with the formula $COCl_2$. A colorless gas, in low concentrations its odor resembles freshly cut hay or grass

89. Mitochondria own another set of DNA molecule that enable it to perform the biological functioning inside the cell body at an optimum level i.e. why it is also known as the powerhouse of the cell.

90. Photosynthesis is the name given to the set of chemical reactions performed by plants to convert energy from the sun into chemical energy in the form of sugar. Specifically, plants use energy from sunlight to react carbon dioxide and water to produce sugar (glucose) and oxygen.

91. All options are correct.

92. Cranial nerves are the nerves that emerge directly from the brain (including the brainstem).

The cranial nerves are considered components of the peripheral nervous system (PNS), although on a structural level the olfactory (I), optic (II), and trigeminal (V) nerves are more accurately considered part of the central nervous system (CNS)

93. Electromagnetic waves consist of electric and magnetic waves which change sinusoidally and are perpendicular to each other and the direction of propagation of the wave. These waves do not require any medium to travel and thus are able to travel in vacuum. All other options are correct except option C.

94. Antacid is a substance which neutralizes stomach acidity and is used to relieve heartburn, indigestion or an upset stomach.

Antibiotic : A drug used to treat bacterial infections. Antibiotics have no effect on viral infections. Originally,

An analgesic or painkiller is any member of the group of drugs used to achieve analgesia, relief from pain. Analgesic drugs act in various ways on the peripheral and central nervous systems

Antiseptics are used to kill or eliminate microorganisms and/or inactivate virus on living tissues

95. $Ca(OCl)2 + 2H2O \rightarrow Ca(OH)2 + Cl2$

96. Producer gas is a fuel gas made from coke, anthracite and mainly constitutes carbon monoxide and nitrogen

97. Kurie plot (also known as a Fermi–Kurie plot) is a graph used in studying beta decay developed by Franz N. D. Kurie, in which the square root of the number of beta particles whose momenta (or energy) lie within a certain narrow range, divided by the Fermi function, is plotted against beta-particle energy.

98. The buckling loads depend upon cross-sectional area, slenderness ratio, modulus of elasticity.

99. The SI unit of power is the watt (W), which is equal to one joule per second.

100. If an egg with shell is placed in a microwave oven, the egg shell will explode. It is because there is no control on the rise of temperature while heating in microwave and the water content in albumen (actually yolk also contains water but it is mainly fat. Albumen has relatively more water content) gets converted into steam and the pressure inside the shell increases. Hence it explodes

Mathematics

Q.1 D and E are the mid-points of AB and AC of ΔABC, BC is produced to any point P; DE, DP and EP are joined. then, area of:

A. ΔPED = ¼ ΔABC

B. ΔPED = ΔBEC

C. ΔADE = ΔBEC

D. ΔBDE = ΔBEC

Q.2 One side other than the hypotenuse of right angle isosceles triangle is 6 cm. The length of the perpendicular on the hypotenuse from the opposite vertex is:

A. 6 cm

B. $6\sqrt{2}$ cm

C. 4 cm

D. $3\sqrt{2}$ cm

Q.3 The speeds of two trains are in the ratio 3 : 4. They are going in opposite directions along parallel tracks. If each takes 3 seconds to cross a telegraph post, find the time taken by the trains to cross each other completely?

A. 1 seconds

B. 3 seconds

C. 5 seconds

D. 7 seconds

Q.4 A mother is 3 times faster than her daughter. If the daughter completes a piece of work in 15 days, how long will it take for both mother and daughter to complete the same work?

A. 13/4 days

B. 15/4 days

C. 17/4 days

D. 19/4 days

Q.5 Study the following table carefully to answer the questions that follow.

Number of soldiers (in thousands) joining five different forces during six different years.

Academics→ years↓	Air force	Army	Navy	Coast Guard	BSF
2004	2.4	4.2	0.6	1.7	4.6
2005	1.7	5.1	0.9	2.9	4.1
2006	3.9	7.7	1.2	1.3	4.7
2007	3.4	5.6	1.8	4.7	5.2
2008	4.3	6.5	2.9	5.5	6.4
2009	5.7	7.9	3.5	3.7	6.1

Total number of soldiers joining BSF in the years 2004, 2005 and 2006 was approximately what percent of the total number of soldiers joining Navy over all the years together?

A. 123

B. 145

C. 113

D. 95

Q.6 Study the following table carefully to answer the questions that follow.

Number of soldiers (in thousands) joining five different forces during six different years.

Academics→ years↓	Air force	Army	Navy	Coast Guard	BSF
2004	2.4	4.2	0.6	1.7	4.6
2005	1.7	5.1	0.9	2.9	4.1
2006	3.9	7.7	1.2	1.3	4.7
2007	3.4	5.6	1.8	4.7	5.2
2008	4.3	6.5	2.9	5.5	6.4
2009	5.7	7.9	3.5	3.7	6.1

What was the ratio of the number of soldiers joining Army in the year 2008 to the number of soldiers joining coast guard in the year 2006?

A. 5 : 2

B. 3 : 7

C. 4 : 3

D. 5 : 1

Q.7 If tan (5x – 10°) = cot (5y + 20°), then the value of (x+y) is:

A. 20°

B. 15°

C. 16°

D. 24°

Q.8 If a train, with a speed of 60 km/hr, crossed a pole in 30 second, the length of the train (in meters) is:

A. 1000

B. 900

C. 750

D. 500

Q.9 The supplement of an angle is one-fourth of itself. Determine the angle and its supplement.

A. 132°, 48°

B. 156°, 24°

C. 118°, 62°

D. 144°, 36°

Q.10 3 years ago the average age of a family of 5 members was 17 years. A baby having been born, the average age of the family is the same today. The present age of the baby is

A. 1 year

B. 5 years

C. 2 year

D. 3 year

Q.11 A ladder leans against a vertical wall. The top of the ladder is 8 meter above the ground. When the bottom of the ladder is moved 2 meter farther away from the wall, the top of the ladder rests against the foot of the wall. What is the length of the ladder?

A. 20 meter

B. 16 meter

C. 18 meter

D. 17 meter

Q.12 The length of a Rectangular plot is decreased by 33.33%. By how much % the breadth of the plot will be increased so that the area remains constant?

A. 50%

B. $33\dfrac{1}{3}\%$

C. 25%

D. None of these

Q.13 A man deposited a certain amount in a fixed deposit at r % p.a., interest being compounded annually. If the interest accrued for the fourth and fifth years are Rs 13310 and Rs 14641. what is the total interest accrued for the first three years?

A. Rs. 33,100

B. Rs. 33,000

C. Rs. 23,100

D. None of these.

Q.14 A person earns Rs. 5000 as an interest in 5/2 years on a certain sum invested with a company at the rate of 10% per annum. Find the sum invested by a person in the company?

A. Rs. 16,000   **B.** Rs. 17,000
C. Rs. 19,000   **D.** Rs. 20,000

Q.15

The value of $\dfrac{cot40°}{tan50°} - \dfrac{1}{2}\dfrac{cos\,35°}{sin\,55°}$ is:

A. 1   **B.** - 1   **C.** 1/2   **D.** $-\dfrac{1}{2}$

Q.16 A is twice as fast as B and B is one third as fast as C. If they together can complete work in 30 days. In how many days, A, B and C individually can do the same work?

A. 60, 180, 240   **B.** 60, 180, 90
C. 180, 90, 60   **D.** None of these

Q.17 If ab= 25, then the minimum value of a+ b is:

A. 10   **B.** 8   **C.** 24   **D.** 16

Q.18 If a + b + c = 1, then Find (1+a) (1+b) (1+c)?

A. 1.47   **B.** 2.87   **C.** 55 / 27   **D.** 2.37

Q.19 The price of a shirt is ₹260 but the shopkeeper successively discount 15% & 20%. The net sales price is subject to a sales tax of 5%. What does the buyer pay?

A. ₹ 172.64   **B.** ₹ 183.64   **C.** ₹ 194.64   **D.** ₹ 185.64

Q.20 A cistern from inside is 12.5 m long, 8.5 m broad and 4 m high and is open at top. Find the cost of cementing the inside of a cistern at Rs. 24 per sq. m

A. Rs. 6582   **B.** Rs. 8256   **C.** Rs. 7752   **D.** Rs. 8752

Q.21 A goat is tied to a pole fixed at a corner outside a room with a square base in a grass field. It is tied using a 14 m long rope. The side of the base of the room is 21 m. Find the area of the field over which the goat can graze (in sq. m).

A. 484   **B.** 440   **C.** 418   **D.** 462

Q.22 An article is sold at a loss of 10%. Had it been sold for Rs. 9 more, there would have been a gain of

$12\dfrac{1}{2}$ % on it. The cost price of the article is :

A. ₹ 40   **B.** ₹ 45   **C.** ₹ 50   **D.** ₹ 35

Q.23 A water tank is 6 m long, 5 m broad and 3.4 m high. Find the capacity of the tank in litres?

A. 8.2 litre   **B.** 10.2 litre   **C.** 12.2 litre   **D.** 6.2 litre

Q.24 The ratio of the area of a square to that of the square drawn on its diagonal is :

A. 1:1   **B.** 1:2   **C.** 2:3   **D.** 1:3

Q.25 If sec θ + tan θ = p, the

$$\dfrac{p^2 - 1}{p^2 + 1} =?$$

A. sin θ   **B.** cos θ   **C.** sec θ   **D.** tan θ

Q.26 In the given figure, if ∠ABC = 90°, and ∠A = 30°, then ∠ACD=

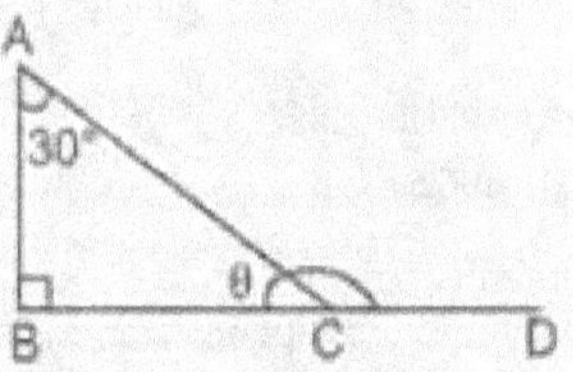

A. 120°   **B.** 100°   **C.** 110°   **D.** 130°

Q.27 A certain sum of money yields ₹ 1261 as compound interest for 3 years at 5% per annum. The sum is

A. ₹ 9000   **B.** ₹ 8400   **C.** ₹ 7500   **D.** ₹ 8000

Q.28 If $2^{x-1} + 2^{x+1}$ = 320, then x =?

A. 4   **B.** 5   **C.** 6   **D.** 7

Q.29 The value of $(sin^2\,25° + sin^2\,65°)$ is

A. $\dfrac{\sqrt{3}}{2}$ **B.** 1   **C.** 0   **D.** $\dfrac{2}{\sqrt{3}}$

Q.30 A is twice as good as workman as B. Together, they finish the work in 14 days. In how many days can it be done by each separately?

A. A = 19 days, B = 38 days
B. A = 15 days, B= 30 days
C. A = 21 days, B = 42 days
D. A = 14 days, B = 28 days

General Intelligence & Reasoning

Q.31 What should come at the place of question mark?
KM5, IP8, GS11, EV14, ?

A. BX17   **B.** GY17   **C.** CY17   **D.** CY18

Q.32 In the given sequence how many such symbols and numbers are there which are either immediately preceded or immediately followed by the letters which is from the first half of the English alphabet?

2 L K @ 8 $ P B 1 V # 6 % G W 9 J C D 4 © 7 F R 4 A

A. 6   **B.** 7   **C.** 5   **D.** 8

Q.33 The question given below consists of five figures marked 1,2,3,4, and 5 named as the problem figures and is followed by five answer figures marked (a), (b), (c), and (d). Select a figure from the answer figures which will continue the series as established by the five problem figures.

Problem Figure

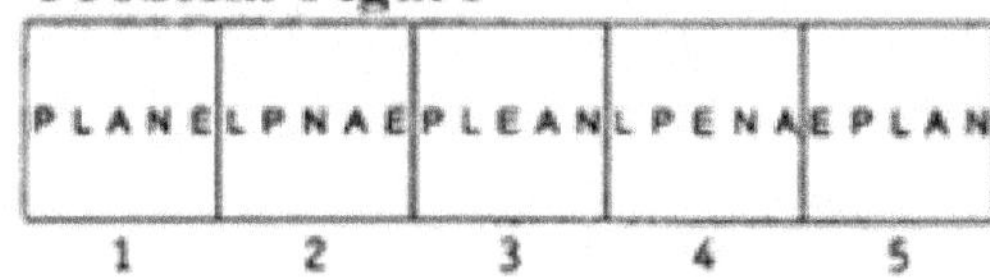

Answer Figures

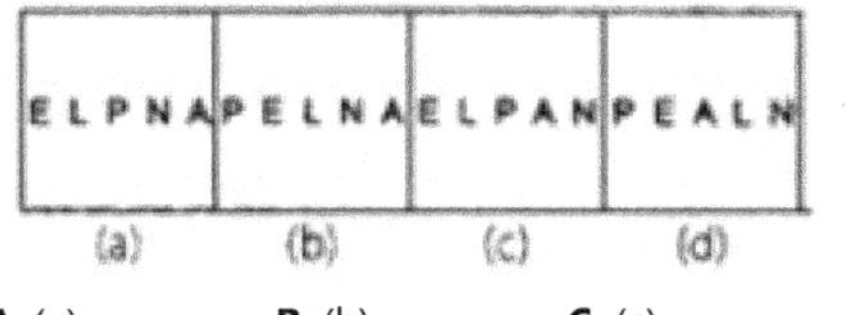

A. (a) **B.** (b) **C.** (c) **D.** (d)

Q.34 A husband and a wife had five married sons and each of them had four children. How many members are there in the family?

A. 32 **B.** 36 **C.** 30 **D.** 40

Q.35 Find the odd one out from the given alternatives.

A. IJNR **B.** ZCFI **C.** QTWZ **D.** GJMP

Q.36 In the given question, the letter sequence is formed by skipping 3 letters in the forward direction. Identify from the following alternatives which one of them cannot be formed using the above principle.

A. GKOS **B.** TXBF **C.** MPSW **D.** AEIM

Q.37 If 'white' is called 'rain', 'rain' is called 'green', 'green' is called blue', 'blue', is called 'cloud', 'cloud' is called 'red', 'red' is called 'sky', 'sky' is called 'yellow' and 'yellow' is called' 'black', what is the colour of 'blood'?

A. Red **B.** Blue **C.** Cloud **D.** Sky

Q.38 Select the related letter/word/number from the given alternatives.

A. NOQT **B.** DEIIK **C.** BCEH **D.** RSUX

Q.39 If P means 'division', T means 'addition', M means 'subtraction' and D means 'multiplication', then what will be the value of the expression 12 M 12 D 28 P 7 T 15?

A. -30 **B.** -15
C. 15 **D.** None of these

Q.40 Which one of the following figures represents the relationship among Shirts, Bed sheets and Towels?

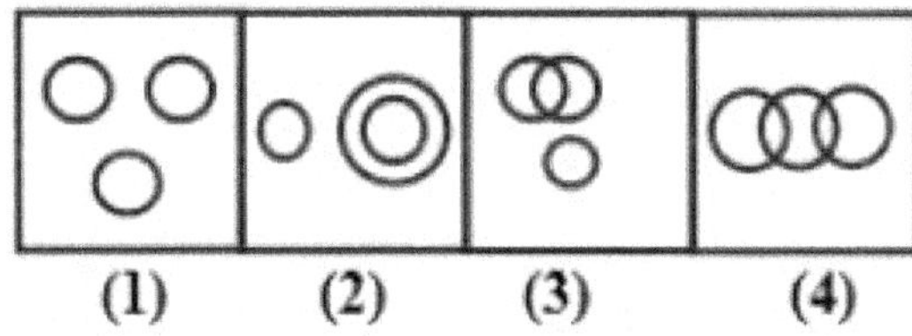

A. 1 **B.** 2 **C.** 3 **D.** 4

Q.41 Arrange the following words according to the English dictionary.

(a) Fraudulent (b) Fraught (c) Fraternity (d) Franchise (e) Frantic

A. (b), (e), (a), (d), (c) **B.** (e), (c), (a), (d), (b)

C. (a), (e), (c), (d), (b) **D.** (d), (e), (c), (a), (b)

Q.42 Mohan is the son, of Arun's father's sister. Prakash is the son of Reva, who is the mother of Vikas and grandmother of Arun. Pranab is the father of Neela and the grandfather of Mohan. Reva is the wife of Pranab. How is the wife of Vikas related to Neela?

A. Sister **B.** Sister-in-law
C. Niece **D.** None of these

Q.43 Which of the following diagram shows the best relation between Patiala, Bhagalpur, Bihar, and India?

A.

B.

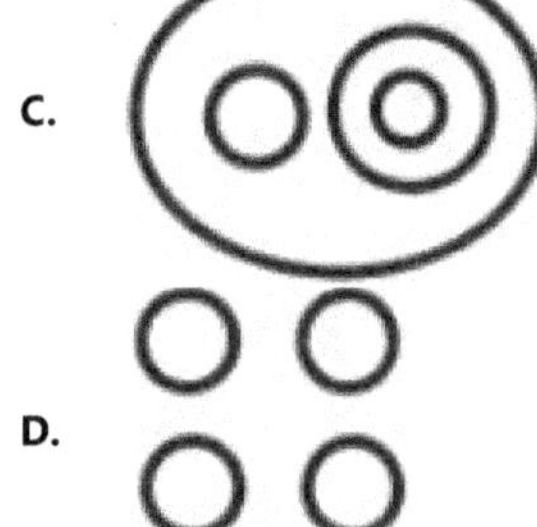

C.

D.

Q.44 Vishal walks 2 kms towards South. He then turns right and walks 3 kms, he now turns left and walks 5 kms. Further, he moves 2 kms after turning to the left. In which direction is he facing?

A. West **B.** East **C.** North **D.** South

Q.45 Arrange the following in a logical order.

1. Puberty
2. Adulthood
3. Childhood
4. Infancy
5. Senescence
6. Adolescence

A. 2, 4, 6, 3, 1, 5 **B.** 4, 3, 1, 6, 2, 5
C. 4, 3, 6, 2, 1, 5 **D.** 5, 6, 2, 3, 4, 1

Q.46 Find the odd one out from the given alternatives.

A. 32-41 **B.** 62-44 **C.** 46-28 **D.** 33-56

Q.47 A man pointing to a photograph says, The lady in the photograph is my nephew's maternal grandmother and her son is my sister's brother-in-law. How is the lady in the photograph related to his sister who has no other sister?

A. Mother
B. Cousin
C. Mother-in-law
D. Sister-in-law

Q.48 In the question below, there are few statements followed by few conclusions. You have to take the given statements to be true even if they seem to be at variance with commonly known facts and then decide which of the given conclusion logically follow(s) from the given statements.

Statements:

Some bulbs are canes.

Some canes are books.

All books are lanterns.

Conclusions:

I. Some lanterns are canes.

II. Some lanterns are bulbs.

A. If only Conclusion I follows.
B. If only Conclusion II follows.
C. If either Conclusion I or II follows.
D. If neither Conclusion I nor II follows.

Q.49 In the questions given below, some relationship has been expressed through symbols as shown below. Based on the meaning of these symbols and choose the correct answer.

φ means 'less than'

Δ means 'not greater than'

- means 'equal to'

+ means 'not equal to'

× means 'not less than'

= means 'greater than'

X - Y + Z implies

A. X + Y + Z
B. X φ Y - Z
C. X - Y φ Z
D. X Δ Y - Z

Q.50 In a certain code 'SENSITIVE' is written as 'QHLVGWGYC'. How is 'MICROSOFT' written in that code?

A. KGAPMQMDT
B. QKETQUQHV
C. KLAUMVMIR
D. LKBTNUNHS

Q.51 If '+' means '÷', '-'means '+', 'x' means '– ' and '÷' means '×', what will be the value of the following expression?

$$\left[\{(17 \times 12) - \left(\frac{4}{2}\right)\} + (23 - 6)] \right] \over 0$$

A. Infinite
B. 0
C. 118
D. 219

Q.52 How many squares are there in this figure?

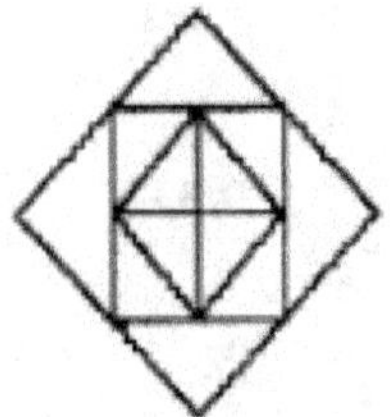

A. 4
B. 7
C. 6
D. 8

Q.53 Which figure from the given options can replace the question mark?

Problem Figures

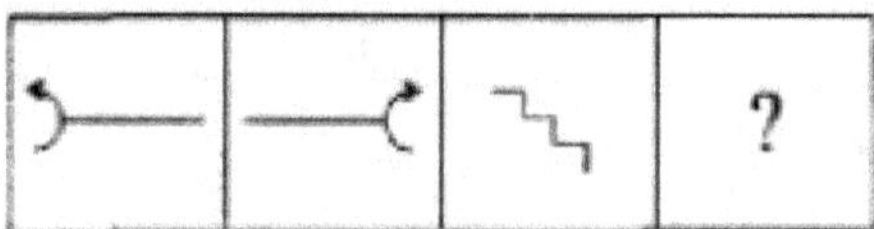

Answer Figures

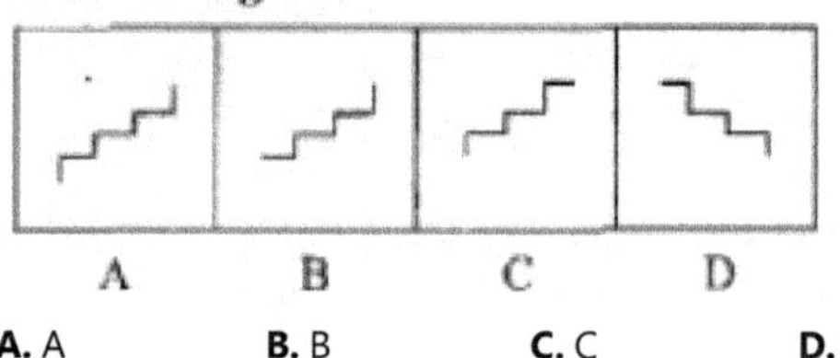

A. A
B. B
C. C
D. D

Q.54 Which one of the following responses would be a meaningful order of the following?

1. Adolescence

2. Prenatal

3. Adulthood

4. Infancy

A. 2 4 1 3
B. 2 1 4 3
C. 1 3 2 4
D. 4 2 1 3

Q.55 Read the following information carefully and answer the questions given below.

A word is represented by only one set of numbers as given in any one of the alternatives. The set of numbers given in the alternatives are represented by two classes of alphabets as in the two matrices given below. The columns and rows of Matrix I are numbered from 0 to 4 and that of Matrix II from 5 to 9. A letter can be represented first by its row and next by its column number. e.g., 'N' can be represented by 03, 21, etc. 'O' can be represented by 65, 96 etc. Similarly, you have to identify the correct set for the word given in each question.

Matrix I

	0	1	2	3	4
0	P	W	N	I	S
1	I	S	P	W	N
2	W	N	I	S	P
3	S	P	W	N	I
4	N	I	S	P	W

Matrix II

	5	6	7	8	9
5	A	E	R	O	H
6	O	H	A	E	R
7	E	R	O	H	A
8	H	A	E	R	O
9	R	O	H	A	E

A. 85, 41, 24, 11   **B.** 78, 34, 23, 04
C. 67, 41, 24, 42   **D.** 66, 21, 24, 11

General Awareness

Q.56 Who is the Prime Minister of Bhutan?
A. Dr. Lotay Tshering   **B.** Dr. Kehing Rijiju
C. Dr. Malal Dablu   **D.** Dr. Krewing Ghau

Q.57 Which of the following passes through India?
A. Tropic of Cancer   **B.** Tropic of Capricorn
C. Equator   **D.** None of these

Q.58 Swadesh Darshan scheme was launched by Union Tourism Ministry in-
A. 2014   **B.** 2015   **C.** 2016   **D.** 2017

Q.59 The moon revolve round the earth in—
A. 30 days   **B.** 29 days
C. 28½ days   **D.** 27 days

Q.60 Which state Government has launched One District, One Product scheme recently?
A. Uttar Pradesh   **B.** Rajasthan
C. Gujrat   **D.** Madhya Pradesh

Q.61 Home ministry extends ban on eight extremist groups for how many years?
A. 3   **B.** 4   **C.** 5   **D.** 6

Q.62 What is the capital of Uganda?
A. Kigali   **B.** Entebbe   **C.** Jinja   **D.** Kampala

Q.63 Which of the following sets of Articles deals with 'Emergency Provisions'?
A. Articles 32 and 226
B. Articles 350 and 351
C. Articles 352, 356 and 360
D. Articles 335, 336 and 337

Q.64 Who has been appointed as the 21st Chairman of Law Commission of India?
A. S. Sivakumar   **B.** Abhay Bhardwaj
C. Ravi R. Tripathi   **D.** B.S. Chauhan

Q.65 The first Sultan of Delhi to issue regular currency and declare Delhi as the capital of his empire was?
A. Alam Shah.   **B.** Iltumish.
C. Qutubudin Aidak.   **D.** Balban.

Q.66 The first Indian selected For Indian Civil Service was:
A. Satyandra nath tagore.
B. Sarojani Naidu.
C. Lala Lajpat Rai.
D. C.R. Das.

Q.67 Who was the first Indian to become member of British Parliament?
A. W.C. Bannerjee.
B. Behramji M. Malabari.
C. D.N. Wacha.
D. Dadabhai Naoroji.

Q.68 Who is the new Director General of Indo-Tibetan Border Police?
A. R K Pachnanda   **B.** S.S. Deswal
C. Rajiv Jain   **D.** Alok Verma

Q.69 'Mohiniyattam' is a classical dance from the Indian State of
A. Asom   **B.** Kerala
C. Odisha   **D.** Arunachal Pradesh

Q.70 Because of which one of the following factors, clouds do not precipitate in deserts ?
A. Low pressure   **B.** Low humidity
C. High wind velocity   **D.** High temperature

General Science

Q.71 The two elements that are frequently used for making transistors are ___ and ___.
A. Boron and Aluminium
B. Silicon and Germanium
C. Silicon and Germanium
D. Niobium and Columbium

Q.72 The metal used in storage batteries —
A. Iron   **B.** Copper   **C.** Lead   **D.** Zinc

Q.73 What is the orbital speed of a satellite rotating near the surface of earth?
A. 7.9 km/sec   **B.** 7.4 km/sec
C. 6.8 km/sec   **D.** 6.3 km/sec

Q.74 Which of the following has the smallest atomic radius?
A. Sodium   **B.** Potassium
C. Caesium   **D.** Rubidium

Q.75 What should be the Mach number of a body for being hypersonic?

A. More than 3   **B.** More than 4
C. More than 5   **D.** More than 6

Q.76 Shearing stress that acts on a body affects its—

A. Length   **B.** Width   **C.** Volume   **D.** Shape

Q.77 A light year is nearest to:

A. 10^8 m   **B.** 10^{12} m   **C.** 10^{16} m   **D.** 10^{20} m

Q.78 Which of the following gases is lighter than air ?

A. Carbon dioxide   **B.** Oxygen
C. Ammonia   **D.** Chlorine

Q.79 The element required for Solar energy conversion is ___.

A. Beryllium   **B.** Silicon
C. Tantalum   **D.** Ultra pure carbon

Q.80 A moving body of mass 20 kg has 40 joules of kinetic energy Calculate its speed?

A. 1 m/s   **B.** 1.5 m/s   **C.** 2 m/s   **D.** 2.5 m/s

Q.81 Ex situ conservation is carried out in

A. Sanctuary   **B.** Not park
C. Biospehere reserve   **D.** Zoo

Q.82 The behaviour of a perfect gas, undergoing any change in the variables which control physical properties, is governed by

A. pressure exerted by the gas
B. volume occupied by the gas
C. temperature of the gas
D. All of these

Q.83 Light Year is a unit to measure -

A. Time   **B.** Distance
C. Luminous Intensity   **D.** Magnetic Field

Q.84 Which of the following belongs to the 18th group of the Periodic Table?

A. Fluorine   **B.** Selenium
C. Antimony   **D.** Radon

Q.85 Who was the first person to describe plants?

A. Aristotle   **B.** Linnaeus
C. John Ray   **D.** Leeuwenhoek

Q.86 In screw jack, effort required to lift a load is given by:

A. P = w tan $(\alpha+\varphi)$ **B.** P = w tan $(\alpha-\varphi)$
C. P = w tan $(\varphi-\alpha)$ **D.** None of these

Q.87 Which of the following is used for removing air bubbles from glass during its manufacture ?

A. Fledspar
B. Arsenic oxide
C. Potassium Carbonate
D. Soda Ash

Q.88 Deficiency of vitamin D causes —

A. Rickets   **B.** Beri-beri
C. Scurvy   **D.** Night blindness

Q.89 Which one of the following is the reason for small liquid drops assuming spherical stage?

A. The liquid tends to have minimum surface area due to surface tension.
B. The development of pressure from all sides.
C. Adhesion.
D. All the above.

Q.90 A plant used to treat bone fractures

A. H brasiliensis
B. Lawsonia inermis
C. Digitalis purpurea
D. Cissus quadrangularis

Q.91 The most abundant metal in the earth's crust is-

A. Zinc   **B.** Copper
C. Aluminium   **D.** Iron

Q.92 Kanha National Park is located in

A. Assam   **B.** Rajasthan
C. Uttar Pradesh   **D.** Madhya Pradesh

Q.93 What changes will happen to a bowl of ice water kept at exactly zero degree Celsius?

A. All ice will melt
B. All water will become ice
C. No change will happen
D. Only some ice will melt

Q.94 Hard Water contains which of the following?

A. Aluminum   **B.** Chlorine
C. Calcium   **D.** Zinc

Q.95 A hydrogen balloon floats up because of:

A. Air pressure decreases with decrease in height.
B. Air pressure decreases with decrease in weight.
C. Weight of the balloon is less than the weight of air displaced by it.
D. The pressure inside the balloon is more than the pressure outside it.

Q.96 If an object is placed at between F and 2F in front of a Convex Lens, then the image formed will be

A. Beyond 2F   **B.** Diminished
C. Both of them   **D.** None of these

Q.97 Which one of the following denotes inertial mass?

A. W /g.   **B.** M /V.   **C.** F/a.   **D.** v x d.

Q.98 A machine having an efficiency less than 50%, is known as:

A. reversible machine
B. non-reversible machine
C. neither (1) nor (2)
D. ideal machine

Q.99 L.P.G. is a hydrocarbon consisting of a mixture of:

A. Methane and Butane
B. Propane and Butane
C. Ethane and Propane

D. Ethane and Butane

Q.100 In an atomic nucleus, neutrons and protons are held together by —

A. Gravitational forces **B.** Magnetic forces

C. Exchange forces **D.** Coulombic forces

// Smart Answer Sheet //

Correct — Percentage of students who answered correctly.   **Skipped** — Percentage of students who skipped.

Q.	Ans.	Correct / Skipped
1	A	88.26 % / 11.68 %
2	D	89.03 % / 10.95 %
3	B	79.21 % / 18.12 %
4	B	86.41 % / 12.92 %
5	A	79.72 % / 18.19 %
6	D	76.48 % / 21.94 %
7	C	84.66 % / 13.88 %
8	D	80.97 % / 18.99 %
9	D	78.07 % / 15.09 %
10	C	76.41 % / 18.4 %
11	D	87.34 % / 12.35 %
12	A	83.03 % / 14.61 %
13	A	76.96 % / 18.07 %
14	D	77.84 % / 21.86 %
15	C	77.55 % / 19.07 %
16	D	89.41 % / 10.15 %
17	A	86.21 % / 10.35 %
18	D	78.79 % / 13.48 %
19	D	88.54 % / 10.95 %
20	A	80.15 % / 11.55 %
21	D	84.52 % / 14.78 %
22	A	88.29 % / 10.71 %
23	B	76.49 % / 14.99 %
24	B	77.97 % / 18.71 %
25	A	88.2 % / 10.94 %
26	A	88.63 % / 10.76 %
27	D	82.75 % / 11.88 %
28	D	85.06 % / 10.56 %
29	B	80.2 % / 17.25 %
30	C	78.19 % / 20.93 %
31	C	89.32 % / 10.36 %
32	D	85.63 % / 14.34 %
33	A	82.57 % / 15.99 %
34	A	78.23 % / 10.37 %
35	A	88.94 % / 10.41 %
36	C	76.23 % / 14.36 %
37	D	85.68 % / 10.34 %
38	B	83.98 % / 13.3 %
39	D	86.93 % / 12.15 %
40	A	76.43 % / 15.78 %
41	D	77.5 % / 21.06 %
42	B	79.65 % / 17.79 %
43	C	77.16 % / 21.2 %
44	B	76.32 % / 10.93 %
45	B	78.88 % / 16.4 %
46	D	78.29 % / 12.22 %
47	C	86.29 % / 13.65 %
48	A	80.72 % / 15.27 %
49	C	83.14 % / 11.4 %
50	C	84.22 % / 12.58 %
51	B	78.83 % / 16.48 %
52	B	77.59 % / 12.16 %
53	C	84.39 % / 10.24 %
54	A	89.07 % / 10.24 %
55	A	83.95 % / 15.94 %
56	A	87.2 % / 11.74 %
57	A	86.57 % / 12.27 %
58	B	86.7 % / 12.13 %
59	D	77.24 % / 17.9 %
60	A	85.07 % / 12.81 %
61	C	76.14 % / 22.88 %
62	D	82.14 % / 13.23 %
63	C	86.68 % / 12.42 %
64	D	83.42 % / 16.09 %
65	B	79.22 % / 13.65 %
66	A	82.58 % / 14.06 %
67	D	83.1 % / 10.75 %
68	B	76.05 % / 22.51 %
69	B	87.78 % / 10.9 %
70	B	88.31 % / 11.44 %
71	B	89.97 % / 10.01 %
72	C	83.37 % / 12.08 %
73	A	77.62 % / 19.2 %
74	A	76.81 % / 13.99 %
75	C	80.06 % / 18.4 %
76	D	84.71 % / 10.04 %
77	C	89.77 % / 10.09 %
78	C	88.48 % / 11.13 %
79	B	80.23 % / 13.81 %
80	C	87.34 % / 10.62 %

Q.	Ans.	Correct		Q.	Ans.	Correct		Q.	Ans.	Correct		Q.	Ans.	Correct		Q.	Ans.	Correct
		Skipped				Skipped				Skipped				Skipped				Skipped
81	D	77.88 %		85	D	84.86 %		89	A	81.05 %		93	C	78.8 %		97	C	80.84 %
		21.78 %				10.95 %				18.76 %				18.44 %				17.3 %
82	D	88.86 %		86	A	86.24 %		90	D	84.46 %		94	C	83.42 %		98	B	78.63 %
		10.87 %				11.16 %				14.51 %				15.69 %				11.52 %
83	B	84.79 %		87	B	76.27 %		91	C	88.17 %		95	C	79.97 %		99	B	82.79 %
		14.2 %				12.95 %				10.11 %				17.29 %				16.68 %
84	D	86.17 %		88	A	89.64 %		92	D	87.07 %		96	A	82.3 %		100	C	81.87 %
		12.31 %				10.25 %				11.05 %				17.35 %				16.71 %

//Hints and Solutions//

1. (By mid-point theorem)

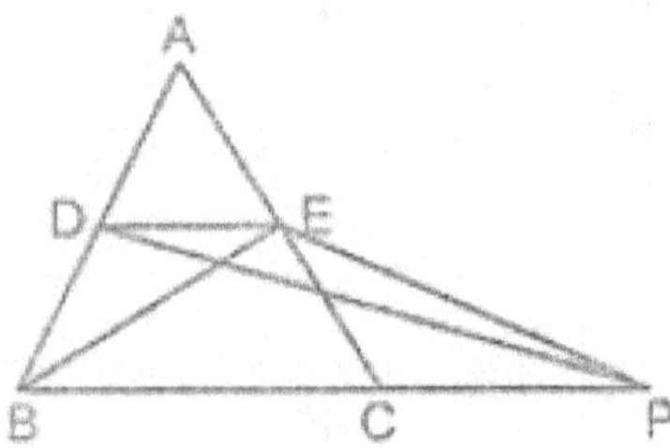

DE ∥ BC

DE = 1/2 BC

$\Rightarrow$ ar($\triangle$BDE) = 1/4 × ar($\triangle$ABC)

And $\triangle$BDE = $\triangle$PED

[∵ both triangles lie on the same base DE and between two parallel lines DE and BP.]

∴ ar($\triangle$PED) = 1/4 × ar($\triangle$ABC)

2.

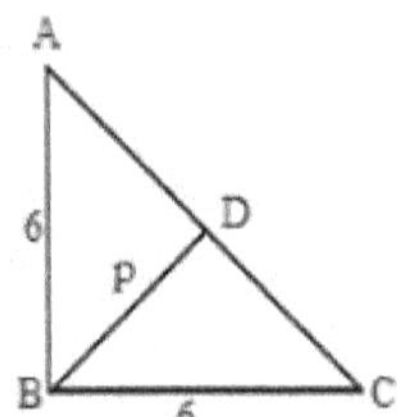

Let $\angle$B be right angle in $\triangle$ABC

and BD be perpendicular on hypetenuse AC then

$$\frac{1}{P^2} = \frac{1}{6^2} + \frac{1}{6^2}$$

$$P^2 = \frac{6^2}{2} \Rightarrow p = 3\sqrt{2}$$

3.

Speed of both trains = 3 : 4

× 3 ↓ : ↓ × 3 → time

Length = 9m : 12 m.

$$\text{Time} = \frac{D}{S} = \frac{L_1 + L_2}{S_1 + S_2} = \frac{9+12}{4+3} = \frac{21}{4+3}$$

= 3 sec.

4. Daughter's one day work = 1/15

Mother's one day work = 1/5

Both can complete their work = 1/5+1/15 = (3+1)/15 = 4/15

Hence, required days= 15/4 days .

5. Total no. of soldiers joining BSF in 2004, 2005, 2006

= 13400

Total no. of soldiers joining in Navy = 10900

Required Percentage= (13400/10900)×100 = 123%

6. Required ratio = 6.5/1.3 = 5/1 = 5:1

7. tan (5x – 10°) = cot (5y + 20°)

tan (5x – 10°) = tan (90° – {5y + 20°})

5x – 10° = 90° – (5y + 20°)

5x + 5y = 90° + 10° – 20°

5x + 5y = 80°

x + y = 16°

8.

Speed = 60 km/hr.

$$S = 60 \times \frac{5}{18} \text{ m./sec.} = \frac{50}{3} \text{ m./sec.}$$

T = 30 sec.

$$\text{Length} = S \times T = \left(\frac{50}{3} \times 30\right) \text{ m.}$$

l = 500m.

9. Let the measure of the angle be x°

Then, the measure of its supplementary angle is (180 - x°).
It is given that,

$$180° - x = \frac{1}{4} \times x$$

$\Rightarrow$ (180° - x) = x

$\Rightarrow$ 720 - 4x = x

$\Rightarrow$ 5x = 720

$\Rightarrow$ x = 144

Thus, the measure of the angle is 144° and the measure of its supplement
= 180° - 144° = 36°.

10. Total age of 5 members, three years ago

= 17 × 5 = 85 years

Three years hence,

Total age of 5 members = 85+3x5 = 85+15 = 100 years

Sum of present ages of 6 members = 17 × 6 = 102 years

Present age of baby= 102 – 100 = 2 years

11.

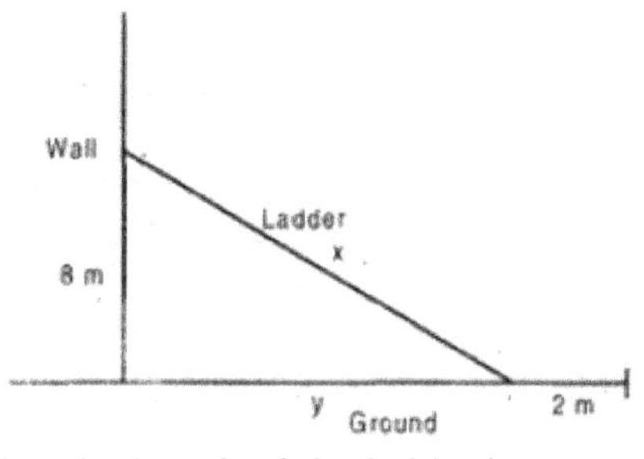

Let the length of the ladder be x meter. We have

$8^2 + y^2 = x^2$ and $(y + 2) = x$

Hence, $64 + (x - 2)^2 = x^2$

$\Rightarrow 64 + x^2 - 4x + 4 = x^2$

$\Rightarrow 68 = 4x \Rightarrow x = 17$ meter

12.

$$33.33 = \frac{1}{3} \rightarrow \frac{1}{2} = 50\% \left[\frac{1}{2} = \frac{1}{3-1}\right]$$

13.

The interests accrued each year on compound interest form a geometric progression with I, as the first year interest and common ratio of $(1 + \frac{r}{100})$.

Therefore, interests for 1st, 2nd, 3rd, 4th and 5th years will be:

$I, I(1 + \frac{r}{100})^1, I(1 + \frac{r}{100})^2, I(1 + \frac{r}{100})^3, I(1 + \frac{r}{100})^4$ respectively.

Given, $(1 + \frac{r}{100})^3 = 13310$ ——————(1)

and $(1 + \frac{r}{100})^4 = 14641$ —————— (2)

(2) divided by (1), we get

$\left(1 + \frac{r}{100}\right) = \frac{14641}{13310} = 1.1$

∴ Sum of the first three years interests

$= \frac{13310}{(1.1)^3} + \frac{13310}{(1.1)^2} + \frac{13310}{(1.1)^1}$

$= \frac{13310}{1.331} + \frac{13310}{1.21} + \frac{13310}{1.1}$

$= 10000 + 11000 + 12100$

$= Rs. 33100$

14.

$$P = \frac{5000 \times 100 \times 2}{10 \times 5}$$

P = Rs. 20,000

15.

$\cot \theta = \tan (90 - \theta)$ and $\cos \theta = \sin(90 - \theta)$

Hence $\dfrac{\tan 50^\circ}{\tan 50^\circ} - \dfrac{1}{2} \dfrac{\sin 55^\circ}{\sin 55^\circ}$

$1 - \dfrac{1}{2} = \dfrac{1}{2}$

16. Condition 1- A is twice as fast as

B, means their ratio is 2: 1.

Condition 2- B is one third as fast

as C, means their ratio is 1: 3. Then we can say, the ration of A, B and C is as follows

According to condition 1,

A : B = 2 : 1

According to condition 2;

B : C = 1 : 3

Thus, Ratio of A : B : C = 2 : 1 : 3

This ratio denotes the working efficiency of A, B and C which means;

A, B and C can do = (2 + 1 + 3 = 6) work/day

Now we can calculate total work i.e.

Total work = Total days × Per day work

Total work = 30 × 6 = 180

A can do the same work in;

= (Total work / Efficiency of A) = 180 / 2 = 90 days

B can do the same work in;

= (Total work / Efficiency of B)

180 / 1 = 180 days

C can do the same work in;

= (Total work / Efficiency of C) = 180 / 3 = 60 days

Thus, A, B and C can individually complete the same work in 90, 180 and 60 days, respectively.

17. Minimum value of (a+ b) can be obtained when a= b

Then a + b = 5 + 5 (∵ ab= 25 and a=b)

=10

18.

Given, $a + b + c = 1$

Let observe the value of a, b, c

$a = \frac{1}{3}$, $b = \frac{1}{3}$, $c = \frac{1}{3}$

$a + b + c = 1$

$\frac{1}{3} + \frac{1}{3} + \frac{1}{3} = 1$

$\frac{3}{3} = 1$

$1 = 1$

put the value of a, b, c

$(1 + a)(1 + b)(1 + c)$

$(1 + \frac{1}{3})(1 + \frac{1}{3})(1 + \frac{1}{3})$

$\frac{4}{3} \times \frac{4}{3} \times \frac{4}{3}$

$\frac{64}{27} = 2.37$

19.

1st discount

S.P = Rs.260 – 15% Rs.260

$= 260 – 39 = 221$

2nd discount

S.P= Rs.221 – 20% Rs.221

$= 221 – 44.2 = 176.8$

Sales tax $= \dfrac{5}{100} \times \dfrac{1768}{10}$

$= \dfrac{8840}{1000}$

$= Rs.8.84$

Amount paid by buyer

$= Rs.176.8 + Rs.8.84$

$= Rs.185.64.$

20. Area of surface to be cemented = 2 x (l+b) x h + (lxb)

i.e, area of four walls + area of the floor

= 2 x (21) x 4 + (106.25)

= 274.25 m²

∴ cost of cementing = 24 x 274.25 = Rs. 6582

21.

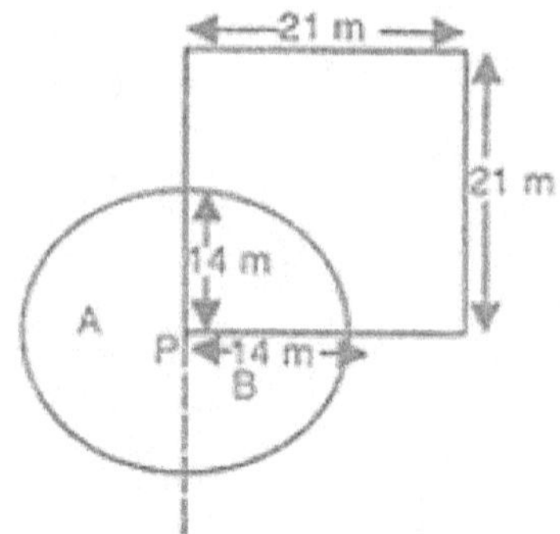

Let the goat be tied at P.

The area over which the goat could graze = sum of the areas of the regions A and B = Area of a

sector of radius 14 m and central angle 270°

$= \dfrac{270°}{360°} \pi(14)^2 sq.\,m$

$= \dfrac{3}{4}\,\dfrac{22}{7}\,196 sq.\,m$

$= \dfrac{3}{4}\,616 sq.\,m = 462 sq.\,m.$

22.

Let the cost price of the article = Rs. x

S.P. at 10% loss = Rs 0.9x

According to question if it is sold by Rs 9 more there will be gain of 25/2 %

$$0.9x + 9 = x \times \frac{100 + 12\frac{1}{2}}{100}$$

$$0.9x + 9 = \frac{225x}{200}$$

$$\Rightarrow 180x + 1800 = 225x$$

$$\Rightarrow 225x - 180x = 1800$$

$$\Rightarrow 45x = 1800$$

$$\therefore x = Rs.\,40$$

Alternate solution,
Let the CP of the article = 100

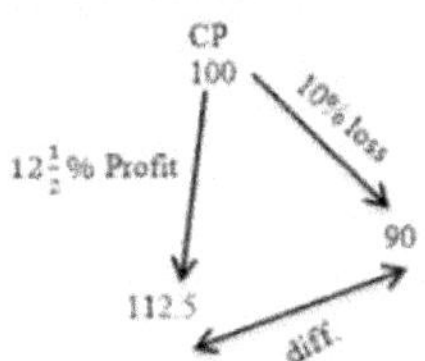

$$x \times 22.5 = 9$$
$$x = \frac{9}{22.5}$$
$$= \frac{18}{45}$$
Required,
$$\Rightarrow CP \times x$$
$$\Rightarrow 100 \times \frac{18}{45}$$
$$\Rightarrow 40$$

23.

Volume = 6 x 5 x 3.4

Volume = 102 cu. cm

1 cu. m = 100 cu. cm

102 cu. m = 102 x 100

= 10200 cu. cm

1000 cu. cm = 1 litre

$$1 \text{ cu. cm} = \frac{1}{1000}$$

$$10200 \text{ cu. cm} = \left(\frac{1}{1000}\right) \times 10200$$

= 10.2 litres

24. Let the side of the square be 'α'

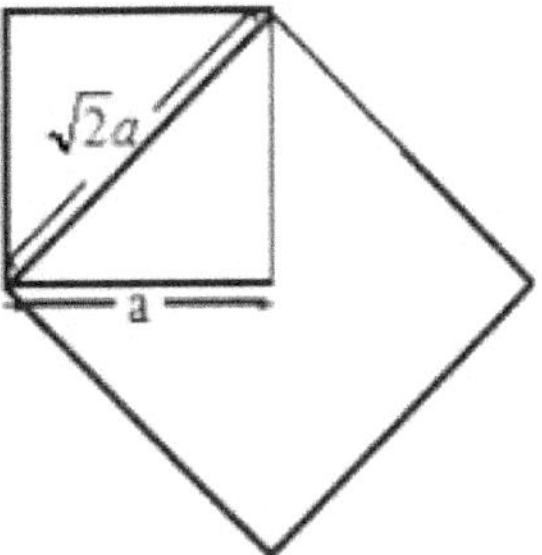

Its area = a^2

Area of square on the diagonal $= (\sqrt{2}a)^2 = 2a^2$

Required ratio $= \dfrac{a^2}{2a^2} = 1:2$

25.

$$\frac{p^2 - 1}{p^2 + 1} = \frac{(\sec\theta + \tan\theta)^2 - 1}{(\sec\theta + \tan\theta)^2 + 1}$$

$$= \frac{\sec^2\theta + \tan^2\theta + 2\sec\theta\tan\theta - 1}{\sec^2\theta + \tan^2\theta + 2\sec\theta\tan\theta + 1}$$

$$= \frac{(\sec^2\theta - 1) + \tan^2\theta + 2\sec\theta\tan\theta}{\sec^2\theta + 2\sec\theta\tan\theta + (1 + \tan^2\theta)}$$

$$= \frac{\tan^2\theta + \tan^2\theta + 2\sec\theta\tan\theta}{\sec^2\theta + 2\sec\theta\tan\theta + \sec^2\theta}$$

$$= \frac{2\tan^2\theta + 2\tan\theta\sec\theta}{2\sec^2\theta + 2\sec\theta\tan\theta}$$

$$= \frac{2\tan\theta\,(\tan\theta + \sec\theta)}{2\sec\theta\,(\sec\theta + \tan\theta)}$$

$$= \frac{\tan\theta}{\sec\theta} = \frac{\sin\theta}{\cos\theta.\sec\theta} = \sin\theta$$

26. ∠ACD = ∠B + ∠A

= 90° + 30°

= 120° (exterior angle)

27. Let the principal , compound interest rate and time be x, R and T respectively

$$C.I. = P\left[\left(1 + \frac{R}{100}\right)^T - 1\right]$$

$$\Rightarrow 1261 = x\left[\left(1 + \frac{5}{100}\right)^3 - 1\right]$$

$$\Rightarrow 1261 = x\left(\frac{9261}{8000} - 1\right)$$

$$\Rightarrow 1261 = x\left(\frac{9261 - 8000}{8000}\right)$$

$$= \frac{1261x}{8000}$$

$$\Rightarrow x = \frac{1261 \times 8000}{1261}$$

$$= Rs.\ 8000$$

28.

$$2^{x-1} + 2^{x+1} = 320$$
$$2^{x-1}(1 + 2^2) = 320$$
$$2^{x-1} = 320$$
$$2^{x-1} = \frac{320}{5} = 64$$
$$2^{x-1} = 2^6$$
$$x - 1 = 6$$
$$x = 7$$

29.

$$\sin^2 25° + \sin^2 65 = \sin^2 25° + \sin^2(90° - 25°)$$

$$= \sin^2 25° + \cos^2 25° = 1$$

30. As per the question, A do twice the work as done by B.

So A:B = 2:1

Also (A+B)'s one-day work = 1/14

To get days in which B will finish the work,

let's calculate work done by B in 1 day

=(1/14)x(1/3) = 1/42

So B will finish the work in 42 days and A will finish the work in 21 days.

31.

$$K \xrightarrow{-2} I \xrightarrow{-2} G \xrightarrow{-2} E \xrightarrow{-2} [C]$$
$$M \xrightarrow{+3} P \xrightarrow{+3} S \xrightarrow{+3} V \xrightarrow{+3} [Y]$$
$$5 \xrightarrow{+3} 8 \xrightarrow{+3} 11 \xrightarrow{+3} 14 \xrightarrow{+3} [17]$$

32. Such combinations are :

2L, K@, B1, %G, 9J, D4, 7F, 4A

33. From problems figure (1) to (3) and (3) to (5) last letter comes two place left and other letters have been written in same order. Similar rule follows from problem figure (2) to (4) to answer figure.

34. Husband ⇒ One

Wife ⇒ One

Five married sons

⇒ 5 × 2 = 10

Number of children

⇒ 5 × 4 = 20

Total number of members

= 1 + 1 + 10 + 20 = 32

35.

$$I \xrightarrow{+1} J \xrightarrow{+4} N \xrightarrow{+4} R$$
$$Z \xrightarrow{+3} C \xrightarrow{+3} F \xrightarrow{+3} I$$
$$Q \xrightarrow{+3} T \xrightarrow{+3} W \xrightarrow{+3} Z$$
$$G \xrightarrow{+3} J \xrightarrow{+3} M \xrightarrow{+3} P$$

36.

$$M \xrightarrow{+3} P \xrightarrow{+3} S \xrightarrow{+4} W$$

So, here in option (c), three letters are skipped.

37. We know colour of blood is red. Here, red is called sky. Therefore, our correct answer is 'sky'.

38. In all other groups of words there is a gap of one letter as in the alphabet between second and third letter.

39. The given expression is 12 M 12 D 28 P 7 T 15

Using the symbols correctly as given in the above question, the above expression becomes

12 − 12 × 28 ÷ 7 + 15

Using BODMAS RULE, we get

12 - 12 × 4 + 15 = 12 − 48 + 15 = 27 − 48 = -21

40. Shirts, Bedsheets and Towels are different from one another. Therefore, these can be represented by three distinct circles.

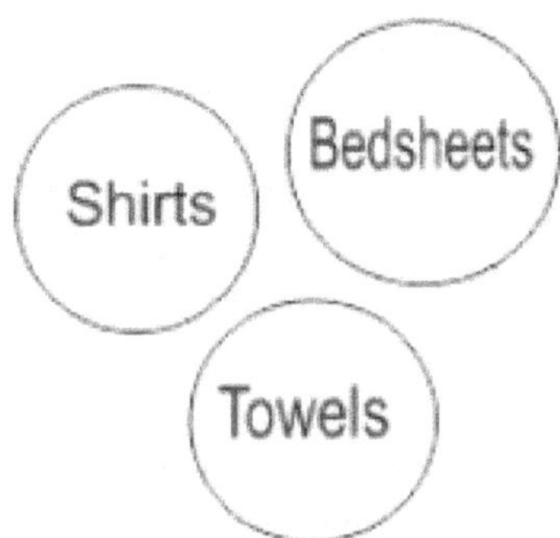

41. The correct arrangement is:

(d) Franchise (e) Frantic (c) Fraternity (a) Fraudulent (b) Fraught

42. The relations describe in the question can be represented as follows:

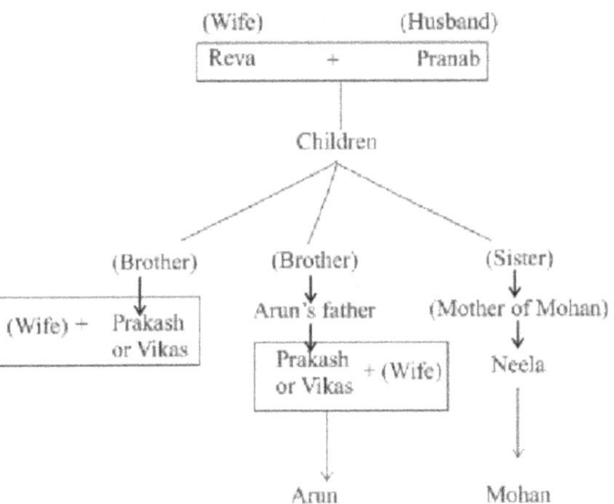

Thus wife of either Vikas or Prakash is sister in-law of Neela.

43.

44.

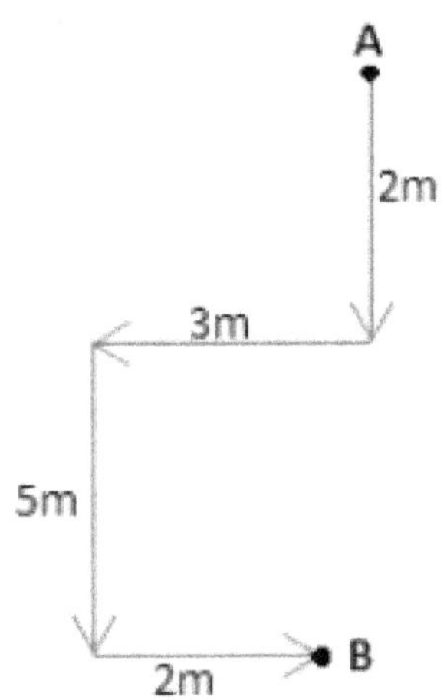

He is facing towards east.

45.

Infancy → Childhood → Puberty → Adolescence → Adulthood → Senescence

  4   3   1   6   2   5

46. Except in pair 33- 56, in all others the sum of digits of one number is equal to the sum of digits of all the second number.

47.

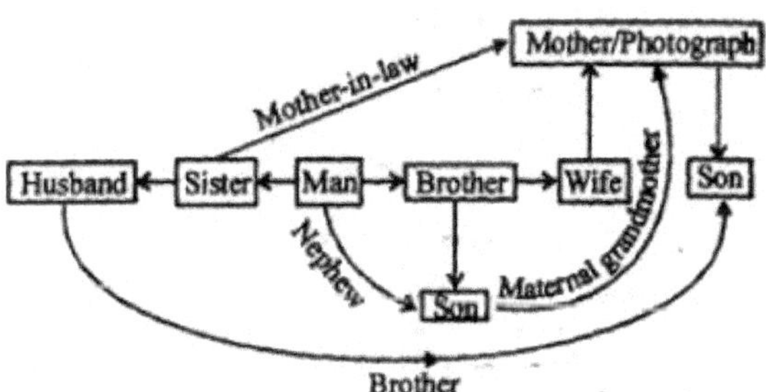

48.

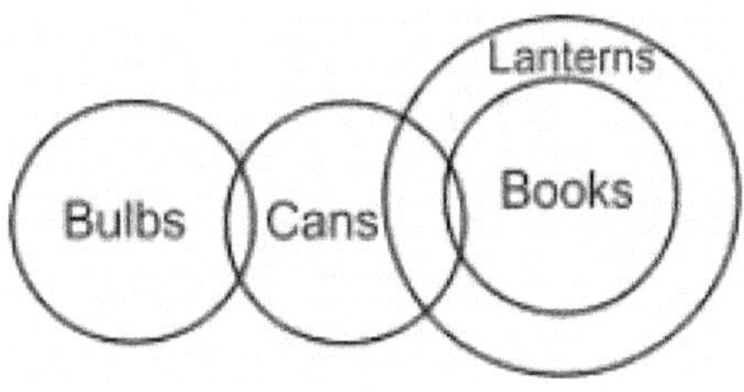

If only Conclusion I follows.

49. Clearly, the meaning of the given symbols

X - Y + Z ⇒ X = Y ≠ Z

Using the proper notations/symbols in option (c), we get

X - Y φ Z ⇒ X = Y < Z ⇒ X = Y ≠ Z

Therefore, X - Y + Z ⇒ X - Y φ Z.

50. The letters at odd-numbered positions move two letters backward. While those at even numbered positions move three letters forward.

51. The given expression is

$$\frac{\left[\{(17 \times 12) - \left(\frac{4}{2}\right)\} + (23 - 6)\right]}{0}$$

Using the symbols correctly as given in the above question, the above expression becomes

[{(17 - 12) + (4 × 2)} ÷ (23 + 6)] x 0 = 0

52.

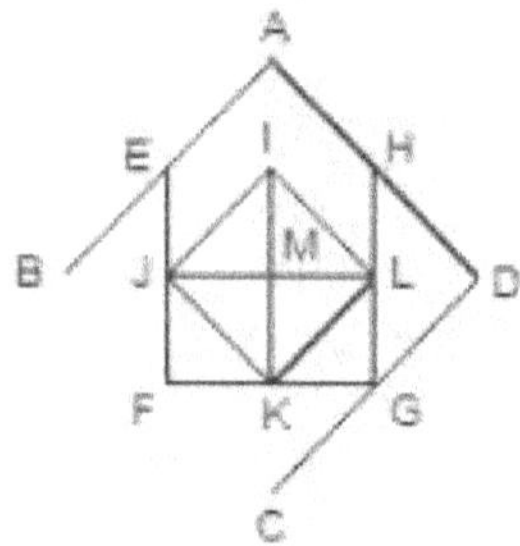

There are 7 squares -

ABCD, EFGH, IJKL, EIMJ, IHLM, JMKF, MLGK.

53. Second figure is the mirror image of first figure.

54. (a) 2 4 1 3

55. According to the matrices,

H — 59, 66, 78, (85), 97

I — 03, 10, 22, 34, (41)

P — 00, 12, (24), 31, 43

S — 04, (11), 23, 30, 42

HIPS ⇒ 85, 41, 24, 11

56. Prime Minister of Bhutan Dr. Lotay Tshering today called on President Ram Nath Kovind at Rashtrapati Bhavan.

57. Tropic of Cancer passes through India.

58. Swadesh Darshan scheme was launched by Union Tourism Ministry in 2015.

59. The Moon orbits Earth in the prograde direction and completes one revolution relative to the stars in approximately 27.322 days (a sidereal month).

60. Uttar Pradesh state Government has launched One District, One Product scheme recently.

61. The Ministry of Home Affairs has extended the ban on eight Meitei extremist organisations active in Manipur for five more years for their continued involvement in unlawful and violent activities.

62. Kampala is the capital of Uganda.

63. The Emergency Provisions are mentioned from Article 352 to Article 360 of the Indian Constitution. Article 352 : Proclamation of Emergency – due to external instruction or war, Article 356: Provisions in case of failure of constitutional as to financial emergency.

64. Justice B.S. Chauhan has been appointed as the 21st chairman of Law Commission of India in March,2018.

65. Iltutmish was the first Sultan of Delhi to issue regular currency and declare Delhi as the capital of his empire before it Badayun (1210–1214) was the capital. He introduced the silver tanka and copper jital.

66. Satyendranath Tagore was the Indian to join the indian civil services.June, 1863. The ICS Act of 1861 established the Indian Civil Service. The Act of 1853 had already established the practice of recruiting covenanted civilians through competitive examinations.

67. Dadabhai Naoroji.

68. The Indo-Tibetan Border Police (ITBP) is one of the five Central Armed Police Forces of India, raised on 24 October 1962, under the CRPF Act, in the wake of the Sino-Indian War of 1962. The ITBP was intended for deployment along India's border with China's Tibet Autonomous Region.

69. Kerala

70. There are often no clouds at all in many desert regions because there is low humidity.

71. Silicon and Germanium : Transistors are made of semiconductor chemical elements, usually Silicon, which belongs to in Group IV in the periodic table of elements. Germanium, another group-IV element, is used together with silicon in specialized transistors.

72. Lead

73. The orbital speed of a satellite rotating near the surface of earth is 7.9 km/sec

74. The atomic size increases down the group.

75. The Mach number should be more than 5, i.e. more than 5 times the speed of sound

76. A shearing stress that acts on a body affects its shape

77. 1 Light Year = 9.4607×10^{15} m almost equal to 10^{16} m

78. Ammonia: Anhydrous ammonia gas is lighter than air. However, in the presence of moisture (such as high relative humidity), the liquefied anhydrous ammonia gas forms vapors that are heavier than air. Methane, Hydrogen and helium Nitrogen are also lighter than air.

79. Silicon is required for the conversion of solar energy.

80. its speed is 2 m/s

81. Zoo

82. All of these are correct

83. Light Year is a unit to measure distance.

84. Radon belongs to the 18th group of the Periodic Table

85. Leeuwenhoek

86. In screw jack, effort required to lift a load is given by P = w tan $(\alpha+\varphi)$

87. Arsenic oxide

88. Rickets

89. The liquid tends to have minimum surface area due to surface tension. Small liquid drop from spherical shape because it wants to have less area due to the application of the surface tension.

90. Cissus quadrangularis

91. Almost 99% of the minerals making up the Earth's crust are made up of just eight elements.

Element name	Symbol	Percentage by weight of the Earth's crust
Oxygen	O	47
Silicon	Si	28
Aluminium	Al	8
Iron	Fe	5
Calcium	Ca	3.5
Sodium	Na	3
Potassium	K	2.5
Magnesium	Mg	2
All other elements		1

92. Madhya Pradesh

93. No change will happen

94. Hard water is generally found in areas where groundwater is in contact with limestone, chalk and dolomite and gets higher amount of calcium and magnesium dissolved in it.

95. Weight of the balloon is less than the weight of air displaced by it.

96. The image formed will be beyond 2F, enlarged, real and inverted.

97. F/a. Inertial mass is a mass parameter giving the inertial resistance to acceleration of the body when responding to all types of force.

$$M = \frac{F}{q}$$

98. A machine having an efficiency less than 50%, is known as non-reversible machine.

99. L.P.G. is a hydrocarbon consisting of a mixture of Propane and Butane.

100. Exchange forces

Mathematics

Q.1 A canal is 5 m wide at bottom and 8 m wide at top. The depth of water is 4 m. Water is flowing in the canal with the speed of 10 m/s. How much cubic m. of water will flow in 1 minute?

A. 7800 **B.** 15,600 **C.** 23,400 **D.** 11,700

Q.2 In how many years will a sum of Rs. 3,500 yield an interest of Rs. 2,100 at 15% per annum?

A. 2 Years **B.** 3 Years **C.** 4 Years **D.** 5 Years

Q.3 The average of all the prime and composite numbers up to 100 is:

A. 51 **B.** 49.50 **C.** 100 **D.** 385

Q.4 A, B and C can do a work in 6, 8 and 12 days respectively. Doing that work together they get an amount of Rs. 1350, the share of B in that amount is:

A. Rs. 450 **B.** Rs. 440 **C.** Rs. 400 **D.** Rs. 430

Q.5 The cost price of an article is ₹ 3,90 and sold at a profit of 3.12%, how much would be its approximate selling price?

A. ₹ 410 **B.** ₹ 402 **C.** ₹ 417 **D.** ₹ 420

Q.6 The two chords AB and CD of a circle cut each other perpendicularly at point O. OA = 2 cm, OC = 3 cm and OB = 6 cm, then what will be the diameter of the circle?

A. $\dfrac{\sqrt{145}}{2}$ **B.** $\sqrt{130}$

C. $\dfrac{\sqrt{130}}{2}$ **D.** $\sqrt{65}$

Q.7 17 articles were bought for ₹ 3,910 and sold for ₹ 4,590. How much was the approximate profit percentage per article?

A. 17% **B.** 12% **C.** 9% **D.** 21%

Q.8 If cos A + cos 2A = 1, then sin 2A + sin 4A = ?

A. 1 **B.** 1/2 **C.** 0 **D.** -1

Q.9 If θ is a positive acute angle and tan 2θ.tan 3θ = 1, then what will be the value of $(2\cos^2 5\theta/2 - 1)$?

A. -1/2 **B.** 0 **C.** 1 **D.** 1/2

Q.10 A mixture contains spirit and water in the ratio 3:2. If it contains 3 liters more spirit than water, the quantity of spirit in the mixture is?

A. 10 liters **B.** 12 liters **C.** 8 liters **D.** 9 liters

Q.11 What will be the compound interest on a sum of Rs. 25,000 after three years at the rate of 12% per annum?

A. Rs. 10123.20 **B.** Rs. 9000.30

C. Rs. 83.20 **D.** Rs. 9720

Q.12 A round balloon of radius r subtends an angle α at the eye of an observer while the angle of elevation of its center is β. The height of the center of the balloon is:

A. r sin β. cosec α/2 **B.** r cos β. Cosec α/2
C. r cosec α. sin β **D.** r^2 sin β/2. cos α/2

Q.13 The largest and the second largest angles of a triangle are in the ratio of 3 : 2 respectively. The smallest angle is 20% of the sum of the rest two angles. What is the sum of the smallest and the second largest angles?

A. 80° **B.** 60° **C.** 100° **D.** 90°

Q.14 Study the following Pie Chart carefully and answer the questions given below:

Budget estimated by by a family for their monthly expenses

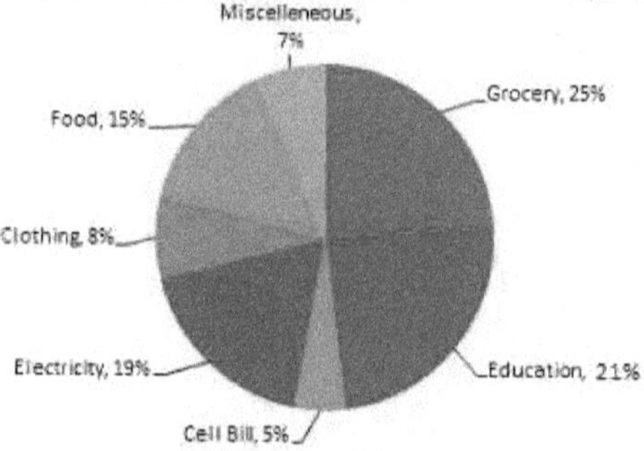

What is the budget estimated by the family on Clothing and Grocery together?

A. ₹ 8,960 **B.** ₹ 8,550 **C.** ₹ 8,780 **D.** None

Q.15 Study the following Pie Chart carefully and answer the questions given below:

Budget estimated by by a family for their monthly expenses

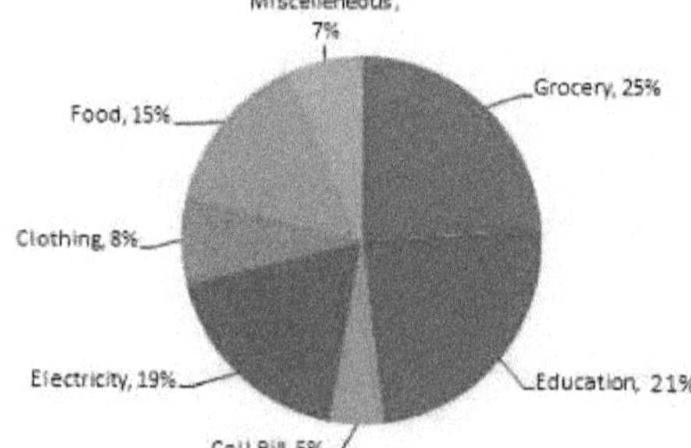

Due to a sudden marriage, the family incurs Miscellaneous expenditure of ₹ 3,040. How much is the increase in the amount under this head from that of the budgeted?

A. ₹ 2,240 **B.** ₹ 304 **C.** ₹ 800 **D.** ₹ 224

Q.16 PQ is a direct common tangent of two circles of radii r_1 and r_2 touching each other externally at A. Then the value of PQ^2 is:

A. r_1r_2 **B.** $2r_1r_2$ **C.** $3r_1r_2$ **D.** $4r_1r_2$

Q.17 20% of the 4/5th of a number is 60, find the number?

A. 275   **B.** 375   **C.** 325   **D.** 400

Q.18 If a number x is 10% less than another number y and y is 10% more than 125, then x is equal to

A. 150   **B.** 143   **C.** 140.55   **D.** 123.75

Q.19 If A, B, C, D are four points in a straight line such that distance from A to B is 10, B to C is 5, C to D is 4 and A to D is 1, then their correct sequence is:

A. A - B - C- D   **B.** C- D -A - B
C. A - D -C - B   **D.** C- B - A - D

Q.20 The ratio between the speeds of a truck, car and train is 3 : 8: 12. The car moved uniformly and covered a distance of 1040 km in 13 hours. What is the average speed of the truck and the train together?

A. 74 km/h
B. 60 km/h
C. 48 km/h
D. Cannot be determined

Q.21 A, B and C contract a work for Rs. 550 together. A and B are supposed to do 7/11 of the work. The amount that C gets is:

A. Rs. 100   **B.** Rs. 210   **C.** Rs. 200   **D.** Rs. 150

Q.22 The radius of a cylinder is the same as that of a sphere. There volumes are equal. The height of the cylinder is how many times of its radius?

A. 1   **B.** 2   **C.** 2/3   **D.** 4/3

Q.23 A train traveling at 65 kmph leaves Mumbai at 10 A.M. and another train travelling at 75 kmph starts at 12 Noon in the same direction. How many k.m. away from Mumbai will they be together?

A. 1050 km.   **B.** 1000 km.
C. 975 km.   **D.** 925 km.

Q.24 If the angles of a pentagon are in the ratio 1 : 3 : 6 : 7 : 10, then the smallest angle is:

A. 30°   **B.** 32°   **C.** 27°   **D.** 20°

Q.25 A bob of length 50 cm makes an arc of 16 cm during its motion. What will be the measure of the angle thus formed (approx.)?

A. 18°25'   **B.** 18°35'   **C.** 18°20'   **D.** 18°08'

Q.26 If the radius of a cylinder is tripled and the height is halved, what is the ratio between the new volume and the previous volume?

A. 3:2   **B.** 4:5   **C.** 6:2   **D.** 9:2

Q.27 Find the value of

$$\frac{1}{3-\sqrt{8}} - \frac{1}{\sqrt{8}-\sqrt{7}} + \frac{1}{\sqrt{7}-\sqrt{6}} - \frac{1}{\sqrt{6}-\sqrt{5}} + \frac{1}{\sqrt{5}-2}$$

A. 0   **B.** 1   **C.** 5   **D.** 6

Q.28 The sides of a triangle are 24 cm, 32 cm and 40 cm. What is the height of the perpendicular drawn on the longest side?

A. 25 mtr.   **B.** 21.33 mtr.
C. 19.2 mtr.   **D.** 20 mtr.

Q.29 If $x \sin^3 \theta + y\cos^3 \theta = \sin \theta.\cos \theta$ and $x\sin \theta = y\cos \theta$, $\sin \theta \neq 0$, $\cos \theta \neq 0$, then $x^2 + y^2$ is:

A. $\dfrac{1}{\sqrt{2}}$ **B.** 1/2   **C.** 1   **D.** $\sqrt{2}$

Q.30 If $42x = 1/32$ then x is:

A. 5/4   **B.** 4/5
C. 3/5   **D.** None of the above

General Intelligence & Reasoning

Q.31 In the following question, select the related word from the given alternatives.

PARTS : STRAP :: WOLF : ?

A. FOX   **B.** ANIMAL
C. WOOD   **D.** FLOW

Q.32 DIRECTIONS: In the question below, there are few statements followed by few conclusions. You have to take the given statements to be true even if they seem to be at variance with commonly known facts and then decide which of the given conclusion logically follow(s) from the given statements.

Statements:

All books are pins.

Some pins are desks.

Conclusions:

I. Some desks are books.

II. All desks are pins.

III. No desk is book.

A. Only either I or II follows.
B. Only either I or III follows.
C. Only either II or III follows.
D. Only I follows.

Q.33 DIRECTIONS: Read the following information carefully and answer the questions given below it.

'X + Y' means 'X is the father of Y'.

'X – Y' means 'X is the mother of Y'

'X x Y' means 'X is the brother of Y'

'X ÷ Y' means 'X is the sister of Y'.

Which of the following symbols should replace question mark in the given expression in order to make the relation 'P is the niece of M' definitely true?

M x N ? R – P÷S

A. x   **B.** +
C. ÷   **D.** Either x or ÷

Q.34 DIRECTIONS: In the question below, there are few statements followed by few conclusions. You have to take the given statements to be true even if they seem to be at variance with commonly known facts and then decide which of the given conclusion logically follow(s) from the given statements.

Statements:

All books are pins.

Some pins are desks.

Conclusions:

I. Some desks are books.

II. All desks are pins.

III. No desk is book.

A. Only either I or II follows.

B. Only either I or III follows.

C. Only either II or III follows.

D. Only I follows.

Q.35 DIRECTIONS: In the questions given below, some relationship has been expressed through symbols as shown below. Based on the meaning of these symbols and choose the correct answer.

φ means 'less than'

Δ means 'not greater than'

- means 'equal to'

+ means 'not equal to'

× means 'not less than'

= means 'greater than'

X φ Y + Z implies

A. X − Y = Z   **B.** X ×Y − Z

C. X Δ Y φ Z   **D.** X + Y = Z

Q.36 DIRECTIONS: In the following question, continuous pattern series is given. Some of the letters of the series are missing. These missing letters are given in that order as one of the four alternatives below the series. Find out the correct alternatives.

jk_ljkk_ljj_klljk_ljk_ll

A. jkkll   **B.** kjjkl   **C.** klkkk   **D.** kljjl

Q.37 Roy walks 2 km to East, then turns North-West and walks 3 km. Then he turns South and walks 5 km. Then again he turns West and walks 2 km. Finally he turns North and walks 6 km. In which direction, is he from the starting point?

A. South-West   **B.** South-East

C. North-West   **D.** North-East

Q.38 If' A' is coded as 1, 'B' as 3, 'C' as 5 and so on, which of the following is the numerical value of the word 'FAZED'?

A. 81   **B.** 79   **C.** 77   **D.** 80

Q.39 If 'MATCH' is coded as 'NCWGM' and 'BOX' as 'CQA', then which of the following is coded as 'OQWIGUVS'?

A. NOTEBOOK   **B.** NOTEBOKE

C. NOTFBOPE   **D.** NOTFBOPE

Q.40 In the question which one of the given choices would be a meaningful order of the following words?

1. Bibliography 2. Contents 3. Title 4. Chapters 5. Introduction

A. 3, 2, 5, 1, 4   **B.** 2, 3, 4, 5, 1

C. 5, 1, 4, 2, 3   **D.** 3, 2, 5, 4, 1

Q.41 A word is represented by only one sequence of numbers as given in any one of the alternatives. The sets of numbers given in the alternatives are represented by two classes of alphabets as in two matrices given below. The columns and rows of Matrix – I are numbered from 0 to 3 and that Matrix – II are numbered from 4 to 7. A letter from these matrices can be represented first by its row and next by its column. e.g., 'A' can be represented by 00, 12 etc. and 'L' can be represented by 46, 54, 67 etc. Similarly, You have to identify the set for the word given below. **"TUBULE"**

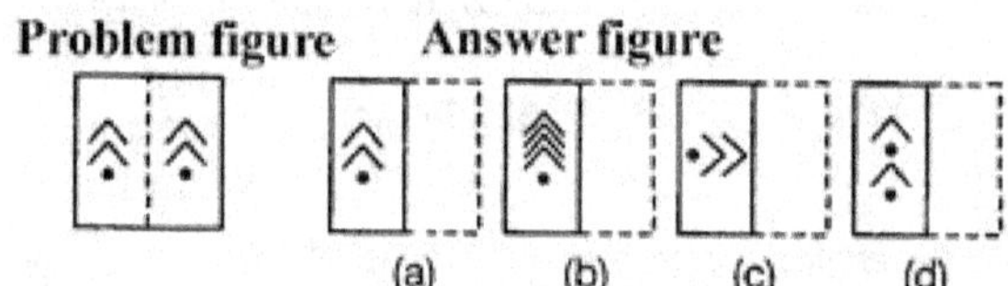

Matrix – I

	0	1	2	3
0	A	M	T	I
1	T	I	A	M
2	I	A	M	T
3	M	T	I	A

Matrix- II

	4	5	6	7
4	E	B	L	U
5	L	U	E	B
6	U	E	B	L
7	B	L	U	E

A. 10, 47, 57, 64, 75, 46

B. 23, 55, 67, 47, 46, 77

C. 02, 64, 45, 55, 66, 77

D. 31, 76, 57, 47, 67, 56

Q.42 DIRECTIONS: Choose the missing terms out of the given alternatives.

QPO, SRQ UTS, WVU, ?

A. XVZ   **B.** YXW   **C.** ZYA   **D.** VWX

Q.43 Find out missing number:

9 : 81 :: 12 : ?

A. 124   **B.** 104   **C.** 134   **D.** 144

Q.44 DIRECTIONS: A piece of paper is opened after being cut as shown below in the questions figure. From the given answer figures, indicate how it will appear when closed?

Problem figure   Answer figure

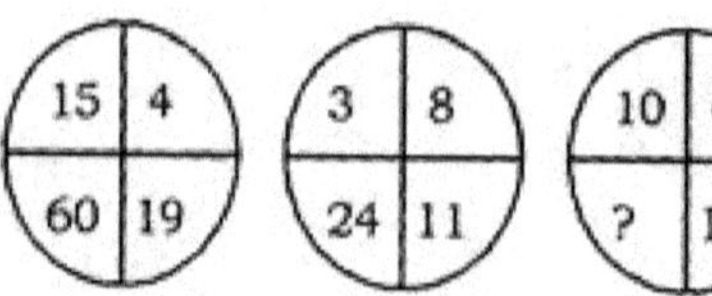

(a)   (b)   (c)   (d)

A. a   **B.** b   **C.** c   **D.** d

Q.45 DIRECTIONS: Choose the missing terms out of the given alternatives.

B M f q J U ? ?.

A. N y   **B.** m X   **C.** M x   **D.** n y

Q.46 DIRECTIONS: Find out missing number from the following given figures.

15	4		3	8		10	4
60	19		24	11		?	14

A. 117 **B.** 40 **C.** 61 **D.** 81

Q.47 The given alternative choose the one who is different from other three alternatives.

A. Blackmail **B.** Smuggling.
C. Snobbery. **D.** Forgery.

Q.48 DIRECTIONS: Select from answer choices a number to replace the question mark.

5 11 8
11 13 12
6 ? 7

A. 9 **B.** 8 **C.** 7 **D.** 10

Q.49 Choose the correct water image of the figure from responses given below?

Question Figure:

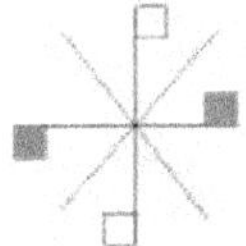

Answer Figures:

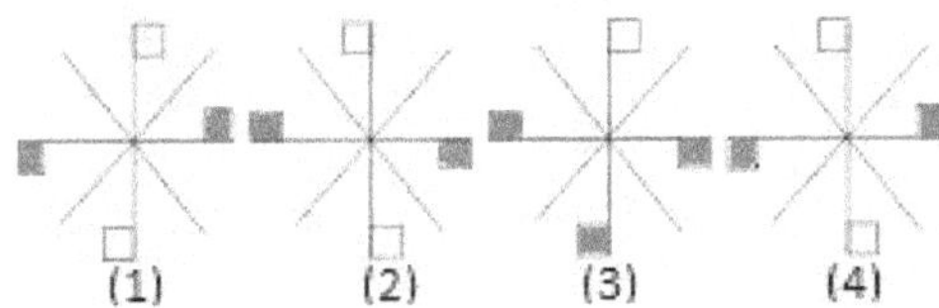

(1) (2) (3) (4)

A. 1 **B.** 2 **C.** 3 **D.** 4

Q.50 A, B, C, D, E, F and G are members of a family consisting of 4 adults and 3 children, two of whom, F and G are girls. A and D are brothers and A is a doctor. E is an engineer married to one of the brothers and has two children. B is married to D and G is their child. Who is C?

A. G's brother **B.** F's father
C. E's father **D.** A's son

Q.51 DIRECTIONS: Study the following diagram and answer the questions that follow.

a. The rectangle represents men.

b. Circle represents graduates.

c. Triangle represents skilled persons.

d. Square represents employed persons.

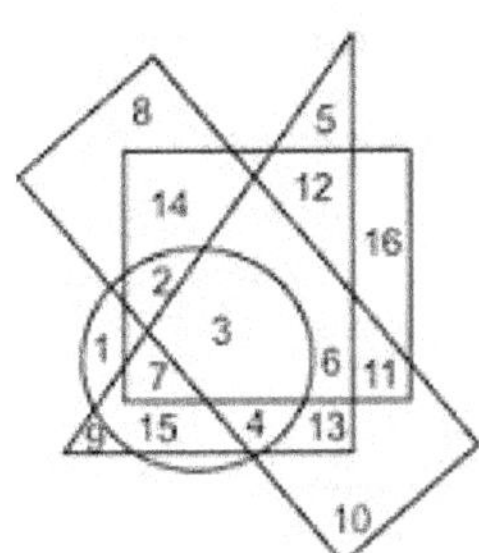

The skilled employed men who are not graduates are-

A. 3 and 11 **B.** Only 6 **C.** Only 12 **D.** 6 and 9

Q.52 Three of the following four are alike in certain way and so form a group. Which is the one that does not belong to that group?

A. Yajur veda **B.** Atharva veda
C. Rig veda **D.** Ayurveda

Q.53 DIRECTIONS: Arrange the following words according to the english dictionary.

(a) Assistant (b) Assessment (c) Asbestos (d) Asterisk (e) Ass

A. (b), (e), (a), (d), (c) **B.** (c), (e), (b), (a), (d)
C. (a), (e), (c), (d), (b) **D.** (c), (e), (a), (d), (b)

Q.54 Kannan walked 10 kms towards North. From there the he turned back and walked 6 kms towards South. Then he walked 3 km towards East. How far was he from the starting point?

A. 3 km **B.** 6 km **C.** 7 km **D.** 5 km

Q.55 DIRECTIONS: Choose the odd one out from the given alternatives.

A. DINHI **B.** LAMIA
C. ENICSCE **D.** OGRAGEPHY

General Awareness

Q.56 Which of the following is not the border state of Punjab?

A. Rajasthan
B. Uttaranchal
C. Himachal Pradesh
D. Jammu and Kashmir

Q.57 Where does the heat come from in the atmosphere?

A. Insolation **B.** Condensation
C. Radiation **D.** Convection

Q.58 Genghis Khan invaded India in:

A. 1240 **B.** 1221 **C.** 1248 **D.** 1223

Q.59 The financial bill deals with:

A. Article 111 **B.** Article 112
C. Article 116 **D.** Article 117

Q.60 Who has the legislative council in the following states?

A. Bihar **B.** Odisha
C. West Bengal **D.** Punjab

Q.61 Till Which year was Ahmedabad's the capital Gujarat?

A. 1960 **B.** 1965 **C.** 1970 **D.** 1975

Q.62 Who is currently the Minister of Electronics and Information Technology?

A. Prakash Javadekar
B. Arun Jaitley
C. Sushma Swaraj
D. Ravi Shankar Prasad

Q.63 Whose tomb is the tomb of a wife

A. Nurjahan **B.** Aurangzeb's wife
C. Humayun's sister **D.** Mumtaz Mahal

Q.64 According to the Indian Constitution, the Union Minister who lives in the office during the funeral?

A. President.

B. Prime minister.

C. Speaker.

D. Chief Justice of the Supreme Court of India

Q.65 Who was the last Sultan of Delhi?

A. Daulat Khan Lodhi   **B.** Rana Sanga

C. Ibrahim Lodhi   **D.** Sikandar Lodhi

Q.66 The inland Salt Lake is located in _______

A. Himachal Pradesh   **B.** Karnataka

C. Madhya Pradesh   **D.** Rajasthan

Q.67 When the Battle of Haldighati was fought?

A. 1539   **B.** 1556   **C.** 1565   **D.** 1576

Q.68 The first players to honor "Bharat Ratna" are:

A. Milkha Singh   **B.** Sunil gavask

C. Dara Singh   **D.** Sachin Tendulkar

Q.69 Ram Nath Kovind inaugurated the first Jnana Kumbh, which was billed as a major event of higher education in _______ .

A. Himachal Pradesh   **B.** Uttarakhand

C. Arunachal Pradesh   **D.** Delhi

Q.70 Which of the following soil is suitable for paddy cultivation?

A. Laterite soil   **B.** Red soil

C. Alluvium   **D.** black soil

General Science

Q.71 What is the SI unit of Force?

A. Dyne   **B.** Erg   **C.** Newton   **D.** Joule

Q.72 Which of the following is the hottest planet?

A. Jupiter.   **B.** Venus.   **C.** Earth.   **D.** Moon.

Q.73 At high attitude water boils at a lower temperature because —

A. There is much more water vapour in the upper atmosphere than earth.

B. There is less water vapour in the upper atmosphere than earth.

C. The temperature of the atmosphere decrease with altitude

D. pressure of the atmosphere decreases with altitudes.

Q.74 Clear nights are colder than cloudy nights because of _______

A. conduction   **B.** condensation

C. radiation   **D.** isolation

Q.75 A particle performing a simple harmonic motion during passage through the mean position of rest has—

A. Maximum K.E. and maximum P.E.

B. Minimum K.E. and minimum P.E.

C. Maximum K.E. and minimum P.E.

D. Minimum K.E. and maximum P.E.

Q.76 Which of the following cannot be recharged?

A. Primary cell

B. Secondary cell

C. Both can be recharged

D. both cannot be recharged

Q.77 Which of the following is the best source of vitamin 'A' ?

A. Apple   **B.** Honey   **C.** Carrot   **D.** Peanut

Q.78 The element with the highest electrical conductivity is -

A. Aluminium   **B.** Diamond

C. Graphite   **D.** Silver

Q.79 Commercial name of Sodium bicarbonate is

A. Washing soda   **B.** Baking soda

C. Bleaching powder   **D.** Soda ash

Q.80 Which of the following explains the dual nature of electron?

A. Plum Pudding Model

B. Rutherford's experiment

C. De-Broglie's equation

D. Schrodinger's wave equation

Q.81 The presence of which of the following salts in water causes corrosion in steam boilers ?

A. Sodium Chloride

B. Magnesium Chloride

C. Calcium bicarbonate

D. Potassium bicarbonate

Q.82 Stem in ferns is-

A. Rhizome   **B.** Corm   **C.** Bulb   **D.** Sucker

Q.83 The temperature at which the volume of a gas becomes zero is called

A. absolute temperature

B. absolute zero temperature

C. absolute scale of temperature

D. None of these

Q.84 A boat will submerge when it displaces water equal to its own:

A. Volume   **B.** Weight

C. Surface area   **D.** Density

Q.85 Which of the following is not a neutral oxide ?

A. Carbon Monoxide   **B.** Sulphur Dioxide

C. Water   **D.** Nitric Oxide

Q.86 The Mach number needs to be more than .... to be hypersonic

A. 3   **B.** 4   **C.** 5   **D.** 6

Q.87 Which of the following is used as lubricant?

A. Graphite   **B.** Silica

C. Diamond   **D.** Iron Oxide

Q.88 What is true of National Park

A. Tourism is allowed in buffer zone

B. No human activity is allowed
C. Cattle grazing is allowed in buffer zone
D. Hunting is allowed in core zone

Q.89 Largest tiger population occurs in
A. Kanha National Park
B. Corbett National Park
C. Sunderbans National Park
D. Ranthambor National Park

Q.90 The Doppler's Effect is applicable for -
A. Light wave   **B.** Sound wave
C. Space wave   **D.** Both a and b

Q.91 If the supply curve is a straight line passing through the origin, then the price elasticity of supply will be?
A. Infinitely large.   **B.** Greater than unity.
C. Equal to unity.   **D.** Less than unity.

Q.92 The gas used to extinguish fire is —
A. Neon   **B.** Nitrogen
C. Carbon dioxide   **D.** Carbon Monoxide

Q.93 Tooth enamel is made of________ .
A. Calcium phosphate   **B.** Calcium silicate
C. Calcium carbonate   **D.** Calcium sulphate

Q.94 Which of the following relations is incorrect?
A. Power factor = Real power Apparent power
B. Power factor = kW/kVA
C. Power factor = Resistance Impedance
D. Power factor = Conductance/Susceptance

Q.95 A television channel is characterised by
A. frequency of transmitted signal
B. velocity of transmitted signal
C. physical dimension of television screen
D. size of picture tube

Q.96 Paper is manufactured by —
A. Wood and resin
B. Wood, Sodium and Bleaching powder
C. Wood and bleaching powder
D. Wood, Calcium, hydrogen sulphate and resin

Q.97 Permanent hardness of water can be removed by adding
—
A. Potassium Permanganate
B. Chlorine
C. Bleaching Powder
D. Washing Soda

Q.98 Decibel is the unit used for measuring?
A. Speed of light
B. Intensity of heat
C. Intensity of sound
D. Radio waves frequency

Q.99 A carnot engine receiving heat at 400 K has an efficiency of 25%. The C.O.P. of a carnot refrigerator working between the same temperature limit s:
A. 1   **B.** 2   **C.** 3   **D.** 4

Q.100 Endangered plant species are conserved through
A. Herbarium   **B.** Gene library
C. Gene Bank   **D.** Reducing pollution

// Smart Answer Sheet //

Correct Percentage of students who answered correctly.   **Skipped** Percentage of students who skipped.

Q.	Ans.	Correct / Skipped	Q.	Ans.	Correct / Skipped	Q.	Ans.	Correct / Skipped	Q.	Ans.	Correct / Skipped	Q.	Ans.	Correct / Skipped
1	B	78.01 % / 21.77 %	17	B	82.27 % / 12.04 %	33	D	89.65 % / 10.26 %	49	B	76.66 % / 21.78 %	65	C	88.23 % / 11.63 %
2	C	85.95 % / 10.7 %	18	D	82.27 % / 11.73 %	34	B	88.23 % / 11.2 %	50	D	89.86 % / 10.05 %	66	D	83.38 % / 16.4 %
3	A	88.81 % / 10.98 %	19	C	87.8 % / 10.31 %	35	C	85.72 % / 14.01 %	51	B	85.88 % / 13.2 %	67	D	79.37 % / 11.95 %
4	A	83.23 % / 12.67 %	20	C	79.16 % / 20.76 %	36	C	81.62 % / 11.35 %	52	D	78.41 % / 16.76 %	68	D	80.91 % / 13.83 %
5	B	86.03 % / 12.76 %	21	C	85.06 % / 13.02 %	37	C	79.38 % / 18.58 %	53	B	80.94 % / 12.99 %	69	B	85.92 % / 13.75 %
6	D	84.75 % / 10.51 %	22	D	86.24 % / 12.24 %	38	B	84.33 % / 10.9 %	54	D	89.43 % / 10.51 %	70	C	87.73 % / 11.97 %
7	A	88.06 % / 10.31 %	23	C	80.63 % / 12.07 %	39	A	82.39 % / 15.54 %	55	B	81.63 % / 13.83 %	71	C	88.76 % / 10.94 %
8	A	77.67 % / 16.21 %	24	D	79.11 % / 11.23 %	40	D	80.4 % / 14.73 %	56	B	79.59 % / 16.08 %	72	B	89.23 % / 10.53 %
9	B	81.27 % / 12.14 %	25	B	77.28 % / 22.56 %	41	D	78.2 % / 21.02 %	57	C	78.85 % / 18.85 %	73	D	88.56 % / 10.84 %
10	D	79.39 % / 18.37 %	26	D	78.68 % / 13.11 %	42	B	77.2 % / 12.39 %	58	B	84.44 % / 11.29 %	74	C	77.25 % / 11.59 %
11	A	84.11 % / 15.27 %	27	C	77.85 % / 19.02 %	43	D	89.32 % / 10.57 %	59	D	83.71 % / 11.39 %	75	C	84.8 % / 13.15 %
12	A	81.75 % / 16.85 %	28	C	84.62 % / 12.13 %	44	A	83.56 % / 11.87 %	60	A	81.54 % / 10.27 %	76	A	85.33 % / 12.8 %
13	D	78.01 % / 14.27 %	29	C	86.55 % / 11.22 %	45	D	89.7 % / 10.18 %	61	C	85.51 % / 13.17 %	77	C	89.0 % / 10.91 %
14	D	86.24 % / 11.58 %	30	D	84.9 % / 12.26 %	46	B	87.65 % / 11.86 %	62	D	87.11 % / 12.71 %	78	D	82.48 % / 14.6 %
15	C	77.19 % / 12.22 %	31	D	84.26 % / 14.86 %	47	C	78.75 % / 16.22 %	63	B	79.02 % / 18.14 %	79	B	77.27 % / 21.83 %
16	D	86.8 % / 11.62 %	32	B	82.39 % / 13.49 %	48	B	82.7 % / 13.91 %	64	A	87.65 % / 10.55 %	80	C	78.92 % / 17.49 %

Q.	Ans.	Correct / Skipped
81	B	89.7 %
		10.2 %
82	A	86.22 %
		13.74 %
83	B	82.1 %
		12.79 %
84	B	84.86 %
		12.1 %

Q.	Ans.	Correct / Skipped
85	B	83.67 %
		11.34 %
86	C	77.26 %
		21.75 %
87	A	80.38 %
		17.86 %
88	B	86.71 %
		12.83 %

Q.	Ans.	Correct / Skipped
89	C	81.75 %
		13.85 %
90	D	89.18 %
		10.71 %
91	D	76.13 %
		15.15 %
92	C	84.06 %
		15.17 %

Q.	Ans.	Correct / Skipped
93	A	77.2 %
		13.32 %
94	D	88.95 %
		11.02 %
95	A	79.02 %
		13.05 %
96	D	79.97 %
		17.08 %

Q.	Ans.	Correct / Skipped
97	D	87.42 %
		11.92 %
98	C	86.18 %
		12.32 %
99	D	88.76 %
		10.18 %
100	C	87.4 %
		12.24 %

//Hints and Solutions//

1. Area of the base 1/2 (sum of parallel sides) × Height

= 1/2(8+5)×4 = 26 m²

∵ Speed of water = 10 m/sec.

∴ Volume of water = 26 × 10 × 60 = 15600 m³

2. T = 2100×100/3500×15

T = 4 Years

3. Since 1 is neither prime nor composite number. Thus there are only 99 number viz.

2, 3, 4, 5, 6, ... 99, 100.

Hence $\left(\dfrac{2+3+4+5+6+...100}{99}\right)$

$= \left(\dfrac{(1+2+3+4+...100)-1}{99}\right)$

$= \dfrac{5050-1}{99} = \dfrac{5049}{99} = 51$

4. A's one day work = 1/6

B's one day work = 1/8

C's one day work = 1/12

A's share: B's share: C's share = 1/6:1/8:1/12

= 4 : 3 : 2

∴ B's share = 1350×3/9 = ₹ 450

5. S.P. = 390 + 3.12% of 390 = ₹ 402.168

6.

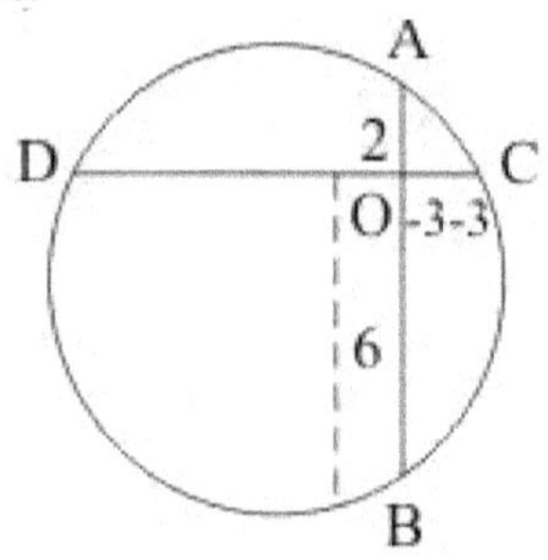

Alternate solution

∵ AB ⊥ CD at O

∴ CO × OD = OA × OB

$\Rightarrow 3 \times OD = 2 \times 6$

$\Rightarrow OD = 4$

Now, diameter $= \sqrt{\left(OA^2 (OB)^2 + (OC)^2 + (OD)^2\right)}$

$= \sqrt{(2)^2 + (6)^2 + (3)^2 + (4)^2}$

$= \sqrt{4+36+9+16}$

Diameter $= \sqrt{65}$ cm

7. Profit = 4590 - 3910

= Rs. 680

Profit percentage = 680/3910 x 100

= 17.39%

= 17% approximately.

8. cos A = 1 – cos² A

= sin² A

Now, since

sin² A + cos² A = 1

$\Rightarrow$ sin² A + (sin² A)² = 1

$\Rightarrow$ sin² A + sin⁴ A = 1

9. Given:

$\tan 2\theta.\tan 3\theta = 1$

$\tan 2\theta = \cot 3\theta$

$\tan 2\theta = \tan(90° - 3\theta)$

$\Rightarrow 5\theta = 90°$

$\Rightarrow \theta = 18°$

$\therefore 2\cos^2 \dfrac{5\theta}{2} - 1 = 2\cos^2 45° - 1 = 0$

10. Let the amount of water be x liters

∴ x+3/x = 3/2

or 2x + 6 = 3x or, x= 6

∴ The quantity of spirit in the mixture = x + 3= 6+3

= 9 liters

11.

$$A = P\left(1 + \frac{r}{100}\right)^t$$

$P = 25000,\ r = 12\%,\ t = 3$ years

$$\therefore A = 25000\left(1 + \frac{12}{100}\right)^3 = ₹35123.20$$

$\therefore$ interest $= A - P = ₹(35123.20 - 25000)$

$= ₹10123.20$

12. Let O be the center of balloon of radius r. The observer's eye is at C.

$\angle ACB = \alpha$ and $\angle OCD = \beta$ clearly, CA and CB are tangents to the circle. So

$\angle ACO = \angle BCO = \alpha/2$

In right angled $\triangle OBC$,

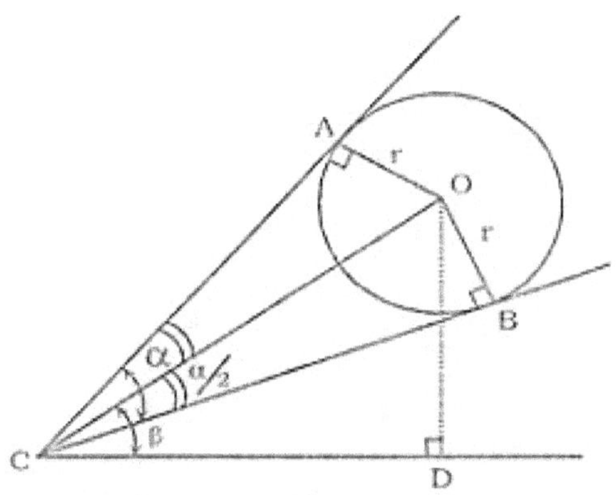

$\sin\dfrac{\alpha}{2} = \dfrac{OB}{OC} \Rightarrow OC = \dfrac{OB}{\sin\alpha/2} = r\operatorname{cosec}\dfrac{\alpha}{2}$

In right angled $\triangle OCD$,

$\sin\beta = \dfrac{OD}{OC} \Rightarrow OD = OC\sin\beta = r\operatorname{cosec}\dfrac{\alpha}{2}\cdot\sin\beta$

$\therefore$ Height of the center of the balloon is

$r\sin\beta.\operatorname{cosec}\dfrac{\alpha}{2}$

13. If the largest and the second largest angles be 3x and 2x respectively then, third angle = x

$\therefore x + 2x + 3x = 180°$

$\Rightarrow x = 30°$

$\therefore$ Required sum

$= x + 2x = 3x = 90°$

14. Budget estimated on Clothing and Grocery together= (25 + 8)% of ₹ 32,000

$= (33/100) \times 32000 = ₹ 10,560$

15. Budget estimated on miscelleneous 7% of ₹ 32,000

$= (7/100) \times 32000 = ₹ 2240$

Required change= 3040-2240 = 800

16.

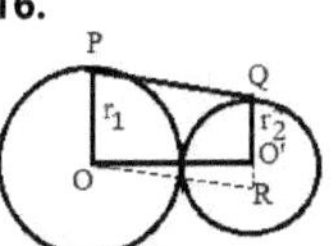

Since opposite sides are parallel and interior angles are 90° therefore OPQR is a rectangle.

$OP = QR = r_1$

In $\triangle OO'R$,

$\angle ORO' = 90°$

By Pythagoras theorem,

$OR^2 + O'R^2 = OO'^2$

$OR^2 + (r_1 - r_2)^2 = (r_1 + r_2)^2$

$OR^2 = 4r_1r_2$

$OR = \sqrt{4r_1r_2}$

$\therefore PQ^2 = OR^2 = 4r_1r_2$

17.

20% of $\dfrac{4}{5}x = 60$

$\therefore x = 60 \times \dfrac{5}{4} \times \dfrac{100}{20} = 375$

18. x = y - 10% of y

x = 9/10 y

New, y = 125 + 10% of 125

$= 110/100 \times 125$

$\therefore$ x = 9/10 × 110/100 × 125 = 123.75

19. Given that the distance from A to B = 10 and B to C = 5 and C to D = 4, D to A = 1

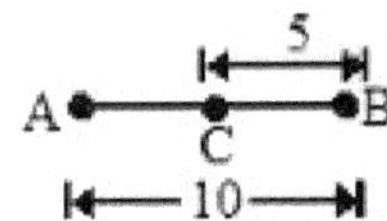

$\therefore$ The correct sequence is A - D - C - B which is in increasing order.

20. The ratio between the speeds of the truck, car and train is 3:8:12

Given that the car covers 1040 km in 13 hours, the speed of the car 80 km/h

Also, if we assume that the speeds of the truck, car and train are 3x, 8x and 12x

respectively, then

x = 10

Therefore, speed of truck 30 km/h

Speed of train = 120 km/h

Average speed of truck and train is calculated as:

2×30×120/30+120 = 48 km/h

21.

$(A+B)$ did $\dfrac{7}{11}$ work and C did $\left(1-\dfrac{7}{11}\right)=\dfrac{4}{11}$ work

$\therefore$ $(A+B)$'s share : C's share $=\dfrac{7}{11}:\dfrac{4}{11}=7:4$

$\therefore$ C's share $=\dfrac{550}{11}\times4=₹200$

22. Radius of cylinder = Radius of sphere and volume of cylinder = volume of sphere

so $\qquad \pi r^{2}h=\dfrac{4}{3}\pi r^{3}$

$\Rightarrow \qquad 4r=3h \Rightarrow h=\dfrac{4}{3}r$

23.

In two hours, the first train is 2×65 kms i.e., 130 kms ahead of the second train. The second train moves 10 kms faster

so it will meet the first train in $(130\div10)$ i.e., 13 hours

$\therefore$ Distance travelled by the second train $=13\times75$ km $=975$ km

Therefore after 975 km both train will meet.

24. Suppose the angles of a pentagon are

x°, 3x°, 6x°, 7x°, 10x°

But x° + 3x° + 6x° + 7x° + 10x° = (2x5 -4) x 90°

or 27x° = 6 x 90°

or x = 20°

25. Radius = 50 cm

Arc = 16 cm

Let the angle be θ.

16 = θ/360×2×π×50 ⇒ θ = 8×36×7/5×22 ≈ 18°33 ≈ 18°35'

26. Let the initial radius and height of the cylinder be r cm and h cm respectively.

Then, $V_1 = \pi r^2 h$ and $V_2 = \pi.(3r).2.h/2 = 9/2\, \pi r^2 h$

NewVolume/Previousvolume = $9/2\pi r^2h/\pi r^2h$ = 9/2 = 9:2

27.

$$\dfrac{1}{3-\sqrt{8}}-\dfrac{1}{\sqrt{8}-\sqrt{7}}+\dfrac{1}{\sqrt{7}-\sqrt{6}}-\dfrac{1}{\sqrt{6}-\sqrt{5}}+\dfrac{1}{\sqrt{5}-2}$$

$$\dfrac{1}{\sqrt{9}-\sqrt{8}}-\dfrac{1}{\sqrt{8}-\sqrt{7}}+\dfrac{1}{\sqrt{7}-\sqrt{6}}-\dfrac{1}{\sqrt{6}-\sqrt{5}}+\dfrac{1}{\sqrt{5}-\sqrt{4}}$$

Rationalized

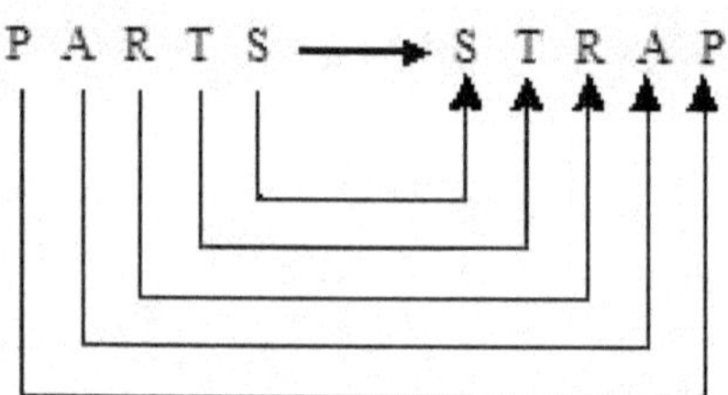

$$\Rightarrow \left(\dfrac{1}{\sqrt{9}-\sqrt{8}}\times\dfrac{\sqrt{9}+\sqrt{8}}{\sqrt{9}+\sqrt{8}}\right)-\left(\dfrac{1}{\sqrt{8}-\sqrt{7}}\times\dfrac{\sqrt{8}+\sqrt{7}}{\sqrt{8}+\sqrt{7}}\right)+\left(\dfrac{1}{\sqrt{7}-\sqrt{6}}\times\dfrac{\sqrt{7}+\sqrt{6}}{\sqrt{7}+\sqrt{6}}\right)-\left(\dfrac{1}{\sqrt{6}-\sqrt{5}}\times\dfrac{\sqrt{6}+\sqrt{5}}{\sqrt{6}+\sqrt{5}}\right)+\left(\dfrac{1}{\sqrt{5}-\sqrt{4}}\times\dfrac{\sqrt{5}+\sqrt{4}}{\sqrt{5}+\sqrt{4}}\right)$$

$$\Rightarrow \sqrt{9}+\sqrt{8}-\sqrt{8}-\sqrt{7}+\sqrt{7}+\sqrt{6}-\sqrt{6}-\sqrt{5}+\sqrt{5}+\sqrt{4}$$

$$\Rightarrow \sqrt{9}+\sqrt{4}\Rightarrow 3+2=5$$

28. The triangle thus formed is a right-angled triangle.

Thus, the length of perpendicular on the largest side

= 32×24/40 = 19.2 meter.

29.

Take θ = 45°

$\therefore x.\left(\dfrac{1}{\sqrt{2}}\right)^{3}+y\left(\dfrac{1}{\sqrt{2}}\right)^{3}=\dfrac{1}{\sqrt{2}}.\dfrac{1}{\sqrt{2}}$

or $x+y=\sqrt{2}$ ....(i)

and $\dfrac{x}{\sqrt{2}}=\dfrac{y}{\sqrt{2}}$ or $x=y$ ....(ii)

$\therefore$ from (i) & (ii)

$x+x=\sqrt{2}$ or $2x=\sqrt{2}$ $\Rightarrow x=\dfrac{1}{\sqrt{2}}$

$\therefore y=\dfrac{1}{\sqrt{2}}$

$\therefore x^{2}+y^{2}=\dfrac{1}{2}+\dfrac{1}{2}=1$

30. $4^{2x} = 1/32$

or $(2^2)^{2x} = 1/2^5$

or 24x = 2^-5

$\therefore$ 4x = -5

or x = −5/4

31.

P A R T S ⟶ S T R A P

similarly,

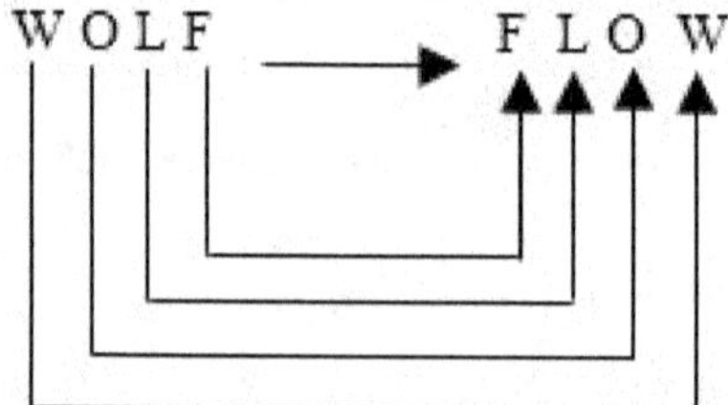

W O L F ⟶ F L O W

32.

Only either I or III follows.

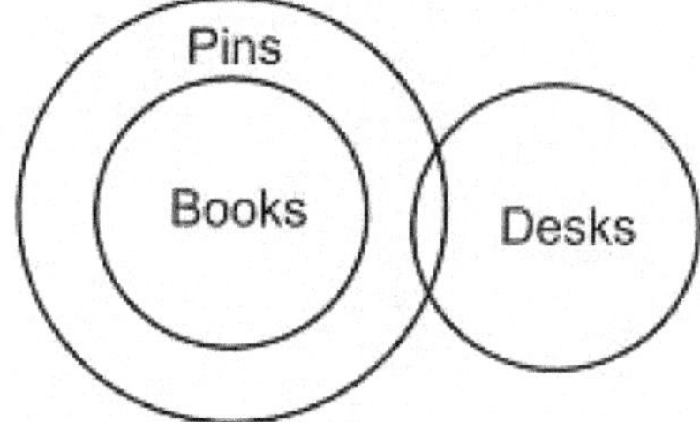

33.

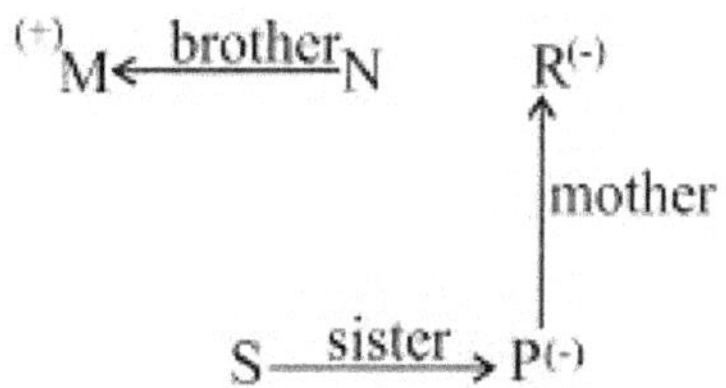

M and R must be siblings. So, their intermediary sibling N should be either a brother or a sister of both. Therefore, either x or ÷ can be placed.

34.

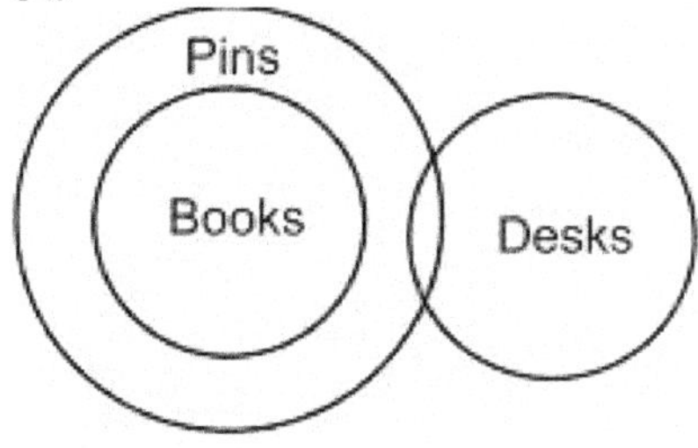

35. Clearly, the meaning of the given symbols

X φ Y + Z ⇒ X < Y ≠ Z

Using the proper notations/symbols in option (c), we get

X △ Y φ Z

⇒ X< Y< Z.

⇒ X< Y ≠ Z.

Therefore, X φ Y + Z = X △ Y < φ Z.

36. Series pattern is : jkkl/jkkll/jjkkll/jkkl/jkkll

∴ Required answer = klkkk

37.

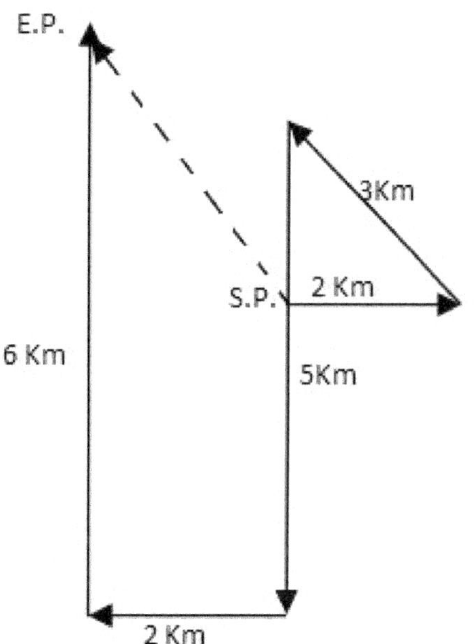

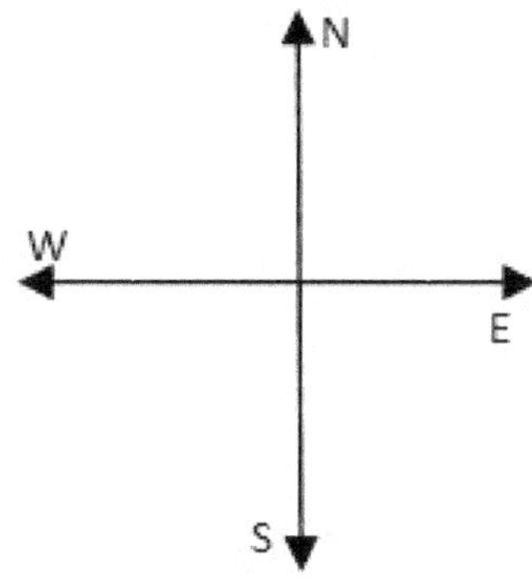

Now Roy is in the North-west direction from starting point.

38. Given that;

A	B	C	D	E	F	G	H	I	J	K	L	M	N	O	P	Q	R	S	T	U	V	W	X	Y	Z
1	3	5	7	9	11	13	15	17	19	21	23	25	27	29	31	33	35	37	39	41	43	45	47	49	51

So from the above table, numerical value of FAZED= 11 +1 + 51 + 9 + 7 =79.

39.

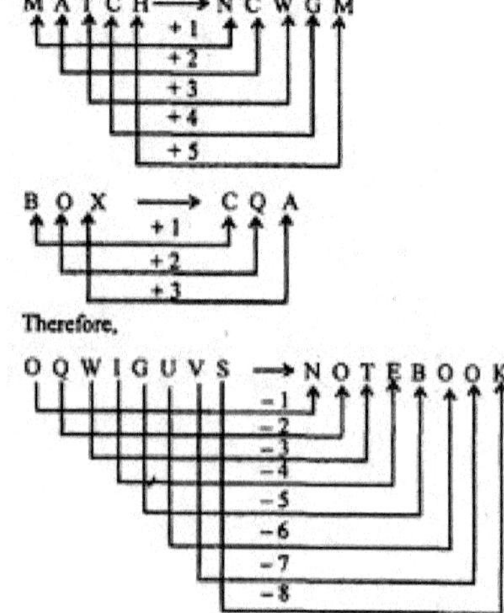

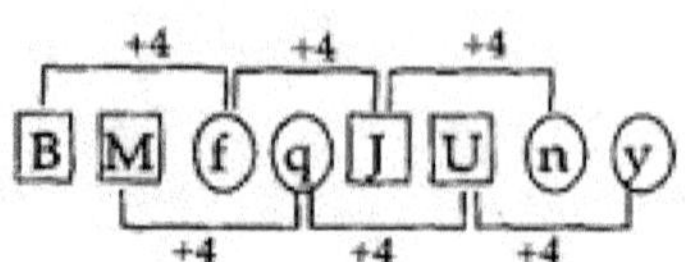

Therefore, missing letters =

40. 3. Title "Because it is the first thing a person wants to know about a book".

2. Contents "Because, it shows what is in the book".

5. Introduction "Because it introduces the book".

4. Chapters "Because after the introduction we go on to read the chapters".

1. Bibliography "Because this lists the references of the content at the end."

41. TUBULE

Possible code for T : 02/10/23/31

Possible code for U: 47/55/64/76

Possible code for B: 45/57/66/74

Possible code for L: 46/54/67/75

Possible code for E : 44/56/65/77

Hence, the code for TUBULE = 31, 76, 57, 47, 67, 56

42. The given sequence of group of letters follows the pattern:

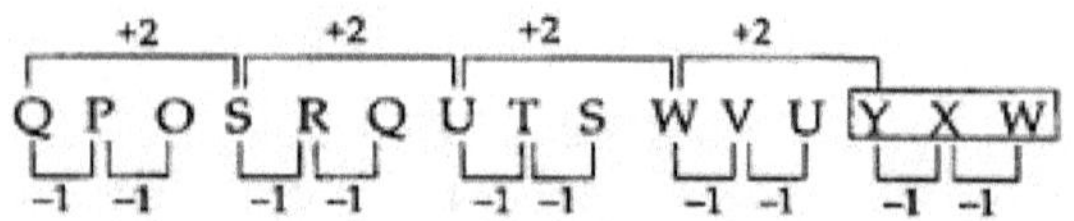

Therefore, missing group of letters = YXW.

43. $9 : (9)^2 :: 12 : (12)^2$

$= 9 : 81 :: 12 : 144.$

44. When we will open problem figure, it will be look like answer fig. (a)

45. The given sequence is a combination of small-cap letter that follows the pattern:

46. In figure I = 15 × 4 = 60,

15+4=19

In figure II = 3 x 8 = 24,

3 + 8=11

Then missing number is = 10 × 4

=40

47. All other terms except snobbery are related to crimes.

48. (right term × 2) – left term = middle term

(8 × 2) – 5 = 11

(12 × 2) – 11 = 13

So,

(7 × 2) – 6 = 8

49. 2

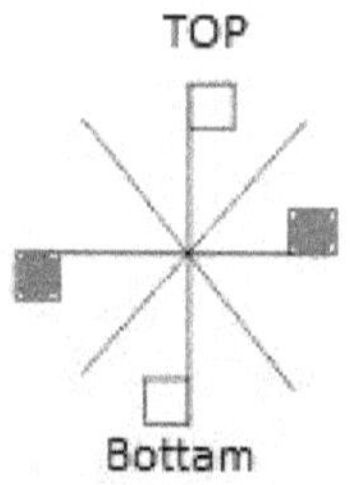

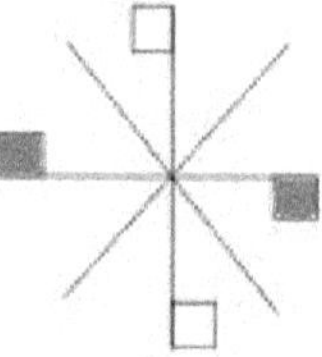

50. '↔' → brothers, '=' → couple, '↓' → offspring, '‴' → male, 'O' → female, 'X' → unknown

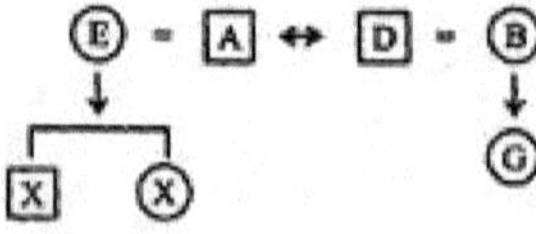

Clearly, C and F are the remaining members to be adjusted in place of two x. since, there are 3 children out of which two are

girls, i.e. G and F, so clearly the third children C is a boy. So C is the son of E and A.

51. only 6

52. Except Ayurveda, all others are Vedas. 'Ayurveda' is the branch of medicine.

53. The correct arrangement is:

(c) Asbestos (e) Ass (b) Assessment (a) Assistant (d) Asterisk

54.

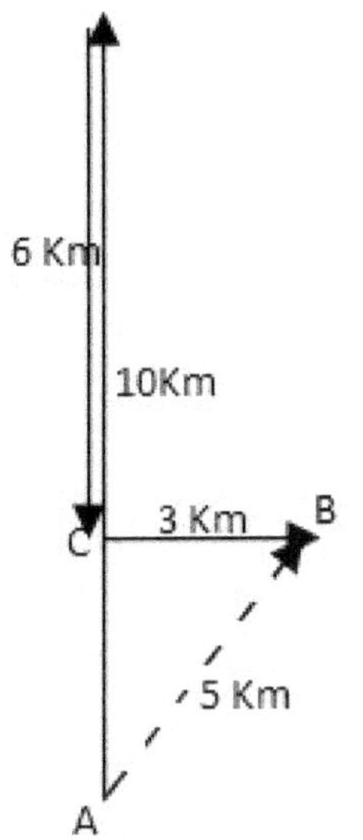

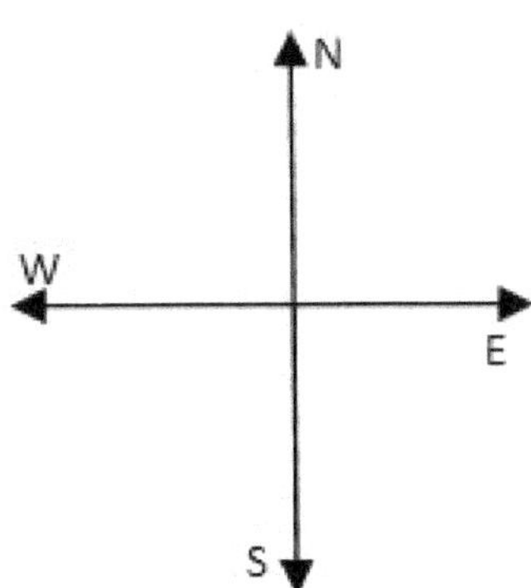

From the figure its clear that Kannan is 5 Km from the starting point.

55. Except LAMIA, all other groups of letters, if arranged form study subject, i.e. HINDI, SCIENCE, and GEOGRAPHY respectively.

56. Uttaranchal is not a border state of Punjab

57. Sun is the ultimate source of heat and light for the earth. As the soil goes hot and warm. It becomes a radiative body and emits long waves of radiation. This energy makes the environment warm. This process is known as terrestrial radiation. These radiations are absorbed by atmospheric gases like carbon dioxide and other greenhouse gases. Thus the atmosphere is heated by this terrestrial radiation.

58. Genghis Khan invaded India in 1221.

59. The Financial Bill (I) is related to Article 117 (1) and the Financial Bill (II) Article 117 (3)

60. The Legislative Council (or Legislative Council) is a High House in those states of India who have a bicameral legislature. As of 2011, there is a legislative council in twenty six (out of twenty-nine) states. The State Government also expressed its opposition to the revival of the Council.

61. Ahmedabad was the capital of Gujarat from 1960 to 1970. The current capital is Gandhinagar

62. Currently Ravishankar Prasad is the Minister of Electronics and Information Technology.

63. The tomb of the wife is the tomb of Aurangzeb's wife

64. A member of any House of Parliament belonging to any political party, which is declared disqualified for being a member of that House under Article 2 of the Tenth Schedule, under clause (1) for the period of commencement of the period. Will be disqualified for appointment as a minister. From the date of his disqualification till that date, the term of his office shall be terminated as the member, or where he fights for any House of Parliament either before the expiry of such period,

By the date she is declared elected, whichever is earlier. During the pleasure of the President, he will hold the post of minister. The Council of Ministers will be collectively responsible for the Lok Sabha. If a minister enters his office, the President will take oath of office and secrecy as per the prescribed forms for the third position.

65. Ibrahim Lodhi was the last sultan.

66. India's largest inland salt lake, Sombre Salt Lake, is located 96 km northeast of Ajmer with 96 km southwest of Jaipur city and National Highway 8 in Rajasthan. It is India's largest saline lake and makes Rajasthan the third largest salt producing state in India.

67. It was fought in 1576.

68. Sachin Tendulkar

69. President Rama Nath Kovind today inaugurated the first knowledge Kumbha in the form of a major event of higher education in Uttarakhand.

70. Alluvial soil contains organic material, which is suitable for paddy cultivation.

71. Newton is the SI unit of Force.

72. Venus is the second planet from the Sun, orbiting it every 224.7 Earth days. It has no natural satellite. It is named after the Roman goddess of love and beauty.

73. At high attitude water boils at a lower temperature because pressure of the atmosphere decreases with altitudes.

74. radiation

75. A particle performing a simple harmonic motion during passage through the mean position of rest has Maximum K.E. and minimum P.E.

76. Primary cell cannot be recharged

77. carrot

78. The element with the highest electrical conductivity is Silver.

79. Baking soda

80. It is described by the de-Broglie equation

81. Magnesium Chloride:

Corrosion of the water side of the boiler may occur in three ways, by oxidation, by electrolytic dissolution and by acid attack.

The corrosion reactions occurring in a boiler are complex but may be summarized by saying that they are caused directly or indirectly by oxygen, carbon dioxide or certain salts, e.g. magnesium chloride, in the boiler water.

82. Rhizome

83. The temperature at which the volume of a gas becomes zero is called absolute zero temperature

84. Weight

A boat will float when the weight of water it displaces equal the weight of the boat and anything will float if it is shaped to displace its own weight.

85. Sulphur Dioxide:

Neutral oxides are oxides which are neither acidic nor basic.

When Sulphur dioxide is dissolved in water (neutral medium) form sulphurous acid (H_2SO_3) which became able to donate hydrogen ion.

86. The Mach number needs to be more than 5 to be hypersonic

87. Graphite:

Graphite contains layers of carbon atoms. The layers slide over each other easily because there are only weak forces between them, making graphite slippery.

90. The Doppler's Effect is applicable for both light waves and sound waves.

91. Less than unity.

92. Carbon dioxide :

Sodium bicarbonate, regular or ordinary used on class B and C fires, was the first of the dry chemical agents developed. In the heat of a fire, it releases a cloud of carbon dioxide that smothers the fire. That is, the gas drives oxygen away from the fire, thus stopping the chemical reaction.

93. Tooth enamel, the clear outer layer of the tooth above the gum line, is the hardest substance in the human body. Tooth enamel is made of calcium phosphate.

94. Power factor = Conductance/Susceptance

95. A television channel is a physical or virtual channel' over which a television atation or television network Is distributed. Channel numbers represent actual frequencies used to broadcast the television signal. For example. In North America. "channel 2" refers to the broadcast or cable band of 54 to 60 MHz, with carrier frequencies of 55.25 MHz for NTSC analog video (VSB} and 59.75 MHz for an alog audio (PM), or 55.31 MHz for digital ATSC (8VSB).

96. Wood, Calcium, hydrogen sulphate and resin

97. Washing Soda

98. Intensity of sound

99. (d) 4

100. Gene Bank

Mathematics

Q.1 If $\sin\theta + \sin^2\theta = 1$, then the value of $\cos^{12}\theta + 3\cos^{10}\theta + 3\cos^8\theta + \cos^6\theta - 1$ is:

A. 0   **B.** 1   **C.** 2   **D.** 3

Q.2 The height of an equilateral triangle is $4\sqrt3$ cm, then what will be the area of the equilateral triangle?

A. $16\sqrt3$ **B.** 16   **C.** $48\sqrt3$ **D.** 50

Q.3 If 10 men can do a work in 6 days and 15 women can do the same in 5 days, Then 8 men and 5 women can together do the work in :

A. 7 days   **B.** 6 days   **C.** 5 days   **D.** 4 days

Q.4 The average of two numbers is 8 and that of another three numbers is 3. The average of these five numbers is-

A. 7   **B.** 5.5   **C.** 6   **D.** 5

Q.5 Which of the following is obtained after the rationalization of the expression $1/(\sqrt2+\sqrt3+\sqrt5)$?

A. $(2\sqrt2+3\sqrt3-\sqrt{30})/12$ **B.** $(2\sqrt2-3\sqrt2+\sqrt{30})/12$

C. $(2\sqrt3+3\sqrt2-\sqrt{30})/12$ **D.** $(2\sqrt2+3\sqrt3+\sqrt{30})/12$

Q.6 If $\sin\theta=8/17$, where $0°<\theta<90°$, then $\tan\theta+\sec\theta$ is:

A. 1/3   **B.** 2/3   **C.** 4/3   **D.** 5/3

Q.7 OA, OB, OC are 3 lines in a plane which meet at O. If the angles $\angle AOB$, $\angle BOC$, $\angle COA$ are 2x, 5x, 8x respectively (where x is a positive angle), then x equals:

A. 24°   **B.** 18°   **C.** 15°   **D.** 12°

Q.8 The value of tan 31° tan 33° ... tan 59° is equal to:

A. -1   **B.** 0   **C.** 1   **D.** 2

Q.9 If x = 81, then the value of $(x^{1/4}-1)(x^{1/4}+1)$ is:

A. 4   **B.** 6   **C.** 0   **D.** 8

Q.10 A man sells two scooters for Rs.12000 each. He makes a profit of 20% on one and a loss of 20% on the other. The profit/loss, on the whole, is

A. Rs.1000 profit   **B.** Rs.1000 loss

C. Rs.960 profit   **D.** Rs.960 loss

Q.11 A train covers a certain distance in 50 minutes, if it runs at a speed of 48 km/hr on an average. The speed at which the train must run so that time of journey becomes 40 minutes?

A. 10 km/hr   **B.** 20 km/hr   **C.** 40 km/hr   **D.** 60 km/hr

Q.12 The pie chart given here shows expenditures incurred by a family on various items and their savings, which amount to Rs. 8,000 in a month.

Study the chart and answer the questions based on the pie chart.

How much expenditure is incurred on education?

A. Rs.3,000   **B.** Rs. 5,000

C. Rs. 4,000   **D.** Rs. 7,000

Q.13 The pie chart given here shows expenditures incurred by a family on various items and their savings, which amount to Rs. 8,000 in a month.

Study the chart and answer the questions based on the pie chart.

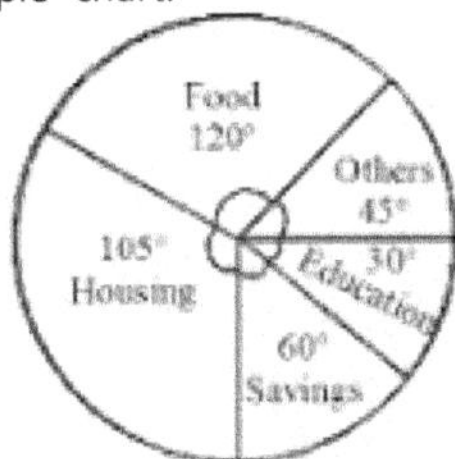

The ratio of the expenditure on food to the savings is:

A. 3:1   **B.** 2:1   **C.** 4:3   **D.** 3:4

Q.14 A solid metallic cone of height 10 cm and radius of base 20 cm is melted to make spherical balls each of 4 cm diameter. How many such balls can be made?

A. 25   **B.** 50   **C.** 125   **D.** 75

Q.15 Sum of the lengths of any two sides of a triangle is always greater than

A. The third side of the triangle

B. Bigger side of the triangle

C. Lesser side of the triangle

D. None of these

Q.16 If D is a point on the side AB of triangle ABC and DE is a line through D meeting AC at E such that $\angle ADE = \angle ACB$, then AB. AD is equal to:

A. AE.BC   **B.** AC.DE   **C.** AE.AC   **D.** AB.BC

Q.17 A man can row 15 km per hour downstream and 9 km per hour upstream. The speed (in km/hour) of the boat in still water is:

A. 8   **B.** 10   **C.** 12   **D.** 15

Q.18 If x : y = 3 : 4, then the value of $(5x - 2y)/(7x+2y)$

A. 7/25   **B.** 7/23   **C.** 7/29   **D.** 7/17

Q.19 The sum of the numberator and denominator of certain fraction is 8. If 2 is added to both the numerator and the denominator the value of the fraction increased by 4/35, then the fraction is:

A. 1/7
B. 3/5
C. 5/3
D. Can not be determinted

Q.20 The simple interest on a certain principal at the rate of 9.5 percent per annum is Rs 950 for two year. How much will be the additional interest on the same amount for the same period at the rate of 10.5 percent per annum?

A. Rs 75
B. Rs 150
C. Rs 100
D. None of these

Q.21 If the angle of elevation of the top of a tower from two points at the distance x and y meter from the base and in the same straight line with it are complementary, then the height of the tower is?

A. $\sqrt{(x/y)}$
B. $\sqrt{xy}$
C. $\sqrt{(x+y)}$
D. $\sqrt{(x-y)}$

Q.22 Kamya purchased an item of 46,000 and sold it at a loss of 12%. With that amount she purchased another item and sold it at a gain of 12%. What was her overall gain/loss?

A. Loss of ₹ 662.40
B. Profit of ₹662.40
C. Loss of ₹ 642.80
D. Profit of ₹642.80

Q.23 The owner of a cell phone shop charges his customer 23% more than the cost price. If a customer paid Rs.7,011 for a cell phone, then what was the cost price of the cell phone?

A. Rs.5,845
B. Rs.6,750
C. Rs.5,900
D. None of these

Q.24 The cost of an article was Rs.75. The cost was first increased by 20% and later on it was reduced by 20%. The present cost of the article is:

A. Rs. 72
B. Rs. 60
C. Rs. 75
D. Rs. 90

Q.25 A rectangular box measures internally 1.6 m long, 1 m broad and 60 cm deep. The number of cubical block each of edge 20 cm that can be packed inside the box is:

A. 60
B. 53
C. 30
D. 120

Q.26 The diameter of the curved surface of a bucket are 28 decimeter and 14 decimeter and its height is 12 decimeter. Find its volume.

A. 4312 demi.^{3}
B. 3412 demi.^{3}
C. 534 demi.^{3}
D. 4132 demi.^{3}

Q.27 What will be the area of a rhombus, whose one side is 20 cm and one diagonal is 24 cm?

A. 240 cm^2
B. 480 cm^2
C. 384 cm^2
D. 386 cm^2

Q.28 The ratio of two unequal sides of a rectangle is 1 : 2. If its perimeter is 24 cm, then the length of diagonal in cm is:

A. $2/\sqrt{5}$
B. $4/\sqrt{5}$
C. $2\sqrt{5}$
D. $4\sqrt{5}$

Q.29 8 hours work of a woman is equal to 6 hours work of a man or 12 hours work of a boy. If 9 men working 6 hours daily can complete a work in 6 days, then in how many days 12 men, 12 women and 12 boys working 8 hours daily will complete the same work?

A. 5/2 days
B. 3/2 days
C. 7/2 days
D. 3 days

Q.30 In an examination, the average marks was found to be 50. For deducting marks for computational errors, the marks of 100 candidates had to be changed from 90 to 60 each and so the average of marks came down to 45. The total number of candidates, who appeared at the examination, was:

A. 600
B. 300
C. 200
D. 150

General Intelligence & Reasoning

Q.31 In the following question, select the related letter/word/number from the given alternatives.

MUSIC : TUNE

A. Game : Player
B. Poetry: Poet
C. Dance : Rhythm
D. Religion : God

Q.32 Find out similar set of the given set:

(64, 216, 125)

A. (26, 144, 163)
B. (55, 126, 80)
C. (8, 27, 64)
D. (45, 134, 154)

Q.33 Pointing to a boy Neha said, 'He is the son of my grandfather's only child. How is she related to that boy?

A. Sister.
B. Aunt
C. Cannot be determined.
D. None of these.

Q.34 In a code language 'S1357' means 'SWe are very happy', 'S2639' means 'Sthey are extremely lucky' , and 'S794' means 'SHappy and lucky'. Which digit in that code language stands for 'Svery'?

A. 1
B. 5
C. 7
D. Data inadequate

Q.35 In a certain code language the word 'FUTILE' is written as 'HYVMNI'. How will the word 'PENCIL' be written in that language?

A. OIFRLT
B. OIFRLS
C. OLFRIT
D. इनमें से कोई नहीं

Q.36 Laxman start walking from his house and went 15 km to North then he turned West and covered 10 kms. Then he turned South and covered 5 kms. Finally turning to East he covered 10 kms. In which direction he is from his house?

A. East
B. West
C. North
D. South

Q.37 Given below are two Matrices of Twenty-five Cells, each containing two classes of alphabets. The columns and rows of Matrix I are numbered form 0 to 4 and that of Matrix II from 5 to 9. A letter from these Matrices can be represented first by its row number and next by its column number. In each of the following questions, identify one set of number pairs out of (1),

(2), (3) and (4) which represents the given word.

MATRIX-I

	0	1	2	3	4
0	A	E	F	G	C
1	H	B	I	J	K
2	M	A	C	B	C
3	D	E	F	D	L
4	H	I	J	K	E

MATRIX-II

	5	6	7	8	9
5	N	S	R	S	T
6	Q	O	T	U	X
7	W	X	P	U	V
8	Y	Z	Y	Q	X
9	Z	W	R	S	R

RUST
A. 57, 78, 96, 56
B. 97, 68, 55, 56
C. 97, 68, 56, 59
D. 57, 68, 97, 66

Q.38 Arrange the following in a meaningful order:
1. Curd
2. Grass
3. Butter
4. Milk
5. Cow
A. 2, 5, 4, 3, 1
B. 4, 2, 5, 3, 1
C. 5, 2, 3, 4, 1
D. 5, 2, 4, 1, 3

Q.39 In the questions given below, some relationship has been expressed through symbols as shown below. Based on the meaning of these symbols and choose the correct answer.

φ means 'less than'
Δ means 'not greater than'
- means 'equal to'
+ means 'not equal to'
× means 'not less than'
= means 'greater than'
X φ Y - Z implies
A. X × Y– Z
B. X - Y × Z
C. X + Y × Z
D. X × Y = Z

Q.40 Choose the odd one out from the given alternatives.
A. SUNDAY : YADSUN
B. MOTHER : TMPRHD
C. PARENT : TNEPAR
D. MOSTLY : YLTMOS

Q.41 Find the odd one out from the given alternatives.
A. 32-41
B. 62-44
C. 46-28
D. 33-56

Q.42 In the question below, there are few statements followed by few conclusions. You have to take the given statements to be true even if they seem to be at variance with commonly known facts and then decide which of the given conclusion logically follow(s) from the given statements.
Statements:
All horses are rivers.
All rivers are jungles.
No Jungle is flower.
Conclusions:
I. No horse is flower.
II. No flower is horse.
A. If only Conclusion I follows.
B. If only Conclusion II follows.
C. If either Conclusion I or II follows.
D. If both Conclusions I and II follow.

Q.43 Choose the missing terms out of the given alternatives.
ef_h_gfe_hef_ehgefg_
A. egffh
B. ghgfh
C. ehhfg
D. ggfhe

Q.44 What should come next in the following letter sequence:
A A B A B C A B C D A B C D E A B C D E F A B C D E F G A B C D E F G
A. A
B. I
C. H
D. B

Q.45 In the given figure, circle represents youths, triangle represents the persons who are in job and rectangle represents illiterate person.

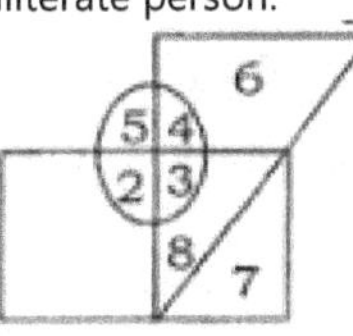

Which of the following number depicts, illiterate youths who have job?
A. 5
B. 4
C. 3
D. 10

Q.46 What comes in place of question mark ?

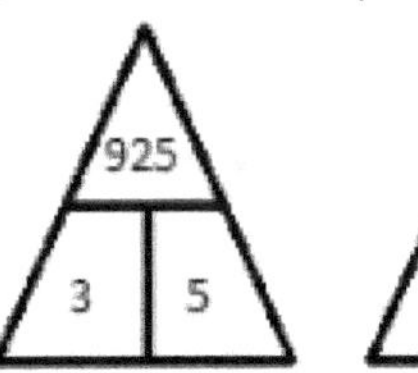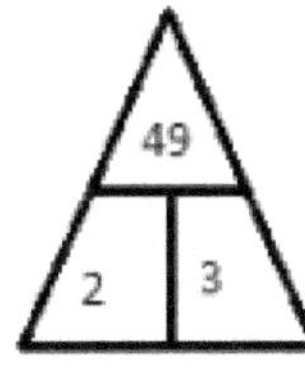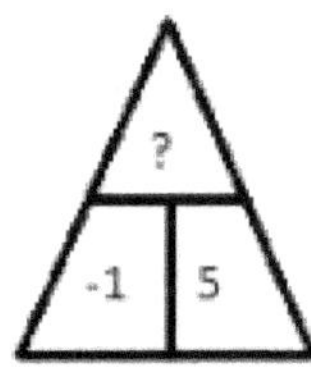

A. 125
B. 215
C. 251
D. 512

Q.47 what comes in place of ?

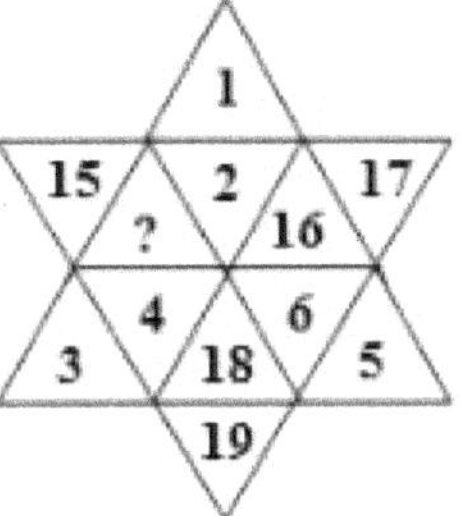

A. 13
B. 14
C. 20
D. 21

Q.48 Find the water image of the object given in the question figure.

T⊥FW

A. ⊥TⱢW   **B.** ⊥TⱢM   **C.** ⊥TFM   **D.** ⊥TFW

Q.49 A Piece of paper is folded and cut as shown below in the question figure. From the given answer figures, indicate how it will appear when opened.

Question Figure :

Answer Figures :

(1)   (2)   (3)   (4)

A. 1   **B.** 2   **C.** 3   **D.** 4

Q.50 In the following questions, four/five figures are given. Three/four are similar in a certain way and so form a group. Find out which one of the figures does not belong to that group.

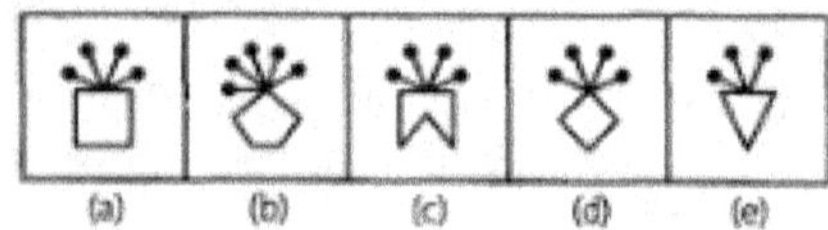
(a)   (b)   (c)   (d)   (e)

A. a   **B.** b   **C.** c   **D.** d

Q.51 Which of the following words cannot be formed from 'GENERALIZATION'?

A. NOTE   **B.** RATION   **C.** LIZARD   **D.** GOAT

Q.52 If '+' stands for multiplication, 'x' stands for division, '−' stands for addition and '÷' stands for subtraction, what is the answer for the following equation?

$20 − 5 ÷ 18 x (3 + 2) = ?$

A. 20   **B.** 18   **C.** 108   **D.** 22

Q.53 The day on 18.09.1977 was Sunday. A couple was married on this date. In the next 15 years, there how many marriage anniversaries would fall on Sunday?

A. 1   **B.** 2   **C.** 5   **D.** 9

Q.54 In a row of girls, if Rohini who is 12th from the left and Mihika who is 9th from the right, if they interchange their seats then Rohini becomes 18th from the left. How many girls are there in the row?

A. 17   **B.** 20   **C.** 22   **D.** 26

Q.55 Study the diagram given below and answer the question.

Which part represents those clerks who are graduates and have government job?

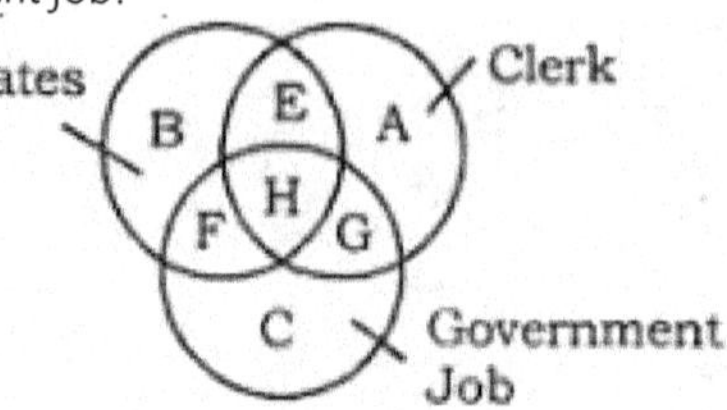

A. E   **B.** H   **C.** G   **D.** F

General Awareness

Q.56 See Solution In:
The first Viceroy of India was.
A. Lord.   **B.** Lord Canning.
C. Lord Curzon.   **D.** Lord Minto.

Q.57 15th edition of Pravasi conference will be held in:
A. Varanasi   **B.** Delhi
C. Mumbai   **D.** Benaras

Q.58 How many members of the Anglo-Indian community can be nominated by the President of India to the Parliament?
A. 1   **B.** 2   **C.** 5   **D.** 8

Q.59 Which Amendment of the Constitution deals with Political defections?
A. 44th   **B.** 50th   **C.** 52nd   **D.** 60th

Q.60 Which is the highest peak of India?
A. Kangchenjunga   **B.** Nanda Devi
C. Kamet   **D.** None of the above

Q.61 Where will be the two new Indian Institutes of Science Education & Research (IISERs) established?
A. Tirupati and Berhampur
B. Vijayawada and Bhubaneswar
C. Guntur and Berhampur
D. Visakhapatnam and Tirupati

Q.62 The older alluvium is called
A. Bhangar   **B.** Bhabhar   **C.** Khadar   **D.** Tarai

Q.63 In Shivaji's Council of ministers the Prime minister was called.
A. Peshwa.   **B.** Sachiv .
C. Mantri.   **D.** Samanta.

Q.64 Which river of India is called Dakshin Ganga?
A. Krishna   **B.** Godavari
C. Kaveri   **D.** Narmada

Q.65 Money Bills are described in the Article ________.
A. 109   **B.** 110   **C.** 111   **D.** 112

Q.66 Who was the First Indian Nobel Prize winner?
A. Sir C.V. Raman
B. Mother Teresa
C. S. Chandrashekar

D. Rabindra Nath Tagore

Q.67 Iltutmish established a centre of learning at:

A. Multan   **B.** Kolkatta   **C.** Alwar   **D.** Patna

Q.68 The Tapti river rises from the—

A. Vindhyan range   **B.** Satpura range
C. Maikal range   **D.** Mahadev hills

Q.69 World Tsunami Awareness Day being observed on

_________.

A. 5th november   **B.** 6th November
C. 4th November   **D.** 3th November

Q.70 Where was 46th "Know India Programme" in March, 2018 held?

A. Coimbatore   **B.** Jaipur
C. Mumbai   **D.** New Delhi

General Science

Q.71 If the gravitational acceleration at any place is doubled, then the weight of body will be

A. g/2   **B.** g   **C.** $\sqrt{2}g$ **D.** 2g

Q.72 If at high altitudes, birds become rare, the plants likely to disappear are

A. Pine   **B.** Orchids
C. Oak   **D.** Rhododendron

Q.73 In blanking operation clearance is provided on

A. die
B. punch
C. half on punch and half on die
D. either on punch or die

Q.74 In graphite, electrons are ______

A. Localized on every third carbon
B. Present in antibonding orbitals
C. Localized on each carbon atom
D. Spread out between the structure

Q.75 Focal length of a convex lens is maximum for

A. Blue light   **B.** Yellow light
C. Green light   **D.** Red light

Q.76 The hardest substance available in earth is ____

A. Platinum   **B.** Silicon
C. Diamond   **D.** Gold

Q.77 Which of the following is a non-metal that remains liquid in room temperature ?

A. Bromine   **B.** Chlorine
C. Helium   **D.** Phosphorus

Q.78 The formula of Plaster of Paris is _____

A. $CaSO_4$ **B.** $CaSO_4, 2H_2O$
C. $2CaSO_4, 4H_2O$ **D.** $2CaSO_4, H_2O$

Q.79 A body moving in a circular path with constant speed has

A. radially outward acceleration

B. constant retardation
C. constant acceleration
D. variable acceleration

Q.80 In a National Park protection is provided to

A. Entire ecosystem   **B.** Flora and fauna
C. Fauna only   **D.** Flora only

Q.81 If we throw a Stone with some speed in a horizontal direction it follows a .... path as it falls to the ground.

A. Straight   **B.** Curved   **C.** Zig-Zag   **D.** Circular

Q.82 Radar is used to

A. Locate submerged submarines
B. Receive signal from radio receivers
C. Detect and locate distant objects
D. Locate geostationary satellites

Q.83 Which of the following has maximum metallic character?

A. Silicon   **B.** Tin
C. Lead   **D.** Germanium

Q.84 The purest form of iron is ____

A. Steel   **B.** Pig iron
C. Cast iron   **D.** Wrought iron

Q.85 Molecular mass of sulphurous acid is ____.

A. 82   **B.** 98   **C.** 96   **D.** 84

Q.86 Caustic Soda is ____

A. Nacl   **B.** $Na2CO_3$
C. NaOH   **D.** $NaHCO_3$

Q.87 In wind power, which form of energy is converted into electrical energy?

A. Kinetic energy   **B.** Potential energy
C. Solar energy   **D.** Radiant energy

Q.88 Which instrument is used for measuring relative humidity?

A. Barometer   **B.** Hydrometer
C. Hygrometer   **D.** Manometer

Q.89 Which one of the following has maximum genetic diversity in India

A. Tea   **B.** Teak   **C.** Wheat   **D.** Mango

Q.90 What is key ingredient of Vinegar that you use in diet ?

A. Acetic acid   **B.** Ascorbic acid
C. Benzoic Acid   **D.** Nicotinic Acid

Q.91 If petrol is used in a diesel engine, then

A. low power will he produced
B. Efficiency will be low
C. Higher knocking will occur
D. Dark and black smoke will be produced

Q.92 Electricity is produced through dry cell from

A. Chemical energy   **B.** Thermal energy
C. Mechanical energy   **D.** Nuclear energy

Q.93 X-rays were discovered by -

A. Roentgen   **B.** H.Davy
C. Lavoisier   **D.** Faraday

Q.94 Electron was discovered by:-
A. Mosale   **B.** Milicon
C. Thomson   **D.** Rutherford

Q.95 The unit of solid angle is
A. 9.46×10^{12} km   **B.** 8.46×10^{12} km
C. 9.46×10^{8} km   **D.** 8.46×10^{8} km

Q.96 Which of the following roofs provide better protection against fire ?
A. Cement slab   **B.** Asbestos sheet
C. Reinforced concrete   **D.** None of these

Q.97 'Piped Natural Gas(PNG) Is used for
A. Mining   **B.** Welding
C. Anaesthesie   **D.** Cooking

Q.98 The ionosphere is mainly composed of
A. Nitrogen and Oxygen
B. Ozone
C. Electrons and positive ions
D. None of these

Q.99 What principle/law explains the working of the hydraulic brakes in automobiles?
A. Bernoulli's law
B. Posieulle's principle
C. Pascal's law
D. Archimedes' principle

Q.100 is called the Power house' of cell—
A. Mitochondria   **B.** Lisosome
C. Ribosome   **D.** Golgi Body

// Smart Answer Sheet //

Correct Percentage of students who answered correctly. **Skipped** Percentage of students who skipped.

Q.	Ans.	Correct / Skipped	Q.	Ans.	Correct / Skipped	Q.	Ans.	Correct / Skipped	Q.	Ans.	Correct / Skipped	Q.	Ans.	Correct / Skipped
1	A	89.16 % / 10.18 %	17	C	78.72 % / 16.51 %	33	A	80.54 % / 19.06 %	49	D	77.94 % / 20.28 %	65	B	87.81 % / 12.03 %
2	A	76.43 % / 13.44 %	18	C	84.66 % / 14.43 %	34	D	86.89 % / 13.04 %	50	C	81.36 % / 17.96 %	66	D	83.13 % / 15.01 %
3	C	82.33 % / 13.79 %	19	B	82.13 % / 12.4 %	35	D	87.1 % / 12.45 %	51	C	80.7 % / 10.41 %	67	D	88.69 % / 11.02 %
4	D	78.93 % / 11.71 %	20	C	80.83 % / 10.55 %	36	C	89.4 % / 10.01 %	52	D	89.69 % / 10.25 %	68	B	83.0 % / 15.18 %
5	C	82.1 % / 13.24 %	21	B	87.06 % / 11.32 %	37	C	86.26 % / 12.09 %	53	B	82.19 % / 16.46 %	69	A	80.27 % / 18.35 %
6	D	82.69 % / 14.39 %	22	A	81.31 % / 13.6 %	38	D	78.26 % / 11.65 %	54	D	86.15 % / 11.67 %	70	D	77.55 % / 17.42 %
7	A	84.19 % / 14.75 %	23	D	88.45 % / 11.09 %	39	C	86.87 % / 10.34 %	55	B	79.08 % / 18.73 %	71	D	89.74 % / 10.24 %
8	C	87.18 % / 11.96 %	24	A	79.11 % / 10.05 %	40	B	79.64 % / 19.23 %	56	B	85.58 % / 11.35 %	72	D	86.74 % / 11.81 %
9	D	83.77 % / 10.66 %	25	D	78.79 % / 20.06 %	41	D	87.57 % / 12.23 %	57	A	87.04 % / 11.29 %	73	B	84.74 % / 14.62 %
10	B	80.96 % / 12.64 %	26	A	77.83 % / 18.5 %	42	D	77.39 % / 13.1 %	58	B	88.83 % / 10.01 %	74	D	89.1 % / 10.72 %
11	D	84.1 % / 12.73 %	27	C	80.08 % / 17.76 %	43	B	86.94 % / 12.26 %	59	C	79.03 % / 19.8 %	75	D	86.11 % / 12.27 %
12	C	78.62 % / 17.77 %	28	D	85.44 % / 10.87 %	44	C	77.55 % / 17.28 %	60	A	84.58 % / 14.68 %	76	C	85.32 % / 10.89 %
13	B	86.4 % / 12.38 %	29	B	85.45 % / 14.48 %	45	C	85.45 % / 12.6 %	61	A	84.71 % / 10.22 %	77	A	87.17 % / 10.73 %
14	C	80.26 % / 13.72 %	30	A	86.36 % / 10.39 %	46	A	89.04 % / 10.21 %	62	A	78.11 % / 13.7 %	78	D	80.58 % / 15.16 %
15	A	82.87 % / 14.44 %	31	C	88.64 % / 10.86 %	47	B	81.06 % / 15.35 %	63	A	87.78 % / 11.52 %	79	D	79.69 % / 16.83 %
16	C	88.54 % / 10.78 %	32	C	79.23 % / 13.25 %	48	B	86.62 % / 10.33 %	64	B	85.9 % / 12.78 %	80	B	80.2 % / 10.42 %

Q.	Ans.	Correct	Skipped
81	B	76.67 %	10.7 %
82	C	81.83 %	15.17 %
83	C	83.03 %	12.33 %
84	D	88.5 %	11.4 %

Q.	Ans.	Correct	Skipped
85	A	87.14 %	10.87 %
86	C	82.27 %	12.43 %
87	A	76.41 %	14.55 %
88	C	81.47 %	11.61 %

Q.	Ans.	Correct	Skipped
89	D	79.01 %	10.39 %
90	A	77.01 %	10.92 %
91	D	77.65 %	21.72 %
92	A	86.73 %	11.89 %

Q.	Ans.	Correct	Skipped
93	A	87.24 %	10.64 %
94	C	79.38 %	17.95 %
95	C	88.35 %	10.95 %
96	B	83.84 %	11.69 %

Q.	Ans.	Correct	Skipped
97	D	81.01 %	18.35 %
98	C	80.86 %	14.49 %
99	C	81.48 %	16.07 %
100	A	81.5 %	15.86 %

//Hints and Solutions//

1. $\sin\theta + \sin^2\theta = 1 \Rightarrow \sin\theta = \cos^2\theta$

Given : $\cos^{12}\theta + 3\cos^{10}\theta + 3\cos^8\theta + \cos^6\theta - 1$

$= (\cos^4\theta + \cos^2\theta)^3 - 1 = (\sin^2\theta + \cos^2\theta)^3 - 1 = 1 - 1 = 0$

2. Height = $4\sqrt{3}$ cm

Thus, side of equilateral triangle = 8 cm

$$\left(\tan 60^\circ = \frac{h}{side/2}\right)$$

Area of equilateral triangle = $\dfrac{\sqrt{3}}{4} \times 8^2 = 16\sqrt{3}$ cm²

3. 10 Men can do the work in 6 days

If the work is to be finished in 5 days, number of women required = 15

If the work is to be finished in 6 days, number of women required = [15×5]/6 = 25/2

So that 10 men = 25/2 women

or 5 women = 4 men

8 men + 5 women = 8 men + 4 men = 12 men

Now 10 men can finish the work in = 6 days

∴ 12 men can finish the work in [6×10]/12=5 days

4.

$$\frac{n_1 A_1 + n_2 A_2}{n_1 + n_2}$$

$$= \frac{2 \cdot 8 + 3 \cdot 3}{2 + 3} = \frac{16 + 9}{5}$$

$$\Rightarrow \frac{25}{5} = 5.$$

5.

$$A = \frac{1}{\sqrt{2}+\sqrt{3}+\sqrt{5}}$$

$$= \frac{(\sqrt{2}+\sqrt{3})-\sqrt{5}}{(\sqrt{2}+\sqrt{3}+\sqrt{5})(\sqrt{2}+\sqrt{3}-\sqrt{5})}$$

$$= \frac{\sqrt{2}+\sqrt{3}-\sqrt{5}}{(\sqrt{2}+\sqrt{3})^2-(\sqrt{5})^2}$$

$$= \frac{(\sqrt{2}+\sqrt{3})-\sqrt{5}}{(2\sqrt{6})}$$

$$= \frac{\sqrt{12}+\sqrt{18}-\sqrt{30}}{12}$$

$$= \frac{2\sqrt{3}+3\sqrt{2}-\sqrt{30}}{12}$$

6.

Using pythagorus theorem

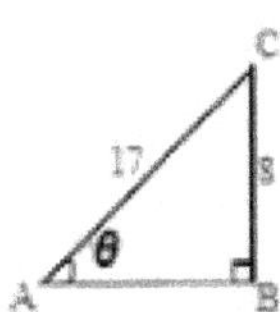

$AC^2 = AB^2 + BC^2$

$(17)^2 = AB^2 + (8)^2$

$AB^2 = 289 - 64$

$AB = \sqrt{225}$.

$AB = 15$

$\therefore \tan\theta = \dfrac{8}{15}$ and $\sec\theta = \dfrac{17}{15}$.

$\therefore \tan\theta + \sec\theta = \dfrac{8}{15} + \dfrac{17}{15} = \dfrac{25}{15} = \dfrac{5}{3}$

7.

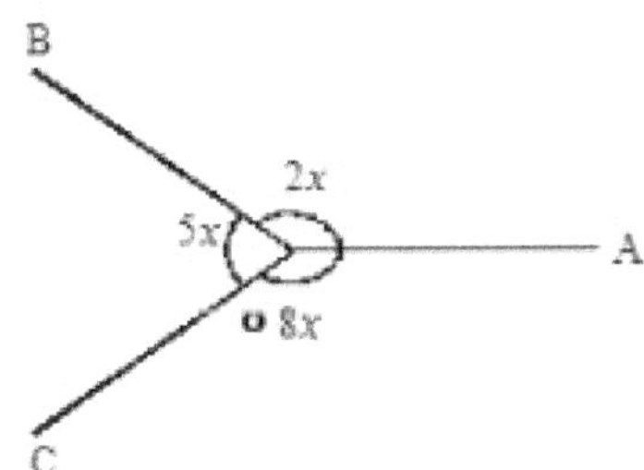

$2x + 5x + 8x = 360^\circ$

$15x = 360^\circ$

$x = \dfrac{360^\circ}{15} = 24^\circ$

8. tan 31°. tan 32°. tan 33° .... tan 59°
= tan 31°.tan 32°. tan 33° ... tan 57°. tan 58°. tan 59°= tan 31°. tan 32°. tan 33° ... cot 33°. cot 32°. cot 31° = 1[tan (90°-θ) = cotθ and tanθ cotθ =1]

9.

$$\left(x^{\frac{1}{4}}-1\right)\left(x^{\frac{1}{4}}+1\right)=\left(x^{\frac{1}{4}}\right)^2 -(1)^2$$

$$x^{\frac{1}{2}} -1=(81)^{\frac{1}{2}} -1=9-1=8$$

10. SP1 = 12000

profit = 20%

∴ CP1 = 12000/120 x 100 = Rs.10,000

SP2 = 12000

Loss % = 20%

∴ CP = 12000/80 x 100 = Rs.15,000

Total CP = 25000

Total SP = 24000

Loss = Rs.25000 − Rs.24000 = Rs.1000

(or)

If the selling price of the two items is equal and the percentage of profit on one equals the percentage of loss on the other, then, the result is always loss and the percentage of loss is (loss%2/100).

Hence, in the present case, loss percentage = (20)2/100 percent = 4%.

Loss = 4/96 × Rs.24000 = Rs.1000

11.
Distance travelled in one hour = 48 km.

∴ Distance travelled in 50 minutes $= \dfrac{48}{60} \times 50 = 40$ km.

Time to be reduced is 40 min. $= \dfrac{40}{60}$ hr

Required speed $= \dfrac{40}{40/60} = \dfrac{40 \times 60}{40} = 60$ km/hr

12.
∴ $60° = ₹8000$

∴ Total expenditure

$300° = \dfrac{8000}{60} \times 300 = ₹40,000$

Expenditure on education

$= \dfrac{30}{300} \times 40,000 = ₹4000$

13. Expenditure on food

=(120/300)×40,000=₹16,000

Required ratio = 16000 : 8000 ⇒ 2 : 1

14. Volume of cone = 1/3πr2h

=(1/3)×π×(20)²×10

=400×10

=(π/3)×4000=(4000/3)π

Volume of spherical balls = 4/3πr³

=(4/3)×π×(2)²

= 32/3π

∴ Spherical balls are formed from the cones.

∴ Total volume of all spherical cones = Volume of cones.

∴ No. of spherical balls = Volume of cone/Vol of 1 spherical ball

=4000/3

=32/3

=4000/32=125

15. The sum of the other two sides of a triangle is always greater than the third side.

16.

Clearly △ADE and △ABC are similar

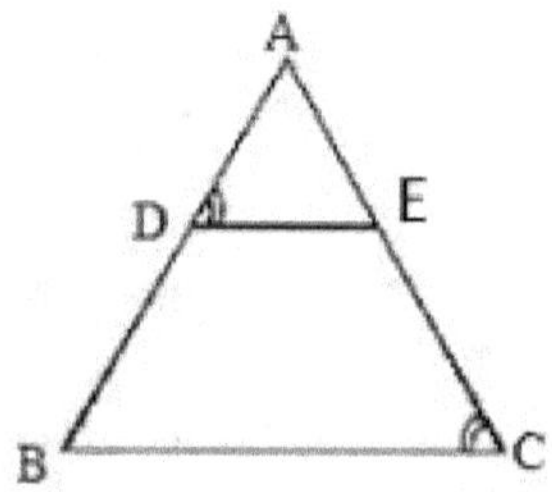

∴ $\dfrac{AD}{AC} = \dfrac{AE}{AB}$

AD. AB = AE. AC

17.
The speed of boat in still water$= \frac{1}{2}$(Rate downstream + Rate upstream)

The speed of boat in still water $= \frac{1}{2}(15+9) = \dfrac{24}{2} = 12$ km/hr.

18.
$\dfrac{x}{y} = \dfrac{3}{4}$ (Given)

$\dfrac{5x-2y}{7x+2y} = \dfrac{5\left(\frac{x}{y}\right)-2}{7\left(\frac{x}{y}\right)+2}$

$= \dfrac{5\times\frac{3}{4}-2}{7\times\frac{3}{4}+2} = \dfrac{\frac{15-8}{4}}{\frac{21+8}{4}} = \dfrac{7}{29}$

19. Let fraction be x/y by given condition

$$x + y = 8 \qquad \dots\dots\dots (i)$$

and $\dfrac{x+2}{y+2} - \dfrac{x}{y} = \dfrac{4}{35}$

or $\dfrac{2x + 2y - xy - 2x}{y(y+2)} = \dfrac{4}{35}$

or $\dfrac{2(y-x)}{y(y+2)} \quad \dfrac{4}{35}$

or $35\ (y - x) = 2y\ (y + 2) \qquad \dots\dots (ii)$

from (i)

x = 8 - y

substituting this value in (ii)

35 (y - 8 + y) - 2y (y + 2)

35 (y - 4) = y (y + 2)

$y^2 - 33y + 140 = 0$

y= 28 or 5

We cant take 28, taking y=5, x will become 3

Therefore x/y = 3/5

20. S.I. = Rs 950, rate = 9.5%

time – 2 years

∴ sum =(950×100)/(9.5×2)=5000

If rate of interest is 10.5% then

Simple Interest=(5000×2×10.5)/100=Rs 1050

∴ additional interest due to change in rate of interest =Rs 100

21.

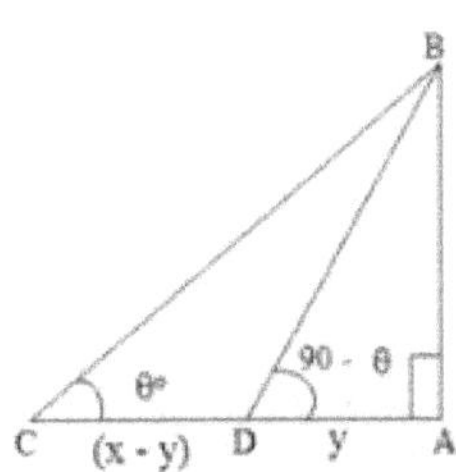

Let AB be tower and C and D be the point of observation on AC.
$\angle ACB = \theta$, $\angle ADB = 90 - \theta$, AB = h m
AC = X m, AD = Y m
So, CD = x – y m.
$\tan \theta = \dfrac{h}{x}$
And $\tan (90 - \theta) = \dfrac{h}{y}$
$\Rightarrow \dfrac{h}{x} \times \dfrac{h}{y} = 1$
$\Rightarrow h^2 = xy$
$\Rightarrow h = \sqrt{xy}$ m.

22. SP of first article = (46000×88)100=₹40,480

SP for second article = (40480×112)/100=₹45,337.60

∴ Loss = 46000 - 45337.60 = ₹662.40.

23. Let the cost price of cell phone be Rs. x

According to the question,

[(100+23)/100] × x = 7011

Or, x = (7011×100)/123 = 5700

24. Effective decrease

= [20 – 20 – 20×(20/100)] % = -4%

∴ Present cost of the article = 96% of Rs.75

= (75×96)/100 = Rs.72

25. Volume of rectangular box = 160 x 100 x 60 cm³

and volume of one cubical block = 20 x 20 x 20 cm³

∴ Required number of cubical block =
(160×100×60)/(20×20×20)   = 120 blocks

26. Volume

$= \dfrac{1}{3}\pi(r_1^2 + r_2^2 + r_1 r_2)\,h$

$= \dfrac{1}{3}\pi(14^2 + 7^2 + 98)\times 12$

$= \dfrac{1}{3} \times \dfrac{22}{7} \times \dfrac{12}{10}(14^2 + 7^2 + 98)$

$= 22 \times 4 \times 49 = 4312$ decimeter³

27.
Let length of another diagnol = 2x

Diagnols of rhombus intersect at right angles , so by using pythagorus theorem,

$x^2 + 12^2 = 20^2$

Therefore x = 16 , So diagonal = 2*16 =32

Area of rhombus

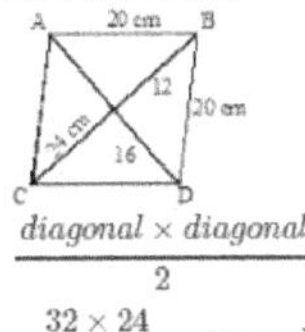

$\dfrac{diagonal \times diagonal}{2}$

$= \dfrac{32 \times 24}{2}$ = 384 cm²

28. Let the sides of rectangle be 2x, x cm

∴ Perimeter of rectangle = 2 (2x+x)

2 (2x+x) = 24

or 6x = 24

∴ x = 4 cm

hence length of diagonal = √[(2x)²+x²]

= √5x²

= √(5×16)

$=\sqrt{80}$

$= 4\sqrt{5}$

29. 1 man done work in 6×6×9 hours

Since 8W=6M=12B

therefore 12M+12W+12B=27M

therefore 27 men will do work in (6×6×9/27)=12 hours

=12/8=1.5 days

30. Let total number of candidates be x.

$\therefore$ 50x - 30 × 100 = 45x

$\Rightarrow$ 5x = 3000

$\Rightarrow$ x = 3000/5 = 600

31. As tune is in music; rhythm is in dance.

32. The given question set (64, 216, 125) is the perfect cube of (4, 6, 5). Similarly (8, 27, 64) is the perfect cube of (2, 3, 4).

33. Grandfather's child is father and son of a girl's father will be her brother.

34. 01357 → we are very happy   ....(i)

2639 → they are extremely lucky   ......(ii)

794 → happy and lucky   ......(iii)

from (i) and (ii)

3 → are

from (ii) and (iii)

9 → lucky

from (i) and (iii)

7 → happy

from (iii)

4 → and

from (i)

1, 5 → we, very

Hence, we cannot find exact code for 'very'.

35. Odd-placed letters are coded as two places forward and even-placed letters are coded as four places forward as in English alphabet.

36.

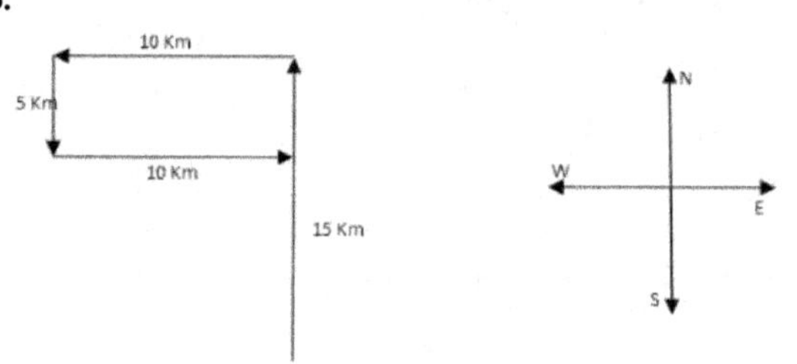

From the figure its clear that Laxman is in north of his house.

37. RUST

R– 57, 97, 99

U– 68, 78

S– 56, 58, 98

T– 59, 67

Therefore, the correct answer is option (3) i.e. 97, 68, 56, 59

39. Clearly, the meaning of the given symbols

X φ Y - Z ⇒ X < Y = Z

Using the proper notations/symbols in option (c), we get

X + Y × Z ⇒ X ≠ Y > Z ⇒ X < Y = Z

Therefore, X φ Y - Z ⇒ X + Y × Z.

40. Except MOTHER: TMPRHD, the rest of the group, follow the arrangement given below.

Pattern is-

S	U	N	D	A	Y
1	2	3	4	5	6

Y	A	D	S	U	N
6	5	4	1	2	3

41. Except in pair 33- 56, in all others the sum of digits of one number is equal to the sum of digits of all the second number.

42.

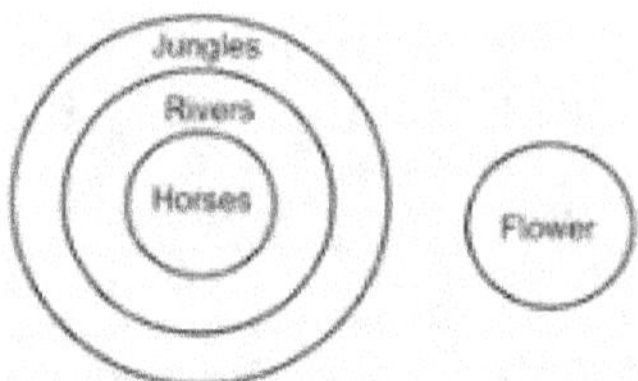

If both Conclusions I and II follow.

43. The given cyclic order series follows the pattern:

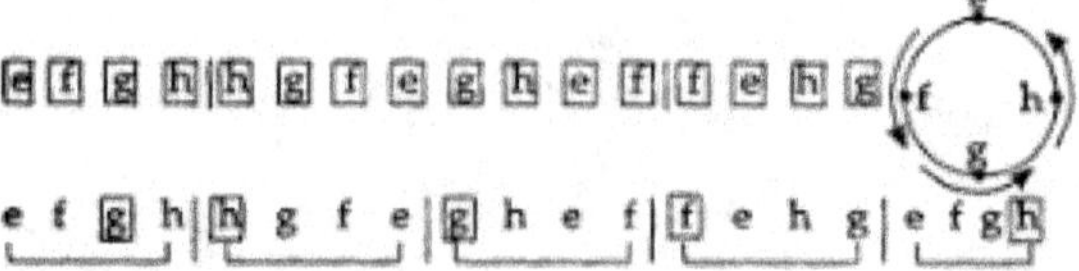

44. The sequence is A AB ABC ABCD.........

45. The number of illiterate youths and who have a job are three.

46. The numbers obtained by squaring the numbers at the bottom are combined together physically to get the number in the upper part.

47. The given figure contains numbers 1 to 6 in three alternate segments, the smaller number being towards the outside and the numbers 14 to 19 in the remaining three alternate segments with the smaller number towards the inside.

48.

T L F W water

L T F M (water image)

49.

50. In all other figures, the number of pins at the top of the figure are equal to the number of sides of the figure.

51. Using the letters of the given word, the word 'LIZARD' cannot be formed.

52.

+	=	×		×	=	÷
−	=	+		÷	=	−

Given expression is

$$20 - 5 \div 18 \times (3 + 2) = ?$$

After conversions:

$$? = 20 + 5 - 18 \div (3 \times 2)$$
$$\text{or, } ? = 20 + 5 - 18 + 6$$
$$\text{or, } ? = 20 + 5 - 3$$
$$\text{or, } ? = 25 - 3 = 22$$

53. 1977 is an ordinary year. We know that the calendar of an ordinary year repeats after 6 yrs or 11 yrs.

Year	Number of odd days
1978	1
1979	1
1980	2
1981	1
1982	1
1983	1
1984	2
1985	1
1986	1
1987	1

1988	2

Therefore,

Number of odd days from 18.09.1977 to 18.09.1983=7, i.e., 0 odd day

It means that in 1983, 18th September would fall on Sunday.

and number of odd days from 18.09.1977 to 18.09.1988 = 14, i.e., 0 odd day.

Now, it is clear that 2 marriage anniversaries would fall on Sunday in the next 15 yr.

54. When Rohini and Mihika interchange their places, then Rohini becomes on 18th place, it means Rohini who was on the 12th place comes at the 6th place after crossing 5 places. Therefore, there are 5 girls between Rohini and Mihika. So, the total number of the girls in the row = (18 + 9) -1 = 26 or (15 + 12) − 1 = 26.

55. 'H' represents those clerks who are graduates and have government job.

56. The first viceroy of India was lord Cannings. After the mutiny of 1857, the title of viceroy was created in 1858. Before 1858, it was East India Company who was ruling large parts of India and the head of administration of the East India Company was called Governor general. This office was created in 1773 (by regulating act)

57. 15th edition of Pravasi conference will be held in Varanasi close to the site of 'Ardh Kumbh'.

58. The Constitution provides that the maximum strength of the House be 552 members. up to 525 members represent of the territorial constituencies in States, up 20 members represent the Union Territories and no more than two members from Anglo-Indian community can be nominated by the President of Indian if he or she feels that the community is not adequately represented.

59. The fifty-second Amendment 1985, inserted the Tenth Schedule in the constitution regarding provisions as to disqualification on the grounds of defection.

60. Kangchenjunga is the highest peak of India.

61. The Union Cabinet chaired by the Prime Minister Shri Narendra Modi has approved establishment and operationalistion of permanent campuses of the two new Indian Institutes of Science Education & Research (IISERs) at Tirupati (Andhra Pradesh) and Berhampur (Odisha).

62. The older alluvium is called the Bhangar

63. The Ashta Pradhan was a council of minisless that administered the Maratha empire.

64. Godavari is considered the Dhakshin (Southern) Ganga and it is the largest river of the peninsular India. It rises near Nasik in Maharashtra.

65. Money Bills are described in the Article 110

66. Rabindranath Tagore (1861-1941) was a poet, philosopher, educationist, artist and social activist. In 1913, he was awarded the Nobel Prize in Literature. He was the first person of non-Western heritage to be awarded a Nobel Prize.

67. Iltutmish established a centre of learning at Patna.

68. Mahadev hills

The Tapti River is one of the major rivers of peninsular India with a length of around 724 kilometres (450 mi). It is one of only three rivers in peninsular India that run from east to west - the others being the Narmada River and the Mahi River. The river rises in the eastern Satpura Range of southern Madhya Pradesh state, and flows westward, draining Madhya Pradesh's Nimar region, Maharashtra's Kandesh and east Vidarbha regions in the northwest corner of the Deccan Plateau and south Gujarat, before emptying into the Gulf of Cambay of the Arabian Sea, in the Surat District of Gujarat. The river, along with the northern parallel Narmada River, form the boundaries between North and South India. The Western Ghats or Sahyadri range starts south of the Tapti River near the border of Gujarat and Maharashtra. The Tapti (Tapi) River empties into the Gulf of Khambhat near the city of Surat in Gujarat.

69. World Tsunami Awareness Day is being observed today across the world, including Pakistan, aiming at minimizing the number of people affected by disasters worldwide.

70. The 46th "Know India Programme" in March, 2018 was held in New Delhi.

71. If the gravitational acceleration at any place is doubled, then the weight of body will be 2g

72. Rhododendron /ˌroʊdəˈdɛndrən/ (from Ancient Greek ῥόδον rhódon "rose" and δένδρον déndron "tree") is a genus of 1,024 species of woody plants in the heath family (Ericaceae), either evergreen or deciduous, and found mainly in Asia, although it is also widespread throughout the highlands of the Appalachian Mountains of North America. It is the national flower of Nepal as well as the state flower of West Virginia and Washington. Most species have brightly coloured flowers which bloom from late winter through to early summer.[Rhododendron /ˌroʊdəˈdɛndrən/ (from Ancient Greek ῥόδον rhódon "rose" and δένδρον déndron "tree") is a genus of 1,024 species of woody plants in the heath family (Ericaceae), either evergreen or deciduous, and found mainly in Asia, although it is also widespread throughout the highlands of the Appalachian Mountains of North America. It is the national flower of Nepal as well as the state flower of West Virginia and Washington. Most species have brightly coloured flowers which bloom from late winter through to early summer.
If at high altitudes, birds become rare, the plants likely to disappear are Rhododendron

73. In blanking operation clearance is provided on punch

74. In graphite, electrons are generally spread out between the structure.

75. Focal length of a convex lens is maximum for Red light.

76. Diamond is very hard. The hardness of diamond is due to the structure of its carbon atoms. In diamond each carbon atom is bonded to four other carbon atoms which forms giant, three dimensional structure.

77. Room temperature usually taken as being 25°C, at this temperature, fluorine and chlorine are gases, bromine is a liquid, and iodine and astatine are solids.

78. The formula of Plaster of Paris is $2CaSO_4, H_2O$

79. A body moving at constant speed in a circular path experience an acceleration directed towards the centre of the circular path. This acceleration is called a centripetal acceleration and is provided by a centripetal force. In the circular motion situation, even if the speed is constant the acceleration changes all the time as the direction keeps on changing.

80. In a National Park protection is provided to flora and fauna

81. If we throw a Stone with some speed in a horizontal direction it follows a curved path as it falls to the ground.

82. Radar is used to Detect and locate distant objects.

83. As we move down the group in the periodic table, metallic character increases.

84. Wrought iron:

Wrought Iron is the purest form Iron. It contains 0.12–0.25 carbon.

85.

Molecular mass of H_2SO_3 sum of individual atomic masses

$$= 2 \times 1 + 1 \times 32 + 3 \times 16 = 82$$

86. Caustic soda is a solution of Sodium hydroxide (NaOH) in water. It is a strong base with a wide range of applications in different industries. We produce caustic soda together with chlorine and hydrogen from the electrolysis of salt brine.

87. In wind power, Kinetic energy form of energy is converted into electrical energy.

88. Hygrometer is used for measuring relative humidity

90. Acetic acid : Vinegar is a liquid consisting of about 5–20% acetic acid (CH3COOH), water, and other chemicals, which may include flavorings.

91. Diesel doesn't ignite so well, but burns much better through compression. Petrol engines inject the air/fuel mixture and then use spark plugs to ignite the mixture just after a piston reaches top dead centre. Diesel engines compress air, and then add air/fuel mixture. As a result they run hotter. So Dark and black smoke will be produced

92. Electricity is produced through dry cell from Chemical energy.

93. X-rays were discovered by Wilhelm Conrad Roentgen

94. Electron was discovered by J J Thomson

95. The unit of solid angle is 9.46×10^8 km

96. Asbestos sheet roofs provide better protection against fire

97. PNG is mainly methane'CH4 with a small percentage of other higher hydrocarbons. The ratio of carbon to hydrogen is least in methane hence it burns almost completely making, it the cleanest fuel. Domestic 'PNG customers, also known as

Residential customers, use gas for cooking purpose and also for heating water tough gas geysers.

98. The ionosphere is mainly composed of Electrons and positive ions.

99. Hydraulic brakes work on the principle of Pascal's law which states that "pressure at a point in a fluid is equal in all directions in space". According to this law when pressure is applied on a fluid it travels equally in all directions so that uniform braking action is applied on all four wheels. The hydraulic brake is an arrangement of braking mechanism which uses brake fluid, typically containing ethylene glycol, to transfer pressure from the controlling unit, which is usually near the operator of the vehicle, to the actual brake mechanism, which is usually at or near the wheel of the vehicle.

100. Mitochondria is called the Power house' of cell.

Mathematics

Q.1 DIRECTIONS: The pie-chart, given here, shows various expenses of a publisher in the production and sale of a book. Study the chart and answer question based on it.

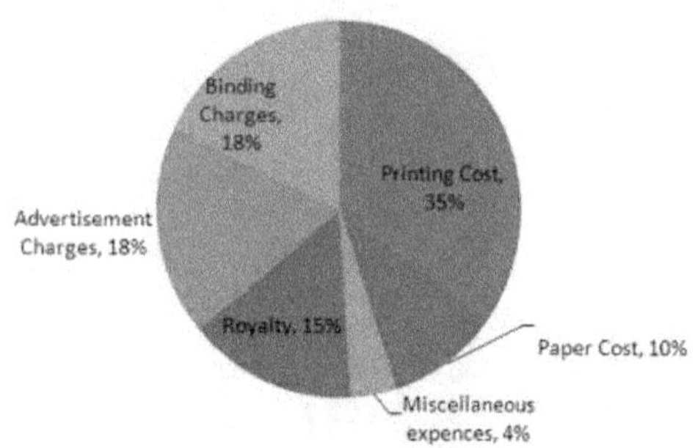

The measure of central angle for the sector on 'Printing cost' is:

A. 126°   **B.** 70°   **C.** 63°   **D.** 35°

Q.2 DIRECTIONS: The pie-chart, given here, shows various expenses of a publisher in the production and sale of a book. Study the chart and answer question based on it.

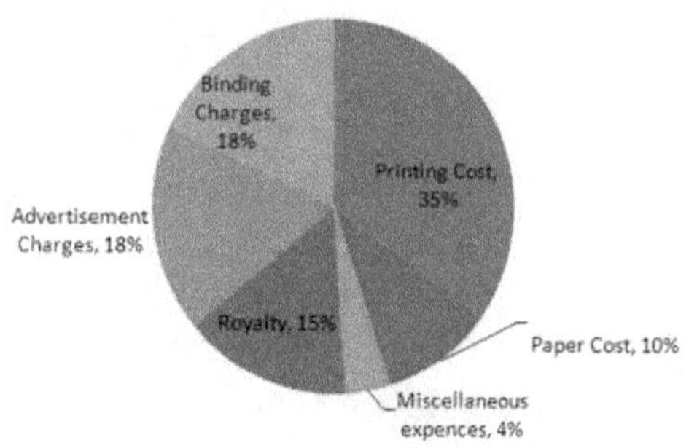

The difference between the measures of central angles of sectors for binding charges and advertisement charges is:

A. 180°   **B.** 90°   **C.** 18°   **D.** 0°

Q.3 Find the angle of elevation of the sun, if the length of the shadow of a pole is $1/\sqrt3$ times its height?

A. $\pi/6$ **B.** $2\pi/3$ **C.** $\pi/9$ **D.** $\pi/3$

Q.4 If the point (x, y) (1, 2) and (-3, 4) are collinear, then :

A. x + 2y - 5 = 0   **B.** x+y - 1 = 0
C. 2x+y-4 = 0   **D.** 2x - y + 10 = 0

Q.5 The dimensions of a piece of iron in the shape of a cuboid are 270 cm x 100 cm x 64 cm. If it is melted and recast into a cube, then the surface area of the cube will be :

A. 14400 cm²   **B.** 44200 cm²
C. 57600 cm²   **D.** 86400 cm²

Q.6 The average age of a family of five persons is 20 years. If the youngest member is 8 years old then, what was the average age of the family at the birth time of the youngest member.

A. 12 years   **B.** 15 years   **C.** 18 years   **D.** 16 years

Q.7 If a train takes 1.75 sec to cross a telegraph pole and 1.5 sec to a cyclist travelling in opposite direction at 10 m per second, then the length of the train is:

A. 135 m   **B.** 125 m   **C.** 115 m   **D.** 105 m

Q.8 The semi-perimeter of a right angled triangle ABC is 12 cm and the shortest median is 5 cm. What is area of the triangle which has the largest median of triangle ABC as its longest side?

A. $\sqrt{(73)}$ cm²   **B.** 10 cm²
C. 12 cm²   **D.** None of these

Q.9 If $4 \sin^2 x - 3 = 0, 0 < x < 2\pi$, then the values of x are:

A. 30°, 120°, 210°, 330°
B. 30°, 150°, 240°, 300°
C. 60°, 120°, 240°, 300°
D. 60°, 150°, 270°, 330°

Q.10 Sum of the lengths of any two sides of a triangle is always greater than

A. The third side of the triangle
B. Bigger side of the triangle
C. Lesser side of the triangle
D. None of these

Q.11 If 391 bananas were distributed among three monkeys in the ratio 1/2:2/3 :3/4, how many bananas did the first monkey get?

A. 102   **B.** 108   **C.** 112   **D.** 104

Q.12 A is twice as good as B and is therefore able to finish a piece of work in 30 days less than B. In how many days they can complete the whole work working together?

A. 18   **B.** 19   **C.** 20   **D.** 25

Q.13 A dishonest fruit seller sells fruits at 5% loss. If he uses 850 gm weight in place of 1 kg weight, then what is his profit percent?

A. 11(13/17)%   **B.** 11(12/17)%
C. 11.5%   **D.** 12%

Q.14 A man calculates his loss% as 16 (2/3)% on S.P. What is the actual loss percent?

A. 14(2/7)%   **B.** 15(2/7)%
C. 20(1/7)%   **D.** 18(1/7)%

Q.15 In the figure, OP ⊥ OA and OQ ⊥ OB.
Find ∠POQ if ∠AOB = 200

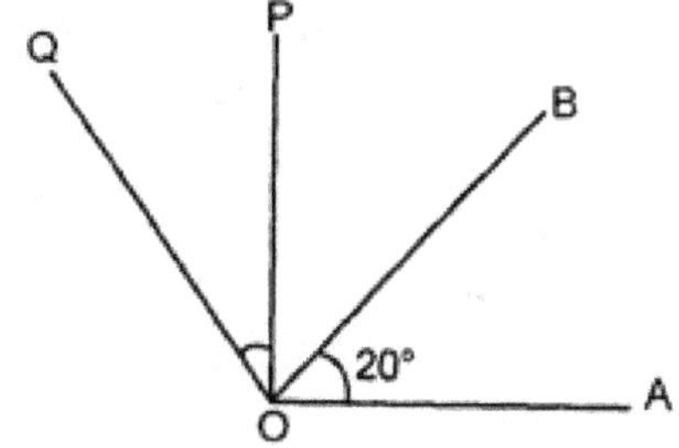

A. 20°

B. 30°

C. 40°

D. None of these

Q.16 If 2 men and 3 women can do a piece of work in 8 days and 3 men and 2 women in 7 days. In how many days can the work be done by 5 men and 4 women working together?

A. 4 days **B.** 5 days **C.** 10 days **D.** 15 days

Q.17 If the volume of a cube is 729 cm³, then the total surface area of the cube will be :

A. 486 cm² **B.** 476 cm² **C.** 466 cm² **D.** 456 cm²

Q.18 Two pipes A and B can fill a tank in 60 minutes and 75 minutes respectively. There is also an outlet C. If A, B and C are opened together, the tank is full in 50 minutes. How much time will be taken by C to empty the full tank?

A. 90 minutes **B.** 100 minutes

C. 120 minutes **D.** 110 minutes

Q.19 If 10 persons can do a job in 20 days. Then 20 persons with the twice efficiency can do the same job in:

A. 10 **B.** 20 **C.** 5 **D.** 15

Q.20 A sum of Rs.1,075 is divided among Aman, Anu and Aradhya such that Aman receives 25% more than Aradhya and Aradhya receive 25% less than Anu. What is Aman's share in the amount?

A. Rs.375 **B.** Rs.425 **C.** Rs.400 **D.** Rs.450

Q.21 The horizontal distance between two towers is 90 m and the angular depression of the top of the first as seen from the top of the second is 30o. Find the difference of the heights of the two towers.

A. 30 meters. **B.** 30√4meters.

C. 30√3meters. **D.** 90 meters.

Q.22 If the ratio of the areas of two squares is 16 : 1, then the ratio of their perimeters is?

A. 4 : 1 **B.** 16 : 1 **C.** 1 : 3 **D.** 3 : 4

Q.23 If the ratio areas of two squares is 225 : 256, then the ratio of their perimeters is?

A. 225 : 256 **B.** 256 : 225

C. 15 : 16 **D.** 16 : 15

Q.24 The time duration of 1 hour 45 minutes is what percent of a day?

A. 7.218 **B.** 7.291 **C.** 8.3 **D.** 8.24

Q.25 Two circles of radii 4 cm each cuts each other such that each circle passes through the centre of each other. Thus, what is the length of the common chord?

A. 2√3 cm **B.** 4√3 cm **C.** 2√2cm **D.** 8 cm

Q.26 In ΔABC, medians BE and CF intersect at G. If the straight line AGD meets BC at D in such a way that GD = 1.5 cm, then, length of AD is:

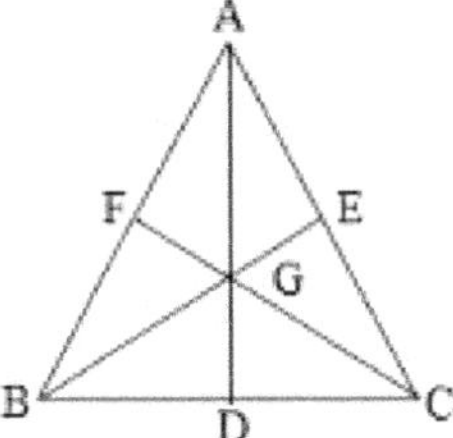

A. 2.5 cm **B.** 3 cm **C.** 4 cm **D.** 4.5 cm

Q.27 If two person A and B start at the same time in opposite direction from two points and after passing each other they complete the journey in a and b hours respectively, then the ratio of A's and B's speed will be:

A. √a : √b **B.** √b: √a

C. √a + √b: √a - √b **D.** None of these

Q.28

If $\sqrt{\dfrac{x}{0.0064}} = \sqrt[3]{0.008}$, the value of x is :

A. 0.256 **B.** 0.0256

C. 0.000256 **D.** 0.00256

Q.29 Students of a class stand in a queue. If Ramesh is 19th in order from both ends. How many students are there in the queue?

A. 20 **B.** 37 **C.** 38 **D.** 39

Q.30

If $\left(\dfrac{a}{b}\right)^{x-1} = \left(\dfrac{b}{a}\right)^{x-3}$,then the value of x is:

A. 1 **B.** 2 **C.** 3 **D.** -1

General Intelligence & Reasoning

Q.31 If in the word EMBLAZONER the position of the first and the sixth letters are interchanged, the second and seventh letters are interchanged and so on upto the fifth and the tenth letters. Then which will be the fourth letter from the left end after interchange ?

A. M **B.** E **C.** O **D.** L

Q.32 The diagram given below represents owner-broker and worker. Identify the region which represents all the three i.e. owner, broker and worker.

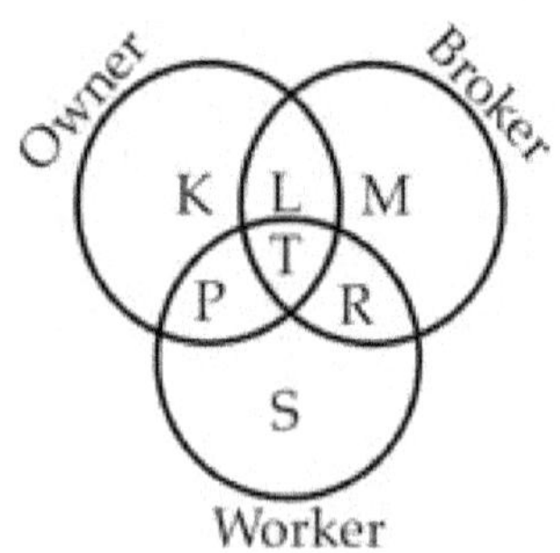

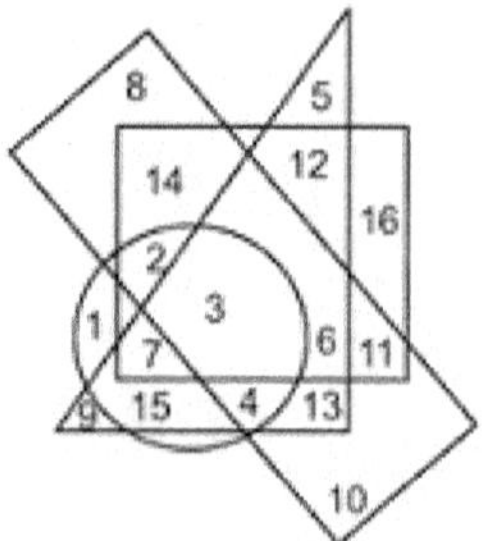

A. L   **B.** T   **C.** P   **D.** R

Q.33 DIRECTIONS: A jeweler has five diamond stones, each having a different weight.

Statement (a): Stone D weighs twice as much as stone E.

Statement (b): Stone E weighs four and one-half times as much as stone F.

Statement (c): Stone F weighs half as much as stone G.

Statement (d): Stone G weighs half as much as stone H.

Statement (e): Stone H weighs less than stone D but more than stone F.

Which of the following is the lightest in weight?

A. Stone D   **B.** Stone E   **C.** Stone F   **D.** Stone G

Q.34 In the following question, select the related letter/word/number from the given alternatives.

QDXM: SFYN :: UIOZ:

A. PAQM   **B.** LPWA   **C.** QNLA   **D.** WKPA

Q.35 DIRECTIONS: In the question below, there are few statements followed by few conclusions. You have to take the given statements to be true even if they seem to be at variance with commonly known facts and then decide which of the given conclusion logically follow(s) from the given statements.

Statements:

All books are eyes.

Some eyes are pens.

All pens are pencils.

Conclusions:

I. Some pencils are books.

II. Some pencils are eyes.

A. If only Conclusion I follows

B. If only Conclusion II follows

C. If either Conclusion I or II follows.

D. If neither Conclusion I nor II follows.

Q.36 DIRECTIONS: Study the following diagram and answer the questions that follow.

a. The rectangle represents men.

b. Circle represents graduates.

c. Triangle represents skilled persons.

d. Square represents employed persons.

The skilled employed men who are graduates are-

A. Only 12   **B.** Only 3   **C.** Only 9   **D.** 3 and 11

Q.37 Ram went 15 km to the West from my house then turned left and walked 20 km. He then turned East and walked 25 km and finally turning left covered 20 km. How far was he from my house ?

A. 5 km   **B.** 10 km   **C.** 40 km   **D.** 80 km

Q.38 There are 30 plants of Badam, Banana, Apple and Pomegranate in a row. There is one pair of Pomegranate plants after Badam and Banana and Pomegranate plants are followed by one Badam and one Apple plant and so on. If the row begins with a plant of Badam, then which of the following will be the last in the row?

A. Banana   **B.** Pomegranate

C. Badam   **D.** Apple

Q.39 Three of the following four are alike in a certain way and so form a group. Which is the one that does not belong to that group?

A. 115   **B.** 161   **C.** 253   **D.** 345

Q.40 A cage has 21 rabbits .All but 14 died. How many rabbits were left in the cage?

A. 7   **B.** 14   **C.** 9   **D.** Nil

Q.41 Find the missing term:

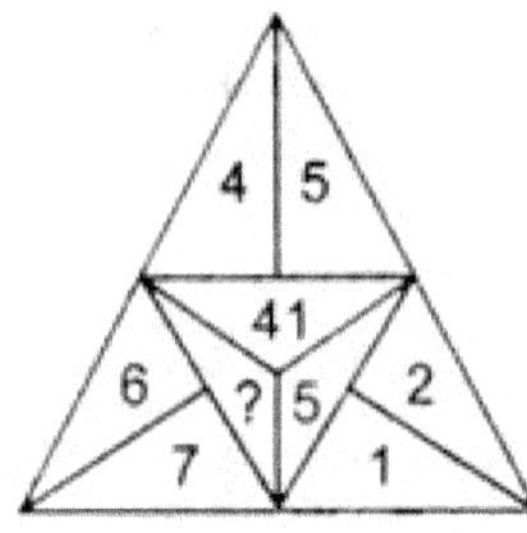

A. 16   **B.** 9   **C.** 85   **D.** 112

Q.42 In the following question, select the related letter/word/number from the given alternatives.

MUTE : MOUNTAIN

A. Roaring: Ocean   **B.** Drizzle: Stream

C. Sound : Reflection   **D.** Affection: Mother

Q.43 DIRECTIONS: A word is represented by only one set of numbers as given in anyone of the alternatives. The set of numbers given in the alternatives are represented by two classes of alphabets as in the 2 matrices given below. The columns and rows of Matrix I are from 0 to 4 and that of Matrix II from 5 to 9. A letter can be represented first by its row and next by its column number. e.g., 'C' can be represented by 02, 21, etc. 'T' can be represented by 65, 96 etc. Similarly, you have to identify the correct set for the word given below.

"ADJUST"

Matrix I

	0	1	2	3	4
0	D	V	C	P	M
1	P	M	D	V	C
2	V	C	P	M	D
3	M	D	V	C	P
4	C	P	M	D	V

Matrix II

	5	6	7	8	9
5	S	A	U	T	J
6	T	J	S	A	U
7	A	U	T	J	S
8	J	S	A	U	T
9	U	T	J	S	A

A. 87, 31, 66, 69, 54, 89
B. 68, 12, 66, 58, 86, 65
C. 87, 31, 66, 69, 86,89
D. 75, 43, 97, 69, 86,79

Q.44 DIRECTIONS: Study the following information to answer the given questions
In a certain code:
'swords hidden in area' is written as 'white black yellow red'
'ready swords for attack' is written as 'grey pink red green'
'hidden for own safety' is written as 'silver grey violet white'
'own area under attack' is written as 'violet blue pink black'
'black pink yellow' could be a code for which of the following?
A. area in attack
B. swords for safety
C. under in area
D. own area safety

Q.45 Sanjay says, "I have as many sisters as brothers." Sarita says, "Each of us sisters has only half as many sisters as brothers." Assuming that Sanjay and Sarita are brother and sister, how many brothers and sisters are there in the family?
A. 6 brothers and 4 sisters
B. 4 brothers and 6 sisters
C. 3 brothers and 4 sisters
D. 4 brothers and 3 sisters

Q.46 DIRECTIONS: Read the following information carefully to answer the questions that follow.
A is the father of C, but C is not his son. E is the daughter of C. F is the spouse of A. B is the brother of C. D is the son of B. G is the spouse of B. H is the father of G.

Who is the son of F?
A. B
B. E
C. C
D. D

Q.47 DIRECTIONS: In the following question, continuous pattern series is given. Some of the letters of the series are missing. These missing letters are given in that order as one of the four alternatives below the series. Find out the correct alternatives.

n_pps_nsp_sn_sp_sn
A. pnpsn
B. nspnp
C. snnpn
D. snpnp

Q.48 DIRECTIONS:Solve the following series?
B2F, G4K, L12P, Q38U, ?
A. V118Z
B. V108Z
C. U118Z
D. Z108V

Q.49 DIRECTIONS: Choose the missing terms out of the given alternatives.
cx fu ir ? ol ri
A. lo
B. mn
C. no
D. op

Q.50 DIRECTIONS: Each of the following questions consists of five figures marked A, B, C, D and E if called the Problem figures followed by five other figures marked 1, 2, 3, and 4 called the 'Answer figures. Select a figure from amongst the Answer Figures which will continue the same series as established by the five Problem Figures.

Problem Figure

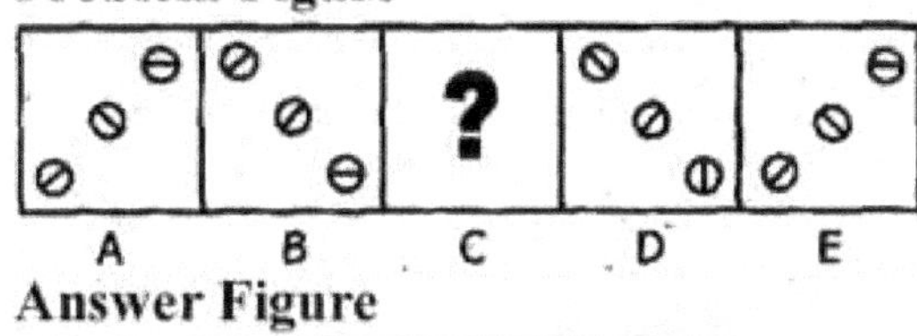

Answer Figure

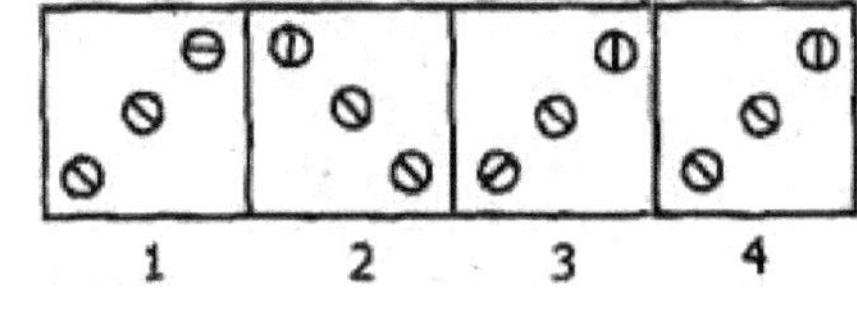

A. 1
B. 2
C. 3
D. 4

Q.51 DIRECTIONS: Find the Mirror image of the figure:

Main figure

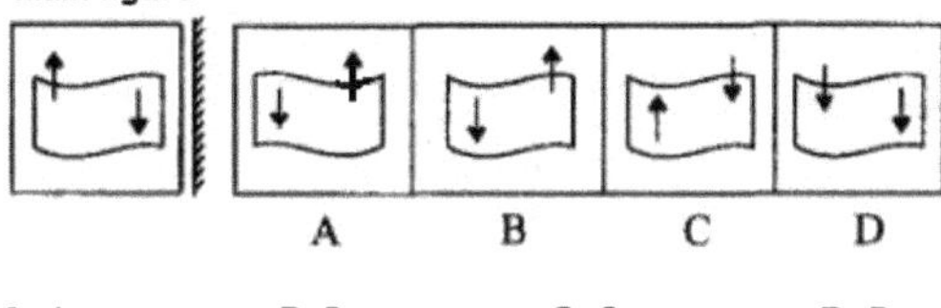

A. A
B. B
C. C
D. D

Q.52 DIRECTIONS: Each of the following questions consists of five figures marked A, B, C, D and E if called the Problem figures followed by five other figures marked 1, 2, 3, and 4 called the 'Answer figures. Select a figure from amongst the Answer Figures which will continue the same series as established by the five Problem Figures.

Problem Figure

T	⊣	?		
A	B	C	D	E

Answer Figure

1	2	3	4

A. 1   **B.** 2   **C.** 3   **D.** 4

Q.53 DIRECTIONS: Arrange the following words according to the English dictionary.
(a). Nature (b). Native (c). Narrate (d). Nascent (e). Naughty
A. (b), (d), (c), (a), (e)   **B.** (c), (d), (b), (a), (e)
C. (d), (a), (c), (e), (b)   **D.** (d), (b), (c), (e), (a)

Q.54 Arrange the following words according to the english dictionary.
(a) Haste (b) Haphazard (c) Host (d) Hang (e) Handkerchief
A. (b), (d), (a), (e), (c)   **B.** (e), (d), (b), (a), (c)
C. (d), (b), (a), (e), (c)   **D.** (b), (e), (a), (c), (d)

Q.55 How many pairs of letters are there in the word 'DABBLE' each of which has as many letters between them in the word as in the alphabet?
A. One   **B.** Two
C. Three   **D.** More than three

General Awareness

Q.56 Through which of the following states does the river Chambal flow?
A. U.P., M.P., Rajasthan
B. M.P., Gujarat, U.P.
C. Rajasthan, M.P., Biha
D. Gujarat. M.P., U.P

Q.57 Radcliffe Line was the boundary demarcation line between India and _________
A. China   **B.** Myanmar
C. Pakistan   **D.** None of the above

Q.58 How many members of the Rajya Sabha retire from the house every 2 years?
A. 1/6 of the total members
B. 1/3 of the total members
C. 1/12 of the total members
D. 5/6 of the total members

Q.59 Sports Minister Rajyavardhan Rathore and Minister of Culture, Sports and Tourism of South Korea _________ signed the MoU on cooperation in sports in New Delhi.
A. Do Jong-hwan   **B.** Ahn Do-hyun

C. Kim Hyun-mee   **D.** Shijo abe

Q.60 Which of the following sultans used to patronize Minhaj-us-Siraj?
A. Ruknuddin   **B.** Iltutmish
C. Balaban   **D.** Jalaluddin Khilji

Q.61 Whom does the President of India send his resignation to if he wants to quit his office?
A. Chief Justice of India
B. Prime Minister
C. Vice-President of India
D. Any of these

Q.62 Sultana Razia Begum was the daughter of :-
A. Balban
B. Qutub-ud-din Aibak.
C. Iltutmish
D. Rukh-ud –din

Q.63 The book "The God of small things" is written by :
A. Pupul Jayakar   **B.** Sobha De
C. Shekhar Kapoor   **D.** Arundhati Roy

Q.64 What is the rank of TCS in 100 most valuable U.S. brands
A. 58th   **B.** 59th   **C.** 60th   **D.** 61th

Q.65 Who was the Chairman of the first Finance Commission?
A. K C Niyogi   **B.** A K Chanda
C. K Santhanam   **D.** Y B Chavan

Q.66 Which of the following gases has the highest concentration in the atmosphere after nitrogen?
A. Oxygen   **B.** Nitrogen
C. Argon   **D.** Carbon dioxide

Q.67 Which of the following countries has become the second country to legalize the use of cannabis?
A. Uruguay   **B.** Canada   **C.** Australia   **D.** India

Q.68 The Qutub Minar was completed by the famous ruler.
A. Qutub-ud –din Aibak.
B. Iltutmish
C. Firoz shah Tuglaq.
D. Alauddin Khilji.

Q.69 Who has signed a MoU for establishing ROSHNI-Centre of Women Collectives led Social Action with Deendayal Antyodaya Yojana – National Rural Livelihood Mission (DAY-NRLM) and Ministry of Rural Development?
A. University of Delhi
B. Chandigarh College of Architecture
C. Indian Institute of Mass Communication
D. Lady Irwin College

Q.70 Jama Masjid was was built by -
A. Shah Jahan   **B.** Akbar
C. Jahangir   **D.** None of these

General Science

Q.71 Glass is made from the mixture of —
A. Quartz and mica **B.** Sand and salt
C. Sand and silicate **D.** None of these

Q.72 The unit of electrical power is
A. Volt **B.** Watt
C. Kilowatt hour **D.** Ampere

Q.73 RNA is found in—
A. Animal cell **B.** Plant cell
C. Virus **D.** All of the above

Q.74 Biodiversity act of India was passed by Parliament in
A. 1992 **B.** 1996 **C.** 2000 **D.** 2002

Q.75 Jim Corbette National Park is known for
A. Lions **B.** Tigers
C. Black Buck **D.** Rhino

Q.76 Which of the following is the best conductor of electricity ?
A. Copper **B.** Mica **C.** Zinc **D.** Silver

Q.77 According to Newton's .... law of motion - To every action there is an equal and opposite reaction.
A. First **B.** Second **C.** Third **D.** Fourth

Q.78 Foreign materials entering the cell, such as bacteria or food, as well as old organelles end up in the __________.
A. Vacuoles **B.** Mitochondria
C. Plastids **D.** Lysosomes

Q.79 Piezometer is used to measure
A. atmospheric pressure
B. very low pressure
C. very high pressure
D. difference in pressure between two points

Q.80 What is dry ice?
A. Liquid nitrogen
B. Water ice
C. Solid carbon dioxide
D. Frozen ethanol

Q.81 Rust is _
A. A mixture of $Fe2O_3$ and $Fe(OH)_2$
B. A mixture of FeO and $Fe(OH)_2$
C. FeO only
D. A mixture of Fe_2O_3, $3H_2 O$ and FeO

Q.82 The atmospheric gas which cannot produce green house effect is _____
A. N_2 **B.** H_2O **C.** CO_2 **D.** O_3

Q.83 Which of the following is not a bleaching agent?
A. Sulphur dioxide
B. Carbon dioxide
C. Sodium hypochlorite
D. Chlorine

Q.84 What is the Normal Blood Volume in human adult?
A. One litre **B.** Three litres
C. Five litres **D.** Seven litres

Q.85 Cotton fibers are made of —
A. Cellulose **B.** Starch
C. Protein **D.** Fats

Q.86 Wildlife is destroyed most when
A. There is lack of proper care
B. Mass scale hunting for foreign trade
C. Its natural habitat is destroyed
D. Natural calamity

Q.87 In drilling operation. the feed is expressed in:-
A. mn **B.** mm/sec
C. mm/minute **D.** mm/revolution

Q.88 Consider the group of atoms - O2-, F-, Ne, Na+
This group is an example of -
A. Isotopes **B.** Isobars
C. Isotones **D.** Isoelectronic

Q.89 What is laughing gas ?
A. Carbon dioxide **B.** Sulphur dioxide
C. Nitrogen Dioxide **D.** Nitrous oxide

Q.90 1A° is equal to
A. 10^{-7} mm **B.** 10^{-13} mm
C. 10^{-10} mm **D.** 10^{-6} mm

Q.91 The waves used in sonography are:
A. Micro waves **B.** Infra-red waves
C. Sound waves **D.** Ultrasonic waves

Q.92 The colours of stars depend on their
A. Temperature
B. Distance
C. Atmospheric pressure
D. Radius

Q.93 Which of the following is the most stable element?
A. Uranium **B.** Hydrogen
C. Oxygen **D.** Lead

Q.94 What is black hole?
A. Vacuum in space **B.** A dead star
C. A shooting star **D.** A spot in sun

Q.95 Who stated the equation $E = mc^2$?
A. Issac Newton **B.** Michael Faraday
C. Albert Einstein **D.** Marie Curie

Q.96 The electric field intensity on the surface of a charged conductor is
A. Zero
B. Directed normally to the surface
C. Directed tangentially to the surface
D. Directed along 45^0 to the surface

Q.97 The amount of light entering an eye is regulated by the-
A. Retina **B.** Optic nerve

C. Pupil   **D.** Cornea

Q.98 The nucleus of an atom consists of:-

A. Protons

B. Neutrons

C. Protons and neutrons

D. Protons, neutrons and electrons

Q.99 The capacitance unit of convenient size is

A. Farad   **B.** Microfarad

C. Kilo farad   **D.** Mega farad

Q.100 The amount of variation permitted in the size of a part is called

A. Allowance   **B.** Tolerance

C. Both (1) and (2)   **D.** Neither (1) nor (2)

// Smart Answer Sheet //

Correct Percentage of students who answered correctly. **Skipped** Percentage of students who skipped.

Q.	Ans.	Correct / Skipped	Q.	Ans.	Correct / Skipped	Q.	Ans.	Correct / Skipped	Q.	Ans.	Correct / Skipped	Q.	Ans.	Correct / Skipped
1	A	86.78 % / 10.2 %	17	A	86.68 % / 11.51 %	33	C	83.26 % / 15.51 %	49	A	80.53 % / 15.87 %	65	A	88.25 % / 10.82 %
2	D	81.8 % / 11.95 %	18	B	81.62 % / 13.87 %	34	D	86.79 % / 11.12 %	50	D	79.1 % / 20.79 %	66	A	78.69 % / 15.69 %
3	D	76.74 % / 18.08 %	19	C	87.47 % / 10.73 %	35	B	77.59 % / 11.84 %	51	A	84.17 % / 11.88 %	67	B	85.51 % / 10.69 %
4	A	83.2 % / 14.84 %	20	A	81.77 % / 16.73 %	36	B	78.76 % / 10.85 %	52	C	85.48 % / 14.32 %	68	B	86.26 % / 13.68 %
5	D	83.1 % / 11.22 %	21	C	79.31 % / 13.6 %	37	B	82.89 % / 11.95 %	53	B	87.38 % / 10.81 %	69	D	87.8 % / 11.69 %
6	B	79.41 % / 16.36 %	22	A	81.61 % / 15.43 %	38	D	89.07 % / 10.63 %	54	B	83.58 % / 15.99 %	70	A	86.96 % / 11.41 %
7	D	89.69 % / 10.15 %	23	C	89.53 % / 10.24 %	39	D	83.44 % / 15.84 %	55	D	80.83 % / 16.21 %	71	C	86.42 % / 10.01 %
8	C	82.3 % / 17.1 %	24	B	78.81 % / 19.0 %	40	B	88.55 % / 11.18 %	56	A	81.53 % / 11.03 %	72	B	80.97 % / 16.83 %
9	C	81.13 % / 11.43 %	25	B	79.91 % / 16.28 %	41	C	82.69 % / 10.31 %	57	C	77.38 % / 21.54 %	73	D	85.62 % / 10.82 %
10	A	76.4 % / 10.31 %	26	D	82.49 % / 15.8 %	42	A	88.04 % / 11.77 %	58	B	88.91 % / 10.16 %	74	D	78.38 % / 10.35 %
11	A	76.9 % / 13.93 %	27	B	82.71 % / 13.29 %	43	C	84.14 % / 11.75 %	59	A	85.52 % / 11.45 %	75	B	87.75 % / 10.5 %
12	C	76.4 % / 20.46 %	28	C	82.67 % / 14.36 %	44	A	86.32 % / 12.19 %	60	B	82.66 % / 11.25 %	76	D	76.1 % / 22.21 %
13	A	81.88 % / 11.8 %	29	B	82.67 % / 15.71 %	45	D	87.74 % / 12.25 %	61	C	84.39 % / 12.4 %	77	C	77.35 % / 10.64 %
14	A	85.83 % / 10.5 %	30	B	85.97 % / 11.59 %	46	A	76.26 % / 14.99 %	62	C	80.36 % / 13.93 %	78	D	79.97 % / 11.91 %
15	A	86.87 % / 10.33 %	31	B	89.53 % / 10.44 %	47	D	85.96 % / 13.82 %	63	D	88.37 % / 10.77 %	79	D	76.9 % / 11.78 %
16	A	83.57 % / 10.22 %	32	B	86.42 % / 13.35 %	48	A	82.15 % / 10.91 %	64	A	83.41 % / 10.64 %	80	C	81.61 % / 15.7 %

Q.	Ans.	Correct	Skipped
81	D	87.64 %	12.06 %
82	A	77.53 %	13.5 %
83	B	86.94 %	12.63 %
84	C	82.08 %	10.42 %

Q.	Ans.	Correct	Skipped
85	A	78.8 %	15.35 %
86	C	84.76 %	12.82 %
87	D	81.15 %	17.79 %
88	D	86.72 %	11.2 %

Q.	Ans.	Correct	Skipped
89	D	80.74 %	14.89 %
90	A	79.35 %	10.43 %
91	D	78.92 %	16.3 %
92	A	77.93 %	14.13 %

Q.	Ans.	Correct	Skipped
93	D	83.84 %	11.53 %
94	B	82.46 %	17.43 %
95	C	76.47 %	22.76 %
96	B	77.22 %	16.96 %

Q.	Ans.	Correct	Skipped
97	C	87.83 %	10.88 %
98	C	80.81 %	13.59 %
99	B	86.72 %	10.94 %
100	B	88.25 %	11.35 %

//Hints and Solutions//

1. According to question $360 \times 35/100 = 126°$

3.

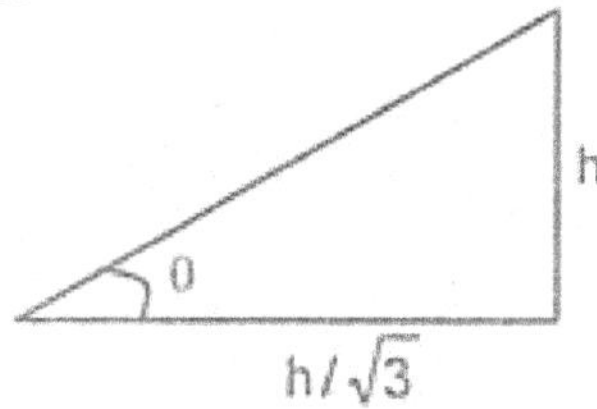

$$\tan\theta = \dfrac{h}{\dfrac{h}{\sqrt{3}}} = \sqrt{3} \Rightarrow \theta = 60° = \dfrac{\pi}{3}$$

4. If (x, y) (1, 2) and (-3, 4) are collinear then the triangle formed by points should be zero

$\therefore 1/2 [2x + 4 - 3y - 4x + 6 -y] = 0$

$-2x - 4y + 10 = 0$

$x + 2y - 5 = 0$

5. Volume of cube = volume of cuboid

$= 270 \times 100 \times 64 = 1728000$ cm^3

$\therefore$ Length of one side of the cube = 120 cm

$\therefore$ Surface area of cube $= 6 \times 120 \times 120 = 86400$ cm^2

6.
Sum of the age of family $= 5 \times 20 = 100$ years

8 years before, sum of Ages $= 100 - 8 \times 5 = 60$ years

Average age $= \dfrac{Sum}{Total\ person} = \dfrac{60}{4} = 15$ years

7.

Suppose speed of train = x m/s

or length of train = l m

Time taken by trains to cross a telegraph cost

$$= \dfrac{Length\ of\ train}{Speed\ of\ train}$$

$\therefore 1.75 = \dfrac{l}{x}$

or $x = \dfrac{l}{1.75}$ .... (i)

$\therefore 1.5 = \dfrac{l}{x + 10}$

or $x + 10 = \dfrac{l}{1.5}$ .... (ii)

Using (i) and (ii)

$\dfrac{l}{1.75} + 10 = \dfrac{l}{1.5}$

or $\dfrac{l}{1.5} - \dfrac{l}{1.75} = 10$

or $0.25\ l = 10 \times 1.5 \times 1.75$

$\therefore \dfrac{10 \times 1.5 \times 1.75}{0.25} - 105$ m

8.

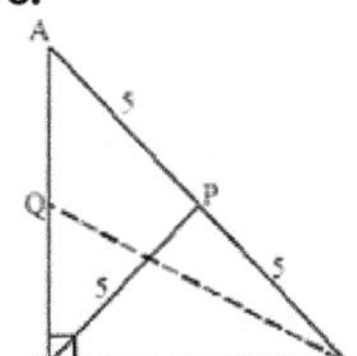

Given: S = 12 cm & BP = 5 cm

$\therefore$ AP = PC = BP = 5 cm

$\therefore$ AC = 10 cm

We know the ratio of Right triangle like (3:4:5)

then we assume the ratio, (6:8:10)

So, the other two sides = 8 cm, 6 cm

$\therefore$ Area of $\triangle$QBC $= \dfrac{1}{2} \times$ QB $\times$ BC $= \dfrac{1}{2} \times 4 \times 6 = 12$ cm^2

9.

$4 \sin^2 x - 3 = 0$

or $\sin^2 x = \dfrac{3}{4}$

$\therefore \ \sin x = \pm \dfrac{\sqrt{3}}{2}$

since $0 < x < 2\pi$

$\therefore \ \sin x = \pm \dfrac{\sqrt{3}}{2} = \sin 60°, \sin 120°, \sin 240°, \sin 300°$

10. The sum of the other two sides of a triangle is always greater than the third side.

11. The ratio: 1/2 :2/3 : 3/4

Converts to 6 : 8 : 9 (on multiplying by 12)

Thus, the first monkey would get (391/23) × 6 = 102 bananas.

12. Let A can complete the work in x days.

So, B can complete the work in 2x days.

A.T.Q., $2x - x = 30 \Rightarrow x = 30$ days

A ⟶ 30 days ⟍
           60 ⟋ 2 per day
B ⟶ 60 days ⟋   ⟍ 1 per day

They both can complete in = $\dfrac{60}{2+1}$ = 20 days.

13.

Let C.P. of 1000 gms = 100

S.P. of 850 gms

= 100 - L

= 100-5=95 (as 5% on 100 = 5)

S.P. of 1000 gms = $\dfrac{1000 \times 95}{850}$

$= \dfrac{1900}{17}$

$P\% = \dfrac{P}{C.P.} \times 100$

$= \dfrac{\dfrac{1900}{17} - 100}{100} \times 100$

$= \dfrac{1900 - 1700}{17} = \dfrac{200}{17} = 11\dfrac{13}{17}\%$

14.

$\text{Loss}\% = 16\dfrac{2}{3}\% = \dfrac{50}{3 \times 100} = \dfrac{1}{6} \rightarrow L$

S.P. = 6

LOSS = 1

then C.P. = 7 (as C.P. = S.P. + L)

$= \dfrac{1}{7} \times 100 = 14\dfrac{2}{7}\%$

15. ∠BOP = 90⁰ - ∠AOB

= 90⁰ - 70⁰

= 20⁰

∴ ∠POQ = 90⁰ - ∠BOP

= 90⁰ - 70⁰

=20⁰

16. |2 x 8 - 3 x 7| men's work = |3x 8 - 2 x 7| women's work.

∴ 5 men's work = 10 women's work

∴ 1 men's work = 2 women's work

2 men's work = 4 women's work

∴ Days taken by 5 men + 4 women = 14 women are = 7×8/14 = 4 days

Alternate method-

=> (2 M + 3W) 8 = (3M + 2W)7

=> 16M + 24W = 21M + 14 W

=> 10W = 5M

=> 2W = M

=> 14W × (x) = 7W × 8

= (x) = 4 days

17. Volume of the cube = 729 cm³

∴ Length of one side of the cube = 9 cm

∴ surface are of the cube = 6 x 9 x 9 = 486 cm²

18.

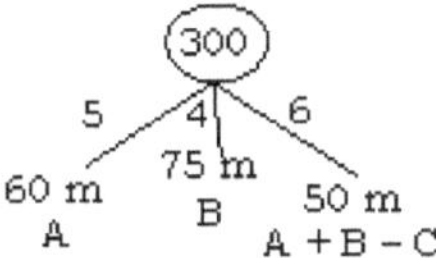

(A + B) eff = 9

(A + B – C) eff = 6

So, C eff = 3 units

C will empty the tank = $\dfrac{300}{3}$ = 100 min

19.

Let the number of days be x.
Here efficiency is 2 : 1
Person 20 : 10
Number of days 20 : x

$$\therefore \quad x = \dfrac{1 \times 10 \times 20}{20 \times 2} = 5 \text{ days}$$

20. Let Anu get x, then Aaradhya get 75% of x and Aman gets 125% amount of 75% of x

75% of x + 125% of 75% of x + x = 1075

x = 400

125/100 × 75/100 × 400

= Rs.375.

21.

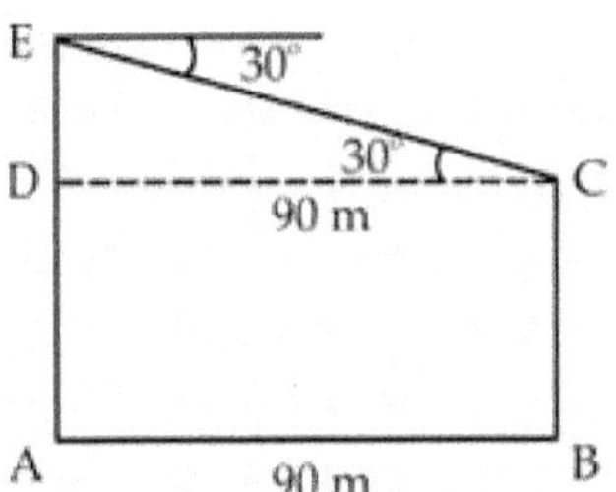

Difference between the height of tower = DE

Again AB = DC

From ΔCDE

$$\tan 30^\circ = \dfrac{DE}{DC}$$

$$\dfrac{1}{\sqrt{3}} = \dfrac{DE}{90}$$

$$DE = \dfrac{90}{\sqrt{3}}$$

= 30$\sqrt{3}$ meters.

22. Area of square = (side)²

Ratio of sides of two square = 4 : 1

Perimeter of square = 4 x side

Ratio of perimeter of two squares = 16 : 4 = 4 : 1

23.

$$\dfrac{a_1^2}{a_2^2} = \dfrac{225}{256}$$

$$\dfrac{a_1}{a_2} = \sqrt{\dfrac{225}{256}} = \dfrac{15}{16}$$

Ratio of their perimeters-

$$\dfrac{4a_1}{4a_2} = \dfrac{a_1}{a_2} = \dfrac{15}{16}$$

15 : 16

24. 1 hours 45 minutes = 7/2 hours

= [7/(4×24)]×100 = 7.291%

25.

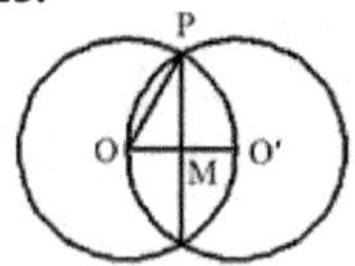

Let the centres be O & O'.

In △OPM,

OP^2 = OM^2 + PM^2

16 = 4 + PM^2

PM = $\sqrt{12}$

∴ Length of the commom chord = $2\sqrt{12} = 4\sqrt{3}$ cm

26. GD = 1/3 AD

or AD = 3 GD

AD = 3 × 1.5 = 4.5 cm

27.

Let total distance be D km. and A's speed be x km/hr and B's speed be y km/hr.

$$\frac{v_1}{v_2} = \sqrt{\frac{t_2}{t_1}} \Rightarrow \frac{x}{y} = \sqrt{\frac{b}{a}} \Rightarrow \frac{x}{y} = \frac{\sqrt{b}}{\sqrt{a}}$$

28.

$$\sqrt{\frac{x}{0.0064}} = \sqrt[3]{0.008}$$

$$\Rightarrow \frac{\sqrt{x}}{0.08} = \sqrt[3]{\frac{8}{1000}} \Rightarrow \sqrt{x} = 0.08 \times \frac{2}{10}$$

$$\Rightarrow \sqrt{x} = 0.016 \Rightarrow x = (0.016)^2 = 0.000256$$

29. Ramesh is 19th from both ends.

∴ There are 18 student on his each side

∴ Total students in the queue = 18 × 2 + 1 = 37

30.

$$\left(\frac{a}{b}\right)^{x-1} = \left(\frac{b}{a}\right)^{x-3} = \left(\frac{a}{b}\right)^{-(x-3)} = \left(\frac{a}{b}\right)^{3-x}$$

∴ x - 1 = 3 - x or 2x = 4

∴ x = 2

31. E M B L A Z O N E R ⇒ Z O N E R E M B L A

Hence, E is the fourth letter from the left end after interchange.

32. T is the common to all the regions

33. ⇒ D= 2E

⇒ E = 4.5 F

⇒ E=1/2 G

⇒ G =1/2 H

⇒ D > H > F

So, the order of weights can be D > H > G>E > F.

34. WKPA

35.

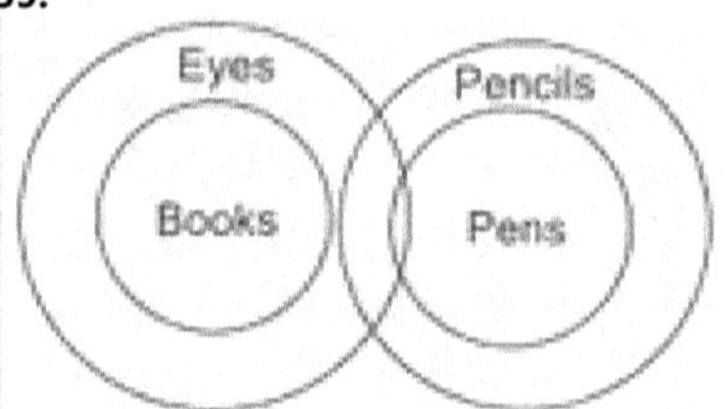

If only Conclusion II follows.

36. Only 3

37.

Suppose my house is at P. from P Ram walks 15 km towards West and reaches Q. At Q he turns left and walks 20 km to reach R. At R, he turns east and walks 25 km to reach S. At S, he turns left and walks 20 km to reach T. It is evident from the figure that:

TP=TQ-PQ and TQ=RS

TP= RS-PQ = 25-15=10 km

38.

Badam	Banana	Pomegranate	Pomegranate	Banana	Apple
1	1	1	1	1	1

39. 115 = 23 × 5

161 = 23 × 7

253 = 23 × 11

391 = 23 × 17

345 = 23 × 5 × 3

40. All but 14 died means all died except 14.So,left rabbits = 14.

41. The pattern in the question is:

42 + 52 = 16 + 25 = 41,

22 + 12 = 4 + 1 = 5

72 + 62 = 49 + 36 = 85

Hence option (c) is the correct answer.

42. Mute is the character of mountain similarly roaring is the character of ocean.

43. According to the question,

A = 75, 56, 87, 68, 99

D = 00, 31, 12, 43, 24

J = 85, 66, 97, 78, 59

U = 95, 76, 57, 88, 69

S = 55, 86, 67, 98, 79

T = 65, 96, 77, 58, 89

So, ADJUST = 87, 31, 66, 69, 86, 89

44. From 1 & 2

swords = red

From 1 & 3

hidden = white

From 3 & 4

own = violet

From 1 & 4

area = black

From 1

in= yellow

From 2 & 3

for= grey

From 2

ready = green

From 3

safety = silver

From 4

under = blue

So, 'black pink yellow' is 'Area in attack'

45. Let there are 'b' brothers and 's' sisters, then according to Sanjay.

b-1 = s   ..... (i)

According to Sarita, b = 2 (s-1)   ...... (ii)

On solving Eqs. (i) and (ii) b = 4 and s = 3

Thus, there are 4 brothers and 3 sisters

46. B is the son of A and F is the spouse of A, so B is the son of F.

47. Series pattern is : nsp/psn/nsp/psn/nsp/psn

∴ Required answer = snpnp

48.

The series is as follows:

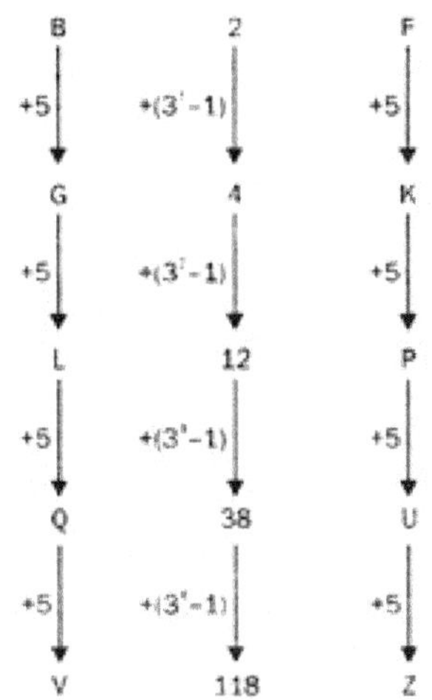

V118Z will come in place of '?'.

49. The first letter of each term is moved three steps forward and the second letter is moved three steps backward to obtain the corresponding letters of the next term.

50. The circles get arranged along the two diagonals alternately. The diameter of the uppermost circle rotates 45° ACW each step, of the middle circle rotates 90° and that of the lowermost circle rotates 45° CW in each step.

51.

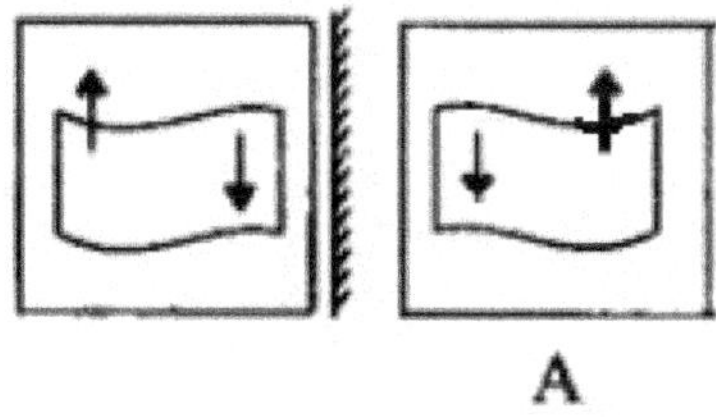

A

52. The T moves 90° OW

↑ moves 90° AGW and every new symbol has its head upwards.

53. The correct arrangement is:

(c). Narrate (d). Nascent (b). Native (a). Nature (e). Naughty

54. The correct arrangement is:

(e) Handkerchief (d) Hang (b) Haphazard (a) Haste (c) Host

55.

Letters in the word	Letters in the alphabet
D A B	D C B
B B L E	B C D E
A B	A B
A B B L E	A B C D E

56. The river Chambal flows through U.P., M.P., Rajasthan

57. Radcliffe Line was the boundary demarcation line between India and Pakistan.

58. The Rajya Sabha is also known as "Council of States" or the upper house. Rajya Sabha is a permanent body and is not subject to dissolution. However, one third of the members retire every second year, and are replaced by newly elected members.

59. Sports Minister Col. Rajyavardhan Rathore and Minister of Culture, Sports and Tourism of South Korea Do Jong-hwan signed the MoU.

60. Iltutmish had patronized Minhaj-us-Siraj

61. President of India send his resignation to Vice-President of India if he wants to quit his office

62. She was the sultan of Delhi from 1236 - 1240. Razia Sultan was the only women ruler of both sultanate & Mughal period.

63. Arundhati Roy (born 24 November, 1961) is an Indian author and political activist who was best known for the 1998 Man Booker Prize for 'Fiction winning novel The God of Small Things (1997) and for her involvement in environmental and human rights causes. Roy's novel became the biggest-selling book by a non-expatriate Indian author. Roy began writing her first novel, The God of small Thins, in 1992, completing it in 1996. The book is semi-autobiographical and a major part captures her childhood experiences in Aymanam. The publication of The God of Small Things catapulted Roy to instant international fame. It received the 1997 Booker Prize for Fiction and was listed as one of the New York Times Notable Books of the Year for 1997. It reached fourth position on the New York Times Bestsellers list for Independent Fiction.

64. Tata Consultancy Services Ltd (TCS) has been ranked among the top 100 most valuable U.S. brands (58th) for the fourth consecutive year by Brand Finance, a leading brand valuation firm.

65. K C Niyogi was the Chairman of the first Finance Commission from 1952-57

66. After nitrogen, oxygen has the highest concentration of 20.95 percent in the Earth's atmosphere

67. Canada has become the second country after Uruguay to legalise possession and use of recreational cannabis.

68. The Construction of Qutub Minar was started by Qutub-ud-din Aibak. Construction of Qutub Minar was started by Qutub ud-din Aibek, the first ruler of Delhi Sultanate. In the memory of Qutbuddin Bakhtiar kaki, the famous Sufi saint. But after his sudden death his son- in-law Illtutmish completed it. In 1368 A.D., the topmost storey was damaged by lightning and was rebuilt by Firoz Shah Tughlaq.

69. Deendayal Antyodaya Yojana – National Rural Livelihood Mission (DAY-NRLM), Ministry of Rural Development and Lady Irwin College, have signed a Memorandum of Understanding (MoU) for establishing ROSHNI – Centre of Women Collectives led Social Action.

70. Jama Masjid was was built by Shah Jahan.

71. glass is made from liquid sand. You can make glass by heating ordinary sand (which is mostly made of silicon dioxide) until it melts and turns into a liquid. You won't find that happening on your local beach: sand melts at the incredibly high temperature of 1700°C (3090°F).

72. The unit of electrical power is Watt.

73. Ribonucleic acid is a polymeric molecule essential in various biological roles in coding, decoding, regulation and expression of genes. RNA and DNA are nucleic acids, and, along with lipids, proteins and carbohydrates, constitute the four major macromolecules essential for all known forms of life

74. Biodiversity act of India was passed by Parliament in 2002.

75. Jim Corbette National Park is known for Tigers.

76. Silver also has the highest thermal conductivity of any element and the highest light reflectance. Although it is the best conductor, copper and gold are used more often in electrical applications because copper is less expensive and gold has a much higher corrosion resistance.

77. According to Newton's third law of motion - To every action there is an equal and opposite reaction

78. Lysosomes are basically a class of waste disposal system of the cell that helps to maintain the cleanness of the cell by digesting any strange material as well as useless cell organelles.

79. Piezometer is used to measure difference in pressure between two points

80. Dry Ice is the common name for solid carbon dioxide (CO_2). It gets this name because it does not melt into a liquid when heated; instead, it changes directly into a gas.

81. Rusting is the common term for corrosion of iron and its alloys . It is an iron oxide. It is a chemical reaction between iron and oxygen in the presence of water or air moisture. Rust consists hydrated iron(III) oxide Fe_2O_3 and H_2O and iron(III) hydroxide $FeO(OH)$, $Fe(OH)_3$.

82. The atmospheric gas which cannot produce green house effect is Nitrogen

83. Chlorine is the basis for the most common bleaches: for example, the solution of sodium hypochlorite, which is so ubiquitous that most simply call it "bleach", and calcium hypochlorite, the active compound in "bleaching powder". Most bleaches are oxidizing agents, some are reducing agents such as sodium dithionite and sodium borohydride, Sulphur dioxide .

84. The average adult has a blood volume of roughly 5 liters. which is composed of plasme and several kinds of cells. By volume, the red blood cells constitute about 45% of whole blood, the plasma about 54.3%, and white cells about 0.7%.

85. Cotton is a soft, fluffy staple fiber that grows in a boll, or protective case. The fiber is almost pure cellulose.

86. Wildlife is destroyed most when Its natural habitat is destroyed.

87. In drilling operation. the feed is expressed in is mm/revolution

88. These atoms are having the same number of electrons. Hence they are isoelectronic.

89. Nitrous oxide, commonly known as laughing gas or nitrous is a chemical compound, an oxide of nitrogen with the formula N_2O.

90. 10^{-7} mm

91. Ultrasound imaging, also called ultrasound scanning or sonography, involves the use of a small transducer (probe) and ultrasound gel placed directly on the skin. High-frequency sound waves are transmitted from the probe through the gel into the body.

92. The colours of stars depend on their Temperature.

93. the most stable element is Lead.

94. A dead star is black hole

95. Albert Einstein stated the equation $E = mc^2$.

96. The electric field intensity on the surface of a charged conductor is Directed normally to the surface.

97. The iris consists of two sheets of smooth muscle with contrary actions: dilation (expansion) and contraction (constriction). These muscles control the size of the pupil and thus determine how much light reaches the sensory tissue of the retina.

98. The nucleus of an atom consists of Protons and neutrons.

99. The capacitance unit of convenient size is Microfarad.

100. The amount of variation permitted in the size of a part is called tolerance

Mathematics

Q.1 if x+y = 25 and $x^2y^3 + y^2x^3 = 25$, what is the value of xy?

A. 0   **B.** ±1   **C.** 5   **D.** 4

Q.2 A horse takes 212 seconds to complete a round around a circular field. If the speed of the horse was 66 m/s, then the radius of the field is :[Given π=227]

A. 25.62 m   **B.** 26.52 m   **C.** 25.26 m   **D.** 26.25 m

Q.3 One man or two women or three boys can do a piece of work in 88 days. One man, one woman and one boy will do it in ____.

A. 44 days   **B.** 24 days   **C.** 48 days   **D.** 20 days

Q.4 If the numerator of a fraction is increased by 200% and the denominator is increased by 350%, the resultant fraction is 512. What was the original fraction?

A. 5/9   **B.** 5/8   **C.** 7/12   **D.** 11/12

Q.5 A car travels 120 km from A to B at 30 kmph. but returns the same distance at 20 kmph. The average speed for the round tip is closest to:

A. 33 kmph.   **B.** 24 kmph.
C. 25 kmph.   **D.** 36 kmph.

Q.6 A sum of Rs. 210 was taken as a loan. This is to be paid back in two equal installments. If the rate of interest be 10% compounded annually, then the value of each installment is

A. Rs.127   **B.** Rs.121   **C.** Rs.210   **D.** Rs.225

Q.7 If p = cosec θ + cot θ, then the value of p + 1p=

A. 2/sinθ   **B.** 2sinθ   **C.** 2/cosθ   **D.** 2cotθ

Q.8 In what time period Rs.100, 000,000 will amount to Rs.104,060,401 at 2% per annum at compound interest, interest being compounded half yearly?

A. 1 Years.   **B.** 2 Years.   **C.** 3 Years.   **D.** 4 Years.

Q.9 Find the measures of an angle which is complement of itself.

A. 40°   **B.** 30°
C. 45°   **D.** None of these

Q.10 ABC is a right-angled triangle, right angled at B. The external bisector of ∠A meets CB produced at D. If AC = 25 cm, BC = 7 cm, find the length, of CD.

A. 78 cm   **B.** 112 cm   **C.** 168 cm   **D.** 175 cm

Q.11 We have to divide a sum of Rs.13,950 among three persons A, B and C. B must get the double of A's share and C must get Rs.50 less than the double of B's share. The share of A will be:

A. Rs.1950   **B.** Rs.1981.25
C. Rs.2000   **D.** Rs.2007.75

Q.12 Mohan purchased a bike for Rs 800/- including sales tax of 20%. Find the actual price of the bike?

A. Rs.666.67   **B.** Rs.600
C. Rs.1000   **D.** Rs.900

Q.13 $\sin^6 A + \cos^6 A$ is equal to:

A. 1-3 sin2 Acos2 A   **B.** 1-3 sin A cos A
C. 1+3 sin2 A cos2 A   **D.** 1

Q.14 A man can row 15 kmph in still water and hefinds that it takes him twice as much time to row up than as to row down thesame distance in the river. The speed of the current is :

A. 6 kmph   **B.** 6.5 kmph
C. 4.5 kmph   **D.** 5 kmph

Q.15 The sum of the internal angles of a regular polygon is 1440°. The number of sides is:

A. 6   **B.** 8   **C.** 10   **D.** 12

Q.16 If 5 girls can embroider a dress in 9 days, then the number of days taken by 3 girls will be ____.

A. 14 days   **B.** 10 days   **C.** 20 days   **D.** 15 days

Q.17 The angle of elevation of the top of a tower at a point on the ground is 30o on walking 16 meters towards the tower, the angle of elevation becomes 60°. Find the height of the tower.

A. 11.75 meters   **B.** 12.82 meters
C. 13.856 meters   **D.** 14.57 meters

Q.18 A child reshapes a cone made up of clay of height 24 cm and radius 6 cm into a sphere. The radius (in cm) of the sphere is

A. 6   **B.** 12   **C.** 24   **D.** 48

Q.19 The difference in selling price of a radio at gains of 10% and 15% is Rs.30. Find the price of the radio?

A. 660   **B.** 670   **C.** 680   **D.** 600

Q.20 What should come in place of the question mark (?) in the following question?

(36)12×(64)13÷(8)13=?

A. 24   **B.** 12   **C.** 3   **D.** 36

Q.21 For what value of m, the system of equations mx + 2y =2 and 3x + y = 1 will be coincident?

A. 2   **B.** 3   **C.** 5   **D.** 6

Q.22 In a mixture of 60 litres, the ratio of milk and water is 2 : 1. What amount of water must be added to make the ratio of milk and water as 1 : 2?

A. 42 litres   **B.** 56 litres   **C.** 60 litres   **D.** 77 litres

Q.23 △ABC is a right angled at A and AD is thealtitude to BC. If AB= 7cm and AC= 24cm. Find the ratio of AD is to AM if M isthe mid-point of BC:

A. 25:41   **B.** 32:41   **C.** 336/625   **D.** 625/336

Q.24 An equilateral triangle circumscribes all the six circles, each with radius 1 cm. What is the perimeter of the equilateral triangle?

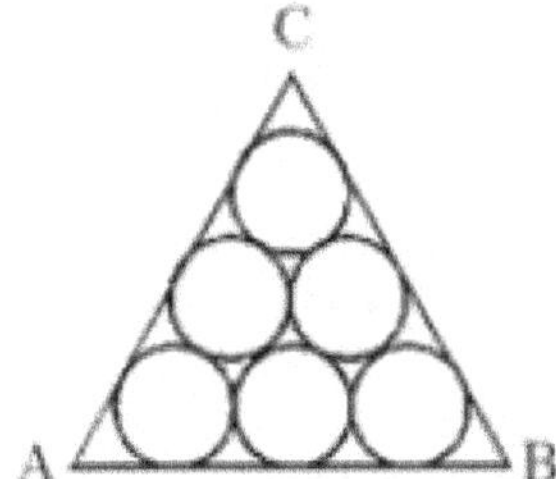

A. 6(2+√3)cm
B. 3(√3+ 2) cm
C. 12(√3 +4)cm+4) cm
D. None of the above

Q.25 If the average weight of 6 students is 50 kg, average weight of 2 students is 57 kg, and average weight of 2 students is 55 kg, then the average weight of all students is?
A. 61 kg **B.** 51.5 kg **C.** 52.4 kg **D.** 51.2 kg

Q.26 DIRECTION: Study the table carefully to answer the questions that follow.

Production of two types of items by four different companies in the different months								
Company	K		L		M		N	
Months	Type- 1	Type- 2	Type- 1	Type- 2	Type- 1	Type- 2	Type- 1	Type- 2
January	234	452	432	654	434	324	435	564
February	545	543	534	335	532	450	652	54
March	756	670	864	654	765	565	564	765
April	634	765	643	454	665	933	875	80
May	568	656	789	654	424	666	565	54
June	875	426	908	767	568	958	574	546

What was the average number of items of type-2 produced by all the companies together in the month of January?
A. 498.5 **B.** 489.5 **C.** 469.5 **D.** 496.5

Q.27 If θ lies in the second quadrant, then
1−sinθ1+sinθ−−−−−−−−√+1+sinθ1−sinθ−−−−−−−−√ is equal to:
A. - 2sec θ
B. 2 sec θ
C. 2cosec θ
D. 2 tan θ

Q.28 Heena and meena start walking from a fixed point in the opposite direction at an average speed of 2 Kmph. and 4 Kmph. respectively. How many Km. will they be apart from each other in 5 hours?
A. 25km
B. 30 Km
C. 32 Km
D. 34 Km

General Intelligence & Reasoning

Q.29 DIRECTIONS:Choose the odd one out from the given alternatives.
A. ADBEC
B. FIGJH
C. KNLOM
D. PRTSQ

Q.30 Arrange the words given below in a meaningful sequence.
1. Key
2. Door
3. Lock
4. Room
5. Switch on
A. 5, 1, 2, 4, 3
B. 4, 2, 1, 5, 3
C. 1, 3, 2, 4, 5
D. 1, 2, 3, 5, 4

Q.31 Pointing to a girl in a photograph, Sunita said, "She is the mother of Renu, whose father is my son". How is Sunita related to that girl?
A. Mother
B. Aunt
C. Cousin
D. None of these

Q.32 DIRECTIONS:Choose the odd one out from the given alternatives.
A. SUNDAY : YADSUN
B. MOTHER : TMPRHD
C. PARENT : TNEPAR
D. MOSTLY : YLTMOS

Q.33 DIRECTIONS:In the question below are given few statements followed by few conclusions. Youhave to take the given statements to be true even if they seem to be atvariance from commonly known facts. Read all the conclusions and then decidewhich of the given conclusion logically follows from the given statementsdisregarding commonly known facts.
Statements:
Allkings are queens.
Somequeens are soldiers.
Allsoldiers are strong.
Conclusions:
I. Somestrong are kings.
II.Some queens are strong.
A. If only Conclusion I follows
B. If only Conclusion II follows
C. If either Conclusion I or II follows
D. If neither Conclusion nor II follows

Q.34 Solve the given letter series
W64X49, M100N81, O144P121, ?
A. T196R169.
B. R196S169.
C. B161R196.
D. Z161R196.

Q.35 DIRECTIONS: In the question given below, an unfolded dice is given in the left side while in the right side, four answer choices are given in the form of complete dices. You have to select the correct answer choice(s) which is are formed by folding the unfolded dice.

Unfolded Dice   Answer Choice

A. a
B. b
C. c
D. d

Q.36 How many triangles are there in the following figure?

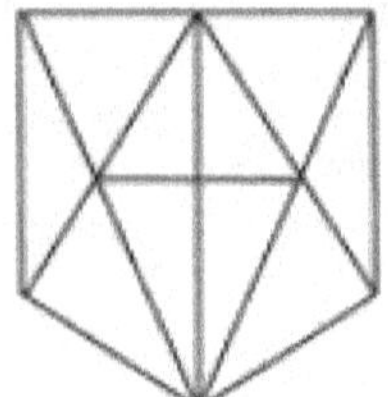

A. 30   **B.** 23   **C.** 18   **D.** 20

Q.37 Select the correct order of the letters as indicated by the numbers to form a meaningful word.

E L B M A G
1 2 3 4 5 6

A. 2,1,6,3,5,4   **B.** 3,1,6,4,5,2
C. 4,5,6,3,1,2   **D.** 6,5,4,3,2,1

Q.38 In a certain code language 'POULTRY' is written as 'PRQXNVTY'. How is 'TREASON' written in that code?

A. TVSGCUQN   **B.** TVTGCUQN
C. TTVGCUQN   **D.** TVTHCUQN

Q.39 Rihana walks 3 km from her house in the East direction to reach the bus stop. She takes a bus and goes 17 km ahead. After getting down from the bus, she walks 2 km on the left side, to reach the spot where she meets Santa. Santa and Rihana take a right from that point and travel 3 km to reach the market place. After shopping, they turn right from the market place and walk 2km to reach Sanita house for a cup of tea. What is the straight line distance between Rihana's house and Sanita house?

A.   24 km
B.   23 km
C.   25 km
D.   Cannot be determined

Q.40 DIRECTIONS: Find the odd one out from the given alternatives.

A. 343   **B.** 64   **C.** 75   **D.** 27

Q.41 DIRECTIONS: Select the related word from the given alternatives.

BDGK : CEHL :: ???? : DFIM

A. EHKO   **B.** FHKO   **C.** FGHI   **D.** FIGO

Q.42 DIRECTIONS: Which of the words in the following options can be formed using the letter of the given word?

DETERMINATION

A. DECLARATION   **B.** NATIONAL
C. TERMINATED   **D.** DEVIATION

Q.43 DIRECTIONS: Which of the words in the following options can be formed using the letter of the given word?

CORRESPONDING

A. CORRECT   **B.** DISCERN
C. REPENT   **D.** RESPONSE

Q.44 Select the correct combination of mathematical signs to replace * signs and to balance the given equation:

15 * 24 * 3 * 6 * 17

A. − ÷ + =   **B.** + ÷ − =   **C.** + × = ÷   **D.** − × = +

Q.45 Arrange the following words according to the English Dictionary.

(1)Save2)Sausage(3)Saviour(4)Savour(5)Savage

A. 5, 4, 2, 3, 1   **B.** 2, 5, 1, 3, 4
C. 2, 3, 4, 1, 5   **D.** 3, 2, 1, 5, 4

Q.46 DIRECTIONS: The following questions are based on the diagram given below.

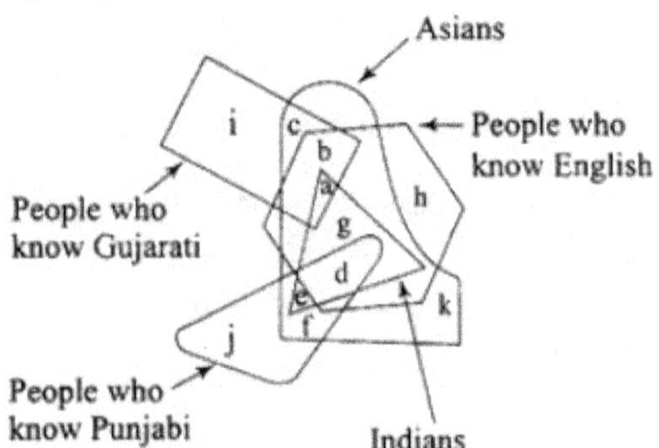

The non-Asians who know English are represented by:

A. i   **B.** j   **C.** k   **D.** h

Q.47 DIRECTIONS: What will come in place of question marks?

20, 20, 19, 16, 17, 13, 14, 11, ?, ?

A. 15, 14   **B.** 10, 10   **C.** 12, 14   **D.** 10, 11

Q.48 In a certain code language 'POETRY' is written as 'QONDSQX' and 'OVER' is written as 'PNUDQ'. How is 'MORE' written in that code language?

A. NNNQD   **B.** NLPQD   **C.** NLNQD   **D.** LNNQD

Q.49 DIRECTIONS: Solve the following letter series.

adb _ ac _ da _ cddcb _ dbc _cbda

A. bccba   **B.** cbbaa   **C.** ccbba   **D.** bbcad

Q.50 Which of the given answer figure will be the correct mirror image of the problem figure?

Problem Figure

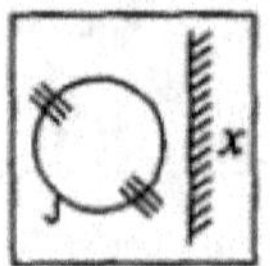

Answer Figures

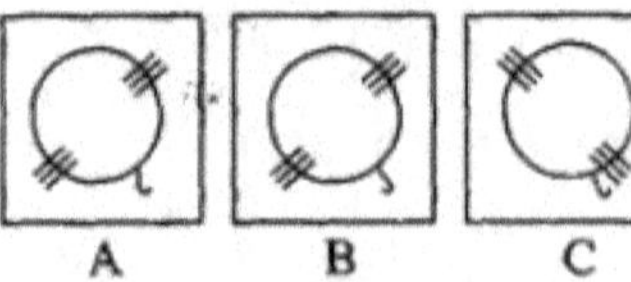

A. A   **B.** B   **C.** C   **D.** D

Q.51 DIRECTIONS: What should come at the place of question mark?

N5V, K7T, ?, E14P, B19N

A. H9R   **B.** H10Q   **C.** H10R   **D.** I10R

Q.52 Which of the answer figure is embedded in the problem figure?

Problem Figure

Answer Figures

A   B   C   D

A. A   **B.** B   **C.** C   **D.** D

Q.53 In the question, select the related digit from the given alternatives.

24 : 60 :: 120 : ?

A. 160   **B.** 220   **C.** 300   **D.** 108

General Awareness

Q.54 Who is the current Governor of Haryana?

A. Satyadev Narayan Arya

B. Anandiben Patel

C. Om Prakash Kohli

D. None of these

Q.55 When the East India Company was formed, the Mughal emperor in India was_____ .

A. Jahangir   **B.** Humayun

C. Aurangzeb   **D.** Akbar

Q.56 The Bhakra Nangal dam is built on the river ?

A. Ravi   **B.** Beas   **C.** Sutlej   **D.** Yamuna

Q.57 Which one of the following countries shares the shortest boundary with India?

A. Bangladesh.   **B.** China.

C. Nepal.   **D.** Myanmar.

Q.58 By which name/names is our country mentioned in the Constitution?

A. India and Bharat

B. India and Hindustan

C. Bharat Only

D. India, Bharat and Hindustan

Q.59 Who founded the Mughal dynasty in India?

A. Akbar   **B.** Babur

C. Shah Jahan   **D.** Jehangir

Q.60 The maximum canal irrigated area is in the state of:

A. Haryana.   **B.** Madhya Pradesh.

C. Punjab.   **D.** Uttar Pradesh

Q.61 Under the Ayushman Bharat Yojana, Prime Minister Narendra Modi has inaugurated the first Health and Wellness Centre in -

A. Gulbarga   **B.** Bidar

C. Bijapur   **D.** Hubli

Q.62 Third Battle of Panipat was fought between–

A. Babar and Ibrahhn Lodi

B. Ahmed Shah Abdali and the Marathas

C. Shivaji and Mughals

D. Akbar and Hemu

Q.63 Who has been appointed as Finance Secretary?

A. Shri A.N.Jha   **B.** Shri Prakash Kumar

C. Shri Mukesh Yadav   **D.** Saleem Khan

Q.64 The first meeting of the India and ___________ Joint Committee on Border Haats was held in Agartala recently.

A. China   **B.** Bhutan

C. Nepal   **D.** Bangladesh

Q.65 The DRDO was established in:

A. 1928   **B.** 1944   **C.** 1954   **D.** 1958

Q.66 'Dudhwa National Park' is situated in-

A. Bihar.   **B.** Uttar Pradesh.

C. Madhya Pradesh.   **D.** Jharkhand.

Q.67 Buland Darwaza was built by -

A. Akbar   **B.** Babur

C. Shah Jahan   **D.** None of these

Q.68 Part III of the Constitution of India relates to?

A. Fundamental Rights.

B. Directive Principles of State Policy.

C. Fundamental Duties.

D. Citizenship.

General Science

Q.69 A boat will submerge when it displaces water equal to its own ______

A. volume   **B.** weight

C. surface area   **D.** density

Q.70 Gamma rays were discovered by -

A. Rontgen   **B.** Paul Villard

C. Ritter   **D.** Marcony

Q.71 The measurement of the gravitational pull on an object is its

A. volume   **B.** weight   **C.** mass   **D.** length

Q.72 First biosphere reserve was established is 1986 at-

A. Nilgiri

B. Nanda Dew
C. Little Rann of Kutch
D. Sunderbans

Q.73 What is the atomic number of Iron?
A. 21   **B.** 22   **C.** 24   **D.** 26

Q.74 The atomic number of an element is the number of -
A. Protons
B. Electrons + Protons
C. Neutrons
D. Neutrons + Protons

Q.75 Friction is a
A. Gravitational force
B. Magnetic force
C. Contact force
D. Non-contact force

Q.76 Weight of the body is?
A. Minimum at the equator.
B. Maximum at the equator.
C. Minimum at the poles.
D. Same everywhere.

Q.77 Modulus of elasticity is defined as the ratio of:
A. Shear stress to shear strain
B. Linear stress to linear strain
C. Linear stress to lateral strain
D. Lateral stress to linear strain

Q.78 Light Year is a unit to measure -
A. Time
B. Distance
C. Luminous Intensity
D. Magnetic Field

Q.79 Two richest known sources of edible protein are ______.
A. groundnut and milk
B. milk and vegetables
C. soyabean and groundnut
D. some type of algae and other micro-organisms

Q.80 Scurvy is caused by the deficiency of?
A. Vitamin-B
B. Vitamin-C
C. Vitamin-A
D. Vitamin-E

Q.81 NSC (National Savings Certificates) are issued in the denominations of :
A. Rs.500
B. Rs.1000
C. Rs.5000 & Rs.10,000 only
D. All the above

Q.82 Smallpox is caused by:
A. Virus   **B.** Bacteria   **C.** Fungi   **D.** Protozoa

Q.83 Which of the following is a Compound?
A. Air   **B.** Sulphur   **C.** Water   **D.** Gold

Q.84 Diamond is -
A. An element
B. A compound
C. A mixture
D. A liquid

Q.85 Which instrument is used to measure wind speed?
A. Lux meter
B. Geiger counter
C. Anemometer
D. Altimeter

Q.86 The SI unit of the universal gravitational constant G is:
A. $N\ m^2kg^2$ **B.** $N\ m/kg$ **C.** $N\ kg/m$ **D.** Nm^2/kg^2

Q.87 Which of the following is a vector?
A. Power
B. Displacement
C. Work
D. Potential

Q.88 Which vitamin is prepared by our body in the presence of sunlight?
A. Vitamin A.
B. Vitamin B-complex.
C. Vitamin C.
D. Vitamin D.

Q.89 The shape of a rain drop is spherical due to
A. Viscosity
B. Surface tension
C. Elasticity
D. Gravitation

Q.90 Which of the following is an example of Newton's Third Law?
A. Recoil of a Gun
B. Swimming
C. Both of these
D. None of the these

Q.91 Who invented the aeroplane?
A. Pascal
B. Charles Babbage
C. Wright Brothers
D. Charles Darwin

Q.92 Charle's Law describes the relation between -
A. Volume and Temperature
B. Volume and Pressure
C. Pressure and Temperature
D. Volume and number of molecules

Q.93 Which one of the following has greatest mass?
A. electron
B. proton
C. neutron
D. hydrogen nucleus

Q.94 Which of the following is not a fossil fuel?
A. Oil
B. Natural gas
C. Geothermal
D. Coal

Q.95 For a missile launched with a velocity less than the earth's escape velocity, the total energy is
A. Zero
B. Negative
C. Either positive or negative
D. Positive

Q.96 Where does the oxygen that keeps us alive come form?
A. Carbon dioxide
B. Carbonates absorbed from soil
C. Oxides of minerals
D. Water

Q.97 What is the number of periods in the modern periodic table?
A. 2   **B.** 6   **C.** 7   **D.** 8

Q.98 J J Thomson is credited with the discovery of -
A. Electron   **B.** Proton   **C.** Neutron   **D.** Neutrino

// Smart Answer Sheet //

Correct — Percentage of students who answered correctly.   **Skipped** — Percentage of students who skipped.

Q.	Ans.	Correct / Skipped
1	B	84.34 % / 13.36 %
2	D	76.64 % / 21.1 %
3	C	87.24 % / 11.79 %
4	B	84.38 % / 10.74 %
5	B	85.17 % / 12.35 %
6	B	88.36 % / 10.8 %
7	A	89.41 % / 10.49 %
8	B	82.8 % / 10.1 %
9	C	76.31 % / 12.48 %
10	D	76.41 % / 15.18 %
11	C	84.66 % / 15.27 %
12	A	89.62 % / 10.3 %
13	A	89.48 % / 10.33 %
14	D	78.59 % / 10.64 %
15	C	85.91 % / 11.71 %
16	D	79.77 % / 11.24 %
17	C	82.01 % / 16.73 %
18	A	80.97 % / 10.48 %
19	D	86.08 % / 13.04 %
20	B	78.14 % / 21.09 %
21	D	81.21 % / 15.72 %
22	C	87.98 % / 10.18 %
23	C	87.09 % / 11.4 %
24	A	84.68 % / 14.65 %
25	C	79.89 % / 10.43 %
26	A	80.81 % / 18.41 %
27	D	89.22 % / 10.3 %
28	B	86.79 % / 11.3 %
29	B	82.01 % / 15.76 %
30	B	76.08 % / 20.86 %
31	D	79.74 % / 11.25 %
32	C	87.18 % / 10.29 %
33	D	78.96 % / 18.68 %
34	B	80.42 % / 11.27 %
35	B	83.88 % / 12.29 %
36	B	79.87 % / 12.45 %
37	D	88.28 % / 10.75 %
38	B	79.51 % / 20.19 %
39	D	79.63 % / 14.64 %
40	D	81.75 % / 14.81 %
41	B	78.76 % / 20.2 %
42	C	78.72 % / 12.89 %
43	B	88.83 % / 10.44 %
44	C	77.03 % / 21.65 %
45	B	76.01 % / 13.81 %
46	B	86.2 % / 12.02 %
47	B	89.2 % / 10.17 %
48	D	78.71 % / 12.22 %
49	B	76.13 % / 19.98 %
50	C	76.04 % / 21.31 %
51	B	78.43 % / 17.4 %
52	A	80.46 % / 11.83 %
53	C	81.93 % / 14.66 %
54	A	77.25 % / 15.52 %
55	C	87.81 % / 12.13 %
56	A	78.06 % / 12.02 %
57	D	80.72 % / 12.93 %
58	C	76.61 % / 19.91 %
59	D	83.73 % / 13.45 %
60	A	87.7 % / 10.84 %
61	B	86.42 % / 11.97 %
62	D	85.29 % / 11.92 %
63	C	83.62 % / 11.06 %
64	B	81.36 % / 14.49 %
65	A	77.96 % / 14.5 %
66	D	88.52 % / 10.39 %
67	D	82.86 % / 13.38 %
68	B	80.26 % / 12.97 %
69	A	84.39 % / 15.03 %
70	A	83.26 % / 11.32 %
71	B	83.08 % / 12.27 %
72	B	84.5 % / 11.46 %
73	B	77.62 % / 15.19 %
74	A	79.74 % / 15.92 %
75	D	87.18 % / 10.66 %
76	A	80.89 % / 14.82 %
77	C	83.78 % / 10.99 %
78	A	89.73 % / 10.15 %
79	B	84.4 % / 13.67 %
80	B	86.53 % / 10.66 %

Q.	Ans.	Correct		Q.	Ans.	Correct		Q.	Ans.	Correct		Q.	Ans.	Correct		Q.	Ans.	Correct
		Skipped				Skipped				Skipped				Skipped				Skipped
81	C	82.8 %		85	C	81.09 %		89	B	78.37 %		93	C	86.1 %		97	B	79.27 %
		15.12 %				11.43 %				13.39 %				11.44 %				18.46 %
82	B	79.18 %		86	A	84.14 %		90	D	87.98 %		94	A	81.8 %		98	D	82.56 %
		16.28 %				11.28 %				11.83 %				12.3 %				17.38 %
83	D	79.88 %		87	C	76.14 %		91	B	79.53 %		95	C	85.29 %		99	C	89.37 %
		19.94 %				12.23 %				13.74 %				13.33 %				10.1 %
84	A	89.92 %		88	D	82.23 %		92	C	83.3 %		96	B	82.43 %		100	A	87.05 %
		10.0 %				16.84 %				13.6 %				10.99 %				10.77 %

//Hints and Solutions//

1. $x^2y^3 + y^2x^3 = 25$

$\Rightarrow x^2 y^2 (x + y) = 25$

$\Rightarrow (xy)^2 (x + y) = 25$

$\Rightarrow (xy)^2 = 1$

$(\because x + y = 25)$

$\Rightarrow xy = \pm 1$

2. Distance covered in one round

= Circumference of circle

= $2\pi r$

Speed = 66 m/s

$$Time = \frac{5}{2}$$

$$S = \frac{D}{T}$$
$$D = S \times T$$

$$= 66 \times \frac{5}{2}$$
$$D = 165 \ m$$
$$2\pi r = 165$$

$$= 2 \times \frac{22}{7} \times r = 165$$

$$r = \frac{165 \times 7}{44} = 26.25 \ m.$$

3. 1 man + 1 woman + 1 boy

$$= \left(3 + \frac{3}{2} + 1\right) \text{boys} = \frac{11}{2} \text{boys}$$

$$M_1 D_1 = M_2 D_2$$

$$\Rightarrow 3 \times 88 = \frac{11}{2} \times D_2$$

$$D_2 = \frac{3 \times 2 \times 88}{11}$$

$$= 3 \times 2 \times 8 = 48 \text{ days}$$

4. Let the original fraction be xy

$x \times (100+200)\% y \times (100+350)\%$ = 512

$\Rightarrow x \times 300 y \times 450$ = 512 $\Rightarrow 5 \times 45012 \times 300$ then xy = 58

5. Average Speed = 2xyx+y

$= 2 \times 30 \times 2030 + 20$

$= 24$

6. Let x be the value of installment.

Principal = Present value of x for 1 year + Present value of x for 2 years

$$210 = \frac{x}{\left(1 + \dfrac{R}{100}\right)} + \frac{x}{\left(1 + \dfrac{R}{100}\right)^2}$$

$$\Rightarrow 210 = \frac{x}{1 + \dfrac{1}{10}} + \frac{x}{\left(1 + \dfrac{1}{10}\right)^2}$$

$$\Rightarrow 210 = \frac{x}{\dfrac{11}{10}} + \frac{x}{\left(\dfrac{11}{10}\right)^2}$$

$$\Rightarrow 210 = \frac{10x}{11} + \frac{100x}{121}$$

$$210 = \frac{110x + 100x}{121}$$

$$210 = \frac{210x}{121}$$

$$121 = \frac{210}{210}x$$

$$x = 121.$$

7. Given p = cosec θ + cot θ

$\Rightarrow 1p - \text{cosec } 0 - \text{cot } 0$

P + 1p = cosec θ + cot θ + cosec θ - cot θ = 2cosec θ

= 2sinθ

8. 104,060,401 = 100,000,000 (1 + (1/100))2t104,060,401/100,000,000 = (101/100) 2t(101)4/(100)4 = (101/100) 2t(101/100)4 = (101/100) 2t2t = 4t = 2 years

9. Let the measure of angle = x°
measure of its complement = x°∴ x°+x°= 90° ⇒ x° = 45°

10.

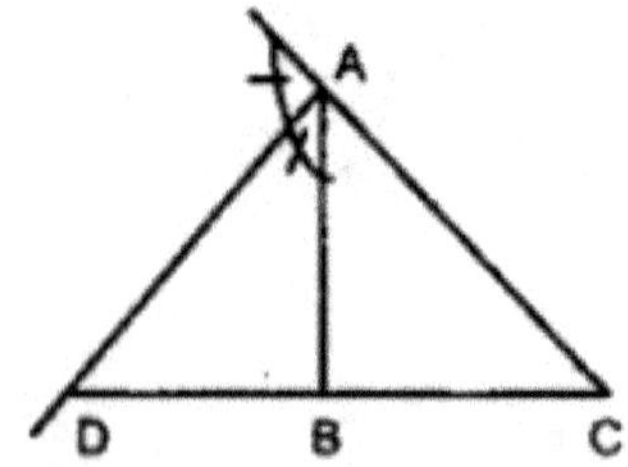

$$\sqrt{AC^2 - BC^2} = \sqrt{25^2 - 7^2} = 24$$

Now, $\dfrac{AC}{AB} = \dfrac{CD}{BD}$

$\Rightarrow CD/BD = 25/24 \Rightarrow CD = \dfrac{25}{24}\, BD$

$BC = CD - BD = \dfrac{25}{24}\, BD - BD \Rightarrow 1/24\, BD = 7$

$\therefore BD = 7 \times 24 = 168$ cm

$\therefore CD = 7 + 168 = 175$ cm

11. Let Rs. x be the part of A, then
x+ 2x + 4x - 50 = 139507x = 14000x = 2000

12. 800×100120=20003 = 666.67

13. a3 + b3 = (a+b)3 −3ab (a+b)

Let a = sin2A, b = cos2A, so that

a + b = sin2A+ cos2A = 1

$\Rightarrow$ sin6A+cos6A = 1- 3 sin2 A cos2 A

14. Let the speed of current be x kmph

$\therefore$ Down stream speed = 15 + x kmph

Up stream speed = 15 - x kmph

Let the distance be d km.

$\therefore$ Down stream time = d15+x

Upstream time = d15−x

According to question,

2d15+x=d15−x

$\Rightarrow$ 2(15 - x) = (15 + x)

$\Rightarrow$ 30 - 2x = 15 + x

$\Rightarrow$ 15 = 3x

$\Rightarrow$ x = 153=5

$\therefore$ speed of current = 5 kmph

15. Let the number of sides of regular polygon be n.

(n − 2) × 180 = 1440° $\Rightarrow$ n = 10

16. Days taken by 5 girls to embroider a dress = 9 days

Days taken by 1 girl to embroider a dress = 9 x 5 days

Days taken by 3 girls to embroider a dress = 9×53 days = 15 days

17.

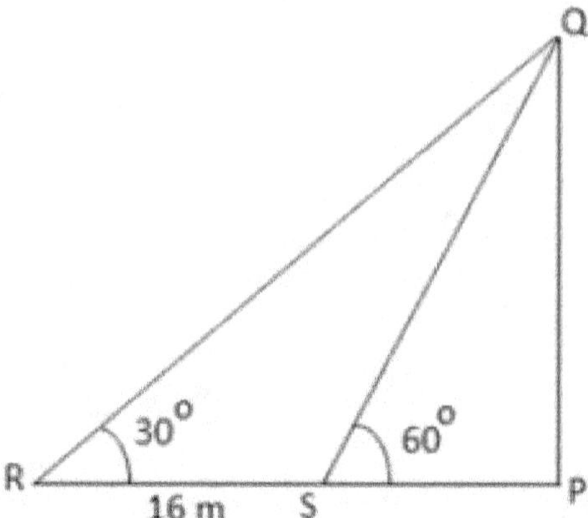

$\dfrac{PQ}{PS} = \tan 60^\circ$

$\Rightarrow PS = \dfrac{PQ}{\tan 60^\circ}$

$PS = \dfrac{h}{\sqrt{3}}$

$\dfrac{PQ}{PR} = \tan 30^\circ$

$\dfrac{PQ}{PR} = \dfrac{1}{\sqrt{3}}$

$\Rightarrow PR = h\sqrt{3}$

$Rs = PR - PS$

$16 = h\sqrt{3} - \dfrac{h}{\sqrt{3}}$

$16 = h\left(\sqrt{3} - \dfrac{1}{\sqrt{3}}\right)$

$16 = h\left(\dfrac{2}{\sqrt{3}}\right)$

$\dfrac{16 \times \sqrt{3}}{2} = h$

$h = 13.856$ m.

18.

Volume of the cone $= \dfrac{1}{3}\pi r^2 h$

$= \dfrac{\pi}{3} \times 6 \times 6 \times 24 \ cm^3$

= Volume of the sphere
If the radius of the sphere be r cm, then

$\dfrac{4}{3}\pi r^3 = \dfrac{\pi}{3} \times 6 \times 6 \times 24$

$\Rightarrow r^3 = 6 \times 6 \times 6$

$\therefore \ r = \sqrt{6 \times 6 \times 6} = 6 \ cm.$

19. 15 - 10 = 5% =30

Then100% = (100×30)5 = 600

20. (36)12×(64)13÷(8)13=?

6 x 4 ÷ 2 = ?

(6×4)2 = 12

21. Two linear equations will coincide if there are infinite number of solutions,

i.e. a1a2=b1b2=c1c2

for a1 x +b1 y = c1

and a2x +b2y = c2

$\therefore$ m3=21=21

⇒ m = 6

22. Milk in the original mixture is (2/3)×60= 40 litres and water= 20 litres.

In the new mixture, the ratio of milk to water is 1 : 2.

if milk is 40 litres, water should be 80 litres;

Thus 60 litres of water must be added.

23.

$\because$ AM is the median of a right angled triangle.

$\therefore \qquad AM = \dfrac{BC}{2} = \dfrac{25}{2}$

And $\qquad AD = \dfrac{AB \times AC}{BC} = \dfrac{7 \times 24}{25}$

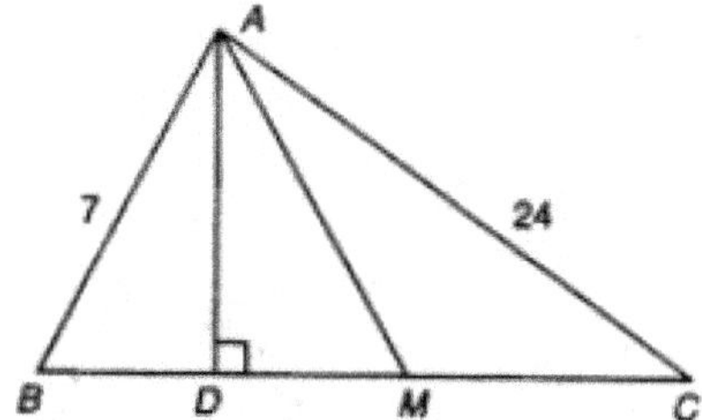

$\therefore \ \dfrac{AD}{AM} = \dfrac{7 \times 24 \times 2}{25 \times 25} = \dfrac{336}{625}$

24.

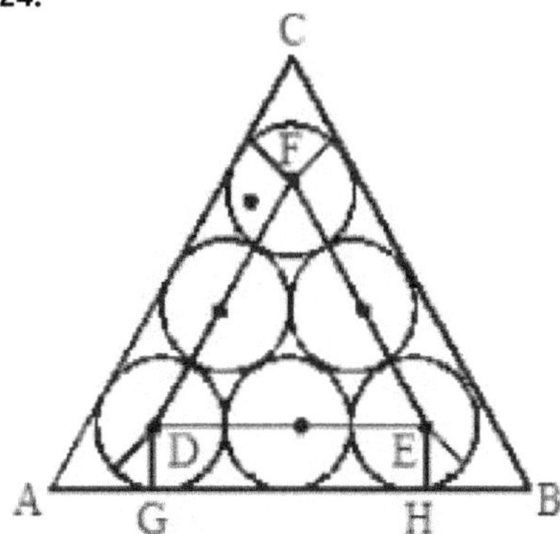

DE = GH = 4, ∠ADG = 60°

Then from 30 - 60 - 90 theorem

AG = 3√, BH =3√, then

AB = AG+GH+BH

Then perimeter of △ABC = 3×(3√+4+3√)=3×(23√+4)=6(3√+2)

25. Required average weight

= (50×6+57×2+55×2)   10

= 300+114+110   10   =524 10 = 52.4 kg.

26. Required average= (452 + 654 + 324 + 564)/4

= 1994/4 = 498.5.

27.

$$\sqrt{\dfrac{1-sin\theta}{1+sin\theta}} + \sqrt{\dfrac{1+sin\theta}{1-sin\theta}} = \dfrac{(1-sin\theta)+(1+sin\theta)}{cos\theta}$$

$= 2sec\,\theta$

28. Distance covered by Heena = 2 x 5 = 10 Km

Distance Covered by Meena = 4 x 5 = 20 Km

Total distance = (10 + 20) = 30Km

29. Except PRTSQ in all other groups, the consecutive letters are written alternately.

30. The correct order is :

Key Lock Door Room Switch on

1 3 2 4 5

31. If the woman in the picture is Renu's mother, and Renu's father is Sunita's son, that means Sunita is the mother-in-law of the woman in the photo.

33.

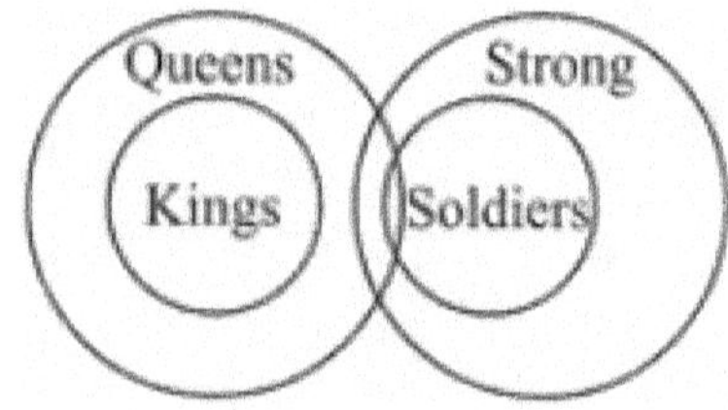

∴ only Conclusion II follows

∴ only Conclusion II follows

34.

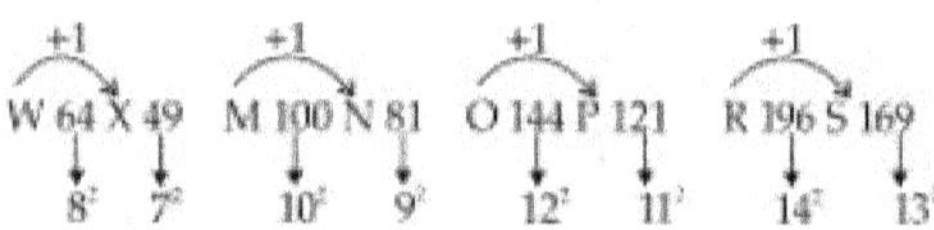

35. According to the unfolded dice,

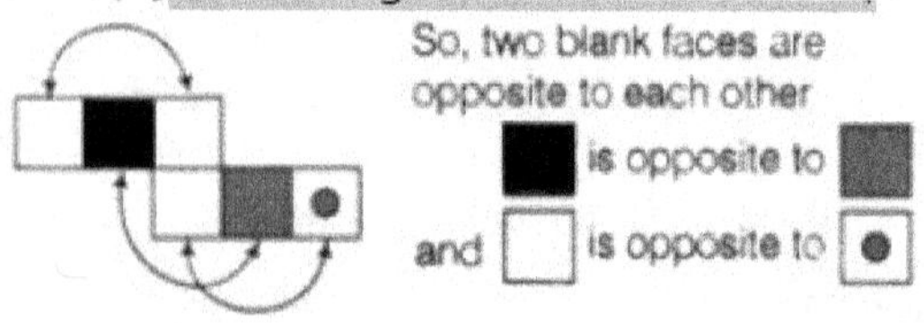

Hence, only option (d) is correct.

36.

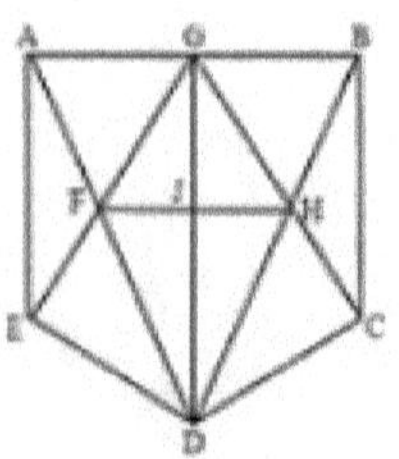

Thus there are 23 triangles.

AEF, AGF,DEF,
AED,AEG,GJF,
GJH,GFH,FGD,
FDH,FJD,JHD,
GHD,GBH,BHC,
GBC,BCD,DCH,
GED,GDC,ADB,
AGD,BGD

37. GAMBLE

38. There is one letter more in the code as compared to the letters of the given word. The pattern of coding is as follows.

As,

$$P \xrightarrow{+2} P$$
$$P \xrightarrow{+2} R$$
$$O \xrightarrow{+2} Q$$
$$U \xrightarrow{+3} X$$
$$L \xrightarrow{+2} N$$
$$T \xrightarrow{+2} V$$
$$R \xrightarrow{+2} T$$
$$Y \longrightarrow Y$$

Similarly,

$$T \xrightarrow{+2} T$$
$$T \xrightarrow{+2} V$$
$$R \xrightarrow{+2} T$$
$$E \xrightarrow{+3} H$$
$$A \xrightarrow{+2} C$$
$$S \xrightarrow{+2} U$$
$$O \xrightarrow{+2} Q$$
$$N \longrightarrow N$$

39.

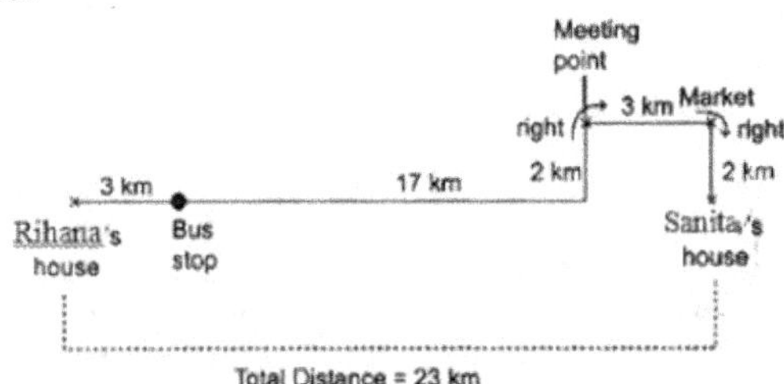

$$20 \xrightarrow{-1} 19 \xrightarrow{-2} 17 \xrightarrow{-3} 14 \xrightarrow{-4} 10$$

2nd series:

$$20 \xrightarrow{-4} 16 \xrightarrow{-3} 13 \xrightarrow{-2} 11 \xrightarrow{-1} 10$$

40. Except 75 all other numbers are perfectcubes.

$343 = 7 \times 7 \times 7$

$64 = 4 \times 4 \times 4$

$27 = 3 \times 3 \times 3$

41.

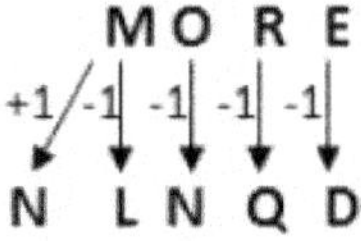

$$B \xrightarrow{+2} D \xrightarrow{+3} G \xrightarrow{+4} K$$

$$C \xrightarrow{+2} E \xrightarrow{+3} H \xrightarrow{+4} L$$

SAME WAY

$$F \xrightarrow{+2} H \xrightarrow{+3} K \xrightarrow{+4} O$$

$$D \xrightarrow{+2} F \xrightarrow{+3} I \xrightarrow{+4} M$$

48.

As,

```
        P O E T R Y           O V E R
    +1 -1 -1 -1 -1 -1 -1    +1 -1 -1 -1 -1
        Q O N D S Q X        P N U D Q
```

Similarly,

```
        M O R E
    +1 -1 -1 -1 -1
        N L N Q D
```

49. The series is

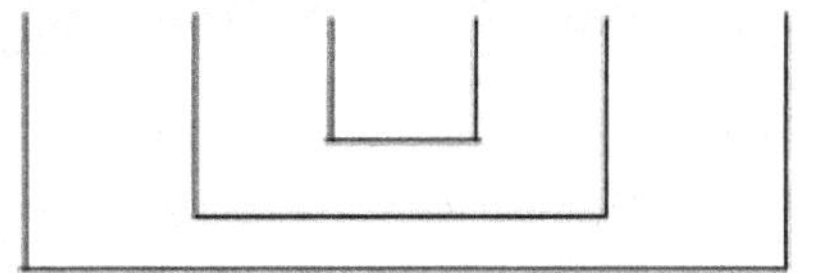

42. There is no 'C' in the given word.So, DECLARATION cannot be formed.

There is no 'I' in the given word.So, NATIONAL cannot be formed.

There is no 'V' in the given word.So, DEVIATION cannot be formed.

43. There is no 'T' in the given word. So, CORRECT and REPENT cannot be formed.

There is only one 'S' in the given word. So, RESPONSE cannot be formed.

44. Given that:

$15 * 24 * 3 * 6 * 17$

After applying, $+ \div - =$

$15 + 24 \div 3 - 6 = 17$

$\Rightarrow 15 + 8 - 6 = 17$

$\Rightarrow 23 - 6 = 17$

$\Rightarrow 17 = 17.$

45. Sausage, Savage, Save, Saviour, Savour

47. There are two series.

1st series:

50. A is the correct mirror image.

51. $N - \rightarrow -3K - \rightarrow -3[H] - \rightarrow -3E - \rightarrow -3B$

$5 - \rightarrow +27 - \rightarrow +3[10] - \rightarrow +414 - \rightarrow +519$

$V - \rightarrow -2T - \rightarrow -2[R] - \rightarrow -2P - \rightarrow -2N$

52. answer figure A is embedded in problem figure.

53. $24 \times 5 = 120$
Similarly, $60 \times 5 = 300$

54. Satyadev Narayan Arya is the current Governor of Haryana.

55. The English East India Company was founded in 1600. Akbar was Mughal Emperor from 1556 until his death in 1605.

56. Bhakra Dam is built on the river Satluj in Bilaspur, Himachal Pradesh, northern India.

57. Myanmar.

58. (a) The constitution states: India, also known as Bharat, is a Union of States. It is a Sovereign Socialist Secular Democratic Republic with a parliamentary system of government. The Republic is governed in terms of the Constitution of India which was adopted by the Constituent Assembly on 26th November, 1949 and came into force on 26th January, 1950. The Constitution provides for a Parliamentary form of government which is federal in structure with certain unitary features. The constitutional head of the Executive of the Union is the President.

59. Babur had founded the Mughal rule in India in 1526 AD.

60. Uttar Pradesh.

61. Prime Minister Narendra Modi inaugurated the first Health and Wellness Centre in Bijapur, Chhattisgarh to mark the launch of Ayushman Bharat Yojana- National Health Protection Mission (AB-NHPM).

62. Third Battle of Panipat was fought between Ahmed Shah Abdali and the Marathas

63. Shri A. N. Jha appointed as Finance Secretary.

64. The first meeting of the India and Bangladesh Joint Committee on Border Haats was held in Agartala recently.

65. The DRDO was established in 1958 with just 10 laboratories to enhance the research work in defence sector.

66. Uttar Pradesh.

67. Buland Darwaza was built by Akbar.

68. (a) Fundamental Rights are mentioned part III of the Indian Constitution.

69. A boat will float when the weight of the water it displaces equals the weight of the boat and anything will float if it is shaped to displace its own weight of water before it reaches the point where it will submerge. Floating of the boat works on the principle of buoyancy force which is an upward force exerted by a liquid, gas or other fluid, that opposes the weight of an immersed object. In a column of fluid, pressure increases with depth as a result of the weight of the overlying fluid. Thus a column of fluid, or an object submerged in the fluid, experiences greater pressure at the bottom of the column than at the top. This difference in pressure results in a net force that tends to accelerate an object upwards.

70. It was discovered by Paul Villard

71. weight-the measurement of the gravitational pull on an object is its weight.

72. First biosphere reserve was established is 1986 at Nilgiri .

73. The atomic number of Iron is 26.

74. Atomic number is the number of electrons or protons.

75. The force responsible for changing the state of motion of objects in contact is called the force of friction. It always acts on all moving objects.

76. Minimum at the equator.

While standing at the equator you are further away from the bulk of Earth's mass than at the poles, so the planet exerts less pull on you. An object at the equator weighs a mere 0.5 percent less than at the poles less than a pound for anyone under 200 pounds.

77. Modulus of elasticity is defined as the ratio of Linear stress to linear strain

78. Light Year is a unit to measure distance.

79. The richest sources of protein are animal foods such as chicken, meat, fish, cheese and eggs. However, plant proteins are believed to be healthier because of their lower fat content. Plant protein is found (e.g.) in beans (esp. soy beans), lentils, nuts, quorn and seeds. Fish and seafood are some of the richest sources of protein. One-half of a typical fillet of halibut or salmon provides approximately 41g of protein. Soybeans are legumes that provide a valuable protein-rich food option for vegetarians and non-vegetarians alike. One cup of boiled soybeans provides over 28g of protein.

80. Scurvy is caused by the deficiency of Vitamin C

81. All the above

82. Smallpox is caused by two virus variants-Variola major and Variola minor.

83. Sulphur and Gold are element while air is mixture of various compound made of element Hydrogen and Oxygen and its Chemical formula is H_2O.

84. Diamond is an element.

85. Anemometer is a measuring instrument used in meteorology to measure wind speed. The first anemometer was invented by Leon Battista Alberti in 1450.

86. The SI unit of the universal gravitational constant G is Nm^2/kg^2

87. Displacement is a vector quantity while the rest are scalar

88. Vitamin D.-Vitamin D can be made by our body itself. Our skin uses sunlight to produce vitamin D.

89. High surface tension binds the raindrop from all corners from inside and that is why the raindrop is spherical in shape

90. Newton's Third Law states that "To every action, there is an equal and opposite reaction". When a gun is fired, it thus recoils and while we swim we exert force on the water which exerts force on us, due to which we move forward.

91. The Wright Brothers had invented the aeroplane.

92. Charle's Law describes the relation between Volume and Temperature

93. Mass of proton is $1.672621777(74) \times 10^{-27}$ kg. An electron has a mass ($9.10938291(40) \times 10^{-31}$ kg) that is approximately 1 / 1836 that of the proton. The mass of neutron is slightly larger than that of a proton. The mass of the hydrogen nucleus is 1.7×10^{-27} kg. The heaviest of these particles is the neutron.

94. Natural gas

95. When a missile is launched with a velocity less than the escape velocity of the earth, the sum of its kinetic energy and potential energy is negative.

96. Since water and carbon dioxide are both compounds which contain oxygen, it is possible to obtain oxygen from either. The oxygen produced from photosynthesis is not released into the air. It is not until cellular respiration that oxygen is released. the oxygen comes from water. The water molecules are split at the "beginning" of photosynthesis for the electrons. These electrons eventually make their way to the electron transport chain, where oxygen is the final electon accept, and then released into the air. Scientists agree that there's oxygen from ocean plants in very breath we take. Most of this oxygen comes from tiny ocean plants – called phytoplankton-that live near the water's surface and drift with the currents. Like all plants, they photosynthesize-that is, they use sunlight and carbon dioxide to make food. A byproduct of photosynthesis is oxygen.

97. There are 7 periodic in the Periodic Table

98. He had discovered electrons

Mock Test 12

Mathematics

Q.1 If a,b,c, are the distinct positive numbers then (a+b+c) (ab+bc+ca) is:

A. greater than 9abc
B. less than 8 abc
C. equal to 10 abc
D. greater than 25 abc

Q.2 A is thrice as fast as B and is therefore able to finish a work in 60 days less than B. The time in which they can do it working together is:

A. 45/2
B. 44/2
C. 43/2
D. 47/2

Q.3 A mixture of 70 litres contains milk and water in ratio of 3 :4. How many litres of milk must be added to mixture so as to make the ratio 5 : 4?

A. 10 litres
B. 15 litres
C. 20 litres
D. 25 litres

Q.4 The selling price of 12 objects is equal to the cost price of 9 objects. Find the loss or profit percentage?

A. 28% profit
B. 25% loss
C. 23% profit
D. 31% loss

Q.5 If tan θ = 2 - $\sqrt{3}$, then tan (90 - θ)is equal to:

A. $2 + \sqrt{3}$
B. $2 - \sqrt{3}$
C. $3 + \sqrt{2}$
D. $3 - \sqrt{2}$

Q.6 Two pipes can separately fill a tank in 20 hrs and 30 hrs respectively. Both the pipes are opened to fill the tank but when the tank is 1/3 full a leak develops in the tank through which 1/3 of the water supplied by both the pipes per hour leak out. What is the total time taken to fill the tank?

A. 12 hrs
B. 14 hrs
C. 16 hrs
D. 18 hrs

Q.7 Two poles of the height 15 m and 20 m stand vertically upright on a plane ground. If the distance between their feet is 12 m, find the distance between their tops.

A. 11 m
B. 12 m
C. 13 m
D. 14 m

Q.8 A shopkeeper earns a profit of 12% on selling a book at 10% discount on the printed price. The ratio of the cost price and the printed price of the book is

A. 45 : 56
B. 45 : 51
C. 47 : 56
D. 47 : 51

Q.9 In the given figure, BO and CO are the bisector of ∠CBD and ∠BCE respectively and ∠A = 40°, then ∠BOC is equal to:

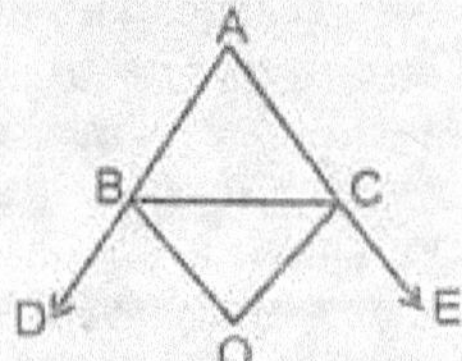

A. 60°
B. 65°
C. 75°
D. 70°

Q.10 The sum of two numbers is 40 and their difference is 4. The ratio of the numbers is :

A. 21 : 19
B. 22 : 9
C. 11 : 9
D. 11 : 18

Q.11

If A + B = 90°, then $\sqrt{\dfrac{tanA\,tanB + tanA\,cotB}{sinA\,secB} - \dfrac{sin^2 B}{cos^2 A}}$ = ?

A. tan A
B. sin A
C. cot A
D. cosec A

Q.12 If O is the orthocentre of ΔABC, then ∠BOC + ∠BAC is equal to:

A. 90°
B. 120°
C. 135°
D. 180°

Q.13 For which of the following value of m the equation $x^2 - 6x + m = 0$ has equal roots?

A. 3
B. 1/2
C. 9
D. 5

Q.14 The difference between the circumference and diameter of a circle is 150 m. The radius of that circle is (Take π=22/7)

A. 25 metres
B. 35 metres
C. 30 metres
D. 40 metres

Q.15 Area of circle is equal to the area of a rectangle having perimeter of 100 cm and length is more than the breadth by 6 cm. What is the diameter of the circle?

A. 14 cm
B. 28 cm
C. 22 cm
D. 24 cm

Q.16 The average monthly income of A and B is ₹7760. The average monthly income of B and C is ₹10990 and that of C and A is ₹9070. What is the annual income of B?

A. ₹120240
B. ₹124480
C. ₹112360
D. ₹116160

Q.17 The simple interest on a sum of money is 1/25 of the principal and the number of years is equal to the rate percent per annum. Find the rate percent per annum.

A. 1%
B. 2%
C. 3%
D. 4%

Q.18 If 3 tan θ - 4 = 0 and 180° < θ < 270° then cosec θ = _______

A. 5/4
B. 4/5
C. -5/4
D. -4/5

Q.19 In the given figure, ABCD is a trapezium such that AD II BC and P, Q are the points on AB and CD respectively such that PQ II AD and AP: PB = 5 : 3. Then PQ is:

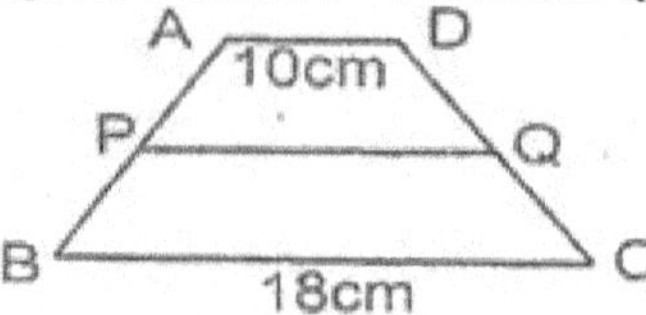

A. 12.5 cm
B. 15 cm
C. 17.5 cm
D. 20 cm

Q.20 The area of a square park is 25 sq.km. The time taken to complete around of the field once, at a speed of 3 km/hour is

A. 4 hours 60 minutes
B. 4 hours 50 minutes
C. 6 hours 40 minutes
D. 5 hours 40 minutes

Q.21 The total area of a circle and a square is equal to 5450 sq.cm. The diameter of the circle is 70 cms. What is the sum of the circumference of the circle and the perimeter of the square?

A. 360 cm
B. 380 cm
C. 270 cm
D. Cannot be determined

Q.22 A rectangle with one side of length 12 cm is inscribed in a circle of diameter 15cm.Find the area of rectangle.

A. 120 cm²   B. 102 cm²
C. 108 cm²   D. 100 cm²

Q.23 What is the difference between the simple interest on a principal of ₹600 being calculated at 4% per annum for 3 years and 3 % per annum for 3 years?

A. ₹14   B. ₹16   C. ₹18   D. ₹20

Q.24 1% of 1% of 25% of 1000 is?

A. 0.025   B. 0.0025
C. 0.25   D. 0.000025

Q.25 A tank is filled by pipe A in 32 minutes and by pipe B in 36 minutes. When it is full, it can be emptied by a pipe C in 20 minutes. If all the three pipes are opened simultaneously, half of the tank will be filled in how many minutes?

A. 51312   B. 5335   C. 55513   D. 56413

Q.26 The average age of 30 students is 9 years. If the age of their teacher is included, it becomes 10 years. What is the age of teacher?

A. 30 year   B. 35 year   C. 25 year   D. 40 year

Q.27 If 100 men can do 100 work in 100 days, then 1 man will do 1 work in how many days?

A. 1 days   B. 10 days   C. 100 days   D. 200 days

Q.28 The average of all the perfect squares up to 100 is:

A. 38.5   B. 1000   C. 100   D. 385

Q.29 DIRECTIONS: Study the following table carefully and answer the questions that follow.

The table represents the total number of students studying courses P, Q, K, S and T, across eight Institutes i.e., A, B, C, D, E, F, G and H.

Courses	Institutes							
	A	B	C	D	E	F	G	H
P	520	410	550	450	570	210	750	450
Q	410	540	610	580	380	550	570	310
R	430	210	590	530	730	510	530	480
S	350	280	570	320	410	480	610	460
T	370	480	380	250	180	370	590	660

What is the respective ratio between the total number of students studying in institute A and the total number of students studying in institute H?

A. 52 : 59   B. 52 : 55   C. 55 : 59   D. 59: 61

Q.30 DIRECTIONS: Study the following table carefully and answer the questions that follow.

The table represents the total number of students studying courses P, Q, K, S and T, across eight Institutes i.e., A, B, C, D, E, F, G and H.

Courses	Institutes							
	A	B	C	D	E	F	G	H
P	520	410	550	450	570	210	750	450
Q	410	540	610	580	380	550	570	310
R	430	210	590	530	730	510	530	480
S	350	280	570	320	410	480	610	460
T	370	480	380	250	180	370	590	660

What is the total number of students who are studying course T across all institutes?

A. 3480   B. 3280   C. 3420   D. 3840

General Intelligence & Reasoning

Q.31 Ram is facing North-West. He turns is clockwise direction by 900, then 1800 in the anti-clockwise direction and 900 in the same direction. Which direction is he facing now?

A. South-West   B. West
C. South   D. South-East

Q.32 The last day of a century cannot be either

I. Tuesday.
II. Thursday.
III. Saturday.
IV. Sunday.

A. I and II.   B. I and IV.
C. I, II and III.   D. III and IV.

Q.33 A piece of paper is folded and cut as shown below in the questions figure. From the given answer figures, indicate how it will appear when opened?

Problem Figure

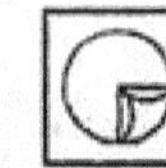

Answer Figure

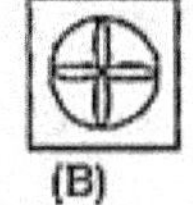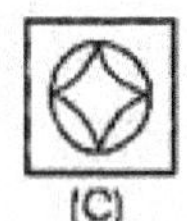

(A)   (B)   (C)   (D)

A. A   B. B   C. C   D. D

Q.34 Complete the given series:

6, 12, 30, 56, ?

A. 132   **B.** 102   **C.** 98   **D.** 108

Q.35 If the 3rd day of a month is Monday, which day will fall on the 5th day after the 21st of that month?

A. Thursday   **B.** Monday
C. Wednesday   **D.** Tuesday

Q.36 Find the Mirror image of the figure given below.

Question Figure

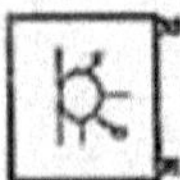

Answer Figures

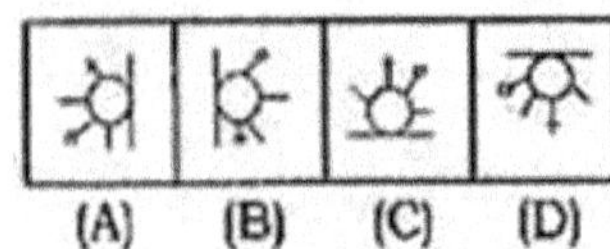

(A)   (B)   (C)   (D)

A. A   **B.** B   **C.** C   **D.** D

Q.37 In questions given below select the related letters from the given alternatives.
NLO:RPS::VTW:?

A. XVY   **B.** VTR   **C.** TRP   **D.** VUW

Q.38 Read the following information carefully and answer the questions given below it.

'X + Y' means 'X is the father of Y'.

'X – Y' means 'X is the mother of Y'

'X x Y' means 'X is the brother of Y'

'X ÷ Y' means 'X is the sister of Y'.

If L + M x N÷P – R then L is R's?

A. Paternal Grandfather.
B. Uncle.
C. Maternal uncle.
D. Maternal grandfather.

Q.39 Identify the diagram that best represents the relationship among Profit, Dividend and Bonus.

A. A   **B.** B   **C.** C   **D.** D

Q.40 Find the odd one out from the given alternatives.

A. 9 : 80   **B.** 5 : 24   **C.** 6 : 35   **D.** 10 : 91

Q.41 Select the answer figure in which the questions figure is embedded.

Question Figure :

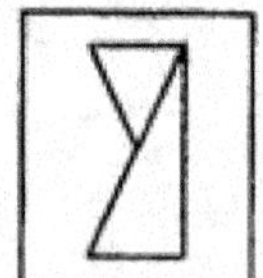

Answer Figures :

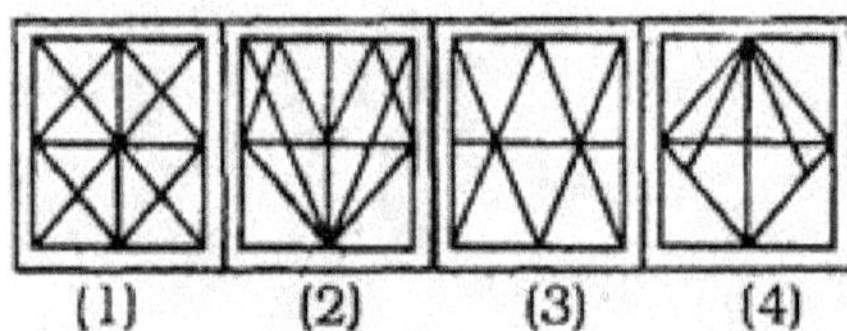

(1)   (2)   (3)   (4)

A. 1   **B.** 2   **C.** 3   **D.** 4

Q.42 Four of the following five pair have same relation between their elements and hence form a group. Which one does not belong to that group?

A. Bull-Calf   **B.** Cat-Kitten
C. Chitah-Cub   **D.** Tiger-Tigress

Q.43 Four kids P, Q, R and S are up on the ladder. P is further up the ladder than Q, Q is between P and R. If S is further up than P, who is the third from the bottom?

A. Q   **B.** P   **C.** R   **D.** S

Q.44 Arrange the following words according to the english dictionary.
(1) Repoint (2) Reptile (3) Repent (4) Repute (5) Report

A. 3, 1, 5, 2, 4   **B.** 3, 5, 1, 2, 4
C. 5, 1, 4, 3, 2   **D.** 5, 4, 1, 3, 2

Q.45 In the following questions a word is followed by five other words, one of which cannot be formed by using the letters of the given word. Find this word
CONCENTRATION

A. CONCERN   **B.** NATION
C. TRAIN   **D.** CENTRE

Q.46 What should come at the place of question mark?
N5V, K7T, ?, E14P, B19N

A. H9R   **B.** H10Q   **C.** H10R   **D.** I10R

Q.47 What should come at the place of question mark?
Q1F, S2E, U6D, W21C, ?

A. Y44B   **B.** Y66B   **C.** Y88B   **D.** Z88B

Q.48 If A means '+', B means '—' C means 'x' and D means ÷, then

18 C 14 A 6 B 16 D 4 ?

A. 254   **B.** 238   **C.** 188   **D.** 258

Q.49 Arrange the following in a logical order:
1. Butterfly   2. Cocoon   3. Egg   4. Worn

A. 1, 3, 4, 2,   **B.** 1, 4, 3, 2,
C. 2, 4, 1, 3   **D.** 3, 4, 2, 1

Q.50 Six friends P, Q, R, S, T and U are standing around a circular park facing towards centre. The angle made at the centre of the circle by a straight line from P and Q is 180o, from Q and R is 120o, from R and S 180o. T is not standing on the immediate left of R while R is not on the immediate right of P. On the basis of the above information which of the following statements is definitely true?

A.   R is standing between P and S
B.   T is standing between P and U
C.   Q is standing between S and U
D.   T and R are standing opposite each other

Q.51 Below are given letters A to Z. Under each capital letter, a small letter is written which is to be used as a code for the Capital Letters:

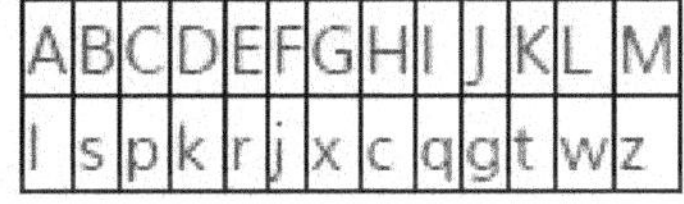

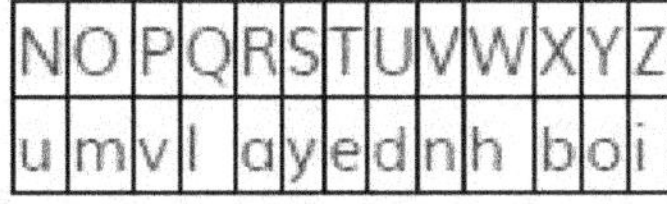

In each of the following questions, a group of six Capital Letters is given and its code equivalent is given below. Select the response containing the correct code.

Find the code for 'CHWCLS'

A. lkcvmf   **B.** lbvseo   **C.** afdber   **D.** pchpwy

Q.52 From the given responses, find the missing number in the series.
YW, US, ?, MK
A. RP   **B.** BD   **C.** FH   **D.** QO

Q.53 Choose the odd one out from the given alternatives.
A. Carrot   **B.** Potato   **C.** Ginger   **D.** Cabbage

Q.54 If in a code language RUSTUM is written in INWANZ and RASTOGI is written as IXWAVJK, how would RUSSIA be written in that code ?
A.   INNWKJ   **B.**   INNWKT
C.   INWWKX   **D.**   INNWNX

Q.55 Choose the odd one out.
A. (18, 45)   **B.** (23, 14)   **C.** (29, 82)   **D.** (36, 27)

General Awareness

Q.56 What is the number of spokes in the Dharmachakra in the National Flag of India?
A. 16   **B.** 18   **C.** 22   **D.** 24

Q.57 By what name is the Ganga known in Bangladesh?
A. Padma   **B.** Bhagirathi
C. Rupnarayan   **D.** Nubra

Q.58 Which of the following states is not a member of the 'Seven Sisters'?
A. Nagaland   **B.** Arunachal Pradesh
C. Sikkim   **D.** Manipur

Q.59 Consumer Protection Act was passed by Indian parliament in:
A. 1982   **B.** 1984   **C.** 1986   **D.** 1989

Q.60 ISI is presently known as:
A. ISO   **B.** Agmar   **C.** Mark   **D.** BIS

Q.61 India born Gita Gopinath has joined _________as its chief economist.
A.   World Bank
B.   IMF
C.   World Economic Forum
D.   NDB

Q.62 The Nagarjuna sagar dam is constructed on the river-
A. Krishna   **B.** Chambal   **C.** Kosi   **D.** Sutlej

Q.63 Central Institute of Medicinal and Aromatic Plants (CIMAP) has signed MoU with which US-based for improving the quality of fragrant oils?
A.   Research Institute for Fragrant Materials (RIFM)
B.   Fragrance & Flavour Development Centre (FFDC)
C.   International Fragrance Association
D.   ISIPCA

Q.64 'Mohiniattam' is a dance form of?
A. Kerala.   **B.** Tamil Nadu.
C. Karnataka.   **D.** Tanjavur.

Q.65 Booker prize is given in the field of :
A. Medicine   **B.** Adventure
C. Fiction writing   **D.** Science

Q.66 Daulatabad was constructed by.
A.   Razia Sultan.
B.   Ibrahim Lodi.
C.   Mohamniad bin Tughlaq.
D.   Sikander Lodhi.

Q.67 Who is the current CM of Chasttisgarh?
A. Bhupesh Baghel   **B.** Kamalnath
C. Sushant Sharma   **D.** Baldev Singh

Q.68 The minimum age of the member of Rajya Sabha is :
A. 25 years   **B.** 21 years   **C.** 30 years   **D.** 35 years

Q.69 Which is the second largest planet in a solar system is-
A. Jupiter   **B.** Saturn   **C.** Venus   **D.** Neptune

Q.70 The position of India in the world on the scale of size (area) Is-
A. Second   **B.** Fifth   **C.** First   **D.** Seventh

General Science

Q.71 A mixture of water and alcohol can be separated by —

A. Filtration	**B.** Evaporation
C. Distillation	**D.** Decantation

Q.72 Oxidation number of sodium in sodium amalgam is _____

A. +1   **B.** 0   **C.** -1   **D.** +2

Q.73 If the length of a simple pendulum is halved then its period of oscillation is:
A. Doubled
B. Halved
C. Increased by a factor $\sqrt{2}$
D. Decreased by a factor $\sqrt{2}$

Q.74 Enzymes are
A. Carbohydrates   **B.** Proteins
C. Lipids   **D.** Steroids

Q.75 Which of the following scientists first gave the Quantam Theory?
A. W. F. Talbot   **B.** Sir J. S. Fleming
C. Max Planck   **D.** Albert Einstein

Q.76 The weight of an object would be minimum when it is placed at
A. north place   **B.** south place
C. equator   **D.** centre of the earth

Q.77 An atom of an element with mass number 23 and atomic number 11 will have —
A. 11 neutrons, 12 protons and 11 electrons
B. 11 protons, 12 neutrons and 11 electrons
C. 11 protons, 12 electrons and 11 neutrons
D. 23 protons and 11 electrons

Q.78 On which of the following is the working of the Venturimeter based on?
A. Bernoulli's theorem   **B.** Boltzmann equation
C. Faxen's law   **D.** Poiseuille's law

Q.79 Why do we feel comfortable under a fan?
A. It throws down cool air
B. It evaporates the sweat
C. It produces convection current
D. None of these

Q.80 A catalyst _____
A. increases the free energy change of the reaction
B. decreases the free energy change of the reaction
C. neither increase nor decrease the free energy of the reaction
D. may increase or decrease the depending upon the nature of the catalyst

Q.81 Weightlessness experienced while orbiting the earth is a result of which one of the following?
A. Zero gravity.   **B.** Inertia.
C. Center of gravity.   **D.** Acceleration.

Q.82 In an automobile, the power is transmitted from the gear box to the differential through:

A. Knuckle joint   **B.** Bevel gears
C. Hooke's joint   **D.** Oldham's coupling

Q.83 At very high pressure a real gas, as compared to an ideal gas, occupies:
A. same volume   **B.** less volume
C. more volume   **D.** Any of these

Q.84 If steel is heated bright red hot and is then cooled slowly, the process is called:
A. Annealing   **B.** Tempering
C. Smelting   **D.** Quenching

Q.85 The nuclear particle having no mass and no charge, but only spin is:
A. proton   **B.** neutrino   **C.** meson   **D.** electron

Q.86 Which of the following has the smallest wavelength?
A. red   **B.** blue   **C.** green   **D.** violet

Q.87 pH value of X is 14. X is_____ .
A. weak acid   **B.** strong acid
C. weak base   **D.** strong base

Q.88 Animal proteins are also called _______.
A. First class protein
B. Second class protein
C. essential proteins
D. Important proteins

Q.89 The principle on which a jet engine works is?
A. Conservation of energy.
B. Bernoulli's principles.
C. Newton's law of action and reaction.
D. None of the above.

Q.90 Pyrometer is used to measure -
A. Low Temperature   **B.** Low Pressure
C. High Temperature   **D.** High Pressure

Q.91 which of the following types of radiation has the highest energy?
A. α-particles   **B.** β-particles
C. γ-rays   **D.** visible light

Q.92 The Barometer is used to measure the -
A. Altitude
B. Heat
C. Atmospheric pressure
D. Angles

Q.93 Identify the chemical change in the following list.
A. Gold metal is formed from gold chloride in solution.
B. was is melted out of a mold in a kiln.
C. plaster of paris is ground to a powder for making a mold.
D. A gold ring is resized to fit a new owner.

Q.94 J. J. Thomson received the Nobel Prize in physics for the discovery of _____.
A. protons   **B.** neutrons   **C.** electrons   **D.** positrons

Q.95 Which of the following is formed by an electrovalent bond?

A. NaCl
B. CH$_4$
C. SO$_2$
D. None of these

Q.96 A man jumping out of a moving train due to inertia is thrown

A. Backward
B. Forward
C. Sideward
D. Falls flat.

Q.97 Typhoid fever is caused by

A. Bacteria   **B.** Virus   **C.** Protozoa   **D.** Fungi

Q.98 Which among the following is poorest source of Fat?

A. Curd.   **B.** Egg.   **C.** Fish.   **D.** Milk.

Q.99 The amount of heat required to raise the temperature of 1 kg of water through 1°C is called

A. specific heat at constant volume
B. specific heat at constant pressure
C. kilocalorie
D. None of these

Q.100 Chromosomes are made up of

A. DNA
B. Protein
C. DNA and Protein
D. RNA

// Smart Answer Sheet //

Correct	Percentage of students who answered correctly.	Skipped	Percentage of students who skipped.

Q.	Ans.	Correct / Skipped	Q.	Ans.	Correct / Skipped	Q.	Ans.	Correct / Skipped	Q.	Ans.	Correct / Skipped	Q.	Ans.	Correct / Skipped
1	A	84.11 % / 10.32 %	17	B	82.75 % / 15.34 %	33	B	86.42 % / 10.79 %	49	D	80.66 % / 12.77 %	65	C	78.97 % / 11.5 %
2	A	82.91 % / 13.46 %	18	C	88.88 % / 11.09 %	34	A	87.3 % / 11.13 %	50	C	80.66 % / 16.38 %	66	C	83.84 % / 14.99 %
3	C	87.84 % / 11.08 %	19	B	78.16 % / 16.78 %	35	C	86.94 % / 10.01 %	51	D	84.2 % / 11.88 %	67	A	83.64 % / 12.5 %
4	B	88.33 % / 11.31 %	20	C	85.26 % / 10.75 %	36	A	85.46 % / 13.27 %	52	D	76.18 % / 17.76 %	68	C	87.32 % / 10.59 %
5	A	76.02 % / 12.44 %	21	B	78.14 % / 14.32 %	37	A	84.85 % / 13.12 %	53	D	87.81 % / 11.3 %	69	B	81.72 % / 15.83 %
6	C	76.96 % / 18.0 %	22	C	78.58 % / 17.54 %	38	D	77.12 % / 21.83 %	54	C	77.63 % / 11.89 %	70	D	89.6 % / 10.39 %
7	C	84.5 % / 14.71 %	23	C	76.49 % / 17.98 %	39	D	81.69 % / 12.49 %	55	C	83.2 % / 10.73 %	71	C	86.11 % / 11.41 %
8	A	76.51 % / 21.29 %	24	A	85.74 % / 14.24 %	40	D	85.63 % / 10.56 %	56	D	87.18 % / 10.88 %	72	B	83.14 % / 16.7 %
9	D	87.89 % / 11.06 %	25	C	82.95 % / 12.82 %	41	C	79.39 % / 14.35 %	57	A	81.56 % / 18.17 %	73	B	89.29 % / 10.35 %
10	C	88.58 % / 10.17 %	26	D	85.28 % / 12.47 %	42	D	80.9 % / 10.12 %	58	C	87.61 % / 10.55 %	74	B	84.99 % / 13.09 %
11	A	76.41 % / 17.29 %	27	C	79.63 % / 17.4 %	43	B	82.71 % / 17.14 %	59	C	89.63 % / 10.29 %	75	C	88.85 % / 11.09 %
12	D	82.45 % / 11.3 %	28	A	89.19 % / 10.21 %	44	A	89.09 % / 10.54 %	60	C	87.47 % / 10.64 %	76	D	79.06 % / 10.79 %
13	C	82.83 % / 12.2 %	29	A	88.04 % / 11.34 %	45	D	82.97 % / 14.12 %	61	B	84.89 % / 11.18 %	77	B	76.03 % / 18.1 %
14	B	79.6 % / 12.0 %	30	B	81.72 % / 13.57 %	46	C	86.02 % / 10.2 %	62	A	77.58 % / 15.84 %	78	A	77.16 % / 11.03 %
15	B	79.23 % / 19.13 %	31	D	85.73 % / 10.42 %	47	C	77.71 % / 11.31 %	63	A	79.14 % / 20.02 %	79	B	87.67 % / 10.4 %
16	D	80.0 % / 13.96 %	32	C	76.64 % / 16.99 %	48	A	86.4 % / 10.55 %	64	A	85.78 % / 13.33 %	80	C	86.77 % / 11.22 %

Q.	Ans.	Correct		Q.	Ans.	Correct		Q.	Ans.	Correct		Q.	Ans.	Correct		Q.	Ans.	Correct
		Skipped				Skipped				Skipped				Skipped				Skipped
81	D	85.62 % 13.22 %		85	B	83.87 % 13.45 %		89	C	87.69 % 12.01 %		93	A	84.22 % 10.22 %		97	A	85.06 % 12.89 %
82	A	86.6 % 12.56 %		86	D	77.11 % 19.53 %		90	C	78.7 % 16.24 %		94	C	83.8 % 10.32 %		98	C	86.34 % 11.36 %
83	B	78.87 % 16.58 %		87	D	81.33 % 14.85 %		91	C	81.92 % 12.8 %		95	A	85.4 % 10.66 %		99	C	82.19 % 15.78 %
84	A	87.98 % 10.47 %		88	A	76.65 % 16.23 %		92	C	84.96 % 14.69 %		96	B	86.98 % 10.83 %		100	C	77.7 % 14.15 %

//Hints and Solutions//

1. This is the standard inequality formula.

2. Let B finish the work in 3x days

∴ A will finish the work in x days

Also 3x-x=60

x=30 days.

∴ A's one day work =1/30

B"s one day work=1/90

(A+B)'s one day work=1/30+1/90=4/90

∴ Time taken to Finish the work

while (A+B) working together = 90/4

=45/2 days.

3. Milk   : Water

New ratio 5 : 4

Old ratio   3 : 4

Difference 2 : 0

Sum of old ratios = 3 + 4 = 7

∴ Milk added = 2/7×70=20 litres

4. S.P. of 12 objects = C.P. of 9 objects

Clearly there is a loss as 12 articles are sold for what 9 articles are bought.

L% = L/C.P.×100 = 3/12 × 100 = 25%

5.

$$\tan(90-\theta)=\cot\theta=\frac{1}{\tan\theta}$$

$$=\frac{1}{2-\sqrt{3}}\times\frac{2+\sqrt{3}}{2+\sqrt{3}}$$

$$\frac{2+\sqrt{3}}{4-3}=2+\sqrt{3}$$

6.

Time taken by the two pipes to fill the tank

$=\frac{20\times30}{20+30}$ hrs = 12hrs.

∴ $\frac{1}{3}$ of tank if filled in $\frac{12}{3}$ = 4 hrs.

Now, $\frac{1}{3}$ of the supplied water leaks out

⇒ the filler pipes are only $1-\frac{1}{3}=\frac{2}{3}$ as efficient as earlier.

⇒ the work of (12 - 4 =) 8 hrs will be completed now in

$8\div\frac{2}{3}=\frac{8\times3}{2}$ = 12 hrs

∴ total time = 4 + 12 = 16 hrs.

7.

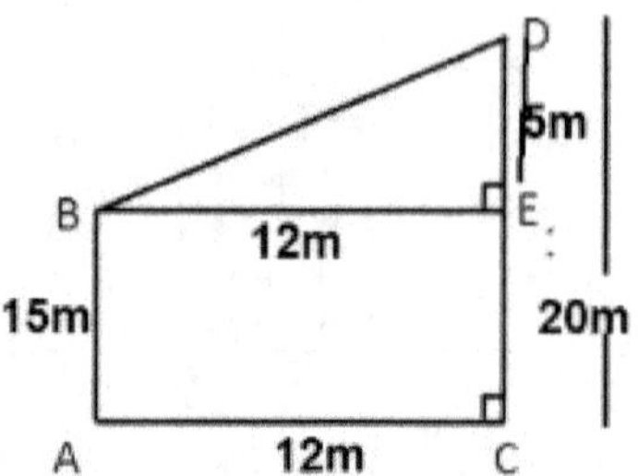

Applying Pythagoras theorem in triangle BDE

$$BD^2 = BE^2 + DE^2$$

$$= 5^2 + 12^2$$

$$= 25 + 144 = 169$$

BD = 13m

8.

Let the CP be Rs. 100.

∴ SP = Rs. 112

If the marked price be Rs. x, then

90% of x = 112

$$x = \frac{112\times100}{90} = Rs.\ \frac{1120}{9}$$

Required Ratio $= 100 : \frac{1120}{9}$

$$= 900 : 1120 = 45 : 56$$

9. ∠BOC

= 90° - 1/2 ∠A = 90° - 1/2 (40) =70°

10. Let the two numbers be x and y. Then according to question

x+y=40

x-y=4

so x=22 and y=18

therefore required ratio=22/18=11 : 9

11.

$A + B = 90° \Rightarrow B = 90° - A$

$$\sqrt{\frac{\tan A \tan B + \tan A \cot B}{\sin A \sec B} - \frac{\sin^2 B}{\cos^2 A}}$$

$$= \sqrt{\frac{\tan A \tan(90°-A) + \tan A \cot (90°-A)}{\sin A \sec(90°-A)} - \frac{\sin^2(90°-A)}{\cos^2 A}}$$

$$= \sqrt{\frac{\tan A \cot A + \tan A \tan A}{\sin A \ cosec\ A} - \frac{\cos^2 A}{\cos^2 A}}$$

$$= \sqrt{1 + \tan^2 A - 1} = \sqrt{\tan^2 A} = \tan A$$

12.

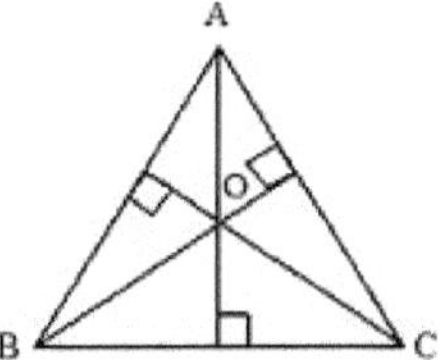

$\angle BOC + \angle BAC = 180°$

Orthocentre is the intersecting point of altitudes.

13. When equation has equal roots then

$b^2 - 4ac = 0$

$\therefore (-6)\,2 - 4\,(1)\,(m) = 0$

$36 - 4m = 0$

$-4m = -36$

$4m = 36$

$m = 9$

14.

(Circumference of a circle − Diameter) = 150

$\pi d - d = 150$

$d\left(\dfrac{22}{7} - 1\right) = 150$

$\left(\dfrac{22}{7} - 1\right) d = 150$

$d = \dfrac{150 \times 7}{15} = 70$

Radius $= \dfrac{70}{2} = 35\text{m}.$

15. Let breadth = x, then length

$= (x + 6)$

$\therefore 2(x + x + 6) = 100$

$\Rightarrow 2x + 6 = 50$

$\Rightarrow x = 22$ cm

$\therefore$ breadth = x = 22 cm & length

$= 22 + 6 = 28$ cm

$\therefore$ Area of circle = Area of rectangle

$\Rightarrow \pi r^2 = 22 \times 28$

$\Rightarrow r^2 = 22 \times 28 \times 22 / 7 = 7 \times 4 \times 7$

$\Rightarrow 7 \times 2 = 14$ cm

$\therefore$ Diameter = 2r = 28 cm

16. Total income of A and B = 2 x 7760

$\Rightarrow A + B = 15520 \quad ...(i)$

Similarly,

$B + C = 10990 \times 2 = 21980 ...(ii)$

and $A + C = 9070 \times 2 = 18140 ...(iii)$

Adding Eqs. (i), (ii) and (iii),

$2(A + B + C) = 55640$

$\Rightarrow A + B + C = 27820 \qquad ,..(iv)$

Subtracting Eq. (iii) from Eq. (iv),

$B = 27820 - 18140 = 9680$

Hence, annual income of

$B = 9680 \times 12 = ₹116160$

17.

$$\frac{P}{25} = \frac{P \times R \times R}{100} \Rightarrow R^2 = 4 \Rightarrow R = 2\%.$$

18.

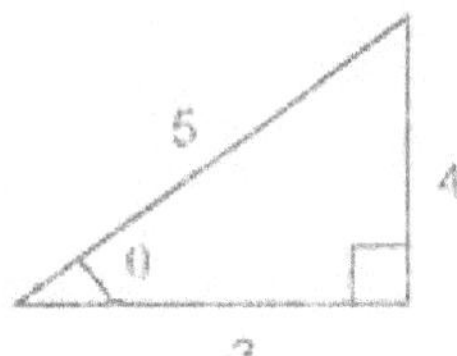

$3\tan \theta - 4 = 0$

$$\Rightarrow \tan \theta = \frac{4}{3}$$

$$\therefore \csc \theta = -\frac{5}{4}$$

$(\because 180° < \theta < 270°)$

19.

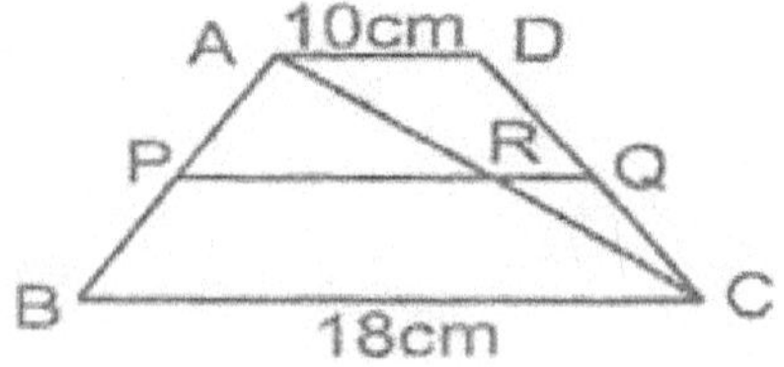

Now In $\triangle APR$ and $\triangle ABC$

$\angle APR = \angle ABC$ ($\because$ PQ II AD II BC)

And $\because$ APR = $\angle ACB$ ($\because$ PQ I I BC)

$\therefore \triangle APR \sim \triangle ABC$

$\therefore \dfrac{AP}{AB} = \dfrac{PR}{BC} \Rightarrow PR = \dfrac{AP}{AB} \times BC$

$= \dfrac{AP}{AP+PB} \times BC$

$\Rightarrow PR = \dfrac{5}{8} \times 18 = \dfrac{45}{4}$ cm

And $\dfrac{AP}{PB} = \dfrac{AR}{RC} = \dfrac{5}{3}$

Similarly, $\triangle RCQ \sim \triangle CAD$

$\therefore \dfrac{RQ}{AD} = \dfrac{RC}{AC}$

$\Rightarrow RO = \dfrac{RC}{AR+RC} \times AD = \dfrac{3}{8} \times 10$

$= \dfrac{15}{4}$ cm

$\therefore PQ = PR + RO = \dfrac{45}{4} + \dfrac{15}{4} = 15$ cm

20. Area = 25 km2

Side = $\sqrt{25}$ = 5 km

Perimeter = 4 × 5 = 20 km

S = D/T

Time taken in completing one round

= (Distance)/(Speed)

=203 hrs = 623 hrs

6 hours 23 × 60 = 6 hours 40 minutes.

21.

If the side of the square be x cm then,

$\pi \times 35 \times 35 + x^2 = 5450$

$\Rightarrow \dfrac{22}{7} \times 35 \times 35 + x^2 = 5450$

$\Rightarrow x^2 = 5450 - 3850 = 1600$

$\therefore$ x = 40 cm

$\therefore$ Required sum = $\pi \times d + 4x$

$= \left(\dfrac{22}{7} \times 70 + 4 \times 40\right)$ cm.

= 380 cm.

22.

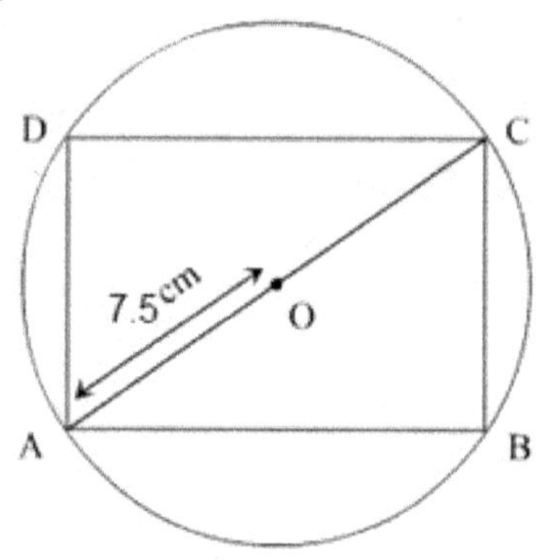

Now, OA=OC=7.5 cm[Radius of circle]

$\Rightarrow$ AC=OA+OC=7.5+7.5=15 cm

In right triangle ABC, by pythagoras theorem

$(AC)^2 = (AB)^2 + (BC)^2$

$\Rightarrow 15^2 = 12^2 + (BC)^2$

$\Rightarrow (BC)^2 = 225 - 144 = 81$

=BC=9 cm

$\therefore$ Area of rectangle= AB × BC=12 × 9=108 cm^2

23. 4% for 3 years (S.I.) = 12% of the amount

3% for 3 years (S.I.) = 9% of the amount

The difference between the two is 3% of amount.

3% of 600 = 3/100× 600

=₹18

24. 1% of 1% of 25% of 1000

(1/100)×(1/100)×(25/100) × 1000 = 0.025.

25.

A + B + C fill the tank in:

$$\frac{32 \times 36 \times 20}{36 \times 20 + 32 \times 20 - 32 \times 36} = \frac{32 \times 36 \times 20}{208}$$

$$= \frac{1440}{13} \text{ min}$$

A + B + C fill half the tank in $\frac{720}{13}$ min

$$= 55\frac{5}{13} \text{ min}$$

Alternate method

$$= \frac{1}{32} + \frac{1}{36} - \frac{1}{20}$$

$$= \frac{1440}{13}$$

half of the tank will be filled in:

$$= \frac{720}{13}$$

$$या = 55\frac{5}{13}$$

26. Total number of students = 30*9 = 270

When teacher's age is included then total age = 31*10=310

therefore, Required answer = 310- 270 = 40 years

27.

Men	Work	Days
100 ↑	100 ↓	100 ↓
1 ↑	1 ↓	x ↓

∴ Time taken = 100×100 1×11 00 = 100 days

28.

$$\frac{1+4+9+16+\cdots 100}{10}$$

$$= \frac{10 \times 11 \times 21}{6 \times 10}$$

$$\left[\because 1^2 + 2^2 + \cdots n^2 = \frac{n(n+1)(2n+1)}{6} \right]$$

$$= 38.5$$

29. Total number of students studying in institute A

= 520 + 410 + 430 + 350 + 370

= 2080

Total number of student studying in institute H

= 450 + 310 + 480 + 460 + 660

= 2360

Now, required ratio = 2080/2360 = 52/59 = 52 : 59

30. Total number of required students

= 370 + 480 + 380 + 250 + 180 + 370 + 590 + 660

= 3280

31.

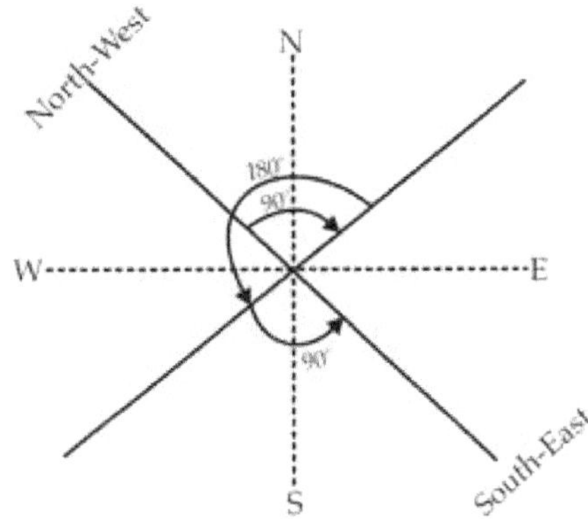

He is facing in South-East direction.

32. The last day of century cannot be either Tuesday, Thursday or Saturday.

33.

34. The given series follows the pattern:
(prime number)^2 + (prime number)So,
$2^2+2=4+2=6$, $3^2+3=9+3=12$, $5^2+5=25+5=30$, $7^2+7=49+7=56$, $11^2+11=121+11=132$.Hence required term will be 132.

35. The 3rd day is Monday. So, the 10th and 17th days are also Mondays.
Thus, the 21st day is Friday..'. The fifth day from the 21st will be Wednesday.

37.

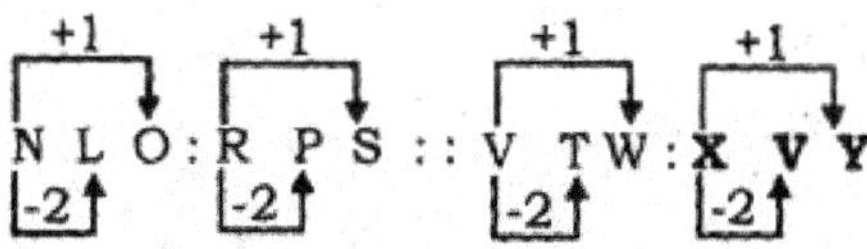

38.

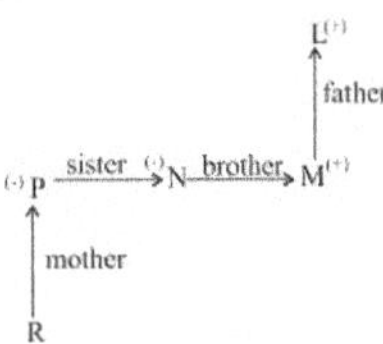

L is the father of P who is the mother of R. Thus, L is the maternal grandfather of R.

39. Bonus and Dividend are different from each other. But both these are parts of profit.

40. Second number is one less than the square of first number.

41.

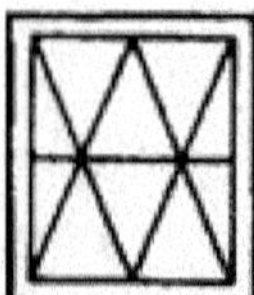

42. Only the tiger and the tigress hold the male and female relationship, while the remaining hold the parent and offspring relationship.

43.

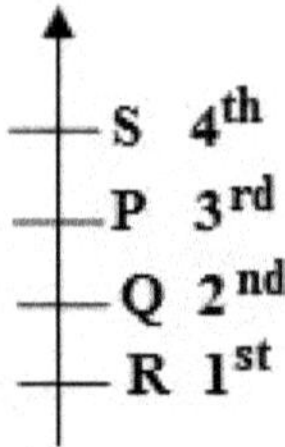

P is third from bottom.

44. 3, 1, 5, 2, 4

45. As there is only one 'E' in the given word

46.

$$N \xrightarrow{-3} K \xrightarrow{-3} [H] \xrightarrow{-3} E \xrightarrow{-3} B$$
$$5 \xrightarrow{+2} 7 \xrightarrow{+3} [10] \xrightarrow{+4} 14 \xrightarrow{+5} 19$$
$$V \xrightarrow{-2} T \xrightarrow{-2} [R] \xrightarrow{-2} P \xrightarrow{-2} N$$

47.

$$Q \xrightarrow{+2} S \xrightarrow{+2} U \xrightarrow{+2} W \xrightarrow{+2} [Y]$$
$$1 \xrightarrow{\times 1+1} 2 \xrightarrow{\times 2+2} 6 \xrightarrow{\times 3+3} 21 \xrightarrow{\times 4+4} [88]$$
$$F \xrightarrow{-1} E \xrightarrow{-1} D \xrightarrow{-1} C \xrightarrow{-1} [B]$$

48. According to the question,

$$? = 18 \underset{\times}{\downarrow} C \ 14 \underset{+}{\downarrow} A \ 6 \underset{-}{\downarrow} B \ 16 \underset{\div}{\downarrow} D \ 4$$

=18 x14+ 6—16÷4 (using BODMAS rule)=18x14+6—4=252+6—4=258—4=254

49. The logical arrangement of the occurrence of various steps in a process :

Egg →	Worn →	Cocoon →	Butterfly
3	4	2	1

50. So, Q is standing between S and U

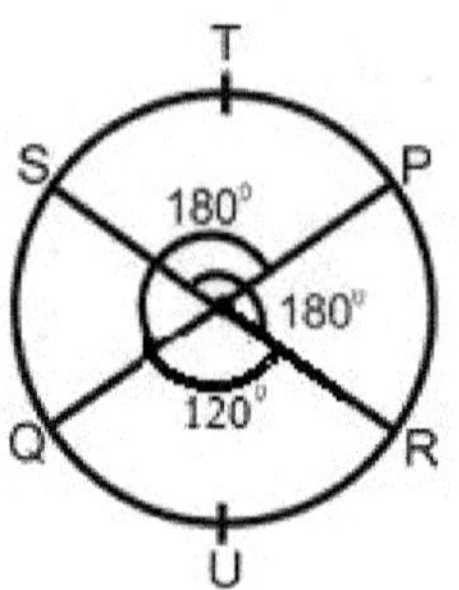

51.

C	H	W	C	L	S
↓	↓	↓	↓	↓	↓
p	c	h	p	w	y

52. The pattern is as follows

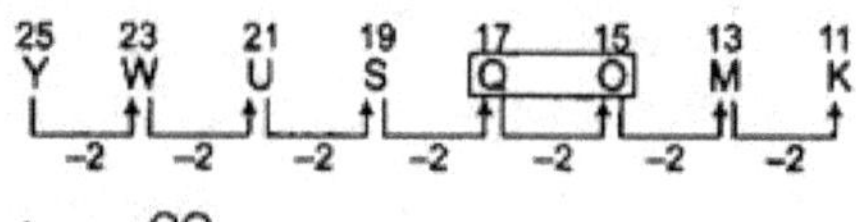

∴ = QO

53. All except Cabbage grow under-ground.

54.

R	U	S	T	U	M
↓	↓	↓	↓	↓	↓
I	N	W	A	N	Z

R	A	S	T	O	G	I
↓	↓	↓	↓	↓	↓	↓
I	X	W	A	V	J	K

Therefore,

R	U	S	S	I	A
↓	↓	↓	↓	↓	↓
I	N	W	W	K	X

56. The Ashoka Chakra is a depiction of the dharmachakra; represented with 24 spokes. It is so called because it appears on a number of edicts of Ashoka, most prominent among which is the Lion Capital of Ashoka. The most visible use of the Ashoka Chakra today is at the centre of the Flag of India (adopted on 22 July 1947), where it is rendered in a navy-blue colour on a white background, replacing the symbol of charkha (spinning wheel) of the pre-independence versions of the flag.

57. Padma

58. The Seven Sisters of India: Meghalaya, Arunachal Pradesh, Nagaland, Tripura, Assam, Manipur, and Mizoram cover a huge area of 255,511 square kilometres.

59. 1986.

The Consumer Protection Act, 1986 was enacted to provide a simpler and quicker access to redressal of consumer grievances. The Act for the first time introduced the concept of 'consumer' and conferred express additional rights on him.

60. ISI mark is a certification mark for industrial products in India. The mark certifies that a product confirms to the Indian Standard,mentioned as IS:xxxx on top of the mark, developed by the Bureau of Indian Standards (BIS), the national standards body of India. The ISI mark is by far the most recognized certification mark in the Indian subcontinent. The name ISI is an abbreviation of Indian Standards Institute, the former name of the Bureau of Indian Standards.

61. India born Gita Gopinath has joined International Monetary Fund as its chief economist.

62. Nagarjuna Sagar Dam is a masonry dam built across Krishna River in Nagarjuna Sagar, Andhra Pradesh. It is the largest dam in India.

63. Central Institute of Medicinal and Aromatic Plants (CIMAP) has signed MoU with US-based Research Institute for Fragrant Materials (RIFM) for improving the quality of fragrant oils. It was signed at conclusion of two-day annual conference of International Fragrance Association (IFA) in Paris, capital city of France.

64. Kerala. Mohiniyattam or Mohiniattam is a classical dance form of Kerala, developed by the Tamil nattuvanar (dance master) Vadivelu,one of the Thanjavur Quartet. It is one of the eight Indian classical dance forms. It is considered a very graceful dance meant to be performed as a solo recital by women.

65. The Man Booker prize for fiction is a literary prize that is awarded each year for the best original full-length novel, written in the English language, by a citizen of the commonwealth of Nations, Ireland or Zimbabwe. It is one of the awards given in the field of fiction writing.

66. Mohamniad bin Tughlaq-Muhammad Salman Khan also known as Jauna Khan , was the Turkic Sultan of Delhi through 1324 to 1351. He was the eldest son of Ghiyas-ud-din Tughlaq. Muhammad bin Tughlaq founded a new city, called Jahanpannah which connected older Delhi with Sin. Later, he ordered that the capital of his Sultanate be moved from Delhi to Deogir in Maharashtra (renaming it to Daulatabad). The capital move failed because Daulatabad was arid and did not have enough drinking water to support the new capital. The capital then returned to Delhi.

67. Five days after the Congress party swept the Chhattisgarh polls, State Congress chief Bhupesh Baghel has been named as the next Chief Minister.

68. Article 84 of the Constitution lays down the qualifications for membership of Parliament. As per that Article,"The minimum age requirement for a person to become a member of Rajya Sabha is 30 years."

But, minimum age for rajya sabha chairman (vice president of india) is 35 years."

69. The biggest planet in the Solar System is Jupiter. But the title for the second biggest planet in our Solar System goes to Saturn.

70. India is the seventh-largest country by area, the second-most populous country (with over 1.2 billion people), and the most populous democracy in the world.

72. Sodium amalgam is a homogeneous mixture of Na and Hg and as such Na exists in the elemental state and hence its O.N is zero.

74. Enzymes are large molecules that speed up the chemical reactions inside cells. Each type of enzyme does on specific job. Enzymes are a type of protein, and like all proteins, they are made from long chains of different amino acids.

75. Max Planck first gave the Quantam Theory

76. The weight of an object would be minimum when it is placed at centre of the earth

78. The working of the venturimeter is based on the Bernoulli's theorem

79. When the fan is turned on, it circulates the air, which evaporates the sweat on our body. This creates a cool feeling and we feel comfortable.

80. $dG = G_{products} - G_{Reactants}$ Hence , it does not change in the presence of a catalyst

81. Acceleration. weight lessens experienced while orbiting the Earth in because it will develop the centripetal force due to the center of gravity.

82. In an automobile, the power is transmitted from the gear box to the differential through Knuckle joint

83. At very high pressure a real gas, as compared to an ideal gas, occupies less volume

84. Annealing, in metallurgy and materials science, is a heat treatment that alters the physical and sometimes chemical properties of a material to increase its ductility and reduce its hardness, making it more workable.

85. neutrino

86. Violet has the smallest wavelength

87. Values less than 7 on the pH scale represent an acidic solution. As the pH value increases from 7 to 14, it represents an increase in OH" ion concentration in the solution, that is, increase in the strength of base.

88. Animal proteins are also called First class protein.

89. Newton's law of action and reaction-A jet engine is a machine for turning fuel into thrust (forward motion). The thrust is produced by action and reaction—a piece of physics also known as Newton's third law of motion. The force (action) of the exhaust

gases pushing backward produces an equal and opposite force (reaction) called thrust that powers the vehicle forward. Exactly the same principle pushes a skateboard forward when you kick backward with your foot.

90. It is used to measure high temperature

91. y-rays-Electromagnetic radiation (EM radiation or EMR) is a form of radiant energy released by certain electromagnetic processes. Visible light is one type of electromagnetic radiation; other familiar forms are invisible electromagnetic radiations such as X-rays and radio waves.

92. Barometers are used to measure atmospheric pressure

93. Gold metal is formed from gold chloride in solution-gold metal is formed from gold chloride in solution.

94. electrons

95. NaCl is formed by an ionic or electrovalent bond

96. A man jumping out from a moving train thrown forward due to inertia.

97. Typhoid fever, also known simply as typhoid, is a bacterial infection due to Salmonella typhoid.

98. Fish provides the least amount of fat. Apart from that one of the best sources of the essential omega-3 fats eicosapentaenoic acid, or EPA, and docosahexaenoic acid, or DHA. These omega-3 fats may lower the risk for heart disease, which is why it is also recommended by the American Heart Association to eat fish at least twice a week

99. The small calorie or gram calorie (symbol: cal) is the approximate amount of energy needed to raise the temperature of one gram of water by one degree Celsius, thus 1 kilo calorie is the amount of heat required to raise the temperature of 1 kg of water through $1{\circ}$C

100. Chromosomes are a thread-like structure of nucleic acids and protein found in the nucleus of most living cells, carrying genetic information in the form of genes.

Mathematics

Q.1 Solve the following expression: 452 - 35 * 68 - 58 + 60% of 730.

A. 3^2 **B.** 4^2 **C.** 5^2 **D.** 6^2

Q.2 The angles of elevation of the top of a tower 90 m high, from two points on the level ground on its opposite sides are 45° and 60°. What is the distance between the two points (rounded off to the nearest integer)?($\sqrt{3}$ = 1.732)

A. 133m **B.** 142m **C.** 150m **D.** 167m

Q.3 Two quadratic equations: $16x^2$ - Ax + 25 and Bx^2 + Ax + 4 = 0 have real and equal roots, then what is the value of $\sqrt{B}$?

A. 15 **B.** 10 **C.** 8 **D.** 20

Q.4 Roshan deposited Rs 17500 in bank which offers compound interest at 8% per annum. What is the interest obtained on the sum after 2 years?

A. Rs 2800 **B.** Rs 2912 **C.** Rs 2842 **D.** Rs 2878

Q.5 Length of a rectangle is increased by 10% and breadth is decreased by 10%. Find the percent effect in area.

A. 2% increase **B.** 1% decrease
C. 2% decrease **D.** 1% increase

Q.6 One of the angles of a triangle is half the larger angle of a parallelogram. The respective ratio between the adjacent angles of the parallelogram is 14 : 31 . The smallest angle of the triangle Is half the smaller angle of the parallelogram. What is the value of the largest angle of the triangle?

A. 110° **B.** 80°
C. 70° **D.** None of these

Q.7 Aman donated 10% of his Savings to Charity and gave 15% of his savings to his sister. Of the remaining savings his gave 60% to his son and gave 80% of the still remaining saving to his daughter. If the sum of the money given to sister and the money left with Aman finally is Rs 84,000, what was his savings?

A. Rs 3,60,000 **B.** Rs 4,00,000
C. Rs 4,20,000 **D.** Rs 3,00,000

Q.8 The ratio of 4th and 2nd term of an A.P of positive terms is 5:3 and the product of the 1st and the 3rd terms is 72. what is the product of the 5th and 6th terms of the AP?

A. 378 **B.** 366 **C.** 346 **D.** 384

Q.9 Three pipes A, B and C can fill a cistern in 10 hrs. After working together for 4 hours, C is closed and A and B fill the cistern in 9 hrs. Then find the time in which the cistern can be filled by pipe C?

A. 35 hrs **B.** 40 hrs **C.** 30 hrs **D.** 90 hrs

Q.10 If the average of twelve consecutive even numbers be 113, then find the sum of 3rd and 8th number among them?

A. 252 **B.** 242 **C.** 232 **D.** 222

Q.11 What approximate value should come in the place of the question mark in the following question ?

$(72)^2 \div \sqrt[3]{46656} = ?$

A. 169 **B.** 196 **C.** 128 **D.** 144

Q.12 Ranjan purchases an article at Rs.660 and marks up the price by 25% and after allowing the discount of Rs.99 he gains __% profit on the sale.

Given below are the steps involved. Arrange them in the sequential order.

A) Per cent profit = (66/660) * 100 = 10%

B) Selling price of the item after discount of Rs.99 = 825 - 99 = Rs.726

C) Profit amount earned on the item = 726 - 660 = Rs.66

D) Cost price of the article is Rs.660 and marked price = 125% of 660 = Rs.825

A. DBCA **B.** BCAD **C.** ABCD **D.** DCBA

Q.13 Study the following table carefully and answer the related question.

Following table represents the three types of products A, B and C manufactured in a company during Five months.

Month	A	B	C
January	18	22	25
February	20	12	32
March	40	10	13
April	21	22	24
May	25	21	16

In which of the following month there is a maximum percentage increase/decrease in the manufacturing of all three types of products together?

A. April **B.** February **C.** may **D.** march

Q.14 Two trains 140 m and 160 m long run at the speed of 60 kmph and 40 kmph respectively in opposite directions on parallel tracks. The time (in seconds) which they take to cross each other is :

A. 9 **B.** 9.6 **C.** 10 **D.** 10.8

Q.15 $a^2 + b^2 = 5$ and $a^3 + b^3 = 9$. If ab = 2, what is the value of $a^4 + b^4$?

A. 17 **B.** 21 **C.** 23 **D.** 27

Q.16 The average weight of 24 students in a class is 40 kg. if the weight of the teacher is included, the average is increased by 500 gms. Find The weight of the teacher?

A. 52 kgs **B.** 52.5 kgs **C.** 60 kgs **D.** 53.5 kgs

Q.17 A shopkeeper makes a profit of 20% by selling a T.V. What would be the new profit percent if the shopkeeper paid 15% less for the T.V and the customer paid 10% more for the T.V?

A. 48.2%   **B.** 58.4%   **C.** 55.3%   **D.** 60.2%

Q.18 Solve the following expression: (13/8) of (15/32) of 45% of 3072.

A. 1072   **B.** 1053   **C.** 1081   **D.** 1093

Q.19 Following Pie Chart shows the percentage distribution of people of different ages in a Building. The table shows the ratio of Male and Female people in each age group. There is a total of 800 people in the building.

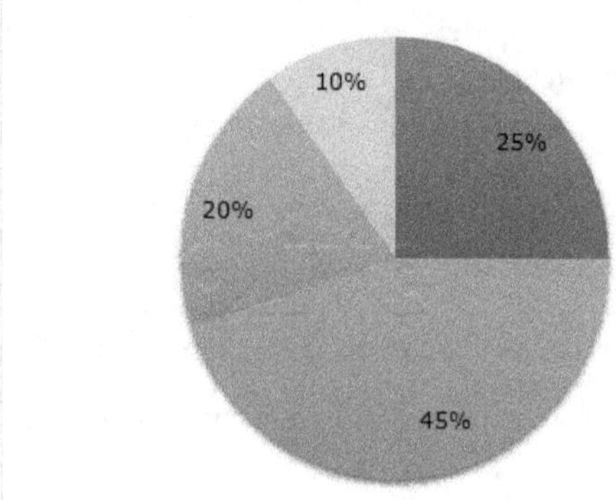

Age Group	Ratio
Less than 20	3:2
20 to 40	7:5
40 to 60	3:1
More than 60	1:1

What is the difference between the total number of Males of age 20 to 60 and the total number of Females of age 20 to 60?

A. 120   **B.** 130   **C.** 140   **D.** 150

Q.20 The population of a village is 6000. The next year, the number of male increases by 10% and the number of female increases by 20% and the population becomes 6840. What is the initial population of Male?

A. 3600   **B.** 4800   **C.** 1200   **D.** 2400

Q.21 The average age of a Sheela and her sister is 16 years. The respective ratio of their ages is 7:1 respectively. Find Sheela's age?

A. 28   **B.** 24
C. 12   **D.** None of these

Q.22 20% of x% of 60 is equal to y% of 60% of 40, what is the value of the ratio x:y?

A. 2:1   **B.** 3:2   **C.** 3:1   **D.** 4:1

Q.23 What is the remainder when $x^{20} + x^{19} + x^{18} + x^{17} + x^{16} + x^{15} + x^{14} + x^{13} + x^{12} + x^{11}$ is divided by $x^9 + x^8 + x^7 + x^6 + x^5 + x^4 + x^3 + x^2 + x + 1$

A. 1   **B.** 5   **C.** 3   **D.** 0

Q.24 A person invested equal amounts in two scheme A and B at the same rate of interest. Scheme A offers simple interest while scheme B offers compound interest. After two years he got Rs. 1920 from the Scheme A as interest and Rs. 2112 from scheme B. If the rate of interest is increased by 4%, what will be the total interest after two years both schemes ?

A. Rs. 4884.48   **B.** Rs. 4888.48
C. Rs. 4884.84   **D.** Rs. 4384.48

Q.25 How many litres of a solution containing milk and water in the ratio 2:3 should be added to 30 litres of 70 % milk solution in order to get 60% milk solution?

A. 15 liters   **B.** 12 liters   **C.** 25 liters   **D.** 20 liters

Q.26 If 12% of a is equal to 15% of b. Find the respective ratio of a and b.

A. 4:5   **B.** 2:3   **C.** 5:4   **D.** 3:2

Q.27 Downstream speed of boat A is 20% more than the downstream speed of boat B whose upstream speed is 6 km/hr less than upstream speed of boat A. What is the speed of boat A in still water? The stream for both boat is moving with 10 km/hr.

A. 28km/hr   **B.** 26km/hr   **C.** 24km/hr   **D.** 22km/hr

Q.28 If monthly income of a person is increased by 20% and his expenditures are increased by 40%, then his savings are decreased by what percent? (ratio of income and expenditure is 4: 3 respectively.)

A. 45%   **B.** 40%   **C.** 35%   **D.** 30%

Q.29 A and B can finish a work in 2 days, B and C in 3 days and A and C in 4 days. Find the ratio of time taken by A alone and C alone to finish the work?

A. 2:5   **B.** 2:7   **C.** 3:7   **D.** 1:5

Q.30 Which of the following is irrational?

A. Product of $(3 - \sqrt{27})$ and $(\sqrt{9} + 3\sqrt{3})$
B. Sum of $(5 - 4\sqrt{2})$ and $4(6 + \sqrt{2})$
C. Sum of $\sqrt{4761}$ and $\sqrt{5175}$
D. Product of $\sqrt{16875}$ and $\sqrt{27}$

General Intelligence & Reasoning

Q.31 There are several chickens and rabbits in a cage (with no other types of animals). There are 72 heads and 200 feet inside the cage. How many chickens and rabbits are there?

A. 44 chickens and 28 rabbits
B. 28 chickens and 44 rabbits
C. 44 chickens and 20 rabbits
D. 20 chickens and 44 rabbits

Q.32 Find the next term in the given series?
BY, DW, GT, KP, ?

A. PJ   **B.** QJ   **C.** OK   **D.** PK

Q.33 Read the following statements. The conclusions are given in the options, you have to read the conclusions and then decide which one of them among the options definetly does not follow.

Statements:

1. Some tables are chairs.

2. No Chair is a couch.

3. All sofas are couch.

A. Some sofas are not chairs

B. All couch are not sofas

C. Some tables are not couch

D. Some tables being sofa is not a possibility

Q.34 Which of the following will be the mirror image of the given question figure (x), if the mirror is placed along the line MN. Choose the correct mirror image among (I), (II), (III) and (IV) given

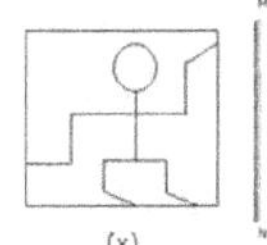

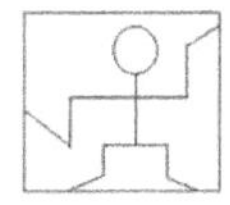 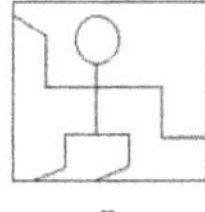 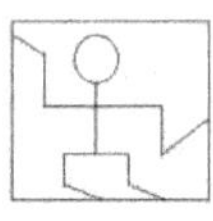 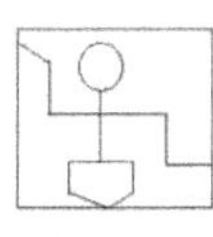

A. II   **B.** I   **C.** IV   **D.** III

Q.35 If in a certain code, GLACIER is coded as 6293017 and FRUIT is coded as 47806, then how will FILTER be coded as in the same code?

A. 402617   **B.** 148706   **C.** 302617   **D.** 745617

Q.36 Harish is standing to the north-west of Kishore. Raju is standing to the south-east of Prem. Prem is standing to the south-east of Kishore. Manu is standing to the east of Kishore. What is the direction of Raju with respect to Harish?

A. South-west   **B.** South-east

C. East   **D.** North-east

Q.37 In the following question, select the related numbers from the given alternatives.

9246 : 1926 :: 3968 : ?

A. 4927   **B.** 2649   **C.** 2850   **D.** 2754

Q.38 Arrange the given words in the sequence in which they occur in the dictionary and then choose the correct sequence.

1- Arraign 2- Arrest 3- Arrive 4- Array

A. 1,4,3,2   **B.** 1,4,2,3   **C.** 4,1,2,3   **D.** 4,1,3,2

Q.39 In order to complete the set, which one of the following set of letters should be placed at the gaps sequentially?

QOMKI

A. S G   **B.** R F   **C.** S F   **D.** R G

Q.40 A Faulty watch loses 5 minutes in 2 hours. It was set right at 6 o' clock in the morning. At 6 o' clock in the morning on the next day, what was the time shown in the faulty watch?

A. 05:00 a.m.   **B.** 04:00 a.m

C. 05:30 a.m.   **D.** 04:30 a.m.

Q.41 In a certain code, BOTANY is written as Q3M. How is RHYTHM written in that code?

A. Z9U   **B.** Z9I   **C.** P9U   **D.** P9I

Q.42 Each question given below consists of a statement, followed by two arguments numbered I and II. Decide which of the arguments is a 'strong' argument and which is a 'weak' argument and choose the corresponding option as your answer.

Should the age of drinking be reduced from 21 years to 18 years?

I. Yes, because alcohol is not as harmful to health as smoking is.

II. Yes, because if an 18-year old adult can have the right to vote and get married, he can also have the right to drink

A. Only I is strong

B. Only II is strong

C. Both I and II are strong

D. Neither I nor II are strong

Q.43 Each question given below consists of a statement, followed by two arguments numbered I and II. You have to decide which of the arguments is a 'strong' argument and which is a 'weak' argument.

Statement: Should luxury hotels be banned in India?

Arguments:

I. Yes. They are places from where international criminals operate.

II. No. Affluent foreign tourists will have no place to stay.

A. If only argument I is strong.

B. If only argument II is strong.

C. If either I or II is strong.

D. If neither I nor II is strong.

Q.44 P remembers that his joining date in office is after 18th October, but not on any odd-numbered date. Q remembers that P is joining in October. R, who is P's friend remembers that P is joining before 21st October. Then, on which date is P joining?

A. None of these   **B.** 18th अक्टूबर

C. 19th अक्टूबर   **D.** 20th अक्टूबर

Q.45 Identify the diagram that best represents the relationship among the given classes.

Human, children, Male

(1)

(2)

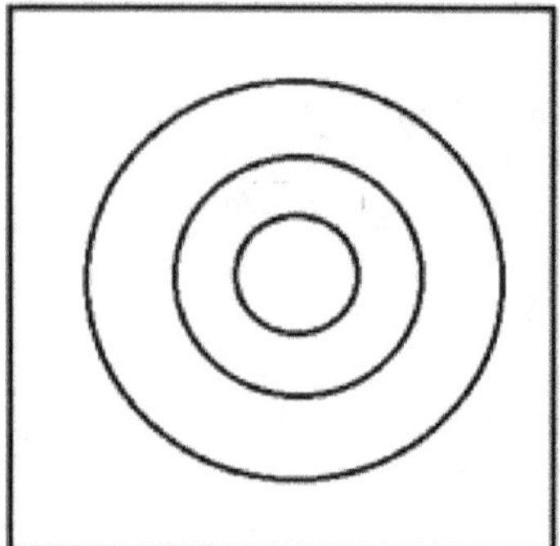

(3)

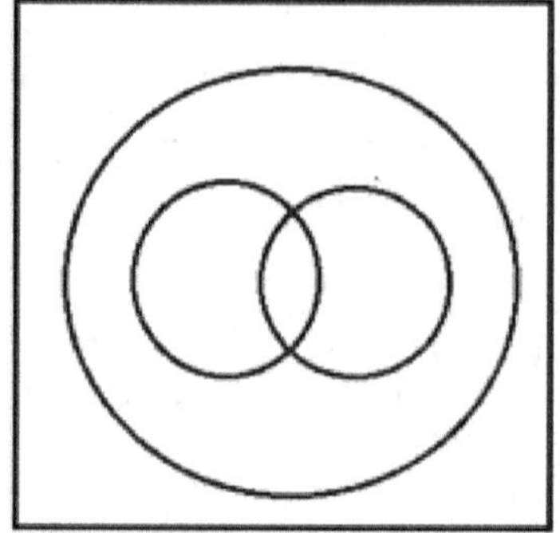

(4)

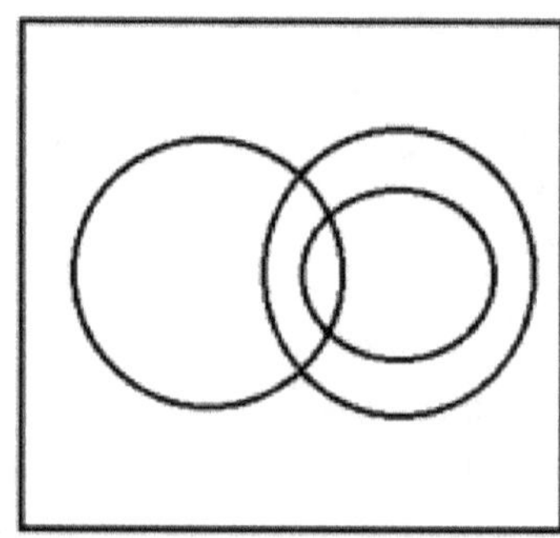

A. 1   **B.** 2   **C.** 3   **D.** 4

Q.46 In the following question, select the odd letters from the given alternatives.

A. GNO   **B.** DHI   **C.** IRS   **D.** MYZ

Q.47 Select the related letters/words/numbers from the given alternatives

AK : FP : EO : ?

A. BM   **B.** IS   **C.** CR   **D.** JS

Q.48 Find the odd one out.

A. 842   **B.** 444   **C.** 284   **D.** 624

Q.49 In the following question, a figure (x) is given having a pattern, whose two portions marked as A and B are missing. Below the figure, four patterns (i), (ii), (iii) and (iv) are given, among which two of them fit A and B correctly. Select the option which matches both A and B correctly.

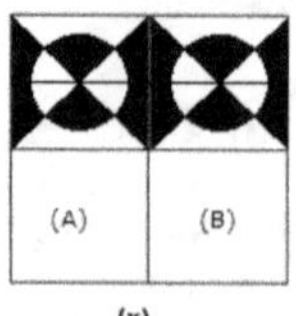

(x)

  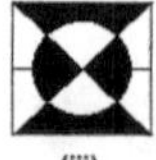  

(i)   (ii)   (iii)   (iv)   (v)

A. (A) - (i); (B) - (iii)   **B.** (A) - (iv); (B) - (ii)

C. (A) - (i); (B) - (i)   **D.** (B) - (i); (A) - (v)

Q.50 How many triangles are present in the given figure?

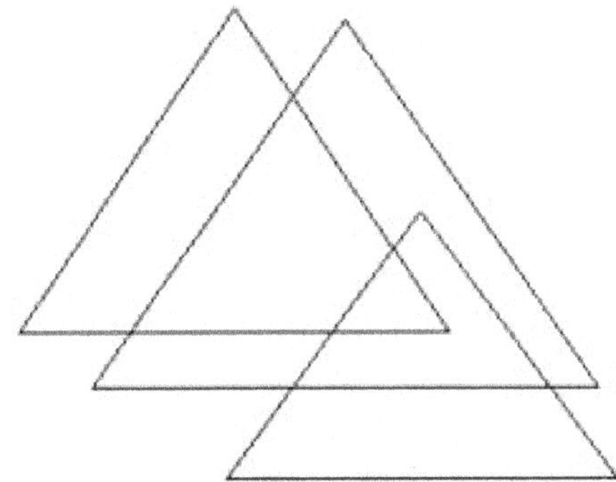

A. 4   **B.** 5   **C.** 7   **D.** 6

Q.51 Find out from amongst the four alternatives as to how the pattern would appear on the sheet when the sheet is folded at the dotted line and is punched as given

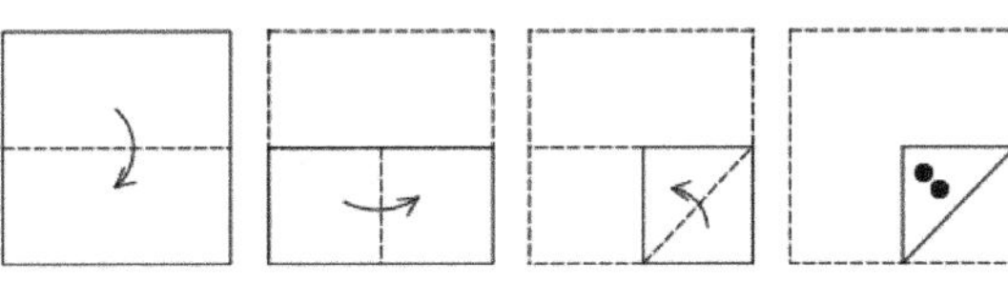

a)

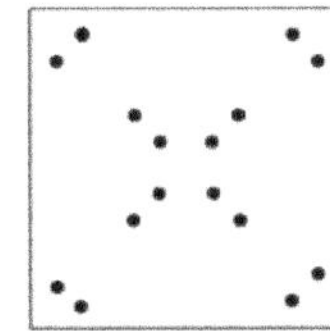

b)

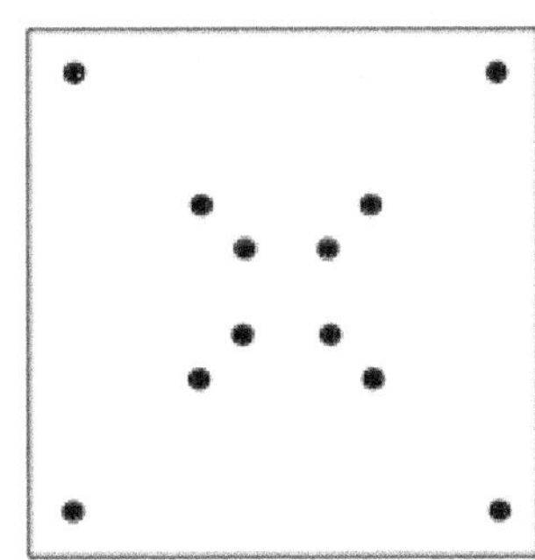

c)

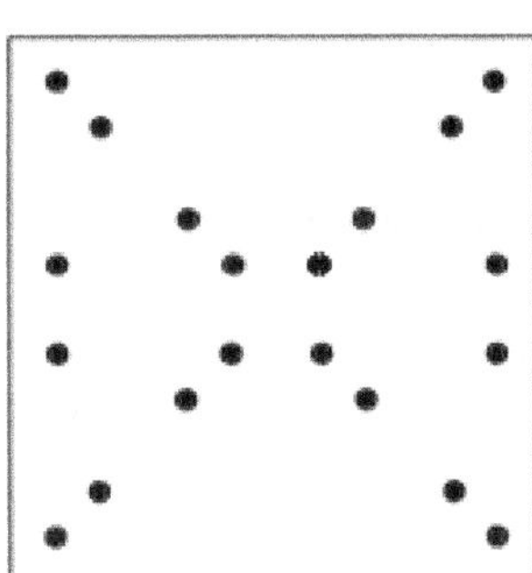

d)

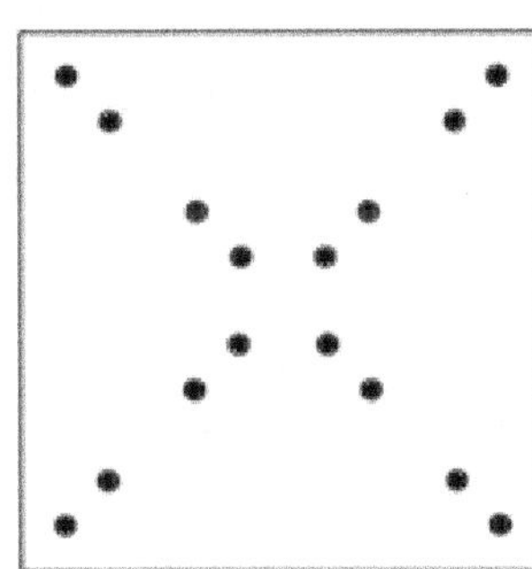

A. a   **B.** b   **C.** c   **D.** d

Q.52 Each question given below consists of a statement, followed by two arguments numbered I and II. Decide which of the arguments is a 'strong' argument and which is a 'weak' argument and choose the corresponding option as your answer.

Should sex education be made compulsory at all schools?

I. Yes, because parents are not capable of educating their children.

II. No, because this leads students astray.

A. Only I

B. Only II

C. Both I and II

D. Neither I nor II

Q.53 In a queue, Tina is standing 8th from the left and 9th from the right. Pooja is to the immediate left of Sara, who is 8th towards right of Tina. What is the position of Pooja from the right side?

A. 3   **B.** 10   **C.** 15   **D.** 2

Q.54 Three positions of a same cube are shown below. Which number appears on the face opposite to '5'?

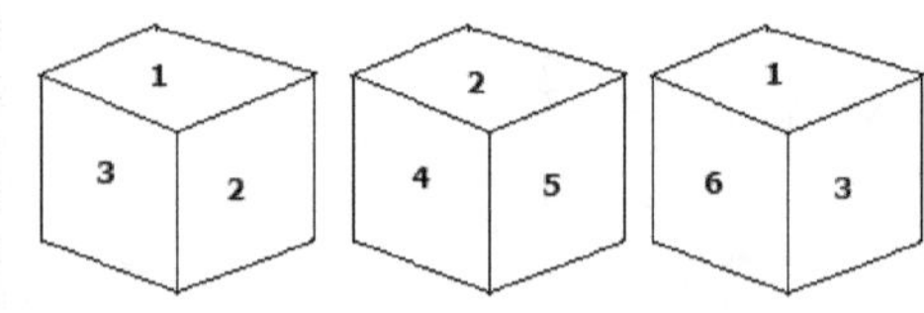

A. 1   **B.** 6   **C.** 3   **D.** 2

Q.55 C is wife of B and B is son of K. F is brother of C and A is nephew of F. J is father of F. Q is daughter of F. How is C related to K?

A. Sister

B. Mother in law

C. Sister in law

D. Daughter in law

General Awareness

Q.56 Who replaced Hasmukh Adhia as the new Revenue Secretary in the Finance Ministry recently?

A. Shatikanta Das

B. Urjit Patel

C. Ajay Bhushan Pandey

D. Sriram Jaggi

Q.57 Daranghati Wildlife Sanctuary is situated in which Indian state?

A. Uttarakhand

B. Rajasthan

C. Chhattisgarh

D. Himachal Pradesh

Q.58 "Hand-in-Hand" is an annual military exercise that takes place between ________ & ________

A. India, Russia

B. India, Nepal

C. India, Bangladesh

D. India, China

Q.59 What is the capital of Vietnam, one of the members of ASEAN?

A. Hong Kong

B. Hanoi

C. Jakarta

D. Colombo

Q.60 Bonn Convention is associated with which of the following?

A. Sustainable Development

B. Conservation of Migratory species

C. Poverty Alleviation

D. Controlling NPAs

Q.61 To connect with Direct Benefit Transfer (DBT), an online portal ________ was recently launched by Ministry of Agriculture & Farmer's Welfare

A. SAMPURN

B. ENSURE

C. SECURE

D. DIRECT-PASS

Q.62 "Hornbill Festival" is an annual celebration that takes place in which of the following Indian States?

A. Manipur

B. Sikkim

C. Nagaland

D. Mizoram

Q.63 Prime Minister Narendra Modi inaugurated India's first multi modal terminal on the Ganga river in ______ & received the country's first container cargo transported on inland waterways from Kolkata.

A. Patna

B. Allahabad

C. Varanasi

D. Lucknow

Q.64 Recently, President Ram Nath Kovind launched "One District, One Product" Summit in which Indian state?

A. Maharashtra

B. Kerala

C. Manipur

D. Uttar Pradesh

Q.65 "Adopt a Heritage" initiative is a collaborative effort between which of the following?

A. Ministry of Tourism

B. Ministry of Culture

C. Archaeological Survey of India

D. All of the above

Q.66 In the history of Indian Freedom Struggle, Round Table conferences play a vital role. The ________ Round Table Conference convened from 12 November 1930 to 19 January 1931.

A. Second   **B.** First   **C.** Third   **D.** Fourth

Q.67 Where did PM Modi recently inaugurated National Rail and Transport University, India's first Railway University?

A. Surat, Gujarat

B. Vadodara, Gujarat

C. Indore, Madhya Pradesh

D. Pune, Maharashtra

Q.68 Recently, 10 News organisations out of 87 were selected from India for________, for enhancing digital journalism capabilities.

A. Facebook News Initiative

B. Microsoft News Initiative

C. Google News Initiative

D. The Hindu News Initiative

Q.69 Recently Shri Ananth Kumar passed away. He was holding which portfolio in the Union government?

A. Ministry of Health & Family Affairs

B. Ministry of Power

C. Ministry of Agriculture & Farmer Welfare

D. Ministry of Chemicals & Fertilizers

Q.70 Ramon Magsaysay Award is presented to winners in formal ceremony, which take place in__________ every year.

A. Bangkok, Thailand   **B.** Seoul, South Korea
C. Hong Kong, China   **D.** Manila, Philippines

General Science

Q.71 Rusting of iron happens when a layer of _______ forms on the surface of iron material.

A. Ferrous Oxide
B. Ferric Dioxide
C. Hydrated Ferric Oxide
D. Ferric Oxide

Q.72 Which of the following is/are the characteristics of a common salt?

A. They are Tetrahedral crystals
B. They have Pungent Odour
C. They are insoluble in water
D. None of the above

Q.73 Which of the following is/are NOT a characteristic of a solid?

A. High Rigidity   **B.** Regular Shape
C. High Density   **D.** None of the above

Q.74 The frequency range of hearing for a normal young person is __________ hertz.

A. 20 to 50000   **B.** 20 to 40000
C. 20 to 20000   **D.** 10 to 40000

Q.75 Which of these is/are example(s) of Newton's 3rd Law of Motion?

A. Recoil of a gun   **B.** Motion of a rocket
C. Swimming   **D.** All of the above

Q.76 ____________ are tiny organelles inside cells that are involved in releasing energy from food hence, gaining the tag, "Power house of Cell".

A. Cerebrum   **B.** Cell Wall
C. Mitochondria   **D.** Nuclei

Q.77 Which of the following is/are a stage in the Nitrogen Cycle?

A. Assimilation   **B.** Ammonification
C. Denitrification   **D.** All of the above

Q.78 Atomic Number of Chlorine is ____.

A. 12   **B.** 14   **C.** 17   **D.** 22

Q.79 ____________ is the process of conversion of a solid directly into vapour.

A. Humidity   **B.** Sublimation
C. Fusion   **D.** Hoarfrost

Q.80 Which of the following are generally used as fuel for Nuclear reactors?

A. Potassium   **B.** Argon
C. Uranium   **D.** None of the above

Q.81 The boiling point of water is _______ at 1 atmospheric pressure that is, at sea level.

A. 80 °C   **B.** 100 °C   **C.** 160 °C   **D.** 200 °C

Q.82 Which of the following are properties of a sound wave?

A. Reflection   **B.** Refraction
C. Diffraction   **D.** All of the above

Q.83 Pleural Membrane is associated with which organ in Human body?

A. Brain   **B.** Heart
C. Lungs   **D.** Large Intestine

Q.84 Which of the following is responsible for floating of the brain in the Human skull?

A. Cerebro-Membrane Fluid
B. Cerebrospinal Fluid
C. Augmented Grey Fluid
D. Pancreatic Fluid

Q.85 Iron, Silver are examples of __________ of electricity whereas wood, glass are examples of _________ of electricity.

A. conductor, insulator
B. insulator, conductor
C. perfect insulator, perfect conductor
D. None of the above

Q.86 _______ is a softer and flexible than bone in the human body and is a connective tissue found in many areas of the body.

A. Bone marrow   **B.** Spinal cord
C. Thyroid   **D.** Cartilage

Q.87 Mass of an electron is _______.

A. 3.6×10^{-36} kg   **B.** 4.2×10^{-33} kg
C. 9.1×10^{-31} kg   **D.** 3.5×10^{-34} kg

Q.88 Who is credited with discovery of X-Rays in the year 1895?

A. Julius Caesar   **B.** Wilhelm Roentgen
C. Thomas Edison   **D.** Albert Einstein

Q.89 The ash formed from burning of a Magnesium ribbon is _______ in colour.

A. Pink   **B.** Red   **C.** Yellow   **D.** White

Q.90 Chemical Formulae of Chloroform is _________

A. $CHCl_2$ **B.** $CHCl_3$ **C.** $CHCl_5$ **D.** $CHCl_4$

Q.91 Near-sightedness (myopia) is a common vision condition in which you can see objects _______ to you clearly, but objects _______ are blurry.

A. Far, nearer
B. Near, farther
C. Near, of certain colour
D. Far, of certain colour

Q.92 Speed of light in vacuum is approximately ____________.

A. 40×10^6 m/s   **B.** 10×10^7 m/s
C. 5×10^8 m/s   **D.** 3×10^8 m/s

Q.93 __________carry blood from the tissues of the body back to the heart.

A. Plasma

B. Arteries

C. Haemoglobin

D. Veins

Q.94 Which of the following is the strongest acid?

A. Sulphuric Acid

B. Hydrochloric Acid

C. Nitric Acid

D. Carbonic Acid

Q.95 __________ is the device used for detecting the presence of small current and voltage or for measuring their magnitude.

A. Delta meter

B. Altimeter

C. Galvanometer

D. Voltmeter

Q.96 First Law of thermodynamics is equivalent to principle of __________ of energy.

A. Destruction

B. Conservation

C. Pluralism

D. Creation

Q.97 The de Broglie wavelength associated with an electron moving with a speed of 200 m/s is ______.

A. 6450 nanometres

B. 3600 nanometres

C. 2600 nanometres

D. 6500 nanometres

Q.98 Which is the eye's outermost layer which is a clear, dome shaped surface covering the front of the eye?

A. Retina

B. Cornea

C. Pupils

D. Eyebrow

Q.99 A body initially at rest moves with a constant acceleration of 15 m/s2. At what time from the initial point will it have travelled 3 kilometres?

A. 15 seconds

B. 25 seconds

C. 20 seconds

D. 35 seconds

Q.100 __________ is a long, muscular tube that connects the mouth to stomach.

A. Oesophagus

B. Large Intestine

C. Small Intestine

D. Rectum

// Smart Answer Sheet //

Correct — Percentage of students who answered correctly. **Skipped** — Percentage of students who skipped.

Q.	Ans.	Correct / Skipped
1	C	84.99 % / 13.75 %
2	B	87.83 % / 10.22 %
3	B	78.86 % / 12.66 %
4	B	86.43 % / 12.56 %
5	B	85.35 % / 10.41 %
6	D	86.27 % / 13.32 %
7	B	85.98 % / 11.39 %
8	A	77.4 % / 16.34 %
9	C	87.54 % / 11.52 %
10	D	88.33 % / 10.46 %
11	D	76.42 % / 15.03 %
12	A	85.79 % / 10.59 %
13	C	89.05 % / 10.12 %
14	D	89.17 % / 10.62 %
15	A	87.74 % / 12.12 %
16	B	82.76 % / 10.74 %
17	C	82.83 % / 11.36 %
18	B	88.83 % / 10.09 %
19	C	80.52 % / 18.56 %
20	A	87.44 % / 11.55 %
21	A	80.37 % / 11.48 %
22	A	89.69 % / 10.09 %
23	D	89.58 % / 10.17 %
24	A	85.61 % / 11.48 %
25	A	88.28 % / 10.77 %
26	C	88.9 % / 10.54 %
27	B	80.48 % / 15.62 %
28	B	85.77 % / 10.56 %
29	D	77.62 % / 20.81 %
30	C	80.22 % / 11.79 %
31	A	82.78 % / 11.14 %
32	D	76.03 % / 21.59 %
33	D	80.14 % / 10.32 %
34	A	84.23 % / 13.57 %
35	A	81.3 % / 11.62 %
36	B	83.16 % / 13.71 %
37	C	76.03 % / 23.58 %
38	B	77.61 % / 21.78 %
39	A	81.82 % / 17.16 %
40	A	89.11 % / 10.07 %
41	A	81.16 % / 17.99 %
42	B	81.63 % / 10.89 %
43	B	76.36 % / 22.23 %
44	D	76.92 % / 20.27 %
45	C	86.85 % / 10.72 %
46	D	88.76 % / 10.54 %
47	B	77.68 % / 18.42 %
48	D	88.21 % / 11.16 %
49	C	82.69 % / 13.5 %
50	D	81.48 % / 14.31 %
51	D	80.45 % / 14.31 %
52	D	76.93 % / 18.9 %
53	D	89.76 % / 10.15 %
54	C	77.67 % / 16.16 %
55	D	79.26 % / 16.33 %
56	C	81.88 % / 15.82 %
57	D	86.7 % / 12.64 %
58	D	81.16 % / 10.98 %
59	B	88.58 % / 10.27 %
60	B	83.34 % / 12.0 %
61	B	83.51 % / 14.9 %
62	C	80.33 % / 10.74 %
63	C	77.92 % / 12.93 %
64	D	81.55 % / 12.16 %
65	D	80.58 % / 10.14 %
66	B	76.78 % / 11.42 %
67	B	89.53 % / 10.01 %
68	C	87.81 % / 11.79 %
69	D	77.58 % / 15.77 %
70	D	83.11 % / 13.18 %
71	C	85.28 % / 14.12 %
72	D	81.86 % / 14.32 %
73	D	76.86 % / 13.44 %
74	C	78.04 % / 21.38 %
75	D	79.75 % / 17.34 %
76	C	88.29 % / 10.29 %
77	D	89.33 % / 10.57 %
78	C	86.67 % / 13.31 %
79	B	81.87 % / 10.55 %
80	C	89.12 % / 10.47 %

Q.	Ans.	Correct	Skipped
81	B	79.32 %	16.57 %
82	D	82.2 %	16.07 %
83	C	86.04 %	10.58 %
84	B	89.45 %	10.18 %

Q.	Ans.	Correct	Skipped
85	A	79.77 %	13.99 %
86	D	81.9 %	11.06 %
87	C	85.17 %	11.51 %
88	B	87.25 %	11.12 %

Q.	Ans.	Correct	Skipped
89	D	86.72 %	12.54 %
90	B	85.44 %	13.22 %
91	B	84.95 %	14.26 %
92	D	87.08 %	10.94 %

Q.	Ans.	Correct	Skipped
93	D	83.3 %	15.99 %
94	A	86.06 %	11.94 %
95	C	77.28 %	14.01 %
96	B	84.06 %	10.49 %

Q.	Ans.	Correct	Skipped
97	B	83.46 %	15.68 %
98	B	87.39 %	11.78 %
99	C	77.87 %	12.36 %
100	A	82.81 %	16.64 %

//Hints and Solutions//

1. $= 45^2 - 35 * 68 - 58 + 60\%$ of 730

$= 2025 - 2380 - 58 + 438$

$= 2463 - 2438$

$= 25$

$= 5^2$

2.

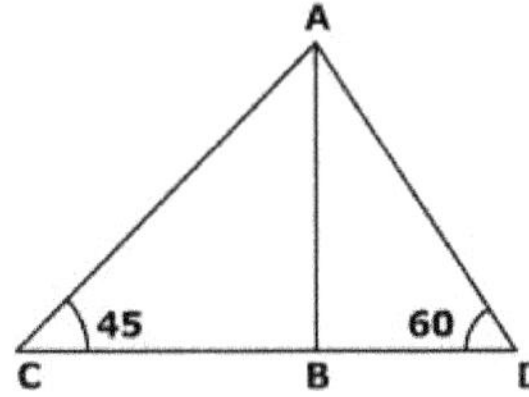

Let AB be the tower and C and D the two points.

Now $AB/BC = \tan 45° = 1$

$AB = BC = 90$

Also $AB/BD = \tan 60° = \sqrt{3}$

$BD = 90/\sqrt{3} = 30\sqrt{3}$

Hence $CD = CB + BD = 90 + 30\sqrt{3} = 90 + 51.96 = 141.96 \approx 142$ m

3. $16x^2 - Ax + 25$ has real and equal roots

$(-A)2 = 4 * 16 * 25$

$A = 40$

$Bx^2 + Ax + 4 = 0$ has real and equal roots

$(A)2 = 4 * B * 4$

$(40)^2 = 4 * B * 4$

$B = 100$

$\sqrt{B} = \sqrt{100}$

$\sqrt{B} = 10$

4. Amount after two years $= 17500 \times (1 + 8/100)^2$

$= 17500 \times 1.08 \times 1.08 = 20412$

Interest $= 20412 - 17500 = $ Rs 2912

5. Let length $= l$

And breadth $= b$

Area $= lb$

After increment, length $= l \times (100 + 10)/100 = l \times 110/100 = l \times 11/10$

After decrement, breadth $= b \times (100 - 10)/100 = b \times 90/100 = b \times 9/10$

Area $= l \times 11/10 \times b \times 9/10$

$= 99lb/100$ lb

% decrease $= (lb - 99lb/100)/lb \times 100$

$= (100lb - 99lb)/100 \times 1/lb \times 100$

$= lb/100 \times 1/lb \times 100$

$= 1\%$

6. We know that the sum of the adjacent angles of a parallelogram $= 180$o

Let the adjacent angles of the parallelogram be 14x and 31x

Therefore, $14x + 31x = 180$o

$45x = 180$o

$X = 4$

7. Let his savings be Rs 100x

Money donated to charity = Rs 10x and Money given to sister = Rs 15x

Money left with Aman = 100x - 10x - 15x = Rs 75x

Money left with him after giving to son = (40/100)*75x = Rs 30x

Money left with him after giving to daughter = (20/100)*30x = Rs 6x

Given, 15x + 6x = 84000

=> 21x = 84000

=> x = 4000

His Savings = Rs 4,00,000

8. Let the first term be 'a' and the common difference be 'd'.

Given, $(a + 3d)/(a + d) = 5/3$

$\rightarrow 3a + 9d = 5a + 5d$

=> 2a = 4d

=> a = 2d

Also, $a(a + 2d) = 72$

=> 2d(2d + 2d) = 72

=> $8d^2 = 72$

=> d2 = 9

=> d = 3

$\therefore a = 2*3 = 6$

$d \neq -3$ as the 1st term will become $a = 2(-3) = -6$ but all terms are positive.

5th term = a + 4d = 6 + 4*3 = 18

6th term = 18 + 3 = 21

Required product = 18*21 = 378

9. A, B and C can fill in 1 hour = 1/10 of cistern

A, B and C can fill in 4 hour= 4/10 =2/5 of cistern

Remaining part = 1 - 2/5 =3/5 of cistern

3/5 of cistern is filled by A+B in 9 hours

Therefore, A and B can fill the cistern in 9*5/3 = 15 hrs

Hence in one hour C filled the cistern = 1/10 - 1/15 = 1/30 of cistern

Hence C can fill the cistern in 30 hrs.

10. Let the 1st number = x

According to question,

x + (x+2) + (x+4) + ... + (x+22) = 113*12

12x + 132 = 1356

12x = 1224

x = 102

Therefore 3rd number = 102 + 4 = 106

8th number = 102 + 14 = 116

Hence the required answer = 106 + 116 = 222

11. ? = $(72)^2 \div \sqrt[3]{46656}$

? = $(72)^2 \div \sqrt[3]{(36 \times 36 \times 36)}$ = $(72)^2 \div 36$

? = (72 X 72)/36 = 144

12. The correct arrangement is:

D) Cost price of the article is Rs.660 and marked price = 125% of 660 = Rs.825B) Selling price of the item after discount of Rs.99 = 825 - 99 = Rs.726

C) Profit amount earned on the item = 726 - 660 = Rs.66

A) Per cent profit = (66/660) * 100 = 10%

13. Total products manufactured:

In January = 18 + 22 + 25 = 65

In February = 20 + 12 + 32 = 64

In March = 40 + 10 + 13 = 63

In April = 21 + 22 + 24 = 67

In May = 25 + 21 + 16 = 62

Percentage increase/decrease:

In February = ((65 - 64)/65) x 100 = 1.54%

In March = ((64 - 63)/64) x 100 = 1.56%

In April = ((67 - 63)/63) x 100 = 6.35%

In May = ((67 - 62)/67) x 100 = 7.46%

14.

$$time = \frac{Distance}{Velocity}$$

Distance = $140 + 160 = 300m = 0.3km$

Relative velocity = $60 + 40 = 100$ kmph (opp. direction)

$$Time = \frac{0.3}{100} h$$

$$or \; \frac{0.3}{100} \times 3600 = 10.8 \; sec.$$

$$Time = 10.8 \; sec.$$

15. Let (a+b) = c

$c^2 = (a+b)^2 = a^2+b^2 + 2ab = 5 + 4 = 9$

=> a + b = 3

Now, $(a+b)(a^3+b^3) = a^4+b^4+ab(a^2+b^2)$

=> $3 \times 9 = a^4+b^4 + 2 \times 5$

=> $a^4+b^4 = 17$

16. 25*40.5 - 24*40 = 52.5

Hence, the answer is option (2).

17. Let the price at which T.V was purchased by shopkeeper = Rs 100a

Hence the price at which T.V was sold by shopkeeper = Rs 120a

If shopkeeper paid 15% less than the previous amount hence new cost price of the T.V = Rs (100a X 0.85) = Rs 85a

New selling price of the T.V = Rs (120a X 1.1) = Rs 132a

Profit % = (132a-85a)/85a X 100 = 55.3%

18. = (13/8) of (15/32) of 45% of 3072

= (13/8) * (15/32) * (45/100) * 3072

= (13/8) * (3/32) * (9/4) * 307

= 13 * 3 * 9 * 3

= 1053

19. Calculating the number of Male and Females of each age group:

Age Group	Total	Male	Female
Less than 20	0.25*800 = 200	(3/5)*200 = 120	200 - 120 = 80
20 to 40	0.45*800 = 360	(7/12)*360 = 210	360 - 210 = 150
40 to 60	0.20*800 = 160	(3/4)*160 = 120	160 - 120 = 40
More than 60	0.10*800 = 80	(1/2)*80 = 40	80 - 40 = 40

total number of Males of age 20 to 60 = 210 + 120 = 330

total number of Females of age 20 to 60 = 150 + 40 = 190

Required difference = 330 - 190 = 140

20. Let the initial population of Males and Females be 100x and 100y respectively.

Given, 100x + 100y = 6000

=> x + y = 60..(i)

And, 110x + 120y = 6840

=> 11x + 12y = 684..(ii)

12*(i) - (ii), gives

x = 36

Initial population of Males = 3600

21. Sum of their ages = 2 X 16 = 32

Let 7x and x be their respective ages, then, 8x = 32 and x = 4

So, Sheela's age = 7x = 7 X 4 = 28 years . Hence, option 1.

22. 20% of x% of 60 = y% of 60% of 40

x = 2y

x:y = 2:1

23. Numerator = x11 $(x^9 + x^8 + x^7 + x^6 + x^5 + x^4 + x^3 + x^2 + x + 1)$ = x11 times the denominator.

The denominator divides the numerator, so the answer is 0.

24.

C.I - S.I = 192

S.I for 1 year = 960

Interest on RS 960 for 1 year is 192

so rate is $= \frac{192 \times 100}{960 \times 1} = 20\%$

so the principal is $= \frac{960 \times 100}{20} = 4800$

when interest is increased is 4% then new rate of interest is 24%

So simple interest after two years will be $= \frac{4800 \times 2 \times 24}{100} = 2304$

and compound interest rate after two years will be $= 24 + 24 + \frac{24 \times 24}{100} = 53.76\%$

Compound interest after two years $= \frac{53.76 \times 4800}{100} = 2580.48$

So total interest is = 2304+2580.48 = Rs. 4884.48

25. Let the number of liters of solution added be: x

The initial ratio of milk (m) to water (w) is:

=> m/w = 2/3

=> m = 2/5 of the solution

=> m = 40% of the solution

Acc. to the question, after adding x liters of 40% milk solution to 30 liters of 70% milk solution, we get 60% of (x+30) liters milk solution.

Hence, the equation becomes:

=> 40x + 30 * 70 = (x+30) * 60

=> 40x + 2100= 60x + 1800

=> 20x = 300

=> x = 15

26. 12% of a = 15% of b

=> a/b = 15/12

=> a/b = 5/4

=> a:b = 5:4

27. Stream speed = 10 km/hr

Downstream speed of boat A = (6/5) x downstream speed of boat B

Upstream speed of boat A - upstream speed of boat B = downstream speed of boat A - downstream speed of boat B = 6

(6/5) x downstream speed of boat B - downstream speed of boat B = 6

Downstream speed of boat B = 30 km/hr

Downstream speed of boat A = 30 + 6 = 36 km/hr

Speed of boat A in still water = 36 - 10 = 26 km/hr

28. Let income and expenditure are 'a' and 'b' respectively.

Savings = a - b = a - 3a/4 = a/4

When income and expenditure are increased by 20%. Then,

New income = 120% of a = 1.2a

New expenditure = 140% of b = 1.4 x 3a/4 = 2.1a/2

New savings = 1.2a - 2.1a/2 = 3a/20

Decrement in savings = (a/4) - (3a/20) = a/10

Percentage = a/10)/(a/4 x 100 = 40%

29. Suppose A, B and C take A, B and C days respectively to finish the work on their own.

1/A + 1/B = 1/2 (1)

1/B + 1/C = 1/3 (2)

1/A + 1/C = 1/4 (3)

(1)+(2)+(3) => 2(1/A+1/B+1/C) = 13/12

=> 1/A + 1/B + 1/C = 13/24 (4)

(4) - (2) => 1/A = 5/24

Thus A takes 24/5 = 4.8 days.

(4) - (1) => 1/C = 1/24

Hence C takes 24 days.

Required ratio = 4.8: 24 = 1:5

30. Product of (3 - √27) and (√9 + 3√3)

= (3 - 3√3)(3 + 3√3)

= - 18 (which is not irrational)

Option (2):

= Sum of (5 - 4√2) and 4(6 + √2)

= (5 - 4√2) + 4(6 + √2)

= 5 - 4√2 + 24 + 4√2

= 29 (which is not irrational)

Option (3):

= Sum of √4761 and √5175

= 69 + 15√23 (which is irrational)

Option (4):

= Product of √16875 and √27

= 75√3 x 3√3

= 675 (which is not irrational)

31. No. of chicken = x

No. of rabbit = y

No. of legs = 2x + 4y = 200

x + 2y = 100 → 1

No. of heads = x + y = 72 → 2

1 - 2

y = 100 - 72 = 28

= 72 - 28 = 44

Hence the correct answer is option A

32. The first letter is increased by 2, 3, 4, 5 and the second letter is decreased by 2, 3, 4, 5. Hence the next term is K+5, P-5 = PK

33. The venn diagram of the statements are shown below:

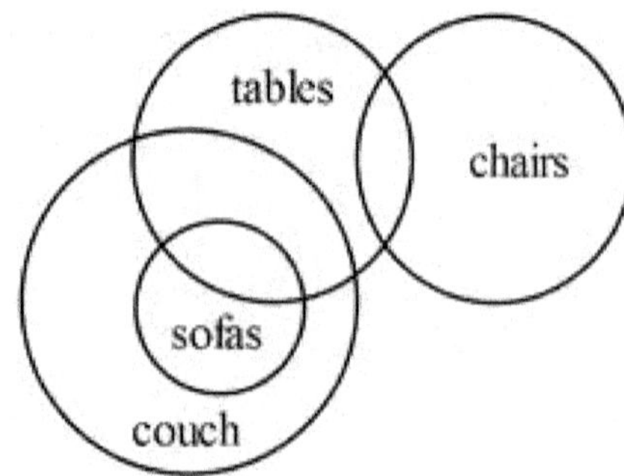

All sofas are not chairs. So some sofas being not chairs is true.

So Option 1 is true.

Option 2 is also true

Option 3 is also true.

Option 4 is false.

34. Image II is the correct image of (x).

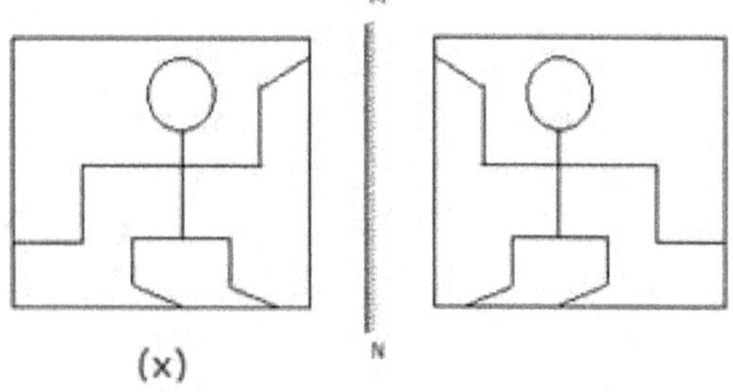

35.

Here, the letters of the word are coded as certain number. For solving this, we find out the codes for letters from the given codes of the words as follows.

G	L	A	C	I	E	R
6	2	9	3	0	1	7

And,

F	R	U	I	T
4	7	6	0	6

So, we get,

F	I	L	T	E	R
4	0	2	6	1	7

36. The positions are shown in the figure

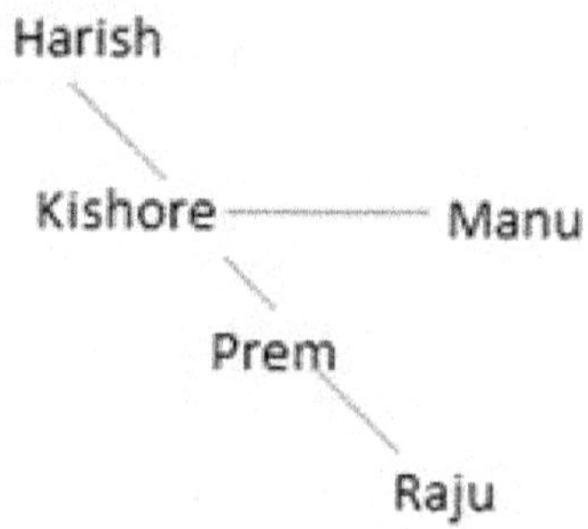

Raju South-east of Harish

37. 9*2=18 → 18+1= 19

4*6=24 → 24+2= 26

Becomes 1926.

Similarly,

3*9=27 → 27+1= 28

6*8=48 → 48+2= 50

Becomes 2850.

38. The correct order is arraign, array, arrest, arrive.

39. The sequence is letters arranged in reverse alphabetical order, skipping a letter: S, Q, O, M, K, I, G.

40. Time duration = 24 hours

In 2 hours, the faulty watch loses 5 minutes

In 24 hours, the faulty watch loses 60 minutes or 1 hour

Time shown in the faulty watch will be 05:00 a.m.

41. In this code,

B (2) + O (15) = 17 → Q

T (20) + A (1) = 21 = 2 + 1 = 3

N (14) + Y (25) = 39 = 26 + 13 = M

So, R (18) + H (8) = 26 = Z

Y (25) + T (20) = 45 = 4 + 5 = 9

H (8) + M (13) = 21 → U

Hence, the required code is Z9U

42. I is not a strong argument as the statement has not talked about smoking, which is out of scope here. II is a strong argument as both voting and marrying are rights that one gains after turning 18, so being an adult, one must also be able to drink. B is the right answer.

43. The luxury hotels are a mark of country's standard and a place for staying for the affluent foreign tourists. So, argument II holds. Argument I is not a strong reason because ban on hotel is not a way to do away with the activities of international criminals.

44. P's joining is on even numbered date between 18th and 21st, hence, 20th October.

45. All children are human, and some children are males, all males are humans, thus, 3rd shows the right relationship.

46. The position value of 2nd alphabet is twice as that of the 1st alphabet. The 3rd alphabet comes just after the 2nd alphabet in the alphabet series

G(7) N(14) O(15)

D(4) H(8) I(9)

I(9) R(18) S(19)

M(13) Y(25) Z(26)

47. In this sequence of alphabets, the difference between the numerical value of the 2 alphabets is 10 .i.e.(1 11),(6 16),(5 15), (9 19).

48. 8x4x2=64

4x4x4=64

2x8x4=64

6x2x4=64 not 48

49. Complete figure is -

50. There are 6 triangles in the given figure

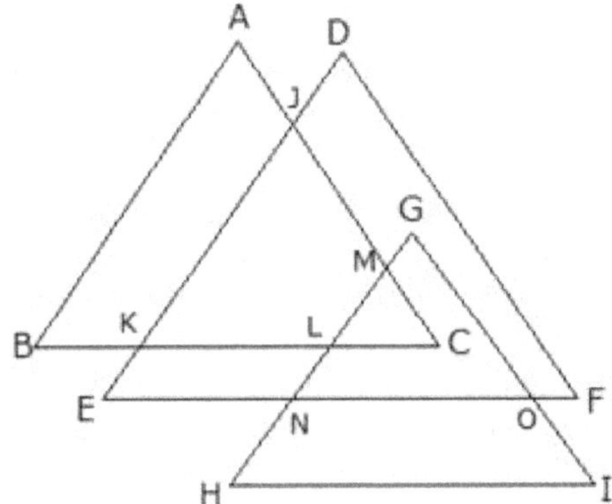

Triangles are - ABC, CLM, CKJ, DEF, GHI, GNO.

51. The paper when opened would look like the one given in figure d

52. Neither of the two arguments give valid arguments in favour or against this step, which makes D the right answer.

53. Number of students =Position of Tina from left+ Position of Tina from right -1=8+9-1=16

Position of Sara =8+8=16th from left

Position of Pooja =16-1=15th from left

Position of Pooja from right =16-15+1=2 from right

54. '3' appears opposite to '5'.

We get -

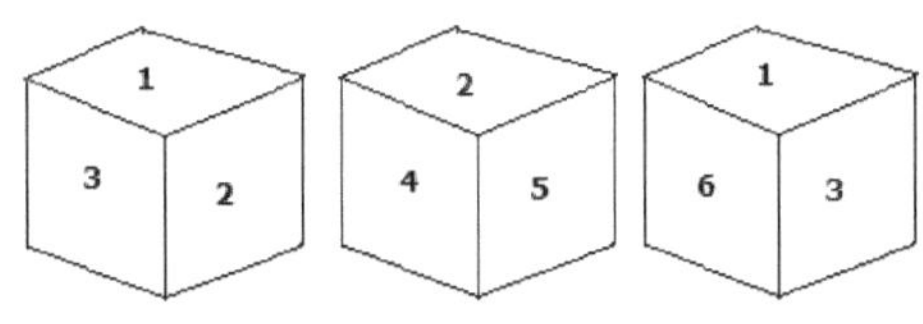

55. C is wife of B and K is mother of B. therefore, C is daughter in law of K.

56. Ajay Bhushan Pandey took over as the Revenue Secretary in the Ministry after Hasmukh Adhia retired recently.

Pandey would continue to head the Unique Identification authority of India (UIDAI) as its CEO, where he had a remarkable stint of over eight years playing a key role in establishing and steering Aadhaar across the country.

57. Daranghati Wildlife Sanctuary is situated in Shimla, Himachal Pradesh. It lies on the Dhauladhar Mountain. Bandli Wildlife Sanctuary, Nargu Wildlife Sanctuary, Shilli Wildlife Sanctuary, Talra Wildlife Sanctuary are also situated in Himachal Pradesh.

58. The Hand-in-Hand exercise between India & China convened from December 11 to 23 2018 (7th in the series) in Chengdu, China.

The aim of the exercise is to build and promote close relations between armies of both the countries and to enhance ability of joint exercise commander to take military contingents of both nations under command.

The exercise will involve tactical level operations in an International Counter Insurgency/ Counter Terrorist environment under UN mandate.

59. Hanoi is the capital of Vietnam, and also its second largest city, is a fascinating blend of East and West, combining traditional Sino-Vietnamese motifs with French flair.

60. Bonn Convention is about Convention on the Conservation of Migratory Species of Wild Animals. It aims to conserve terrestrial, marine and avian migratory species throughout their range.

Founded: 1 November 1983

Membership: 127 Parties

Headquarters: Bonn, Germany

61. Union Minister of Agriculture and Farmers' Welfare Shri Radha Mohan Singh recently launched a portal ENSURE- National Livestock Mission-EDEG developed by NABARD and operated under the Department of Animal Husbandry, Dairying & Fisheries.

Under the Mission's component called Entrepreneurship Development and Employment Generation (EDEG), subsidy payment for activities related to poultry, small ruminants, pigs etc. through Direct Benefit Transfer (DBT) goes directly to the beneficiary's account.

62. The Government of Nagaland organizes the Hornbill Festival every year to encourage inter-tribal interaction and to promote cultural heritage of Nagaland.

It showcases a mélange of cultural displays under one roof.

All the tribes of Nagaland take part in this festival. The aim of the festival is to revive and protect the rich culture of Nagaland and display its extravaganza and traditions.

63. Prime Minister Narendra Modi inaugurated India's first multi modal terminal on the Ganga river in Varanasi & received the country's first container cargo transported on inland waterways from Kolkata.

It is the first of three multi-modal terminals on the river under the Jal Marg Vikas Project (JMVP).

It is being implemented by the Inland Waterways Authority of India (IWAI).

64. President of India, Shri Ram Nath Kovind, inaugurated the 'One District One Product' Summit recently in Lucknow, Uttar Pradesh.

'One District One Product' scheme will enhance skills of local people as well as increase the reach to products. And it will result in economic progress of artisans of Uttar Pradesh.

65. "Adopt a Heritage: Apni Dharohar, Apni Pehchaan", is a collaborative effort between the Ministry of Tourism, Ministry of Culture and Archaeological Survey of India (ASI), and State/UTs Governments. The Project aims to develop synergy among all partners to effectively promote "responsible tourism".

It aims to involve public sector companies, private sector companies and corporate citizens/individuals to take up the responsibility for making our heritage and tourism more sustainable through development, operation and maintenance of world-class tourist infrastructure and amenities at ASI/ State heritage sites and other important tourist sites in India.

66. In response to the inadequacy of the Simon Report, the Labour Government, which had come to power under Ramsay MacDonald in 1929, decided to hold a series of Round Table Conferences in London. The first Round Table Conference convened from 12 November 1930 to 19 January 1931

67. Prime Minister Narendra Modi recently inaugurated the National Rail and Transport University, NRTU in Vadodara, Gujarat.

The institute will provide human resources training and build the capability of Indian Railways by offering 2 courses currently- BBA Transportation Management and BSc Transportation Technology in order to give education on latest technology applications like- Radio frequency Identification, Artificial Intelligence and satellite-based tracking.

68. Global search giant Google has selected 10 Indian media companies for funding under its Google News Initiative, as part of its YouTube-specific funding to support media companies.

Google News Initiative will build efforts and deepen Google's commitment to a news industry facing dramatic shifts in how journalism is created, consumed, and paid for.

It's focused on three objectives: elevate and strengthen quality journalism, evolve business models to drive sustainable growth; and empower news organisations through technological innovation.

69. He was Minister of Chemicals & Fertilizers under the current government in 16th Lok Sabha.

Ananth Kumar began his parliamentary career when he was elected to the Lok Sabha in 1996 from Bangalore South, the constituency which remained his strong fort till his passing away, by winning it for six consecutive times.

70. The Ramon Magsaysay Award, Asia's premier prize and highest honour, celebrates greatness of spirit and transformative leadership in Asia.

The trustees of the Ramon Magsaysay Award Foundation annually select the awardees. Awardees are presented with a certificate and a medallion with an embossed image of Ramon Magsaysay facing right in profile.

The Award is presented to them in formal ceremonies in Manila, Philippines on August 31st, the birth anniversary of the much-esteemed Philippine President whose ideals inspired the Award's creation in 1957.

71. iron + water + oxygen → hydrated iron(III) oxide (hydrated ferric oxide)

Rust forms when oxygen reacts with iron in presence of water/moisture.

The iron oxide reacts with oxygen to yield red rust, $Fe_2O_3.H_2O$

72. Physical properties of table salt are:

1. Salt is a white cubic crystals. When the salt is pure it clear. It also appear in white, grey or brownish color depending upon the purity.

2. It is odourless but has strong salty taste.

3. Solubility in water is different at different temperatures.

4. Hygroscopic(ability of a substance to attract and hold water molecules from the surroundings)

73. The solids are characterized by incompressibility, rigidity and mechanical strength.

The molecules, atoms or ions in solids are closely packed, i.e., they are held together by strong forces and cannot move about at random. Hence solids have definite volume, shape, slow diffusion, low vapour pressure and possess the unique property of being rigid.

74. The frequency range of a young person is about 20 to 20,000 hertz.

The human ear is capable of hearing many of the sounds produced in nature. Any frequency that is below the human range is known as infrasound.

Bats, whales, porpoises, and dolphins use ultrasound for navigation. Most bats can detect frequencies as high as 100,000 Hz.

75. A force is a push or a pull that acts upon an object as a result of its interaction with another object.

According to Newton, whenever objects A and B interact with each other, they exert forces upon each other. These forces are called action and reaction forces and are the subject of Newton's third law of motion. Formally stated, Newton's third law is:

For every action, there is an equal and opposite reaction.

All the above given options are examples of the stated law.

76. Mitochondria are tiny organelles inside cells that are involved in releasing energy from food and the process is known as cellular respiration.

It is for this reason that mitochondria are often referred to as the powerhouses of the cell. Cells that need a lot of energy, like muscle cells, can contain thousands of mitochondria.

When the breakdown products from the digestion of food find their way into the cell, a series of chemical reactions occur in the cytoplasm.

This allows some of the energy locked up in these products to be released and incorporated into the universal energy supplier in cells known as ATP (adenosine triphosphate).

ATP → ADP + P + energy for bodily function.

77. The nitrogen cycle helps to explain as to how nitrogen flows between animals, bacteria, plants, the atmosphere, and the soil on earth.

Processes of the Nitrogen Cycle

Nitrogen fixation is the process of converting the atmospheric nitrogen (N_2) into biological state nitrogen.

Nitrification is the process where the ammonium ions (NH_4) are converted into nitrides, first into nitrites (NO^{2-}) then into nitrate (NO^{3-}) which is done by the nitrogen-fixing bacteria.

Assimilation refers to how plants and animals obtain nitrogen. Plant roots absorb nitrates from the soil into the roots then into the entire plant system.

Ammonification is also termed as the decaying process. It occurs when the plant or animal dies then decomposers such as fungi and bacteria decompose the tissues and transforms the nitrogen back into ammonium.

Denitrification is the process that changes nitrate to nitrogen gas, hence returning it into the atmosphere. This process releases the excess nitrogen in the soil back into the atmosphere

78. Chlorine (Cl) is a member of the halogen group with an atomic number of 17.

It is the second most common halogen on Earth.

Chlorine in its pure form is yellowish-green, but its common compounds are typically colourless

Chlorine is vital for living organisms although highly concentrated pure chlorine is dangerous to living beings.

Chlorine has two stable isotopes, Cl-35 and Cl-37 while Cl-36 is radioactive.

79. Sublimation is conversion of a substance from the solid to the gaseous state without its becoming liquid.

An example is the vaporization of frozen carbon dioxide (dry ice) at ordinary atmospheric pressure and temperature. The phenomenon is the result of vapour pressure and temperature relationships.

Hoarfrost is formed by direct condensation of water vapour to ice at temperatures below freezing and occurs when air is brought to its frost point by cooling.

80. Uranium is a naturally-occurring element in the Earth's crust. Traces of it occur almost everywhere, although mining takes place in locations where it is naturally concentrated.

The uranium ore requires to make fuel for nuclear. Uranium is to be extracted from the rock in which it is found, then enriched in the uranium-235 isotope, before being made into pellets that are loaded into assemblies of nuclear fuel rods.

81. The boiling point of water is 100 °C at 1 atmospheric pressure that is, at sea level.The boiling point of water depends on the atmospheric pressure, which changes according to elevation.

The boiling point of water depends on the purity of the water, atmospheric pressure. Water that contains impurities (such as salted water) boils at a higher temperature than pure wate.

82. when a wave travels from one medium to another, a part of the wave undergoes reflection. The reflection of sound waves can end up with any of the two phenomena either it's an echo or reverberation.

Refraction of waves is the change in direction of waves as they pass from one medium to another.

Diffraction is the phenomena known for the bending of a wave towards the small obstacles that spreads out as a wave fronts beyond the openings.

83. The pleural membranes enclose a fluid-filled space surrounding the lungs.

The membranes and associated fluid serve to protect the lungs and to provide lubrication. Lung tissue is delicate and easily damaged compared to muscle, bone, or connective tissue.

Protecting the lungs from damaging interactions with other tissues is important. The lungs are also constantly expanding and contracting. The pleural membranes and fluid allow the lungs to easily move within the body cavity with minimal friction from other organs.

84. In the human skull, the brain "float" in the cerebrospinal fluid. It is found within the skull and spine. This cushioning fluid is produced by the choroid plexus tissue, which is located within the brain, and flows through a series of cavities (ventricles) out of the brain and down along the spinal cord.

The cerebrospinal fluid is kept separate from the blood supply by the blood-brain barrier

85. Iron, Silver, Copper etc. are considered to be a conductor because they conduct the electron current or flow of electrons fairly easily. Most metals are good conductors of electrical current.

Insulators are materials that have the opposite effect on the flow of electrons. They do not let electrons flow very easily from one atom to another. These electrons are not free to roam around and be shared by neighbouring atoms.

Some common insulator materials are glass, plastic, rubber, air, and wood.

86. Cartilage is an important structural component of the human body, a firm tissue which is softer and much more flexible than bone.

Cartilage is a connective tissue found in many areas of the body including:

• Joints between bones e.g. the elbows, knees and ankles

• Ends of the ribs

• Between the vertebrae in the spine

• Ears and nose

87. According to the Committee on Data for Science and Technology, mass of the electron, or the electron's mass is 9.109 38356 x 10^{-31} kg.

Mass of proton: Mass of proton is 1.6726 x 10^{-27} kg.

Mass of neutron: Mass of neutron is 1.6749 x 10^{-27} kg.

88. In 1895, German physicist Wilhelm Roentgen while working in his laboratory in Würzburg, accidentally discovered the X-rays.

Roentgen was conducting experiments with a Crookes tube - basically a glass gas bulb that gives off fluorescent light when a high-voltage current is passed through it - when he noticed that the beam turned a screen 9 feet away a greenish fluorescent color, despite the tube being shielded by heavy black cardboard.

89. When the magnesium metal burns it reacts with oxygen found in the air to form Magnesium Oxide. A compound is a material in which atoms of different elements are bonded to one another. Oxygen and magnesium combine in a chemical reaction to form this compound. After it burns, it forms a white powder of the magnesium oxide.

$2Mg(s) + O_2(g) \rightarrow 2MgO(s) + energy$

90. Chloroform (IUPAC name of trichloromethane) is an organic solvent very used in chemical and pharmaceutical industries. Chloroform chemical formula is $CHCl_3$ and its molar mass is 119.37 g mol-1

The molecule has the typical structure of a methane, which is the most related molecule due to chloroform is a methane where 3 hydrogen atoms has been substituted by 3 chloride atoms.

The molecular structure is tetrahedral.

91. Near-sightedness (myopia) is a common vision condition in which you can see objects near to you clearly, but objects farther away are blurry.

Near-sightedness symptoms may include:

• Blurry vision when looking at distant objects

• The need to squint or partially close the eyelids to see clearly

• Headaches caused by eyestrain

• Difficulty seeing while driving a vehicle, especially at night (night myopia)

92. In vacuum the speed of light is 2.997 x 10^8 m/s.

When light is in a vacuum, its speed has that exact value, no matter who measures it. Even if the vacuum is inside a box in a rocket traveling away from earth, both an astronaut in the rocket and a hypothetical observer on earth will measure the speed of light moving through that box to be exactly c. No one will measure a faster speed. Indeed, c is the ultimate speed limit of the universe

93. Veins have following characteristics-

• carry blood from the tissues of the body back to the heart

• are usually positioned closer beneath the surface of the skin

• are less muscular than arteries, but contain valves to help keep blood flowing in the right direction, usually toward the heart

Haemoglobin (Hb) is a protein found in the red blood cells that carries oxygen in your body and gives blood its red colour.

94. Sulphuric Acid has the lowest pH compare to other acids which were mentioned in options. So, it is the strongest acid

Acid Name	pH
Sulphuric Acid	2.75
Hydrochloric Acid	3.01
Nitric Acid	3.01
Carbonic Acid	4.68

95. The galvanometer is the device used for detecting the presence of small current and voltage or for measuring their magnitude.

The galvanometer is mainly used in the bridges and potentiometer where they indicate the null deflection or zero current.

An altimeter or an altitude meter is an instrument used to measure the altitude of an object above a fixed level.

Ammeter is an instrument for measuring either direct or alternating electric current, in amperes.

A voltmeter is an electronic instrument used to measure potential between any two points in an electric or electronic circuit in volts.

96. Conservation of energy, principle of physics according to which the energy of interacting bodies or particles in a closed system remains constant.

For example, when a pendulum swings upward, kinetic energy is converted to potential energy. When the pendulum stops briefly at the top of its swing, the kinetic energy is zero, and all the energy of the system is in potential energy. When the pendulum swings back down, the potential energy is converted back into kinetic energy. At all times, the sum of potential and kinetic energy is constant.

This version of the conservation-of-energy principle, expressed in its most general form, is the first law of thermodynamics.

97. The de Broglie equation is an equation used to describe the wave properties of matter, specifically, the wave nature of the electron: $\lambda = h/mv$, where λ is wavelength, h is Planck's constant (6.6×10^{-34} J s), m is the mass of a particle (mass of electron= 9.1×10^{-31} kg), moving at a velocity v

Putting the values in the formulae,

$\lambda = h/mv$; $\lambda = 6.6 \times 10^{-34} / (9.1 \times 10^{-31} \times 200)$

$\lambda \approx 3600$ nanometre

98. The cornea is the transparent part of the eye that covers the front portion of the eye.

It covers the pupil, iris, and anterior chamber.

The cornea's main function is to refract, or bend, light. The cornea is responsible for focusing most of the light that enters the eye.

The retina is a light-sensitive layer that lines the back of the eye. The retina contains photoreceptors that absorb light and then transmits those signals through the optic nerve to the brain.

99. Using the distance-time equation for a body moving with constant acceleration, $S = ut + 1/2at^2$ where, S = distance travelled, u= initial velocity, a=acceleration, t= time taken for body to travel distance s.

Since, body was initially at rest, u= 0 m/s,

Hence, Putting the values in the equation, $S = ut + 1/2at^2$

$3000 = 0 + \frac{1}{2} (15 \times t^2)$

Or, t = 20 seconds

100. Oesophagus is part of the digestive system, which is sometimes called the gastro-intestinal tract (GI tract). It's around 25cm (10in) long in adults.

When we swallow our food, the walls of the oesophagus squeeze together (contract) and helps to move the food down the oesophagus to the stomach.

Mathematics

Q.1 If $x^4 - 3x^3 + 5x^2 - 6x + 2k$ is divisible by $(x - 4)$, then what is the value of k?

A. 20   **B.** -60   **C.** -40   **D.** 30

Q.2 In a pet shop, number of 9 different types of pets are given below. Find the median of number of pets of different types in the shop.
12, 7, 8, 18, 14, 21, 5, 7 and 16

A. 8   **B.** 14   **C.** 12   **D.** 7

Q.3 A boatman can row 2 km against the stream in 20 minutes and return in 18 minutes. Find the rate of current ?

A. 2/3 km/hr   **B.** 1/3 km/hr
C. 5/3 km/hr   **D.** None of these

Q.4 A boat goes 60 km. downstream in 4 hr. If the speed of boat is double of the speed of river, then tell how much distance it travels upstream in 2hr.

A. 30 km   **B.** 10 km   **C.** 13 km   **D.** 20 km

Q.5 In a $\triangle ABC$, ratio of AB: BC: AC = 5: 8: 7 and perpendicular drawn from A to BC is $(5\sqrt{3})$ cm long. What is the circum-radius of $\triangle ABC$?

A. $(28/\sqrt{3})$ cm   **B.** $(14/\sqrt{3})$ cm
C. $(14\sqrt{3})$ cm   **D.** $(28\sqrt{3})$ cm

Q.6 The simple interest on a certain sum is Rs.240 for 3 years at 8% per annum. The corresponding compound interest is

A. Rs. 160   **B.** Rs. 220   **C.** Rs. 260   **D.** Rs. 275

Q.7 If $(x + 1/x) = 4$ and 'x' is less than 2, then what is the value of $(x^2 - 4x + 6)$?

A. 14   **B.** 15   **C.** 4   **D.** 5

Q.8 A fraction is equivalent to 4/5. If 8 is added to the numerator and 6 is subtracted from the denominator, the resultant fraction is equivalent to 4/3. Find the difference between the numerator and the denominator of the original fraction.

A. 5   **B.** 6   **C.** 8   **D.** 4

Q.9 What is the value of 25% of 40% of [{($\sqrt{16} - \sqrt{9}$) X 5 ÷ 2.5} - 2 + $\sqrt{(80\% \text{ of } 27 \div 3 \times 5)}$]?

A. 1/5   **B.** 2/3   **C.** 1/3   **D.** 3/5

Q.10 A series is given: 167, 98, 23, A, 67, 217, B and 134 and mean of all the numbers is 100 and mean of first 4 numbers is 84, then what is the difference between A and B?

A. 4   **B.** 5   **C.** 3   **D.** 2

Q.11 A watch which gains 5 seconds in 3 minutes was set right at 7 a.m. In the afternoon of the same day, when the watch indicated quarter past 4 O'clock, the true time is -

A. 4 p.m.
B. 59(7/12) minutes past 3
C. 58(7/11) minutes past 3
D. 2(3/11) minutes past 4

Q.12 A certain number is factorized into 4 parts such that all the parts are in an increasing AP and sum of first and last number is 12 and multiplication of those two numbers is 27, then what is that number?

A. 945   **B.** 780   **C.** 1240   **D.** 650

Q.13 In what time a cistern be filled by three pipes whose diameters are 1cm, 1(1/3) cm and 2 cm running together, when the largest alone will fill it in 61 minutes. It is found that the amount of water flowing in each pipe is proportional to the square of the diameter?

A. 36 minutes   **B.** 40 minutes
C. 60 minutes   **D.** 25 minutes

Q.14 (a+b)% of (a-b) is equal to 2% of the average of a and b. If a^2 is 44% more than b^2. Then (a+b) is what percent more than (a-b) where a and b both are positive numbers?.

A. 100%   **B.** 500%   **C.** 2000%   **D.** 1000%

Q.15 If A:B = 2/3:1/4, B:C = 1/5:1/3, C:D = 1/6:1/7, then (A+B+D):(B+C+D) is equal to

A. 107:86   **B.** 23/44:33/53
C. 118:89   **D.** 11/25:17/27

Q.16 Following is the data regarding the percentage distribution of the number of students in 5 Colleges. Total number of students in all 5 Colleges combined = 12000. First year and Second year students are known as Junior Year Students and Third year and Fourth year students are known as Senior Year students. The ratio of the number of Junior year and Senior Year students in College A and College B is 5:4 and 3:2.

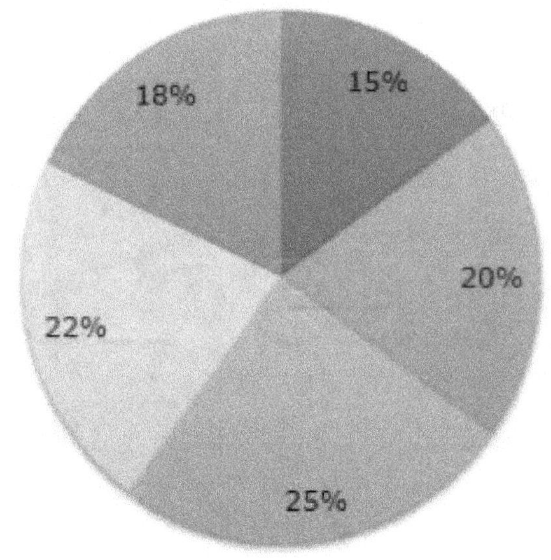

What is the sum of the number of Junior Year students in College A and the number of Senior Year students in College B?

A. 2300 **B.** 1400 **C.** 2500 **D.** 1960

Q.17 There is a town named Ratanpur. In this town the number of shops are 1/4 of the number of house. The total population of the town is 5 times of the total number of houses. Out of total population 3/5 of the population is adult. The total numbers of females are 7/12 of the total adult population. What is the ratio between number of houses to the number of females in the given town?

A. 1 : 7 **B.** 1 : 1 **C.** 4 : 7 **D.** 7 : 4

Q.18 If three numbers are in the ratio 1:3:5 and one-third the sum is 18, then the half the sum of their squares is?

A. 730 **B.** 630 **C.** 930 **D.** 530

Q.19 The sum of two numbers is 216 and their H.C.F is 27. What are those two numbers?

A. 27, 189 **B.** 154, 62 **C.** 24, 92 **D.** 88, 128

Q.20 An accurate clock shows 8 o'clock in the morning. Through how many degrees will the hour hand rotate when the clock shows 2 o'clock in the afternoon?

A. 144° **B.** 150° **C.** 168° **D.** 180°

Q.21 The Speed of a boat in still water is 15 km/hr and the rate of current is 3 km/hr. The distance travelled downstream in 12 minutes is ?

A. 3.6 km **B.** 1.2 km **C.** 1.8 km **D.** 1.7 km

Q.22 If the nature of roots of two equations: $4x^2 - 21x + 35 = 0$ and $Ax^2 + 2x + C = 0$ are same, then which of the following can be a value of 'AC'?

A. $\sqrt{2}$ **B.** $\sqrt{(1/2)}$ **C.** $\sqrt{0.8}$ **D.** 1

Q.23 In an ODI cricket match Rohit scored 132 runs which included 12 boundaries and 3 sixes. What percents of his runs

he made by running between wickets? (1 boundary = 4 runs and 1 six = 6 runs)

A. 45% **B.** 55% **C.** 50% **D.** 60%

Q.24 $3\cos A + 2\sin^2 A = 0$, what is the value of $\cos^3 A$?

A. −1/8 **B.** 1/8 **C.** 1 **D.** 0

Q.25 Solve and Arrange the following in the proper sequence and mark the answer.Two articles A and B are marked at Rs.400 and Rs.500 respectively. Discount given on A is 15% while amount of discount on B is double than that given on A. What is the profit per cent if the cost price of both the articles is Rs.300 each?Given below are the steps involved. Arrange them in the sequential order.

(A) Amount of discount given on B = 2 * 60 = Rs.120

(B) Profit per cent = [(720 - 600)/600] * 100 = 20%

(C) Amount of discount given on A = 15% of 400 = Rs.60

(D) Total cost price = 300 + 300 = Rs.600 and Total selling price = (400 - 60) + (500 - 120) = Rs.720

A. CBAD **B.** CDAB **C.** CADB **D.** CBDA

Q.26 What is the value of [5 X {25 ÷ (2.5 ÷ 0.5)}] ÷ 2.5 X 2 - 16 ÷ 4 + 16 ÷ 2?

A. 12 **B.** 18 **C.** 24 **D.** 30

Q.27 Six men and four boys working together, can complete a piece of work in 8 days. The same piece of work can be completed by four men in 'd' days only and by eight boys in (d +5) days only. By what percentage is the work efficiency of a boy less than that of a man?

A. 33.33% **B.** 37.5% **C.** 62.5% **D.** 66.67%

Q.28 Which among the following is irrational number: $\sqrt[4]{(7.2^2 * 20^2)}$, $\sqrt[3]{(5^2 * 135)}$, $(\sqrt{43.2})/5$ and $\sqrt{(8^2 + 3^2 + 2^3)}$?

A. $\sqrt[4]{(7.2^2 * 20^2)}$ **B.** $\sqrt[3]{(5^2 * 135)}$
C. $(\sqrt{43.2})/5$ **D.** $\sqrt{(8^2 + 3^2 + 2^3)}$

Q.29 A student gets an aggregate of 60% marks in five subjects in the ratio 10:9:8:7:6. If the passing marks are 50% of the maximum marks and each subject has the same maximum marks, in how many subjects did he pass the exam?

A. 2 **B.** 3 **C.** 4 **D.** 5

Q.30 Ages of A and B after 2 years will be in the ratio 2: 3 respectively, ages of B and C before two years were in the ratio 7: 8 respectively and present ages of A and C are in the ratio 5: 9 respectively. Find the present age of B.

A. 12 years **B.** 16 years
C. 18 years **D.** None of these

General Intelligence & Reasoning

Q.31 T is the sister of B. K is the brother of R and the father of T. M is the wife of R. G is the father of K. S is the mother-in-law of M. Q is the sister-in-law of R. How is Q related to T?

A. Mother **B.** Grandmother
C. Aunt **D.** Father

Q.32 Sonu walked a certain distance and rode back taking a total time of 37 minutes. Sonu could walk both ways in 55 minutes. How long would it take Sonu to ride both ways?

A. 20 minutes   **B.** 17 minutes

C. 15 minutes   **D.** 19 minutes

Q.33 Which of the following are the amphibious animals, that is creatures who survive both on territorial land and water ecosystems?

A. Frog   **B.** Snakes

C. Turtles   **D.** All of the above

Q.34 Each question given below consists of a statement, followed by two arguments I and II. You have to decide which of the arguments is a 'strong' argument and which is a 'weak' argument.**Statement:** Should one close relative of a retiring government employee be given a job in government in India?**Arguments:**

I. Yes, where else will the relative get a job like this?

II. No, it will close doors of government service to competent and needy youth.

A. if only argument I is strong.

B. if only argument II is strong.

C. if either I or II strong.

D. if neither I nor II strong.

Q.35 Select the odd one out: $\sqrt[4]{0.0256}$, [16 * 10^{-2}], [8^3 ÷ (12^3 - 448)] and [(0.2)^2 * 10].

A. $\sqrt[4]{0.0256}$ **B.** [16 * 10^{-2}]

C. [8^3 ÷ (12^3 - 448)]   **D.** [(0.2)^2 * 10]

Q.36 In a certain code language PRINCE is coded as IGPJVT the MOTHER is coded as

A. LJFQTG   **B.** LJEQTG

C. LEJTQG   **D.** LEJQUG

Q.37 In each of the following questions, you are given a figure (X) followed by four alternative figures (a), (b), (c) and (d) such that figure (X) is embedded in one of them. Trace out the alternative figure which contains fig. (X) as its part.

 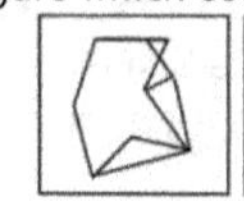  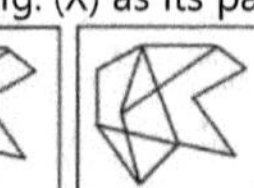 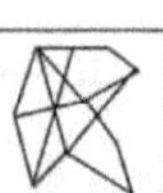

A. a   **B.** b   **C.** c   **D.** d

Q.38 Find the odd option from given alternatives.

A. ABCDEF   **B.** GHIJKL

C. MNOPQR   **D.** STUVWX

Q.39 Each of the following figure consists of a 3x3 matrix. The matrix consists of 9 different figures. The figures are such that 3 of them bear a similar relation and from group 1, another 3 figures bear a relation and form group 2 and similarly the rest 3 bear another relationship and form group 3. Find the option which shows all three groups in the correct sequence.

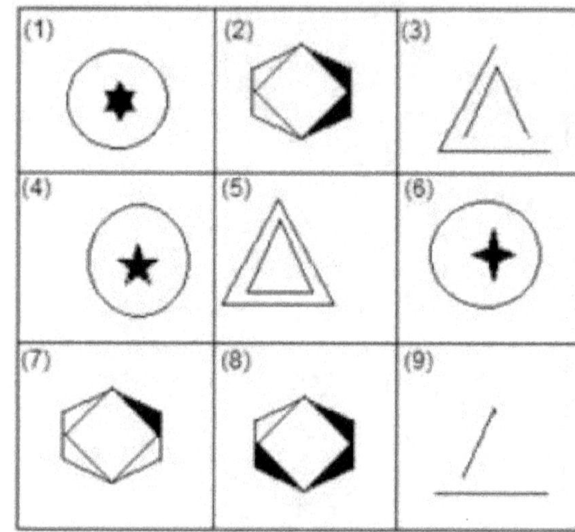

A. (4, 6, 1); (3, 9, 5); (7, 8, 2)

B. (6, 1, 4); (9, 5, 3); (8, 7, 2)

C. (1, 4, 6); (5, 3, 9); (7, 2, 8)

D. (1, 3, 4); (5, 6, 9); (7, 8, 2)

Q.40 Identify the diagram that best represents the relationship among the given classes.Train, vehicle, bus

A.

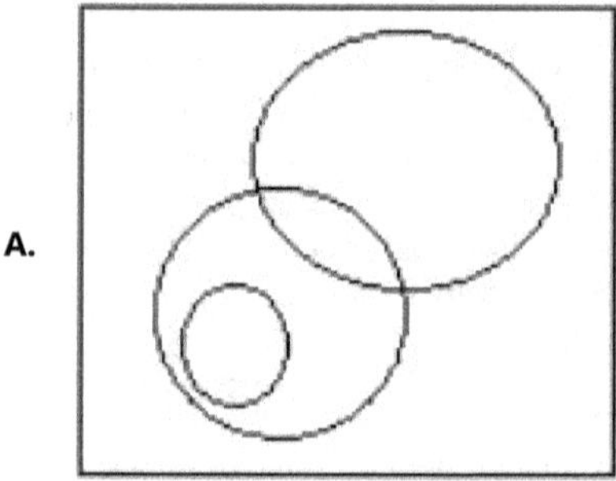

B.

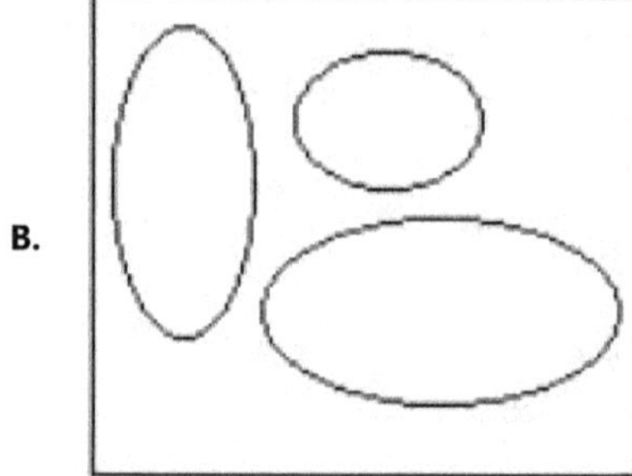

C.

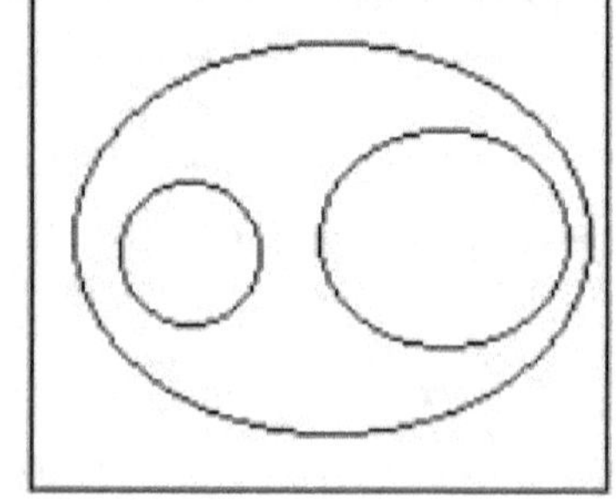

D. 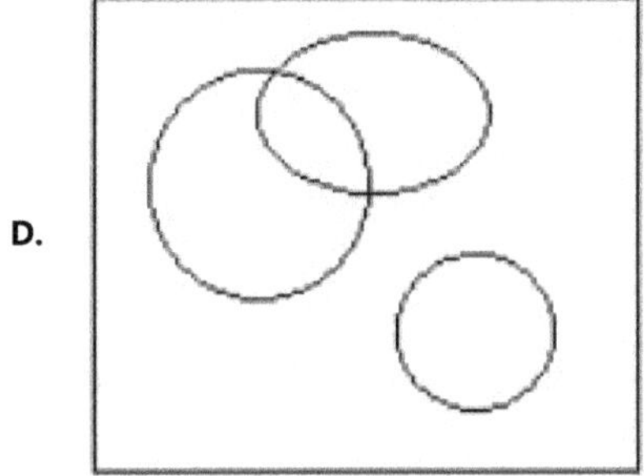

Q.41 Each of the questions below consists of a question and two statements numbered I and II given below it. You have to decide whether the data provided in the statements are sufficient to answer the question.What does '$' mean in a code language?

I. '5 $ # 3' means 'flowers are really good'.

II. '7 # 3 5' means 'good flowers are available'.

A. if the data in statement I alone are sufficient to answer the question, while the data in statement II alone are not sufficient to answer the question.

B. if the data in statement II alone are sufficient to answer the question, while the data in statement I alone are not sufficient to answer the question.

C. if the data given in both the statements I and II together are not sufficient to answer the question, and

D. if the data in both the statements I and II together are necessary to answer the question.

Q.42 100-degree Fahrenheit is equal to ______degree Celsius.

A. Around 37
B. Around 50
C. Around 100
D. Around 0

Q.43 Each of the questions below consists of a question and two statements numbered I and II given below it. You have to decide whether the data provided in the statements are sufficient to answer the question:On which day Ravi got promoted?I. His friend correctly remembers he got promoted after 12th and before 20th while his mother correctly remembers that he got promoted after 15th.

II. His father correctly remembers that he got promoted after Monday but before Friday.

A. If the data in Statement I alone is sufficient to answer the question, while the data in Statement II alone is not sufficient to answer the question.

B. If the data in Statement II alone is sufficient to answer the question, while the data in Statement I alone is not sufficient to answer the question.

C. If the data either in Statement I alone or in Statement II alone is sufficient to answer the question.

D. If the data in both the Statements I and II together are not sufficient to answer the question.

Q.44 Find the next term in the series.194, 219, 283, 404, 600, ?

A. 1071   **B.** 889   **C.** 950   **D.** 821

Q.45 In each of the questions below, an assertion (A) is given, followed by a reason (R) which may or may not explain the assertion. From the given options, choose the right answer.

A: Vaccines help to diagnose diseases.

R: Vaccines must be given to children.

A. Both A and R are true, and R is the correct explanation for A

B. Both A and R are true, but R is not the correct explanation for A

C. A is true, while R is false

D. A is false, while R is true

Q.46 K starts walking straight and then turns right and walks some distance. Then he takes left to face north and walks some distance. D starts walking at the same time and at the same starting point as K but facing the opposite direction of K. D also walks in the directions exactly opposite to the one K takes every time. M is 15 meters to the west of K's starting point. What is the position of D's final position with respect to M?

A. South-west
B. South-east
C. South
D. North

Q.47 Expansion of DNA is________.

A. Deoxyribo Nucleic Acid
B. Dehydrated Nuclear Acid
C. Dematerialised Nucleic Acid
D. Dihydride Nucleic Acid

Q.48 In order to complete the set, which one of the following set of letters should be placed in the gaps sequentially?

b y d w _ u _ _ _

A. k t h j   **B.** f h s j   **C.** m w l c   **D.** f q v z

Q.49 Find out from amongst the four alternatives as to how the pattern would appear on the sheet when the sheet is folded at the dotted line and is punched as given.

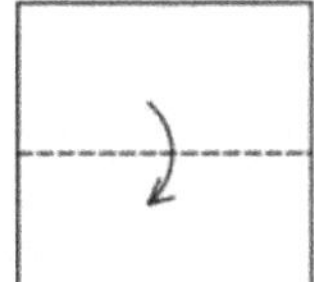 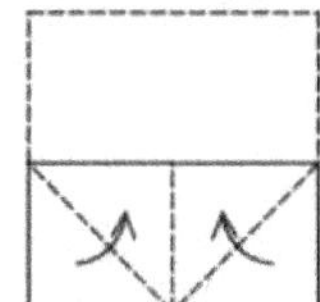 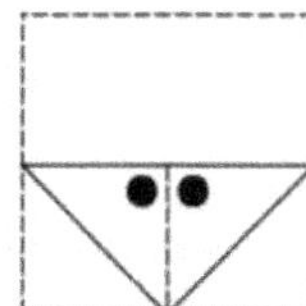

A. 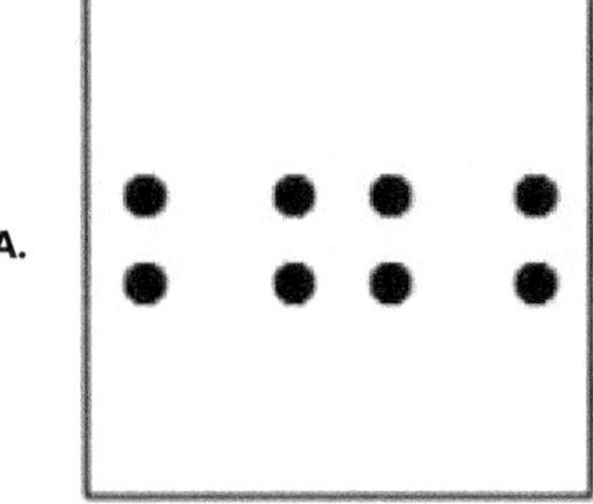

B.

C.

D.

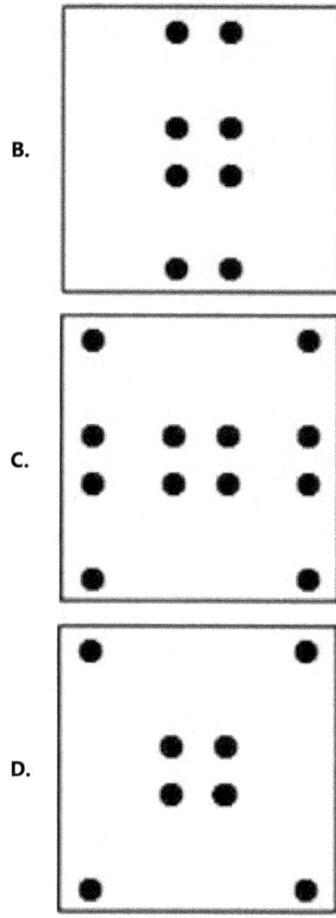

Q.50 In each of the questions below, one statement is given, followed by two conclusions which may or may not follow. From the options below, choose the one that reflects the correct choice of conclusion(s) that follows/follow.

Bullying has always been a problem for young people, but it is only recently that bullying could be done over a long distance and potentially without knowing who the bully is. Bullying through the internet or phones, cyberbullying, has however with the spread of first the internet and then smartphones become as much of a problem and one that is harder to deal with than offline bullying.

I. Some countries do have jail time as a potential punishment for cyberbullying.

II. Harassment online can be a crime just like harassment offline is widely accepted but there is less consensus about what to do to punish extreme cases.

A. Only I

B. Only II

C. Both I and II

D. Neither I nor II

Q.51 In each of the questions below, a statement/passage is given. From the options below, choose the one that reflects the correct choice of assumption(s) that follows/follow.

South Africa should be given a chance to host the Summer Olympic Games in the future.

I. South Africa has a track record of successfully hosting major sporting events.

II. The climate of South Africa suits most of the games which are a part of Summer Olympic Games.

A. Only I

B. Only II

C. Both I and II

D. Neither I nor II

Q.52 P's height is less than T's as well as S's height. Q's height is less than P's height. R's height is less than T's height. T is not the tallest. U's height is less than R's height. Who is taller than only two persons, among the given persons?

A. R

B. U

C. P

D. Cannot be determined

Q.53 How many triangles are present in the given figure?

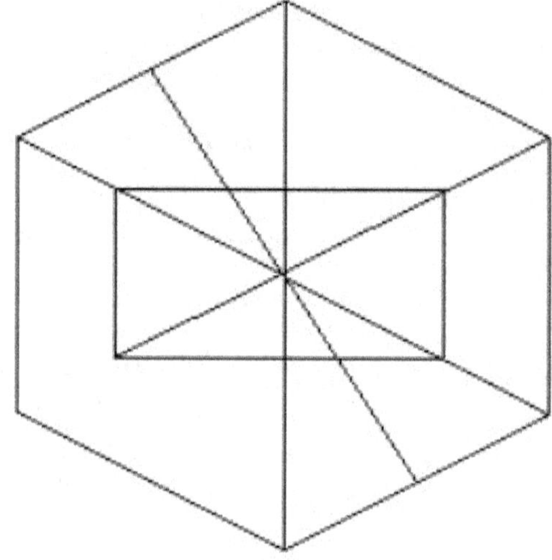

A. 25   **B.** 26   **C.** 23   **D.** 24

Q.54 In each of the questions below are given some statements followed by some conclusions. You have to take the given statements to be true even if they seem to be at variance from commonly known facts. Read all the conclusions and then decide which of the given conclusions logically follows from the given statements disregarding commonly known facts.

Statements:

All arcs are tangents.

No tangent is a secant.

All secants are circles.

Conclusions:

I. No arc is a circle.

II. Some secants being arcs is a possibility.

A. If only conclusion I follows.

B. If only conclusion II follows.

C. If either conclusion I or conclusion II follows.

D. If neither conclusion I nor conclusion II follows.

Q.55 In the following question select the related number from the given alternatives.102:2601::?:2401

A. 75   **B.** 94   **C.** 98   **D.** 78

General Awareness

Q.56 2023 ICC Cricket World Cup will be hosted completely in which of the following countries?

A. West Indies   **B.** South Africa
C. Australia   **D.** India

Q.57 Arrange the given words in a meaningful sequence.
1. Ploughing
2. Harvesting
3. Sowing
4. Germinating
5. Selling

A. 4, 3, 1, 2, 5   **B.** 3, 1, 4, 5, 2
C. 4, 1, 3, 2, 5   **D.** 1, 3, 4, 2, 5

Q.58 In each of the following questions, select a figure from amongst the four alternatives, which when placed in the blank space of figure (X) would complete the pattern.

Identify the figure that completes the pattern.

A.

B.

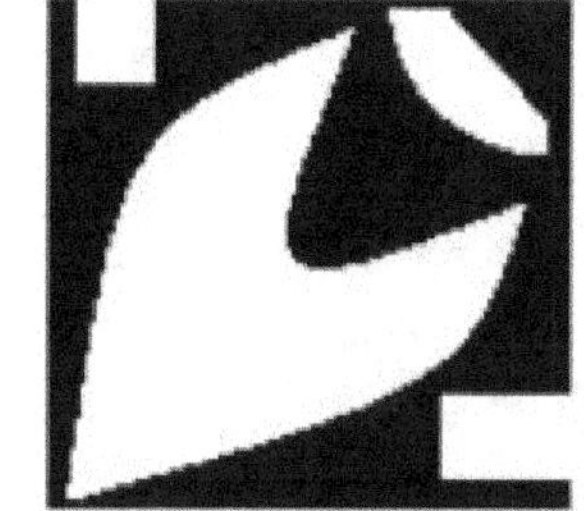

C.

D.

Q.59 Indian Space Research Organisation launched _________ to engage with students on Space Science.

A. SAMPADA   **B.** SAMWAD
C. SOOCHNA   **D.** SAMADHAN

Q.60 ___________ recently joined International Monetary Fund as its chief economist, becoming the first woman to occupy the top IMF post.

A. Sumitra Krishnan
B. Indira Nooyi
C. Anindita Chakraborty
D. Gita Gopinath

Q.61 Artificial Pacemaker is used to cure which of these affected parts in the body?

A. Heart   **B.** Lungs   **C.** Bones   **D.** Liver

Q.62 The upcoming General Elections to be held in 2019 will lead to formation of the ________ Lok Sabha for Republic of India.

A. 14th   **B.** 16th   **C.** 18th   **D.** 17th

Q.63 Headquarters of the Indian Space Research Organisation is in _____________

A. Pune   **B.** Hyderabad
C. Bengaluru   **D.** Visakhapatnam

Q.64 "Hampi ruins" is the Heritage architecturally important monumental site in India which is situated in which Indian state?

A. Kerala

B. Assam

C. Madhya Pradesh

D. Karnataka

Q.65 _____________ is a security force of India entrusted with protecting railway passengers, passenger area and railway property of the Indian Railways

A. Railway Indian Guards

B. Railway Police Association

C. Railway Police Force

D. Railway Armed Force

Q.66 Government of India launched __________ mobile App for Freight Managers which provides features for monitoring and managing freight business using Geographic Information System (GIS) Views and Dashboard.

A. SPURTI

B. SMRITI

C. SAFAR

D. SFOORTI

Q.67 Ranji trophy is associated with which sport?

A. Squash

B. Snooker

C. Cricket

D. Badminton

Q.68 2+2 Ministerial Dialogue is a Bilateral diplomatic conference between India and _________

A. Japan

B. China

C. United States of America

D. Bangladesh

Q.69 The first railway on Indian sub-continent ran over a stretch of 21 miles from _________ to ___________ in the 19th century

A. Surat, Gandhinagar

B. Bhandup, Thane

C. Bombay, Thane

D. Madras, Mysore

Q.70 Indian economy is expected to grow at _____ in 2018-19 according to the Central Statistics Office.

A. 7.2%   **B.** 6.7%   **C.** 7.8%   **D.** 7.9%

General Science

Q.71 Which of the following Metallic element would you find in a 'Clinical Thermometer'?

A. Tungsten

B. Mercury

C. Molybdenum

D. Quartz

Q.72 'Swinging of a pendulum' is an example of which type of motion?

A. Straight line motion

B. Circular motion

C. Oscillatory motion

D. Zig-zag motion

Q.73 Which of the following IS NOT an abiotic component of the ecosystem?

A. Algae

B. Rock

C. Moses

D. Both a & c

Q.74 In a Distance Vs. Time plot for a vehicle moving at a 'constant speed', graph would look like which of the following?

A. A straight line parallel to time axis

B. A straight line making certain degree angle with either axis but with constant slope

C. A straight line parallel to the distance axis

D. A set of point anywhere in the graph depending upon the acceleration

Q.75 Which of these is/are parts of the Human brain?

A. Cerebrum

B. Thalamus

C. Medulla

D. All of the above

Q.76 Which of the following element is in liquid state at room temperature?

A. Molybdenum

B. Cobalt

C. Mercury

D. Phosphorus

Q.77 Which of the following is/are the example(s) of a 'Magnetic material'?

A. Iron bar

B. Nickel bar

C. Rubber

D. Both 1 & 2

Q.78 __________ objects are the ones which do not allow light to pass through them.

A. Translucent

B. Transparent

C. Opaque

D. Luminous

Q.79 Which of the following phenomenon is an example of Total Internal Reflection?

A. Sparkling of Diamond

B. Mirage and Looming

C. Shining of Air bubble in water

D. All of the above

Q.80 Remotely Piloted Aircraft (RPAs) - commonly known as __________ are used for commercial and defence activities.

A. Sigma crafts

B. Drones

C. Auto-Pilot crafts

D. Remote pilot crafts

Q.81 Rainbow formation is a meteorological phenomenon that takes place due to which of the following?

A. Diffraction of Light

B. Dispersion of Light

C. Higher content of noble gases in air

D. Higher water vapour presence in air

Q.82 Rubbing of an inflated balloon surface against a fabric leads to creation of which kind of energy?
A. Centrifugal Energy
B. Centripetal Energy
C. Electrodynamic Energy
D. Electrostatic Energy

Q.83 Largest gland in human body is ___________.
A. Spleen
B. Liver
C. Pancreas
D. Lungs

Q.84 ____________ is the branch of physics that deals with heat and temperature and their relation to energy and work in a system.
A. Dynamic Physics
B. Static Physics
C. Thermodynamics
D. Metallurgy

Q.85
S.I. unit for 'acceleration' is __________.
A. Meter/second
B. Meter/second^3
C. Kilogram meter/second
D. Meter/second^2

Q.86 C_6-H_6 is the chemical formulae for ____________.
A. Ethanol
B. Chloroform
C. Benzene
D. Teflon

Q.87 Which of the following Quantitative instruments working on phenomenon of Physics would you find in a moving vehicle?
A. Barometer & Odometer
B. Barometer & Speedometer
C. Cosmo meter & speedometer
D. Speedometer & Odometer

Q.88 A body of mass 45 kg is travelling at a constant velocity of 30 m/s, what is the momentum of the moving mass?
A. 1350 kg m/s
B. 650 kg m/s
C. 1200 kg m/s
D. 900 kg m/s

Q.89 Which of the following is NOT an example of 'Liquid Solution'?
A. Aerated water drinks like Pepsi, Coke etc,
B. Sugar in Water
C. Alcohol in water
D. Humidity in Air

Q.90 Formation of Sodium Chloride (NaCl) salt is a classic example of an acid-base reaction forming a salt. In this, Na (sodium) gets _________ whereas Cl (Chloride) gets __________.
A. Oxidised, Oxidised
B. Reduced, Reduced
C. Oxidised, Reduced
D. Reduced, Oxidised

Q.91 Which of the following IS NOT a part of Circulatory system in Human body.
A. Heart
B. Arteries

C. Blood
D. Ligaments

Q.92 White light is composed of _________ distinct visible colours.
A. 4
B. 9
C. 7
D. 6

Q.93 Electron was first experimentally discovered by___________
A. J Rutherford
B. S Coulomb
C. J.J Thomson
D. Audrey Huxley

Q.94 Find the charge in Coulomb on 1 g-ion of O_2^-
A. 1.9264 x 10^5 Coulomb
B. 192.64 x 10^5 Coulomb
C. 2.642 x 10^5 Coulomb
D. 26.42 x 10^5 Coulomb

Q.95 Who proposed that 'all species of life have descended over time from common ancestors' which is now widely accepted and considered as a foundational concept in science.
A. Charles Babbage
B. Charles Darwin
C. Yogi Mahesh
D. Seth Godwin

Q.96 A bond formed by the complete transfer of one or more electrons from one atom to another is called ___________.
A. Ionic bond
B. Covalent bond
C. Electrostatic bond
D. Neutral bond

Q.97 Which of these is Not an example of an Acid from the given solutions?
A. Vinegar
B. Coffee
C. Lemon Juice
D. Milk of Magnesia

Q.98 What is the scientific name of peacock?
A. Pavo cristatus
B. Nelumbo nucifera
C. Orzya Sativa
D. Panthera tigris

Q.99 A fog is an aerosol of ______ particles.
A. Solid
B. Liquid
C. Gas
D. None of the above

Q.100 One-watt hour is equivalent to_______ Joule.
A. 746
B. 3600
C. 6.67 × 10^{11}
D. 1800

// Smart Answer Sheet //

Correct Percentage of students who answered correctly.   **Skipped** Percentage of students who skipped.

Q.	Ans.	Correct / Skipped	Q.	Ans.	Correct / Skipped	Q.	Ans.	Correct / Skipped	Q.	Ans.	Correct / Skipped	Q.	Ans.	Correct / Skipped
1	B	85.16 % / 11.63 %	17	C	77.66 % / 11.95 %	33	D	77.97 % / 16.8 %	49	D	89.87 % / 10.09 %	65	C	80.4 % / 16.93 %
2	C	77.95 % / 15.51 %	18	B	86.66 % / 13.09 %	34	B	79.36 % / 18.87 %	50	D	82.3 % / 14.43 %	66	D	81.88 % / 17.8 %
3	B	88.04 % / 10.28 %	19	A	88.53 % / 11.26 %	35	A	76.01 % / 23.93 %	51	C	78.86 % / 16.48 %	67	C	85.22 % / 13.1 %
4	B	85.26 % / 13.97 %	20	D	85.65 % / 11.78 %	36	B	83.93 % / 12.5 %	52	D	88.77 % / 10.04 %	68	C	78.9 % / 18.37 %
5	B	77.76 % / 22.09 %	21	A	80.93 % / 11.66 %	37	C	83.63 % / 10.92 %	53	A	85.24 % / 10.08 %	69	C	78.68 % / 21.3 %
6	C	83.06 % / 13.36 %	22	A	86.92 % / 10.66 %	38	A	89.07 % / 10.22 %	54	D	78.5 % / 12.67 %	70	A	85.01 % / 13.2 %
7	D	80.56 % / 14.8 %	23	C	76.88 % / 22.11 %	39	C	85.03 % / 11.2 %	55	C	88.8 % / 10.14 %	71	B	85.66 % / 11.73 %
8	B	85.25 % / 13.88 %	24	A	77.75 % / 16.11 %	40	C	82.1 % / 16.47 %	56	D	88.59 % / 10.23 %	72	C	78.24 % / 11.62 %
9	D	78.46 % / 14.35 %	25	C	78.37 % / 18.6 %	41	D	82.59 % / 11.13 %	57	D	82.75 % / 15.77 %	73	D	80.28 % / 17.35 %
10	D	82.18 % / 10.97 %	26	C	84.79 % / 14.99 %	42	A	89.57 % / 10.32 %	58	B	83.51 % / 14.93 %	74	B	88.15 % / 11.18 %
11	A	82.26 % / 15.7 %	27	C	87.52 % / 11.77 %	43	D	77.41 % / 16.66 %	59	B	78.62 % / 11.6 %	75	D	88.21 % / 11.5 %
12	A	77.22 % / 12.41 %	28	C	88.62 % / 11.16 %	44	B	86.72 % / 10.71 %	60	D	77.32 % / 15.47 %	76	C	82.27 % / 12.78 %
13	A	88.8 % / 10.27 %	29	C	81.77 % / 12.65 %	45	D	82.79 % / 14.02 %	61	A	76.23 % / 16.65 %	77	D	76.38 % / 15.0 %
14	D	89.1 % / 10.81 %	30	B	85.44 % / 13.86 %	46	B	77.86 % / 11.31 %	62	D	82.84 % / 14.82 %	78	C	78.61 % / 18.25 %
15	A	80.35 % / 10.22 %	31	A	76.16 % / 10.23 %	47	A	81.74 % / 11.84 %	63	C	79.75 % / 13.99 %	79	D	85.46 % / 11.21 %
16	D	89.59 % / 10.26 %	32	D	76.25 % / 12.25 %	48	B	76.27 % / 18.99 %	64	D	79.43 % / 15.27 %	80	B	89.99 % / 10.01 %

Q.	Ans.	Correct		Q.	Ans.	Correct		Q.	Ans.	Correct		Q.	Ans.	Correct		Q.	Ans.	Correct
		Skipped				Skipped				Skipped				Skipped				Skipped
81	B	77.92 %		85	D	86.78 %		89	D	84.39 %		93	C	88.42 %		97	D	79.04 %
		21.63 %				12.01 %				11.27 %				10.73 %				11.19 %
82	D	89.88 %		86	C	83.55 %		90	C	86.09 %		94	A	83.06 %		98	A	76.84 %
		10.04 %				16.27 %				10.64 %				11.19 %				20.7 %
83	B	89.34 %		87	D	85.94 %		91	D	85.47 %		95	B	87.1 %		99	B	84.21 %
		10.63 %				12.63 %				12.73 %				10.51 %				13.57 %
84	C	79.23 %		88	A	77.0 %		92	C	89.66 %		96	A	86.55 %		100	B	84.95 %
		17.68 %				13.48 %				10.09 %				12.81 %				11.98 %

EDUGORILLA PUBLICATION

//Hints and Solutions//

1. Since, $x^4 - 3x^3 + 5x^2 - 6x + 2k$ is divisible by $(x - 4)$
$x = 4$ must satisfy the given equation $4^4 - 3(4)^3 + 5(4)^2 - 6(4) + 2k$
$= 0256 - 192 + 80 - 24 + 2k = 0 => 120 + 2k = 0 => 2k = -120 =>$
$k = -60$

2. Ascending order of number of pets of different types-

5, 7, 7, 8, 12, 14, 16, 18, 21

Total terms = 9(Odd)

Median = $[(n + 1)/2]^{th}$ term

=> $[(9 + 1)/2]^{th}$ term = 5th term = 12

3. Speed of the boatman upstream = 2/20 x 60 = 6 km/hr.

Speed of the boatman downstream = 2/18 x 60 = 20/3 km/hr

Rate of current = 1/2 (DownstreamSpeed–UpstreamSpeed)

= (1/2) (20/3 - 6) = 1/3 km/hr

4. Relative Speed in downstream

(x+y)= 60/4=15

x=2y

y=5Km/h

x=10Km/h

Distance Travelled in 2 hrs going Upstream

= 2×5=10km

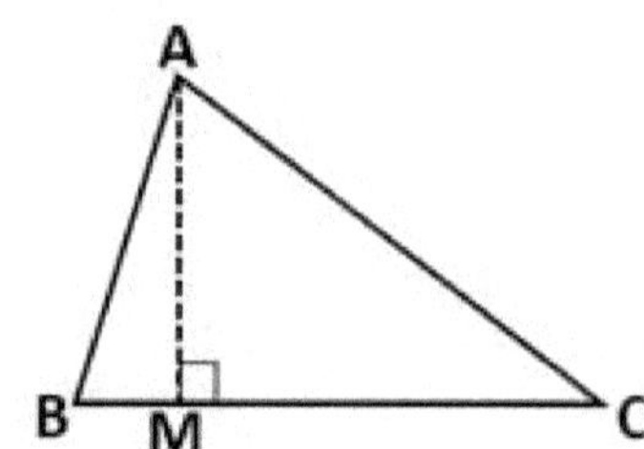

5.

AM = 5√3 cm

Let AB, BC and AC are 5x, 8x and 7x respectively.

s = (a + b + c)/2 = (5x + 8x + 7x)/2 = 10x

Area of △ABC = √[s(s - a)(s - b)(s - c)] = (1/2) * BC * AM

= √[10x(10x - 5x)(10x - 8x)(10x - 3x)] = (1/2) * 8x * (5√3)

= $10x^2$ * √3 = 4x * 5√3

= x = 2

Hence, AB, BC and AC are 10 cm, 16 cm and 14 cm respectively.

Area of △ABC = (1/2) * 16 * 5√3

= 40√3 cm²

Circum-radius = R = (abc)/4△

= (10 * 16 * 14)/(4 * 40√3)

= (14/√3) cm

6. Sum = (240 x 100) / (3 x 8) = 1000

Compound interest = $1000(1+0.08)^3$ - 1000 = 1259.712 - 1000 ≈ Rs. 260

7. (x + 1/x) = 4

(x^2 + 1) = 4x

(x^2 - 4x) = -1

(x^2 - 4x + 6)

-1 + 6 = 5

= 5

8. Let the fraction be 4a/5a

New fraction = (4a+8)/(5a-6) = 4/3

=> 12a + 24 = 20a - 24

=> 8a = 48

=> a = 6

Hence the fraction is 24/30

Difference between numerator & denominator = 30 - 24 = 6

9. 25% of 40% of [{((√16 − √9) X 5 ÷ 2.5} - 2 + √(80% of 27 ÷ 3 X 5)]

= (1/4) of (2/5) of [{(4 − 3) X 2} - 2 + √(21.6 ÷ 3 X 5)]

= (1/4) of (2/5) of [2 - 2 + √(7.2 X 5)]

= (1/4) of (2/5) of [√36]

= (1/4) X (2/5) X 6

= 3/5

10. Sum of all the given numbers = (167 + 98 + 23 + A + 67 + 217 + B + 134)/8 = 100

(A + B) = 94 .... (1)

Sum of first four numbers = (167 + 98 + 23 + A)/4 = 84

288 + A = 336

A = 48

From equation (1)-

48 + B = 94

B = 46

Required difference = 48 - 46 = 2

11.

(a) Time from 7 a.m. to quarter pas 4
= 9 hours 15 min.=555 min.

Now, $\frac{37}{12}$ min. of this watch = 3 min. of the correct watch.

555 min. of this watch = $\left(\frac{3\times12}{37}\times555\right)$ min.

= $\left(\frac{3\times12}{37}\times\frac{555}{60}\right)$ hrs. = 9 hrs. of the correct watch.
Correct time is 9 hours after 7 a.m. i.e., 4 p.m.

12. Let the four parts are 'a', 'a + d', 'a + 2d' and 'a + 3d' respectively.

According to question-

a + (a + 3d) = 12

(2a + 3d) = 12 ...... (1)

a(a + 3d) = 27 .... (2)

a + (27/a) = 12

a^2 - 12a + 27 = 0

(a - 9)(a - 3) = 0

a = 3 and 9

From equation (1) when a = 3

6 + 3d = 12

d = 2

From equation (2) when a = 9

18 + 3d = 12

d = -2 [Not possible as numbers are in increasing AP]

Required number = a * (a + d) * (a + 2d) * (a + 3d) = 3 * 5 * 7 * 9
= 945

13. Portion of the cistern filled by pipe of diameter 2cm= 1/61

Portion of the cistern filled by pipe of diameter 1cm= 1/61 X $(1/2)^2$=1/61 X 1/4

Portion of the cistern filled by pipe of diameter 1(1/3cm) = 1/61 X 1/4 X $(4/3)^2$=1/61 X 4/9

When all the three pipes are open, the portion of the cistern filled is = 1/61+1/61 X 1/4+ 1/61 X 4/9

1/61+1/61 X 1/4+ 1/61 X 4/9= 1/36

Therefore the time taken is 36 minutes.

14. (a+b)/100 x (a-b) = 2/100 x (a+b)/2........(i)

Or

a-b = 1 ....(ii)

also

a^2 = 1.44 b^2 ....(iii)

So,

a = 1.2 b ....(iv)

Using (ii) and (iv)

0.2b = 1

b= 5

a= 6

So, a+b = 11

Required percentage = (11 - 1)/1 x 100 = 1000%

15. A:B = 2/3:1/4 = 8:3

B:C = 1/5:1/3 = 3:5

C:D = 1/6:1/7 = 7:6

A:B:C = 8:3:5

C:D = 7:6

A:B:C:D = (8*7):(3*7):(5*7):(6*5) = 56:21:35:30
Therefore (A+B+D):(B+C+D) = (56+21+30):(21+35+30) = 107:86

16. Total number of students in College A = 15% of 12000 = 1800

Junior Year students in College A = (5/9)*1800 = 1000

Total number of students in College B = 20% of 12000 = 2400

Senior Year students in College B = (2/5)*2400 = 960

Required sum = 1000 + 960 = 1960

17. Let the numbers of houses in the town be 4p.

So total population = 5 X 4p = 20p

And number of adults = 3/5 of 20p = 12p

Total number of females = 7/12 of 12p = 7p

So the required ratio = 4p : 7p = 4 : 7

18. Given (x+3x+5x)/3=18

x = 6

The sum of their squares = 6^2 + 18^2 + 30^2 = 1260

Half the sum of their square = 630

Required answer = 630

19. Since the H.C.F of two numbers are 27 then we can write both numbers as 27a and 27b where a and b must be co-primes.

Then, 27a + 27b = 216

=> a + b = 8

Now, co-primes with sum 8 are (1, 7) and (3, 5).

∴ Required number are (27 X 1, 27 X 7) and (27 X 3, 27 X 5) i.e.

(27, 189) and (81, 135);

Out of these, the one given in the answer choices is the pair (27, 189).

20.

Angle traced by the hour hand in 6 hours

$$= \left(\frac{360}{12} \times 6\right)^\circ = 180°$$

21. Speed downstream = (15 + 3) kmph = 18 kmph Distance travelled = 18×12 / 60 = 3.6

22. $4x^2 - 21x + 35 = 0$

$b^2 = (-21)^2 = 441$

$4ac = 4 * 4 * 35 = 560$

Since, $b^2 < 4ac$. So, roots of this equation are imaginary.

Similarly, roots of the equation: $Ax^2 + 2x + C = 0$ will also be imaginary.

$b^2 < 4ac$

$(2)^2 < 4 * A * C$

$AC > 1$

23. Total runs scored by Rohit from Boundaries and sixes = (12 X 4) + (6 X 3) = (48 + 18) = 66 runs

Hence total runs scored from Rohit by running between wickets = (132 - 66) runs = 66 runs

Therefore required % = 66/132 X 100 = 50%

24. $3\cos A + 2\sin^2 A = 0$

$=> 3\cos A + 2(1 - \cos^2 A) = 0$

$=> 2\cos^2 A - 3\cos A - 2 = 0$

$=> 2\cos^2 A + \cos A - 4\cos A - 2 = 0$

$=> \cos A(2\cos A + 1) - 2(2\cos A + 1) = 0$

$=> (2\cos A + 1)(\cos A - 2) = 0$

$\therefore \cos A = -1/2$ or 2

$\cos A \neq 2$ [$-1 \leq \cos A \leq 1$]

$\therefore \cos^3 A = (-1/2)^3 = -1/8$

25.

The correct order is:
(C) Amount of discount given on A = 15% of 400 = Rs.60
(A) Amount of discount given on B = 2 * 60 = Rs.120
(D) Total cost price = 300 + 300 = Rs.600 and Total selling price = (400 - 60) + (500 - 120) = Rs.720
(B) Profit per cent = [(720 - 600)/600] * 100 = 20%

26. [5 X {25 ÷ (2.5 ÷ 0.5)}] ÷ 2.5 X 2 - 16 ÷ 4 + 16 ÷ 2

= [5 X {25 ÷ 5}] ÷ 2.5 X 2 - 4 + 8

= [5 X 5] ÷ 2.5 X 2 - 4 + 8

= 25 ÷ 2.5 X 2 - 4 + 8

= 10 X 2 - 4 + 8

= 20 - 4 + 8

= 24

27. Let us assume that a man does 'm' units of work in a day, and a boy does 'b' units of work in a day.

Together six men and four boys can complete a piece of work in 8 days.

Thus the total work = 8(6m + 4b)

Also the same piece of work can be completed by two men in 'd' days only and by eight boys in (d + 5) days only.

Thus 8(6m + 4b)/8b - 8(6m + 4b)/4m = (d + 5) - d

or (6m/b + 4) - (12 + 8b/m) = 5

or 6(m/b) - 8(b/m) = 13

On solving, we get the value of m/b = 8/3

Thus the efficiency of a boy is 3/8 times that of a man, and hence a boy's efficiency is 62.5% less than that of a man.

28. $\sqrt[4]{(7.2^2 * 20^2)} = \sqrt[4]{20736} = 12/1 = $ (Rational)

$\sqrt[3]{(5^2 * 135)} = \sqrt[3]{3375} = 15/1 = $ (Rational)

$(\sqrt{43.2})/5 = (\sqrt{43.2/25}) = \sqrt{1.728} = \sqrt{1.2^3} = 1.2\sqrt{1.2} = $ (Irrational)

$\sqrt{(8^2 + 3^2 + 2^3)} = \sqrt{(64 + 9 + 8)} = \sqrt{81} = 9/1 = $ (Rational)

29.

c) Let maximum marks be 100
Hence his average = 60
Let his marks be 10x, 9x, 8x, 7x, 6x respectively in 5 subjects
i.e. 10x + 9x + 8x + 7x + 6x=60% of 5 x 100
=60/100 x500=60 x 5 ......(i)
Solving we get his marks were 75, 67.5, 60, 52.5, 45 Since passing marks are 50
He passed in 4 subjects

30. Let present ages of A, B and C are a, b and c respectively.

Ages of A and B after 2 years will be in the ratio 2: 3 respectively, i.e.

(a + 2): (b + 2) = 2: 3

a = (2b - 2)/3

Ages of B and C before two years were in the ratio 7: 8 respectively, i.e.

(b - 2): (c - 2) = 7: 8

c = (8b - 2)/7

Present ages of A and C are in the ratio 5: 9 respectively, i.e.

a: c = 5: 9

9 x (2b - 2)/3 = 5 x (8b - 2)/7

b = 16 years

31. Q is the mother of T.

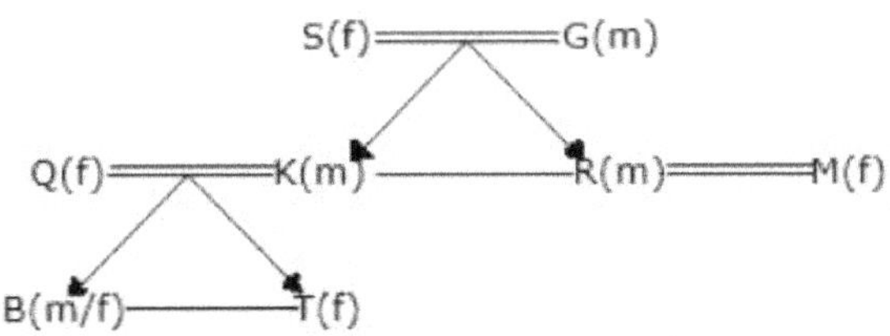

32. Let the distance be 'x' km

(Time taken to walk x km) + (Time taken to ride x km) = 37 min

(Time taken to walk 2x km) + (Time taken to ride 2x km) = 37*2 = 74 min

But, the time taken to walk 2x km = 55 min

Hence, the time taken to ride 2x km = 74 - 55 = 19 minutes

33. Amphibians inhabit a wide variety of habitats with most species living within terrestrial, arboreal or freshwater aquatic ecosystems. Thus, amphibians typically start out as larvae living in water, but some species have developed behavioural adaptations to bypass this. The young generally undergo metamorphosis from larva with gills to an adult air-breathing form with lungs.

34. I is weak because we can't vitiate the system for one individual. II is strong. As the seats will be filled by close relatives of government employees, competent and other needy youths won't get entry for govt. services.

35. $\sqrt[4]{0.0256} = 0.4$

$[16 * 10^{-2}] = 0.16$

$[8^3 \div (12^3 - 448)] = [512 \div 1280] = 0.4$

$[(0.2)^2 * 10] = 0.04 * 10 = 0.4$

36. If we take A=1, B=2, C=3, and so on, the nth letter is replaced by (25-n).

e.g. A by X, B by W, C by V, D by U, E by T and so on.

37.

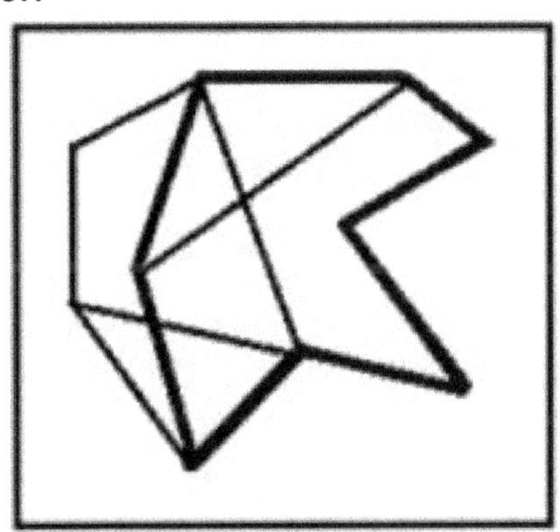

38. Option A has 2 vowels A and E.

Option B, C and D has only one vowel.

39. Group 1: (1, 4, 6) - the number of spokes of star inside the circle decrease in each step.

Group 2: (5, 3, 9) - two sides are removed in each step.

Group 3: (7, 2, 8) - one part is filled/shaded in each step.

40. The correct representation is option (c) as, all trains are vehicles and all buses are vehicles but, trains and buses are not related to each other.We get,

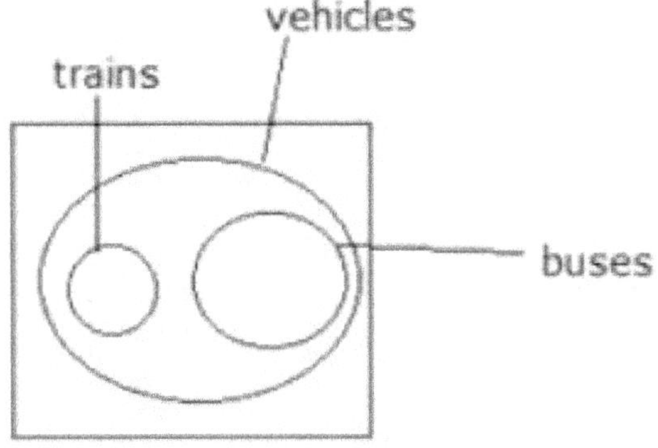

41. From I and II both, # 3 5 means 'flowers are good'.

Thus $ stands for really.

42. (100°F − 32) X 5/9 = 37.778°C (Here, F= Fahrenheit, C=Celsius)

So, 100-degree F is around 37-degree Celsius.

43. Friend: 13,14,15,16,17,18,19

Mother: 16, 17, 18......

So, we can't find exact date.

Hence, statement I is not sufficient.

44. The pattern is as follows:

$194 + 5^2 = 219$

$219 + 8^2 = 283$

$283 + 11^2 = 404$

$404 + 14^2 = 600$

$600 + 17^2 = 889$

45. Vaccines help to prevent and not diagnose diseases; therefore, statement A is incorrect while statement R is correct as vaccines will help children avoid diseases; hence, are a must. Therefore, (d) is the right answer.

46.

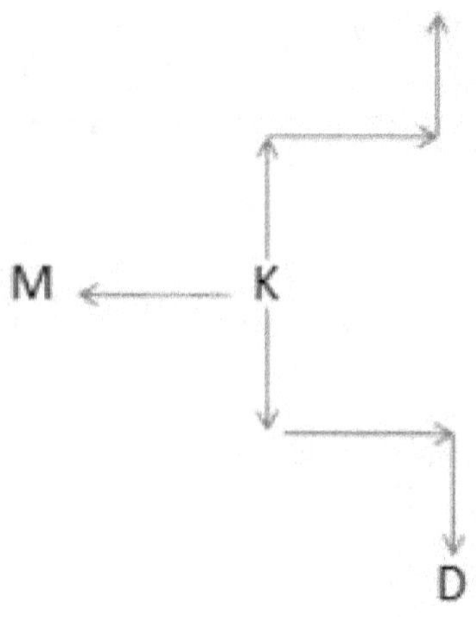

47. DNA or Deoxyribonucleic acid is a molecule composed of two chains that coil around each other to form a double helix carrying the genetic instructions used in the growth, development, functioning, and reproduction of all known living organisms and many viruses.It is found in the nucleus of the cell.

48. The series follows the pattern 2nd letter, 25th letter, 4th letter, 23rd letter, 6th letter, 21st letter..

Hence the series is: b y d w f u h s j

49. The paper when opened would look like the one given in figure d

50. Nothing in particular has been talked about online harassment as a crime and its potential punishment; therefore, none of the statements can be concluded from the main statement. Hence, (d) is the right answer.

51. Both statements I and II are strong assumptions for South Africa to be given a chance to host Summer Olympics Games; hence, (c) is the right answer.

52. P's height is less than T's as well as S's height.

i.e.

Case I:

P < S < T

Case II:

P < T < S

Now,

Q's height is less than P's height.

Case I:

Q < P < S < T

Case II:

Q < P < T < S

Now,

R's height is less than T's height.

R < T

And, U's height is less than R's height.

U < R < T

Since,

T is not the tallest, so, case I will become invalid.

From case II, there can be multiple possibilities as there is no relation given between U/R and P or, U/R and Q.

Q < P < U < R < T < S

Or

Q < U < P < R < T < S

Or

Q < U < R < P < T < S

Or

U < R < Q < P < T < S

Or

U < Q < R < P < T < S

Or

U < Q < P < R < T < S

Thus, either U or P or R or Q, is taller than only two persons, among the given ones. Hence, cannot be determined.

53.

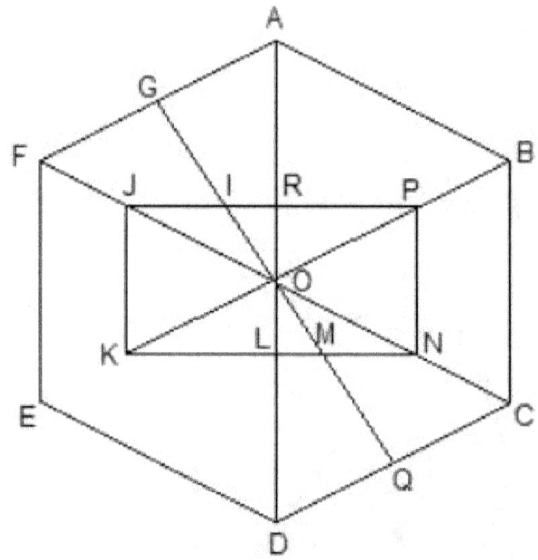

There are 25 triangles in the given figure.

Triangles are - AOB, ROP, BOC, PON, COD, COQ, QOD, NOM, NOL, LOM, LOK, KOJ, IOJ, GOF, AOG, AOF, ROI, ROJ, NOK, JOP, PJN, KJN, PJK, PKN ,KOM.

54.

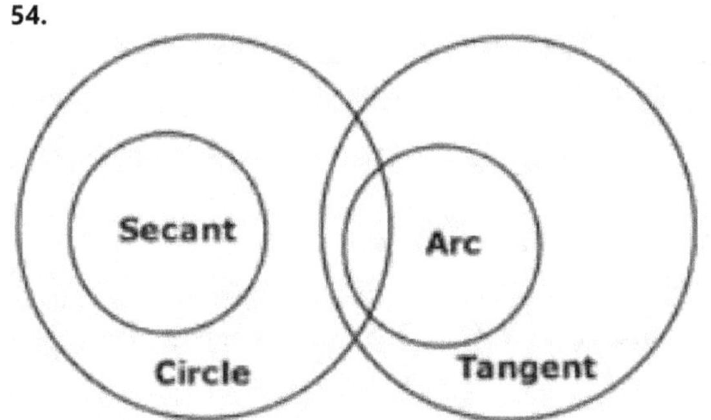

Some secants cannot be arcs as in that case, they will be tangents which contradicts the given statement.

55. When we look at the question we can interpret it as follows

$102 => 102/2 = 51 => 51*51 = 2601$

Similarly, $2401^{1/2} = 49 => 49*2 = 98$

56. The 2023 Cricket World Cup will be the 13th edition of the Cricket World Cup, scheduled to be hosted by India, from 9 February to 26 March 2023.

This will be the first time the competition is held completely in India.

58.

62. The current Lok Sabha is 16th since formation of Indian Republic.

The General elections of 2019 will elect members for the formation of **17th** Lok Sabha.

63. The Indian Space Research Organisation is the space agency of the Government of India headquartered in the city of **Bengaluru**.

It was founded in 1969 by Dr Vikram Sarabhai

Its current Chairman is K Sivan.

64. Hampi monuments are a subset of the wider-spread Vijayanagar ruins situated in the Indian state of Karnataka.

It is designated as a UNESCO world heritage site.

65. Under the Authority of Ministry of Railways, Railway Police Force (RPF), has the power to arrest, investigate and prosecute criminals.

Its duty is towards protecting railway passengers, passenger area and railway property of the Indian Railway.

66. With the use of SFOORTI application, movement of freight trains on Geographic Information System (GIS) view can be tracked. Both passenger and freight trains can be tracked over Zones/Divisions.

Freight Business will get a boost due to the application monitoring.

67. The Ranji Trophy is a domestic first-class cricket championship played in India between teams representing regional and state cricket associations.

The competition currently consists of 37 teams, with all 29 states in India and two of the seven union territories having at least one representation.

68. 2+2 Ministerial Dialogue is a Bilateral Annual conference between **USA and India.**

It was conceptualised in 2017 following the Official visit of PM Modi to the United States.

The dialogue pans wide range of Strategic issues including Defence, Economy, Trade etc.

69. Asia's first railway train chugged out from Bori Bunder, **Bombay and reached faraway Tannah** (today's Thane) on April 16, 1853.

Headquartered in New Delhi, today The Indian Railway manages the fourth-largest railway network in the world by size with 121,407 kilometres of total track over a 67,368-kilometre route.

70. Releasing the first advance estimates of National Income for 2018-19, the CSO said, "The growth in GDP during 2018-19 is estimated at **7.2%** as compared to the growth rate of 6.7% in 2017-18."

72. Oscillatory motion can be termed as the repeated motion in which an object repeats the same movement over and over.

In the absence of friction, the oscillatory motion would continue forever; but in the real world, the system eventually settles into equilibrium.

So, 'swinging of a pendulum' is an **Oscillatory type** of motion

Other examples are Playground swing or humming of a string in any musical instrument.

73. In an Ecosystem, Abiotic components are non-living chemical and physical parts of the environment that affect living organisms and the functioning of ecosystems.

Algae and Mosses exhibit the characteristics of Biotic components in the Ecosystem

74. Constant speed means that the distance traversed in a time is constant throughout the motion.

This means the plot for motion at any given point of time is constant and at equal distance from each of the axis. This gives the resultant plot as **'A straight line making 45-degree angle with either axis'**

75. The Human brain consists of -

Fore Brain- Cerebrum, Thalamus and Hypothalamus

Mid Brain Corpora Quadrigemina

Hind Brain- Cerebellum, Pons, Medulla

76. Mercury is the only metallic element which is liquid at room temperature.

Phosphorus, Cobalt and Molybdenum all exist is solid state at room temperature.

77. The materials which get attracted to magnets like iron, nickel and cobalt etc. are called "Magnetic materials".

The materials which are not attracted towards a magnet are non-magnetic like rubber, plastic, cotton etc.

78. Transparent objects allow light to pass through them to make us see the object on the other side clearly

Translucent objects allow light to pass through them but partially it make us see the object on the other side unclearly

Opaque objects do not allow light to pass through them at all.

Luminous is a property of an object emitting light.

79. If light is propagating from denser towards rarer medium and angle of incidence is more than the critical angle, then the light incident on the boundary is reflected in the denser medium obeying the laws of reflection.

All the above given options are an example of the phenomenon of Total Internal Reflection.

80. India has a Drone policy 1.0 which allows RPAs to be used commercially and it came into effect on December 1, 2018. It defines drones as a technology platform, classifies RPAs, fly zones, and the required approvals are needed to operate them commercially and otherwise.

As per the regulation, RPAs have been categories as Nano, Micro, Small, Medium and Large based on weight.

81. A rainbow is a meteorological phenomenon that is caused by reflection, refraction and **dispersion of light in water droplets resulting in a spectrum of light** appearing in the sky.

It takes the form of a multicoloured circular arc. Rainbows caused by sunlight always appear in the section of sky directly opposite the sun.

his rainbow is caused by light being refracted when entering a droplet of water, then reflected inside on the back of the droplet and refracted again when leaving it.

82. Rubbing the balloon with a piece of fabric gives it a negative charge, also known as static electricity.

Enough static electricity will force the balloon to stick to neutrally charged surfaces, such as walls, by attracting the positive charge to the surface.

This is a typical example of an Electrostatic energy force.

83. Liver is the largest gland in the human body.

It is also the largest (internal) organ in our body and can even weigh up to 1.5-1.6 kg for a human adult. That is, almost about 1/50th of the body weight is because of liver.

84. Dynamics is the branch of classical mechanics concerned with the study of forces and their effects on motion.

"Static" means stationary or at rest.

Thermodynamics is the branch of physics that deals with heat and temperature and their relation to energy and work in a system.

Metallurgy is a domain of materials science and engineering that studies the physical and chemical behaviour of metallic elements.

85. S.I. unit for acceleration is Meter/second^2.

S.I. unit for Speed is meter/second.

86. Benzene is an important organic chemical compound with the chemical formula C_6-H_6.

The benzene molecule is composed of six carbon atoms joined in a ring with one hydrogen atom attached to each.

As it contains only carbon and hydrogen atoms, benzene is classed as a hydrocarbon.

87. Speedometer in a vehicle measures the speed at which the vehicle is moving, usually shown in km/hr.

Along with speedometer, you also find Odometer, indicating the distance traversed by the vehicle, usually shown in Km(s).

88. Momentum of a mass (M), moving with velocity (V), is calculated as

Momentum(p)= M x V

According to the question, p= 45 x 30

P= 1350 kg m/s

89. Humidity in Air is an example of Gaseous Solution like also iodine vapours in air or any other mixture of gases where solvent is Gas.

Rest all are examples of Liquid solutions where the solvent is Water (a liquid).

90. In classic NaCl salt formation reaction, Na gets oxidised by losing an electron whereas Cl gets reduced by gaining the electrons lost by Na.

Thus, this is a case of Ionic bond formation.

91. The Circulatory system in the Human body has four parts- Heart, Arteries, Veins, Blood.

Mammals have double circulation, that is, blood crosses two times from the heart before circulating throughout the body.

92. Isaac Newton (1642-1727) was a well-known scientist had conducted research on the sun, light, and colour.

Through his experiments with prisms, he was the first to authoritatively demonstrate that white light is composed of the colours of the spectrum.

Seven colours constitute white light: red, orange, yellow, green, blue, indigo, and violet.

93. In 1897, Sir Joseph John Thomson who was an English physicist and Nobel Laureate,

was credited with the discovery and identification of the electron; and with the discovery of the first subatomic particle.

94. Charge of a g-ion = No. of electron x charge of a single electron x mole number

1 Mole = 6.02×10^{23}; Charge of an Electron in Coulomb = 1.6×10^{-19}

According to the question, Charge on one g-ion of $O_2^- = 2 \times 1.6 \times 10^{-19} \times 6.02 \times 10^{23}$

$= 1.92 \times 10^5$ Coulomb

95. Charles Robert Darwin was an English naturalist, geologist and biologist, best known for his contributions to the science of evolution. In his works, "Origin Of Species", he proposed that all species of life have descended over time from common ancestors which is now widely accepted, and considered a foundational concept in science.

96. In **Ionic bond**, there is complete transfer of one or more electrons from one atom to another. Example, formation of NaCl.

In Covalent bond, there is no actual transfer but mutual sharing/contribution of electrons.

97. pH values of >7 indicate basic nature whereas pH values of <7 indicate acidic nature.

pH values of the given options are

Vinegar- 3.0

Coffee- 5.0

Lemon Juice- 2.5

Milk of Magnesia- 10.5

98. Pavo cristatus is the scientific name of peacock.

Lotus- Nelumbo nucifera

Rice- Orzya Sativa

Tiger- Panthera tigris

99. A fog is an aerosol of **liquid particles,** in particular a low cloud.

Aerosols are dispersions in gases. In aerosols the particles often exceed the usual size limits for colloids. If the dispersed particles are solid, it is called aerosols of solid particles, if they are liquid, they are called aerosols of liquid particles.

100. One-watt hour is equivalent to **3600 Joule**. The watt-hour (Wh) is a unit of energy equivalent to one watt (1 W) of power expended for one hour (1 h) of time. It is commonly used in electrical applications.

1 Kilowatt hour=3.6×10^6

Mock Test   15

Mathematics

Q.1 The ratio of number of Matches played by Rohit and Kohli is 6:5. Kohli scored an average of 52 runs per match and Rohit's average is 25% less than that. If the total runs scored by Kohli is 546 more than Rohit, what is the number of matches Kohli has played?

A. 95   **B.** 100   **C.** 105   **D.** 110

Q.2 What is the value of

$$\sqrt{1233 + \sqrt{3969} + \sqrt{1225}} \, ?$$

A. 71   **B.** 97   **C.** 93   **D.** 90

Q.3 For what value of 'k', quadratic equation $4x^2 - 3m\sqrt{2}x + k = 0$ (where, m>0) has equal roots? (Given: $2m^2 + 7m - 60 = 0$)

A. 15   **B.** 17   **C.** 16   **D.** 18

Q.4 Study the following table carefully and answer the related question.

Following table represents the marks of top four students of class in four subjects.

Students	Hindi (100)	English (100)	Chemistry (150)	Physics (150)
Rakhi	78	60	96	124
Jay	56	80	88	92
Amit	95	90	80	75
Urvi	70	70	120	105

Who got approximately 71.5% percentage in the class?

A. jay   **B.** rakhi   **C.** urvi   **D.** amit

Q.5 A sum of money at simple interest amounts to Rs 2240 in 2 years and to Rs 2600 in 5 years. What is the principal amount?

A. Rs 1520   **B.** Rs 1880

C. Rs 2120   **D.** none of these

Q.6 Number of kids in 10 families is given below. Find the median of number of kids.

3, 4, 2, 1, 0, 2, 4, 0, 1 and 2

A. 1,5   **B.** 2   **C.** 2,5   **D.** 3

Q.7 There are four persons A, B,C and D, and ratio of present age of A to C is 4: 3, C is 7 years younger to E who is 16 years old at present. Present age of B is 75% of present age of D and B is 6 years elder to A, what is the average of present age of persons B, C and D?

Given below are the steps involved. Arrange them in the sequential order.

Let the age of A = 4A

(A) Age of A and C is 12 years and 9 years respectively.

(B) Present age of E = (3A + 7) = 16 => A = 3

(C) Required average = (18 + 9 + 24)/3 = 17 years

(D) Present age of B = 12 + 6 = 18 years and present age of D = 18 * (100/75) = 24 years

(E) Present age of C = 4A * (3/4) = 3A

A. EABDC   **B.** EDBAC

C. EBADC   **D.** EBAACD

Q.8 The average age of a man and his son is 54 years. The ratio of their ages is 23:13. What will be the ratio of their ages after 6 years?

A. 10.7   **B.** 5.3   **C.** 4.3   **D.** 3.2

Q.9 Out of 5 numbers, whose average is 36, the first one is one fifth of the sum of the last four. The first number is?

A. 42   **B.** 38   **C.** 32   **D.** 30

Q.10 What value we get when: $\sqrt{(9^2 - 4^3 + 3)}$ is multiplied by $\sqrt{(2^5 * 10^{-1})}$?

A. 4^2 **B.** 2^3 **C.** 3^3 **D.** 5^2

Q.11 Following graph shows number of questions attempted and number of correct questions in preliminary and mains exams by 5 persons.

{[376.PNG}}

What is the ratio of total number of non-correct questions out of total number of questions attempted by all 5 persons in preliminary exam to the total number of non-correct questions out of total number of questions attempted by all 5 persons in mains exam?

A. 33:125   **B.** 35:126   **C.** 31:123   **D.** 31:129

Q.12 If n is the greatest number that will divide the three numbers 1236, 3708 and 4944 leaving the same remainder in each case. What is the product of digits of 'n'?

A. 36   **B.** 45   **C.** 16   **D.** 24

Q.13 LCM of three numbers is 840 and their ratio is 2: 3: 5 respectively. What will be the HCF of these numbers?

A. 24   **B.** 28   **C.** 30   **D.** 32

Q.14 A discount of 30% on one article is the same as a discount of 35% on another article. The marked prices of two articles can be (in ₹.)

A. 1548 and 1754   **B.** 2093 and 2154

C. 1734 and 2023   **D.** 1526 and 1650

Q.15 A boat takes 4 more hours to travel 180 km upstream than to travel the same distance downstream. If the still water speed of the boat is 28 km/hr, what is the stream speed?

A. 6 km/hr   **B.** 8 km/hr   **C.** 10 km/hr   **D.** 12 km/hr

Q.16 The ratio of heights of Asif and Bharat is 3:4 and the ratio of heights of Bharat and Chatur is 6:7. If the average of their heights is 175 cm, what is the height of Asif?

A. 125 cm   **B.** 130 cm   **C.** 135 cm   **D.** 140 cm

Q.17 A alone can do a piece of work in 20 days, B alone in 40 days and C alone in 60 days. Everyone begin to do the work together, but A leaves after 4 days and B leaves 6 days before the completion of the work. How many days did the work last?

A. 22 days **B.** 21 2/5 days
C. 22 4/5 days **D.** 25 days

Q.18 A faulty watch gains 5 minutes every 40 minutes. After how many days will it show the correct time again?

A. 8 days **B.** 10 days **C.** 5 days **D.** 6 days

Q.19 If x/y + y/x + 1 = 0, what is the value of $(x - y)^6/9x^3y^3$?

A. -3 **B.** -2 **C.** 2 **D.** 3

Q.20 A TV costs Rs.20000 and the shopkeeper announces that the price of the TV will reduce at 10% per annum. What will be the cost price of the item after 2 years?

A. Rs 12050 **B.** Rs 13150
C. Rs 16200 **D.** Rs 14200

Q.21 In the following diagram ABCD is a square inscribed in a circle of centre O. If perimeter of the square ABCD is 40 cm, then what is the area of the blue portion?(take π = 3.14)

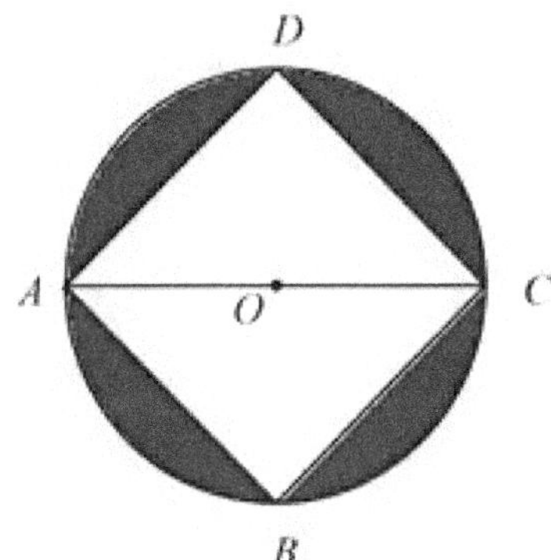

A. 50 cm² **B.** 57 cm²
C. 60 cm² **D.** none of these

Q.22 Ramesh salary got 2 salary hikes, one of 10%, the next one of 25%. If the total increase in Ramesh salary was 24000, what is the increase in his salary from the first hike to the second Hike?

A. Rs 16700 **B.** Rs 17600
C. Rs 14800 **D.** Rs 18400

Q.23 Which of the following is irrational?
A. Product of 3rd root of 2197 and √6889
B. Product of 4th root of 4096 and √1377
C. Product of 3rd root of 3375 and √5929
D. Product of 4th root of 2401 and √1444

Q.24 A car wiper can clean 693 sq. inch area in its one sweep. If its length is decreased by 3.5 inch, then how much area will it clean in one sweep? (Car wiper covers a semi-circle in one sweep)

A. 481.25 sq. inch **B.** 461.5 sq. inch
C. 475.75 sq. inch **D.** none of these

Q.25 A bus reached Nagpur to Amravati in 2:30 hr with the average speed of 70 km/hr. If the average speed increased by 30 km/hr. How much time it will take to cover the same distance.

A. 105 min **B.** 115 min **C.** 95 min **D.** 180 min

Q.26 Two poles of equal heights are on either side of a 100 m wide road. From a point on the road, the angles of elevation of their tops are 30° and 60°. Find the height of each pole.

A. 25√3 m **B.** 20√3 m **C.** 25 m **D.** 20 m

Q.27 The sales for the month of January was 500 units. Sales increased by 50 units every month for the next 11 months. Find the average monthly sales for the year?

A. 775 **B.** 750 **C.** 800 **D.** 825

Q.28 Select the odd one from the following options.

a = 2.5 x 2.4 - 8 x 0.5
b = 12 x 4 x 0.5 - 16
c = 21 - 30 x 0.5

A. 2c **B.** 3a+c **C.** 2a+b **D.** 2b-a

Q.29 A grocer bought two types of rice A and B at Rs.20 per kg and Rs.25 per kg. If no profit and no loss occurs on selling both the items together at Rs.24 per kg, then find the ratio of quantity of rice A and B.

A. 1:2 **B.** 2:5 **C.** 3:7 **D.** 1:4

Q.30 In an election contested by two candidates, a candidate who got 54% of total votes won by a margin of 288 votes. Total votes is..

A. 3000 **B.** 3600 **C.** 4000 **D.** 4800

General Intelligence & Reasoning

Q.31 The series is given, with one term missing. Choose amongst the given responses and complete the series.
ABZ, CDY, EFX, GHW, __.
A. IJU **B.** IJV **C.** JKV **D.** JKU

Q.32 Each of the questions below consists of a question and two statements numbered I and II given below it. You have to decide whether the data provided in which of the statements are sufficient to answer the question. Choose your answer from the options based on this.

What can be the code for '12'?
I. If 'For your sake' is written as '13 12 21'.
II. If 'Don't leave for tomorrow' is written as '31 13 14 11'.

A. If the data in statement I alone are sufficient to answer the question, while the data in statement II alone are not sufficient to answer the question.
B. If the data in statement II alone are sufficient to answer the question, while the data in statement I alone are not sufficient to answer the question
C. If the data in both the statements I and II together are not sufficient to answer the question.
D. If the data in both the statements I and II together are necessary to answer the question.

Q.33 If ANIMAL is coded as 321435 and ELEPHANT is coded as 65609328, then METAL is coded as

A. 83564 **B.** 46453 **C.** 35648 **D.** 46835

Q.34 T is to the north-east of D and east of S. How is D related to H, if H is to the east of T?

A. South **B.** South-west
C. West **D.** Can't be determined

Q.35 In the following question, which one set of letters when sequentially placed at the gaps in the given letter series shall complete it?

a _ b d _ b _ c a b _ _ a b b _

A. babbdc **B.** bbacdc **C.** ababac **D.** bacbdc

Q.36 Which of the following will be the mirror image of the given question figure (x), if the mirror is placed along the line MN. Choose the correct mirror image among (I), (II), (III) and (IV) given.

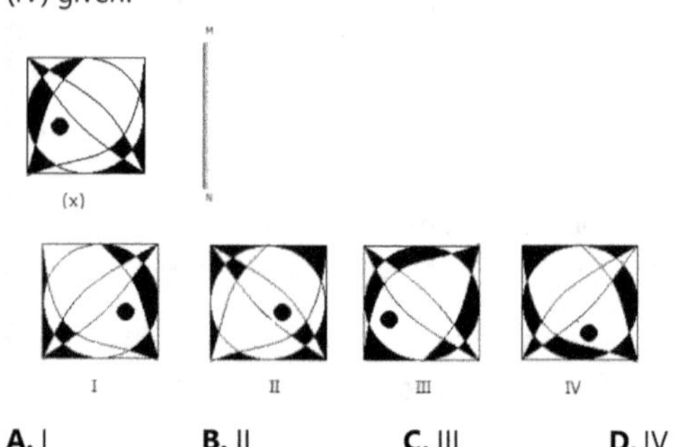

A. I **B.** II **C.** III **D.** IV

Q.37 Arrange the given words in a meaningful sequence.
1. Kilogram
2. Gram
3. Ton
4. Quintal

A. 4,3,1,2 **B.** 3,4,1,2 **C.** 3,4,2,1 **D.** 4,3,2,1

Q.38 Pointing to a photograph, Prakash said "Her father's only son is the father of my brother". How is that person in the photograph related to Prakash's father?

A. Aunt **B.** Daughter
C. Sister **D.** Sister-in-law

Q.39 In a certain code language, " play your good game" is coded as " ad pd cd md" , "play game run fast" is coded as " zd cd md td" , "run speed end game" is coded as " fd zd ld md". Find out what will be the code for " your good"?

A. pd cd **B.** pd md **C.** cd ad **D.** ad pd

Q.40 Each question below is followed by two arguments numbered I and II. You have to decide which of the argument is a 'strong' argument and which is a 'weak' argument. 'Strong' arguments are those which are both important and directly related to the question. 'Weak' arguments are those which are of minor importance and also may not be directly related to the question.

Statement: Should young entrepreneurs be encouraged?
Arguments: I. Yes. They will help in industrial development of the country.

II. Yes. They will reduce the burden on employment market.

A. If only argument I is strong.
B. If either argument I or II is strong.

C. If neither argument I nor II is strong
D. If both arguments I and II are strong.

Q.41 In each of the questions below are given some statements followed by some conclusions. You have to take the given statements to be true even if they seem to be at variance from commonly known facts. Read all the conclusions and then decide which of the given conclusions logically follows from the given statements disregarding commonly known facts.

Statements:

All knots are ships.

No ship is a lip.

All lips are hips.

Conclusions:

I. Some hips are lips

II. No lip is knot.

A. If only Conclusion II follows.
B. If either Conclusion I or II follows.
C. If neither Conclusion I nor II follows.
D. If both Conclusions I and II follow.

Q.42 In the following question, select the number which can be placed at the sign of question mark (?) from the given alternatives.

	3				1				3	
7	8	8		5	13	9		6	?	7
	2				4				5	

A. 19 **B.** 12 **C.** 11 **D.** 17

Q.43 In each of the questions below, one statement is given, followed by two conclusions which may or may not follow. From the options below, choose the one that reflects the correct choice of conclusion(s) that follows/follow.

National curriculums don't always work for rural and regional schools.

I. Curriculums should be tailor-made for rural and regional schools as per their requirements and specifications.

II. While formulating national curriculums, authorities don't always take diversity of rural and regional schools into consideration.

A. Only I **B.** Only II
C. Both I and II **D.** Neither I nor II

Q.44 Each of the questions below consists of a question and two statements given below it. You have to decide whether the data provided in the statements are sufficient to answer the question.

Among M, P, K, J, T and W, who is lighter than only the heaviest?

I. P is heavier than M and T.

II. W is heavier than P but lighter than J who is not the heaviest.

A. if the data in statement I alone are sufficient to answer the question, while the data in statement II alone are not sufficient to answer the question.

B. if the data in statement II alone are sufficient to answer the question, while the data in statement I alone are not sufficient to answer the question.

C. if the data given in both the statements I and II together are not sufficient to answer the question, and

D. if the data in both the statements I and II together are necessary to answer the question.

Q.45 If S=19 and SON=24 then SIT=?

A. 24   **B.** 22   **C.** 20   **D.** 28

Q.46 Select the suitable figure from the Answer figures that would replace the question mark (?).

Problem Figure

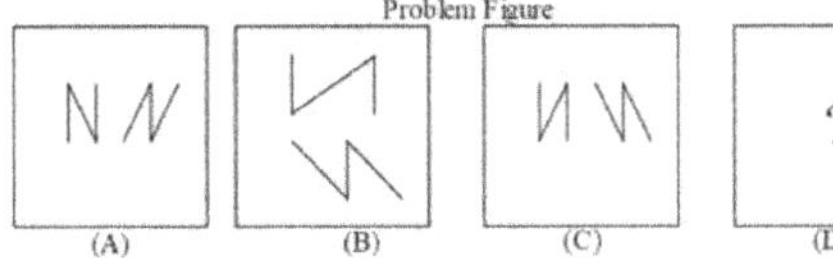

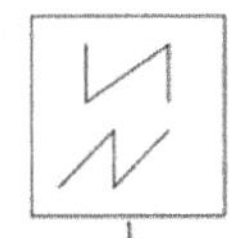   

Answer Figures

A. 1   **B.** 2   **C.** 3   **D.** 4

Q.47 Find out the odd term in the given series.

21,24, 81, 36, 6, 4

A. 81   **B.** 24   **C.** 4   **D.** 6

Q.48 In the following question select the related word from the given alternatives.

Tuberculosis:Lungs :: Jaundice: ?

A. eyes   **B.** liver   **C.** nails   **D.** nerves

Q.49 Z is older than only two persons. T is younger to both W and V. Y is younger to neither Z nor T, who is older than both S and Z. U is younger to at least three persons, none of whom is S. Who among the given persons is older than as many persons as is younger to?

A. U   **B.** W

C. T   **D.** none of these

Q.50 In the following question, select the related numbers from the given alternatives.

7834 : 499 :: 5271 : ?

A. 50   **B.** 2514   **C.** 490   **D.** 49

Q.51 In each of the questions given below, there are two statements followed by an inference. Mark the correct option accordingly.

(a) Collection of frequent flyer miles is not useful at all.

(b) All the airlines have their respective frequent flyer programmes.

Inference: It's okay not to enrol under frequent flyer programmes of any airline.

A. The inference is definitely true

B. The inference is definitely false

C. The inference is probably false or true

D. The inference cannot be drawn

Q.52 Identify the diagram that best represents the relationship among the given classes.

Children, naughty, energetic

(1)

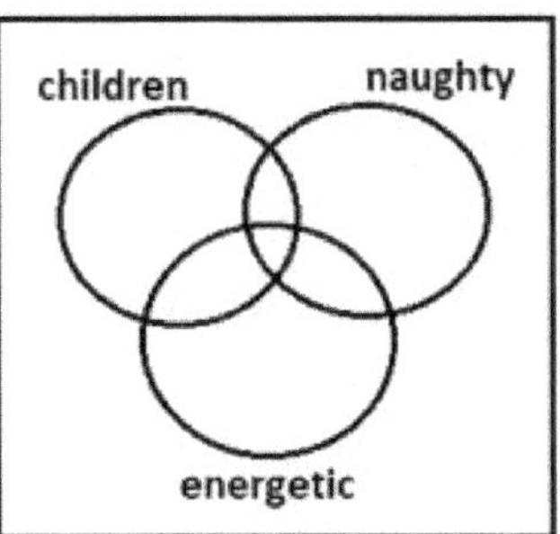

(2)

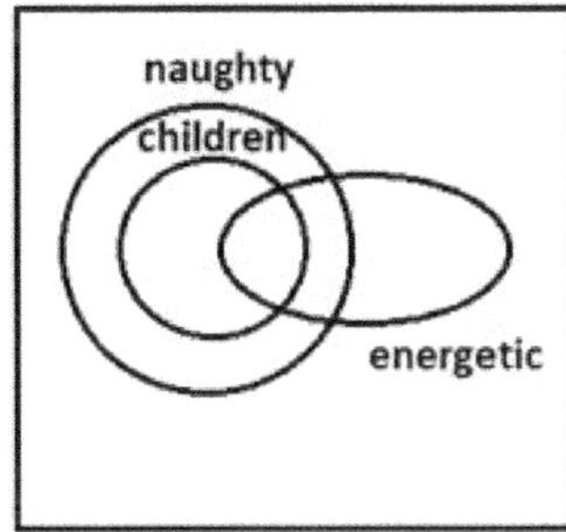

(3)

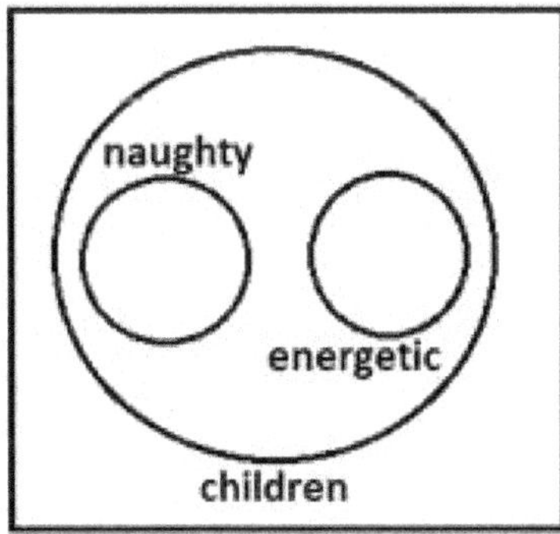

(4)

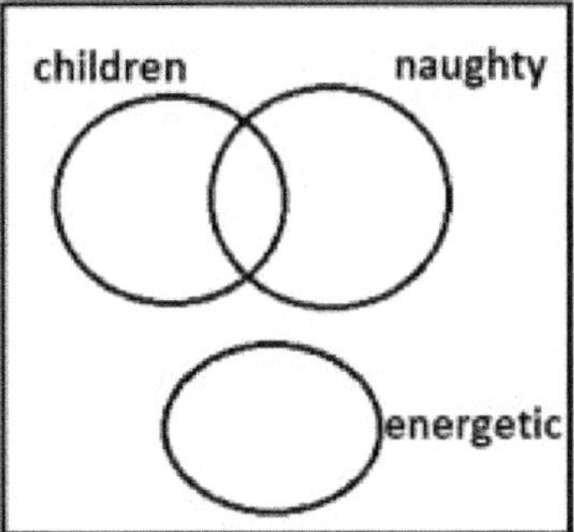

A. 1   **B.** 2   **C.** 3   **D.** 4

Q.53 A series is given, with one term missing. Choose the correct alternative from the given ones that will complete the series.

EHF, ILJ, MPN, ?

A. QTS   **B.** PSR   **C.** QTR   **D.** RVU

Q.54 Which one set letters when sequentially placed at the gaps in the given letter series shall complete it?

MNO_MMN_OO_MM_NNN_OOO

A. OONOO   **B.** MMOON
C. ONOMO   **D.** NMMOO

Q.55 BANKER is coded as SFLOBC, how CLERK will be coded?

A. EJKFG   **B.** EFLKG   **C.** DMFSL   **D.** LSFMD

General Awareness

Q.56 Who was recently elected as the Deputy Chairman of the Rajya Sabha in the Parliament?

A. Jai Dev Singhal
B. Venkaiah Naidu
C. Sitaram Yechury
D. Harivansh Narayan SIngh

Q.57 Recently, Ministry of External Affairs organised 11th World Hindi Conference at which of the following Indian ocean states?

A. Sri Lanka   **B.** Mauritius
C. Maldives   **D.** Bangladesh

Q.58 Right to Information, an important legislative act to promote transparency & strengthen the democracy of India came into being on which year?

A. 2001   **B.** 2005   **C.** 2010   **D.** 2015

Q.59 Which Indian state excelled to be the top performer in the recently released 'Ease of Living Index 2018' by Ministry of Housing & Urban Affairs?

A. Karnataka   **B.** Tamil Nadu
C. Kerala   **D.** Andhra Pradesh

Q.60 Which of the following government entity started 'Seva Bhoj Yojna' - a scheme to reimburse central share of CGST and IGST on food, prasad, langar etc. offered by religious and charitable institutions?

A. Ministry of Finance
B. Ministry of Culture
C. Ministry of Housing & Urban Affairs
D. Ministry of Commerce

Q.61 Google recently, unveiled __________ which will quickly render any PDF with Indian language content into editable text using Artificial Intelligence.

A. Project Samskriti   **B.** Project Navlekha
C. Project Aryabhata   **D.** Project Vaad-Vivad

Q.62 Which of the following Indian states launched a scheme, 'Kanyashree', to incentivize adolescent girl child education to combat issue of child marriages?

A. Uttar Pradesh   **B.** Chhattisgarh
C. Maharashtra   **D.** West Bengal

Q.63 Which of the following government institution launched "Pitch to MOVE", a business opportunity platform for budding entrepreneurs?

A. Department of Science & Technology
B. Prime Minister's Office
C. NITI Aayog
D. Ministry of MSME

Q.64 Ghoomar is a popular traditional folk dance from which region in India?

A. Rajasthan   **B.** Punjab
C. Uttar Pradesh   **D.** Odisha

Q.65 Which of the following International Organisations are headquartered in Washington D.C., USA?

A. International Atomic Energy Agency
B. International Monetary Fund
C. World Bank
D. Both 2 & 3

Q.66 Match the following trophies with their respective sports

Aga Khan Cup	Hockey
Durand Trophy	Football
Sharjah Cup	Cricket
Yonex Cup	Badminton

A. A-d, B-a, C-c, D-b   **B.** A-d, B-c, C-a, D-b
C. A-a, B-c, C-d, D-b   **D.** A-b, B-c, C-a, D-d

Q.67 Dhauladhar National Park is situated in which of the following Indian state?

A. Rajasthan   **B.** Odisha
C. Himachal Pradesh   **D.** Haryana

Q.68 Daman & Diu is Union territory of India comprising 2 different areas separated by which of the following?

A. Arabian Sea   **B.** Indian Ocean
C. Bay of Bengal   **D.** Narmada River

Q.69 Recently, BOMBAY NATURAL HISTORY SOCIETY opened its regional centre at which of the following important Wetland in India?

A. Sambhar Lake   **B.** Pulicat Lake
C. Chilika Lake   **D.** Kanji Lake

Q.70 With which of the following Financial Institution would you associate 'Prompt Corrective Action'?

A. International Monetary Fund
B. Reserve Bank of India
C. Export Import Bank of India
D. Bombay Stock Exchange

General Science

Q.71 In case of spherical mirrors, focal length is ______ of its radius of curvature image.

A. Twice   **B.** Half   **C.** Same as   **D.** Thrice

Q.72 Lemon contains Citric acid in the same way Vinegar contain __________.

A. Abscisic Acid   **B.** Lactic Acid
C. Acetic Acid   **D.** Carbonic Acid

Q.73 When a pendulum is at either side of the peak in its oscillation, its potential energy is ______ while kinetic energy is ______.

A. maximum, minimum
B. minimum, minimum
C. maximum, maximum
D. minimum, maximum

Q.74 ______________ are a species of plant which are adapted to life in a dry or physiologically dry habitat.

A. Xerophytes   **B.** Phylum
C. Exotic   **D.** Harsh plants

Q.75 Which of the following are examples of polymers?

A. Nylon   **B.** Polyvinyl Chloride
C. Teflon   **D.** All of the above

Q.76 Which of the following are examples of Natural Gas Liquids?

A. Propane   **B.** Butane
C. Bromine   **D.** Both a & b

Q.77 Glucose, essential to a living being, has a molecular formula of __________.

A. $C_3H_6O_6$ **B.** $C_6H_{12}O_6$
C. $C_6H_6O_6$ **D.** $C_3H_2O_3$

Q.78 Nephron is the functional unit of the________ in the human body.

A. Lungs   **B.** Kidney
C. Liver   **D.** Large Intestine

Q.79 Marie Curie was awarded Nobel Prize in Chemistry in 1911 for her discovery of _________ and Polonium.

A. Strontium   **B.** Sodium
C. Helium   **D.** Radium

Q.80 Kirchhoff's 1st law states that current flowing into a node (or a junction) must be __________to current flowing out of it.

A. greater than   **B.** less than
C. equal   **D.** null

Q.81 Atomic Number of Carbon is ______whereas its Mass number is _____.

A. 6,12   **B.** 6,8   **C.** 7,15   **D.** 4,8

Q.82 New blood cells in human body is produced in _________.

A. Bone Marrow   **B.** Heart
C. Spinal cord   **D.** Lungs

Q.83 A sitar changes _________ energy to ______ energy whereas a microphone changes __________ energy to ___________ energy.

A. mechanical, sound, sound, electrical
B. sound, mechanical, electrical, sound
C. sound, electrical, mechanical, electrical
D. electrical, sound, sound, mechanical

Q.84 Which of the following are true regarding Geosynchronous satellite?

A. Geosynchronous orbit synchronizes with the rotation of the Earth
B. Geosynchronous satellites are particularly useful for telecommunications
C. An observer on ground, would see the satellite as if it's in a fixed position without movement.
D. All of the above

Q.85 Which of the following statements are true regarding the element, SODIUM?

A. Atomic Number = 11
B. Low melting point
C. Used in manufacturing glass
D. All of the above

Q.86 Sun, stars, electric bulbs are examples of _______ bodies whereas moons, trees, rocks are examples of _________ bodies.

A. Transparent, Luminous
B. Opaque, Transparent
C. Luminous, Non-Luminous
D. Transparent, Opaque

Q.87 How much electrical charge passes through an electrical appliance with a resistance of 50 ohm and a power consumption of 1800 watts.

A. 8 Ampere   **B.** 7 Ampere
C. 6 Ampere   **D.** 4 Ampere

Q.88 An __________ process is one in which no heat is gained or lost by the system.

A. Isothermal   **B.** Isobaric
C. Adiabatic   **D.** Isochoric

Q.89 A body with an initial velocity of 10 m/s gets displaced 9 m while moving with an acceleration of 2 m/sec². What is the final velocity?

A. 16 m/s²   **B.** 18 m/s²   **C.** 8 m/s²   **D.** 6 m/s²

Q.90 _________ are fibrous indigestible substance that are essential in human diet for aiding digestion

A. Proteins   **B.** Carbohydrates
C. Roughages   **D.** Weed

Q.91 S.I. unit for acceleration is ______.

A. m/s   **B.** m/s²   **C.** m²/s³   **D.** m³/s

Q.92 Chemical elements which belong to the group 18 of periodic table are called_________.

A. Fluorides   **B.** Noble gases
C. Metals   **D.** None of the above

Q.93 Statement: Refrigerators work on the principle of reverse heat engine.
A. Always true
B. Always false
C. True only if efficiency is 100%
D. False only if efficiency is 100%

Q.94 Which of the following is the semi fluid substance upon with organelles of the animal cell are found?
A. Cytoplasm
B. Keratoplasm
C. Mitochondria
D. Cell wall

Q.95 Alexander Fleming was a Scottish physician & pharmacologist who is best known for his discovery of _________.
A. Polio Vaccine
B. AIDS virus
C. Penicillin
D. Homeopathy medicine

Q.96 Bronchitis is an ailment related to which of the following internal organ of the Human body?
A. Liver
B. Lungs
C. Oesophagus
D. Stomach

Q.97 Which of the following process take place in a blast furnace in a metallic extraction industry?
A. Soldering
B. Forging
C. Smelting
D. Rolling

Q.98 _________ is the act or process of making soap.
A. Listerization
B. Saponification
C. Saturation
D. Vulcanisation

Q.99 Which of the following is a 2-terminal diode which stores electrical energy and used in everyday appliances?
A. Semiconductor
B. Capacitor
C. Voltmeter
D. Odometer

Q.100 Which of the following is responsible for floating of the brain in the Human skull?
A. Cerebro-Membrane Fluid
B. Cerebrospinal Fluid
C. Augmented Grey Fluid
D. Pancreatic Fluid

// Smart Answer Sheet //

Correct — Percentage of students who answered correctly.   **Skipped** — Percentage of students who skipped.

Q.	Ans.	Correct	Skipped
1	C	87.91 %	11.72 %
2	A	77.89 %	19.96 %
3	D	86.86 %	10.42 %
4	B	77.13 %	17.23 %
5	D	84.84 %	12.06 %
6	B	87.05 %	10.72 %
7	C	88.43 %	11.12 %
8	B	82.79 %	16.58 %
9	D	88.59 %	10.27 %
10	B	83.86 %	10.64 %
11	B	76.81 %	22.95 %
12	A	89.04 %	10.05 %
13	B	82.8 %	11.72 %
14	C	89.6 %	10.31 %
15	B	77.99 %	12.8 %
16	C	89.3 %	10.7 %
17	C	80.81 %	10.86 %
18	A	80.03 %	15.07 %
19	A	86.36 %	12.44 %
20	C	87.22 %	10.7 %
21	B	83.08 %	10.57 %
22	B	84.48 %	12.35 %
23	B	89.65 %	10.1 %
24	A	82.43 %	13.93 %
25	A	82.44 %	13.98 %
26	A	86.38 %	10.95 %
27	A	83.82 %	12.91 %
28	D	86.92 %	10.78 %
29	D	81.26 %	12.76 %
30	B	89.01 %	10.54 %
31	B	78.28 %	16.73 %
32	C	76.02 %	18.44 %
33	D	87.88 %	10.05 %
34	B	82.44 %	15.66 %
35	A	76.63 %	18.07 %
36	A	77.98 %	20.94 %
37	B	76.42 %	18.67 %
38	C	83.01 %	15.27 %
39	D	80.04 %	11.82 %
40	D	85.04 %	10.06 %
41	D	88.53 %	10.63 %
42	B	86.27 %	12.0 %
43	C	78.01 %	11.58 %
44	D	78.91 %	14.99 %
45	A	86.52 %	11.27 %
46	B	84.46 %	12.03 %
47	C	87.48 %	11.72 %
48	B	76.78 %	17.18 %
49	C	85.25 %	10.01 %
50	A	82.19 %	16.68 %
51	C	87.63 %	10.36 %
52	A	83.46 %	13.86 %
53	C	87.17 %	10.62 %
54	C	81.21 %	12.64 %
55	D	86.43 %	10.2 %
56	D	76.04 %	14.7 %
57	B	87.05 %	12.5 %
58	B	80.82 %	14.11 %
59	D	87.69 %	10.73 %
60	B	78.59 %	14.95 %
61	B	87.15 %	11.8 %
62	D	82.42 %	16.35 %
63	C	87.78 %	11.4 %
64	A	78.43 %	13.01 %
65	D	79.64 %	17.97 %
66	B	87.08 %	12.43 %
67	C	82.85 %	12.94 %
68	A	89.69 %	10.18 %
69	C	83.92 %	10.89 %
70	B	77.33 %	17.03 %
71	B	86.56 %	11.16 %
72	C	88.42 %	10.72 %
73	A	84.43 %	11.02 %
74	A	83.29 %	13.25 %
75	D	89.43 %	10.2 %
76	D	87.86 %	12.03 %
77	B	84.73 %	14.42 %
78	B	79.35 %	11.47 %
79	D	81.57 %	18.13 %
80	C	87.64 %	12.01 %

Q.	Ans.	Correct	Skipped
81	A	84.89 %	13.41 %
82	A	79.06 %	19.74 %
83	A	87.64 %	11.83 %
84	D	89.04 %	10.25 %

Q.	Ans.	Correct	Skipped
85	D	78.94 %	14.08 %
86	C	88.84 %	10.03 %
87	C	87.69 %	10.11 %
88	C	82.95 %	10.1 %

Q.	Ans.	Correct	Skipped
89	C	87.14 %	10.58 %
90	C	81.1 %	11.54 %
91	B	82.14 %	13.05 %
92	B	82.61 %	11.3 %

Q.	Ans.	Correct	Skipped
93	A	78.01 %	16.94 %
94	A	76.0 %	22.9 %
95	C	84.22 %	12.5 %
96	B	81.07 %	15.37 %

Q.	Ans.	Correct	Skipped
97	C	89.79 %	10.15 %
98	C	76.3 %	12.61 %
99	B	84.85 %	12.87 %
100	B	87.59 %	11.73 %

//Hints and Solutions//

1. Let the number of matches played by Rohit and Kohli be 6k and 5k respectively.

Average runs scored in a match by Rohit = 52(1 - 25/100) = 39

Given, 52*5k - 39*6k = 546

=> 26k = 546

=> k = 21

Number of Matches played by Kohli = 5*21 = 105

2.

$$= \sqrt{1233 + \sqrt{3969} + \sqrt{1225}}$$

= √(1233+63)+35

= 36 + 35

= 71

3. For $2m^2 + 7m - 60 = 0$:

$2m^2 - 8m + 15m - 60 = 0$

m = -15/2,

Quadratic equation $4x^2 - 3m\sqrt{2}x + k = 0$ has equal roots, therefore,

$D = 0 = (-3m\sqrt{2})^2 - 4 \times 4 \times k$

For m = 4:

$18 \times (4)^2 = 16 \times k$

k = 18

4. Total marks = 100 + 100 + 150 + 150 = 500

Total marks of Rakhi = 78 + 60 + 96 + 124 = 358

Rakhi's percentage = (358/500) x 100 = 71.6%

Total marks of Jay = 56 + 80 + 88 + 92 = 316

Jay's percentage = (316/500) x 100 = 63.2%

Total marks of Amit = 95 + 90 + 80 + 75 = 340

Amit's percentage = (340/500) x 100 = 68%

Total marks of Urvi = 70 + 70 + 120 + 105 = 365

Urvi's percentage = (365/500) x 100 = 73%

5. Interest for 3 years = Rs 2600 - Rs 2240 = Rs 360

=> Interest for 2 years = 360x2/3 =Rs 240

Hence, principal = (2240 - 240) = Rs 2000

6. Ascending order of number of kids in the family-

0, 0, 1, 1, 2, 2, 2, 3, 4, 4

Total terms = 10 = Even

Median = [(n/2)th term + {(n/2) + 1} th term]/2

=> [(10/2)th term + {(10/2) + 1}th term]/2

7. The correct order is:

(E) Present age of C = 4A * (3/4) = 3A

(B) Present age of E = (3A + 7) = 16 => A = 3

(A) Age of A and C is 12 years and 9 years respectively

(D) Present age of B = 12 + 6 = 18 years and present age of D = 18 * (100/75) = 24 years

(C) Required average = (18 + 9 + 24)/3 = 17 years

8. Let their ages be 23x and 13x respectively.

Average age is 54 years which means the sum of their ages = 108 years

i.e. 36x = 108

or x = 3

Hence their ages are 69 and 39 years respectively.

After 6 years, their ages would be 75 and 45 years

So the required ratio = 75:45 = 5:3

9. Let the five numbers be a, b, c, d and e

Given, (a+b+c+d+e)/5=36

a+b+c+d+e = 180

a = (b+c+d+e)/5

a = (180-a)/5

a = 30

10. = √(9² - 4³ + 3) * √(2⁵ * 10⁻¹)

= √(81 - 64 + 3) * √(32 ÷ 10)

= √20 * √3.

= √(20 * 3.2)

= √64

= 8

11. Total number of non-correct questions out of total number of questions attempted by all 5 persons in preliminary exam

= (10 +5 +5 +10 +5)

= 35.

Total number of non-correct questions out of total number of questions attempted by all 5 persons in mains exam

= (30 +15 +11 +30 +40)

= 126

Required ratio= 35/126

12. n = HCF of (3708 - 1236), (4944 - 3708) and (4944 - 1236)

= HCF of 2472, 1236 and 3708

= 1236

Product of digits of n = 1 x 2 x 3 x 6 = 36

13. Let the three numbers be 2a, 3a and 5a respectively.

According to the question:

840 = 2a x 3a x 5a

a = 28

Therefore, the numbers are (2 x 28), (3 x 28) and (5 x 28) respectively.

Hence, HCF of these numbers = 28

14. Since discounts are 30 % and 35 % respectively, Therefore, discounts are 0.3x and 0.35y, where x and y are the marked prices respectively.

Further, it is given that these discounts are equal, so 0.3x = 0.35y=> x: y = 7: 6

i.e. marked price ratio is 7:6.

Now, check for all the given options.

15. Let the stream speed be 'r' km/hr.

180/(28 - r) = 4 + 180/(28 + r

45/(28 - r) - 45/(28 + r) = 1

$90r/(784 - r^2)$ =

$r^2 + 90r - 784 = 0$

(r - 8)(r + 98) = 0

r = 8

16. Ratio of heights of Asif and Bharat = 3:4 = 9:12

Ratio of heights of Bharat and Chatur = 6:7 = 12:14

Ratio of heights of Asif, Bharat and Chatur = 9:12:14

Sum of parts of the ratio = 9 + 12 + 14 = 35

Asif's height =(9/35)*175*3 = 135 cm

17. Total work in 1 day by A, B and C = 1/20 + 1/40 + 1/60 = 11/120

In 4 days = 44/120

By C in last 6 days = 6/60 = 1/10

Total = 44/120 + 1/10 = 56/120

Work left = 1 - 56/120 = 64/120

Work done by B and C in one day = 1/40 + 1/60 = 5/120

Work left is done by B and C. Number of days it takes = (64/120)*(120/5) = 64/5

Total time = 10 + 64/5 = 22 4/5

18. It will show the correct time again when it gains 24 hours.

It gains 5 minutes in 40 minutes

It gains 1 minute in 8 minutes

It gains 1 hr in 480 minutes

It gains 24 hr in 480*24 minutes or (480*24)/(60*24) or 8 days

19. x/y + y/x + 1 = 0

$=> x^2 + y^2 + xy = 0$

$=> x^2 - 2xy + y^2 + 3xy = 0$

$=> (x - y)^2 = -3xy$

$=> (x - y)^6 = -27x^3y^3$

$(x - y)^6/9x^3y^3$

$\therefore = (-27x^3y^3)/9x^3y^3$

= −3

20. Whenever the dimensions of the quantity are decreased by 'x' percentage then the overall percentage change = (-x%)+(-x%)+₋ ₓ%)(- x%)/100

Overall change in the price of the TV = -10-10+100/100=-19%

Cost Price of the TV after two years = 20000-(19/100 X 20000)=Rs.16200

21. Side of the square = Perimeter/4 = 40/4 =10 cm

Diagonal AC of square = Side x √2 =10√2 cm

AC is also diameter of circle.

Radius of circle = 5√2 cm

Area of circle = 3.14 x (5√2)² = 3.14 x 50 = 157 cm²

Area of square = 100 cm²

Area of blue portion = 157-100 = 57 cm²·

22. Let Ramesh's initial salary be Rs 100x

His salary after 1st Hike = (110/100)*100x = Rs 110x

His salary after 2nd Hike = (125/100)*110x = Rs 137.5x

Given 137.5x - 100x = 24000

=> 37.5x = 24000

=> x = 640

increase in his salary from the first hike to the second Hike

= 137.5x - 110x

= 27.5x

= Rs 17,600

23. Option (1):

= Product of 3ʳᵈ root of 2197 and √6889

= 13 x 83

= 1079

Option (2):

= Product of 4ᵗʰ root of 4096 and √1377

= 8 x 9√17

= 72√17 (irrational)

Option (3):

= Product of 3rd root of 3375 and $\sqrt{5929}$

= 15 x 77

= 1155

Option (4):

= Product of 4th root of 2401 and $\sqrt{1444}$

= 7 x 38

= 266

24. Let original length a car wiper be L inch.

Area cleaned by the car wiper in 1 sweep

= (1/2) x (22/7) x (L)^2

L^2 = 693 x (7/11) = 63 x 7

L = 21 inch.

Area cleaned by car wiper in a sweep if its length decreased by 3.5 inch.

= (1/2) x (22/7) x (17.5) x (17.5)

= 481.25 sq. inch.

25. Distance = speed *time

= (70 * 150)/60 min

= 175 km

New speed = (70 + 30) km/hr = 100 km/hr

Time = (Distance)/speed

− (175 * 60)/100

= 105 min

26. Let the height of poles be h m.

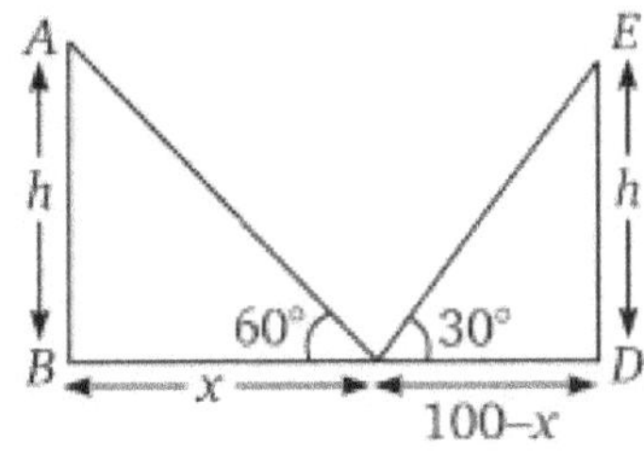

Tan 60 = h/x

=> $\sqrt{3}$ = h/x

Or h = $\sqrt{3}$ x

Similarly,

1/$\sqrt{3}$ = h/(100-x)

=> 100-x = $\sqrt{3}$ h = 3x

=> x = 25

Therefore, h = 25$\sqrt{3}$ m

27. Total sales for the year = 500 + 550 + 600 + 650 +700 +750 + 800 +850 +900+ 950 + 1000 +1050 = 9300

Average monthly sales for the year = 9300/12 = 775

28. a = 2.5 x 2.4 - 8 x 0.5 = 2

b = 12 x 4 x 0.5 - 16 = 8

c = 21 - 30 x 0.5 = 6

29. Let quantity of rice A and B are a and b respectively.

Total selling price = 20a + 25b

Total cost price = 24a + 24b

No profit no loss occurred. So,

Total selling price = total cost price

20a + 25b = 24a + 24b

4a = b

a: b = 1: 4

30. Let total number of votes cast = x

54% of x = 46% of x + 288

8% of x = 288

x = 288 x 100/8 = 3600. Hence, the answer option is (2).

31. A and B are first and second letters respectively as per alphabetical order.

Z is the last letter as per alphabetical order.

C and D are 3rd and 4th letter respectively as per alphabetical order.

Y is the 2nd last letter as per alphabetical order.

Following the similar pattern, we get IJV.

32. Neither of the statement alone is sufficient to answer and even if we combine the two statements, we get that 13 = for. But, 12 = '?'. Hence, answer is (4).

33. As per the codes given in the question,

M is coded as 4, E is coded as 6, T is coded as 8, A is coded as 3, L is coded as 5.

34. D is south-west of H.

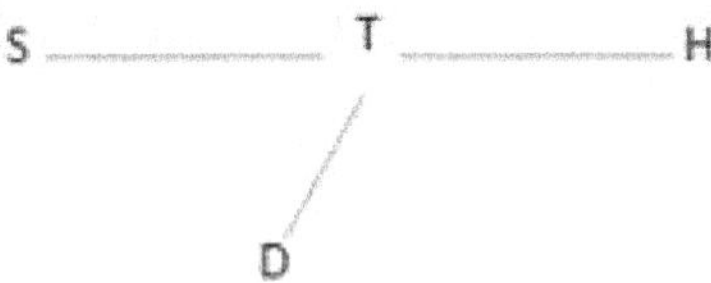

35. a **b** b d/ **a** b b **c**/ a b **b d**/ a b b **c**

36. Image I is the correct mirror image of (x).

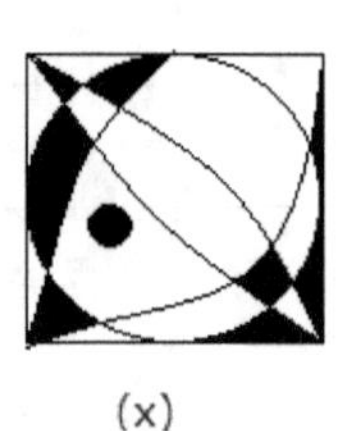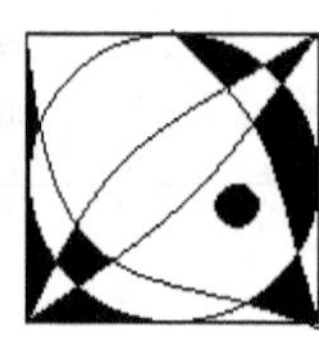

(x)

37. With respect to the values -

Ton (1000 kgs) > Quintal (100 Kgs) > Kilogram (1000 grams) > Gram

38.

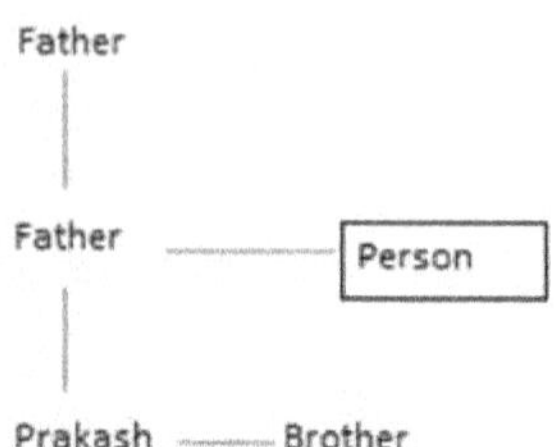

The person in the photograph is the sister of Prakash's father.

39. " play your good game" is coded as " ad pd cd md"..(I)

"play game run fast" is coded as " zd cd md td"..(II)

"run speed end game" is coded as " fd zd ld md"..(III)

From I, and III, we get: game= md

Then, from II and I we get: play= cd

So, "your /good" = "ad/ pd" in any order.

40. Encouraging the young entrepreneurs will open up the field for the establishment of new industries. Thus, it shall help in industrial development and not only employ the entrepreneurs but also create more job opportunities for others as well. So, both the arguments hold strong.

41.

The statements can be represented as:

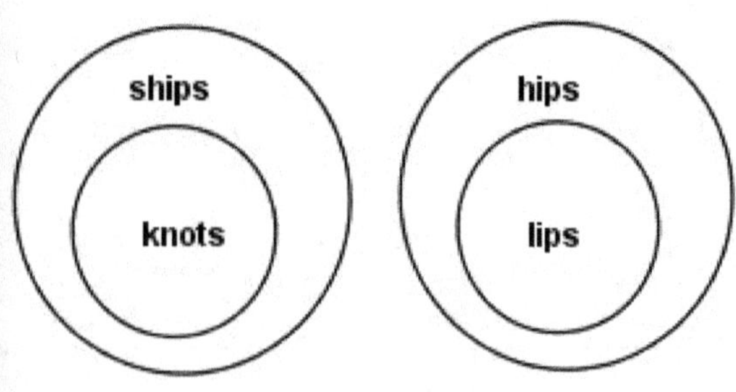

Both conclusions I and II follow

42. We have,

In fig (i) → 7*8 + 3*2 = 56+6 = 62 → 6+2 = 8

In fig (ii) → 5*9 + 1*4 = 45+4 = 49→ 4+9 = 13

Similarly,

In fig (iii) → 6*7 + 3*5 = 42+15= 57 → 5+7= 12

43. Both statements I and II are valid conclusions of the main statements. I- it talks about curriculums to be tailor-made since they don't always work for rural and regional schools as mentioned in the main statement. II talks about neglecting the diversity while formulating national curriculums which can be a reason for them not working.

44. rom statement I, P > M, T

from statement II, J>W>P

From both the statements, J>W>P> M, T. Therefore K is the heaviest. So J is lighter than only the heaviest.

45. The average of the position values is taken

SIT= (19+9+20)/2 =24

46. Option b is the correct answer.

Option a, c are incorrect as the object on top is wrongly drawn.

Option d is incorrect as object at the bottom is wrongly drawn.

47. Each term is a multiple of 3, except 4. Hence answer option is (3).

48. Tuberculosis affects lungs and jaundice affects liver.

49. Z is older than only two persons.

We get,

__ < __ < Z

Then,

T is younger to both W and V.

We get,

T < W, V

Since,

Y is younger to neither Z nor T, who is older than both S and Z.

We get,

__ < __ < Z < T < W, V, Y

Only S and U are left and, we know,

U is younger to at least three persons, none of whom is S.

So, we get,

S < U < Z < T < W, V, Y

Hence, T is the one who is younger to as well as elder to same number of persons i.e. 3 persons.

50. 7*(8-1)= 49

3*(4-1) = 9

We get, 499.

Similarly,

5*(2-1) = 5

7*(1-1) =0

We get, 50.

51. There can be other benefits of frequent flyer programme of an airline apart from frequent flyer miles; hence, it wouldn't be completely correct to say the statement mentioned in inference; hence, (c) is the right answer. (If frequent flyer miles were the only benefit of frequent flyer programme; in that case, the inference is definitely true).

52. Some children are naughty, some children are energetic, some energetic may be naughty

53. E---+4--- I ----+4--- M ----+4--- Q

H---+4--- L ----+4--- P ----+4--- T

F---+4--- J ----+4--- N ----+4--- R

54. Pattern is - MNOOMMNNOOOMMMNNNOOOO

55. Reverse the letters and then +1 to each letter.

56. Harivansh Narayan Singh Rajya Sabha MP from Bihar since 2014 was recently elected as the new Deputy Chairman of Rajya Sabha in the Parliament.

Earlier in his career he was a journalist with 'Prabhat Khabar' and then was chosen as the media advisor to former Prime Minister Chandra Shekhar.

57. 11th edition of World Hindi Conference was organised in Swami Vivekanand International Convention Centre, Pailles Mauritius.

Theme of the Conference: "Hindi Vishwa Aur Bharatiy Sanskriti". It was organised by the Ministry of External Affairs, Government of India in association with the Government of Mauritius

58. On October 12, 2005, Right To Information came into being after passage of an Act in the Indian parliament to bring in transparency in governmental procedures and end corruption

Using rtionline.gov.in citizens of India can seek information to turn India into a participatory democracy.

According to the government guidelines, 'Any person who desires to obtain information shall submit a written or electronic request in English or Hindi or in the official language of the area to the Central Public Information Officer or his/her counterpart at the state level.'

59. Andhra Pradesh topped the charts among Indian States in terms of "Ease of Living Index 2018" rankings launched by the Ministry of Housing and Urban Affairs, followed by Odisha and Madhya Pradesh.

The Index seeks to assist states in undertaking a 360-degree assessment of their strengths, weaknesses, opportunities, and threat & innovate to perform in the governance, identity and culture, education, health, safety and security, economy, affordable housing, land use planning etc. for its residents.

60. Ministry of culture recently launched the Seva Bhoj Yojna, a scheme to reimburse central share of CGST and IGST on food, prasad, langar etc. offered by religious and charitable institutions.

Institutions like Temples, Gurudwara, Mosque, Church, Dharmik Ashram, Dargah etc. who are established and serving free food for more than 5 years to more than 5000 people every month without any discrimination are the eligible entities.

61. During the 4th edition of 'Google for India' event, the Project Navlekha was unveiled which in Sanskrit means "a new way to write". It will quickly render any PDF with Indian language content into editable text using Artificial Intelligence.

Under the project, The registered publishers will be provided with free web hosting service along with a branded domain for 3 years and having AdSense support to help monetising their content.

62. Kanyashree was launched in 2013 by the West Bengal government to prevent child marriage in economically backward sections with an annual household income of ₹1.2 lakh.

Eligible girls got ₹1,000 a year scholarship from ages 13 to 18 years and a one-time grant of ₹25,000 on remaining unmarried till 18 years. More than 5 million girl children benefitted from the scheme.

Recently the annual income limit was relaxed to any girl child within the age limit.

63. NITI Aayog recently launched "Pitch to MOVE", a business opportunity platform for budding entrepreneurs to promote their business ideas.

It aims to identify and incentivise the start-ups, which will help the Government realize its vision of Shared, Connected, Intermodal and Environment Friendly Mobility for India.

The objective is to harness the latest disruption for generating employment and growth in our country

64. Ghoomar is a traditional dance from Rajasthan's Bhil tribe performed only by the women during celebrations pertaining to Goddess Saraswathi, Diwali, Holi etc.

Attire for women: Ghagharas along with colourful chunaris and heavy embroidery. Works garment.

65.

International Atomic Energy Agency	Vienna, Austria
World Bank	Washington DC
International Monetary Fund	Washington DC

66.

A. Aga Khan Cup	a. Cricket
B. Durand Trophy	b. Badminton
C. Sharjah Cup	c. Football
D. Yonex Cup	d. Hockey

67. Dhauladhar National Park is situated at a distance of 13kms from the city of Palampur in the Indian state of Himachal Pradesh.It is filled with exotic flora and fauna, and is home to

different types of deer, red fox, sambhar, Asiatic lion, angora rabbits, black bears and leopards.It covers an area of 30 acres.

68. Arabian Sea separates the two areas of the union territory, Daman & Diu, bordered by the state of Gujarat.

With an area of only 112 square kms, it is the second smallest UT of India after Lakshadweep.

69. Recently, BOMBAY NATURAL HISTORY SOCIETY opened its regional centre in the premises of The Wetland Research and Training Centre (WRTC) of the Chilika Development Authority (CDA) at Chandrapur in Chilika.

Here, BNHS would be engaged in identifying the air route of the migratory birds flocking the Chilika lake during winter & sample collection, training related to bird census among other important conservatory purposes.

70. The Reserve Bank of India has specified certain regulatory guidelines, as a part of prompt corrective action (PCA) Framework, in terms of 3 parameters,

- capital to risk weighted assets ratio (CRAR),

- net non-performing assets (NPA) and

- Return on Assets (RoA), applicable only to commercial banks and not extended to co-operative banks, non-banking financial companies (NBFCs) & other financial institutes

71. In case of spherical mirrors, focal length is half its radius of curvature image. Radius curvature of a mirror is defined as the radius of that sphere of which the mirror forms a part.

72.

Vinegar	Acetic Acid
Sour milk	Lactic Acid
Carbonated drinks	Carbonic Acid
Plant hormone	Abscisic Acid

73. During the oscillatory motion of a pendulum, energy balance is as follows-

The peak position: its potential energy is maximum while kinetic energy is minimum

The middle rest position: its potential energy is minimum while kinetic energy is maximum

74. Xerophytes are the plant species adapted to life in a dry or physiologically dry habitat like salt marsh, saline soil desert or ice-covered areas by means of mechanisms to prevent water loss or to store available water.

Examples Cacti, Pineapple, Pine trees etc

75. Polymer is any useful chemical made of many repeating units- either 1-dimensional, 2-dimensional or 3-dimensional called monomers.

Nylon, Polyvinyl Chloride & Teflon are all examples of polymers extremely useful in everyday life.

76. Propane - lower boiling point

-Used for central heating, cooking

- Transport fuel and numerous commercial applications.

- Chemical formulae: C_3H_8

Butane - used mainly in cylinders for portable applications in home

- For leisure activities such as boats, caravans and barbecues.

- Used as a propellant, refrigerant or to fuel torches

- Chemical formulae: C_4H_{10}

77. Glucose molecular formulae: $C_6H_{12}O_6$

Glucose comes from foods which are rich in carbohydrates, like rice, bread, potatoes etc. Glucose is released when enzymes act of the food passage through oesophagus to the stomach.

78. Nephron is the functional unit of the kidney. It performs the function of-

Producing urine in the process of removing waste in the body and excess substances from the blood.

The are over a million nephrons present in each human kidney.

79. Marie Curie was awarded The Nobel Prize in Chemistry 1911 in recognition of her services to the advancement of chemistry by the discovery of the elements radium and polonium.

She successfully isolated radium and conducted study upon its nature and characteristics.

80. Kirchhoff's 1st law states that, At any junction in a circuit, the sum of the currents arriving at the junction must be equal to the sum of the currents leaving the junction.

Or The algebraic sum of currents in a network of conductors meeting at a point is zero

81. Carbon atomic no.: 6; Mass No.: 12

Carbon is one of the most abundant elements commonly found in all living organisms. It contains 6 protons in the nucleus as well as 6 neutrons.

82. Bone marrow is the spongy tissue inside the hip and thigh bones containing immature stem cells that produces blood cells

• Bone marrow produces almost 200 bn new red blood cells every day, along with white blood cells and platelets essential to the human body

• Red blood cells (erythrocytes) help in transportation of oxygen around the body

• White blood cells (leukocytes) help fight infection and diseases

83. A sitar changes mechanical energy while strumming to produce sound energy whereas a microphone changes the supplied sound energy to electrical energy for amplification.

84. At any given inclination, a geosynchronous orbit synchronizes with the rotation of the Earth taking exact time of rotation as of the earth. An observer on ground, would see the satellite as if it's in a fixed position without movement.This makes geosynchronous satellites particularly useful for telecommunications and other remote sensing applications.

85. Sodium (Na): Atomic No.: 11; Atomic Mass: 22.9 g.mol-1 ;

- Highly reactive and low melting point

- Used in manufacturing of glass, soap etc.

Sodium is the 6th most abundant element in The Earth's crust.

86. Luminous bodies: Objects which emit light on their own. Example- Sun, stars, electric bulbs.

Non-Luminous bodies- Objects that do not emit light on their own but can be seen when light falls on them. Example- moons, trees, rocks etc.

Transparent- Objects which allow majority of light rays to pass through them. Example- Glass

87. Power equation: $P = I^2R$; P- Power consumption, I- electrical charge, R- Resistance

According to the question,

: $P = I^2R$

Or $1800 = I^2 \times 50$

Or I= 6 Ampere

88. In physics, an adiabatic process is a thermodynamic process in which there is no heat transfer into or out of a system and is generally obtained by surrounding the entire system with a strongly insulating material or by carrying out the process so quickly that there is no time for a significant heat transfer to take place

An isothermal process is a thermodynamic process in which the temperature of a system remains constant. The transfer of heat into or out of the system happens so slowly that thermal equilibrium is maintained.

An isobaric process is one where the pressure of the system (often a gas) stays constant in the thermodynamic system.

An isochoric process is a thermodynamic process in which the volume remains constant.

89. The velocity-displacement equation for a body moving with constant acceleration is $V^2 = U^2 - 2aS$

U= Initial velocity, V= final velocity, a= acceleration and S= displacement

Putting the value in the equation we get,

$V^2 = 102 - 2*2*9$

$V^2 = 64$

Or $V = 8 \ m/s^2$

90. Roughages are a fibrous indigestible compound that human body can't absorb. It aids in the passage of food and waste products through the digestive system.

Roughages are beneficial to overall health of a human body.

Fibre is found in many fruits, vegetables, grains and legumes, nuts and seeds.

91.

Acceleration	m/s^2
Velocity	m/s
Volumetric flow	m^3/s

92. Noble gases are the chemical elements which belong to group 18 of the periodic table.

The elements are- helium, neon, argon, krypton, xenon, and radon.

Having optimum valence electrons in their outer shell, they are the most stable elements found in environment.

93. Reverse heat engine is a device that transfers energy from an object at a lower temperature to an object at a higher temperature by doing work on the system which is essentially reverse of the process that takes place inside a heat engine, in which energy flows from a higher to a lower temperature and work is generated as a result.

Refrigerators and Air conditioners are typical example of reverse heat engines.

Efficiency does not play any role in the simple working of any of these processes.

94. Cytoplasm is the semi fluid substance enclosed within the cell membrane of an animal cell.

Its constituents are- water (80 - 85%), proteins (10 - 15%), lipids (2 - 4%) and rest are polysaccharides and nucleic acids.

All the organelles like Ribosomes, Mitochondria, golgi apparatus etc. are found in this.

95. In 1928 Alexander Fleming discovered penicillin, and after successful decades of its vital use and importance received the Nobel Prize in Medicine in 1945.

Fleming's discovery of penicillin occurred in 1928, while he was investigating a common type of bacteria that causes boils and infections in patients with weakened immune systems.

96. Bronchitis occurs when bronchial tubes, which essentially carry air to the lungs in the human system, gets infected and swollen causing a massive build-up of mucus

Same viruses that causes cold or the flu also cause bronchitis.

97. Smelting is a process to mix and melt metallic ores in order to control the pure metallic content according to specification in an industry.

Soldering is a process in which two or more metal items are joined together by melting and then flowing a filler metal into the joint - the filler metal having a relatively low melting point. Soldering is used to form a permanent connection between electronic components.

Forging is an after-extraction process where metal is given its desired shape.

98. Saponification is an organic chemical reaction utilized to make soap.

Saponification is a process by which triglycerides are reacted with sodium or potassium hydroxide (lye) to produce glycerol and a fatty acid salt, called "soap."

There are 2 compounds involved in this process- Fat and an Alkali.

99. The capacitor is made of two closely place conducting plates which are separated by a dielectric material.

The plates accumulate electric charge when connected to power source. One plate accumulates the positive charge and the other plate accumulates negative charge.

The capacity of a capacitor to store electrical energy is called Capacitance.

100. In the human skull, the brain "float" in the cerebrospinal fluid. It is found within the skull and spine. This cushioning fluid is produced by the choroid plexus tissue, which is located within the brain, and flows through a series of cavities (ventricles) out of the brain and down along the spinal cord.

The cerebrospinal fluid is kept separate from the blood supply by the blood-brain barrier

// Notes //

// Notes //